Discovering
Christ
In All The
Scriptures

Discovering Christ In All The Scriptures

Donald S. Fortner

Go *publications*

Go Publications
The Cairn, Hill Top, Eggleston, Co. Durham, DL12 0AU, ENGLAND
web: http://www.go-publications.com

© Go Publications 2006
First Published 2006

British Library Cataloguing in Publication Data available

ISBN 0 9548 6241 4

Printed and bound in Great Britain
by Lightning Source UK Ltd

This book is dedicated to:

Pastor Henry Mahan
Ashland, Kentucky

From whom I learned that

"Christ is all"

Contents

Discovering Christ In All The Scriptures

Old Testament

Discovering Christ In All The Scriptures

Discovering Christ In All The Scriptures

Foreword

The Bible is a daunting book. As a thirteen year old, armed with an unregenerate heart and not much idea of the Word of God, I resolved to read the Scriptures from cover to cover. I was reasonably diligent for a time, getting through Genesis and Exodus, but in Leviticus I found myself completely flummoxed. Here was a world of animals, food laws, blood sacrifices, holy days, priests, and a tabernacle – things that might have almost come from another planet.

About halfway through the book, my resolve failed, and I switched to the New Testament for a time. I am not altogether sure that I fared much better there, until in my early twenties, God spoke to my soul through the book of Romans, and there I came to see something of His wondrous and sovereign grace to sinners in Christ Jesus.

The two disciples at Emmaus were treated to a sermon by our Lord Himself, who chided them for their slowness and folly, but then opened up the whole of the Old Testament – which constituted the whole Bible at that stage – and showed how all 39 books of it testified of a suffering and glorified Messiah (Luke 24:25-27).

My friend, Don Fortner, rejoices in the fact that Christ is revealed in all of Scripture, and he has written a simple but most helpful survey of the whole of the Bible which highlights this wonderful truth. It is still true that the Bible is a daunting book, but Don Fortner's guide will surely be used to help many a pilgrim on the way to the Celestial City. May the Lord greatly bless it to that end!

Peter Barnes
Revesby Presbyterian Church, Sydney

Chapter 1

Genesis

I want to take you through the entire volume of holy scripture, book by book, showing you the message of each book and its relation to the whole Word of God. That will be the easy part. Here is the tough part. I plan to cover one entire book in each of the succeeding chapters. We will begin, of course, with Genesis, the book of beginnings.

What I hope to do in these studies is to give you a zoom-lens view of holy scripture. I trust the Lord will use this approach to help you see clearly that the message of the Bible from beginning to end is Jesus Christ and him crucified, and that you will be able to grasp more fully the whole truth of God, the whole of divine revelation.

We read in Genesis 1:1-3 'In the beginning God created the heaven and the earth. And the earth was without form, and void; and darkness was upon the face of the deep. And the Spirit of God moved upon the face of the waters. And God said, Let there be light: and there was light'. This is a picture of redemption.

In chapter 50, verses 24-26, we read, 'And Joseph said unto his brethren, I die: and God will surely visit you, and bring you out of this land unto the land which he sware to Abraham, to Isaac, and to Jacob. And Joseph took an oath of the children of Israel, saying, God will surely visit you, and ye shall carry up my bones from hence. So Joseph died, being an hundred and ten years old: and they embalmed him, and he was put in a coffin in Egypt'. This is a promise of redemption.

Thus we see the book of Genesis opens with a picture of redemption; and it closes with a promise of redemption; and everything between Genesis 1:1 and 50:26 shows either our desperate need of redemption or God's marvellous method of redemption and grace by Christ.

There is no greater wonder, no greater miracle in the world than the book you hold in your hand. The Lord God, in great mercy and grace, has given us his Word in one blessed, holy, inspired volume, and has given it to us in our language, so that we can read it, hear him speak, and learn of him.

The book of God is a great, tremendous, miraculous book. Let us honour it as God who gave us his Word honours it (Psalm 138:2). Surely, we to whom it is given, we who are made to profit by it, ought to honour it. Honour the book of God by reading it, believing it, seeking to understand it, and living by it. In doing so, we will honour our God.

Evidence of Inspiration

One of the most powerful and unanswerable evidences of the inspiration of the Bible is its unity. One message runs through its pages: redemption. One Person is portrayed, prophesied, presented, and proclaimed throughout the book of God, the Lord Jesus Christ. Yet, the scriptures were written over a period of hundreds of years by numerous men, most of whom never knew one another, written under extremely diverse conditions, containing neither error nor contradiction of any kind. That fact cannot be explained except by one thing; God did it. 'For the prophecy came not in old time by the will of man: but holy men of God spake as they were moved by the Holy Ghost' (2 Peter 1:21).

Divinely Authoritative

The Word of God alone is authoritative as our rule, our only rule of faith and practice. 'All scripture is given by inspiration of God, and is profitable for doctrine, for reproof, for correction, for instruction in righteousness: That the man of God may be perfect, thoroughly furnished unto all good works' (2 Timothy 3:16-17).

Let us wisely use and appreciate the writings of faithful men about the scriptures. But we must always interpret the writings of men by the Word of God, not the other way around. The Word of God, and the Word of God alone, is profitable to teach us doctrine to believe and preach, to reprove our errors, to correct our evils, and to instruct us in righteousness. Only the Bible can, by the blessing of God's Holy Spirit, make us complete 'and throughly furnished unto all good works'.

How Old?

We are so accustomed to reading it and hearing it, that we seldom consider how old Genesis actually is. Herodotus is called 'the father of history', because he was the first historian whose writings have been preserved for us. He was a Greek philosopher and teacher who lived 300 years before the incarnation of our Saviour. But Moses, who wrote the first five books of the Bible, had finished his work and was with Christ in glory a thousand years before Herodotus was born!

That's how old the book of Genesis is. It is the book of beginnings. It takes us back into the very dawn of human history. Yet, as we read it, it is as up-to-date as this morning's newspaper. As I read about Adam and Abel, Enoch and Noah, Abraham, Isaac and Jacob, and Joseph and his brothers, I tend to think of them as men I once knew. Their lives seem to mingle with mine. Do you find that to be the case? The scriptures bring us close to them and bring them close to us

More Than History

But the book of Genesis is not merely a history book. If that were the case, it would have little significance to us and would have little influence over us. It would just be facts recorded on paper. The book of Genesis was written to give us a specific message from the Lord our God. The message is as clear and simple as it is painful. It is as obvious as it is humbling. Without Christ, man is utterly sinful, helpless, inadequate, useless, insignificant, and vain. In revealing God's grace, the message of redemption also exposes our need.

The word 'genesis' means 'beginning'. Every foundational doctrine of the Bible has its beginning in the book of Genesis. Here we see all the doctrines of holy scripture in seed. The rest of the sacred volume expands and opens them. But the seed is in this first book.

The Word of God begins with this message: Man without Christ is utterly sinful, helpless, inadequate, useless, insignificant and vain. That is the message of Genesis. And, as the book of Beginnings, it sets the direction for all the subsequent revelation of our God.

Creation

Our inadequacy and insignificance is seen in the fact that we would have no existence at all without Christ. He is our Creator. This is what the Holy Spirit shows us in Genesis 1 and 2. 'All things were created by him and for him: and he is before all things, and by him all things consist' (Colossians 1:16-17).

'In the beginning was the Word, and the Word was with God, and the Word was God. The same was in the beginning with God. All things were made by him; and without him was not any thing made that was made' (John 1:1-3).

'In the beginning God created the heaven and the earth. And the earth was without form, and void; and darkness was upon the face of the deep. And the Spirit of God moved upon the face of the waters' (Genesis 1:1-2).

In these opening verses of Genesis the great need of redemption is typically set forth. 'In the beginning God created the heaven and the earth'. Like everything else that comes from the hand of God, the original creation of the world was perfect, beautiful, and glorious. That was the original condition of man. Adam was made in the image of God. He was endowed with life by the breath of the Almighty. God said, concerning him, he was 'very good'.

Then something happened. In verse 2 we read, 'And the earth was (became) without form and void'. The earth became a ruin. Between Genesis 1:1 and 1:2 some terrible thing happened which resulted in the ruin of the earth. This is not a matter of theory or speculation. The word translated 'was' in verse two should have been translated 'became'.

'This globe, at some undescribed period, having been convulsed and broken up, was a dark and watery waste for ages perhaps, till out of this chaotic state, the present fabric of the world was made to arise'. (Jamieson, Fausset and Brown Commentary).

No one can say with certainty, because it is not revealed, but perhaps this was the time of Satan's fall, the time when sin first entered God's universe.

This much is certain: Satan, the mightiest and most excellent of God's creatures, was filled with pride. Lucifer dared to oppose the will of his Creator. 'The anointed cherub that covereth' dared to defy God's right to be God. As the result of his sin, Satan was cast out of heaven, cast down to the earth. This fall of Satan had far reaching consequences. The earth, originally created by God fair and beautiful, became 'without form and void', a desolate place of ruin. 'And darkness was upon the face of the deep'.

This is a tremendous picture of what happened in the garden. Man, who was created in the image and likeness of God, fell into sin; and his fall had far reaching consequences. The effects of Adam's sin reached all his posterity. Humanity became a ruin. All future generations were cursed, spiritually dead, incapable of bringing forth life, as the result of Adam's fall. 'By one man sin entered into the world, and death by sin, for all have sinned' (Romans 5:12).

'And darkness was upon the face of the deep'. Darkness is the opposite of light. God is light. Satan is darkness. And man under sin, being void of all light, is engulfed in total, spiritual darkness. Separated from God, morally blind, spiritually dead, darkness is the condition of all unregenerate men and women. This is the black background upon which the holy Lord God chose to display the glory of his grace in redemption by Christ. 'Where sin abounded, grace did much more abound' (Romans 5:21). As the Lord God restored creation from ruin in those first six days of time, so he restores his elect from the ruin of the fall by his redemptive works in Christ.

Experimentally this restoration begins with the work of God the Holy Spirit in effectual grace. The work of redemption and justification was done when Christ died as our Substitute upon Calvary's cursed tree. But we knew nothing about it until 'the Spirit of God moved upon the face of the waters, and God said let there be light; and there was light' (John 16:8-14; 2 Corinthians 4:4-6).

Ruin

The inadequacy and insignificance of our race is displayed in the fact that we are a fallen, ruined, sinful and cursed race whose only hope of eternal life is the free grace of God in Christ.

That is the message of Genesis 3:1-6:8. During those days, from Adam to Noah, men lived for hundreds of years. What opportunities for advancement they had! I am certain that we have no idea how brilliant and advanced the people who walked on the earth in those days had become, in the knowledge of all things earthly. But, when we read what God has to say about the human race, it is obvious that they had only become more and more corrupt through the ages of time.

'And God saw that the wickedness of man was great in the earth, and that every imagination of the thoughts of his heart was only evil continually. And it repented the LORD that he had made man on the earth, and it grieved him at his heart. And the LORD said, I will destroy man whom I have created from the face of the earth; both man, and beast, and the creeping thing, and the fowls of the air; for it repenteth me that I have made them' (Genesis 6:5-7).

Few believed God. Few followed the example of Abel. Few, very few, knew the grace of God. Indeed, when human civilization had reached its highest achievements and greatest potential, the whole race was a mass of iniquity, a running sore of corruption, with its vileness covering the earth. The slime of the serpent's trail was found wherever man breathed

God's air. There was not a single exception, except one; and that one exception was an exception that God himself made by the special, supernatural intervention of his sovereign grace. 'But Noah found grace in the eyes of the LORD' (Genesis 6:8).

Redemption and Restoration

We are inadequate, insignificant, meaningless vanity. But, blessed be his holy name, he who is our God is infinitely adequate! As the Apostle Paul put it, when he was explaining the meaning of this book, 'Where sin abounded, grace did much more abound!' That is the message of the rest of the book of Genesis (6:9-50:26).

Man chose sin; but long before that God chose to save sinful men. Man broke God's covenant in the Garden; but before ever man rebelled, the Lord God had made a covenant on behalf of chosen sinners that can never be broken. It was typified in his covenants with Noah and Abraham. Man is filled with, inspired, and motivated (in every thought of his mind, desire of his heart, decision in life, and deed he performs) by his hatred of God. But God is filled with, inspired and motivated (in every thought of his mind, desire of his heart, determination of his being, and deed of his hand) by his mercy, love, and grace to fallen men! We deserved God's wrath; but God promised all the blessedness of his covenant to the chosen seed. And he found a way to give us that blessedness and still maintain his own holiness, justice, and truth (Job 33:24; Isaiah 45:20). The way is substitution, as typified throughout the book of Genesis, and clearly stated by Abraham in his response to Isaac on the mountain of sacrifice (Genesis 22). 'My son, God will provide himself a lamb for a burnt offering!' Little wonder that he called the name of that place, 'Jehovah-jireh!'

He who is our God always accomplishes his great purpose of grace! Nothing can hinder it. Nothing can prevent it. Indeed, all things are instruments in the hands of our God by which he performs it. Adam's fall did not take God by surprise. Rather, it provided the background and opened the way for Christ's redemption. Lot's drunken incest was overruled by the hand of our God to bring Ruth the Moabitess into the world, through whom Christ came to save us from our sins. The same is true regarding Judah's sin with Tamar and Joseph's ill-treatment by his brothers (Psalm 76:10).

Six Men

Really, the whole history of the book of Genesis (a period of 4000 years) revolves around six men. There is a reason for the prominence of these six men. They are representative of the whole experience of grace.

If you remember the lives of these six men and what they mean, you will have the book of Genesis at your fingertips. They are Adam, Noah, Abraham, Isaac, Jacob, and Joseph.

Adam displays our ruin, our depravity, our sin, and our need of grace. He was also a type of our Saviour in his federal headship (Romans 5:12-19). Adam was 'the figure of him that was to come'.

Noah portrays our redemption by Christ. As Noah built an ark to the saving of his house, so the Lord Jesus obtained eternal redemption for his house. As Noah suffered all the fury of God's wrath in the ark and was never touched by it, so all God's elect suffered all the fury of God's holy wrath in Christ to the full satisfaction of divine justice, but are never touched or harmed in any way by it.

Abraham is the eminent example in the Bible of justification by faith. Here was a man who lived by faith. Everything that he had was given to him by God, not by any merit in him, not by any effort on his part, but by God's free and sovereign grace. God chose Abraham. God revealed himself to Abraham. God called Abraham. God gave Abraham faith in Christ. And God ordered every step of his life. Eight times Abraham's faith was dramatically tried. When God tries your faith, read the life of Abraham. You will find your own experiences in his. Abraham shows us what it is to live by faith, what it is to live in this world as the friend of God.

Isaac exemplifies sonship, our relationship to our God as his own dear children. If there ever was a boy that was spoiled, pampered, and petted by his father, it was Isaac. He was Abraham's son, pre-eminently so. Abraham did everything for Isaac. He sacrificed everything for Isaac. In the glimpses this book gives us of Isaac we see what it means to be the darling of our heavenly Father's heart. What a blessed message this is! Our great God looks upon us as the darlings of his heart (1 John 3:1-2).

Jacob shows us how God's sanctifying grace keeps us and causes us to grow in the grace and knowledge of our Lord Jesus Christ, even as we live in this body of flesh. Jacob was a scoundrel, a schemer, a man who thought he could live on his own, by his own wits, and get anything he desired by his own efforts. He deceived almost everyone who had any dealings with him; but he ended up being deceived. (But Jacob was in the grip of grace!) What a picture he is of the indestructibility of God's purpose and grace!

He clearly shows us that sanctification is altogether the work of God. Anyone who is made holy in justification is made holy because the righteousness of Christ is imputed to him. And any who are made holy in sanctification are made holy because the righteousness of Christ is imparted to him in divine regeneration. We, in our folly, try to live by our own wits and steal God's blessing by the efforts of our flesh. But God uses the very things which ought to forever bar us from his grace to corner us, hedge us about, and drive us into utter desperation and hopelessness, as he did Jacob. At last, as the angel of the Lord wrestled with Jacob until he conquered him, the Lord God graciously forces the chosen object of his love to surrender to Christ as Lord, and forces us to surrender willingly! Then, when we give up, when we surrender our lives to the dominion of King Jesus, we begin to live. That is what Jacob did when he gave up at Peniel (Genesis 32:22-32). There God broke him. And as a broken man, limping for the rest of his life, he became Israel, prince of God. Blessed conquest! Oh, how I thank God for the unbreakable grip of his grace (Malachi 3:6).

Joseph represents our ultimate glorification. Without question, Joseph is typical of our Lord Jesus Christ throughout the closing chapters of Genesis. But he is also typical of every believer. This man, beloved of his father and mistreated by his brethren, living through constant conflicts, trials and heartaches, opposed on every hand, was suddenly lifted from the darkness of a prison house into the glory of Pharaoh's throne to reign and rule as the second person in the kingdom. So it shall be with us! When we are at last in the place our God has prepared for us, we will look upon all hell and say exactly what Joseph said to his brethren. 'But as for you, ye thought evil against me; but God meant it unto good, to bring to pass, as it is this day, to save much people alive'.

This is the message of the book of Genesis. Man without Christ is utterly sinful, helpless, inadequate, useless and vain. But, blessed be God, there is in Christ our God and Saviour an infinite, superlative adequacy of mercy, love and grace for our immortal souls!

Chapter 2

Exodus

Divine Deliverance

Someone once said, 'The Old Testament is the New Testament concealed; and the New Testament is the Old Testament revealed'. The Old Testament comes alive to us when we see the types and pictures of the Old explained in the New. I used to love to hear Bro. Ferrell Griswold preach Christ from the Old Testament. He seemed to make those types and pictures dance with life before my eyes as he expounded their meaning in the light of the New Testament. Facts and figures, laws, ceremonies and rituals of the Mosaic economy became vibrant, bursting with life. That is what I want to do for you as we look at the book of Exodus. I pray that God the Holy Spirit will cause the things set before us in this second book of the Bible to become vibrant with life in your mind.

Exodus means 'going out'. This book is called 'Exodus' because it reveals God's great work of grace in bringing his covenant people out of Egyptian bondage. It covers a time frame of about 140 years, from the death of Joseph to the construction of the tabernacle.

The Message

The whole book of Exodus is a message of divine deliverance. As such, it portrays the great work of our God in redeeming us from the bondage of sin and death and bringing us into what Paul calls, 'the glorious liberty of the children of God' (Romans 8:21). Even as he gave Israel his law in ten commandments, God told them that his intention in his dealings with them was that they might ever be reminded of this fact, 'I am the Lord thy God, which have brought thee out of the land of Egypt, out of the house of bondage' (Exodus 20:2).

The first six books of the Bible, Genesis through Joshua, display the works of God in the lives of chosen sinners. His wondrous method of grace is the same in your life and mine, as it was in the lives of Adam, Enoch, Noah, Abraham, Moses, and Joshua. He does not change; and his method of grace does not change.

In the book of Genesis we see our great need of redemption and grace. The last words of the book of Genesis are very significant. 'So Joseph died, being an hundred and ten years old: and they embalmed him, and he was put in a coffin in Egypt' (Genesis 50:26). This is just about as needy as it gets. Joseph died. He was embalmed. He was placed inside a coffin in Egypt.

Exodus shows us God's answer to our need, his remedy for our ruin, his deliverance of sinners from sin and death by Christ. As such, it is a tremendous picture and conveys very instructive lessons about redemption: what it is and how it is accomplished. Here we see pictures of what our God has done for us, is doing for us, and will yet do for us in bringing us into 'the glorious liberty of the children of God'. Obviously, the story is not complete in Exodus. It continues in Leviticus, Numbers, Deuteronomy, Joshua and on throughout scripture.

But the thing I want you to see is this: These first books of the Bible were written by divine inspiration to show us how God works in providence and grace, to overrule evil for good, and thereby teach us the gospel (Acts 10:43; Romans 15:4; 1 Corinthians 10:11). The whole book of Exodus revolves around six principle things. It focuses our minds on six great events: the Birth of Moses, the Passover, the Crossing of the Red Sea, the Giving of the Law, the Making of the Tabernacle, the End of Moses' Work.

The Birth of Moses

The book of Exodus begins with the Children of Israel in bondage in the land of Egypt. They had been in bondage for four hundred years. But the time of deliverance had come, and God raised up a deliverer.

The Lord God told Abraham that he would send Israel into a stranger's land where they would be afflicted for four hundred years. Then, he promised to deliver his people (Genesis 15:13-14). Now, the time of deliverance was at hand. The book of Exodus begins with the birth of the deliverer Moses.

Without question, the name 'Moses' represents the law of God and is used, at times, as a synonym for the law (Acts 6:11; 15:21; 21:21; 2 Corinthians 3:15). However as a deliverer of God's people Moses was also a type of Christ (Deuteronomy 18:15-18; John 1:45; Acts 3:22; 7:37). Just as with the incarnation, birth, and life of our Saviour, the Lord Jesus, the hand of God was also remarkably and undeniably manifested in the life of Moses. Like the Lord Jesus, that great Deliverer whom he typified, Moses appeared 'in the fulness of time'. When the 'due time' came, the deliverer arrived. Moses' birth was at a time of great darkness and need. When he was born Pharaoh tried to kill him. But he was wonderfully preserved until the time of his appearing as God's deliverer.

God often turns Satan's devices to accomplish his purposes. We will see this many times as we go through the books of the Bible. As I read the scriptures, I cannot help thinking that our Lord must have a sense of humour. Sometimes I can hardly refrain from laughter, as I read about him turning the tables on his enemies and overruling the evil ploys of men and devils to accomplish his great purpose of grace; the very thing they try to prevent. We see the ways of our God as revealed in Psalm 76:10[1] displayed both in the life of Moses and in the life of our Redeemer.

Though Pharaoh ordered the midwives to murder all the baby boys born among the children of Israel, the child Moses was not only saved but Pharaoh hired his own mother to nurse him and take care of him! He grew up in Pharaoh's house, as his own grandson. He was trained in all the learning of the Egyptians and given the best education in the world at that time. As Pharaoh's adopted son he had every privilege and every advantage of the world.

When he became a man God revealed himself to him and showed him that he was chosen and ordained to be the deliverer of Israel. He went about, trying to do this job, as he thought, and ended up killing an Egyptian and fleeing into the wilderness. He left the land of Egypt and tended sheep for forty years in the wilderness.

Only then was he called, commissioned and sent by God to deliver Israel. The Lord God appeared to him in the burning bush and sent him back to Egypt to deliver Israel at the time appointed (chapter 3). However, Moses was totally unfit for the task before him; and he knew it. He could not deliver Israel; but God could. Moses was only a typical redeemer (3:7-22). The Lord told him, 'I am come down to deliver them' (v. 8).

Moses felt he was not able to speak as clearly as he should as God's spokesman. Therefore the Lord assured him that he would be his tongue

[1] Psalms 76:10 'Surely the wrath of man shall praise thee: the remainder of wrath shalt thou restrain'.

and would speak through him (4:10-12). There was nothing wrong with that. It was commendable humility. God never uses anyone who thinks he is fit for the job. He delights to use nothings and nobodies to do his work (Isaiah 6:1-8; 66:2; 1 Corinthians 1:26-31).

But Moses went too far when he said, 'Lord, can't you get someone else to do this work?' Then 'the anger of the Lord was kindled against Moses' (4:14). We would be wise to lay this to heart. A sense of inadequacy, and personal unworthiness is commendable; but a lack of willingness, or even hesitancy in doing what is clearly God's will, is abhorrent rebellion.

Moses went back to Egypt with nothing but the rod (Word) of God in his hand to deliver Israel from the most powerful king the world had ever known (2 Corinthians 10:4-5). Immediately, he ran into trouble. He came into conflict with Pharaoh. The conflict between Pharaoh and Moses, the representatives of Satan and God, was tremendous. No drama ever conceived by man compares to this bit of history. As you read it you can feel its intensity. Though the Lord God sent plague after plague upon the Egyptians, 'Pharaoh hardened his heart and refused to let the people go'.

There were ten plagues in all. Each plague was directed against one of the gods of Egypt. By sending these plagues God not only judged and punished the Egyptians, he also showed the impotence of their idols and displayed himself as God alone; sovereign, omnipotent, majestic, and holy.

The Passover

Moses was typical and representative of Christ our Saviour. The second great event in the book of Exodus, the Passover (chapter 11 and 12), was typical of our redemption by Christ. It is so obvious that the Passover represents our redemption by Christ that everyone who even claims to believe that the Bible is the Word of God acknowledges it. Few indeed, understand what is taught by this great work of deliverance; but all acknowledge that it is a picture of redemption. Let me call your attention to the highlights.

The Passover, like our redemption by Christ, was an act of God's free, sovereign, covenant mercy. It was God who put a difference between Israel and Egypt (11:7). This shows us God's distinguishing grace (1 Corinthians 4:7). The message was spoken in the ears of God's chosen (11:1). The call of God the Holy Spirit is a particular, distinguishing call (Romans 8:29-30). God promised an effectual, glorious work by which all (Egyptians and Israelites) would know that he is God. The Egyptians thrust Israel out of the land, and they went out with a high hand, spoiling the land of Egypt, taking all the good of the land. Israel was under the special protection of divine providence. God promised, 'Against the children of Israel shall not a dog move his tongue, against man or beast' (11:7). The Lord God raised up Pharaoh and hardened his heart. He specifically says, 'that my wonders may be multiplied in the land of Egypt' (11:9; Romans 9:15-18). Satan is God's servant, not his rival! When God gets done with him, he will dump his carcass in the sea of his fury, just as he did Pharaoh's, and all shall know that he alone is God.

The Passover, like our redemption, was a display of how God saves sinners by blood atonement. It was accomplished at God's appointed time (12:2). It was for Israel the beginning of months (2 Corinthians 5:17). The paschal lamb portrayed Christ our Passover who is sacrificed for us (1 Corinthians 5:7). The blood sprinkled upon the door and lintel speaks of the effectual call of grace in which the Spirit of God applies Christ's atoning blood to the conscience, creating faith in the redeemed sinner (Hebrews 9:12-14). Particular, effectual redemption is displayed in the fact that all for whom a lamb was slain went out of Egypt (12:37). And, as Israel spoiled the Egyptians (12:36), we shall have the spoils of victory in resurrection glory, inheriting the earth.

The Crossing of the Red Sea

But the story does not end there. Beginning in chapter 13, we see the third great event in Exodus: the crossing of the Red Sea. Really, the Passover and the crossing of the Red Sea are two parts of the same thing. They cannot be separated. Israel could never have crossed the Red Sea had the Passover not been kept. The keeping of the Passover would have been a meaningless, useless thing had Israel not crossed the sea.

The crossing of the Red Sea is a picture of our conversion by the power and grace of God the Holy Spirit in effectual calling. This is so closely connected with the sacrifice of Christ as our sin-atoning Substitute that the two cannot be separated. Christ's death effectually secured our conversion. Without the conversion of God's elect, Christ's death would have been a useless, futile, vain, and meaningless thing. Now, watch the type. May God make it dance with life.

The Lord went before them (13:21). He led them through the way of the wilderness (13:18). Israel was brought into terror and fear; but their fear only stirred the rebellion that was in them (14:10-11). Legal conviction is not saving. It takes Holy Spirit conviction to save (John 16:8-11). Yet, it seems to be the common experience of God's elect that a time of legal conviction (the terror of eternal death) precedes the blessed joy of faith.

When Israel was utterly terrified, Moses said, 'Fear ye not, stand still, and see the salvation of the Lord!' (14:13). 'The Lord shall fight for you, and ye shall hold your peace!' (14:14). That is exactly the place to which God brings his own. He graciously forces us to cease from our own efforts and works to save ourselves, and makes us look to Christ alone for salvation.

Israel crossed the sea by the rod of Moses. That rod represented the whole Word of God, mercy and truth, justice and grace, holiness and love. 'By mercy and truth iniquity is purged'. The law of God, being satisfied by the blood and righteousness of Christ, opens the way before us to everlasting salvation, and the grace of God carries us through. Then, standing upon the shores of blessed deliverance looking back upon their slain enemies, they believed, worshipped, gave praise to God, and started on their journey (14:31-16:1).

Baptism

The scriptures (1 Corinthians 10:1-2) tell us plainly that the passage of Israel through the Red Sea was a baptism unto Moses. It signified the same thing as believer's baptism does today. It showed the distinction God put between Israel and Egypt. So does believer's baptism. It was an act of obedience to God's command. Both Israel's baptism unto Moses and the believer's baptism with reference to the finished work of Christ are acts of obedience performed to the command of God with reference to the promise of God (Exodus 14:13-16; Matthew 28:19; Mark 16:16). As Israel followed Moses through the Red Sea, so believers follow Christ through the waters of baptism, symbolically declaring salvation to be the work of God alone by Christ's fulfilling all righteousness as our Representative and Substitute.

Marah

No sooner had they crossed the Red Sea than they came to the bitter waters of Marah (15:23-26). It is so with us. From its very inception, the life of faith is a life of trial. 'We must through much tribulation enter into the kingdom of God'. The Lord showed Moses 'a tree, which when he had cast into the waters, the waters were made sweet'. Then he revealed himself in a singular way, declaring, 'I am the Lord that healeth thee'. Let us ever be assured that whatever trials of bitterness we must endure, as we go through this wilderness of woe, the trials and bitter experiences are but the means by which our God intends to reveal himself more fully. And those trials and bitter waters are made sweet to our souls because they flow to us as blessings of grace from the thrown of our heavenly Father, through the blood of our crucified Mediator who died on the cursed tree for us. The cross sweetens everything. Oh, how it sweetens life's experiences! As Bro. Scott Richardson of Katy Baptist Church, Fairmont, West Virginia says, 'There's no bad news once you get the good news'.

Manna

As they made their journey through the wilderness, the Lord graciously fed the children of Israel with heavenly manna every day (chapter 16), and refreshed their bodies with water flowing from the smitten rock that followed them (chapter 17). These were miraculous provisions for their physical sustenance but they were much more than that. The manna that fell from heaven and the water that flowed from the smitten rock were pictures of God's provision for our souls, for time and eternity, in Christ our crucified Saviour (John 6:48-58; 1 Corinthians 10:1-11).

Amalek

Perhaps the most difficult experience of God's people in this world after being converted is the constant, ever-increasing warfare between the flesh and the spirit. We also see this portrayed in chapter seventeen. Amalek comes and fights with Israel; but God declares unending war with Amalek (Exodus 17:10-16). The fact is, the flesh lusts against the spirit and the spirit against the flesh, so that we can never do the things we would. We can never walk with our God and serve him perfectly without sin while we live in this world. We constantly find ourselves to be wretched sinners (Romans 7:14-23; Galatians 5:17). This warfare will never end, or even abate, until we have dropped these bodies of flesh. We can never make peace with Amalek and Amalek will never cease to assail us. But, blessed be God our Saviour, Amalek shall never prevail! Because the Lord Jesus Christ is our Banner, because the Lord our God fights for us, 'we are more than conquerors', and all our foes shall fall before us, even our sins cannot defeat us!

The Giving of the Law

The fourth thing that stands out in the book of Exodus is the giving of the law at Mount Sinai (Exodus 19-24). In chapters 19-24, we find Israel at Mount Sinai, where the Lord God gave Israel his law in ten commandments and taught them how he must be worshipped. The law was a detailed revelation of God's immutable, unrelenting, perfect, glorious holiness. That is why the law and the giving of the law were terrifying to Israel.

Nothing is so terrifying to sinful men and women as the realization that God almighty is absolutely and unchangeably holy, that nothing can change him. He will never be talked out of anything. He can never be bought off. He will never lower his standards in any degree. The law is the absolute, irrevocable standard of God's character. It is also a declaration of the absolute sovereignty and utter solitariness of his being as God. Because he is who and what he is, the Lord our God demands perfection of all who are accepted of him.

At the very outset the law of God taught Israel and teaches us that the holy, sovereign, unalterable Lord God cannot be worshipped by fallen, sinful, sinning men and women except through a mediator. This mediator must be one that he has ordained, provided, and accepted (20:18-19), upon an altar of his own making, an altar to which man contributes nothing, and can never climb by degrees (20:23-26). In other words, the law drives us away from Sinai to Calvary, away from Moses to Christ for refuge and salvation (Galatians 3:19-26).

The Erecting of the Tabernacle

The fifth thing in Exodus is the erecting of the tabernacle, the place of reconciliation and peace, with its altar, sacrifices, priesthood, and mercy-seat (Exodus 25-40). In chapter twenty-five the Lord begins to give Moses instruction about the tabernacle and priesthood, the sacrifices and ceremonies by which the children of Israel may come to him and find acceptance with him. The tabernacle speaks of Christ and the believer's acceptance with God in Christ (Hebrews 9:1-10:22). We are taught by types and pictures how the Lord our God can be both a just God and a Saviour (Isaiah 45:21). By the sacrifice of Christ the holy Lord God, in complete justice, holiness, and truth, receives redeemed sinners in total reconciliation declaring, 'There is now no condemnation', none whatsoever! Every believing sinner has perfect access to the Father through the Son. God himself, by his Holy Spirit, has taken up his tabernacle in our hearts and lives. He will never leave us, and will never let us leave him! We are forever, immutably 'accepted in the beloved!'

The End of Moses' Work

The last thing we see in Exodus is the end of Moses' work. Once the tabernacle was finished and God and his people were ceremonially reconciled, Moses had finished his work (Exodus 40:33). Once the chosen, redeemed sinner has been brought to faith in Christ, the law of God has finished its work (Romans 6:14-15; 7:1-4; 8:1; 10:4). Once God's elect are brought into the blessedness of reconciliation with him by faith in Christ, the law has nothing more to do with us. It no longer terrifies, condemns, or even frowns upon us. Rather, the law of God cries as fully as the grace of God, 'JUSTIFIED!' This is beautifully portrayed in the last paragraph of Exodus (40:34-38). The Holy Ghost tells us:

> Then a cloud covered the tent of the congregation, and the glory of the LORD filled the tabernacle. And Moses was not able to enter into the tent of the congregation, because the cloud abode thereon, and the glory of the LORD filled the tabernacle. And when the cloud was taken up from over the tabernacle, the children of Israel went onward in all their journeys: But if the cloud were not taken up, then they journeyed not till the day that it was taken up. For the cloud of the LORD was upon the tabernacle by day, and fire was on it by night, in the sight of all the house of Israel, throughout all their journeys.

Hymnwriter Philip Bliss wrote:

> Free from the law, O happy condition!
> Jesus hath bled, and there is remission!
> Cursed by the law and bruised by the fall,
> Grace hath redeemed us once for all.
>
> Now are we free. There's no condemnation!
> Jesus provides a perfect salvation!
> 'Come unto Me'. O hear His sweet call!
> Come, and He saves us once for all.
>
> Children of God! O glorious calling!
> Surely His grace will keep us from falling!
> Passing from death to life at His call,
> Blessed salvation once for all!

As we leave the book of Exodus, seeking to worship, serve, and honour our God in this world, we would be wise and prudent to pray for the very same great boons of mercy and grace that Moses sought from the Lord in chapter 32.

'Now therefore, I pray thee, if I have found grace in thy sight, show me now thy way, that I may know thee, that I may find grace in thy sight'. If the Lord God will be pleased to show us his way, order our steps in his paths, cause us ever to grow in the grace and knowledge of Christ, and ever give us his grace, we shall be blessed throughout our days upon the earth, and forever in heavenly glory.

'Consider that this nation is thy people'. Let us ever pray for the church and kingdom of God in this world. We cannot ask anything greater than that the Lord God ever consider that his people are his people.

After the Lord promised Moses his abiding presence, Moses sought it earnestly. 'And he said unto him, If thy presence go not with me, carry us not up hence'. It is almost as if he felt he had neglected this before, or simply made the presumption that God's presence was his. Certainly every believer is promised the Lord's unfailing presence. But let us never presume upon it or imagine we can function without it. Rather, let us constantly seek it. If the Lord is with us, we have no need unsupplied.

Then Moses prayed, 'I beseech thee, show me thy glory', and the Lord God granted his request. He showed himself to be a just God and a Saviour. Oh, may he be pleased ever to hold before our eyes his glory in the face of the Lord Jesus Christ, that our every thought may be consumed with it, that we may in all things do all for the glory of our God.

Chapter 3

Leviticus

God Demands and Gives Holiness

The book of Exodus concludes with the setting up of the tabernacle for the worship of God. This was the place where God met with his chosen people, the place of divine worship, the place from whence the Lord God gave out his word to his people. This tabernacle, being a picture of our dear Saviour, the Lord Jesus Christ, the incarnate God, was made exactly according to the pattern God gave to Moses. The book of Leviticus gives us the prescribed ordinances and ceremonies of divine worship.

John Gill tells us that, the book of Leviticus was written by Moses 2514 years after the creation, about 1490 years before the coming of Christ. The various sacrifices, rites, and ceremonies here described were typical of Christ, and shadows of those good things to come by him for the everlasting salvation of our souls.

Three Historical Events

There are only three historical events mentioned in the whole book of Leviticus. But those three historical events are very instructive. The first historical event recorded in this book is the consecration of Aaron and his sons as the priests of Israel (chapter 8-9). There is a twofold type here.

First, the Aaronic priesthood represents the priesthood of our Lord Jesus Christ. Specifically, Aaron, as the High Priest of Israel, foreshadowed the Lord Jesus Christ, our great High Priest before God. He was divinely chosen, equipped, anointed, approved and accepted. Only Aaron could make atonement in the holy of holies, because only he represented Christ our great High Priest who alone could and would put away sin by the sacrifice of himself (Hebrews 7:23-28)

Second, Aaron's sons represent the Church and Kingdom of God, as that 'holy priesthood' of believers who serve God in the holy place day and night (1 Peter 2:5-9). Everything about these priests typifies and represents believing sinners in this world. These men were specifically chosen by God, portraying our election unto salvation. They were God's priests because of their relationship to Aaron. Believers are made priests unto God because of our relationship to the Lord Jesus Christ. They wore the garments of the priesthood. God's priests today wear the garments of their priesthood, too, the garments of salvation, the righteousness of Christ. Aaron's sons were accepted as priests because of a slain sacrifice. We are accepted because of Christ's sacrifice. They were anointed with holy anointing oil and washed with pure water. Believers are anointed with the Holy Spirit and washed in the pure water of free grace by the Word of God in the new birth. Aaron's sons were men who deliberately and voluntarily consecrated themselves to God. Believers are people who deliberately and voluntarily consecrate themselves to God. As Aaron's sons lived continually upon the sacrifice of God's altar, God's sons live continually upon Christ. As they served God and his people all the days of their lives, so God's 'holy priesthood' today serves him and his people continually.

The second historic event recorded in Leviticus is the death of Nadab and Abihu by the hand of God for offering 'strange fire before the Lord' (chapter 10). Let all who would worship God understand the powerful lesson set before us in chapter 10. If we would worship God and find acceptance with him, we must come to him with that which he has provided, Christ alone, and no mixture of anything with Christ (Leviticus 10:1-3). God is sanctified (honoured) only by Christ; and the only way he can be sanctified by fallen, sinful men and women is by faith in Christ.

The third historic event recorded in the book of Leviticus is the stoning of Shelomith's son for blasphemy (24:10-16). Those who blaspheme the name of God, cursing and denying him as God alone, shall be destroyed by him. Though this unnamed wretch had a Hebrew mother, his father was an Egyptian; and he preferred both the gods and the people of Egypt to the God of Glory and his people. He was stoned by the people themselves, because they judged him worthy of death. In like manner, though our hearts may break and cause us to weep as we behold lost rebels today under the wrath of God, when the Lord God executes his righteous judgment upon the damned in eternity, all shall consent and say, 'Amen', to it.

All the rest of the book is taken up with the ceremonial laws God gave to Israel by Moses concerning their sacrifices and offerings, meats and drinks, and different washings. By these things God set Israel apart as a people for himself, and distinguished them from other people and nations. All these things were shadows of those good things to come, which are ours in Christ. This book is called Leviticus because it is primarily about the Levitical priesthood (Hebrews 7:11).

The Message

We do not have to guess about the central, dominant message of the book of Leviticus. It is plainly stated in chapters 19 and 20. 'And the LORD spake unto Moses, saying, Speak unto all the congregation of the children of Israel, and say unto them, Ye shall be holy: for I the LORD your God am holy ... And ye shall be holy unto me: for I the LORD am holy, and have severed you from other people, that ye should be mine' (19:1-2; 20:26).

The message of Leviticus is this: God demands holiness and God gives what he demands in Christ. All the types and ceremonies, laws and sacrifices, priests and holy things spoken of in these twenty-seven chapters show us that our only way of access to God is Christ. But, blessed be his holy name, we do have access to God by Christ, because we have that holiness which God demands in him, by his obedience and blood (John 14:6; Hebrews 10:14-22).

Holiness

Please read this verse again and think on it. 'And ye shall be holy unto me: for I the LORD am holy, and have severed you from other people, that ye should be mine ... And the LORD spake unto Moses, saying, Speak unto all the congregation of the children of Israel, and say unto them, Ye shall be holy: for I the LORD your God am holy'.

This is both the command of God and the promise of God to his people. God commands us to be holy. Without holiness no one shall see the Lord (Hebrews 12:14). Yet, that holiness without which we cannot see God is not something we perform. It is something God gives.

The Lord God declares to his chosen, covenant people that they *shall* be a holy people; not partially holy; not mostly holy; but entirely holy.

This is not a recommendation, but a declaration. It is a declaration of grace made to a specific people.

The word 'holy' has two distinct meanings. Both definitions of the word must be understood and applied here. First, to be holy is to be separate, distinct, peculiar, separated and severed from all others. Second, to be holy is to be pure or purified.

The Lord God here declares to his Israel, to all who stand before him as his covenant people, 'You shall be separate, distinct, peculiar, separated and severed from all others, pure and purified before me'. We know that this is the intent and meaning of this statement by comparing scripture with scripture (Exodus 19:6; Leviticus 11:44; 20:7; 1 Thessalonians 4:7; 1 Corinthians 6:9-11; Titus 2:11-14; 1 Peter 2:7-10).

The Lord God almighty, by the work of his sovereign, free, distinguishing grace, takes such things as us, such things as he finds in the dung heap of fallen humanity and makes them holy. God makes sinners holy by the total removal of all sin and guilt from them and the imputation of righteousness to them in free justification by the precious blood of Christ (2 Corinthians 5:17). He makes us holy in sanctification when we are first regenerated by imparting holiness to us (creating a new, holy nature in us) by his almighty grace (Romans 7:14-23; 2 Peter 1:4; 1 John 3:9). Thereafter we shall be made holy in resurrection glory, when our very bodies are changed into the likeness of his glorious body (Romans 8:28-30; Ephesians 5:25-26; Jude 24-25; 1 Corinthians 15:20-28; 49-58).

Without a doubt, the scriptures teach us that God requires holiness and God gives holiness to his people; but what is this holiness? Because we are so universally inundated with false, free will, works religion from our youth up we commonly think that holiness has something to do with what we do. We tend to think of holiness in connection with austere, weird behaviour. We tend to think that 'holy' people are people who look sad and sour, that act as if they were weaned on dill pickles and daily bathed in embalming fluid.

We are like that little city girl who on her first visit to the country saw a mule looking at her over a fence with his long, sad face. She had never seen a mule before, and she said, 'I don't know what you are, but you must be a Christian, you look just like Grandpa'.

Holiness is commonly associated with grimness, strangeness, oddness, even something ugly and unappealing. Frankly, as I have heard it described from the pulpit and read about it in the writings of men, I must acknowledge that such thoughts are justified. But that is not holiness. That is nothing but religious self-righteousness and religious delusion.

The Word of God speaks of holiness in a different way. The Bible speaks of holiness as a beautiful and delightful thing. Four times we are called to worship God in the beauty of holiness (1 Chronicles 16:29; 2 Chronicles 20:21; Psalm 29:2; 96:9).

Wholeness

Holiness has something to do with wholeness. Holiness means wholeness, completion, entirety, perfection of being. There are no degrees to it. Either we are whole or we are broken and unwhole, complete or incomplete, perfect or imperfect. As a general rule when reading the Bible, think wholeness every time you read the word holiness, and you will get a better picture of what holiness is.

That is what the Lord is talking about in Leviticus. He says to his covenant people, 'you shall be whole, because I am whole'. God is complete. He is perfect. There is no blemish in his character. He exists in perfect harmony with himself. He is perfect in beauty. He is perfect wholeness. He looks upon his chosen in great, boundless grace, and says, 'You too, shall be whole'.

I am not suggesting that holiness does not involve separation, distinctness, and peculiarity. It certainly does. What I am saying however, is this. It is not separateness that makes men holy but wholeness which separates God's elect from a ruined race. Wholeness, the blessed wholeness of grace and righteousness in Christ, is our separateness, distinctness, and peculiarity.

Nothing is more desirable, nothing more beautiful, and nothing more rare than wholeness. We long to be a whole people. The whole book of Leviticus, indeed the whole Word of God tells us how that God demands this wholeness and gives it to poor, helpless, broken, ruined sinners. He declares, 'I am the Lord that healeth thee'. He heals us by the sacrifice of his dear Son. It is written, 'with his stripes ye are healed'. God almighty heals the broken, ruined state and condition of his people by the five things described in this great book of Leviticus: sacrifice, priesthood, atonement, restoration, liberty.

Sacrifice

As I have been trying to demonstrate, the purpose of Leviticus is echoed in verses such as 11:44-45, 19:2, and 20:26: 'Be ye holy, for I the Lord your God am holy'. The word 'holy' appears more often in the book of Leviticus than in any other book of the Bible. The book of Leviticus both calls God's people to be holy, and shows us how sinners are made holy by Christ.

In chapters 1-7, God gave Moses specific instructions about the sacrifices and offerings by which his people would be allowed to approach him. In these five sacrifices, Israel was ceremonially provided with everything needed to make them whole and holy. These sacrifices represent the Lord Jesus Christ, in and by whom the Lord God gives us everything needed to make us whole, complete, holy before him (Colossians 2:9-10).

The burnt offering shows us the way to God (1:1-17). We must come to God by faith in Christ, who was consumed by the fire of God's wrath as our Substitute. Let it ever be remembered that our Lord Jesus Christ is that Burnt Offering who, being consumed by the fire of God's wrath, in turn consumed the fire of God's wrath for his people. Because God's fury was poured out like fire upon our Substitute (Nahum 1:6), he declares, 'Fury is not in me' (Isaiah 27:4).

The meat offering portrays the character of Christ, the God-man (2:1-16). He who is our Substitute is most holy unto the Lord. It also speaks of our consecration to God by faith in Christ.

The peace offering speaks of the Lord Jesus who is our Peace (3:1-17). Christ alone can reconcile God and man. Christ alone can speak peace to the guilty conscience. Christ alone is our Peace (Colossians 1:20).

The sin offering, of course, represents Christ our Substitute (4:1-35). Without the shedding of blood there is no remission of sin. There is no forgiveness with God except by the merits of a suitable, slain, sin offering; and that great Sin Offering is Christ.

The trespass offering sets before us a picture of Christ's atonement (5:1-6:7). Our Lord Jesus Christ made atonement for the sins of his people by paying our debt to the full satisfaction of divine justice.

> I hear the Saviour say,
> 'Thy strength indeed is small.
> Child of weakness, watch and pray,
> Find in Me thine all in all'.
> Jesus paid it all! All the debt I owed!
> Sin had left a crimson stain,
> He washed it white as snow!

Priesthood

Here, in Leviticus 8-10, is our unwholeness, our brokenness. Sin has separated us from God. By ourselves we cannot come to God, approach him, and find acceptance with him. Who, then, will bring us to God and enable us to find acceptance with him? We must have a priest, a mediator, a daysman, an advocate. This God has provided in Christ.

None but God's Priest, the Lord Jesus Christ can represent us before the holy Lord God, make sacrifice for us in the presence of God, and bring to us the blessing of God. But our great High Priest, the Lord Jesus Christ is so great, so meritorious, so effectual, so worthy that he makes us priests unto God! Yes, it is true ...

> Near, so very near to God, nearer I cannot be,
> For in the Person of His Son, I am as near as He!

Christ is our unfailing, all-prevailing High Priest and Advocate with the Father (1 John 2:1-2).

Atonement

The Lord Jesus is our great High Priest; but a priest is useless without a sacrifice as we see from Leviticus 11-16. Christ is both our Priest and our sin-atoning Sacrifice, the Lamb of God who has taken away our sins! He has, by his one great sacrifice for sin, forever put away all the sins of all his people (Isaiah 53:6, 9-11; Hebrews 9:26; 1 John 3:5).

Restoration

Leviticus 17-24 shows us typically that which is the result of Christ's sin-atoning sacrifice as our Substitute. Because Christ has made atonement for us and put away our sins by the sacrifice of himself, God almighty sends his Spirit in omnipotent, saving grace and restores us to himself. He reconciles us, and brings us into fellowship with him as the sons of God, causing us to walk with him in the obedience of faith, worshipping him. He says, 'I am the Lord your God, which have separated you from other people' (20:24). In other words, he says to you and me, as we come to him through the sacrifice of Christ, 'I am yours and you are mine!' Even now, he owns us as his! He declares, 'And ye shall be holy unto me: for I the LORD am holy, and have severed you from other people, that ye should be mine' (Leviticus 20:26). The only thing left is that liberty for which Paul longed, when he cried, 'O wretched man that I am! Who shall deliver me from the body of this death?'

Liberty

Leviticus 25 opens with the blowing of the jubilee trumpet. I can hardly wait. Soon, Christ shall come again. Then liberty, the glorious liberty of the sons of God! Then, blessed be his name, then we shall be made whole! (1 Corinthians 15:51,52).

Someone told a story many years ago that illustrates what I am trying to say. Some poor children put on a little skit at a Rescue mission in Chicago, Illinois. A small boy, six or seven years old, was to give a short recitation. It was obvious, as he walked out on the stage, that he was shy and nervous. He had never done such a thing before. What made his situation even more pathetic was that he had a severe physical deformity, a humpback that embarrassed him and, naturally made him more sensitive than other boys his age might be in the same situation.

Two older boys, sitting in the back of the room, laughed out loud as he walked across the stage. One of them yelled out, 'Hey, buddy, where are you going with that pack on your back?' The little boy was devastated. He just stood before the crowd horribly embarrassed, crying, and helpless.

A man got up from his seat, walked to the stage, knelt down beside the boy, and put his arm around him. He said to the audience,

> This is my son. He has a deformity he can do nothing about. But he was trying to do this little part because his mother and I wanted him to do it. We thought it would be good for him; and he was trying to please us. He wanted to make us proud of him. Well, I want everyone to know, (I especially want him to know) that this is my son. He belongs to me. I love him just the way he is. I'm proud of him and proud of his effort to please me.

Then, he led the boy off the stage and took him home.

That is what our heavenly Fathers says to us. He sees our hurt, our embarrassment, our heartache, our brokenness over our horrid, sinful deformities. He sees our longing to be whole; and he says, 'You are mine'. That is not all. Our God declares, 'You shall be healed, made whole. You shall be holy. I will see to it. All your blemishes shall be removed. All your deformities shall be corrected. All your faults shall be fixed. You shall be whole, for I am whole'. That is what the book of Leviticus is about. That is what the Bible is about (Jude 24-25). That is what God's amazing grace in Christ does. It makes sinners whole!

Chapter 4

Numbers

Our Failure and God's Faithfulness

If you read the Old Testament as nothing more than a history of ancient events concerning people who lived a long, long time ago, it is just about as boring as a textbook of logarithims. If you read it as nothing more than a book of hidden prophetic mysteries, it may be more interesting, but it is still a book with little meaning to you personally. However, if you read the Old Testament as a picture of what is happening in your own life and day to day experience of redemption and grace it becomes lively and fascinating. If you see in the Old Testament pictures of Christ and his great work of redemption, pictures of his love for and grace to your soul, it becomes precious beyond description.

When we read and study the history of the nation of Israel in the Old Testament, we must constantly remind ourselves that the Lord our God is not providing us with the history of a quaint little nation in a remote part of the world. God's interest in and purpose for the nation of Israel was singular. He raised up and used that nation as a vehicle for the accomplishment of his purpose of grace and redemption in Christ, no more and no less.

The Pentateuch (the first five books of the Bible) and the book of Joshua symbolically display every believer's experience of grace and salvation in and by the Lord Jesus Christ. In these first six books of inspiration we see how that the Lord our God brings us from the bondage and curse of sin and death into 'the glorious liberty of the sons of God'. The whole Old Testament was written so that we might see in vivid types and shadows what the New Testament declares to be true. All those things that happened to Israel in the Old Testament came to pass and were written down in the book of God for our comfort and edification. This is precisely what the Holy Spirit tells us in Romans 15:4 and 1 Corinthians 10:11. The history of God's revelation to Israel is a picture of the history of grace in the life of a believer. Thus,

Genesis, the book of Beginnings, shows our great need of redemption and grace.

Exodus, the book of Deliverance, displays our experience of grace in redemption.

Leviticus, the book of the Priesthood, typifies our atonement by Christ, which is the basis and effectual cause of deliverance.

Numbers, the book of Numbering, displays our (the believer's) weakness, unbelief, and failure in this world.

Deuteronomy, the book of the Law, shows us God's immutability and his faithfulness to his covenant people in the second giving of his law.

Joshua, the book of Deliverance, displays our entrance into and everlasting possession of all the blessings of grace and glory in eternal, resurrection glory with and by our Lord Jesus Christ.

The fourth book of Moses is called 'Numbers' because it opens with the numbering of the children of Israel (1:1-4:49), and concludes with the numbering of the people again (26:1-65). Both counts were done, not as acts of pride or presumption (2 Samuel 24), but at the command of God.

If you read through the first five books of the Bible at one sitting, it appears that Leviticus might be out of place amongst the others because it interrupts the historic narrative. That is because the book of Leviticus is a parenthetical explanation of God's work with his people. Genesis shows us our great need of redemption and grace. Exodus displays our experience of salvation in time. Leviticus shows us, in type and picture, that God deals with us in grace upon the basis of Christ's finished work of atonement as our Substitute. Then, the book of Numbers picks up the historic narrative again, a narrative portraying our struggle as believers with the world, the flesh, and the devil. But assuring us that God continues to deal with his covenant people in grace upon the basis of Christ's finished work and not upon the basis of our experience.

The book of Numbers covers most of the period of Israel's forty years in the wilderness and the events connected with their wilderness journey. From the opening numbering of the children of Israel it goes on to describe the divine pattern by which the camp of Israel was arranged and the order of their movement from one place to another. The people marched through the wilderness toward Canaan for forty years, until all the adults, those twenty years old and upward, who came out of Egypt died. Someone suggested that Israel's wilderness journey was the longest funeral procession in history.

Those forty years in the wilderness were the result of the nation's unbelief, specifically their refusal to believe the report of Joshua and Caleb after the twelve spies had spied out the land of Canaan. Because they chose to follow the lead of the unbelieving spies, God judged the nation, and that generation entered not into the land of promise, but died in the wilderness because of unbelief. The only adults who left Egypt and entered the land of Canaan were Joshua and Caleb. Once the old generation was dead, God commanded that the new generation, that generation to be led by Joshua into the land of promise, be numbered. So, we have the second numbering of Israel at the close of the book.

Our Unbelief

Now, let us see what the message of this book of Numbers is. I do not mean, let us see what we can use in Numbers to teach the Gospel of Christ. I mean, let us see what the message of the book of Numbers is. How does God the Holy Spirit here teach us the Gospel?

In thirty-five chapters we are confronted with what may be the most difficult thing for us to learn as God's people in this world. We are confronted head-on with what causes more trouble than anything else in this life, our own unbelief! It is always the tendency of our fallen nature to lean on our own understanding, or if not our own on someone else's. The book of Numbers teaches us that we must believe God, that we must trust and follow Christ in all things (Proverbs 3:5-6) and that we should not rely on human reason, be it our own or someone else's!

This is where I struggle most. I suspect it is the same with you. How we dishonour our God by unbelief! We all foolishly imagine that what we want to do and the way we want to do it is the right way. Oh, we say, 'The Lord knows best'. But rarely do we act like he does. Like these ancient Jews, you and I must learn that God really does know best. He knows what he is doing when he acts. He knows what he is talking about when he speaks. What he tells us is the truth. All that he says, all that he does, and all that he requires of us, is always for our good and his glory.

How I wish I could learn to live as a man who really believes that! God's way is always right. Our way is always wrong. With regard to all things, Solomon's word is true, no matter what friends, family, the world, and our own proud flesh may think to the contrary. 'There is a way which seemeth right unto a man, but the end thereof are the ways of death' (Proverbs 14:12). The book of Numbers is a picture of that experience in the believer.

Here we have a picture of a people. It is a picture of people who have come out of Egypt and have crossed the Red Sea believing God. They have seen Pharaoh and his armies drowned in the sea. They are going to the land of Canaan, believing God's promise to give them the land for their inheritance as his covenant people. But they have not yet reached the land. They are pressing toward the mark; but they have not yet attained the prize. They had the faith to follow God out of the bondage and slavery and darkness; but they have not yet come into the fulness of liberty and rest in Christ.

How much like them we are! We believe on the Lord Jesus Christ. We trust him for the forgiveness of our sins. We have seen Satan cast out and our sins drowned beneath the blood of Christ. We are moving toward heavenly glory. Yet we have great trouble trusting our Saviour to provide for, protect, and guide us in our daily lives and through our daily struggles.

Our Faithful God

But, blessed be his name, our God is faithful still! His faithfulness, his mercy, his grace, his provision is never altered by our experience. He deals with us upon the basis of his covenant and the accomplished redemption of our souls by the sacrifice of his dear Son (2 Timothy 2:13, 19; Psalm 103:8-14; Isaiah 43:1-7). Let every ransomed soul proclaim with Jeremiah, 'Great is thy faithfulness!'

We see this fact of God's faithfulness, faithfulness in spite of our horrible unbelief, when we get to the latter part of the book of Numbers (chapters 21-35). Here we see Israel triumphing over their enemies by the hand of God. Many enemies surround them. The outward forces of kings Arad, Sihon, and Og, the king of Bashan, and the attempts of Balaam, the false prophet to try to undermine the purpose of God, all result only in greater blessedness for Israel.

The book of Numbers tells us, in the clearest terms God himself can find, that though we are disobedient, though we are rebellious, though we are so full of unbelief and sin, though we live, it seems, in utter barrenness and emptiness of soul, year after year after year in this waste and howling wilderness, our great God will never leave us nor forsake us (Hebrews 13:5). Even in the midst of our weakness, he is our Strength. Even when we fall, he protects us, lifts us up, and holds us in the hands of his omnipotent mercy and immutable grace!

Pictures of Christ

There are four distinct and direct pictures of our Lord Jesus Christ in this book. Aaron's rod that budded (17:1-13) was a picture of life out of death by which God identified Aaron as his servant. As Aaron was, by the budding of his rod, publicly declared to be God's servant and priest, the Lord Jesus Christ was publicly owned as and declared to be the Son of God with power by his resurrection from the dead (Romans 1:3-4).

The water that flowed from the smitten rock (20:1-13 and 1 Corinthians 10:4) was a vivid picture of Christ and our salvation by him. As the rock brought forth water, only after it was smitten by Moses, so the Son of God yields the water of life to chosen sinners only by being smitten to death, to the full satisfaction of divine justice, by the rod of God's holy law.

The brazen serpent (21:1-9) was another clear type and picture of our great Saviour (John 3:14-16). Because the children of Israel murmured against him, in judgment the Lord God sent fiery serpents upon them. The poisonous venom from those fiery serpents killed many. When Moses prayed for the people the Lord commanded him to make a serpent of brass and lift it up upon a pole, promising, 'everyone that is bitten, when he looketh upon it, shall live ... And it came to pass that if a serpent had bitten any man, when he beheld the serpent of brass, he lived'.

Gospel preachers are like the pole to which Moses fastened the brazen serpent. Our only function is to hold up Christ crucified before sinners. The gospel we preach is Jesus Christ. We do not merely preach a Christ centred gospel. We preach Christ and Christ is the gospel we preach. There is a huge difference.

Pastor Roger Ellsworth, in his excellent book, *The Guide*, suggests that the brazen serpent, God's remedy for Israel's ruin, typified the Lord Jesus in six ways. He wrote ...

The remedy consisted of Moses making a serpent in the form of the poisonous serpents. The Lord Jesus Christ was made in the form of sinful men (Philippians 2:8). As the serpent of brass had no venom, so Christ had no sin (2 Corinthians 5:21). As the serpent of brass was lifted up on a pole, so Christ was lifted up on the cross (John 3:14). All that was necessary for the people to be healed was to look at the brass serpent, and all that is necessary for healing of sin is to look at Christ. As there was only one remedy for the people of Israel, the serpent on the pole, so there is only one way of eternal salvation, Jesus Christ.

Other important points of similarity between Christ and the brazen serpent have been made by others. For example, John Gill, in his commentaries on Numbers and John, gives many excellent comparisons. There is one other comparison that must be added. It is very important, but often overlooked. It is that all who looked upon the brazen serpent were healed at once of their plague, and every sinner who looks to Christ by faith is immediately made whole.

The cities of refuge (35:9-34) were also typical of our Lord Jesus Christ, the refuge of our souls, the refuge of salvation. Believers are men and women who have fled for refuge to Christ, just as the man-slayer in the Old Testament sought safety in one of the cities of refuge. Even the names of the cities were typically significant and instructive (Exodus 21:13; Numbers 35:6, 11, 14; Deuteronomy 21:2, 9; Joshua 20:1-9).

Kedesh means, 'holy'. Christ is holy, both as God and man, and is our holiness before God, that 'holiness without which no man shall see the Lord'. Shechem means, 'the shoulder'. Christ not only bore our sins in his own body on the tree, he bears and carries their persons; and the government of his church and kingdom is on his shoulders. There, on his omnipotent shoulders, we are safe and secure. Hebron means, 'fellowship'. Believers have fellowship with Christ and with the Father in him; and in him we have fellowship with one another. Bezer means, 'a fortified place'. Christ is our stronghold, our high tower, and our place of defence. To him we run; and in him we are safe. Ramoth means, 'exaltations'. Our Lord Jesus Christ is exalted at God's right hand, and in due time he will exalt those that trust in him. Golan means 'manifested'. Christ is God 'manifest in the flesh'. The Son of God was manifest to take away our sins and destroy the works of the devil; he will be gloriously manifest and revealed at the last day.

Our Lord Jesus Christ is spoken of prophetically by the false prophet Balaam (24:17-19 – Cf. John 11:47-52). So great is our God that he uses Balaam's ass and false prophets like Balaam (men far beneath dumb beasts) to deliver his message when it so pleases him. Christ is the Star coming out of Judah and the Sceptre (Law Giver) out of Israel. His birth was announced by a star put in the sky by God (Matthew 2:2). He is called 'the Bright and Morning Star' (Revelation 22:16). He is the Deliverer (the Sceptre) who comes out of Zion for the salvation of his people (Romans 11:26).

The Lessons

Now, let me show you some of the lessons the Spirit of God would have us learn from this book. First, there is nothing so dishonouring to our God and so harmful to us in this world as unbelief. We see this clearly in the major theme of the book of Numbers. God sent Israel in to spy out the land of Canaan, but they believed not God (chapters 13 and 14). Therefore, the Lord God sent upon them forty years of judgment, forty years, a year for each day the spies were in Canaan, of wandering from place to place in the wilderness.

We have seen that God's favour is never determined by our experience or contingent upon our work. Divine favour is altogether gracious, free, and unconditional. Yet, as God judged Israel for their unbelief, he chastens us for ours, to teach us to trust and believe him. It is a great blessing that he does so. Still, the Word of God is clear. We forfeit much of God's goodness and blessedness in this world by our unbelief (Isaiah 48:17-19; John 11:40; Matthew 23:37-38).

Second, God almighty demands that those who speak for him be heard and obeyed (11:1-17:13). The lessons of God's judgment upon the sons of Korah need to be learned. God's ambassadors are the ambassadors of God. Hear them, and you hear God. Refuse and disobey them, and you refuse and disobey God.

Third, many, like the sons of Korah and the mixed multitude in Israel, have a barren familiarity with the things of God. There is an acquaintence with spiritual things without any true experience of them. J. C. Ryle wrote, 'Nothing so hardens the hearts of men as a barren familiarity with the things of God'. Barren familiarity with Christ and his gospel is damning to the souls of men, and will ultimately bring God's most severe wrath in hell.

Fourth, the most deadly thing in this world is the error of Balaam (Jude 11). What was Balaam's error? He served God, or pretended to, for hire (Numbers 22:7). He was a man motivated by covetousness. Being such a man, Balaam taught Israel to mix the worship of God with the worship of idols (Numbers 25:1-3). He did not teach them to abandon the worship of God, or even to alter it. He simply taught them that the way to get along with the heathen, among whom they sojourned, was to compromise with them, accepting their gods as God. That is idolatry of the worst kind.

Fifth, there is but one remedy for human sin, but one way of salvation and eternal life. The only way Israel could be saved from the fiery serpents was by looking to that brazen serpent Moses lifted up before them. The only way you and I can be saved is by looking to Christ, our crucified Saviour (John 12:32; 14:6; Isaiah 45:20-22).

Chapter 5

Deuteronomy

Moses Brings Israel to Joshua

We come now to the book of Deuteronomy, the last of The Five books of Moses. The name 'Deuteronomy' means 'second law'. This book is called 'Deuteronomy' because in this book Moses gives Israel God's law a second time.

Here is something worthy of special notice. Once Moses brought Israel to Joshua, once he put Israel into Joshua's hands, he died, and Joshua brought Israel into possession of their divinely ordained inheritance in the land of Canaan. Even so, the law is our schoolmaster unto Christ. Once the law has served that purpose, once we have come to Christ by faith, we are dead to the law and the law is dead to us, because 'Christ is the end of the law'.

Those who like to cast doubt upon the Word of God question and then openly deny, that Moses wrote these first books of the Bible. I will not honour their blasphemy with comment. There is no question that this book was written by Moses. Not only did Moses claim that he wrote it (Deuteronomy 1:1; 31:9, 24, 30), the Lord Jesus also tells us plainly that Moses was the man used by God the Holy Spirit to write these thirty-four chapters of inspiration (Matthew 19:7-9; John 5:45-47). The last eight verses, those describing Moses' death and his remarkable character, were obviously written by someone else. We are not told by whom, perhaps Joshua or Samuel; but whoever it was, he, too, wrote by divine inspiration.

This is Moses' last word to the people of Israel. The faithful prophet of God now delivers the last word from God he would ever speak on the earth. Unlike most, Moses knew this was his final message. We should not be surprised, therefore, to see in the book of Deuteronomy a much more personal and intimate account, even more passionate language than we have seen in his earlier writings.

This book was written during the very last month of Israel's fortieth year in the wilderness. It begins with a word about Moses (Deuteronomy 1:1-5) and ends with the description of his death (Deuteronomy 34:1-10). Moses is very prominent throughout the book. We find his name mentioned repeatedly in these chapters. But Moses is not the subject of the book. The subject is Christ and Moses is the messenger.

Let me remind you again that what we have before us in these first five books of the Bible are divinely inspired visual aids that illustrate the experiences of our own lives. As God led Israel out of Egypt through the wilderness into the land of Canaan, they endured the same problems, met the same obstacles, faced the same enemies, and had the same trials, temptations and failures as you and I encounter in our pilgrimage through this world.

The Key

The key to this book is in its name. As we have seen 'Deuteronomy' means 'the second law'. The law was first given at Mount Sinai in ten commandments (Exodus 20). Why was it necessary for the Holy Spirit to give the law twice? What need was there for this second law, or second giving of the law? The apostle Paul tells us plainly in the book of Romans and the book of Galatians that the law of God has two functions, two very clearly defined and distinct purposes.

Most people think God gave the law to keep us from doing wrong and to make us do right. If you ask the man on the street what was the purpose of the ten commandments, or ask most any religious legalist why God gave the law, he would probably say, 'It is to keep us from doing wrong', or 'The law was given to teach us how to live'. But that is not the reason God gave the law. It is true that the law (by its threat of punishment) restrains wicked men and women from performing much of the evil that is in them (1 Timothy 1:8-11), but God never intended, or even dreamed for a moment, that the law would keep anybody from doing wrong. 'Wherefore then serveth the law?'

The law was given to identify sin and condemn it in us personally (Romans 3:19; 7:6-9). Paul said, 'I had not known sin, but by the law: for I had not known lust, except the law had said, Thou shalt not covet'.

'Now we know that what things soever the law saith, it saith to them who are under the law: that every mouth may be stopped, and all the world may become guilty before God' (Romans 3:19). The law was given to convince us of our own sinfulness and guilt. That is something of which we must be convinced by God. No one else can do it. We all have an amazing capacity for justifying ourselves and condemning one another. It is called 'self-righteousness'. We never think that what we are doing is wrong. It is always what the other person does that is wrong. Do you not find that to be the case? Let me remind you how this works.

We have a whole stack of words we use to describe the things we do, and another whole stack we use to describe what another person does. Others have prejudices. We have convictions. Other people are stingy. We are very thrifty. Others try to keep up with the Joneses. We are just trying to get ahead. He is a flatterer. I just try to be friendly. She is so flirtatious. I try to be nice to people. That person is so unfriendly. I do not want to intrude.

The law of God steps in and forces us to acknowledge our own guilt. Not only does the law force us to admit our own guilt but the law of God is graciously designed to force us into the arms of Christ. Once we see what we are, guilty, helpless, depraved sinners, sinners who are utterly incapable of altering their condition, we are informed that the cross of Christ meets all our needs before the holy Lord God (Romans 3:19-26).

That is what we see so clearly set forth in the books of Exodus and Leviticus in the sacrifices of the lambs, the goats, the oxen, the calves, and the other animals. They were pictures of the sin-atoning sacrifice of Christ in the shedding his precious blood for many for the remission of sins. There is no way a sinful man and the holy Lord God can be brought together except by a justice satisfying payment being rendered to God for sin. The only one who could make such a payment, the only one who could atone for our sins is the incarnate Son of God. Blessed be his name forever, he has done it (Galatians 3:13; 2 Corinthians 5:21; 1 Peter 3:18). The law is our schoolmaster unto Christ (Galatians 3:19-25). Once the schoolmaster has brought us to Christ, he has no more dominion over us.

Allow me to illustrate this from a personal experience. I have a very good friend in North Carolina called Robert Spencer. He and I became good friends just a few years ago, after I ran into him and his wife (Lib) in an elevator. He was then President of the International Lions Club, on his way to one of their meetings. I was on my way to fulfil a preaching engagement in the same town. I had known Bob many years earlier as Mr Spencer. He was my sixth grade school teacher. I was a young rebel, constantly in trouble. Mr Spencer, on many occasions, with the complete authority of the State and of my parents, inflicted pain on my posterior because it was his job to do so, to bring me to maturity. In those days I dreaded his presence and feared his wrath. Now, he is my friend. I look forward to seeing him and always enjoy his presence. Even if he thought about whipping me today, he would not dare. He no longer has any authority or the power to do so. So it is with the law. Once the sinner has come to Christ, the law has no more dominion over him (Romans 6:14-15; 7:4; 10:4).

Romans 7

In Romans chapter seven Paul takes up the matter of the law again. He had already assured us that we who are born of God are no longer under the law (Romans 6:14-15). Now he tells us that the law is dead to us and we are dead to the law, because we died with Christ. But there is more.

Though we are sinners, not only people who do sinful things, but by nature sinners at the very core of our inmost beings, Christ has forever freed us from all possibility of curse and condemnation. He has made us perfectly righteous before God and his holy law. He has made us free by his Spirit to walk with him in the newness of resurrection life in the Spirit, and assures us of our absolute security and everlasting salvation by his blood and grace (Romans 8:1-4, 32-39; 5:10-11).

Still, there is more. Since Christ has totally and absolutely met every demand of God's holy law for us as our Representative and Substitute, all that he is and has as our resurrected, exalted, glorified Saviour is ours by the gift of God's free grace, upon the grounds of perfect righteousness and strict justice (John 17:5, 22). Here, while we live in this world, we are waiting for, and living in anticipation of resurrection glory (Romans 8:23).

This is what the book of Deuteronomy is all about. As Moses delivered Israel into the hands of Joshua, assuring them that Joshua would carry them into and make them possess all the fulness of Canaan (all that God promised by covenant to Abraham), the law of God delivers believing sinners into the hands of Christ assuring us of everlasting salvation by him. All the blessings of grace and glory that God promised us in his covenant with Christ shall be ours forever.

Two Themes

As we read Deuteronomy we find two themes running throughout the entire book. They are not found in Leviticus or Exodus. The first is our utter weakness and inability. Though cleansed before God through the blood of Christ and the washing of regeneration by the Word, we have absolutely no ability to do anything in ourselves to please God. There is nothing we can do in ourselves. Our most sincere, dedicated efforts to please God avail nothing.

Right along with this is a second wonderful, parallel theme. The Lord our God is ever with us. God himself, in the person of his dear Son, is the answer to the demands of his law; and he dwells with us and in us unconditionally. We no longer live in the flesh, but in the Spirit (Romans 8:8-10). God himself has taken up residence in us. All that he demands of us, he himself supplies.

Go back and look at the book of Deuteronomy. I would like you to see these things for yourself. As the book begins, the children of Israel are once again camped on the border of Canaan. They had been here before. On that occasion they could not enter into the land of promise because of unbelief. Through unbelief, they spent forty long years roaming in the wilderness (Numbers 14:32-35).

A Call to Obedience

In Deuteronomy chapters 1-4 Moses issues a call to obedience. The grace of God is not conditioned upon our obedience to him. Yet, obedience is a matter of personal responsibility. We are to obey our God in all things. Grace experienced in the heart makes obedience the inmost desire of the believing heart. God's people are obedient to him (Ephesians 2:10). His commandments are no longer grievous to us, but joyful (1 John 5:1-3). We should not fail to see three things about this call to obedience.

This call to obedience is issued upon the basis of God's goodness, grace, mercy and love in the experience of salvation. Even back here in the giving of the law, obedience among believing sinners was not a legal duty. It was never God saying, 'Obey me or I'll get you'. Rather, the Lord God says, 'Obey me because I have loved you and done you good'.

Before he says a word about what we are to do, Moses reminds the children of Israel of what the Lord God had done for them (1:5-3:29). He reminds them of God's wonderful, tender, fatherly care. He reminds them how God watched over them as he led them with a pillar of fire by night and the cloud by day, and guided them through the waste, howling desert. He reminds them of how God brought water out of the rock to quench their thirst in a vast and waterless desert. He reminds them of how the Lord had delivered them from their enemies again and again, how he fed them with manna that did not fail, day by day for forty years. Think about that. For forty years God fed more than two million people every day with manna that fell from heaven. What marvellous evidence of his tender concern for this people. He bought them. He brought them out. He cared for them because he loved and chose them to be his own peculiar people!

In effect Moses is saying just the same thing Paul did later. 'The love of Christ constraineth us'. Like Israel of old, we are always motivated to the obedience of faith by gratitude to our God for his great mercy, love and grace revealed and experienced in election, redemption, deliverance, and providence.

Obedience is neither more nor less than faith in and submission to the revealed will of God in holy scripture, worshipping him alone as our God and Lord (4:1-14). The obedience of faith involves a renunciation of all the imaginary gods of men (4:15-40). In this passage, Moses calls for Israel, calls for us, to worship the Lord Jehovah alone as God, because he has proved himself to us to be God alone, sovereign, solitary, and great in grace.

Moses' Exposition of the Law

Beginning in chapter four at verse 44 and going through to chapter twenty-eight, Moses gives us the law of God again. But, in these chapters he does not simply repeat what was given at Sinai, he expounds it. He tells us its meaning. Remember, this exposition was not the same as the preaching of faithful men today, but an exposition given by divine inspiration, an infallible exposition of the law.

Here Moses deals with divorce, remarriage, fornication, idolatry, witchcraft and the like. It is essential to understand that the land of Canaan, into which these people were coming, was inhabited by pagans, morally degenerate idolaters, perhaps much like the society in which we live today. They were utterly given over to lewd and obscene practices. The book of Deuteronomy shows us that God expects his people to live for his glory in the midst of a sex-crazed, sex-saturated society, among people who are idolaters and completely committed to the most vile practices. How does God inspire his people to live worthily in this situation?

In Deuteronomy 6 God shows us our weakness and inability to do the very things required in the law. In verses 20 and 21 we are reminded, 'And when thy son asketh thee in time to come, saying, What mean the testimonies, and the statutes, and the judgments, which the Lord our God hath commanded you? Then thou shalt say unto thy son, We were Pharaoh's bondmen in Egypt; and the Lord brought us out of Egypt with a mighty hand'. God shows us our weakness and His strength.

That is where we began, and that is where we are, sinners entirely dependent upon the goodness and grace of God in Christ. 'And the LORD showed signs and wonders, great and sore, upon Egypt, upon Pharaoh, and upon all his household, before our eyes: And he brought us out from thence, that he might bring us in, to give us the land which he sware unto our fathers' (vv. 22-23). He brought them out so that he might bring them into Canaan. These ceremonies are all symbols by which God constantly reminds us of what it takes to get us out of Egypt and into the promised land. That was the explanation they were to make to their sons.

Then, Moses inspires our devotion and consecration to our God and Saviour by assuring us that we belong to him exclusively, not by anything we have done but by his own work of matchless, free, and sovereign grace (Deuteronomy 7:6-8; 1 Corinthians 6:9-11, 19-20).

In this book Moses constantly reminded Israel that everything God had done for them, was doing for them, and would do for them was by grace alone. The same is true of us. 'Salvation is of the Lord' (Romans 8:28; 11:6; Ephesians 1:3-6; 2:8-9; Philippians 1:29; 2 Timothy 1:9-10).

It was not down to their obedience, but God's good pleasure, that the Children of Israel entered into the land of Canaan. 'Speak not thou in thine heart, after that the Lord thy God hath cast them out from before thee, saying, For my righteousness the Lord hath brought me in to possess this land: but for the wickedness of these nations the Lord doth drive them out from before thee. Not for thy righteousness, or for the uprightness of thine heart, dost thou go to possess their land: but for the wickedness of these nations the Lord thy God doth drive them out from before thee, and that he may perform the word which the Lord sware unto thy fathers, Abraham, Isaac, and Jacob. Understand therefore, that the Lord thy God giveth thee not this good land to possess it for thy righteousness; for thou art a stiffnecked people' (Deuteronomy 9:4-6).

After forty years of receiving grace and being taught of God Moses says, 'As long as you live in this body of flesh, you will never get to the place where you can stand on your own. Never'. Only as we know our weakness can we walk in his strength (2 Corinthians 12:2-10).

Agreement with God

At the end of this section (chapter 27 and 28) Moses commanded the children of Israel to observe a ceremony, not at an appointed time, but from time to time in the land of Canaan. It is very instructive. The children of Israel were to gather upon two mountains, Ebal and Gerizim, six tribes on one and six on the other, with the Levites (the priests) standing in the valley between the two mountains, calling out blessings and cursings. When the Levites called out a blessing in the name of God, as his priests, the tribes on one mountain would shout in unison, 'Amen!' When they called out a curse, the tribes on the other mountain would shout, 'Amen!'

I looked to see if there was any significance to the names of these mountains, and found nothing of importance. So, I have to ask, 'What is the meaning of this ceremony?' Let me show you. God requires that we be in agreement with him, in all his righteous judgments, and we shall. When a sinner is converted he is, like David, made to agree with God's justice, even against himself (Psalm 51:3-5). Believing sinners bow to God's providence and his providential judgments upon men, even their own families (1 Samuel 3:18). I do not suggest that such reconciliation is perfect, or immediate; but the Lord will cause his own to bow to his will. In eternity all men shall acknowledge both Christ's rightful dominion as Lord (Philippians 2:8-11), and the righteousness of his dominion in the exercise of his grace and in the execution of his justice (Revelation 19:11-16).

God has fixed things the way they are, leaving us in this world in this body of flesh, constantly struggling with the world, the flesh, and the devil, just as he did the children of Israel. He has done this that we might be compelled constantly to look to Christ, trusting him alone as our Saviour, and, thereby, stand forever as monuments to his matchless, free, amazing grace, 'that no flesh should glory in his presence'. I will leave it to others to explain this mystery more fully. For my part, I am content to know that this is God's wise and good purpose (Deuteronomy 29:29).

God's Appointed Deliverer

In chapter 18 (vv. 15-21) Moses spoke of Christ as that Prophet God's people would hear and obey. By the effectual teaching of Christ our Prophet we are taught of God (Titus 2:11-14). In chapter 30 (vv. 5-7) he declared that God would circumcise the hearts of all his covenant people, speaking, of course, of the new birth (Philippians 3:3; Colossians 2:12-15).

Circumcision in the Old Testament was the sign and seal of God's covenant with his people. As such, it was a type of the new birth, the seal of the Holy Spirit by which God's elect are given assurance of our interest in the covenant of grace. This is the universal teaching of the New Testament. Circumcision had no reference at all to baptism. In the last part of chapter 30 (vv. 11-20) Moses called the nation to faith in Christ, using the very language Paul used many, many years later in Romans 10:5-13. Then, in chapter 31 Moses tells the people that he must die and turns them over to Joshua, God's appointed deliverer, promising that the Lord

God would, by Joshua, bring them into the land of promise and fulfil all his covenant; and he did (Joshua 21:43-45).

What a picture this is of Christ! He is God's appointed Saviour for his elect. We are assured that he shall save them all (Matthew 1:21); and save them all he shall (Hebrews 2:14; 1 Corinthians 15:24-28). As it is written, 'He shall not fail' (Isaiah 42:4). Again, the scriptures declare, 'All Israel shall be saved'. Christ, 'the Deliverer, shall turn away ungodliness from Jacob' (Romans 11:26).

Once Moses had done this, once he put the people into Joshua's hands, he broke out into a song of praise to God (Deuteronomy 31:30-32:43) that is still being sung by the redeemed in heaven (Revelation 15:3), and blessed the people (Deuteronomy 32:44-33:29). In precisely the same way, the holy law of God, beholding us in Christ (our Joshua), pronounces upon us all the blessedness of heaven and everlasting glory, just as fully as the grace of God.

Moses' Death

Then, Moses died. When he had done everything he was sent to do, when he fulfilled all his purpose, Moses died and was never seen upon the earth again, until he was seen with Christ upon the Mount of Transfiguration. There he talked with the Lord about the death he would soon accomplish at Jerusalem. Once Joshua appeared to Israel as their deliverer, Moses' work was done. Once Christ appears in the hearts of chosen sinners as Saviour, the law's work is done. 'For Christ is the end of the law for righteousness to every one that believeth' (Romans 10:4).

Now saved sinners sing 'There is none like unto the God of Jeshurun, who rideth upon the heaven in thy help, and in his excellency on the sky. The eternal God is thy refuge, and underneath are the everlasting arms: and he shall thrust out the enemy from before thee; and shall say, Destroy them. Israel then shall dwell in safety alone: the fountain of Jacob shall be upon a land of corn and wine; also his heavens shall drop down dew. Happy art thou, O Israel: who is like unto thee, O people saved by the Lord, the shield of thy help, and who is the sword of thy excellency! and thine enemies shall be found liars unto thee; and thou shalt tread upon their high places' (Deuteronomy 33:26-29).

Chapter 6

Joshua

Jesus Saves

The book of Joshua spans the history of Israel from the death of Moses to the time of the judges. It is a great monument, not to Joshua, but to the God he served. It is a declaration of God's great, unfailing faithfulness.

By divine order Joshua assumed the government of the nation of Israel after Moses died and brought the chosen nation into the possession of all the land of Canaan, which God had promised in his covenant with Abraham.

There is much debate among men about whether these twenty-four chapters typify the believer's entrance into and possession of God's salvation in this world, or our entrance into and possession of God's salvation in heavenly glory. In my opinion, the debate is unhelpful. The book of Joshua portrays both.

Some say that the Israelites' possession of Canaan cannot portray heavenly glory because they still had to contend with and overcome their enemies in the land and that will not be true of heavenly glory. Certainly, that is true. Nevertheless, grace given on earth is glory begun; and glory given at last is grace consummated. The two cannot be separated. He who possesses God's salvation here in grace shall possess God's salvation in glory, in the world to come.

The message of this book is set before us in Joshua's very name. Joshua means 'Jehovah is Salvation'. His name in Greek is Jesus. The message of the book is 'Jesus saves' (Matthew 1:21). Throughout this book Joshua stands before us as a magnificent type of the Lord Jesus Christ as our Saviour, as Jehovah's righteous Servant; and, as such, he is held before us as an example of what it is to be God's servant in this world.

A Type of Christ

It is important to see in this book the exact fulfilment of divine prophecy: and it is delightful to see the displays Joshua sets before us of our God's faithfulness in all things. He gave the land of Canaan to Israel according to the promises he made to their fathers. We see the justice of God in punishing the Canaanites for their idolatry and sin after being warned repeatedly of his impending wrath. How wondrous are the displays of God's faithfulness in exercising tender care of his people in this book! His love to the people is also displayed as the everlasting love of the ever-faithful God. He preserved and protected the children of Israel and gave them the good land, all of it, in spite of all their murmurings, ingratitude, and unbelief. Joshua, at last, gave them rest!

Yet the primary thing to be seen here is that Joshua who gave Israel rest is a type and picture of our Lord Jesus Christ who brings the Israel of God into the blessed, true sabbath rest of faith here and of glory hereafter. We know that this is the intent of the Holy Spirit because he tells us that Joshua was typical of our Saviour (Hebrews 4:8).

We have already seen that his name, 'Joshua', marks him as a type of Christ. As Joshua was servant to Moses, Christ was made under the law, and became subject to and obedient to it in all things. As Joshua succeeded Moses, Christ succeeded the law. As Joshua gave Israel what Moses never could, God's promised covenant blessing, so Christ gives us what the law never can, God's salvation (Romans 8:2-4; Galatians 3:23-25). As Joshua was the governor of Israel and the commander of their armies, for which he was well qualified with wisdom, courage, and integrity; Christ is the King of saints, the Leader and Commander of the people. He is the Captain of our Salvation. He has fought our battles for us and won the victory for us. Like Joshua, our Lord Jesus Christ is an abundantly qualified Saviour. God poured out his Spirit upon him without measure. He was bold, courageous, mighty, and pure. Joshua was typical of our Saviour in his deeds, too. He led Israel through the river Jordan, as Christ leads us through baptism and through death. As Joshua saved Rahab and her family, so Christ saves the worst and chief of sinners. As Joshua received the Gibeonites who submitted to him, so the Lord Jesus Christ receives all who come to him. As Joshua conquered the kings of the Canaanites, so Christ has conquered all our spiritual enemies for us; sin, Satan, and the world, making us more than conquerors in him. Joshua brought the children of Israel into the land of Canaan, their rest, and divided it to them by lot. This Moses could not do. So our all-glorious Christ, and he alone, brings God's elect into the true rest, into spiritual rest here, and eternal rest hereafter. In him and by him we obtain God's salvation, all the blessings of his grace, and the inheritance of the heavenly glory.

Let's take a very brief look at this man, Joshua, as the servant of God, and see what we can glean from his life for our souls' good.

Divinely Prepared

When God is about to do something, he prepares a specific person for the work and prepares the work or place of service for that specific person. God spent eighty years preparing Moses to do a forty year work. Our Lord Jesus was prepared by thirty years' experience for the work of three. Joshua, too, like our Saviour, was prepared by God to be Israel's leader and deliverer.

Be sure you get the hint. If we are God's, if we are believers, if we are born of God, we are his servants. If the Lord God ever uses you or me for anything, he will prepare us for that specific thing. He will prepare us just as he did Joshua and just as he did the Lord Jesus as a man. How? How does God prepare his servants for his service? He has many tools that he uses for this purpose.

Suffering

The first tool by which God prepares his own to serve him is suffering and sorrow. Joshua was born into slavery in Egypt. He knew what it was to suffer. Israel's bondage in Egypt was harsh and cruel. Yet, that was part of God's preparation of Joshua for his calling (Exodus 3:7). In the kingdom of God no one ever rises to the place of much usefulness, but by suffering. Abasement is the path to exaltation and sorrow is the path to service. That was the case with Joshua. It was also the case with the Lord Jesus (Hebrews 5:8-10; 1 Peter 1:11).

The Apostle Paul exemplifies this for us in his own experience in 2 Corinthians 12:1-10. Whatever our struggles, sorrows, limitations, and losses in this world, they are according to the wise and good purpose of our heavenly Father. Suffering is God's method of preparing us and maturing us (1 Peter 4:13; 5:10).

And must it, Lord, be so?
And must thy children bear
Such various kinds of woe,
Such soul-perplexing fear?
Are these the blessings we expect?
Is this the lot of God's elect?

[Boast not, ye sons of earth,
Nor look with scornful eyes;
Above your highest mirth,
Our saddest hours we prize;
For though our cup seems filled with gall,
There's something secret sweetens all.]

How harsh soe'er the way,
Dear Saviour, still lead on,
Nor leave us till we say
"Father, thy will be done."
At most we do but taste the cup
For thou alone hast drunk it up.

Shall guilty man complain?
Shall sinful dust repine?
And what is all our pain?
How light compared with thine!
Finish, dear Lord, what is begun;
Choose thou the way, but still lead on.

                                    Joseph Hart

Submission

Another instrument God uses to prepare us for his service is submission. Grace teaches all who experience it to submit to authority. At its very core faith is surrender to the dominion of Christ, submission to divine authority (Luke 14:25-33). Joshua was prepared for his place of service by learning to submit to God's authority, the authority he had invested in Moses.

The Son of God submitted himself to the will of God in all things as a man, as our Mediator, that he might be our Saviour (Isaiah 50:5-7; Hebrews 10:5-14). In Gethsemane, at Calvary, throughout his earthly existence, our great Saviour constantly cried to the Father, from the depths of his inmost soul, 'Not my will, thy will be done ... Father, glorify thy name'. Regardless of personal cost, that was his heart's desire. Truly, he exemplified what it is to be the servant of God.

As Israel's divinely appointed prophet and leader in the wilderness, Moses represented God's authority over the nation in both civil and spiritual matters, much as divinely appointed pastors do today in spiritual things (Hebrews 13:7, 17) and civil magistrates do in civil matters (Romans 13:1-7). Joshua, following Moses' orders, honoured God, served Israel, and defeated the Amalekites (Exodus 17:13). In those days he was known as the servant of Moses, staying with his master and serving him faithfully. Men may have looked upon him as Moses' 'servant', but he was really, in the highest sense possible, God's servant (Joshua 11:15).

Patience

The Lord God prepared Joshua to be his servant and prepares us to serve him, just as he prepared our Saviour in his manhood by causing him to learn patience. We are all terribly impatient by nature. Therefore, God often fixes it so that we have no choice but to wait on him, and learn to prefer waiting on him. It had been forty years since Joshua and Caleb had gone in to spy out the land. For forty years Joshua walked with Israel through the wilderness, patiently waiting for God to give them the land. Now, he takes Israel in to possess it, after forty years of waiting in patient faith.

Blessed are those who are taught to wait on the Lord (Psalm 27:14; 37:7, 34; Proverbs 20:22; Lamentations 3:26). Sometimes I am asked by pastors and others who feel constrained to do something to correct what they perceive as a bad situation, 'What should I do about it? How should I handle this?' My answer is almost always, 'I do not know whether I could do it or not, but I am sure the best thing for you to do is nothing. Just wait on the Lord. He will work it out.' For my own part, I have never yet attempted to fix a problem that I did not make worse, or make something happen I did not soon regret.

Joshua's Character

What kind of man was Joshua? He was a man of faith, a man who believed God. That is what our Lord Jesus exemplified above all else. That is what it takes to serve him. We cannot serve him, except as we believe him. Yet, our believing him is ever the result of him giving us faith and sustaining it by his grace.

Obedient Faith

In chapter 1:8 God says to Joshua, 'This book of the law shall not depart out of thy mouth; but thou shalt meditate therein day and night, that thou mayest observe to do according to all that is written therein: for then thou shalt make thy way prosperous, and then thou shalt have good success.'

In chapter 5, before the battle of Jericho, Joshua found himself walking alone at night in front of the walls. There he was confronted by the pre-incarnate Christ, who identified himself as 'Captain of the host of the Lord'. Immediately, he fell flat on his face before the Lord. Throughout the days of his service we find Joshua praying, seeking the will of God, endeavouring to lead Israel according to the Word of the Lord in all things. After the failure at Ai, knowing that the failure arose, at least in part, from his own sinful self-confidence, we see him on his face again, crying out to the Lord in preparation for the second battle. Faithful men lead God's people by prayer and by his Word. So it was with Joshua, So it was with the Lord Jesus. So it is with God's servants today.

Courageous Faith

Four times in the first chapter the Lord commanded Joshua to be courageous. It takes courage, divinely given courage, to walk with God and serve him. Our Lord Jesus Christ was a man of enormous, perfect courage. We have every reason to be courageous, as we walk with God and seek to do his will.

General Omar Bradley defined courage as 'the capacity to perform properly even when scared half to death'. I do not doubt that Joshua was often fearful. The frequency with which the Lord encouraged him bears this out. The Lord spoke to him and said, 'Be not afraid because of them: for to morrow about this time will I deliver them up all slain before Israel: thou shalt hock their horses, and burn their chariots with fire' (11:6). Yet, he did what the Lord God called him to do. He won battle after battle.

I know that I am often fearful as I think about facing difficulties or assuming weighty responsibilities. I have often spoken to the Lord like David as I endeavoured to obey that which I knew to be his will, saying, 'What time I am afraid, I will trust in thee' (Psalm 56:3).

Obedience often involves risks and demands moral courage, particularly when that obedience involves leading others in the name of Christ. Joshua's courage involved much more than just fighting Israel's enemies, great as that was. He had to deal with sin in the camp of Israel after Achan had taken the cursed things of the Babylonians in chapter 7. With great courage, the courage of faith, he commanded Israel to stop procrastinating and take their inheritance in chapter 17. It took courage to rebuke them as he did in his final message to them in chapter 24. But he did what he knew he had to do for their good and God's glory.

Humble Faith

Joshua was God's servant, doing God's work, for God's glory. As such, he was a truly humble man. Humility, true humility, makes a man bold and courageous. True humility is the recognition that I am weak and helpless, I am nothing in myself; but I am the servant of God. As such, I lean not upon my own wisdom, strength, and ability, but his. With my God nothing is impossible (Philippians 4:13).

Joshua followed God's plans, not his own. The conquest of Canaan was not a haphazard thing. It was very carefully planned and executed. First Joshua captured the central hill country, dividing it in half. Then he led Israel in conquest of the southern territory, then the northern. He conquered the cities first, then the more rural areas. Twice he led his armies in forced marches through the night to take the enemy by surprise. All along the way we find him engaged in prayer, seeking God's direction.

There were two notable exceptions, two instances in which Joshua acted in self-confidence. He did not seek the Lord's direction before Ai, or before entering into the covenant with the Gibeonites. Both times he failed miserably. But even his own failures did not induce him to quit, to give up his responsibilities, or to abandon God's cause and his people.

When he was defeated at Ai he acknowledged the failure, sought the face of the Lord, and went back and won the battle. When he was tricked into making league with the Gibeonites, he admitted the mistake publicly, and then he made it work to the benefit of the nation and to God's glory.

There is a very important lesson here. A person's faithfulness is not to be judged by isolated acts, but by the tenor of his life. Faithful men are still only men at best. They often fall and fail. They do the best they can and keep going when they know they have erred, learning from their failures. Experience is a tough teacher. It always gives the exam first and then teaches the lesson afterward. But there is no teacher like it. Joshua turned to the Lord in his failures, found both forgiveness and renewed strength, and continued serving the Lord God and his people. How gracious God is! He not only uses a crooked stick to draw a straight line, he forgives the crooks in the stick, and gets glory to himself in using it (1 Corinthians 1:26-31).

Being the man he was, humble before God, Joshua enlisted others, and they trusted his spiritual authority as God's servant. They exemplified that which the Holy Spirit teaches believers to practice in reference to their pastors today (Hebrews 13:7, 17). Joshua could not have done the job without the thousands who followed his direction. The conquest of Canaan was not the work of one man. It was the work of all Israel, those whose names stand out in the forefront of the battles and those who served behind the lines, unseen and unknown by most.

Throughout this brief history, Joshua's troops consistently obeyed his orders, not because they were afraid of him but because they respected him and trusted him as God's servant. He commanded their respect and loyalty by his character and by his conduct before them. What a picture he is of what a pastor, or leader of any kind, ought to be. They knew that he was serving the Lord God and serving them. Joshua stands signally before us as a picture of the Lord Jesus Christ, God's righteous Servant, who commands our allegiance to him by his obedience for us (2 Corinthians 5:14). Like our Saviour, Joshua was a truly humble servant of God.

Selfless Faith

Joshua's humility made him a selfless man. I mean by that that he was a man who served others, not himself. He was not moved, motivated, or guided by his own interests, but by the interests of the church and kingdom of God. True faith is a gift of God that makes people self-denying, self-sacrificing, and self-abasing.

Joshua was concerned for Israel. He was not concerned only for their present state, but for their future. His two farewell messages recorded in chapters 23 and 24 display this fact clearly. Men who think only of what they can get today are not faithful servants of God. They are opportunists. God's servants, like Joshua, and like the Lord Jesus of whom he was a type, lay down their lives in the service of eternity bound souls for the glory of God. They are not takers, but givers. They are not users. They are used.

God Honouring Faith

Being a man of faith, a man who believed God, Joshua lived for God's glory. He sought the glory of God above all else. When he served Moses and served God under Moses (Numbers 11:28) he was very zealous in protecting Moses' honour and reputation, because Moses was God's servant. He loved and honoured Moses; but his zeal in honouring Moses arose from his love for his God and his desire to honour him.

When Israel crossed the Jordan river, he gave glory to the Lord. He said, 'Hereby ye shall know that the living God is among you' (Joshua

3:10). Once they had crossed over the Jordan, Joshua erected a monument of stones to the perpetual praise and honour of God (4:1-24), 'That all the people of the earth might know the hand of the Lord, that it is mighty: that ye might fear the Lord your God forever'. Throughout the book of Joshua he repeatedly gave God the glory for everything that happened. He never promoted himself or sought honour for himself. Joshua was God's servant. It was the Lord who fought for them, the Lord who conquered their enemies, the Lord who gave the land to the people. Joshua wanted the name of the Lord to be magnified in all the earth.

In this he was again representative of our Lord Jesus Christ. Our Saviour's unceasing prayer was, 'Father, glorify thy name'. If you and I are truly God's servants, that is the unceasing cry of our hearts as well.

The Message

The message of these twenty-four chapters is very clear, 'Jesus saves!' As Joshua brought Israel into the land of Canaan and gave them rest, so the Lord Jesus Christ will save his people (Matthew 1:21; Hebrews 4:1-11). There is a people in this world who are his people. They are his by his own eternal, sovereign choice. They are a people to whom God has from eternity given all the blessedness of heaven and eternal glory as a covenant promise (Ephesians 1:3-5). Christ shall save them. It is his responsibility and his good pleasure to save them. He shall bring them all into the possession of their inheritance for the glory of God.

Lessons

The book of Joshua teaches us much about our great God as he is revealed in the person and work of his dear Son, the Lord Jesus Christ. Joshua is the central figure in this book. But the book is not about Joshua, or even the greatness of his faith. It is really about Christ and the greatness of his grace and salvation. That is the key to understanding the things recorded in these chapters.

God our Father in Christ is a covenant keeping God. He is the Lord our God distinctly. Yes, he is God over all, 'the Lord of all the earth' (3:11); but he is our God, the God of his people Israel, distinctly. He claims us as his own and declares himself to be ours. He takes a personal interest in us and keeps his covenant forever.

Our great God keeps his promises. He is always faithful to his Word. Every promise he made to Israel in his covenant with Abraham and verified to Isaac and Jacob (Genesis 13:15; 15:18; 26:3; 28:4, 13), he fulfilled (Joshua 21:43-45; 23:14). Those five verses in Joshua 21:43-45 and 23:14,15 alone ought to be sufficient to end all the ranting of modern prophecy gurus who imagine that God has not yet fulfilled his promises to Israel. Joshua declared, by divine inspiration, 'not one thing hath failed of all the good things which the Lord your God spake concerning you'.

How gracious, merciful, and forgiving God is! He who forgave the harlot Rahab, saving her and her house because of the blood of Christ represented in the scarlet cord she hung out her window, still forgives sinners freely through the blood of his dear Son (Ephesians 1:6).

Many look upon the slaughter of the Canaanites by the command of God as being contrary to what I have just said about God's free forgiveness of sin. The question is often raised, 'How can a good, gracious, forgiving God kill people and send them to hell?'

The fact is, God's goodness, justice, and truth demand the punishment of sin. Yet, the goodness and grace of God is seen throughout the book of Joshua. It was the goodness of God that delayed his judgment for centuries before bringing Israel into the land, giving the inhabitants of the land space for repentance. Long before Joshua conquered Canaan, the Lord God sent Abraham into the land as a missionary. There Abraham walked with God, worshipped him, and bore witness to him; but the Canaanites preferred their idols to the God of Abraham.

Before Israel came over Jordan and took Jericho, the Lord graciously sent his reputation ahead of them, provoking fear in the Canaanites. As a result of the gospel being brought into Canaan, by some means or other, Rahab and her family and the entire city of Gibeon believed God.

God's grace is seen in his judgment as well. In wrath he remembers mercy. It was the goodness of God that wiped out that hopelessly decadent, idolatrous society so that another generation could grow up in a land where God was worshiped and honoured. Yes, the Lord God graciously and wisely raises up entire nations and treads down entire nations for the salvation of his elect (Isaiah 43:1-7).

Chapter 7

Judges

Enemies Within

The most shocking thing I discovered as a young believer, shortly after God saved me, was the fact that the raging monster of sin in my heart had not been slain, or even tamed. It is a painful lesson I am learning every day. I am every day made increasingly aware of the depths of my depravity. Yet, I know that I have not even begun to discover the hideous enormity of my sinfulness!

The Flesh and The Spirit

The fact is, when God saves a sinner, he does not change his old nature. He gives us a new nature by his grace. But he does not change the flesh. Flesh is still flesh and our flesh, our old, Adamic nature, is our worst enemy. Believers are a people at war, constant, unceasing war with themselves. 'The flesh lusteth against the spirit and the spirit against the flesh: and these are contrary the one to the other: so that ye cannot do the things that ye would' (Galatians 5:17).

We are forgiven of all sin in Christ. We are accepted in him, justified, sanctified, and holy before God by the blood and righteousness of our all-glorious Christ. We can honestly say with John, 'We love him because he first loved us.' We want, in all things, to honour our God and Saviour. We delight in the law of God in the very core of our beings. Yet, when we would do good, evil is present.

Let me be understood. There is no excuse for our sin. Nor do we make
the grace of God a cloak for our unrighteousness. The evil that is in us
and done by us is just as inexcusable as the evil which is in and done by
the unbeliever. John Newton described this experience clearly and
beautifully in one of his hymns.

> I asked the Lord that I might grow
> In faith, and love, and every grace;
> Might more of his salvation know,
> And seek more earnestly his face.
>
> ['Twas he who taught me thus to pray,
> And he, I trust, has answered prayer;
> But it has been in such a way
> As almost drove me to despair.]
>
> I hoped that in some favoured hour,
> At once he'd answer my request;
> And, by his love's constraining power,
> Subdue my sins, and give me rest.
>
> Instead of this, he made me feel
> The hidden evils of my heart,
> And let the angry powers of hell
> Assault my soul in every part.
>
> Yea, more, with his own hand he seemed
> Intent to aggravate my woe;
> Crossed all the fair designs I schemed,
> Blasted my gourds, and laid me low.
>
> 'Lord, why is this?' I trembling cried;
> 'Wilt thou pursue thy worm to death?'
> ''Tis in this way', the Lord replied,
> 'I answer prayer for grace and faith'.
>
> 'These inward trials I employ,
> From self and pride to set thee free;
> And break thy schemes of earthly joy,
> That thou mayest seek thy all in me'.

This warfare between the flesh and the spirit in the experience of God's elect is what the book of Judges is all about.

Joshua and Judges

In the book of Joshua the land of Canaan and Israel's possession of it is primarily typical of the saints' everlasting rest in heaven. But in the book of Judges the land of Canaan is set before us as a typical representation of our experience of God's grace in this world. This world is our 'Bochim', our valley of weeping. Joshua is primarily a declaration of the ultimate triumph of grace. But Judges is a book about failure, defeat, and shame: the failure, defeat, and shame we experience in this world because of our own sin, rebellion and unbelief.

As you read the book of Judges, if you are like me, you cannot avoid thinking, 'This book is not like any other book in the Bible'. You see a man named Ehud, sent of God to deliver a message to a fat King named Eglon, and the message was a long dagger shoved into his belly. A woman named Jael drives a tent stake through the temples of a man named Sisera, and then cuts off his head. Gideon has a army of 32,000 ready to go to war. But God requires him to whittle the army down to 300 men who are scared to death of their own shadows; and you think, 'That's not real smart'. You are astonished by Jephthah's sacrifice of his daughter, and very disappointed in the weakness of Samson. Then, you find yourself shocked by the Levite cutting his wife's raped body into twelve pieces and sending it to the twelve tribes of Israel.

We read of Israel, God's covenant people, the people he brought out of Egypt by the hand of Moses and to whom he gave the land of Canaan by covenant promise as their inheritance forever by the hand of Joshua, rebelling against God, sinking into idolatry, overcome by enemy after enemy, becoming more and more degraded. In the first verse of chapter one, they asked the Lord, 'Who shall go up for us against the Canaanites, to fight against them?' But, by the time we get to the end of the book (20:18), we see them asking the Lord to lead them as they go up to war against their own brethren in the tribe of Benjamin! How can we understand this book? What happened to these people for whom the Lord God had done so much? The answer to that question is found in the very last verse of the last chapter. 'In those days there was no king in Israel: every man did that which was right in his own eyes' (21:25).

This explanation of Israel's great failure and God's providential judgments upon them is given four times in these twenty-one chapters (17:6; 18:1; 19:1; 21:25). Notice that the Lord does not say, 'Every man did what was wrong in his own eyes', but 'that which was right in his own eyes'. They endeavoured to live in the land of Canaan and endeavoured to serve God being governed by their own wisdom rather than God's revelation. They refused the counsel of wisdom and followed the counsel of folly. Rather than trusting the Lord, they leaned unto their own understanding (Proverbs 3:5-6).

A People Who Knew Not The Lord

As long as Joshua lived, the nation of Israel served the Lord. They continued to do so until another generation arose after them 'which knew not the Lord, nor yet the works which he had done for Israel' (2:10). If you carefully read the first two chapters of Judges, you will see that these two chapters explain the rest of the book.

In chapter one we see that though the Lord specifically commanded the children of Israel to drive out all the inhabitants of the land of Canaan, they chose on several occasions not to do so completely. Instead, they subdued them and made a league with them. In chapter two the Lord explains why he left Israel's enemies in the land.

'And an angel of the LORD came up from Gilgal to Bochim, and said, I made you to go up out of Egypt, and have brought you unto the land which I sware unto your fathers; and I said, I will never break my covenant with you. And ye shall make no league with the inhabitants of this land; ye shall throw down their altars: but ye have not obeyed my voice: why have ye done this? Wherefore I also said, I will not drive them out from before you; but they shall be as thorns in your sides, and their gods shall be a snare unto you. And it came to pass, when the angel of the LORD spake these words unto all the children of Israel, that the people lifted up their voice, and wept. And they called the name of that place Bochim: and they sacrificed there unto the LORD' (Judges 2:1-5).

You would think they had learned from their own experience and would do better in the future; but no. We read in verses 11-15 ...

'And the children of Israel did evil in the sight of the LORD, and served Baalim: And they forsook the LORD God of their fathers, which brought them out of the land of Egypt, and followed other gods, of the gods of the people that were round about them, and bowed themselves unto them, and provoked the LORD to anger. And they forsook the LORD, and served Baal and Ashtaroth. And the anger of the LORD was hot against Israel, and he delivered them into the hands of spoilers that spoiled them, and he sold them into the hands of their enemies round about, so that they could not any longer stand before their enemies. Whithersoever they went out, the hand of the LORD was against them for evil, as the LORD had said, and as the LORD had sworn unto them: and they were greatly distressed'.

Then we read of God's great faithfulness to his covenant people in verse sixteen. 'Nevertheless the LORD raised up judges, which delivered them out of the hand of those that spoiled them'. How gracious, how good, how merciful our great God is! 'Like as a father pitieth his children, so the Lord pitieth them that fear him. For he knoweth our frame; he remembereth that we are dust' (Psalm 103:13-14). Even when he displays his great displeasure against the sins of his people, his purpose is to do them good (Romans 8:28; Hebrews 12:5-13). He tells us plainly that that was the reason he refused to hastily drive out the inhabitants of the land of Canaan. He said,

'Because that this people hath transgressed my covenant which I commanded their fathers, and have not hearkened unto my voice; I also will not henceforth drive out any from before them of the nations which Joshua left when he died: That through them I may prove Israel, whether they will keep the way of the LORD to walk therein, as their fathers did keep it, or not. Therefore the LORD left those nations, without driving them out hastily; neither delivered he them into the hand of Joshua' (Judges 2:20-23).

The Time

These twenty-one chapters cover a period of 229-230 years. But it is a mistake to look at the book of Judges as the complete record of that period of Israel's history known as the time of the Judges. The last judge in Israel was not Samson, but Samuel. Though the book of Judges ends with Israel in a sad, sad condition, brought into utter shame and degradation by her own sin, it ought to always be read in close connection with both Joshua and Ruth. The story of Ruth and Boaz takes place during this time. As you know, the book of Ruth is all about Christ our Kinsman Redeemer. The book of Joshua shows us what God is going to do with us. He is going to bring us into the land of glorious rest, the heavenly Canaan. The book of Judges shows us in our present condition, warring with enemies within, constantly needing grace. The book of Ruth shows us our great Judge (Deliverer), the Lord Jesus Christ (portrayed in Boaz), who has redeemed our inheritance for us, prevailed over all our enemies, and will at last drive them all out of the land and give us glorious rest in the Land of Promise. He has promised, 'I will do to thee all that thou requirest' (Ruth 3:11).

The Message

What is the message of this book? Why was it written? Why does the Lord here give us the sordid details of Israel's constant failure, defeat, and sin? We are told plainly that these things were written for our learning (Romans 15:4; 1 Corinthians 10:10-11).

As I read the things recorded in these chapters, the circumstances, the failures, the stubbornness, the rebellion, the sin, the battles, the sorrows, and the shamefulness of Israel, it appears as though I am reading a detailed biography of my own experience.

It is as obvious as the noonday sun that the nation of Israel, though delivered from Egypt and living in the possession of Canaan, could not have survived one day in that land except for this fact, God kept them. There you have the message of the book of Judges. Though the Lord God has saved us by his almighty grace, you and I are so weak, so sinful, so unbelieving, so stubbornly rebellious that we would not last a second if left to ourselves.

We continue in grace only because our great, gracious, glorious God keeps us in grace. We persevere in faith because he perseveres in grace. We continue to walk in the way because he holds us in the way. We continue to hold him because he holds us.

The Cycle of our Lives

I encourage you to read the entire book of Judges at one sitting. Its twenty-one chapters are full of personal lessons and applications. You will see that it clearly displays the constant cycle of our lives in this world as men and women saved by the grace of God.

Rest

The book begins with Israel in the land of rest. They have, at last, come into the possession of the land by the hand of Joshua. For forty years they had no rest. Then Moses died and Joshua gave them rest.

That is where you and I began this thing we call salvation. The Lord Jesus Christ, our great Joshua, brought us into the blessed possession of grace, salvation, and eternal life, and gave us rest. He called us to rest in him and graciously forced us to do so (Matthew 11:28-30; Psalm 65:4). There is no rest like the rest of faith in Christ. This is our sabbath. We rest in Christ, trusting his righteousness as our only righteousness before God, his redemption as our only atonement for sin, and his rule, his universal dominion and disposition of all things in providence, for our souls' good, as our great King.

Rebellion

No sooner did Israel take possession of the land than they rebelled against the Lord. God told them to drive out the inhabitants of the land; but they chose to do what was right in their own eyes, and drove out most of the inhabitants. Some they could not drive out because they were just too strong (1:18-19). Others they chose not to drive out because they thought they could handle them without great difficulty (1:20-36).

When Israel came to some of these places, instead of going to war against them, they went in and investigated the towns. When the place did not seem particularly dangerous and the people seemed to be people they could get along with, or use to their advantage, they spared them and built a town beside them. They allowed them, their gods, and their 'useful' possessions and talents to stay in the land. Oh, they kept an eye on them; but they did not drive them out of the land. They did what was right in their own eyes.

Have you done that? When God saved you, you quit drinking, smoking, dancing, wearing boots to bed, howling at the moon, eating liver for breakfast on Fridays, and all those other things those bad people out in the world do. Those other things, like envy, gossip, malice, anger, wrath, and covetousness, we do not bother with too much. We vainly imagine that we are so much better than we used to be that we do not need to worry about those things with which weaker people have to be concerned. We think, 'These are just small, trivial matters. Surely, the Lord is not going to make an issue out of these'. We leave those inward things no one else sees (at least not all the time) alone. We even protect them. 'After all, I am of German stock. All Germans are a little stubborn'. Or 'I am only human'. Or 'My whole family is like this. This is just the way I am; and you just have to accept me the way I am.'

That is exactly what Israel did. We might suppose that since Baal and Ashtaroth were the male and female gods of fertility, Israel's decline into idolatry had something to do with their crops. They had been farmers and herdsmen for four hundred years in Egypt. There they were accustomed to raising their crops in well-irrigated, lush fields. Things were different in Canaan. The land was terribly dry. They did not know how to use such land. Perhaps their first crops were puny excuses for crops. But the Canaanites had great harvests. The Jews asked them, 'What is your secret?' 'It is very simple. We worship the gods of fertility, and they bless our crops. If you want to make it here, you will have to acknowledge our gods and adjust to our customs.' The Israelites give in. Who can argue with obvious success or deny such obvious logic?

Of course, the Canaanites would also have told them how to plant their crops, when to plant them, where to plant them, how to fertilize the ground, and how to get the moisture needed to the fields. The next spring, sure enough, after they had bowed down to the gods of the Canaanites, they found the crops were wonderful.

Whatever the case may have been, the gods of the Canaanites became a snare to the children of Israel (Judges 2:30); and Israel abandoned the worship of Jehovah. Oh, they never said so. They did not cease to include God's name and ordinances in their religion. They just incorporated the worship of Baal, Ashtaroth, and the gods of the land into the worship of Jehovah. But God says, 'They forsook the Lord God of their fathers and followed other gods'.

These fertility gods were just that, sex gods, and worshipping them involved, not only bowing down before dumb idols that could not speak, see, act, or think, but also vile immorality. Israel's religion had become nothing but the practice of whoredom (literally and spiritually) in the name of God!

Retribution

Israel's rebellion brought divine retribution. As it was with David later (2 Samuel 11:26-12:18), the Lord God ever shows his displeasure with sin, especially with his own people.

'And they forsook the LORD God of their fathers, which brought them out of the land of Egypt, and followed other gods, of the gods of the people that were round about them, and bowed themselves unto them, and provoked the LORD to anger. And they forsook the LORD, and served Baal and Ashtaroth. And the anger of the LORD was hot against Israel, and he delivered them into the hands of spoilers that spoiled them, and he sold them into the hands of their enemies round about, so that they could not any longer stand before their enemies. Whithersoever they went out, the hand of the LORD was against them for evil, as the LORD had said, and as the LORD had sworn unto them: and they were greatly distressed' (Judges 2:12-15)

Sin always brings retribution. I do not mean that God punishes his own for sin in a way of exacting justice and satisfaction. Thank God, he does not! He punished our sins in Christ and found satisfaction for our sins in the sacrifice of his Son (Romans 8:1). But the Lord God does chasten his children, correcting sin in us, because he loves us (Hebrews 12:5-16). William Cowper described this great, gracious work of our heavenly Father beautifully:

'Tis my happiness below
Not to live without the cross,
But the Saviour's power to know,
Sanctifying every loss.

Trials must and will befall
But with humble faith to see
Love inscribed upon them all
This is happiness to me.

God in Israel sows the seeds
Of affliction, pain, and toil:
These spring up and choke the weeds
That would else o'er spread the soil.

Trials make the promise sweet,
Trials give new life to prayer,
Trials bring me to His feet,
Lay me low and keep me there.

Did I meet no trials here,
No chastisements by the way,
Might I not with reason fear
I should prove a castaway?

Bastards may escape the rod,
Sunk in earthly, vain delight;
But the true born child of God
Must not, would not, if he might.

Restoration

God's chastening is followed by and results in restoration. Blessed be his name, our great God is ever gracious to his people!

'Nevertheless the LORD raised up Judges, which delivered them out of the hand of those that spoiled them. And yet they would not hearken unto their Judges, but they went a whoring after other gods, and bowed themselves them: they turned quickly out of the way which their fathers walked in, obeying the commandments of the LORD; but they did not so. And when the LORD raised them up judges, then the LORD was with the judge, and delivered them out of the hand of their enemies all the days of the judge: for it repented the LORD because of their groanings by reason of them that oppressed them and vexed them' (Judges 2:16-18).

These judges, twelve are named in these chapters, eleven men and one woman, Deborah, were all typical of our Lord Jesus Christ. They were raised up by God to deliver or save his people from their enemies. All were Saviours of Israel. All acted as kings. Samuel was a prophet. Eli was a priest. The Lord Jesus Christ is our unfailing, ever faithful Saviour, our Prophet, our Priest, and our King! He will deliver and save us from all our enemies.

The Lord God will not leave us to ourselves, and he will not leave us alone. He will not leave us; and he will not let us leave him. His covenant he will not break (Jeremiah 32:40; Psalm 89:28-37; 2 Timothy 2:13, 19; 1 John 3:20).

Rebellion

The very next thing we see is more rebellion.

'And it came to pass, when the judge was dead, that they returned, and corrupted themselves more than their fathers, in following other gods to serve them, and to bow down unto them; they ceased not from their own doings, nor from their stubborn way' (Judges 2:19).

When we get to the end of the book that is just where we find Israel. They just get worse and worse. They sink lower, and lower. Flesh is always just flesh, rotting, decaying flesh!

I blush with shame and weep bitterly to confess it, but confess it I must, my name is Israel. This is my life's story (Romans 7:14-23). But, blessed be God, the story is not over yet. My Boaz has promised that he will do all that my soul requires. I have a Saviour, a Deliverer, a Redeemer. By grace I have Christ.

Reason

Why did the Lord do this? Why does he leave us here in this valley of weeping with all these inward enemies? To prove us and to teach us.

'I also will not henceforth drive out any from before them of the nations which Joshua left when he died: That through them I may prove Israel, whether they will keep the way of the LORD to walk therein, as their fathers did keep it, or not. Therefore the LORD left those nations, without driving them out hastily; neither delivered he them into the hand of Joshua' (Judges 2:21-23).

> These inward trials I employ,
> From self and pride to set thee free;
> And break thy schemes of earthly joy,
> That thou mayest seek thy all in me.

The Lord our God could, were it his purpose to do so, completely deliver us from sin in our nature, even while we live in this world; but he has chosen not to do so. I will not attempt to explain his reasons. I simply do not know. He has chosen not to reveal them in his Word. But I do know that while we live in this body of flesh, as long as we are in this present state, he would have us constantly aware of the fact of our personal weakness. As he left the Canaanites in the land to be thorns in the side of his people (Judges 2:3), so he has left these thorns in our flesh (2 Corinthians 12:7), that we might ever be forced to look to Christ alone for everything, confessing that we have no righteousness but his, no strength but his, no atonement, no hope, no acceptance with God but that which is found in our all-glorious, all-sufficient Saviour (1 John 1:7-2:2). That being the case, we ought to ever be kind, forgiving, and patient with one another (Galatians 6:1-2).

Our great God and Saviour will not hastily drive out these enemies; but he will drive them out altogether. When our Saviour brings us into the land of rest, there will be no more sin. Then, and then alone, our warfare will be over.

Chapter 8

Ruth

Christ Our Kinsman Redeemer

We will begin our study in the book of Ruth at chapter three, verse nine, where Boaz said to Ruth, 'Who art thou? And she answered, I am Ruth thine handmaid: spread therefore thy skirt over thine handmaid; for thou art a near kinsman'.

This book, like all the Old Testament scriptures, speaks of Christ our Redeemer, that Judge who saves his people, the One of whom all the other judges were typical. The subject of this book is redemption. The whole book is a picture of our redemption by Christ, our kinsman Redeemer. The key word, used repeatedly in these four chapters, is 'kinsman' (2:1, 20; 3:9, 12; 4:6, 14). The kinsman is the one who has the right to redeem.

The law of the kinsman Redeemer was given in Leviticus 25:25. 'If thy brother be waxen poor, and hath sold away some of his possession, and if any of his kin come to redeem it, then shall he redeem that which his brother sold'. That prophetic law was given to be a picture of Christ and was fulfilled by him. Our father Adam sold us into bondage and sin; but Christ, our kinsman Redeemer, bought us and brought us into liberty, righteousness, and life (Romans 5:19).

The book of Ruth is a beautiful picture of the work of our Lord Jesus Christ as our kinsman Redeemer. It shows us both our need of a kinsman Redeemer and the way we may obtain the blessings of redemption.

Primary Characters

There are some people named in these four chapters, who are the primary characters in the book. Their names are meaningful and important. There was a certain man of Israel called Elimelech of Bethlehem-Judah in the days of the Judges. Elimelech means 'God is King'. Yet, when famine came to Israel, Elimelech took his wife, Naomi, and their two sons, Mahlon and Chilion, and went down into Moab, a heathen country where God was neither known nor worshipped. Naomi means 'sweet and pleasant'. Mahlon means 'weakness'. Chilion means 'consumption'. Orpah means 'stiff-necked and declining'. Ruth means 'companion'.

Elimelech left Israel in weakness and was consumed in Moab. He died in Moab and left his wife and two sons. His two sons married Moabite women, lived with them for ten years, and then they died. Now poor and broken-hearted, Naomi determined to go back to Bethlehem. She told her daughters-in-law to remain with their own people. Orpah did just that. She went back to her people and her gods; but not Ruth. She was 'steadfastly minded to go with' Naomi (Ruth 1:16-17). Naomi and Ruth returned to the land of Israel and to the people of God at the beginning of the harvest season.

Our Ruin

Here is a picture of our ruin by the fall of Adam. When Naomi came back to Bethlehem, everyone gathered around her, looked at her with astonishment, and said, 'Is this Naomi?' To which she replied, 'Do not call me Naomi (sweet and pleasant); but call me Mara (bitter) because God hath dealt bitterly with me!' She went out young, happy, beautiful, and full; but she came back old, bitter, worn, weary, poor, and empty. That is a picture of the ravages of sin and a picture of us by nature!

Looking at our sinful human race, we might ask of fallen man, 'Is this Adam?' Can these poor, dying, corrupt creatures called men be the sons of Adam, who was created in the image of God? (Romans 5:12; 3:10-19). Man was created a prince, but now he is a pauper. He who was created a king in the garden is now just a beggar. Man who was created in pleasantness has fallen into bitterness. Adam was given fulness; but his sons are emptiness. In the beginning the race was blessed; but now Adam's fallen race is cursed and condemned.

Christ's Love

Here too is a picture of Christ's free love to sinners. Naomi and Ruth came to Bethlehem at the beginning of the harvest season. They were poor. Their allotted inheritance in Israel was gone. They had no one to support them and take care of them. But it was required, by God's law in Israel, that the poor people be allowed to follow the reapers through the fields and glean, or pick up what the reapers left behind (Leviticus 19:9-10; Deuteronomy 24:19).

Ruth knew that there was a kinsman who could redeem her. Boaz was a kinsman. He was a mighty man, a leader in the community and a man of great wealth. She went out into the fields to glean with the poor, hoping she might find grace in the eyes of her kinsman. If it were possible for her to have her inheritance with God's people redeemed, Ruth was not willing to perish in poverty.

She went to the place where she was most likely to meet her kinsman, with the hope that he might be gracious to her. As Ruth went to the harvest fields, where she had the greatest prospect of meeting Boaz, so sinners in need of mercy are wise to meet with God's people in the house of worship. There, Christ walks with his brethren and reveals himself to his chosen (Matthew 18:20; Revelation 2:1).

Boaz spotted Ruth and had compassion on her. There were many poor widows gleaning in the fields. But Boaz set his eyes upon Ruth, took notice of Ruth, and had compassion on Ruth before she even knew who he was. Even so, the Lord Jesus Christ took notice of us, loved us, and chose us before the world was made. He loved us freely from eternity. Let men talk as they may about universal benevolence, God's love for his elect is a special, sovereign, distinguishing love (Isaiah 43:3-4).

Divine Providence

Now we have a beautiful picture of God's special providence. As the fields of Bethlehem belonged to Boaz, so this world belongs to the Lord Jesus Christ. It is his by design, by decree, and by his death (Colossians 1:16-17; John 3:35; 17:2; Romans 14:9).

As Ruth's 'hap was to light on a part of the field belonging to Boaz', God graciously brings each of his elect to the place where he will be gracious to them. As Boaz commanded his young men not to touch Ruth, so the Lord Jesus Christ has given commandment to all creation, saying, 'touch not mine anointed'.

Boaz commanded his men to let fall 'handfuls of purpose' for Ruth, so our Saviour takes care to provide for his elect, even throughout the days of their rebellion and unbelief (Hosea 2:8). Indeed, his angels were created to be ministering spirits to those whom he has chosen to be heirs of his salvation (Hebrews 1:14).

According to the law of God given to Israel (Leviticus 25:25), if a man sold his inheritance and he had a near kinsman who was willing and able to do so, the kinsman could buy back his brother's lost inheritance. Boaz had given Naomi and Ruth a reason to hope that he might be willing to redeem them. In chapter 3, Naomi tells Ruth what she must do. She told her to go to the threshing floor where Boaz, the near kinsman, would be. She told her to humble herself, lie down at his feet, and spend the night there, 'And he will tell thee what thou shalt do'. Without pride or self-importance, Ruth did what Naomi told her to do.

True Repentance

In these verses we see a picture of true repentance. Ruth marked the place where Boaz would be and went there. She came in softly and laid herself at his feet. The sinner who needs mercy will always be found at the feet of his Lord (Matthew 8:1-2; 15:21-28; Luke 7:37-38; 10:39). Many are too proud to bow as broken, humbled beggars at the feet of Christ. But this woman risked being scandalized. She risked losing the only thing she had left, her name, that she might obtain Boaz's favour.

Ruth plainly told Boaz what she wanted. In essence, she said, 'Take me. I am your handmaid. Take me for your wife'. Boaz said, 'I will do all that thou requirest'. 'But', he continued, 'there is a kinsman nearer than me. He must be dealt with first'. Even so, Christ will be merciful. Christ will save. But he could never save anyone until first he had dealt with the law and justice of God. God must be just, even in (especially in) justifying sinners (Romans 3:24-26).

Our Kinsman Redeemer

Then comes the last great picture of this book. Boaz is set before us here as a picture of Christ as our kinsman Redeemer. Boaz went up to the gate of the city where men transacted business and met Ruth's nearer kinsman. He said, 'You have first claim upon Elimelech's field. If you want it, buy it'. So the man said, 'I'll buy it!' Then Boaz said, 'If you buy the field, you must also marry Ruth, his daughter-in-law'. Then the man said to Boaz, 'I cannot do that, lest I mar my own inheritance. You redeem her'. So Boaz bought the field and married Ruth.

The Lord Jesus Christ is our kinsman Redeemer. He is our kinsman by his incarnation (2 Corinthians 8:9). He is a great and mighty kinsman, for he is himself God (Colossians 2:9). He is a kinsman of great wealth. All things are his. All the fulness of grace and glory is in him. As Boaz loved Ruth, so Christ Jesus loved us without a cause, freely. 'We love him, because he first loved us!' He says, 'I have loved thee, with an everlasting love ... I have drawn thee with the cords of love'. As Boaz promised to redeem Ruth, so the Son of God promised to redeem us in the covenant of grace before the world began (Hebrews 7:22). However, as with Ruth, there was one who had first claim upon us. The law of God held us as its captors (Job 9:2; 25:4-6). But the law of God says, 'I cannot redeem the fallen one, lest I mar my righteousness'. The law has claim upon us, but not the ability to redeem us. The law is our kinsman condemner, but could never be our deliverer (Romans 3:19-20).

The Lord Jesus willingly paid the price of our redemption, the price demanded by the justice of God. By his life of obedience, he magnified the law and made it honourable, and brought in everlasting righteousness for his people. By his sin-atoning death, he fully satisfied the wrath and justice of God as our Substitute.

As Boaz took Ruth to be his wife, so the Lord Jesus has taken chosen sinners to be his bride. Thank God, he has not left us without a kinsman. Christ is the Restorer of our lives. He is the Nourisher of our old age. Like Boaz, our Lord Jesus will not rest until he has 'finished the thing'. 'Faithful is he that calleth you, who also will do it'. 'He which hath begun a good work in you will perform it'. 'He is able to keep you from falling' and he will. Christ will at last present you who are his holy, unblameable, and unreproveable bride before the presence of his glory.

> O love surpassing knowledge,
> O grace so full and free!
> I know that Jesus loves me,
> And that's enough for me!
>
> O wonderful salvation,
> From sin Christ set me free!
> I feel the sweet assurance,
> And that's enough for me!
>
> O blood of Christ so precious,
> Poured out at Calvary!
> I feel its cleansing power,
> And that's enough for me!

Ruth, the pagan Moabitess, became the wife of Boaz, heir to all his vast estate, great-grandmother of king David, and was placed in the direct lineage of Christ. Even so, all who trust him are married to Christ, heirs of God and joint-heirs with Christ, and are made to be the sons and daughters of God almighty. All by grace! All through Christ our kinsman Redeemer!

Chapter 9

1 Samuel

Christ Our Great Saviour and King

The book of 1 Samuel covers a period of about 115 years. It takes us from the birth of Samuel, the last of the judges, to the death of their first king, Saul. The Children of Israel had been under the direct government of God himself throughout their history. The Lord God himself was their King. For almost 300 years the Lord God had administered his rule as King in Israel through the judges he raised up to deliver them.

But all the nations around them had kings in royal attire, sitting on splendorous thrones. When Samuel was an old man, after faithfully serving the nation as God's prophet and their judge, the men of Israel came to him and said, 'We want to be like these other nations'. 'Give us a king to judge us ... Make us a king to judge us like all the nations'. Samuel was, of course, heart broken. After faithfully serving their souls his entire life, they turned on him and rejected him. That is enough to break any man's heart. But, they had, in fact, turned on God and rejected him. Therefore the Lord said to Samuel ...

'Hearken unto the voice of the people in all that they say unto thee: for they have not rejected thee, but they have rejected me, that I should not reign over them. According to all the works which they have done since the day that I brought them up out of Egypt even unto this day, wherewith they have forsaken me, and served other gods, so do they also unto thee. Now therefore hearken unto their voice: howbeit yet protest solemnly unto them, and show them the manner of the king that shall reign over them. And Samuel told all the words of the LORD unto the people that asked of him a king' (1 Samuel 8:7-10).

Samuel told them exactly the kind of man their king would be, self-serving, cruel, abusive, and destructive. 'Nevertheless the people refused to obey the voice of Samuel; and they said, Nay; but we will have a king over us; That we also may be like all the nations; and that our king may judge us, and go out before us, and fight our battles'.

How often have you wanted something, or wanted something to happen so bad you could taste it, so bad that you just felt you had to have it? You prayed for it, prayed for it, and prayed for it. Then the Lord gave it to you; and you wished you had never received it or ever heard of it. There is a saying, 'Be careful what you wish for'. God often gives us what we think we want, and then makes us live with the consequences for a long, long time. The fact is, we never know what is best for us, and never know how to pray as we ought (Romans 8:26).

Many years ago, William Evans told a story about his daughter. His little girl, who was about eight years old, came home from school and said, 'Daddy, I want to get some ball bearing skates. All the other children have ball bearing skates and that is what I want'. He said, 'But you have a pair of skates'. She replied, 'Yes, I know Daddy, but they are not ball bearing skates. They are roller bearing skates. They won't go as fast as the others will'.

Mr Evans was a preacher. His income was limited. So he said, 'Well, sweetheart, I'm afraid you will have to make do with the roller bearing skates. We simply cannot afford to buy any others right now'. But she would not give up. The next night when he came home from his work, there was a little note at his place on the table. It said. 'Dear Daddy, I still want the ball bearing skates'. When he went to bed that night there was another note pinned to his pillow. It said, 'Daddy, would you please buy me some ball bearing skates?'

Well, he did the same thing you or I might have done. He scraped up the money and got those ball bearing skates. When he gave them to her, she was elated. She threw her arms around his neck and hugged him and kissed him and thanked him. Then she put on those great, new ball bearing skates like all the other children had and took off, out the gate, down the sidewalk, and around the corner. That was the last time they ever saw her alive and well. As she went around the corner, she could not manoeuvre the new skates. She slipped and fell down, hitting her head against the sidewalk. They brought her home in a coma. She died at the hospital that night. 'Since then', Mr Evans said, 'when I want something of God and it seems as though he is not willing that I should have it, but I keep crying out for it, the Spirit of God reminds me, "Are you asking for ball bearing skates?"'

God often gives us what we want, and then makes us live with the consequences for a long, long time. This is what happened in Israel. How often we have experienced it in our own lives. 'Stand thou still a while, that I may show thee the word of God'.

Three Principle Characters

There are three principle characters in this book: Samuel, Saul and David. This piece of Israel's history begins with the birth of Samuel and gives us a pretty detailed description of his life and ministry. He was born in a house where God was honoured. He was a gift of God to his mother, Hannah, who dedicated him to the Lord before he was born. As soon as he was weaned, Hannah brought her boy to the house of God and gave him to the Lord. Soon, the Lord revealed himself to Samuel and made him a prophet. A faithful prophet he was until the day of his death.

Chapters 11-31 describe the sad, sad life and rule of Saul, Israel's first king. Saul was the gift of God's judgment to Israel. They wanted to be like all the other nations. They demanded a king. So God gave them Saul.

David comes on the scene in chapter 16. His noble character and his greatness is set before us and for a while runs parallel with Saul's life. David was the man after God's own heart, the man whom God chose to replace Saul as king over Israel.

Those facts are easily traced through this first of the historical books. But what does the Holy Spirit intend for us to learn from the historic facts recorded in these thirty-one chapters? I cannot give you everything our God would have us learn from these chapters. I make no pretence of knowing myself.

However, there are some very important spiritual lessons to be gleaned from 1 Samuel, lessons that will help you and me as we endeavour to live in this world for the glory of our God, serving the interests of his kingdom. Let's go through these thirty-one chapters together, gleaning the 'handfuls of purpose' left here for us by our God.

Worship

1 Samuel begins with a man by the name of Elkanah, who teaches us something about the worship of our God. This man's name, Elkanah,

means 'possession of God'. Learn this first; worship is, at its core, the acknowledgement that we are God's possession. I cannot say this often enough. Faith in Christ involves giving up self to the rule and dominion of Christ our God, acknowledging him as our Lord (Mark 8:34-35; 1 Corinthians 6:19-20). That person who is possessed of God possesses God. What a swap we make when we give up ourselves for Christ and to Christ! We give up our death for his life, our emptiness for his fulness, our sin for his righteousness, our guilt for his atonement, and our way of cursedness for his way of blessedness.

When Elkanah went up to worship God, he brought a sacrifice. If we would worship God, we must come to him with the sacrifice he requires – Christ the Lamb of God, our sin-atoning Substitute. The sacrifice Elkanah brought was a sacrifice involving personal cost. Worship always involves sacrifice. God will not be worshipped and served at our convenience, or upon our terms.

Prayer

Elkanah's wife, Hannah, gives us instruction in the matter of prayer. I do not claim to know much about prayer. I am always embarrassed when people come to me seeking help about prayer, or ask me about how to pray. But I do know this; you will not find richer, more spiritual instruction about prayer than you will read in these first two chapters of 1 Samuel. Listen to this saintly lady's prayer as you read its words, and learn what prayer is.

As Hannah was driven to the throne of grace by the persecution of her adversary, Peninnah, we are often sluggish in prayer until the Lord graciously puts us in desperation. Hannah's prayer arose from her 'bitterness of soul', which caused her to weep sore before the Lord. Prayer is the cry of a child in need to be remembered by our heavenly Father. Thus Hannah cried before God, 'Remember me!'. Nothing is more moving to a loving father than the cry of his needy child. Prayer is a matter of the heart, not the lip. 'She spake in her heart ... I have poured out my soul before the Lord'.

Prayer obtains God's blessing. Hannah came to the throne of grace in her time of need, cast her burden on the Lord and left it there, having obtained the mercy she needed. The Lord our God always honours those who honour him. Prayer gives thanks, praise, adoration, honour, and glory to the Lord God alone. 'Let us therefore come boldly unto the throne of grace, that we may obtain mercy, and find grace to help in time of need' (Hebrews 4:16).

Consecration

In the early chapters of the book Eli stands out, at least to me, as a marvellous example of and lesson about a believer's consecration to God. Eli was the priest in Israel; and he was a man of remarkable faith in God. He also had his faults. He did not restrain his wicked sons, but indulged them in their ungodly behaviour. For that he was chastened of the Lord. Nevertheless, he was a remarkable man. Though he reproved his sons; he did not restrain them when they refused to hear his reproof.

When Samuel told Eli that the Lord was determined to kill his sons and take the priesthood from his house forever, he responded to God's Word and his will with exemplary faith, 'It is the Lord, let him do what seemeth him good'. When the ark of God was taken and his sons were killed by the Philistines, 'his heart trembled for the ark of God'. Eli was more concerned for the cause of Christ and the glory of God than he was for himself, his name, his sons, or his house.

God's Prophet

Samuel exemplifies the prophet of God. There are many, many examples of faithful prophets in the Word of God (Moses, Elijah, Isaiah, Jeremiah, John the Baptist, etc.), but none outshine Samuel. He, too, like Eli, had two sons that were called sons of Belial because of their lawlessness and worthless conduct; but he, too, was a faithful man throughout his life. Samuel faithfully declared God's Word. He plainly told Eli, God's priest and his master, all the Word of God. He declared to Saul the message God gave him to deliver to the king. He withheld nothing of God's revelation from Israel. Being a prophet, he was but the voice by whom God revealed himself, his Word, and his will to Israel. When Israel rejected him, they were not rejecting Samuel, but God (1 Samuel 8:7; 2 Corinthians 5:18-21). The same is true of those who reject the gospel preached to them today. Though the children of Israel rejected him and rejected his message, Samuel was faithful still to their souls and to God.

Our Flesh

Saul stands before us as a very sobering lesson, a lesson we must constantly learn. When we indulge the lusts of our flesh, we bring misery to ourselves. Saul was the product of the flesh. He was exactly what Israel wanted, or thought they wanted. However, he proved to be a source of unceasing pain and misery as long as he lived. Oh, how bitter the experience of this is; but it is a lesson that we must learn. Our flesh is our greatest enemy! The flesh prefers the authority of men to the authority of

God, 'Give us a king'. The flesh craves the approval of flesh, 'A king like the nations'. The flesh seeks to govern the kingdom of God by the opinions of men, rather than the Word of God. The flesh consults with and follows the flesh, rather than the revelation of God. The indulgence of the flesh always disturbs the peace of God's kingdom.

Election

I love the illustration of God's election in David. He teaches us who God's elect are. The Lord God passed by Saul, the great, strong, handsome choice of Israel, and chose David. He passed by all David's brothers, and chose the youngest of Jesse's sons, the runt of the family. The fact is, God's elect are almost always the people we least suspect might be the objects of his grace (1 Samuel 16:10-13). He almost always chooses to use the most unlikely of men to serve the interests of his kingdom and glory (1 Corinthians 1:26-31).

Prevenient Grace

Abigail, Nabal's wife, shows us a lesson about God's prevenient grace. How I adore the wonder of God's providence. Israel's choice of a king was used by our God to accomplish his purpose. He graciously and wisely overruled their evil choice, their rebellion, and their sin to accomplish his own wise purpose for their good (Romans 8:28-30; 11:33-36).

Prevenient grace is another of the mysteries of God's providence, for which we have great reason to praise him with thankful, humbled hearts. Prevenient grace is grace that goes before grace and keeps the objects of grace from much evil, even from the evil we would commit if the Lord would let us (1 Samuel 25:32-39).

The whole book of 1 Samuel is a marvellous display of divine sovereignty. God was in control of everything; and he still is. Blessed be his holy name! Nothing done by Israel, the Philistines, Saul, or anyone else could in any way hinder God's work or thwart his purpose!

Types of Christ

Throughout this book, indeed, throughout the Bible, David stands before us as a great type of our Lord Jesus Christ. Long ago John Gill stated that the Old Testament presents us with three categories of types, by which our Lord Jesus and God's great salvation in him were prefigured: *Institutional Types* such as the ceremonies of the law, *Providential Types* such as the deliverances of Israel, *Personal Types* seen in the experiences of individuals. David was one of the greatest of these personal types.

David was a shepherd in Israel. The Lord Jesus Christ is our good and great Shepherd. David hazarded his life for his sheep; Christ gave his life for his sheep.

Jonathan made a covenant of love with David for the salvation of his house. The Lord God made a covenant of love with Christ for the salvation of his house.

David was anointed and established of God as the king of Israel. Christ is the Lord's anointed King of Zion, established upon his throne forever.

David slew Goliath with the most unlikely of weapons (a shepherd's sling), and cut off his head with the very sword by which Goliath planned to slay him and all of Israel. Our great Saviour defeated sin, Satan, death, and hell, and saved all Israel by his death upon the cross.

All the schemes, plans, and devices by which Saul tried to thwart God's purpose and keep David from the throne only served to establish him and his kingdom. All the schemes of hell to thwart our Saviour and keep him from saving his people and reigning upon the throne of universal monarchy only serve to accomplish God's gracious purpose.

As David recovered all from the Amalekites and rescued his wives from their hands, so the Lord Jesus has recovered all for us and rescued his bride from all harm.

As David made a law concerning the sharing of the spoils so that every man had the same rich reward, so our Lord Jesus has given all his people all his wealth as the God-man our Saviour (John 17:5, 22).

'My heart rejoiceth in the LORD, mine horn is exalted in the LORD: my mouth is enlarged over mine enemies; because I rejoice in thy salvation. There is none holy as the LORD: for there is none beside thee: neither is there any rock like our God. Talk no more so exceeding proudly; let not arrogancy come out of your mouth: for the LORD is a God of knowledge, and by him actions are weighed. The bows of the mighty men are broken, and they that stumbled are girded with strength. They that were full have hired out themselves for bread; and they that were hungry ceased: so that the barren hath born seven; and she that hath many children is waxed feeble. The LORD killeth, and maketh alive: he bringeth down to the grave, and bringeth up. The LORD maketh poor, and maketh rich: he bringeth low, and lifteth up. He raiseth up the poor out of the dust, and lifteth up the beggar from the dunghill, to set them among princes, and to make them inherit the throne of glory: for the pillars of the earth are the Lord's, and he hath set the world upon them. He will keep the feet of his saints, and the wicked shall be silent in darkness; for by strength shall no man prevail. The adversaries of the LORD shall be broken to pieces; out of heaven shall he thunder upon them: the LORD shall judge the ends of the earth; and he shall give strength unto his king, and exalt the horn of his anointed' (1 Samuel 2:1-10).

Chapter 10

2 Samuel

Christ God's King

The book of God has been providentially arranged in the order in which we have it for a purpose. The Lord has not given us a record of the various historic events recorded in holy scripture in a chronological order. To the natural mind, the order in which the various books of the Bible are arranged might appear confusing. If Job was written before Genesis, why does it appear in the middle of the Old Testament rather than nearer the beginning? If 2 Thessalonians was written before Romans, why does Romans appear as the first of Paul's epistles?

Providential Order

I am personally convinced that one reason for the arrangement of scripture in the order in which we have it in the sacred volume is that the order in which the books of the Bible are presented is providentially intended to set before us the progressive order of divine revelation. For that reason it is very helpful, as we read and study holy scripture, to see the connection of each book in its setting with the other books of inspiration.

In Genesis, the book of Beginnings, the Lord God made a covenant with Abraham and his seed in which he promised him an everlasting inheritance of grace in Christ. That inheritance was typically set forth in the land of Canaan.

In Exodus, Leviticus, Numbers, and Deuteronomy God gives us the instructions of his holy law, by which he declares that he will give that inheritance, fulfil his covenant, and bestow his grace only upon a perfectly holy people in a way that is altogether righteous and just, without any compromise of his own holy character. But we are sinful people, a race altogether void of holiness. Does that shut the door of hope against us? Not at all.

Before the books of the Law are closed, Moses who represents God's law throughout the Bible died, declaring that there is no hope of God's covenant and its promises being accomplished by our obedience to the law. Moses could not bring Israel into Canaan. We can never find rest by our obedience to God's holy law, because we have no ability to obey it. Righteousness cannot come by the law (Galatians 2:21). 'By the deeds of the law there shall no flesh be justified in his sight ... Man is justified by faith without the deeds of the law' (Romans 3:20-28).

When Moses died, God raised up Joshua, a great type of the Lord Jesus Christ, to deliver Israel and bring them into the possession of the land of Canaan. In the book of Joshua, Canaan typifies the rest awaiting God's elect in the final consummation of salvation in resurrection glory (Hebrews 4:1-11).

By the hand of Joshua God gave Israel all that he promised to Abraham in covenant mercy (Joshua 21:43-45; 22:4; 23:14). All of that, of course, was typical of the fact that Christ, our Joshua, has obtained for God's elect (the whole Israel of God) all the blessings of grace and glory promised us in the everlasting covenant by the merits of his own blood and righteousness (Hebrews 6:20; 9:12).

The next book of the Bible is Judges. In the book of Joshua the land of Canaan was typical of our heavenly inheritance with Christ. But in the book of Judges, Canaan typifies the believer's present experience of grace. The land was filled with enemies; and throughout the days of the judges Israel was engaged with their enemies. Even now, all the blessings of covenant grace are the rightful property of all who trust Christ. But we have countless enemies within, with whom we have unceasing warfare (Romans 7:14-23; Galatians 5:17-23).

Joshua speaks of heavenly glory. Judges describes our present experience. Then, the book of Ruth shows us how the Lord our God will accomplish his purpose of grace for us by Christ, our lawful, Kinsman Redeemer. Once we lost everything in our Father Adam. Now our great Boaz has recovered all for us in total compliance with and full satisfaction of all the demands of God's holy law.

Then, in 1 and 2 Samuel, the Lord shows us that our Redeemer, our Saviour, that One into whose hands the Lord God has entrusted the everlasting deliverance of his people is the King of Glory, who has all dominion over all flesh, that he might give eternal life to his people. Here David typifies our Saviour as God's great King set upon his throne.

One Man

2 Samuel covers the same time in history as 1 Chronicles. In 1 Samuel three men are prominent: Samuel, Saul, and David. 2 Samuel is a book about one man, God's servant David; but that one man is set before us throughout the scriptures as an eminent type and picture of our Lord Jesus Christ. In fact, many of the passages of inspiration where David's name is used cannot be interpreted as applying to David himself in a strict sense. They apply to David; but they also look beyond David to Another.

Look, for example, at 2 Samuel 7. The repeated use of the word 'forever' in this chapter makes it clear that God's promises concerning the throne, kingdom, and seed spoken of in this chapter cannot be fulfilled in any earthly throne, or kingdom, or man. The promises find their fulfilment in our Lord Jesus Christ, the Son of God and the Son of David, and his Church and Kingdom. David, as God's anointed and enthroned king over all Israel as a nation, was typical of our Lord Jesus Christ, who is God's anointed and enthroned King in Zion, over all the Israel of God, his Church.

I am not suggesting there is no application of the promises in 2 Samuel to David personally and to all God's elect in this world, who are, like David, sinners saved by the grace of God. Clearly, David is representative of all God's people in this world. His life and experiences were representative and typical of ours. But the ultimate fulfilment of David's typical life and dominion as God's anointed king must be found in Christ. This is not my interpretation of this book, but God's. Compare Psalm 16:8-11 and Acts 2:22-36, and this will be obvious. Peter tells us that David's words in Psalm 16 find their ultimate accomplishment in Christ, and that David knew it when he penned that Psalm (Acts 2:30). Yes, the words were David's words. Yes, he spoke of his own hope of the resurrection. They speak of our hope, too. But the Holy Spirit specifically tells us that Psalm 16 finds its ultimate fulfilment in the Lord Jesus Christ.[1]

---

[1] Whenever we read the messianic psalms or any other prophetic portion of holy scripture (Psalm 40; 69; etc.), we must not imagine that the writer is not speaking of his own, present experience. He is. As he does, the passage certainly relates to us and to our experience. However the fuller, more glorious, ultimate message of the passage is the person and work of our Lord Jesus Christ.

Discovering Christ In All The Scriptures

God's King

Let us look at David as a type of our Lord Jesus Christ, God's King. David describes the character of God's King in 2 Samuel 23:1-5. God's King is here described as 'the man who was raised up on high' (Philippians 2:8-11). He is 'the anointed of the God of Jacob'. He is the man by whom the Spirit of God speaks. Christ our King is 'just, ruling over men in the fear of God'.

He is 'as the light of the morning, when the sun riseth, even a morning without clouds, as the tender grass springing out of the earth by clear shining after rain'. Christ is the Light of the world. He sprang out of the earth in humiliation, as the tender grass. He arose from the dead as the Sun of Righteousness, with healing in his wings. Our King is one with whom God has made an everlasting covenant ordered in all things and sure. He has no desire but the fulfilment of that covenant, the glory of God in the salvation of his people.

The King here described is Christ. While David was a man in whom these things were exemplified to a great degree, he was not the King in whom these things are completely found. This King is Christ our Saviour for only in Christ can the prophecies and promises be completely fulfilled.

Abner described the work of God's King in 2 Samuel 3:18. 'By the hand of my servant David I will save my people Israel out of the hand of the Philistines, and out of the hand of all their enemies'. This is what the scriptures everywhere assert concerning Christ (Daniel 7:14; Matthew 1:21; John 17:2; Acts 5:30-32). He has a people, God's Israel, his elect and he will deliver them.

He came into this world, lived, died, arose, and ascended on high to save his people from all their enemies. He is now enthroned with universal power and dominion to give eternal life to his people. Save them he will, by redemption, by regeneration, by resurrection!

God's King is the Man anointed by him to be King. David was anointed as king over Israel three times: first in his father's house, then over Judah, and finally over all Israel. The Lord Jesus Christ is anointed as King by God himself (Psalm 45:7; Hebrews 1:9): first in his Father's house, then at his baptism, and finally in the hearts of chosen sinners.

A King in Exile

Though he was God's anointed king while he was in exile, Saul ruled over the people. Though Christ is King over all his people, he is a despised and rejected King; and the Prince of this world, the Prince of darkness, holds sway over the hearts of the Lord's people until they are saved by his grace.

The King Acknowledged

At God's appointed time all of Judah were gathered to David and gave themselves to their king (2 Samuel 2:4; 1 Chronicles 12:18). This is what happens in the joyful experience of conversion. The Lord God graciously causes chosen sinners to bow to Christ as their Lord and King with gladness, devoting themselves to him in adoration, love, and praise (Psalm 44:4; 110:1-3).

Thank God for our great King, the Lord Jesus Christ. He is a King like no other, King of kings and Lord of lords. Christ our King is himself God almighty. Yet, he is one of us and one with us (Deuteronomy 17:15; Hebrews 2:17). 'The King is near of kin to us' (2 Samuel 19:42).

Christ our King is saving his people from all their enemies. The Lord God promised Israel that David their king would save them from all their enemies. Typically he did so. From the day that he slew Goliath to the day that he went to glory, we never read of David being defeated by any foe. He went forth conquering and to conquer; and conquer he did. So it is with Christ our King. He vanquished Satan, cast out our enemy and accuser, and bound him with the mighty chain of his omnipotence, and has made us more than conquerors by his grace (John 12:31-32; Revelation 20:1-3). He triumphed over death, hell, and the grave as our Substitute. He did it for us.

'Blotting out the handwriting of ordinances that was against us, which was contrary to us, and took it out of the way, nailing it to his cross; And having spoiled principalities and powers, he made a show of them openly, triumphing over them in it' (Colossians 2:14-15).

As 'David took the strong hold of Zion', the Lord Jesus took his place on the throne of God to save his own (Romans 14:9; Hebrews 9:12; 10:9-14). The King of Glory comes to chosen, redeemed sinners in saving mercy, enters their hearts, binds the strong man and casts him out, setting up his throne in their hearts. Christ came 'that we being delivered out of the hand of our enemies might serve him without fear' (Luke 1:74). He never fails to accomplish his purpose (Isaiah 9:6-7; 1 Corinthians 15:25).

He who is the King of Glory reigns upon the throne of grace. In the story of Mephibosheth the Holy Spirit gives us a marvellous picture of the grace of God flowing to sinners through Christ our King. He takes the fallen sons of men, helpless, lame, and poor, men who are his own enemies, and makes us to sit at the King's table as the King's own sons 'to eat bread at his table continually'. This grace, God's boundless, infinite grace comes to us, as it did to Mephibosheth, because of a covenant made with our great King David (Christ) long before we were born.

God's People

As I said before, David is also typical of us, God's people in this world. That is the next thing I want us to see. David was a man after God's own heart (1 Samuel 13:14). He was not such a man by nature. David was, like us all, a fallen, depraved, sinful man by nature. Yet, grace made him a man after God's own heart. When the Lord God looked into David's heart, he saw in that man a man after his own heart.

In spiritual things the heart is the matter of utmost concern. We must not neglect our outward conduct. We must not fail to maintain good works. We must not ignore our responsibilities in outward things. But true religion is an inward thing. We can get everything right on the outside and yet be lost. Things must be made right on the inside. 'The Lord looketh on the heart!' Will we ever learn that? God is not impressed with those things that impress men. Our Lord Jesus said to the Pharisees, 'Ye are they which justify yourselves before men; but God knoweth your hearts: for that which is highly esteemed among men is abomination in the sight of God' (Luke 16:15).

God looks on the heart. God searches the heart. God demands heart faith, heart obedience, heart worship. God requires the heart. He says, 'My son, give me thine heart, and let thine eyes observe my ways' (Proverbs 23:26). God alone knows the heart, and the heart alone knows God. The heart is the matter of primary concern.

When the Lord God looked upon David's heart and declared him to be a man after his own heart, what did he see? What did God see in David's heart that set him apart from other men? When the Lord looked upon David's heart, he saw in David a heart conquered by his grace, ruled by his Spirit, trusting him.

We are not told when, or where David began to believe God, only that he did. At some point in time, when he was still a young man, David committed himself to the Lord God. Like Abraham before him, like his father, Jesse, David believed God, and it was imputed unto him for righteousness. To believe God is simply to trust him, to take him at his word.

Here is the lesson. There is only one way you and I can please God. There is only one way any sinner can ever be pleasing to the holy Lord God; and that is by faith in Christ (Hebrews 11:5-6; Romans 3:31). If we would walk before God accepted and well-pleasing in his sight, we must walk before him in faith, trusting his Son, and his Son alone as our Saviour, trusting Christ alone for the totality of our acceptance with God (1 Corinthians 1:30-31).

David rejoiced in God's electing love. In chapter 6 we see him leaping and dancing before the ark of God. He knew what that ark represented. He knew that that ark represented God's redemption of his people by the blood of Christ, the Lamb of God. He could not get beyond the wonder of God's grace to him. Therefore, he humbled himself before the people, before the Lord, with joy and gladness. His wife, Michal, saw it and despised him for his worship. David told her that the source of his joy was something she could not understand, because she had not experienced it. The source of his joy was God's electing mercy, love and grace (Psalm 65:4).

Throughout his life, David, being a man of faith, a man who believed God, humbly bowed to the will of God. When the Lord killed Uzzah, David acknowledged that the fault was his. 'The Lord our God made a breach upon us, for that we sought him not after the due order' (1 Chronicles 15:13). When he wanted to build a house for God, the Lord refused to allow it; but did permit him to gather the materials with which his son would build the temple. David was overwhelmed by God's goodness to him. He said, 'Do as thou hast said, and let thy name be magnified forever'. When the Lord God killed his infant son, David washed his face and worshipped God. David exemplifies the fact that faith bows to Christ. Faith humbles itself beneath the mighty hand of God. Faith submits to the will of God. Even when his beloved son Absalom was slain because of the evil David had done, and when thousands perished under the judgment of God because of his stubborn pride in numbering Israel, though his heart was broken, though his soul was crushed by the experiences, David bowed to the Lord God. That is called 'faith'.

David's Sin

Though David was a believer, though he was a man after God's own heart, he was a sinner still in constant need of grace. Chapters eleven and twelve tell us the sad story of David's terrible fall and its consequences. Here is a constantly repeated lesson, a lesson we must learn. God's saints in this world are sinners still, sinners saved by grace. Chosen in electing love, forgiven by blood atonement, accepted in the Beloved, and saved and kept by pure, free, sovereign, indestructible, omnipotent grace! Let us make no excuse for our sin or our sins. Let us, instead, acknowledge and confess our sins, and trust our Saviour still, as David did (Psalm 51:1-5). Let us also rejoice in the forgiveness of sin by God's free grace through the blood of his darling Son, as David did (Psalm 32:1-5; Romans 4:8; 1 John 1:7-2:2).

Believing God, David died in peace, falling back and resting upon God's everlasting covenant and its immutability. Dying in the Lord, dying in faith, he was, is, and shall forever be a blessed man. 'Blessed are the dead which die in the Lord from henceforth'. Blessed are all who die as David died, believing God.

The King's Return

Remember when David was anointed as king over Judah, seven years passed before he was anointed king over all Israel. So, after the complete, perfect accomplishment of God's purpose of grace he whom God raised up and exalted shall be acknowledged as King by all in his glorious second advent. We have a picture of our Lord's return in chapter nineteen.

David had been away from Jerusalem for some time because of Absalom's revolt. Now that the rebel was dead, the people longed for David's immediate return. When David heard how they longed for his return, he sent messengers to say he was on his way back. The people said, 'Come!' 'So the king returned, and came to Jordan. And Judah came to Gilgal, to go to meet the king, to conduct the king over Jordan'.

That is a pretty good picture of our Redeemer, our great King and us (Revelation 22:1-13, 20-21). When, at last, our great Saviour and King does return, when our 'Lord the King is come again in peace', we will go out to meet him in the resurrection (1 Thessalonians 4:13-18; 1 Corinthians 15:51-58).

Chapter 11

1 Kings

Christ the Prince of Peace

Salvation is entirely the work and gift of God's free grace in Christ. Our only standing before God is Christ. His blood alone is our atonement. His righteousness alone is our righteousness. We have no other righteousness but his. Our personal obedience or disobedience has absolutely nothing to do with our acceptance before God. Believers are 'accepted in the Beloved', only in the Beloved, and once accepted never unaccepted. 'Blessed is the man to whom the Lord will not impute sin'.

Yet, we must never imagine that obedience and disobedience to the revealed will of God are matters of indifference. Obedience on the part of God's own is so very important (to the honour of our God, the cause of Christ, and our own souls), that the Lord God was determined to kill Moses if he did not circumcise his sons, though his wife was adamantly opposed to it (Exodus 4:24-26).

How foolish and selfish we are when we presume that our behaviour affects no one but ourselves! None of us is an island. We all influence others for good or for evil. This is something we ought to keep in mind all the time. You and I are responsible not only for ourselves, but also for those who are influenced by us. Those to whom God has providentially given positions of authority over others are particularly responsible to lead those who are under them by example.

A nation is morally elevated or debased by the moral character of its government and national leaders. For years following, nations will carry scars for the wickedness and moral debauchery promoted by politicians and lawmakers. A local church usually follows the example of its pastor in doctrine, in behaviour, and in faithfulness. Many local churches, after enjoying the blessings of God through faithful pastors, have been led to spiritual ruin by the unfaithful successors. Children are to a great degree affected for life by their teachers. Mothers and pathers mould the lives of their children by everything they do.

A Kingdom Divided

The importance of our influence upon those around us is set before us dramatically in the life and reign of Solomon as it is described in 1 Kings. Chapters 1-11 give us a picture of Solomon's greatness and glory as the king over all Israel for forty years. Then, chapters 12-22 display the horrible consequences of Solomon's disobedience upon the kingdom. These chapters set before us the first eighty years of the divided kingdom, a kingdom divided because of the evil influence of Solomon's life. The key to understanding the last half of 1 Kings is found in God's Word to Solomon in 1 Kings 11:11. 'Wherefore the Lord said unto Solomon, Forasmuch as this is done of thee, and thou hast not kept my covenant and my statutes, which I have commanded thee, I will surely rend the kingdom from thee, and will give it to thy servant'.

Still, the message of 1 Kings is Christ, of whom Solomon was in many ways a type. If you read Psalm 72, which was 'A Psalm for Solomon', you will immediately see that the things there spoken of Solomon could only find their fulfilment in Christ, the Prince of Peace.

Adonijah

1 Kings begins with David still on the throne. He was old and dying. Solomon's brother, Adonijah tried to seize the kingdom for himself, though David made it clear that Solomon was to succeed him as king. Adonijah's scheme failed and Solomon was established as king. But there are two things connected with the opening of 1 Kings that I cannot fail to mention.

First, David's family suffered as the consequence of his sin in the matter of Uriah and Bathsheba until the very day of his death, and even beyond his death, just as Nathan had told him it would (2 Samuel 12:10). When he sent for Bathsheba, I am sure, the thought never crossed David's mind that he would bring such trouble to his family and God's kingdom by the indulgence of his lust. What a sad, sad bequeathal he made to his family by his behaviour.

Second, when David was dying his servants found a beautiful young woman to come, to lay in his bed, to nourish him, hoping that she might rouse his physical passions, and thereby help their beloved king recover. Needless to say, this incident has raised many eyebrows. But the situation was not as it appears to many. There is no record that Bathsheba disapproved, no record that the Lord disapproved, no record of disapproval of any kind from anyone. This was not a perverse device concocted by perverse men. This young lady, Abishag, married David on his deathbed.

How can that be stated so confidently, when there is no record of the marriage? In chapter two, Adonijah made one last ditch effort to seize the throne from Solomon by deceit, which resulted in his just execution. Adonijah persuaded Solomon's mother, Bathsheba, to ask him to let him marry Abishag. Bathsheba did not see through the thing, but Solomon did. Solomon knew that if Adonijah married Abishag he would have a rightful claim to the throne. That could not have been the case if Abishag had not been married to the King (2:22).

The Importance of Leadership

1 Kings then takes up the reign of Solomon, and carries us through the terrible division of the kingdom under Rehoboam his son. Then, we see the various dynasties within the northern kingdom of Israel, and the lives of the kings of the single dynasty of the house of David in the southern kingdom of Judah.

In each case, the focus is always on the king, because it was the king's relationship with God that determined the condition of the nation. When the king walked with the Lord God prosperity and triumph rested upon the kingdom by God's blessing. The rains came at the right time, the crops grew, and the land flourished. The nation prevailed over their enemies even though the enemies came in allied forces.

But when the king disobeyed God and led the people into the worship of other gods, immediately famines broke out, plagues came, invading armies came, and the kingdom fell into hard times spiritually, morally, and politically. The kings who walked in obedience were types of Christ, such as David, Solomon, Hezekiah, Jehoshaphat, and Josiah. But the kings who walked in disobedience were pictures of the anti-Christ, leading the people away from God and into apostasy.

Solomon

Before his death David called Solomon before him and charged him to walk in the ways of the Lord his God, and to teach his children after him, that the kingdom might endure in safety and prosperity forever. He told Solomon that he must wisely and justly deal with Joab, his brutal and bloody general, and Shimei, who cursed David on the day he fled from Absalom. David kept his word concerning those wicked men by sparing their lives; but they were ultimately executed at the command of Solomon. He also made Zadok the priest, replacing Abiathar and fulfilling the prophecy given to Eli many decades before, by the child Samuel.

As stated before, Solomon was in many ways a magnificent type of our Lord Jesus Christ, the Prince of Peace. His kingdom was a kingdom of peace (1 Chronicles 22:9). His very name means 'Peaceable'. Solomon's peaceable kingdom was the result of David's mighty conquests. It is because of Christ's conquest over all our enemies that we now enjoy the glorious reign of his peace in our hearts. All who are under the dominion of grace, all who are ruled by the grace of the Lord Jesus Christ are ruled in peace. He has made peace for us with God by the blood of his cross. He is our peace. He gives us peace (Romans 14:17).

Solomon was also a king to whom the Lord God gave wisdom beyond measure. His wisdom as the king of Israel also foreshadowed Christ, who is made of God unto us Wisdom, in 'whom are hid all the treasures of wisdom and knowledge'.

Psalm 72 describes the glory of Solomon and the glory of his kingdom. But that Psalm finds its ultimate fulfilment only in our great God and Saviour, the Lord Jesus Christ. Like Solomon, our Mediator is King and possesses his kingdom because the Lord God made him King and gave him his kingdom (1 Kings 5:4; Psalm 2:8; John 17:2).

The Temple

Solomon's most significant achievement was the building of the temple in Jerusalem. He was raised up specifically for that purpose (1 Chronicles 28:5-10). In the fourth year of his reign, he began to build the temple, four hundred and eighty years after the Israelites came out of Egypt. They were now settled in the land of promise, enjoying a season of rest from warfare, and tremendous prosperity. Solomon enlisted the assistance of his father's friend, Hiram the king of Tyre, from whom he obtained huge quantities of cedar and cypress wood as well as skilled artisans in bronze and gold (5: 1-12).

The stones for the temple were quarried from beneath the temple mount and were finished within the quarry so that 'neither hammer nor axe nor any iron tool (was) heard in the house, while it was being built' (6:7). This is a picture of God's work of grace in the building of his spiritual temple, the church (Ephesians 2:20-22). There is no clanging noise of human works heard in the building of God's holy temple. The salvation of God's elect is altogether the work of his free grace in Christ. We contribute nothing to it by our works (Ephesians 2:8-9).

The temple was built along the same pattern as the tabernacle in the wilderness; but it was twice the size and more magnificent than the tabernacle. Like the tabernacle, the temple's beauty and splendour was to be seen from within. Almost everything within was covered with pure gold.

It took Solomon seven years to build the temple. This may seem a long time until we are told, 'Solomon was building his own house thirteen years'. That fact is recorded for a reason. Whenever our time, talents, and possessions are devoted more to our own comfort and pleasure than they are to the cause of Christ, the glory of God and his kingdom, they are misused; and that misuse indicates a horrible self-centredness on our part.

The temple was a picture of God's true house and abode, the church (1 Corinthians 3:16-17; 1 Timothy 3:15). Solomon's temple was costly and glorious. It is set before us throughout the book of Hebrews as a picture of our Saviour's great work of redemption (Hebrews 9:12; 10:11-14, 18-22). When it was finished, the glory of God filled the holy place, so much so that the priests could no longer do their work.

When the temple was complete, it was solemnly dedicated to God. The ark of the covenant was brought out of the tabernacle and installed within the holy of holies in the temple. When the priests pulled out the staves by which the ark was carried for the last time and came out of the holy place after installing the ark in the holy of holies, a cloud of glory from the Lord suddenly filled the temple. When Solomon saw this evidence of God's immediate presence with his people, he was overwhelmed with joy and arose to bless the people.

Then, kneeling before the altar of burnt offering and raising his outstretched hands, Solomon uttered a tremendous, instructive prayer of dedication, recognizing the faithfulness of God and the peril of departing from his ways. His understanding of God's infinite greatness, majesty, and glory was manifest in his words. 'Behold, the heaven and heaven of heavens cannot contain thee; how much less this house that I have builded?' Then, he outlined the many circumstances by which the people might be caused to turn away from the Lord and the method by which they might recover as they turned again to God in repentance, looking to Christ who was symbolized by the ark and mercy seat in the temple.

When Solomon arose from prayer, he pronounced another blessing upon the people and offered thousands of sacrifices. At the close of the day, the joyful people returned to their homes. Never was there a greater day in the history of Israel.

Thereafter, the Lord appeared again to Solomon in a dream and assured him that his prayer had been heard. He assured Solomon that God's promises to David his father were renewed to him, upon the condition that he and his descendants walked before the Lord God in faithful obedience. If they failed to do so, the temple would be torn down and the people would be driven from the land and become a byword and a proverb among the nations. Indeed, that is exactly what happened.

Solomon exceeded all the kings of the earth in riches and in wisdom. He made silver to be as gravel stones in the street. He was truly a remarkable type of Christ our King.

The Queen of Sheba

Chapter ten records the famous, beautiful story of the Queen of Sheba coming to Jerusalem to meet Solomon. 'Behold, a greater than Solomon is here!' What a picture this is of a sinner coming to Christ. The Queen of Sheba heard of Solomon's greatness. 'Faith cometh by hearing and hearing by the Word of God'. She came to him from a country far away. We 'who were sometimes far off are made nigh by the blood of Christ'. She communed with Solomon of all that was in her heart and proved him with many questions. The sinner who comes to Christ in faith pours out all his heart before him (1 John 1:7, 9). Solomon told her everything she wanted to know and gave her all her desire, according to his royal bounty. So the Lord Jesus gives the needy soul all his desire. When the Queen of Sheba saw Solomon for herself, there was no more spirit in her. The glory of our great Saviour withers the pride, breaks the heart, and abases the spirit of all who come to him. Once she had seen, and heard, and learned of Solomon for herself, the Queen of Sheba openly confessed him, his greatness, and his glory.

'And she said to the king, It was a true report that I heard in mine own land of thy acts and of thy wisdom. Howbeit I believed not the words, until I came, and mine eyes had seen it: and, behold, the half was not told me: thy wisdom and prosperity exceedeth the fame which I heard. Happy are thy men, happy are these thy servants, which stand continually before thee, and that hear thy wisdom. Blessed be the Lord thy God, which delighted in thee, to set thee on the throne of Israel: because the Lord loved Israel for ever, therefore made he thee king, to do judgment and justice'.

The gospel of Christ is that true report of the grace and glory of God, which we heard in the land of our alienation from God. It was by the hearing of the gospel that we were brought to Christ. By the glad tidings of the gospel Christ was revealed in us and we were granted life and faith in him by the grace of God (Romans 10:17; 1 Peter 1:23-25). Like Solomon, our Saviour has granted us all that we could desire and has given all the fulness of his royal bounty 'according to his riches in glory'.

Solomon's Great Failure

Solomon was a great king. He was a great man, a man in whom God had put his grace, upon whom the Lord God poured out his Spirit. He was, as we have seen, a great type of Christ, the Prince of Peace. But Solomon was only a man, no more. He was a sinner saved by grace. But he was still a sinner. Solomon went down to Egypt for help. He made a league with Pharaoh. He took Pharaoh's daughter to be his wife. He multiplied horses. He multiplied wives. His wives turned his heart to serve other gods. Therefore the Lord God divided the kingdom, and constantly increasing wars between Israel and Judah ensued. Idolatry became rampant. Moral degeneracy followed. Homosexual prostitutes were advanced in the land! 'Wherefore the Lord said unto Solomon, Forasmuch as this is done of thee, and thou hast not kept my covenant and my statutes, which I have commanded thee, I will surely rend the kingdom from thee, and will give it to thy servant'.

The Lord appeared to Solomon a third time to announce to him that the kingdom would be torn from him and given to another. Yet for David's sake it would occur after Solomon died, during the life of his son. Immediately, adversaries began rising up against Solomon, including Hadad the Edomite on the south, Rezon in the land of Syria on the north, and from within the kingdom itself, Jeroboam the son of Nebat, an Ephraimite who lifted up his hand against the king.

Ahijah the prophet was sent by God to meet Jeroboam outside of Jerusalem. Ahijah took off his new garment and ripped it into twelve pieces. He handed ten pieces to Jeroboam, symbolizing that he would be given ten of Israel's twelve tribes. Only two tribes (Judah and Benjamin) would remain with the house of David.

God's promised blessing to David was extended to Jeroboam, too, upon condition of obedience. If he would walk in the way of David, believing God, he would have David's mercies. When Solomon heard what Ahijah had done he tried to kill Jeroboam, but Jeroboam fled into Egypt and stayed there until Solomon died.

After forty years of unparalleled magnificence and prosperity, Solomon died and was buried in the city of David, his father. What a sad, tragic end to a life that had begun with great promise and possibility. All this happened because he failed to do what he himself declared must be done. He failed to keep his heart. Let us heed his word of wisdom. 'Keep thy heart with all diligence; for out of it are the issues of life'.

A Prophecy Fulfilled

Solomon, by his disobedience, by the disobedience of an erstwhile obedient, believing, faithful man, brought the kingdom into a division from which it never recovered. He stands as a beacon to warn us of the sure, far reaching, and long lasting consequences of disobedience.

When Solomon's son, Rehoboam, came to Shechem to be anointed king, Jeroboam led the people, who had returned from Egypt, to ask that the new king grant them relief from many of the burdens which Solomon had placed upon them. The king sent them away for three days and consulted with both the old men who advised his father and the young men with whom he grew up. With despotic pride he followed the counsel of the young men and told the people that their burdens would be increased. The result was widespread revolt. The ten tribes chose Jeroboam to be their king, fulfilling God's word to Solomon.

Jeroboam

Jeroboam set up his capital at Shechem. Fearing that the people might eventually return to the authority of Rehoboam if they continued to worship at Jerusalem, he made two golden calves and led the northern tribes into idolatry, from which they never recovered. He set one of the calves up in Dan, in the far north, and the other at Bethel, at the border with Judah. Calling Israel to worship, he said, 'Behold thy gods, O Israel, which brought thee up out of the land of Egypt'. This was exactly what Aaron had done at the foot of Mount Sinai, when he made a calf of gold and called Israel to worship the Lord. They called that calf, Jehovah (Exodus 32:5), not openly denying that Jehovah was their God, but foolishly misrepresenting him as no more than the false gods of the idolatrous nations around.

That is exactly what the most deceitful form of idolatry does today. It is but a form of godliness that denies the power of God. It retains the words and phrases and the ordinances of the gospel, but denies the character of God, representing him as one who is pathetically helpless without the aid of men. Every form of freewill, works religion that makes the will and work of God dependent upon the will or work of man for its efficacy follows the deadly sin which Jeroboam, the son of Nebat, introduced to the Northern Kingdom.

From this moment on, David and Jeroboam became representative of two spiritual principles that are seen throughout the rest of the nation's history. In Judah a good king 'walked in the ways of David, his father'. Every good king served the Lord God, tearing down idols, destroying the practice of idolatry, and establishing the worship of God. In Israel the northern kingdom, the evil kings 'walked in all the way of Jeroboam the son of Nebat, and in his sin wherewith he made Israel to sin, to provoke the Lord God of Israel to anger with their vanities'.

It is significant that in Israel, the northern kingdom, there was never even one good king. Israel's throne was occupied by a succession of kings who walked in the idolatrous way of Jeroboam. They frequently gained the throne by murdering their predecessor. Yet, God graciously sent prophet after prophet to the rebel nation. He who is God indeed is God 'who delighteth in mercy!'

In Judah there were a few good kings among many who were evil, but those good kings, who 'walked in the way of David', stand out like lights in the darkness. Among them were Asa, Jehoshaphat, Joash, Hezekiah and Josiah.

When the Lord God sent his prophet to Jeroboam, denouncing his wickedness and announcing the immediate overthrow of his altar, Jeroboam stretched out his hand to order the prophet's arrest. When he did his hand withered; and he could not draw it back. He begged the prophet to pray for him, and he did. The hand was restored; but Jeroboam was yet without repentance toward God.

In chapter thirteen there is a solomn account of what occurred when the prophet left for home. He disobeyed the word of the Lord and accepted hospitality from a deceitful prophet who told him God had sent him. In this man's home he was told that he would die as a result of his disobedience. Sure enough, on the way home a lion killed him. Though no excuse can be made for the lying prophet, there is a solemn lesson here that must never be overlooked. When we know what God would have us do in any circumstance, we must not confer with flesh and blood, and we must not be persuaded to disobedience, even though an angel from heaven or another prophet suggests a change. Learn this, too. Even faithful prophets, like faithful Solomon, are only sinful men at their best.

God's judgment fell upon Jeroboam, just as the faithful prophet had told him it would. Ahijah, the prophet, sent word to Jeroboam by his wife that God who had exalted him to power and made him king over Israel would, because of his sin, remove him from the throne. The sign of it would be the death of his son. As Jeroboam's wife brought the news to her husband the child died. We know nothing else of Jeroboam's twenty-two year reign of wickedness and idolatry. His son, Nadab, took the throne after him.

Rehoboam

Things were not much better in the southern kingdom of Judah where Rehoboam reigned. His seventeen year reign was also characterized by the introduction of idolatry and the reappearance of homosexual prostitutes within the land. God sent the king of Egypt to invade the land in judgment. He took all the treasures of gold out of the temple and the king's palace. Bronze shields and vessels replaced them to remind the king of the deterioration of the worship in the land. War raged continually between Rehoboam and Jeroboam, and ultimately it is recorded that Rehoboam, too, slept with his fathers and was buried in the city of David.

Asa

Abijam, his son reigned in Rehoboam's stead. But he only reigned for three years before he died. Then, one of the good kings, Asa, began a forty-one year reign. Asa eliminated homosexuality in the land and destroyed the idols. He even destroyed his own mother's gods and removed her from the office of queen because of her idolatry. Without question, Asa's bold zeal for God and his people preserved Judah, for the time, from the decay and corruption, which was rampant in Israel.

Israel suffered continually under the rule of wicked, idolatrous kings who 'walked in the way of Jeroboam'. When Ahab, the vilest of them all, ascended the throne with his even viler wife, Jezebel, God sent Elijah, a prophet whose name rings through the Word of God as the type of John the Baptist.

God's Faithfulness

All mere men fail in many ways, as we saw in the example of Solomon. However, man's failure never nullifies God's purpose or prevents his faithfulness. God is ever on his throne, unceasing in goodness, unfailing in faithfulness, and unchanging in his purpose. God intervened in mercy.

By taking Jezebel, the daughter of the king of Sidon, as his wife Ahab brought the worship of Baal into Israel. 'Ahab made a grove; and Ahab did more to provoke the LORD God of Israel to anger than all the kings of Israel that were before him'. Yet, where sin abounded grace abounded more.

Elijah appears on the scene, as out of nowhere (chapter 17). The next four chapters describe the constant, faithful, unflinching boldness of God's prophet Elijah and the constant, stubborn rebellion of Ahab in his defiance of God's right to be God. We know nothing about Elijah's previous life, except the fact that he came out of Gilead. He suddenly appeared on the scene and confronted Ahab with an announcement of divine judgment. He told Ahab that there would be neither dew nor rain for three years; and that when the rain did come it would only be by his word, as the prophet of God.

A Chosen Gentile

Severe drought began immediately. The Lord sent Elijah to the brook Cherith where he was miraculously fed by ravens and protected from the fury of Ahab and Jezebel. Then God sent him to Zarephath on the coast of Sidon, where he lived with a widow and her son.

The Lord Jesus holds this woman before us as a monument of God's unalterable purpose and of his method of grace (Luke 4:24-26). Ahab and all of Israel forsook the Lord God for idols; but God's purpose of grace was unaltered. This poor, Gentile widow was one of God's elect who must be called. So God sent his prophet to her, confronted her with the claims of Christ as her Lord, and she surrendered all to him. However, she lost nothing by giving up her life to Christ. Rather she was constantly supplied with all her need. Even when it appeared that she would lose her only son, he was raised to life again by the power of God. Through this dear, elect lady God's prophet and God's cause were maintained in the world.

What a picture this is of God's saving purpose of grace to us. When the Jews despised Christ and rejected God's revelation of his grace in him, God sent the gospel to the Gentiles. By the preaching of the gospel the Lord God is calling out his elect from among the Gentiles. Bowing to Christ, trusting him, we find in him a constant supply of all our souls' needs (1 Corinthians 1:30), even in this desolate world. Through the fall of Israel, God's elect among the Gentiles are brought to Christ; 'and so all Israel shall be saved' exactly according to the purpose of God. And now, through chosen Gentiles, the purpose and cause of our great God, his gospel, his kingdom, and his glory are maintained in this world (Romans 3:3-4).

Elijah and the prophets of Baal

After three years Elijah was sent back to confront Ahab, who had been looking for Elijah all this time in order to kill him. Ahab came out to meet God's prophet filled with anger. 'And it came to pass, when Ahab saw Elijah, that Ahab said unto him, Art thou he that troubleth Israel? And he answered, I have not troubled Israel; but thou, and thy father's house, in that ye have forsaken the commandments of the LORD, and thou hast followed Baalim'.

Elijah then challenged Ahab to gather all the prophets of Baal on Mount Carmel. There he would show Ahab and all Israel that Jehovah alone is God. Then we have that story that is so familiar. It is a story full of drama, majesty, and instruction.

On one side are four hundred and fifty prophets of Baal and four hundred prophets of the groves. On the other side Elijah stands alone, crying out, 'How long halt ye between two opinions? If the Lord is God, follow him; but if Baal, follow him'. Elijah mocked the prophets and mocked their helpless, useless god, as they vainly cried out for Baal to descend and burn up the sacrifice on the altar. Elijah mocked them by suggesting that perhaps their dumb idol was asleep, or had gone on a journey, or even had gone to find a bathroom to relieve himself.

Then, it was Elijah's turn. After drenching his sacrifice with water, he prayed and God answered by fire from heaven, devouring the sacrifice and licking up the water. In 1 Kings 18:36-39, Elijah's prayer is very short, but remarkably instructive.

'And it came to pass at the time of the offering of the evening sacrifice, that Elijah the prophet came near, and said, Lord God of Abraham, Isaac, and of Israel, let it be known this day that thou art God in Israel, and that I am thy servant, and that I have done all these things at thy word. Hear me, O Lord, hear me, that this people may know that thou art the Lord God, and that thou hast turned their heart back again. Then the fire of the Lord fell, and consumed the burnt sacrifice, and the wood, and the stones, and the dust, and licked up the water that was in the trench. And when all the people saw it, they fell on their faces: and they said, The Lord, he is the God; the Lord, he is the God.'

When it was proved that the prophets of Baal were false prophets, they were put to death. Then, in answer to the prayer of Elijah, the rain, which had not fallen for three years, now came in great torrents. The Lord God kept his Word and preserved his kingdom in spite of everything!

When her prophets were slain and her gods were proved to be nothing but useless idols, Jezebel was enraged. She threatened Elijah with immediate death. Then, Elijah too, proved himself to be nothing more than a man. He was God's true prophet; but, like all God's servants, he was only a sinner saved by grace.

That bold, lion-hearted man, who was so courageous and triumphant on Mount Carmel in the face of eight hundred and fifty false prophets, fled in fear before a single woman. Still, the Lord God graciously met his needs, encouraged his faith, upheld him in grace, made himself known to him anew, and used him as his prophet. Even when we believe not, 'he abideth faithful'.

Being assured that there were yet seven thousand in Israel who had not bowed the knee to Baal, Elijah was sent to anoint Hazael to be king of Syria, Jehu to be king of Israel, and Elisha to be prophet in his own place. The obedient prophet returned to the land and, finding Elisha plowing with oxen, cast his mantle upon him. After offering a sacrifice, Elisha took up his new role as servant to the old prophet.

The Lord God protected Israel from Ben-hadad and the Syrians in chapter twenty, but sent a prophet to Ahab to announce his doom. Ahab returned to his house, 'sullen and vexed'.

The selfish, self-serving king of Israel coveted the vineyard of his neighbour, Naboth. When Naboth refused to sell it to him, Jezebel stole the vineyard for her sulking husband. This base idolater falsely accused Naboth of cursing both God and the king and had him killed. Persecutors never lack for imagination in the appearance of justifying their villainy.

When Ahab went to take possession of Naboth's vineyard, Elijah confronted him again with all the boldness he had in days gone by. When Ahab heard God's message, he showed great outward signs of repentance before the Lord. Though it was only an outward show of repentance, God nevertheless promised not to take the kingdom from his house until after he was dead.

The final chapter in both Ahab's life and the book of 1 Kings is about Jehoshaphat's alliance with Ahab. Ahab, the king of Israel, wanted Jehoshaphat, the king of Judah, to go to war with him against Syria. The two kings sought the will of God by the counsel of four hundred false prophets who cowered before Ahab. The hireling prophets told them what Ahab wanted to hear, and assured them of victory. But Jehoshaphat insisted upon consulting Micaiah, a true prophet of God. Micaiah, being a faithful prophet, told them the mind of God and prophesied that Ahab would be killed in the battle.

True to his cowardly character, Ahab placed Jehoshaphat in a conspicuous place during the battle, hoping that the Syrians would mistake Jehoshaphat for himself and he would be killed. But 'a certain man drew a bow at a venture, and smote the king of Israel between the joints of the harness'. Our God is the God of circumstances. There are no accidents in his world. Ahab's body was brought to Samaria and the dogs licked up his blood from the chariot according to the word of God. The account at the end of 1 Kings briefly summarizes the reign of Jehoshaphat of Judah, who walked in the good way of his father Asa. This story is picked up and continued in 2 Kings.

Elisha's Call

Pause for a moment and reflect upon chapter nineteen. Here we have the record of Elisha's call. Elisha's ministry was a source of healing and of blessing. In that way he was typical of Christ. But Elisha is also representative of all who are called to life and faith in Christ, and representative of all who are called of God to preach the gospel of Christ.

While Elisha was plowing his fields with his servants, he saw the outlawed prophet of Gilead coming toward him. Passing by him, Elijah cast his mantle upon Elisha. Elisha knew the meaning of this sign. Though he was a very wealthy man, he had now been called of God to be Elijah's servant, to follow him, minister to him in lowliness and humility, and perhaps even to die with him. Immediate decisiveness was demanded. Elisha counted the cost and made his choice. After seeking Elijah's permission, he kissed his parents goodbye, burned his oxen, gave everything away, and followed the Lord, serving his prophet Elijah, totally abandoning his former life.

That is exactly what happens when the Lord Jesus Christ, our God and Saviour, passes by chosen, redeemed sinners, and casts over them the skirt of his righteousness, calling them to life and faith. The sinner called by grace willingly forsakes all and follows Christ (Luke 14:25-33).

Likewise, that is exactly what happens when the Lord God calls a man to preach the gospel. The man called of God to the work of the gospel confers not with flesh and blood, but willingly forsakes all for Christ, that he may give himself to the most noble of all callings.

Chapter 12

2 Kings

'Where is the God of Elijah?'

2 Kings picks up the history of Israel's divided kingdom right where 1 Kings ended. It is a sad history of man's rebellion, sin and idolatry.

Israel

After Solomon's death, after the kingdom of Israel was divided, the northern kingdom of Israel was ruled for 250 years by nineteen different men. All of them were wicked, idolatrous, self-serving men. God sent prophet after prophet to them, calling them to repentance. Elijah, Elisha, Amos, Hosea, and Jonah were all sent with God's word to the rebel tribes of the northern kingdom. But Israel and her kings followed Baal and the gods of human invention. Walking after the lusts of their own hearts, they walked in obstinate defiance of God's right to be God, plunging themselves into deeper and deeper moral and spiritual degradation. At last, God gave them up!

Judah

Things were only slightly better in Judah. The southern kingdom of Judah survived for 140 years longer than Israel. She had twenty different kings, all from the family of David. Most of their kings were also wicked men. Few walked in the way of David. They wore his name, but knew nothing of his character or his God. Behold the election of God!

After a long history hearing and despising the Word of God, Israel was taken captive by the Assyrians. One hundred and thirty-six years later, Judah, following the same path of rebellion, idolatry and sin, was also taken away in captivity to Babylon. The reason for both kingdom's troubles is recorded in 2 Kings 17:9-19 ...

'And the children of Israel did secretly those things that were not right against the LORD their God, and they built them high places in all their cities, from the tower of the watchmen to the fenced city. And they set them up images and groves in every high hill, and under every green tree: And there they burnt incense in all the high places, as did the heathen whom the LORD carried away before them; and wrought wicked things to provoke the LORD to anger: For they served idols, whereof the LORD had said unto them, Ye shall not do this thing. Yet the LORD testified against Israel, and against Judah, by all the prophets, and by all the seers, saying, Turn ye from your evil ways, and keep my commandments and my statutes, according to all the law which I commanded your fathers, and which I sent to you by my servants the prophets. Notwithstanding they would not hear, but hardened their necks, like to the neck of their fathers, that did not believe in the LORD their God. And they rejected his statutes, and his covenant that he made with their fathers, and his testimonies which he testified against them; and they followed vanity, and became vain, and went after the heathen that were round about them, concerning whom the LORD had charged them, that they should not do like them. And they left all the commandments of the LORD their God, and made them molten images, even two calves, and made a grove, and worshipped all the host of heaven, and served Baal. And they caused their sons and their daughters to pass through the fire, and used divination and enchantments, and sold themselves to do evil in the sight of the LORD, to provoke him to anger. Therefore the LORD was very angry with Israel, and removed them out of his sight: there was none left but the tribe of Judah only. Also Judah kept not the commandments of the LORD their God, but walked in the statutes of Israel which they made'.

It is disobedience to the revelation of God, wilful, deliberate disobedience of a heart at enmity against God, that brings upon men and women the everlasting wrath and judgment of God (Proverbs 1:23-33; 29:1).

God's Purpose of Grace

Though the Lord God utterly destroyed the northern kingdom and swore that he would destroy Judah as well, he preserved a remnant, even in judgment, by whom Christ would come through the seed of David.

Back in Genesis 49:8-12, God had sworn that he would not destroy Judah until Christ had come. So God refused to cast them off altogether until after the resurrection of Christ. Then, in 70 AD he destroyed the physical seed of Abraham and turned his hand of mercy to the gathering of his elect scattered throughout the world (Romans 11:1-5, 26-29, 33-36).

The Prophets

Yet, rather than focusing our attention on the wickedness of Israel's kings, throughout these twenty-five chapters the Holy Spirit tells a different story of grace and mercy. It is a story that revolves around the lives and ministries of faithful prophets.

In addition to Elijah, Elisha, Amos, Hosea, and Jonah, the history of Israel and Judah described in 2 Kings takes in the ministries Obadiah, Joel, Isaiah, Micah, Nahum, Habakkuk, Zephaniah, Jeremiah, Ezekiel, and Daniel. It is true, there were in Judah a few good kings, a few who enacted laws for the glory of God and the good of his people, a few kings who tore down the idolatrous groves, the high places, the altars, and the images of Baal. There were a few, like Hezekiah, who did 'that which was right in the sight of the Lord'. We do not have to guess what is meant by those words. In 2 Kings 18:4-7, we are told what the faithful man did.

'He removed the high places, and brake the images, and cut down the groves, and brake in pieces the brazen serpent that Moses had made: for unto those days the children of Israel did burn incense to it: and he called it Nehushtan. He trusted in the LORD God of Israel; so that after him was none like him among all the kings of Judah, nor any that were before him. For he clave to the LORD, and departed not from following him, but kept his commandments, which the LORD commanded Moses. And the LORD was with him; and he prospered whithersoever he went forth: and he rebelled against the king of Assyria, and served him not'.

Many today make much of Egypt's boy king, Tutankhamun. But Egypt's king was only a boy pagan, who followed the wickedness of his fathers. Judah also had a boy king by the name of Josiah, who stood head and shoulders above his fathers. In 2 Kings 23:25 we are told, 'And like unto him was there no king before him, that turned to the LORD with all his heart, and with all his soul, and with all his might, according to all the law of Moses; neither after him arose there any like him'.

Josiah was just eight years old when he began to reign. When he was eighteen years old, he undertook to restore the house of God. Hilkiah the priest found the book of God in the ruins of the temple. He gave it to Shaphan the scribe. Shaphan read the book to the king. The young King Josiah went to work for the glory of God and the good of his people. He destroyed the idols, executed false prophets, purged the land of homosexuals, put away the wizards and witches, and kept the Passover. Nevertheless, the story of God's mercy and grace, the story of God's blessings upon his people always revolves around his prophets, those men of God sent to proclaim his Word to his people.

Elijah

Elijah was John the Baptist of the Old Testament. As John the Baptist was the forerunner of Christ, so God's prophets were always the forerunners of either judgment or of mercy. In the second chapter of 2 Kings, Elijah is distinctly set before us as a picture of that blessed hope in which we live, anxiously awaiting our Lord's gracious call by which he will soon fetch us home. 'And it came to pass, as they still went on, and talked, that, behold, there appeared a chariot of fire, and horses of fire, and parted them both asunder; and Elijah went up by a whirlwind into heaven. And Elisha saw it'.

Elijah's translation to heaven is a vivid picture of the believer's death. As Elijah died not, but was translated to glory, so the believer does not die (John 11:26), but merely drops his earthly clay and rises into heaven. Then, in the last day, when Christ comes again, immediately after the resurrection of those saints whose bodies sleep in the earth, all believers living at the time will be instantaneously translated and caught up to meet the Lord in the air (1 Thessalonians 4:13-18).

Elisha

Elisha had faithfully served Elijah from the time the prophet of God had cast his mantle upon him. When the old prophet was about to go home, he asked his faithful servant what he wanted. Look at it. 'And Elisha said, I pray thee, let a double portion of thy spirit be upon me. And he said, Thou hast asked a hard thing: nevertheless, if thou see me when I am taken from thee, it shall be so unto thee; but if not, it shall not be so' (2:9-10).

Elisha's request for a double portion of Elijah's spirit was not, as is commonly thought, a request that he might have twice the power and influence as a prophet that Elijah had. That would have been an absurd, selfish, proud, and ungodly request.

The law of God required that the firstborn son receive a double portion (Deuteronomy 21:17) of his father's estate. What Elisha requested was that he might be received of God and treated by him as Elijah's firstborn son. Elijah knew that what was asked was something only God could grant. If Elisha was permitted to see Elijah's ascension into heaven it would be the sign that his request had been granted. 'And Elisha saw it!' That is exactly what God gives to all his people. He gives all his elect the double portion of his Firstborn Son, all the heritage of Christ (John 17:5, 22; Isaiah 40:1-2, Romans 8:17). This great inheritance of grace and glory is freely bestowed upon every sinner to whom and in whom God reveals his Son in his saving glory. When a sinner receives this great boon of grace, like Elisha when he saw Elijah taken up, tears off his own clothes, takes up the mantle of Christ's righteousness, and walks with God forever in the power of his resurrection (Romans 6). This is exactly what we confess in believer's baptism (Romans 6:4-6).

Waters Healed

As Moses healed the bitter waters of Marah by casting in the tree that pictured the cross of Christ, Elisha healed the waters of Jericho by casting in salt. Before this, the land of Jericho was full of death and barren. Once the waters were healed, it was full of life and abounding with fruit.

The salt Elisha cast into the waters represented much the same thing as the tree at Marah. You will remember that God required Israel, with all their sacrifices, to offer salt. His covenant was called 'a covenant of salt' (Numbers 18:19; 2 Chronicles 13:5).

This is a picture of the gospel and its power in the lives of God's elect. It is the power of God unto salvation. Once the salt of covenant grace has been cast into our deadness and barrenness, life springs up in our very souls and the Spirit of God, by the covenant of salt, makes sinners who were dead in trespasses and sins, sinners who are utterly useless, fruitful unto God (Mark 9:49,50; Colossians 4:6).

Ditches

In chapter three the Lord performed a mighty miracle for Israel, Judah and Edom, when Moab threatened to destroy them. It was a miracle portraying God's great work of grace in chosen, redeemed sinners. Ditches were cut through all the land according to the Word of God. When God the Holy Spirit does a work of grace in the heart of a sinner, his first work is that of breaking up the fallow ground of his sin hardened heart by the Word of God in conviction of sin (John 16:8-9).

Wherever a ditch was cut, the water of life filled the ditch without any effort, or even sound, or even feeling on the part of any man. Wherever God the Holy Spirit comes in conviction, he fills the broken heart with life. The ditches were filled with water in direct connection with the morning sacrifice. Grace and life come to sinners by the power of God as the result of, and only as the result of, Christ's sacrifice.

A Pot of Oil

In chapter four there was a poor prophet's widow, who was left in debt when her husband died. She had two sons and nothing with which to pay her debts. She was terrified that she and her sons might be taken into bondage by their creditor. The Lord God miraculously met her need by the power of his grace in a way that clearly speaks of his method of grace in saving his elect.

She had a little oil in her vessel; but the only way she could get what she needed was to first have her little bit of oil completely poured out. God only fills empty vessels. Once she emptied her little vessel, she never lacked again. When we are emptied of self, God the Holy Spirit fills us. He brings to our souls all the fulness of Christ, by whom all our debt has been paid, and all our needs supplied.

New Birth

Throughout the scriptures, the new birth is portrayed as a resurrection from the dead (John 11; Ephesians 2:4-8; Revelation 20:6). In 2 Kings 4 we have a delightful picture of it in the resurrection of the Shunammite's son. This poor woman ran to the man of God with her dead son. Shall we not run to Christ for mercy for our spiritually dead sons and daughters? Elijah sent his servant running to meet her. The prophet took the dead boy away to his own private room and performed his mighty miracle. He prayed for the child, just as the Lord Jesus Christ intercedes for his elect. He stretched himself upon the child, mouth to mouth, eye to eye, hand to hand, and gave his life (as it were) to the child. That is exactly what our Saviour does for us in the new birth. He gives us his life.

Death in the Pot

At Gilgal, men gathered herbs from the cursed earth, never suspecting that there might be danger in eating them, 'For they knew them not'. They made a huge bowl of pottage for the prophets. But there was death in the pot. Elisha cast meal into the pot and there was no longer any harm or death in the pot. Similarly, when Christ, the Bread of Life, comes into our lives, lives poisoned with sin that would have brought us eternal death, there is no more curse and no more harm for us.

Finally, in the last verses of chapter four, Elisha multiplied the loaves for the feeding of a multitude. They ate all they wanted, and plenty was left over. In like manner, God's free grace in Christ is boundless, ever multiplied, fully satisfying, and there is an infinite abundance of it for sinners.

Naaman

The story of Naaman's healing in chapter five is tremendous and instructive. He was a mighty man of wealth and influence, a captain among Israel's enemies. He was also a leper. But Naaman was a man chosen of God as an object of grace. Because he had purposed to be gracious to him, the Lord God graciously sent a little girl who believed God and who gave him a word of hope. At the appointed time of love, when the Lord would be gracious to him, he crossed Naaman's path, humbled him and healed him, both of the leprosy of his body and the leprosy of his soul.

Axe Head and Fiery Chariots

In chapter six the lost axe head, that was made to swim, is a picture of our constant need of grace being supplied to us by the power and goodness of God. Some men were working with a borrowed tool. Through some carelessness, they lost the axe head. Elisha made it swim and returned it to them.

That grace and power of God's Spirit by which we serve him is his gift to us, but it is his. When we have, through carelessness and sin, lost our Lord's manifest presence and strength, let us pray like David, 'Take not thy Holy Spirit from me. Restore unto me the joy of thy salvation'. Our great Saviour will restore to us the joy of his salvation.

The chariots of fire surrounding God's servants were there to protect and care for his own. But Elisha's servant could not see those chariots until the Lord God opened his eyes. The Lord God is ever with his elect. His angels constantly minister to those he has chosen to be the heirs of salvation (Hebrews 1:14). But the calm assurance of God's presence is known only as our God opens our eyes and gives us faith to behold him.

In chapter seven, four lepers came in desperation to the Syrians, with no rights and little hope. God prepared the Syrian camp for their arrival and there they found bread and life. Once they had found the bread of life, they brought the good news to Israel; and the starving children of Israel were happy to receive the good news even from leprous men.

Like those four lepers, poor, perishing sinners flee to Christ in utter desperation. But fleeing to him, they find life and carry the good news to others. Yes, the Lord God graciously uses leprous sinners, sinners saved by his grace, to carry the good news of grace to other poor, perishing sinners.

Holy Zeal

2 Kings, like all the rest of the book of God, speaks of all those great things Christ has done for his people and the glory of God.

Jehu said to Jehonadab, 'Is thine heart right with mine heart? And Jehonadab said, It is'. Jehonadab gave Jehu his hand, and Jehu took him up into his chariot saying, 'Come with me and see my zeal for the Lord'. Is your heart right with God? 'Dost thou believe on the Son of God?' Give him your hand, trust your life to him; and he will take you unto himself and show you his zeal for God, the zeal by which he has performed your salvation.

Gehazi, Elisha's servant, was commanded of the king saying, 'Tell me, I pray thee, all the great things that Elisha hath done'. Similarly, God's servants are commanded of God to constantly tell eternity bound men and women all the great things Christ has done, to tell it from all the book of God.

Even in death Elisha bore testimony to the resurrection power of Jesus Christ. Elisha died and was buried, but his death brought life to another who was hastily laid in the prophet's sepulchre. So Christ gives life to those who are dead in trespasses and sin. Christ's life-giving touch is all that is necessary for dead sinners.

Hezekiah was sick unto death. Observe how death comes to all men, kings and servants, as the just wages of sin. Hezekiah feared death, as well he might and cried to the Lord. Only Christ can allay the fear of death. Only grace can comfort a needy soul in their darkest hour. Only perfect righteousness can prepare a sin-sick soul for eternity. Hezekiah wept sore.

But God is the God of wonder and miracle and the greatest forces of nature bow to the sovereignty of God. The passage of the sun through the sky cannot continue except the Lord of all creation so dictates. Is it a hard thing that time should stand still? Is it possible that the very course of the sun in heaven be reversed as a demonstration of omnipotent power? See how Christ, the sun of righteousness, stops to comfort a poor sinner. See how the very forces of nature are subject to God's purpose of saving his elect.

Hezekiah sought mercy and the Lord heard his prayer and healed him. God said, 'I have heard thy prayer, I have seen thy tears: behold, I will heal thee'. So the people of God find salvation in their omnipotent Redeemer who accomplished their salvation and declares on their behalf, 'The Lord will do the thing that he has spoken'.

Chapter 13

1 Chronicles

God's King, God's Ark, God's Worship

It is evident that 1 Chronicles was written after Israel had returned from their 70 years of captivity in Babylon. It covers much of the same period of Israel's history that is given in 2 Samuel. But in 1 Chronicles there is a distinct emphasis on instruction, instruction in the worship of God. This book is not so much about Israel's history as it is about God's king, God's ark, and God's worship.

This book might be compared to the gospel of John in the New Testament. We call the first three gospel narratives (Matthew, Mark, and Luke) the synoptic gospels because they give us the historical account of our Lord's earthly life and ministry. But the gospel of John is different. John's gospel was the last book of holy scripture to be written, probably about 90 or 95 A.D. It distinctly teaches us the meaning of our Saviour's accomplishments. John gave us selected incidents in the Lord's earthly life and ministry, and shows us their meaning. He tells us that his purpose was not to give a chronological history of our Lord's life on earth, but to teach us the meaning of it (John 20:30-31)

John made no attempt to cover the whole of the Lord's ministry. Instead, he carefully selected certain things out of Christ's ministry to illustrate the great point that he wanted to make. The Lord Jesus Christ is the Son of God, the Messiah, the King of whom all the prophets spoke. This was his purpose. The book of 1 Chronicles is like that. It gives us selective bits of Israel's history, focusing our attention on God's king, David, God's ark, and God's worship, constantly pointing us to Christ, of whom David and the ark were typical, and in whom alone God is worshipped.

The Genealogies

The first nine chapters read a little laboriously. They give us a long genealogical record of the nation of Israel. 1 Chronicles reaches all the way back to Adam, and takes us through the reign of David and the earliest days of Solomon's reign.

If you are like me, you are tempted to hurry passed these long lists of names and get to the 'important' stuff. We feel sort of like the old preacher who was reading Matthew 1. He started out reading, 'Abraham begat Isaac; and Isaac begat Jacob; and Jacob begat Judah and his brethren'. Then he said, 'They kept on begatting one another all the way down this side of the page and clear on to the other side'. Then he picked up the reading and went on from there. We ought not to do that. The genealogies are very important.

The genealogies give us an indisputable chronological connection and order concerning the various events recorded in Old Testament history. They also show us clearly and indisputably that our Saviour is the seed of Abraham and the seed of David according to the flesh. In fact, he is the only Person now living who is positively known to be of David's seed, possessing a right to David's throne. Of all the things the Jews questioned about our Lord, of all the excuses they made for their refusal to bow to him, of all the accusations they raised of him being an impostor, never once did anyone question our Master's clear genealogy. It was indisputable.

The genealogies display the movement of God's providence toward the goal for which the world was made, the incarnation, redemptive work, and resurrection glory of the Lord Jesus Christ, accomplishing the salvation of God's elect to the praise of the glory of his grace. As they do so, the genealogies give us a picture of God's sovereign electing grace. He includes some in the chosen line, and excludes others, altogether as it pleases him.

The genealogy that begins in 1 Chronicles 1 begins at the dawn of human history. It lists the sons of Adam (Seth, Enosh, Kenan, and Mahalalel). We know that among the sons of Adam were Cain, Abel, and

1 Chronicles   125

Seth, but here Cain is excluded. His brother Abel, whom he murdered, is also excluded. The focus is on the descendants of Seth, because Abraham and Israel came from Seth.

Then the line of Seth is traced down to Enoch and Noah. The three sons of Noah, Shem, Ham and Japheth, are listed; but Ham, and Japheth are dismissed with a brief word and attention is focused on Shem and his family. From Shem we get to Abraham and his family. Ishmael is excluded from the promise and Isaac is chosen. Esau is rejected and Jacob is chosen (Romans 3:3-4). The purpose of God according to election always stands immutable and sure (Romans 9:11-13).

Then the genealogy focuses on Jacob's twelve sons, from whom come the twelve tribes of Israel. In the end, ten of the twelve tribes are rejected. Still, the purpose of God continues. He chose Judah and Levi, the kingly and the priestly lines. David, and Solomon, and the kings of the house of David down to the time of the Babylonian captivity came from the tribe of Judah. The tribe of Levi is traced down to Aaron, the first of the priests, and then to the priests who were prominent in the kingdom at the time of David.

Chapter 10 gives us an account of Saul's miserable reign and of the judgment of God upon him because he despised God and his Word and sought the counsel of a witch.

God's King

Chapter 11 opens with David being established as king over Israel. 'Then all Israel gathered themselves to David unto Hebron, saying, Behold, we are thy bone and thy flesh. And moreover in time past, even when Saul was king, thou wast he that leddest out and broughtest in Israel: and the LORD thy God said unto thee, Thou shalt feed my people Israel, and thou shalt be ruler over my people Israel. Therefore came all the elders of Israel to the king to Hebron; and David made a covenant with them in Hebron before the LORD; and they anointed David king over Israel, according to the word of the LORD by Samuel'.

David is once more set before us as an eminent type of our Lord Jesus Christ, the King of Zion, the King of Glory, whom God has exalted to be our Prince and Saviour to give his salvation to chosen sinners (Acts 5:30-31). All God's Israel shall be gathered to Christ. Even when he is not acknowledged, he is the One who leads, protects and defends his people. As David 'waxed greater and greater: for the LORD of hosts was with him', our great King, the Lord Jesus Christ, is great above all, exalted, pre-eminent, and glorious beyond compare.

God's Ark

Beginning in chapter 13 our attention is focused on the ark of God, the temple of God, and the worship of God. These are things constantly held before us in the book of God as matters of paramount importance. The ark of the covenant represents the Lord Jesus Christ, our propitiation, our sin-atoning substitute, and the salvation he accomplished for his people (Hebrews 9:1-14; 1 John 1:7-2:2). The temple of God represents the church and the kingdom of God. It also represents the whole salvation of God's elect (1 Corinthians 3:16-17; Ephesians 2:20-22). That is the purpose of God accomplished in and by Christ. The worship of God is that which we render to him by faith in Christ.

These things must be paramount in our hearts and in our lives. There is a cathedral in Milan, Italy with three doors and an inscription over each door. Over the right hand door a wreath of flowers is carved and the inscription reads, 'All that pleases is but for a moment'. On the left hand door the inscription is, 'All that troubles is but for a moment'. Over the main entrance are the words, 'Nothing is important but that which is eternal'. This is the lesson of 1 Chronicles. In a sense, it is the lesson of the whole Bible (1 Corinthians 10:31; Colossians 3:1-3, 17).

The Worship of God

Let us see what this instructive book teaches us about the worship of our God and Saviour. May God the Holy Spirit be pleased to inscribe its lessons upon our hearts. One of David's first acts as king was bringing the ark of the Lord back to Zion. It is recorded in chapters 13 and 15.

'And David consulted with the captains of thousands and hundreds, and with every leader. And David said unto all the congregation of Israel, If it seem good unto you, and that it be of the LORD our God, let us send abroad unto our brethren every where, that are left in all the land of Israel, and with them also to the priests and Levites which are in their cities and suburbs, that they may gather themselves unto us: And let us bring again the ark of our God to us: for we inquired not at it in the days of Saul'.

For twenty years the Ark with its mercy-seat, God's appointed meeting-place with his people, was neglected and almost forgotten. The sacrifice, the mercy-seat, the place where God meets with men, all pre-figuring the Lord Jesus Christ had been despised and neglected and ignored. David wanted to re-establish the worship of God in Israel. However, he made several fatal mistakes.

Rather than consulting with God, he consulted with the people. Rather than having the ark carried on the shoulders of the Levites, he made an impressive, ornate cart for the ark. Rather than sacrificing, they made a great, impressive show that pleased everyone, except God. 'They played before God with all their might'.

What a picture that is of what goes on in most churches, in most of what passes for worship today. Men and women, ignoring the gospel and ordinances of God, play before God with all their might, gratifying their own lusts, entertaining themselves nothing more!

Then, suddenly, the oxen that pulled the cart stumbled. Their new cart tipped over and the ark of God appeared to be falling. Almost instinctively, 'Uzza put forth his hand to hold the ark' (13:10). But God required that no man touch that ark. It represented salvation by Christ alone. No man's hand is involved in God's great work of redemption and grace. Uzza dared to defy God. No matter what his intentions were, his act was in defiance of God and for that God killed him on the spot. Now, learn this lesson and learn it well. God almighty still kills men who dare put their hands to his great work of redemption and salvation! All who attempt to put their hand or their will to God's salvation shall perish for their defiance.

Due Order
When the Lord God showed his disapproval of their devices, David became angry with God and was afraid of him. Then, in chapter 15, having learned his lesson, David prepared a place and went to recover the ark and bring it to Jerusalem. This time he did everything by the book, acknowledging that what he had done before was impetuous, wrong and an affront to God. He confessed, 'For because ye did it not at the first, the LORD our God made a breach upon us, for that we sought him not after the due order'.

If we would worship God, we must worship him in the way he has prescribed in his Word, trusting Christ alone, adding nothing to his Word, and taking nothing from his Word. There is no place in the house and worship of God for anything except prayer, praise, preaching, believer's baptism, and the Lord's Table. All the inventions of men, the putting on of religious entertainments, political rallies, debate, infant dedications and sprinklings, all man-made inventions are but an abomination to God. His ordinances must not be perverted. As we worship our God through faith in Christ, giving all honour and glory to him alone, we must expect to be despised by those who do not know our God, just as David was despised by his wife Michal.

'So they brought the ark of God, and set it in the midst of the tent that David had pitched for it: and they offered burnt sacrifices and peace offerings before God. And when David had made an end of offering the burnt offerings and the peace offerings, he blessed the people in the name of the LORD. And he dealt to every one of Israel, both man and woman, to every one a loaf of bread, and a good piece of flesh, and a flagon of wine'.

These burnt offerings and peace offerings speak of Christ, by whom we have peace with God. Once the offerings were accepted, David blessed the people, upon the basis of God's acceptance of the offerings. That is the only way God's blessings come to chosen sinners, upon the basis of Christ's finished work and accepted sacrifice. Not only did he bless them, he gave them each a loaf of bread and a flagon of wine pictures of Christ's sacrifice and of our communion with God by his blood and righteousness.

God's Promise
Next, we read of God's promise to David in chapter seventeen. The great desire of David's heart was to build a temple for the Lord. But the Lord would not allow him to do it because David had 'shed much blood upon the earth'. However, the Lord promised David that a son should be born unto him, who should be 'a man of rest', that he would build his house, and that God would establish his throne forever.

David bowed to God's will without a murmur, and poured forth a song of praise for his great goodness. In the promised son we see Christ our Lord, 'a Greater than Solomon'. 'Thou shalt call his name Jesus. He shall be great, and shall be called the Son of the highest; and the Lord God shall give unto him the throne of his father David: and he shall reign over the house of Jacob forever; and of his kingdom there shall be no end' (Luke 1:31-33).

The preservation of Israel, not the physical nation, but the spiritual Israel of God, was here guaranteed till the end of time, 'as long as the sun and the moon endure' (Jeremiah 31:35-37). David's throne which is Christ's throne, was permanently secured with the added sign, 'and as the faithful witness in the sky', the rainbow (Psalm 89:3, 4, 27-37; Revelation 4:2-3). The bow of God's covenant ever stands before the throne of his grace. All that he does as the Monarch of the universe, he does in fulfilment of his everlasting covenant of grace for the salvation of his people (John 17:2). David's Son, the Lord Jesus Christ, shall sit upon David's throne, answerable to the throne of grace, in that Jerusalem which is above forever.

Israel Numbered
The next very significant and instructive event recorded in 1 Chronicles is David's sin in numbering the people in chapter 21. His sin in

this was, I am sure, at least in part, a display of personal pride because of the greatness of his kingdom. However, there is more to it than that. David's numbering of Israel seems to have conveyed the thought that the success of God's purpose depends upon the number of those who are with us in our efforts. He wanted to see the number of people that were available to him, and thus to glory in the physical strength of his realm.

God never works by a majority. When we begin to think that the cause of Christ is losing out because our numbers are small, we dishonour God and the gospel of God. God's cause does not depend upon us, our strength, or abilities, or our numbers. I cannot help thinking of Gideon and God's deliberate reduction of the number of men from 32,000 to just 300. David slew Goliath and delivered Israel with a sling and a rock from the brook. Samson slew the Philistines with nothing but the jawbone of an ass, hardly an auspicious weapon. God's cause does not depend upon us.

Still, there is more. David's sin displayed a neglect of Christ and his sacrifice. When he numbered Israel, there was no payment of ransom money, or atonement money, as required by God's law.

'And the LORD spake unto Moses, saying, When thou takest the sum of the children of Israel after their number, then shall they give every man a ransom for his soul unto the LORD, when thou numberest them; that there be no plague among them, when thou numberest them. This they shall give, every one that passeth among them that are numbered, half a shekel after the shekel of the sanctuary: (a shekel is twenty gerahs:) an half shekel shall be the offering of the LORD. Every one that passeth among them that are numbered, from twenty years old and above, shall give an offering unto the LORD. The rich shall not give more, and the poor shall not give less than half a shekel, when they give an offering unto the LORD, to make an atonement for your souls. And thou shalt take the atonement money of the children of Israel, and shalt appoint it for the service of the tabernacle of the congregation; that it may be a memorial unto the children of Israel before the LORD, to make an atonement for your soul' (Exodus 30:11-16).

Again, we see a terrible judgment brought upon Israel by the neglect of God's sacrifice, by the neglect of the atonement and by the neglect of Christ. This numbering of the children of Israel and the atonement money they paid so that no plague come upon them was typical of our ransom by Christ. None but Israelites were ransomed. A specific, numbered people were ransomed. The ransom price was the same for all. Those who were ransomed were preserved from any plague (Proverbs 12:21; Psalm 91:10).

Substitution

Yet, against this backdrop, the Lord gives us a blessed picture of that very thing which David had neglected, substitution. That is the message of the whole book of God (21:17).

'And David said unto God, Is it not I that commanded the people to be numbered? even I it is that have sinned and done evil indeed; but as for these sheep, what have they done? let thine hand, I pray thee, O LORD my God, be on me, and on my father's house; but not on thy people, that they should be plagued'.

What a beautiful picture this is of our great, sin-atoning Substitute, the Lord Jesus Christ. He made our sin his own (Psalm 40:12; 69:5). When the Lord God said to the angel of judgment, 'It is enough, stay now thine hand', he had his eye on the substitutionary work of Christ portrayed in the sacrifices offered on Mount Moriah, which David purchased from Ornan. All that transpired there spoke of our Saviour's sacrifice at Calvary.

God's People

When David had finished his work, when all the material for the temple was gathered, he went home. Here, again, our Lord Jesus Christ shines forth brilliantly. When he had finished all his work, when he had brought in everlasting righteousness, when he had put away sin by the sacrifice of himself, when he had magnified the law and made it honourable, when he had done all the will of God, he returned home (John 17:1-4; 19:30). Then all the people worshipped and served God with a willing heart. The Lord God chose them; and they honoured him as his willing servants.

Here is a great thought to cheer our hearts as we seek to serve our great King and Saviour, the Lord Jesus. It brings joy to the heart of our King when we offer willingly to his service, whether it be ourselves, or our substance that we give. David's thanksgiving shows the right attitude of heart, the recognition that all indeed belongs to God. 'Who am I, and what is my people, that we should be able to offer so willingly after this sort? For all things come of Thee, and of Thine own have we given Thee'. God give me such a heart!

Chapter 14

2 Chronicles

'I will never leave thee, nor forsake thee!'

How often, like the children of Israel, we are brought into captivity because of our own sin, because of our disobedience, because we turn aside from the Word of God and walk contrary to the will of God! How often we forsake him! But he never forsakes us! If we had what we deserve, we would be forsaken of him. But, as he swore to Jacob, he has sworn to us, 'I will never leave thee, nor forsake thee!' How I thank God for his word of promise! He says to you and me, 'I am the Lord, I change not: therefore ye sons of Jacob are not consumed'.

He may scatter us, in loving chastisement, and hide his face from us to make us know our need of him. He may bring us, as it were, into bondage and captivity spiritually; but our God will not utterly forsake us. Neither will he let us forsake him. It is written, 'They shall lie down in the evening: for the Lord their God shall visit them, and turn away their captivity' (Zephaniah 2:7). This day of divine visitation is described by the prophet Isaiah in the twelfth chapter of his prophecy.

'And in that day thou shalt say, O LORD, I will praise thee: though thou wast angry with me, thine anger is turned away, and thou comfortedst me. Behold, God is my salvation; I will trust, and not be afraid: for the LORD JEHOVAH is my strength and my song; he also is become my salvation. Therefore with joy shall ye draw water out of the wells of salvation. And in that day shall ye say, Praise the LORD, call upon his name, declare his doings among the people, make mention that his name is exalted. Sing unto the LORD; for he hath done excellent things: this is known in all the earth. Cry out and shout, thou inhabitant of Zion: for great is the Holy One of Israel in the midst of thee'.

The book of 2 Chronicles is a portrayal of God's goodness and grace in visiting, reviving, and refreshing his people after they have forsaken him and have been brought into bondage because of their sin. What is recorded here in these thirty-six chapters of Judah's history is written for our learning and admonition, that God's faithfulness to his people may inspire us to walk faithfully with him.

God's Promise

Let us begin with God's promise to his people in 2 Chronicles 7:14. 'If my people, which are called by my name, shall humble themselves, and pray, and seek my face, and turn from their wicked ways; then will I hear from heaven, and will forgive their sin, and will heal their land'.

I do not know of any one verse in the Old Testament that is more often quoted and more completely misinterpreted than this one. This verse is neither a formula for revival, nor a formula for the healing of any earthly nation's woes. This is a promise from God to his people, the people called by his grace and called by his name, because of his choice of them. Here, the Lord God promises that if we who are his people humbly pray, seek his face, turn from and repent of our wicked ways, he will forgive our sins and heal our land, that is, the land of his heritage, the church and kingdom of God.

The promise appears to be conditional, and, in a sense, it is. God promises forgiveness and healing grace upon condition of our repentance. But, if you will turn back to chapter 6 where we have Solomon's prayer, to which God gives answer in chapter 7, you will see clearly that our repentance is always the result of God's grace and never the cause. Look particularly at verses 26-27. It is the goodness of God that leads us to repentance (Romans 2:4). Christ, our exalted Prince and Saviour, gives repentance and forgiveness of sins to the Israel of God. Clearly, Solomon understood this. In this part of his magnificent prayer he declares plainly that when we have sinned, we will pray and turn again to our God only when the Lord God himself has graciously taught us to walk in the good way wherein we should walk.

'When the heaven is shut up, and there is no rain, because they have sinned against thee; yet if they pray toward this place, and confess thy name, and turn from their sin, when thou dost afflict them; Then hear thou from heaven, and forgive the sin of thy servants, and of thy people Israel, when thou hast taught them the good way, wherein they should walk; and send rain upon thy land, which thou hast given unto thy people for an inheritance.'

The Temple

The first seven chapters of this book are taken up with the building of the temple in Jerusalem. Up to this point in Israel's history there was no fixed, permanent place for the ark of God, no fixed, permanent place of divine worship, no fixed, permanent place to which men and women would gather in solemn assembly to hear from and worship the Lord God. The temple at Jerusalem changed all of that. Still, we must not fail to remember, that the temple itself was but a carnal, physical, temporary type of something far greater, far more magnificent, and far more delightful.

The temple was a picture, a type, a symbol of our Lord Jesus Christ. As we have seen, it typified God's people and God's salvation; but it also typified our Saviour. The New Testament makes this abundantly clear. Our Saviour referred to his body as the temple that must be destroyed and raised again in three days. The whole book of Hebrews relates the temple, its furniture, its priesthood, its sacrifices, and its services to our blessed Saviour and his great work of redemption.

Because the temple represents Christ and his great work of redemption, it also represents his church, the people redeemed by his blood and saved by his grace. Considered as a whole, the church is called the temple of God (1 Corinthians 3:16-17). Because every saved sinner is part of God's church, each particular member of the church, every believer, is also called the temple of God (2 Corinthians 6:16).

As the stones used to build the temple were hewn, shaped, and marked for their place outside the temple itself so that there was no sound of hammer, or saw, or chisel in the temple, so God's elect were chosen from eternity, marked out in divine predestination for their place in the building of God, and made a part of the temple by a work of God's free grace in Christ. In this spiritual temple, the church of God, no jarring sound of human effort is ever heard (Ephesians 2:8-9, 19-22). The building of this house is altogether God's work.

When the temple was finished, God was honoured and worshipped in a solemn ceremony that lasted seven days. It was declared that God had fulfilled his word, that all the people of Israel were 'glad and merry in heart for the goodness that the Lord had shown', and that everything Solomon had set his heart to do 'he prosperously effected'. 'Behold, a greater than Solomon is here!'

Solomon's Prayer

As we read Solomon's prayer of dedication in chapter 6, we must never fail to remember that he, too, was a type of Christ. He made intercession for Israel, and even for the strangers and sojourners, God's elect among the Gentiles, who would be numbered among the children of Israel; and all that he sought on behalf of God's people, the Lord God promised to perform. What a blessed, delightful thing it is for us to know that our God will do all that Christ seeks on our behalf! He who makes intercession for us must and shall prevail.

In his prayer, Solomon, spoke of God's people praying toward the temple. 'Hearken therefore unto the supplications of thy servant, and of thy people Israel, which they shall make toward this place: hear thou from thy dwelling place, even from heaven; and when thou hearest, forgive'. He was not instituting an idolatrous practice, like that of a Mohammedan bowing and praying toward Mecca, or those who build churches to face east. When he spoke of men praying toward Jerusalem, toward the temple, and toward the mercy-seat, he was talking about praying toward heaven, looking to God in heaven through Christ and his finished work, which was portrayed in the temple and the mercy-seat. We see this clearly in the publican's prayer described by our Lord in Luke 18:13. Solomon's request in this verse was but the foreshadowing of our Saviour's promise. 'Whatsoever ye shall ask the Father in my name, he will give it you'.

In his prayer, Solomon specifically mentions numerous situations into which the children of Israel might fall because of their sins: famine, pestilence, captivity, etc. By the exercise of his chastening rod, using these things, the Lord would teach his own to walk in his way, and graciously turn them again to himself, confessing their sins, calling upon his name, turning from the evil, and seeking his face. When they did, Solomon asked God to hear from heaven, forgive their sin, and heal the plague sin had brought upon them. The basis upon which Solomon made this great request was threefold:

1. They are 'thy people'. 2. They look to the mercy-seat, Christ's sin-atoning sacrifice. 3. The honour of God's name is displayed in his grace and salvation of his people. 'That all people of the earth may know thy name and fear thee' (2 Chronicles 6:33; Ephesians 2:7).

The conclusion of this great prayer is humbling, instructive, inspiring, and worth reading again in full. 'If they sin against thee, (for there is no man which sinneth not,) and thou be angry with them, and deliver them over before their enemies, and they carry them away captives unto a land far off or near; Yet if they bethink themselves in the land whither they are carried captive, and turn and pray unto thee in the land of their captivity, saying, We have sinned, we have done amiss, and have dealt wickedly; If they return to thee with all their heart and with all their soul in the land of their captivity, whither they have carried them captives, and pray toward their land, which thou gavest unto their fathers, and toward the city which thou hast chosen, and toward the house which I have built for thy name: Then hear thou from the heavens, even from thy dwelling place, their prayer and their supplications, and maintain their cause, and forgive thy people which have sinned against thee. Now, my God, let, I beseech thee, thine eyes be open, and let thine ears be attent unto the prayer that is made in this place. Now therefore arise, O LORD God, into thy resting place, thou, and the ark of thy strength: let thy priests, O LORD God, be clothed with salvation, and let thy saints rejoice in goodness. O LORD God, turn not away the face of thine anointed: remember the mercies of David thy servant' (2 Chronicles 6:36-42).

Filled with Glory

In chapter 7 the Lord God put his stamp of approval upon the whole thing. Fire fell from heaven and consumed the sacrifices, symbolizing God's acceptance of Christ's sacrifice for us, declaring that justice has been satisfied. Then, 'the glory of the Lord filled the house'.

'And when all the children of Israel saw how the fire came down, and the glory of the LORD upon the house, they bowed themselves with their faces to the ground upon the pavement, and worshipped, and praised the LORD, saying, For he is good; for his mercy endureth for ever'.

That is exactly what happens when God saves a sinner, when he sees the glory of God in the sacrifice of Christ and the Spirit of God, 'the blessing of Abraham', comes upon him (Galatians 3:13-14).

Then the Lord God appeared to Solomon in a dream and said, 'I have heard your prayer and will do all that you have asked'.

Declension and Restoration

Chapters 8 and 9 described the greatness of Solomon, his wisdom, his riches, and his works, picturing Christ. Then we read the history of Judah after Solomon's death. What a chequered history it is! It is the history of a nation favoured of God above any people or nation in the world, a people chosen of God, redeemed and saved by his mighty arm, a people to whom God had revealed himself, a people who continued to live and exist only because God kept them. Yet, it is also the history of a people repeatedly turning from him.

Nevertheless, that is only part of the story. The history of Judah is the history of a people that God would not leave to themselves, a people he would not allow to leave him. As I read the history of Judah, I cannot help thinking, 'This is the history of my own life. It is a picture of my declensions from my God and of my many restorations by his indestructible grace'. Is that not your own experience, as you read these chapters?

Judah's Kings

Chapters 10 through 36 give us the record of Judah's kings up to the time of their captivity. Nine of them were good kings. Eleven were bad. Manasseh, who reigned for fifty-five years on the throne of Judah, started out as the worst king in Judah's history and ended up as one of the best, because God revealed himself to him and saved him.

Rehoboam

As we read through these accounts, these wicked kings reveal a pattern of temptation, sin, and spiritual declension. It begins with Rehoboam following the counsel of his young men, following the counsel of the flesh. A little later, in chapter 12, we find a further lowering of the standards. When the rule of Rehoboam was established and was strong, he forsook the law of the Lord. He turned a deaf ear to God's Word. Thereafter the kingdom was invaded by the Egyptians.

The moment we turn away from the rule of God, the holy scripture, in the temple of God, the church, we invite Satan to take over. It was only by God's goodness that the Egyptians were turned back. When Rehoboam humbled himself and returned to God, the Egyptians were repelled.

Jehoram

The next wicked king, Jehoram, appears in chapter 21. When Jehoram had ascended the throne of his father and was established, he killed all his brothers with the sword, and also some of the princes of Israel. First, there was the refusal to give heed to good counsel. Then a deaf ear was turned to the law. Then, the spirit of jealousy began to assault the kingdom. This is immediately followed, as we read in verse 11, by another downward step. He added human inventions to the worship of God and mingled the worship of God with idolatry. 'He made high places in the mountains of Judah, and caused the inhabitants of Jerusalem to commit fornication, and compelled Judah thereto'.

It might be argued that the high places did not represent open idolatry, just its beginnings. They were high hills where the people of Israel worshipped Jehovah with their neighbours and their neighbours' idols. The problem was that that was not the place where God had told them to worship him. He had put his name in the temple and it was there that they were to worship and offer sacrifice. They were worshipping out on the hills, because that was where their neighbours and friends were worshipping. They were simply down-grading and reducing the true worship of God to a lower level. This, too, was quickly followed by invasion and by disease. As you read, you find that King Jehoram was immediately afflicted by an invasion from the Philistines, who ever represent the lusts of the flesh. Idolatry, you see, is but the exercise of man's carnal lusts and always brings with it the moral degradation of those who practice it (Romans 1:18-32).

Ahaz

The next evil king is King Ahaz in chapter 28. 'Ahaz was twenty years old when he began to reign, and he reigned sixteen years in Jerusalem: but he did not that which was right in the sight of the LORD, like David his father: For he walked in the ways of the kings of Israel, and made also molten images for Baalim'.

Here we see the actual introduction of the vile, despicable practices of idolatry. They were primarily matters of sexual perversion, such as Paul describes in Romans 1, such as we see all around us today. Israel was increasingly afflicted by these practices. The kings were responsible for introducing them, as we read of King Ahaz. Again Judah was invaded and some of her people were taken captive by Syria. What woes we bring upon ourselves, our families, our neighbours, our nation, and the world when we depart from our God, his Word, his worship, and his revealed will!

Good Kings

By contrast, Judah's faithful and good kings reflect the grace of God in cleansing and restoring his people. They also reveal the instruments he uses. There are five great reformations recorded in Israel as God intervenes in grace to keep his people.

Asa

The first of these periods of reformation was under King Asa, found in chapters 14 through 16. We read, 'And Asa did that which was good and right in the eyes of the LORD his God: For he took away the altars of the strange gods, and the high places, and brake down the images, and cut down the groves: And commanded Judah to seek the LORD God of their fathers, and to do the law and the commandment'. Asa destroyed the altars, images, and groves of the gods of the heathen. Then the Lord delivered his people. The first mark of God's visiting his people is the restoration of his worship. As soon as we are turned by his grace to seek him with all our hearts, deliverance is ours (Jeremiah 29:10-14).

Jehoshaphat

Then in the reign of King Jehoshaphat, the next king on the throne of Judah, there is another time of restoration, following a time of failure. Jehoshaphat cleared the land of idols. Later, in great weakness, he made a league with Ammon, Moab, and Edom, typifying the lusts of the flesh. In chapter 20 God graciously delivered him in a way that teaches us exactly how we can and must overcome the lusts of our flesh. We do not overcome our inward lusts by beating ourselves mentally or physically, depriving ourselves of certain foods, or physical pleasure. We overcome our lusts by looking to Christ, by believing God. The battle is not yours, but God's. You do not need to fight in this battle. The Lord will fight for you. As we believe God, we shall see our enemies slain by blood, just as Judah did (Colossians 2:14-16). 'When Judah came toward the watch tower in the wilderness, they looked unto the multitude, and, behold, they were dead bodies fallen to the earth, and none escaped'.

Believe what God has done to the flesh in the cross of Christ (Romans 6:11). We do not have to fight the flesh. Our Saviour nailed it to his cross, rendering it absolutely useless. He conquered our enemies for us and has made us more than conquerors by his grace (Romans 8:32-39). When we believe, when we look to Christ, our enemies wither. They may immediately raise their ugly heads more violently than ever. But they shall just as quickly wither again before our crucified Saviour, and shall one day soon be utterly gone forever (Revelation 21:4).

Joash

Under Joash we see the people of Judah giving for the support of God's cause in chapters 23-24. When God visits his people in grace, reviving their souls, they give themselves to him in renewed consecration. Those who give themselves to the Lord give of their means generously, with willing hearts, for the building of his kingdom and the promotion of his worship.

Hezekiah

Hezekiah's reign in Chapters 29-32, was marked by the cleansing of the temple and the restoration of the Passover. When God visits us in grace, the sacrifice of Christ is prominent. All the garbage brought in by the flesh is taken out of God's house.

Josiah

The last of the good kings in Judah was Josiah in chapters 34-35. His reign is distinctly marked by another thing that always identifies the day of divine visitation. When God visits his people in mercy, when God restores our souls, he brings his Word again to the forefront and makes it precious.

Chapter 15

Ezra

'Our God hath not Forsaken Us'.

The books of Ezra, Nehemiah, and Esther cover the history of Israel immediately following their return from Babylonian captivity to Jerusalem. There was only a remnant, a remnant 'whose spirit God had raised', who returned to Jerusalem. Though there were perhaps three million Jews in Babylon at the time, only around 50,000 returned.

God has a people scattered through all the nations of the world, a people scattered in wrath, yet scattered in mercy, scattered to the place where they shall be preserved in bondage until the day of their calling. These Jews were preserved in Babylon until God raised up Cyrus and Zerubbabel to bring them out of that place. At God's appointed time of love, each of these chosen ones, loved of God with an everlasting love, redeemed by Christ's precious blood, and preserved in him (Jude 1), shall be brought out into the liberty of the City of God. 'And so all Israel shall be saved: as it is written, There shall come out of Sion the Deliverer, and shall turn away ungodliness from Jacob' (Romans 11:26).

The Jews were shepherds when they had first gone down into Babylon. But while they were there they learned the ways of Babylon and became successful businessmen, merchants, and shopkeepers. They became so prosperous, so materialistic, that they did not want to go back to Jerusalem, even though they were still slaves in exile from their own land. They preferred the drudgery of Babylonian bondage, with its wealth, to the liberty of worshipping God in Jerusalem.

Some have suggested that they became a different people while in Babylon. But that was not the case at all. The Lord sent them into captivity to prove them; and there they proved what they really were. So it is with all trials. Trials do not change us, they simply prove what we are.

There was an elect remnant in Babylon whom the Lord reserved, whose spirit he revived. Their seventy-year trial in Babylon made them pine for liberty and the worship of God in Jerusalem. Many of the Jews refused to return when God opened the door. But the Spirit of God stirred up the hearts of some and made them willing in the day of his power. The message of this book is found in chapter 9, verse 9. 'Our God hath not forsaken us'. The book of Ezra is all about God's great grace in keeping, reviving, and restoring his people.

Actually, the book speaks of two returns from Babylon. First, in chapters 1-5, Zerubbabel led about 50,000 back to Jerusalem. After rebuilding the altar of God and relaying the foundation of the temple, there was another long period of languishing. This is the period covered by the book of Esther. Then, in chapters 6-10, Ezra brings another group, even smaller than the first, out of Babylon and back to Jerusalem.

Ezra's Prayer

Chapter 9 records Ezra's prayer, one of the most remarkable prayers of repentance found in the Bible. In this prayer, we see the whole of Israel's problem and the bounteous, enduring grace of God set forth in this book. To grasp the message of the book it is worth here reading the prayer in its entirety. Ezra writes, 'Now when these things were done, the princes came to me, saying, The people of Israel, and the priests, and the Levites, have not separated themselves from the people of the lands, doing according to their abominations, even of the Canaanites, the Hittites, the Perizzites, the Jebusites, the Ammonites, the Moabites, the Egyptians, and the Amorites. For they have taken of their daughters for themselves, and for their sons: so that the holy seed have mingled themselves with the people of those lands: yea, the hand of the princes and rulers hath been chief in this trespass.'

The cause of Israel's trouble

'And when I heard this thing, I rent my garment and my mantle, and plucked off the hair of my head and of my beard, and sat down astonied. Then were assembled unto me every one that trembled at the words of the God of Israel, because of the transgression of those that had been carried away; and I sat astonied until the evening sacrifice'.

Convicted of the seriousness of sin

Astonished and broken hearted, Ezra poured out his soul to God, interceding for his people at the throne of grace.

'And at the evening sacrifice I arose up from my heaviness; and having rent my garment and my mantle, I fell upon my knees, and spread out my hands unto the LORD my God, And said, O my God, I am ashamed and blush to lift up my face to thee, my God: for our iniquities are increased over our head, and our trespass is grown up unto the heavens. Since the days of our fathers have we been in a great trespass unto this day; and for our iniquities have we, our kings, and our priests, been delivered into the hand of the kings of the lands, to the sword, to captivity, and to a spoil, and to confusion of face, as it is this day.

And now for a little space grace hath been showed from the LORD our God, to leave us a remnant to escape, and to give us a nail in his holy place, that our God may lighten our eyes, and give us a little reviving in our bondage. For we were bondmen; yet our God hath not forsaken us in our bondage, but hath extended mercy unto us in the sight of the kings of Persia, to give us a reviving, to set up the house of our God, and to repair the desolations thereof, and to give us a wall in Judah and in Jerusalem.

And now, O our God, what shall we say after this? for we have forsaken thy commandments, Which thou hast commanded by thy servants the prophets, saying, The land, unto which ye go to possess it, is an unclean land with the filthiness of the people of the lands, with their abominations, which have filled it from one end to another with their uncleanness.

Now therefore give not your daughters unto their sons, neither take their daughters unto your sons, nor seek their peace or their wealth for ever: that ye may be strong, and eat the good of the land, and leave it for an inheritance to your children for ever. And after all that is come upon us for our evil deeds, and for our great trespass, seeing that thou our God hast punished us less than our iniquities deserve, and hast given us such deliverance as this; Should we again break thy commandments, and join in affinity with the people of these abominations? wouldest not thou be angry with us till thou hadst consumed us, so that there should be no remnant nor escaping?'

A Ground of Hope for Ezra

Then Ezra throws himself and the people on the faithful mercy of God.

'O LORD God of Israel, thou art righteous: for we remain yet escaped, as it is this day: behold, we are before thee in our trespasses: for we cannot stand before thee because of this.'

Divine Faithfulness

Surely we must ask, 'What gave Ezra any ground of hope for mercy in the face of such serious and acknowledged sin?' Ezra knew something about the prophecies and purpose of the Lord.

In chapter 1 we learned something about the character of our great God. As Cyrus put it in verse 3, 'The Lord God of Israel, he is the God!' Cyrus' decree is one of the greatest displays of the inspiration and infallibility of holy scripture that could be given. Seventy years before it came to pass, Jeremiah had declared that it would come to pass at this very time (Jeremiah 25:11-12; 29:10). Almost two hundred years before that, Isaiah not only spoke of Israel's deliverance out of Babylon, but he named the man who would deliver them and the means by which he would do it (Isaiah 44 and 45).

This is also a marvellous display of God's absolute sovereignty. What could cause a pagan Babylonian king to be so magnanimous to a people who had been the slaves of his kingdom for so long, when he had absolutely nothing to gain and much to lose by such a deed? There is but one answer. 'The king's heart is in the hand of the LORD, as the rivers of water: he turneth it whithersoever he will' (Proverbs 21:1). God still raises up nations and puts them down, raises up kings and puts them down, as he will, for the salvation of his elect.

We here see a great example of God's faithfulness. Our God is always faithful. He promised to bring Judah out of Babylon after 70 years; and he did. Ezra knew the promise and believed in faith. They had forsaken him; but he would not forsake them. Truly, 'the Lord God of Israel, he is the God!'

Divine Chastisement

Here is a lesson in divine chastisement, too. When God sends chastisement, as he does, upon his chosen people, it is not to destroy us, but to refine us. Judah fell captive to Babylon because the people had fallen captive to their own lusts. But the Lord did not destroy them; he restored them. In their restoration, he used even the very thing that had threatened to destroy them to enrich them. God taught his people that he would supply all their needs. Ultimately, all the expenses required for their repatriation and restoration were given out of the king's house in Babylon.

But, learn this too, Once we have fallen into a state of spiritual declension from our God, once we have been drawn away from him, we will never return to him, except he brings us back. The only ones who came back to Jerusalem were those 'whose spirit the Lord had raised'.

Thanksgiving and Worship

When Zerubbabel brought Israel back to Jerusalem, his first act was the building of God's altar. That is always the very first thing that takes place when God restores our souls. He causes us to turn again to Christ and his great sacrifice for us, acknowledging with renewed consecration that we are his (1 Corinthians 6:19-20). The second thing they did was to lay the foundation of the temple. The work was met with mixed feeling.

'And when the seventh month was come, and the children of Israel were in the cities, the people gathered themselves together as one man to Jerusalem. Then stood up Jeshua the son of Jozadak, and his brethren the priests, and Zerubbabel the son of Shealtiel, and his brethren, and builded the altar of the God of Israel, to offer burnt offerings thereon, as it is written in the law of Moses the man of God. And they set the altar upon his bases; for fear was upon them because of the people of those countries: and they offered burnt offerings thereon unto the LORD, even burnt offerings morning and evening' (Ezra 3:1-3).

'And they sang together by course in praising and giving thanks unto the LORD; because he is good, for his mercy endureth for ever toward Israel. And all the people shouted with a great shout, when they praised the LORD, because the foundation of the house of the LORD was laid. But many of the priests and Levites and chief of the fathers, who were ancient men, that had seen the first house, when the foundation of this house was laid before their eyes, wept with a loud voice; and many shouted aloud for joy: So that the people could not discern the noise of the shout of joy from the noise of the weeping of the people: for the people shouted with a loud shout, and the noise was heard afar off' (Ezra 3:11-13).

What a picture this is of the bitter sweetness of true repentance. When the Lord graciously grants us a little reviving in our souls, we weep because of our horrible offences and rejoice because of his great goodness.

Then, a third thing happened. In chapter four, the enemies of Judah and Benjamin tried to turn them away from God again. These adversaries were Samaritans. They pretended to be friends, wanting to help rebuild the house of God. When Zerubbabel and the men of Judah refused to allow them to help, they turned on them fiercely, and for a time delayed the work.

These men were like our flesh. Everything in us, by nature, would turn us from our God. Judah could not allow these Samaritans to have any part in the work, because they had no part in the worship of God. We must never lean to the flesh to do God's work and will!

God's Method of Grace

There is another lesson here that we must not miss. God always accomplishes his purpose of grace; and he does so by the use of human instruments. Many decry this point, so clearly and pointedly made in holy scripture, as a denial of God's absolute sovereignty. But nothing more clearly displays God's sovereignty than his use of the means he chooses for the accomplishment of his predestined purpose. The book before us is an excellent example of this.

Cyrus issued his decree because God put it in his heart to do so (Ezra 1:1); but Cyrus issued the decree. Those who returned, returned because God stirred their hearts to return; but they returned. Ezra succeeded because the good hand of the Lord was upon him; but he succeeded (7:9). Artaxerxes supported the work of rebuilding the temple because the Lord put it in his heart to do so (7:27); but he supported the work. God favoured the nation with repentance because of Ezra's prayer (chapters 9-10). The Lord put the prayer in his heart, but Ezra prayed. God raised up two prophets, Haggai and Zechariah, to prophesy to his people and move them to the work (chapter 5). He always instructs and directs his people by his Word, through the preaching of those sent by him to proclaim his Word (Romans 10:11-17). Consequently, deliverance comes at exactly the time God had purposed and promised.

Grace All-Sufficient

The last thing I want you to see is this. God's grace is sufficient. His grace is sufficient to supply all our needs. God's grace is sufficient to preserve and keep us in all our appointed ways. His grace is sufficient to enable us to perform the work he puts in our hands.

'And now for a little space grace hath been showed from the LORD our God, to leave us a remnant to escape, and to give us a nail in his holy place, that our God may lighten our eyes, and give us a little reviving in our bondage. For we were bondmen; yet our God hath not forsaken us in our bondage, but hath extended mercy unto us in the sight of the kings of Persia, to give us a reviving, to set up the house of our God, and to repair the desolations thereof, and to give us a wall in Judah and in Jerusalem' (Ezra 9:8-9).

Chapter 16

Nehemiah

'Build Thou the Walls of Jerusalem'

As the book of Ezra describes the great work of rebuilding the temple in Jerusalem, the book of Nehemiah describes the rebuilding of the walls of Jerusalem. The book of Nehemiah is really just a continuation of the book of Ezra. The theme in both books is the restoration of divine worship and the restoration of God's people.

These two things always go hand in hand. When there is a revival of true worship, there is revival in the hearts of God's elect. When the Lord sends revival to his people, the worship of God is restored and set in order. This is clearly set before us in David's prayer of repentance in Psalm 51:18-19. 'Do good in thy good pleasure unto Zion: build thou the walls of Jerusalem. Then shalt thou be pleased with the sacrifices of righteousness, with burnt offering and whole burnt offering: then shall they offer bullocks upon thine altar'.

As the temple of God speaks of the place of divine worship and sacrifice, and represents the whole work of salvation, the salvation of God's elect by the sacrifice, intercession, and grace of Christ, the walls of Jerusalem (the city of God, the church) represent another aspect of grace and salvation. The walls represent both the security of God's elect in Christ and that which separates the people of God from all the people of the world (1 Corinthians 4:7). What separates us from others? Grace, nothing but the free, sovereign, saving grace of God, electing grace, redeeming grace, calling grace, and preserving grace. It is the Lord God, and the Lord God alone who makes a difference between Israel and Egypt (Exodus 11:7), between his elect and the rest of the world.

Four times, Sanballat, Tobiah, and Geshem, the leaders of those who conspired against Ezra, Nehemiah, and the people of Judah sent word to Nehemiah to leave off the work of building the walls of Jerusalem to come down and meet them. Though their real purpose was to stop the work, their pretence was that they wanted to work out a plan whereby they could unite in the great work.

Four times Nehemiah gave them the same reply. 'And I sent messengers unto them, saying, I am doing a great work, so that I cannot come down: why should the work cease, whilst I leave it, and come down to you?' (6:3). Like Nehemiah, our concern in this world, the work to which we have been called, is the building of God's church; and we must not allow anything or anyone to turn us aside from that which our God has sent us to do.

There was an interval of about twelve years between the work of Ezra's reforms and the time that Nehemiah obtained permission from King Artaxerxes, to whom he was cup-bearer, to go up to Jerusalem.

Reading the books of Ezra, Nehemiah and Esther, we frequently run across the names of Artaxerxes and Ahasuerus. But really these are not the names of different kings, but the titles given to them. That fact gives us a little difficulty. But it really should not. Many years later, the rulers of Rome were called 'Caesar', but there were several different Caesars. The title 'Artaxerxes' means 'the great king'. 'Ahasuerus' means 'the venerable father'. The titles Artaxerxes in Nehemiah and Ahasuerus in Esther refer to the same king, King Darius, spoken of in the book of Daniel. Then, to add to the confusion, Artaxerxes in the book of Ezra is not the same Artaxerxes spoken of in Nehemiah. That Artaxerxes was opposed to the work Ezra and Nehemiah led Judah to perform. He opposed the building of the temple (Ezra 4:21-24). He was probably Darius' son.

Nehemiah was deeply distressed by the news that his brethren gave him concerning God's people in Jerusalem.

'And they said unto me, The remnant that are left of the captivity there in the province are in great affliction and reproach: the wall of Jerusalem also is broken down, and the gates thereof are burned with fire. And it came to pass, when I heard these words, that I sat down and wept, and mourned certain days, and fasted, and prayed before the God of heaven' (Nehemiah 1:3-4).

The rest of the first chapter records his great prayer of intercession to God. Nehemiah was emminently a man of prayer. Throughout these 13 chapters, he interjects brief prayers. As he worked and laboured in his great cause, he continually sought God's direction and help, depending upon him.

Nehemiah's Prayer

This book is full of lessons for us. Nehemiah confesses his sin and prays to God on behalf of his people. His great concern is for the house of God, the people of God, and the worship of God. He ascribes to God the glory and praise of his greatness as God. Throughout this prayer, he describes God's people in such a way as to move him to be gracious, seeking mercy on the grounds of God's greatness and the desperate need of his people.

'Let thine ear now be attentive, and thine eyes open, that thou mayest hear the prayer of thy servant, which I pray before thee now, day and night, for the children of Israel thy servants, and confess the sins of the children of Israel, which we have sinned against thee: both I and my father's house have sinned. We have dealt very corruptly against thee, and have not kept the commandments, nor the statutes, nor the judgments, which thou commandedst thy servant Moses. Remember, I beseech thee, the word that thou commandedst thy servant Moses, saying, If ye transgress, I will scatter you abroad among the nations: But if ye turn unto me, and keep my commandments, and do them; though there were of you cast out unto the uttermost part of the heaven, yet will I gather them from thence, and will bring them unto the place that I have chosen to set my name there. Now these are thy servants and thy people, whom thou hast redeemed by thy great power, and by thy strong hand. O Lord, I beseech thee, let now thine ear be attentive to the prayer of thy servant, and to the prayer of thy servants, who desire to fear thy name: and prosper, I pray thee, thy servant this day, and grant him mercy in the sight of this man. For I was the king's cupbearer' (vv. 6-11).

Workers Together

Nehemiah's heart was broken. His soul was stirred by the news of the desolate condition of the city with its broken walls. So much so that, as he served King Artaxerxes, the king asked him what was wrong with him.

'Wherefore the king said unto me, Why is thy countenance sad, seeing thou art not sick? this is nothing else but sorrow of heart. Then I was very sore afraid, And said unto the king, Let the king live for ever: why should not my countenance be sad, when the city, the place of my fathers' sepulchres, lieth waste, and the gates thereof are consumed with fire?'

The king then asked him what he wanted and sent him to Jerusalem to build the walls of the city. To put it in Nehemiah's words, 'So it pleased the king to send me ... And the king granted me, according to the good hand of my God upon me'.

He found things in horrible condition at Jerusalem. He gathered the elders together and told them of the good hand of his God upon him, and they said, 'Let us rise up and build. So they strengthened their hands for this good work'.

Nehemiah was sent by the king to do the work; but neither he nor the king thought that this great work would be the work of one man. The work involved all those who feared God. Nehemiah and the people of Judah laboured side by side as 'labourers together with God' (1 Corinthians 3:9). In the church and kingdom of God all his people are his servants. We are workers together with him. Christianity is not a spectator sport. The work of the church is not the work of one man, but of many, working together with God.

Labouring for the Glory of God

As they built the walls of Jerusalem, they began at the Sheep Gate and completely enclosed the city. Priests, rulers, goldsmiths, apothecaries, and merchants all worked side by side, brothers working together in the common cause of God. We are told exactly who set up the various gates, with the locks and the bars. No work done for God's glory is overlooked by him, no matter how small it might appear in our eyes, or in the eyes of others. Our God delights to place on record the humblest service. It is written, 'And I heard a voice from heaven saying unto me, Write, Blessed are the dead which die in the Lord from henceforth: Yea, saith the Spirit, that they may rest from their labours; and their works do follow them' (Revelation 14:13).

That is what we are doing, labouring together for the glory of God, for the worship of God, to build the kingdom of God. Let us be like 'Baruch, the son of Zabbai, (who) earnestly repaired the other piece, from the turning of the wall unto the door of the house of Eliashib the high priest'.

Our Enemies

However, in chapters 4-6 the descendants of the Samaritans, who had harassed Zerubbabel, were relentless in their efforts to hinder the work. First they mocked them: 'What do these feeble Jews? That which they build, if a fox go up, he shall even break down their stone wall'. 'Hear, O our God; for we are despised', was Nehemiah's prayer. 'So built we the wall; and all the wall was joined together unto the half thereof: for the people had a mind to work'.

When their mockery could not stop the faithful from their work, Judah's foes conspired to fight against Jerusalem. But Nehemiah says, 'We made our prayer unto our God, and set a watch day and night'. He armed the workers and gave orders that at the sound of the trumpet they were to run to the place needing help and there defend the city.

That is when Sanballat and his associates sent the messages to Nehemiah, asking him to meet them in the plain of Ono. Nehemiah's reply was, 'I am doing a great work: why should the work cease, whilst I leave it, and come down to you?' Then they accused Judah of rebellion against the law or antinomianism, and sought to weaken their hands and make them afraid; but Nehemiah replied to Tobiah: 'There are no such things done as thou sayest, but thou feignest them out of thine own heart'. As a last resort, one urged Nehemiah to take refuge in the temple, 'for they will come to slay thee'. 'Should such a man as I flee' was Nehemiah's steadfast reply. 'So the wall was finished in fifty and two days'.

Those who oppose Christ and the gospel we preach will employ any means they can to hinder or discourage us from doing God's work. Let us, like Nehemiah, ever remember who has commissioned us, and praying and relying upon our God, completely disregard and utterly ignore their carping.

Christ Our Priest

The register of those who first came from Babylon under Zerubbabel is again repeated in chapter 7. Some of the priests names could not be found in the genealogy, 'Therefore were they, as polluted, put from the priesthood. And the Tirshatha (Governor) said unto the, that they should not eat of the most holy things, till there stood up a priest with Urim and Thummim'.

Here we have one of those instances in the Old Testament when the Face of Christ suddenly shines forth in the most unexpected and unlikely places. This is only a register, and a few priests could not find their place in it. However, our hearts rejoice in the fact that we have a great High Priest, the Lord Jesus Christ, who has the Urim and Thummim, who is the 'Light and Perfection'. He settles the question as to our right to communion with God, symbolized in the eating of the most holy things. He declares that, as those who are made priests unto God by him, we are worthy to partake of the holy things. His blood and righteousness makes us worthy. That, and that alone, makes us worthy to approach our God in the holy place, confess his name in believer's baptism, receive the Lord's Table, and wear the name of the sons of God.

He has, by his own blood, entered in once for all into the holy place, having obtained eternal redemption for us (Hebrews 9:12). And if we trust in his one great sacrifice for sins forever, we also may draw near and have communion with God, not once a year, or once a month, or once a week, but continually!

Christ is our great High Priest, not by genealogy from Aaron, but 'after the order of Melchizedek', who was 'without genealogy' (Hebrews 7:3 RV). Melchizedek's genealogy was, no doubt, omitted to show him as a type of Christ who had no earthly father. God has called us in Christ to be priests unto him, and our right of priesthood depends on whether we have been born again and have our names written, not in an earthly register, but in the Lamb's book of Life. 'He has', A. M. Hodgkin wrote, 'provided for our fitness in the present tenses of John's Epistle. First, "The blood cleanseth", so that there need never be any cloud between our souls and God. Second, "The anointing abideth", so that there need never be any lack of the supply of His Spirit for service.'

The Place of Preaching

When we get to chapter 8 we see that the immediate result of the work of restoration was a great hunger for God's Word. The people gathered themselves together as one man unto Ezra before the Water Gate, and begged him to bring forth the book of the law of Moses.

Here Ezra, now an old man, comes forward again. We see him and Nehemiah uniting in God's service. We are given a striking picture of Ezra's preaching. Already we have seen him as a reformer, and as a man of prayer; and now all his gifts in the Word of the Lord come out as he stands on that pulpit of wood, 'made for the purpose', with thirteen of the leaders of the people standing beside him, and all the people thronging round. He opened the book, and having prayed, read the law distinctly, and gave the sense, and caused the people to understand it. Hour after hour, and subsequently, day after day, they listened, men and women and children, 'all that could understand'.

His preaching stirred Jerusalem as Luther's preaching stirred Germany. The people wept as they acknowledged how far they had fallen and how greatly they had sinned. But Ezra and Nehemiah and the Levites calmed the people, and told them not to weep, and their weeping was turned into joy by the preaching of God's great goodness revealed in his work, which is recorded in his Word. 'And the people went their way ... to make great mirth, because they had understood the words that were declared unto them'. 'Great peace have they that love Thy law'. They kept the feast of the Passover for the first time since the days of Joshua and made a covenant of renewed consecration to the Lord.

In chapter 12 the children of Israel sealed themselves under a solemn covenant to keep the Law, especially with regard to marriages with the heathen, to keeping the sabbath, and to maintaining the worship of God. The dedication of the walls was a joyful occasion, for 'God had made them rejoice with great joy: the wives also and the children rejoiced; so that the joy of Jerusalem was heard even afar off'.

More Decline

Then we see, in chapter 13, that in spite of all the grace and goodness they had experienced, these blessed people show us again that God's people in this world are but sinners saved by grace.

Once more twelve years have passed, and Nehemiah, who had been back at the Court of Shushan, returned to Jerusalem to find all the terms of the covenant broken and the law disregarded. He dealt with all these abuses firmly. Eliashib, the priest, because he was allied to Tobiah the Ammonite, had given a chamber in the Temple to this enemy of the Lord. Nehemiah turned him out immediately. Again, Nehemiah contended with the rulers because he found that the service of the house of the Lord was neglected. Next, he found a wholesale disregard of the sabbath.

Such contempt for the things of God, his honour, his worship, and the blessed rest of faith, symbolized in the sabbath day, must not be tolerated. If it is, it will inevitably lead to utter apostasy. It is a sign of the perilous times of these last days, when 'Men shall be lovers of their own selves ... lovers of pleasure more than lovers of God' (2 Timothy 3:1-4).

Compromise

Nehemiah found that the Jews had married among the heathen. This violation of God's express command is both an act of defiance and idolatry (Exodus 34:14-17). Great evil is sure to follow. The result here was that their children spoke half in the speech of Ashdod, and half in the Jews' language. In other words, their children learned by their compromise to be idolaters.

Believers are to marry 'only in the Lord'. We must 'not be unequally yoked together with unbelievers' in any area of life, but most particularly in marriage. Those who disobey God's revealed will in this matter, marrying unbelievers, can expect nothing but sorrow as a result.

The argument or excuse frequently used is that the believer will be able to win the unbelieving to Christ. But we must never expect God's blessing upon our disobedience. I have seen the Lord graciously intervene; but, more often than not, the result of such a union is that the person professing to be a believer is gradually drawn, it may be almost imperceptibly, to love the things of the world. In time they are found, together with the children of such a marriage, speaking 'half the speech of Ashdod', and unable to speak as a citizen of the heavenly city. The spirit of compromise with the world mars the usefulness for Christ of many homes and churches, just as it did in Solomon's experience.

In all these breaches of God's law Nehemiah 'contended with the Jews'. Whether they were nobles or rulers or the common people, he dealt with them pointedly. He did not rest till all was put right. This was no lack of love on his part, but just the opposite. He was willing to spend and be spent for his people. It is an evidence of true love for the souls of men when a faithful man deals faithfully and pointedly with compromise, false doctrine, and rebellion of any kind. Any church today blessed of God with a pastor who has the boldness, love, and faithfulness Nehemiah had to deal with such things, has reason to give thanks to God for his goodness in giving his church pastors according to his own heart (Jeremiah 3:15).

God's People Still

Having said all that, let us not set ourselves up as judges over one another when the Lord's people are overtaken in a fault, condemning them as unbelieving and reprobate. Evil must be reproved by God's servants by the faithful exposition of holy scripture, as it was by Ezra and Nehemiah. But when our brothers and sisters in Christ are overcome in a fault, let it be ours to fulfil the law of Christ, bearing their burden, doing what we can to restore them in meekness, considering ourselves (Galatians 6:1-4).

The Holy Spirit specifically illustrates the fact that those who are truly beloved of the Lord are yet subject to such evils by using Solomon as an example, both of the sins of the Jews on this occasion, and of the immutability of God's mercy, love, and grace to his elect in Christ (Nehemiah 13:26; Malachi 3:6).

The fall of another reminds us that we are all sinners saved by grace. None of us are beyond temptation. None of us are beyond weakness. None of us are beyond sin. There is nothing we would not do, and completely justify ourselves in doing it, if the Lord left us to ourselves for a moment.

The falls and failings of others gives us opportunity to love and help. These sad events in the lives of God's saints in this world should serve as reminders that salvation is altogether the work of God's free and sovereign grace in Christ, that our only righteousness before God is the righteousness of God in Christ, and that the only thing that makes one to differ from another is God's goodness and grace in Christ. Therefore, it is written 'And be ye kind one to another, tender-hearted, forgiving one another, even as God for Christ's sake hath forgiven you. Be ye therefore followers of God, as dear children; and walk in love, as Christ also hath loved us, and hath given himself for us an offering and a sacrifice to God for a sweetsmelling savour' (Ephesians 4:32-5:2).

Chapter 17

Esther

The Wonder of Divine Providence

As the books of Ezra and Nehemiah display the salvation of our souls in the re-building of the temple and its walls at Jerusalem, the book of Esther shows us a picture of the secret workings of divine providence to accomplish God's purpose of grace for his elect. The book is intended to assure us that our God sovereignly manipulates all things for the salvation of his people, to assure us that no matter how things appear all is well because our God is still on his throne (Psalm 115:3; 135:6).

The book of Esther is a beautifully simple, historic narrative of the events that took place in the king's palace at Shushan in Persia during the days of Ezra, Nehemiah, and Esther when Ahasuerus was king.

Some have suggested that this could not be an inspired book, because there is no mention of God's name in it. Going on that premise, we would have to say the same thing about the Song of Solomon, because there is no mention of God's name in that book either. It is true, God's name is not to be found in this book; but God's finger is everywhere, ruling and over-ruling all things for his chosen people.

Though God's name is not spelled out in the book of Esther, it is present in the book. It is hidden away in the Hebrew text in the form of acrostics five times. Be that as it may, it is certainly hidden in our English

Bible. There is a reason why God's name was hidden in this book. The Lord told Israel that if they forsook him, he would hide his face from them (Deuteronomy 31:16-18). The Lord hid his face from his people, because they had deliberately chosen to stay in the land of their captivity, dwelling among the heathen, instead of returning to Jerusalem, and returning to him, with Zerubbabel. The events of this book took place during the sixty years between the first remnant's returned under Zerubbabel and the second, smaller remnant's return under Ezra.

The Story

There are four principle characters in this book: Ahasuerus, whose name means 'Venerable Father', Mordecai whose name means 'Little Man', Esther whose name means 'Star', and Haman whose name means 'Magnificent'.

Ahasuerus had a great feast to show off his splendor, 'according to the state of the king'. It lasted for many days. One day, when he had had too much to drink, he called for his wife, Vashti whose name means 'Beautiful', to come show herself to his guests, 'for she was fair to look on'. Vashti refused the king's request. She may have been the first feminist in history; but this was not a good idea. The king's request was no mere request! All the king's men were enraged. If the king's wife could exhibit such arrogant defiance, all their wives would try to imitate her. After some discussion of the matter, King Ahasuerus divorced Vashti and in time, he sought a wife to replace her.

In chapter two, the king's servants held a great beauty pageant. The most beautiful women in Persia were summoned and Esther was chosen. Ahasuerus could not have been happier, the old king was about to marry the most beautiful woman in the land. 'The king loved Esther above all the women, and she obtained grace and favour in his sight more than all the virgins; so that he set the royal crown upon her head, and made her queen instead of Vashti. Then the king made a great feast unto all his princes and his servants, even Esther's feast; and he made a release to the provinces, and gave gifts, according to the state of the king'.

Then, in chapter three the king promoted Haman to be prime minister of his great empire. Everybody bowed and scraped before Haman, everybody except one man, Mordecai. 'When Haman saw that Mordecai bowed not, nor did him reverence, then was Haman full of wrath'.

There was some backbone in that old Jew. He was made of stern stuff. He was not about to prostrate himself before one so haughty and so depraved as Haman, even if he was the king's favourite.

Haman was not a man to be snubbed. He hatched a plan to destroy all the Jews, Mordecai included, and convinced Ahasuerus to go along with it. A letter was written, sealed with the king's ring and sent throughout the land, declaring that at a set time all the Jews; men, women, and children, were to be slaughtered and their spoils taken.

Haman's status and prestige continued to grow. He built a huge, high gallows upon which to hang Mordecai. Everything was prepared. The hated Jews were about to be eliminated. Success for Haman would mean destruction of the Jews. It would mean that God's promise could not be fulfilled. It would mean his purposes would be foiled, Christ could not come into the world from the seed of Abraham, none of his chosen people would be redeemed. All God's elect would forever perish.

Divine Providence

All that had transpired, though it appeared to everyone to be against the God of Israel and his purpose of grace to his people, was in fact the secret working of divine providence to accomplish his purpose (Psalm 76:10). Behold the wondrous mystery of God's providence (Romans 8:28-30) and rejoice.

Divine providence is God's absolute rule over, and disposition of, all things animate and inanimate, good and evil according to his unalterable purpose of grace for the salvation of his people and the glory of his own great name. It is the sovereign rule of God in the determination of history. It is the hand of God in the glove of history. Our God is at the steering wheel of the universe. Providence means that God is behind the scene, shifting, directing, controlling, and manipulating everything to accomplish his own agenda (Romans 11:33-36).

Providence is the way God secretly and sovereignly causes all things to do his will. As recorded in the book of Esther, it appeared that the entire Jewish nation was about to be slain. But that was not about to happen. God was keeping watch over his own. In the book of Esther, perhaps more clearly than in any other, the wonder of God's providence is revealed.

God always puts the right person in the right place at the right time to accomplish his purpose. He has his servants exactly where he wants them. He restrains evil and governs his enemies to perform his good pleasure. He arranges the smallest, most minute details to accomplish his great purpose (Matthew 10:30).

One night God arranged that the king could not sleep. In the long quiet hours he had his servant bring out the chronicles of the kingdom and read them. These chronicles contained the official records of one hundred and twenty seven provinces. The servant just happened to read the chronicle of Shushan.

We learn in chapter six that as the servant read he came to a section in the chonicles where it was recorded that Mordecai had saved the king's life when he told of Bigthana and Teresh, two of the king's chamberlains, keepers of the door, who 'sought to lay hand on the king Ahasuerus'. Ahasuerus asked, 'What honour and dignity hath been done to Mordecai for this?' The king's servants replied, 'There is nothing done for him'.

Just at that moment Haman walked in, and the king asked him, 'What shall be done unto the man whom the king delighteth to honour?' Haman, full of pride thought the king meant to honour him. He gave the counsel that would destroy him, exalt Mordecai, and save the Jews.

When the Lord God is about to do a great work for us and with us, he moves his people to seek him (Esther 4:16). But he always accomplishes his purpose. The wonders of his providence are, for the most part, unseen. But 'we walk by faith, not by sight'. We are perfectly safe at all times. Our Father holds the reins of the universe. We have an omnipotent, wise, and good Guardian in the king's palace.

Pictures of Grace

I am aware that typology can sometimes be strained, making passages of scriptures say what they do not say. Yet, we are assured that everything written in the book of God speaks distinctly of our Lord Jesus Christ and the things he has accomplished for us as our Substitute (Luke 24:27, 44-45). Christ crucified is 'all the counsel of God' (1 Corinthians 2:2; Acts 20:27). There are many, instructive pictures of our Saviour in the book of Esther.

Esther's intercession for Israel vividly portrays our Saviour's intercession for us. Here is one willing to lay down her life for her people, interceding before the king as one pure and lovely and delightful in his sight. Our great Mediator was not only willing to lay down his life for his people, he did it; and that which he accomplished in laying down his life for us is the basis of his intercession (1 John 2:1-2).

'And it was so, when the king saw Esther the queen standing in the court, that she obtained favour in his sight: and the king held out to Esther the golden sceptre that was in his hand. So Esther drew near, and touched the top of the sceptre' (Esther 5:2). Here is a picture that should give great encouragement to us in approaching the throne of grace, the throne of Christ our King, to obtain mercy and find grace to help in time of need (Hebrews 4:16).

We urge sinners to venture all at the throne of grace, suing for mercy, with Esther's attitude, 'I will go into the king's presence, and if I perish, I perish'. But it is impossible for a sinner to perish at the throne of grace. No one ever perished confessing his sin and seeking God's forgiveness at the footstool of mercy. God is faithful to his promises, and just to his Son 'to forgive us our sins and to cleanse us from all unrighteousness (1 John 1:9). He 'delighteth in mercy' (Micah 7:18). As we bow before his throne, confessing our sins, trusting his Son, the holy Lord God graciously forgives us, receives us, and accepts us because of the God-Man who sits at his right hand, and ever lives to intercede for sinners. In his name we may come boldly and obtain mercy. Do you have some great need in your soul, a need that only Christ can fill? The king's court stands open; enter and lodge your petition. He will hear the voice of your supplication. The golden sceptre is extended. He will answer with the whole resources of his omnipotence, wisdom, goodness, and grace.

The decree sealed with the king's ring reminds us of the unalterable purpose, and decree of our God (Psalm 89:34; Isaiah 46:9-10; Daniel 4:34-35). The Jews ruling their enemies is symbolic of the fact that God's saints rule over their enemies by his grace (Romans 6:14; Galatians 5:16-23) and shall ultimately rule over all their foes (Romans 16:20; Revelation 20:6). Mordecai seeking the good of his people exemplifies that which every believer ought to practice. May God ever give us grace to live for the good of his people, seeking their peace and prosperity. But there is One greater than Mordecai at the right hand of the Majesty on high, great and 'accepted of the multitude of his brethren, seeking the wealth of his people, and speaking peace to all his seed'.

Chapter 18

Job

Why do the righteous suffer?

The Apostle Paul tells us that 'tribulation worketh patience'. The fact is, we are all such sinful and hard-hearted creatures that we cannot and will not learn patience by any other means. Were you asked to give an example of patience, probably the first name that would come to your mind would be Job. No man is more famous for the exercise of patience. 'Behold, we count them happy which endure. Ye have heard of the patience of Job, and have seen the end of the Lord; that the Lord is very pitiful, and of tender mercy' (James 5:11).

However, patience was no more natural to Job than it is to you and me. It was something he had to learn by tribulation, great tribulation. It was a hard lesson, but a lesson he learned. He expressed the patience the Lord taught him, displaying confident faith in the wisdom and goodness of God. He said, 'He knoweth the way that I take: when he hath tried me, I shall come forth as gold' (Job 23:10).

Poetic books

That which is revealed in the book of Job is a gripping story, a fascinating drama. But it is much more. The book of Job is an inspired narrative of the life and trials of a righteous man in this world. Here we begin a new section of scripture. Genesis through Deuteronomy, the five books of Moses, are commonly referred to as 'the Law'. Joshua through Esther are 'Historic' books. In these we have seen, in the events of history, living parables designed and worked out by God's good providence to explain and illustrate what is going on in our own lives.

Now in the 'Poetic' books (Job to the Song of Solomon, and Lamentations) we see God's saints in worship. Perhaps that is what makes them the most commonly read portions of the Old Testament. In these books, we are allowed to go with God's saints into their private closets, as they pour out their hearts to their heavenly Father, and put into words the very things we often want to say, but simply cannot find either the words or the honesty to speak before the throne of grace. That makes them both precious and instructive as well as comforting and inspiring.

The book of Job is a great poem. Tennyson called it, 'the greatest poem whether of ancient or modern literature'. Martin Luther considered the book of Job 'more magnificent and sublime than any other book of scripture'. It reads like a drama, an epic drama much like those of ancient Greece and Rome.

The book of Job is also historical. Job was an actual, living person and these events actually took place, but God recounts them for us in this beautiful style so that we might have an answer to the age-old question, 'Why do the righteous suffer?'

Job suffered by the assaults of Satan, he suffered by the words of his wife, he suffered by the accusations of his friends. But if you asked Job why he suffered as he did, what the first cause of his sufferings was, he would look past all those secondary sources to the Lord his God.

At the very beginning of the book, we see clearly that the righteous suffer by the hand and will of the God we worship, trust, love and serve. Everywhere we turn in these forty-two chapters, when Job speaks of that which he suffered, he declares that he suffered because the Lord God ordered it. He said to his accusing friends, 'Have pity upon me, have pity upon me, O ye my friends; for the hand of God hath touched me ... But he knoweth the way that I take: when he hath tried me, I shall come forth as gold' (Job 19:21; 23:10)

God's Book

Though the Word of God is neither a book about science or history, whenever it speaks of scientific and historic matters, it is always precise and accurate. We have before us, in the book of Job, that which is probably the very first book of the Bible to be written. Job lived during the days of the patriarchs, probably about the time of Abraham. Therefore this book was written more than 3000 years ago, slightly before the invention of modern scientific technology. Yet, no other book of the Bible contains as much scientific data as Job.

For example, in chapter 26 we are told, 'He stretcheth out the north over the empty place, and hangeth the earth upon nothing.' What could more accurately describe the position and stability of our planet in space? Job's neighbours all believed that the earth was flat, that it rested on the shoulders of one of the gods, or the back of an elephant or giant sea turtle. Not Job. He believed God and worshipped him as the great Creator of all things.

The Lord asked Job in chapter 38, 'Where wast thou ... when the morning stars sang together, and all the sons of God shouted for joy?' I am certain there are spiritual lessons to be gleaned from this passage; but there is also a startling scientific fact spoken of that cannot be explained apart from the fact that the book of Job was written by divine inspiration. Until modern times no one in the world of 'all-wise' science ever dreamed that rays of light give off sound that no human ear can hear, but Job declared it, and it was written down in the book of God, more than 3000 years ago by the Spirit God to whom the morning stars sing praise.

Again, the Lord asked Job, 'By what way is the light parted, which scattereth the east wind upon the earth?' Reading those words in chapter 38, you would think Job had distinct knowledge of spectrum analysis. But this was written more than 3000 years ago!

The Lord God asked Job, 'Canst thou bind the sweet influences of Pleiades, or loose the bands of Orion?' Pleiades is a group of seven stars in the constellation of Taurus. Pleiades and Orion no man can control. Contrary to modern environmentalist thought, the seasons are not to be altered by men. Job was taught by God that it was not in his power to make any change in the dispensations of providence; to turn the winter of adversity into the spring of prosperity, or the spring of prosperity into the winter of adversity. Providence is God's dominion, not man's. All we can do is submit to God's work and walk quietly before him.

The Bible is the Word of God. That fact cannot be denied by any reasonable person. 'The heavens declare the glory of God; and the firmament sheweth his handiwork. Day unto day uttereth speech, and night unto night sheweth knowledge. There is no speech nor language, where their voice is not heard' (Psalm 19:1-3). But it is not my purpose merely to demonstrate the veracity of holy scripture. My purpose is to show how this book speaks of Christ and to set forth some of the lessons it teaches about our Redeemer and our relationship to him.

Behind the Scenes

In the first two chapters of Job we are allowed to look behind the scenes to see what was happening and why. Remember, when you read these chapters, that Job did not have this privilege. It is written here for our learning.

Here we are told, and told by God himself, that Job was a righteous man, a believer, a saved sinner. Many have misjudged Brother Job, asserting that he was a lost, self-righteous hypocrite, as his three friends accused him of being. But the Lord God asserts otherwise (1:1, 8; 2:3; Ezekiel 14:14, 20). He was not a righteous, or perfect man by nature. And we see clearly that he was not perfect in his personal conduct and behaviour. He was, just like you and me, a sinner saved by grace. His only righteousness was the righteousness of Christ imputed to him in free justification and imparted to him in regeneration. Christ was made unto him righteousness; and he had no other righteousness. When Job defended and maintained his righteousness before his friends, he was not boasting of righteousness before God, but simply declaring that he was not guilty of the hypocrisy of which his accusers charged him. Without question, as Elihu declared in chapter 32, Job should have spoken more to justify God before his friends than himself; but God himself verified Job's claims of innocence regarding the things his friends slanderously charged against him.

Job was a man who had been greatly blessed of God with grace and one to whom God had given greater wealth and honour than any other in the East. He worshipped God and interceded for his sons and daughters at the throne of grace continually.

In the first two chapters We see that the Lord God is the absolute Monarch of the universe, ruling and controlling all things in heaven, earth and hell, even Satan. I do not know what to make of or how to explain everything written in these chapters; but I do know that this passage is an assertion of God's dominion and sovereignty. The angels came to give report to God; and Satan came among them. It was God himself, not Satan, who took the initiative in challenging Satan to regard God's servant Job.

It was God who gave Satan permission to do what he did to Job and God who told him exactly what he could and could not do. The devil was allowed to roar against him and afflict him tremendously, but not to harm him. Satan is not a rival to the Almighty, but his servant. He is God's devil. God does with him exactly what he will. When the Lord God gets done with the old serpent, he will cast him into the pit and shut him away forever (Revelation 20:10).

Satan accused Job, as believers are always accused, of serving God for gain. The Lord turned the fiend of hell loose on him both to prove otherwise and to improve his beloved servant Job (1:9-12).

Job's Trials

As we read the first two chapters of this book, it is impossible for us to put ourselves in Job's place and form any right idea of what he felt. One day while all his children were having dinner at the oldest son's house a messenger came to Job and told him the Sabeans had slain all his servants and taken all his oxen and asses, he alone was spared so that he could come tell Job the news. Before he was finished, another messenger arrived to tell Job that lightning had fallen from heaven and killed both his flocks and herdsmen, he alone was spared so that he could come tell Job the news. While he was still talking, a third messenger came to report that the Chaldeans had taken all his camels and slaughtered all his servants who were tending them, he alone was spared so that he could come and tell Job the news. Then, while he was still telling the story, a fourth messenger ran in to tell Job that God had sent a tornado and killed all his children and all his servants who were with them, he alone was spared so that he could come tell Job the awful news. All this happened in one day! How did Job react? What did he do? What did he say? We read Job's response in chapter 1 verses 20-22.

'Then Job arose, and rent his mantle, and shaved his head, and fell down upon the ground, and worshipped, And said, Naked came I out of my mother's womb, and naked shall I return thither: the LORD gave, and the LORD hath taken away; blessed be the name of the LORD. In all this Job sinned not, nor charged God foolishly'.

In chapter two Satan appears with the angels again before the throne of God to give report of what they had been doing. When they did, the Lord God again raises the issue of Job's faith and faithfulness with Satan. 'And Satan answered the LORD, and said, Skin for skin, yea, all that a man hath will he give for his life. But put forth thine hand now, and touch his bone and his flesh, and he will curse thee to thy face. And the LORD said unto Satan, Behold, he is in thine hand; but save his life'. Remember, the fiend of hell can neither roar nor wiggle without our heavenly Father's permission. Furthermore, it is our Father who tells him exactly how loud he can roar and where he can wiggle!

'So went Satan forth from the presence of the LORD, and smote Job with sore boils from the sole of his foot unto his crown. And he took him a potsherd to scrape himself withal; and he sat down among the ashes.

Then said his wife unto him, Dost thou still retain thine integrity? curse God, and die'. Imagine that. No doubt this was the most difficult of all the trials. Job's wife, the woman he loved, the woman who loved him, the one person he had always been able to count on, the one person he knew would stand by him, turned on him in disgust, venting her anger against God and against him for worshipping God. How broken his heart must have been! 'But he said unto her, Thou speakest as one of the foolish women', like one of our idolatrous neighbours who do not know God might speak. 'What? shall we receive good at the hand of God, and shall we not receive evil?' Still, Job persevered in faith. 'In all this did not Job sin with his lips'.

Job's Friends

Beginning at verse 11 in chapter 2 and going through to chapter 31, we see Job's conflict with his friends. What wonderful friends they were! Who has not had more than a few like them? With friends like these, who needs enemies?

When Job's three friends heard about all his woes, they got together to discuss them and set a time to go and see Job and comfort him. Sadly, too often, when friends get together to discuss a friend's troubles his troubles are multiplied. When these three miserable friends came and saw Job, they were utterly astonished at his pain and grief. They sat before him for seven days and nights in astonished silence.

Then, Job's friends went to work on him. Satan's attempt to deconstruct Job's life was nothing compared to the work of these three, self-righteous, reformed legalists. Job's name means persecuted and they made sure he lived up to his name. Their doctrine was not wrong. It was as straight as a steel beam, and just as hard. These three men were severe, judgmental, heartless, religious Pharisees.

Eliphaz, whose name means 'my God is fine gold', was the first to speak. He had a vision in chapter 4, and assumed that his vision gave him authority to sit in judgment over God's servant. Bildad, whose name means 'son of contention', thought himself a scholarly intellectual, and in chapter 8 backed his words with the authority of a long list of forefathers, who could not be mistaken. Zophar, whose name means 'chirping or twitter', was as worthless as a little sparrow. He was described by someone as one of those irksome people we all hope never to meet again, fresh out of Bible college or seminary, who knows everything about everything.

Job described them considerably more pleasantly than I would, as 'miserable comforters'. They were all fully convinced that Job was a hypocrite and that he suffered divine judgment because he was, after all, a man with secret sins which God was determined to expose by his afflictions. There are multitudes like them around the world in every age and in every church.

Roger Ellsworth wrote, 'These three men stand as lasting reminders of the need to handle suffering friends with great care and to refrain from giving quick and easy solutions to complex and trying problems ... to speak little and listen much in our dealings with those stricken by calamity'.

Elihu, whose name means 'he is my God', comes on the scene in chapter 32. Elihu was a young man, but a man with a message from God. He rebuked Job's miserable, tormenting comforters for their accusations and rebuked Job for spending more time justifying himself before them than in justifying God before them. He spoke of God's incomparable greatness. In chapter 33, Elihu gives us a marvellous picture of God's method of grace, by which he delivers chosen sinners from going down to the pit. This is the way God deals with his elect both in effectual calling and in his wise and good chastisements, his fatherly discipline (Hebrews 12:5-11).

First, he tells Job not to strive against God, but to hear his instruction. Then God speaks by his messenger, the pattern for a gospel preacher today. He is one sent of God to interpret his words and his works, who shows us God's uprightness, who opens our ears that we may hear God's voice. This is the way God keeps his chosen from their own devices, breaks our pride, and keeps us from perishing. Such a messenger is truly 'one among a thousand'.

Elihu told Job that God chastens the objects of his mercy with pain upon their beds, sometimes great pain, causing them to abhor all natural, creature comfort, until their flesh is consumed and their souls draw near to the grave. At that point, when all hope is gone, when we are utterly stripped of every hope and refuge but Christ, God's grace appears, he causes us to seek him, causes the glory of God in the face of Christ to shine into our hearts, shows us his favour, and speaks peace to our hearts assuring us that Christ is indeed our Righteousness. Thereby, he delivers his own from going down to the pit, because he found a ransom for our souls in his own dear Son.

'He looketh upon men, and if any say, I have sinned, and perverted that which was right, and it profited me not; He will deliver his soul from going into the pit, and his life shall see the light. Lo, all these things worketh God oftentimes with man, To bring back his soul from the pit, to be enlightened with the light of the living' (Job 33:27-30).

Elihu's instructions in this passage are very much like the instructions given in Psalm 107. 'O give thanks unto the LORD, for he is good: for his mercy endureth for ever. Let the redeemed of the LORD say so, whom he hath redeemed from the hand of the enemy ... Oh that men would praise the LORD for his goodness, and for his wonderful works to the children of men! ... The righteous shall see it, and rejoice: and all iniquity shall stop her mouth. Whoso is wise, and will observe these things, even they shall understand the lovingkindness of the LORD'.

God Confronts His Servant

In chapters 38:1-42:17, the Lord God himself confronts his servant out of the whirlwind, by the irresistible, convincing power and grace of his Holy Spirit. Here, the Lord God effectually applies to Job what his messenger, Elihu had declared (Romans 10:17). The Lord graciously showed Job his greatness, glory, and solitary majesty as God. Job was broken before God, humbled and contrite. He confessed and repented of his sin.

'Then Job answered the LORD, and said, Behold, I am vile; what shall I answer thee? I will lay mine hand upon my mouth. Once have I spoken; but I will not answer: yea, twice; but I will proceed no further'. 'Then Job answered the Lord, and said, I know that thou canst do every thing, and that no thought can be withholden from thee. Who is he that hideth counsel without knowledge? therefore have I uttered that I understood not; things too wonderful for me, which I knew not. Hear, I beseech thee, and I will speak: I will demand of thee, and declare thou unto me. I have heard of thee by the hearing of the ear: but now mine eye seeth thee. Wherefore I abhor myself, and repent in dust and ashes.

Job then forgave and made intercession for Eliphaz, Bildad, and Zophar. Grace experienced makes sinners gracious to one another. Then the Lord blessed Job. When the gold was refined, God took him out of the furnace. His riches and honour were doubled. His children were added in the same number, seven sons and three daughters, as before.

'And the Lord turned the captivity of Job, when he prayed for his friends: also the Lord gave Job twice as much as he had before. Then came there unto him all his brethren, and all his sisters, and all they that had been of his acquaintance before, and did eat bread with him in his house: and they bemoaned him, and comforted him over all the evil that the Lord had brought upon him: every man also gave him a piece of money, and every one an earring of gold. So the Lord blessed the latter end of Job more than his beginning: for he had fourteen thousand sheep, and six thousand camels, and a thousand yoke of oxen, and a thousand she asses. He had also seven sons and three daughters. And he called the name of the first, Jemima; and the name of the second, Kezia; and the name of the third, Kerenhappuch. And in all the land were no women found so fair as the daughters of Job: and their father gave them inheritance among their brethren. After this lived Job an hundred and forty years, and saw his sons, and his sons' sons, even four generations. So Job died, being old and full of days' (Job 42:10-17).

Jemima, Kezia, Kerenhappuch, the names of Job's daughters can be taken to mean, peace, fragrance, and beauty, names that contrast dramatically with Job's previous sufferings and bitter experience.

Gospel Doctrine

Though mistaken in many things, Job's doctrine was pure, gospel doctrine. He acknowledged and trusted the Lord his God as the sovereign Monarch of heaven and earth. He knew and confessed his need of Christ as his Mediator and Kinsman Redeemer (Job 9:29, 32-35).

Job understood and rejoiced in the hope of the resurrection. Too much is made, in my opinion of Job's cursing the day of his birth and expressing a desire to die. I grant, he expressed much self-pity in his words. In that he was wrong. But who has not said much the same thing when enduring great, heart crushing pain, but pain that cannot be compared to Job's? I say that not to justify Job's behaviour or our own, but to express some understanding of his experience. Yet, even while wallowing in self-pity, Job understood that in the grave 'the wicked cease from troubling; and there the weary be at rest'. He knew that the grave is the resting place for the bodies of God's saints. He understood that in the last day our great God will call the bodies of his saints out of the grave and raise us up in resurrection glory (Job 14:13-15). Job had this confident hope because he knew that Christ was his Redeemer.

'Have pity upon me, have pity upon me, O ye my friends; for the hand of God hath touched me. Why do ye persecute me as God, and are not satisfied with my flesh? Oh that my words were now written! oh that they were printed in a book! That they were graven with an iron pen and lead in the rock for ever! For I know that my redeemer liveth, and that he shall stand at the latter day upon the earth: And though after my skin worms destroy this body, yet in my flesh shall I see God: Whom I shall see for myself, and mine eyes shall behold, and not another; though my reins be consumed within me. But ye should say, Why persecute we him, seeing the root of the matter is found in me?' (Job 19:21-28).

Why?

Why do the righteous suffer? The Holy Spirit shows us the answer in these forty-two chapters. Job himself understood the reason. He said, the Lord my God 'knoweth the way that I take: when he hath tried me, I shall come forth as gold'. The apostle Paul gives us the same explanation, more fully in Hebrews 12:5-11. 'And ye have forgotten the exhortation which speaketh unto you as unto children, My son, despise not thou the chastening of the Lord, nor faint when thou art rebuked of him: For whom the Lord loveth he chasteneth, and scourgeth every son whom he receiveth. If ye endure chastening, God dealeth with you as with sons; for what son is he whom the father chasteneth not? But if ye be without chastisement, whereof all are partakers, then are ye bastards, and not sons. Furthermore we have had fathers of our flesh which corrected us, and we gave them reverence: shall we not much rather be in subjection unto the Father of spirits, and live? For they verily for a few days chastened us after their own pleasure; but he for our profit, that we might be partakers of his holiness. Now no chastening for the present seemeth to be joyous, but grievous: nevertheless afterward it yieldeth the peaceable fruit of righteousness unto them which are exercised thereby'.

Chapter 19

Psalms

God's book of Praise

The book of Psalms is the largest book in the Word of God. It is a book about the worship of God. The word 'psalms' means 'praises'. The book of Psalms is 'the book of Praises'. It is God's book of Praise. That which is essential in the praise of God is dominant in these 150 psalms – Worship. 'Worship' means 'prostration'. To worship and praise the Lord our God is to prostrate ourselves before him, taking our place in the dust before him as we acknowledge and adore his supremacy, perfection, and work.

This is where we must begin. After describing Christ as the perfect man in Psalm 1 and declaring him to be the exalted King in Psalm 2, we are called to worship him in Psalm 2:11-12. 'Serve the Lord with fear, and rejoice with trembling. Kiss the Son, lest he be angry, and ye perish from the way, when his wrath is kindled but a little. Blessed are all they that put their trust in him'.

Worship

The book of Psalms teaches us to worship our God, to be ever occupied with him. Just in proportion as our hearts and minds are occupied with Christ, we worship him (Colossians 3:1-3). Here we are taught to treasure his Word, delight in his providence, remember his works, speak of his greatness, trust his care, glory in his gospel, and celebrate his praise continually. We are here taught to find strength for life's labours, comfort for life's troubles, and solace in life's sorrows by continually prostrating ourselves before the throne of grace, seeking mercy and grace from our great God in time of need.

In this book we have 150 psalms, or songs of praise to our great God. As we read these psalms, our hearts often echo the words we are reading, because that which we read here expresses our own feelings, emotions, and experiences as God's people in this world. These inspired psalms express our own doubts and fears, joys and sorrows, sufferings and aspirations, burdens and blessings, as we attempt to worship and serve our God.

Yet, this is a book of praise to our God. If you read the psalms carefully, you cannot avoid noticing the fact that each of the psalms that begin with an expression of sorrow or despondency end with praise to God for his goodness. That is because our sorrows, like our joys, are designed by our God to show us his goodness and bring his goodness to us.

There is one exception, however. Psalm 88, perhaps the oldest of the psalms, is all sorrow. That psalm reveals the inmost sorrow of our Saviour as he suffered the wrath of God for us. When he was made to be sin, when he was made to be the object of God's unmitigated wrath as our Substitute, he found nothing to comfort him. Though he looked for comforters, there were none.

John Gill wrote, 'The subject matter of this book is exceeding great and excellent; many of the psalms respect the person, offices, and grace of Christ; his sufferings and death, resurrection, ascension, and session at the right hand of God; and so are exceeding suitable to the Gospel dispensation. The whole book is a rich mine of grace and evangelical truths, and a large fund of spiritual experience; and is abundantly suited to every case, state, and condition, that the church of Christ, or particular believers, are in at any time'.

Authorship

The New Testament contains two hundred and forty-three quotations from the Old and one hundred and sixteen of these are from the book of Psalms. These 150 psalms were written over a period spanning 900 years. Most of them were written by David, 'the sweet singer of Israel'. One was written by Moses (Psalm 90). One was written by Heman (Psalm 88). One was written by Ethan (Psalm 89). Two were written by Solomon (Psalms 72 and 127). The descendants of Korah wrote ten. Asaph, the chief musician in David's choir, wrote twelve. There are fifty of the psalms to which no author's name is attached. However, it seems certain that David wrote some of these (compare Psalm 2:1 and Acts 4:25).

Divisions

The psalms have been divided into five categories. Each section ends with 'amen' or 'hallelujah'.

Psalms 1-41: Davidic Psalms
Psalms 42-72: Levitical Psalms
Psalms 73-89: Psalms of the Time of Hezekiah
Psalms 90-106: Psalms Before the Captivity
Psalms 107-150: Psalms After the Captivity

Personal Experience

Let us remember that although, as we shall see, the psalms speak of Christ, they are also true expressions of the personal emotions, feelings, and experiences of those who wrote them. When David wrote, 'My God, my God, Why hast thou forsaken me?', He was, without question, speaking prophetically of Christ. But he was also expressing his own soul's lamentation before God. Because the psalms are honest expressions of believing hearts in all the varied experiences of life in this world, they speak the universal language of our souls. Whatever our spiritual state and condition may be, we will find our deepest experiences put into words in the Psalms.

Christ

Yet, it is a mistake to interpret the Psalms in an exclusively historic way, applying the words of the psalms only to mere men. The One of whom the psalms speak is the Lord Jesus Christ himself, our great God and Saviour (Luke 24:25-27, 44-47).

As 'the testimony of Jesus is the spirit of prophecy' (Revelation 19:10), the testimony of Christ is the spirit of the psalms. The Psalms speak of the incarnation of Christ, the deity of Christ, the eternal Sonship of Christ, the offices of Christ as Prophet, Priest and King, the betrayal of Christ, the agony of Christ, the trial of Christ, the rejection of Christ, the crucifixion of Christ, the resurrection of Christ, the ascension and exaltation of Christ, and the second coming of Christ to judge the world (1 Peter 1:10-12).

They tell us of holiness of heart and life, and of Christ, the one perfectly holy man in the history of the world. The Psalms tell us much of the blessedness of righteousness, and of Christ, the only righteous man who ever lived. The Psalms tell us often of the enemies of the righteous, and of Christ who was ever encompassed with enemies who hated him without a cause. The Psalms tell us of the punishment of the wicked, and of Christ the Judge of all. The Lord Jesus Christ is set forth in the Psalms as the Covenant God of his true Israel.

The Gospels tell us about the kingdom of God. The Psalms tell us about Christ the King. God the Father appointed his Son to be King in Zion; and he shall rule the nations with a rod of iron (Psalm 2). David, with his throne in Zion, was typical of Christ who rules from heaven as David ruled on earth. 'For the kingdom is the Lord's; and he is the Governor among the nations'. 'Yea, all kings shall fall down before him; all nations shall serve him. For he shall deliver the needy when he crieth, the poor also; and him that hath no helper'.

The Gospels are a record of the history of our Lord's outer life in this world, his incarnation, his family, his works, his doctrine, his death, his resurrection, his ascension, and his exaltation. The Psalms are a record of our Saviour's inmost Being, the feelings, passions, and experiences of his very heart and soul, the feelings, passions, and experiences of the heart and soul of him who was in all points tempted as we are, yet without sin, that he might be our merciful and faithful High Priest, interceding as One who is touched with the feeling of our infirmities.

Messianic Psalms

Commonly, specific psalms are referred to as 'messianic psalms'. But that is unhelpful because it implies that some of the psalms are not messianic; that some of them do not speak specifically of our Saviour ('In the Psalms concerning me' Luke 24:44).

In these blessed, inspired songs of praise to our all-glorious Christ, we see him in all his offices, in all his works, and in all his accomplishments as Saviour and Lord. He is the Redeemer, the Rock, the Refuge, the Shepherd, the Shield, the Fortress, the High Tower of his people. Christ is the Sun of Righteousness around which the whole book of Psalms revolves.

Behold, here is Christ! Our Good Shepherd (Psalm 23; 77:20; 78:70-72; 80:1; 95:7; 100:3; 119:176). The Rock of our Salvation (Psalm 27:5; 28:1; 31:2-3; 40:2; 61:2-3; 62:2-9; 71:3; 78:20; 89:26; 94:22; 125:1). The Light of the World (Psalm 27:1; 43:3; 118:27). Our Great Redeemer (Psalm 19:14; 69:18; 72:14; 77:15; 78:35; 103:4; 106:10; 107:2; 119:154). The One in Whom and by Whom we have forgiveness (Psalm 32; 51; 130).

Penitential Psalms

There is not, in my opinion, a single psalm in this book that can be applied only to the man who wrote it in the fullest extent of its meaning. Even those psalms referred to as 'Penitential Psalms' are best understood, and most properly understood, when we read them as the words of our great Substitute and Sin-Bearer, the Lord Jesus Christ, when he was made to be sin for us.

As Ezra, Daniel, and Nehemiah confessed the sins of Israel as their own sins, though they were not personally guilty of the crimes they confessed, our great Sin-Bearer took our sins to be his own and confessed them as such. He who bore our sins in his own body on the tree is alone the sacrifice God accepts, finds pleasure in, and upon which he builds his church and blesses his people (Psalm 51:17-19).

Pictures of Christ

Psalm 1—Christ is set before us as the perfect, holy, blessed man, who delights always in God and his will, who walks not in the counsel of the ungodly. He is the Man of whom it is said, 'whatsoever he doeth shall prosper'. The pleasure of the Lord prospers in his hand (Isaiah 53:12).

Psalm 2—Christ, the Son of God, is depicted as the appointed Ruler, the King of kings. 'I will declare the decree: The Lord hath said unto Me, Thou art My Son; this day have I begotten Thee' (v.7).

Psalm 8—Here we see the Son of God becoming the Son of man in order that we might be made the sons of God. 'What is man, that thou art mindful of him? and the son of man, that thou visitest him? For thou hast made him a little lower than the angels, and hast crowned him with glory and honour' (vv. 4-5). The Holy Spirit tells us plainly that these words refer to the incarnation of Christ, his coming into the world to redeem and save his people (Hebrews 2:6-18).

Psalm 16—Christ's deliverance from death is prophesied here. Verses 10 and 11 find their fulfilment in the death and resurrection of our Lord. Peter quoted these words on the day of Pentecost, showing that David was a prophet and that the One of whom he spoke is Christ (Acts 2:25-28).

Psalms 22-24—These songs are examples of divine inspiration in the arrangement of the Psalms. They are filled with Messianic teaching about the life and ministry of the Lord Jesus. We shall return to them shortly.

Psalm 45—Christ is the King who is fairer than the children of men, into whose lips grace has been poured, whom God has blessed forever, the most mighty One who has girded on his sword, riding with glory and majesty, prospering because of his truth, meekness and righteousness. It is of him alone that we sing ...

'Thy throne, O God, is for ever and ever: the sceptre of thy kingdom is a right sceptre. Thou lovest righteousness, and hatest wickedness: therefore God, thy God, hath anointed thee with the oil of gladness above thy fellows. All thy garments smell of myrrh, and aloes, and cassia, out of the ivory palaces, whereby they have made thee glad. Kings' daughters were among thy honourable women: upon thy right hand did stand the queen in gold of Ophir.

Hearken, O daughter, and consider, and incline thine ear; forget also thine own people, and thy father's house; So shall the king greatly desire thy beauty: for he is thy Lord; and worship thou him. And the daughter of Tyre shall be there with a gift; even the rich among the people shall entreat thy favour.

The king's daughter is all glorious within: her clothing is of wrought gold. She shall be brought unto the king in raiment of needlework: the virgins her companions that follow her shall be brought unto thee. With gladness and rejoicing shall they be brought: they shall enter into the king's palace' (vv. 6-15).

Psalm 68—Christ is the Lord God our Saviour who has risen to scatter his enemies (vv. 1, 17-20; Ephesians 4:8-11).

Psalm 40—Hebrews 10 tells us that this psalm speaks of Christ's coming to redeem and save his people.

Psalm 69—The humiliation of Christ is shown in verses 4, 8, 9, 12, and 21. The full meaning of the words used here find their fulfilment only in our Redeemer. 'They that hate me without a cause (John 15:25) are more than the hairs of mine head: they that would destroy me, being mine enemies wrongfully, are mighty: then I restored that which I took not away'. O God, thou knowest my foolishness; and my sins are not hid from thee' (2 Corinthians 5:21). 'I am become a stranger unto my brethren, and an alien unto my mother's children' (Matthew 13:55-56). 'For the zeal of thine house hath eaten me up; and the reproaches of them that reproached thee are fallen upon me' (John 2:17; Romans 15:3). 'They gave me also gall for my meat; and in my thirst they gave me vinegar to drink' (Matthew 27:33-34).

Psalm 110—Christ is our omnipotent Saviour King and everlasting Priest, who makes his people willing in the day of his power (vv. 1-4).

Psalm 118—This psalm is part of the special passage that was used as a prayer on Passover night. It more than likely was sung by the Lord and His disciples at the Lord's Supper, as recorded in Matthew 26:30. Behold Christ is here! 'The stone which the builders refused is become the head stone of the corner' (v. 22; Matthew 21:42; Mark 12:10; Luke 20:17).

The Shepherd Psalms

Psalms 22-24 speak specifically of the Lord Jesus Christ as our Shepherd. Psalm 22 brings us to 'the place called Calvary'. In its light we stand at the foot of the cross. Here and in Isaiah 53 the crucifixion is portrayed more clearly than in any other part of the Old Testament. Isaiah 53 speaks primarily of the sin-atoning aspect of Christ's death. Psalm 22 speaks of his sufferings. It begins with the cry uttered by our Lord in the hour of darkness, 'My God, My God, why hast Thou forsaken me?' It closes with the words 'He hath done it', or 'It is finished', as it stands in the original Hebrew, identical with almost the last cry of our Saviour. It is a psalm of shame, sorrow, and sighing. In the original language there is not a single completed sentence in the opening verses, but a series of short ejaculations, like the gasps of a dying man whose breath and strength are failing, and who can only utter a word or two at a time.

Read Psalms 22 and 69 together, and you will see a tremendous, instructive, prophetic picture of our Redeemer's sufferings. Matthew, Mark, Luke, and John specially and repeatedly call our attention to it. 'I am a worm, and no man; a reproach of men, and despised of the people'. 'All they that see me laugh me to scorn: they shoot out the lip' (22:6, 7). 'The rulers derided Him'. 'The soldiers also mocked Him' (Luke 23:35, 36). 'They shake the head, saying, He trusted on the Lord that he would deliver him: let him deliver him, seeing he delighted in him' (verse 8). 'They that passed by reviled him, wagging their heads. Likewise also the chief priests mocking him, with the scribes and elders, said ... He trusted in God; let him deliver him now, if he will have him' (Matthew 27:39, 41, 43). 'Strong bulls of Bashan have beset me round. They gaped upon me with their mouths' (verses 12, 13). 'Sitting down, they watched him there. The thieves also, which were crucified with him, cast the same in his teeth' (Matthew 27:36, 44).

'They pierced my hands and my feet'. 'All my bones are out of joint'(vv. 16 and 14). The Roman method of death by crucifixion, unknown to Jewish law, is prophesied here. The very action of the soldiers is given in the words, 'They part my garments among them, and cast lots upon my vesture' (v. 18). 'My tongue cleaveth to my jaws' (v. 15). 'In my thirst they gave me vinegar to drink' (Psalm 69:21). 'Jesus ... that the scripture might be fulfilled, saith, I thirst. And they filled a sponge with vinegar, and put it upon hyssop, and put it to his mouth' (John 19:28, 29).

A Broken Heart

'I am poured out like water: My heart is like wax; it is melted' (22:14). 'Reproach hath broken my heart' (Psalm 69:20). Here we are told the immediate cause of our Saviour's death. He died of a broken heart. Six times in Psalm 69 the word 'reproach' appears, reproach and shame and dishonour borne for others. The bearing of our sins, the hiding of his Father's face on account of it, was what broke his heart.

'Jesus, when he had cried again with a loud voice, yielded up the ghost. And, behold, the veil of the temple was rent in twain from the top to the bottom; and the earth did quake, and the rocks rent' (Matthew 27:50, 51). When the soldiers came to break the legs of those that hung upon the cross, they found that the Lord Jesus was dead already, and broke not his legs. 'But one of the soldiers with a spear pierced his side, and forthwith came there out blood and water. And he that saw it bare record, and his record is true; and he knoweth that he saith true, that ye might believe'.

'Therefore doth my Father love me, because I lay down my life that I might take it again. No man taketh it from me, but I lay it down of myself'. By the determinate counsel and foreknowledge of God he was delivered to death. By wicked hands he was crucified and slain. By his own will he laid down his life.

Surely, as mentioned before, we have in Psalm 51 not merely the cry of the penitent sinner, but a prophecy of Christ, the Sacrifice of God. 'The sacrifices of God are a broken spirit: a broken and a contrite heart, O God, Thou wilt not despise' (51:17). The great sacrifice of God is a broken heart. This was the sacrifice our Saviour offered for us. He clothed himself in a human body that he might have it to offer (Hebrews 10:5, 9, 10). He became possessed of a human heart that it might be broken. The way into the holiest is opened up for us through the broken heart of God's own darling Son, our all-glorious Saviour. This is the sinner's Saviour, the sinner's hope, the sinner's gospel.

The New Testament refers to the work of the Lord Jesus Christ as that of a shepherd in three distinct ways. They correspond to Psalms 22, 23, and 24, which present three aspects of our Lord's ministry on earth.

The Good Shepherd

In Psalm 22 we see our Saviour as the good Shepherd, who gave his life for his sheep. He said, 'I am the good shepherd; the good shepherd giveth His life for the sheep' (John 10:11). In the Gospels we read of what he said and did, and what was done to him; in Psalm 22 we are allowed to discover, as well as sinful creatures can discover, what he felt.

The latter part of the psalm (vv. 22-31) is marked by a jubilance that portrays the glory of the salvation obtained by the efficacious merit of his blood. Though the resurrection is not specifically mentioned, we see Christ delivered and his people delivered as well. 'A seed shall serve him; it shall be counted to the Lord for a generation. They shall come and declare his righteousness unto a people that shall be born, that he hath done this' (vv. 30-31). Psalm 22 is the crucifixion psalm. The Good Shepherd has given His life for the sheep.

The Great Shepherd

What tender emotions and thoughts of praise fill our hearts as we read Psalm 23! This is not a song about a dying or a dead shepherd, but of a risen, living, reigning Shepherd. It is in the present tense; it speaks of today. Christ arose from the dead to be our Great Shepherd. 'Now the God of peace that brought again from the dead our Lord Jesus, that great Shepherd of the sheep, through the blood of the everlasting covenant' (Hebrews 13:20). Because my good Shepherd laid down his life for me, I shall never die. Because Christ my great Shepherd sits upon the throne of the universe, 'Surely goodness and mercy shall follow me all the days of my life, and I shall dwell in the house of the Lord forever!'

The Chief Shepherd

Psalm 24 speaks of Christ as the chief Shepherd, who shall bring us with him into his glory, the glory he earned and purchased as our Substitute, the glory he gave us (John 17:5, 22), the glory he holds for us as our Forerunner in heaven (Hebrews 6:20). The apostle Peter wrote, 'And when the chief Shepherd shall appear, ye shall receive a crown of glory that fadeth not away' (1 Peter 5:4).

Listen! Someone is coming! Who is it? Christ, the King of Glory! He is coming to bring his chosen, ransomed people into his kingdom and glory. 'Who shall ascend into the hill of the LORD? or who shall stand in his holy place? He that hath clean hands, and a pure heart; who hath not lifted up his soul unto vanity, nor sworn deceitfully. He shall receive the blessing from the LORD, and righteousness from the God of his salvation' (vv. 3-5). That is Christ.

But these words do not speak of Christ alone. He did not enter and does not stand in the holy place by himself. He entered in for us. He stands there with us. We shall stand there with him in all the perfection of his glory as our Mediator and Substitute. Verse 6 tells us plainly that these words refer just as fully to us, the people he came here to save, as they do to him. 'This is the generation of them that seek him, that seek thy face, O Jacob. Selah'. Pause a while and think about that!

Chapter 20

Proverbs

Christ the Wisdom of God

The Poetic books set before us essential and blessed aspects of life in Christ as it is experienced by God's saints in this world. Job displays the necessity of self-denial, of dying to self that we may live unto God. The Psalms set before us the blessedness of worshipping our God in resurrection life. Ecclesiastes displays the utter vanity of all earthly things, the complete inability of finding satisfaction for our souls in this perishing world of woe. The Song of Solomon displays Christ as that One in whom alone our souls find satisfaction. Lamentations teaches us to set our hearts upon our God and Saviour, finding contentment and satisfaction in him.

Proverbs shows us the blessed wisdom of faith in Christ, wisdom with which to live for God's glory in this present evil world. The first nine chapters of this book are instructions by Solomon to his son, a series of parental admonitions to his son to seek wisdom and shun folly; but there is more here than Solomon's instructions to his son. In this book, we have before us God's instructions to his sons and daughters, teaching us to seek wisdom and shun folly. In the remaining chapters (10-31), we are given 374 proverbs that touch every aspect of life in this world.

Purpose

The purpose of this book is set before us in the opening verses of chapter one. 'The proverbs of Solomon the son of David, king of Israel; To know wisdom and instruction; to perceive the words of understanding; To receive the instruction of wisdom, justice, and judgment, and equity; To give subtlety to the simple, to the young man knowledge and discretion. A wise man will hear, and will increase learning; and a man of understanding shall attain unto wise counsels: To understand a proverb, and the interpretation; the words of the wise, and their dark sayings'.

Wisdom

The Key to the book is found in verse seven. Here we are told plainly what wisdom is. 'The fear of the Lord is the beginning of knowledge: but fools despise wisdom and instruction'. There are many books written by intellectually accomplished men to teach wisdom. The thing that sets this book apart from all others is that it does not teach us about wisdom. It teaches us wisdom. It teaches and reveals Christ who is Wisdom. This fact distinguishes the book of Proverbs from all of the wisdom literature of the world.

There is no wisdom without truth; and there can be no discovery of truth apart from revelation, the revelation of Christ who is the Truth and the Wisdom of God. All the philosophical wisdom of the world, all of it, is utter foolishness, because 'there is no fear of God before their eyes' (Romans 3:18; 1 Corinthians 1:17-25).

Christ is Wisdom. He alone is Wisdom. He alone can make us wise. That is the message of this inspired book of Wisdom. In chapter eight, wisdom is personified. It is obvious that the personification of wisdom spoken of in that chapter is Christ.

'I wisdom dwell with prudence, and find out knowledge of witty inventions ... Counsel is mine, and sound wisdom: I am understanding; I have strength. By me kings reign, and princes decree justice. By me princes rule, and nobles, even all the judges of the earth. I love them that love me; and those that seek me early shall find me. Riches and honour are with me; yea, durable riches and righteousness ... For whoso findeth me findeth life, and shall obtain favour of the LORD' (vv. 12, 14-18, 35).

Christ is the Wisdom spoken of and speaking throughout these thirty-one chapters. This is not a book about moral philosophy. The book of Proverbs is a book about Christ the Wisdom of God and the Truth of God. James said, 'If any of you lack wisdom, let him ask of God, who giveth to all men liberally, and upbraideth not, and it shall be given him' (James 1:5).

The apostle Paul tells us, 'But unto them who are called, both Jews and Greeks, Christ (is) the power of God, and the wisdom of God' (1 Corinthians 1:24). In 1 Corinthians 1:30 we read, 'But of Him are ye in Christ Jesus, who of God is made unto us wisdom'.

This book teaches us that the Lord Jesus Christ, our incarnate God, our crucified Substitute, our risen and exalted Lord, our omnipotent Saviour is the very wisdom of God. 'In all thy ways acknowledge Him, and He shall direct thy paths' (Proverbs 3:6).

A Comparison

Compare what is written in the book of Proverbs about wisdom and what is written elsewhere in the book of God about Christ, and you will see clearly that the Wisdom spoken of here is a person, not an attribute, and that that person is our Lord Jesus Christ.

'Wisdom crieth without; she uttereth her voice in the streets … Turn you at my reproof: behold, I will pour out my spirit unto you, I will make known my words unto you' (1:20, 23). 'And said, Verily I say unto you, Except ye be converted, and become as little children, ye shall not enter into the kingdom of heaven' (Matthew 18:3).

'But whoso hearkeneth unto me shall dwell safely, and shall be quiet from fear of evil' (1:33). 'Come unto me, all ye that labour and are heavy laden, and I will give you rest' (Matthew 11:28).

'If thou seekest her as silver, and searchest for her as for hid treasures' (2:4). 'In whom are hid all the treasures of wisdom and knowledge' (Colossians 2:3).

'Doth not wisdom cry? and understanding put forth her voice? … Unto you, O men, I call; and my voice is to the sons of man' (8:1, 4). 'In the last day, that great day of the feast, Jesus stood and cried, saying, If any man thirst, let him come unto me, and drink' (John 7:37).

'O ye simple, understand wisdom: and, ye fools, be ye of an understanding heart' (8:5). 'In that hour Jesus rejoiced in spirit, and said, I thank thee, O Father, Lord of heaven and earth, that thou hast hid these things from the wise and prudent, and hast revealed them unto babes: even so, Father; for so it seemed good in thy sight' (Luke 10:21).

'Hear; for I will speak of excellent things; and the opening of my lips shall be right things' (8:6). 'And all bare him witness, and wondered at the gracious words which proceeded out of his mouth. And they said, Is not this Joseph's son?' (Luke 4:22).

'Counsel is mine, and sound wisdom: I am understanding; I have strength' (8:14). 'But of him are ye in Christ Jesus, who of God is made unto us wisdom, and righteousness, and sanctification, and redemption' (1 Corinthians 1:30).

'I love them that love me; and those that seek me early shall find me' (8:17). 'I am crucified with Christ: nevertheless I live; yet not I, but Christ liveth in me: and the life which I now live in the flesh I live by the faith of the Son of God, who loved me, and gave himself for me' (Galatians 2:20). 'Ask, and it shall be given you; seek, and ye shall find; knock, and it shall be opened unto you' (Matthew 7:7).

'I lead in the way of righteousness, in the midst of the paths of judgment' (8:20). 'He restoreth my soul: he leadeth me in the paths of righteousness for his name's sake' (Psalm 23:3).

'The LORD possessed me in the beginning of his way, before his works of old' (8:22). 'And he is before all things, and by him all things consist' (Colossians 1:17).

'I was set up from everlasting, from the beginning, or ever the earth was' (8:23). 'In the beginning was the Word, and the Word was with God, and the Word was God' (John 1:1).

'When he prepared the heavens, I was there: when he set a compass upon the face of the depth' (8:27). 'All things were made by him; and without him was not any thing made that was made' (John 1:3).

'Then I was by him, as one brought up with him: and I was daily his delight, rejoicing always before him' (8:30). 'Hath in these last days spoken unto us by his Son, whom he hath appointed heir of all things, by whom also he made the worlds' (Hebrews 1:2). 'And the Holy Ghost descended in a bodily shape like a dove upon him, and a voice came from heaven, which said, Thou art my beloved Son; in thee I am well pleased' (Luke 3:22). 'Father, I will that they also, whom thou hast given me, be with me where I am; that they may behold my glory, which thou hast given me: for thou lovedst me before the foundation of the world' (John 17:24).

'Now therefore hearken unto me, O ye children: for blessed are they that keep my ways' (8:32). 'If ye keep my commandments, ye shall abide in my love; even as I have kept my Father's commandments, and abide in his love' (John 15:10).

'For whoso findeth me findeth life, and shall obtain favour of the LORD' (8:35). 'Verily, verily, I say unto you, He that believeth on me hath everlasting life' (John 6:47).

'Come, eat of my bread, and drink of the wine which I have mingled' (9:5). 'And Jesus said unto them, I am the bread of life: he that cometh to me shall never hunger; and he that believeth on me shall never thirst' (John 6:35).

Faith in Christ

If you would be wise read Proverbs 30 and learn wisdom. The only true wisdom man has is the wisdom of faith, faith in Christ. The man speaking here is Agur, the son of Jakeh. He tells us in verse one that what he is declaring is prophetic. Specifically, it is prophetic of Christ and faith in him.

Wisdom, as faith, begins with a confession of our utter helplessness, unworthiness, and ignorance as fallen, sinful creatures before God. 'Surely I am more brutish than any man, and have not the understanding of a man' (30:2).

This is the cry of repentance and faith, 'God be merciful to me a sinner'. If we are to walk in the path of wisdom, we must acknowledge our own guilt and weakness. Agur goes on to declare, in verse 3, that he has no knowledge of God, no wisdom, no understanding of God. 'I neither learned wisdom, nor have the knowledge of the holy'. The fact is, we will never know God, we will never know Christ, until we are convinced that we do not.

This wisdom, the knowledge of God, which is eternal life (John 17:3), comes by divine revelation. 'For the wisdom of this world is foolishness with God. For it is written, He taketh the wise in their own craftiness' (1 Corinthians 3:19). Even the Greek philosophers could not answer man's quest for the true meaning of life. The best the philosophers on Mars Hill could do was to erect an altar to 'the unknown God' (Acts 17:23). We cannot by searching find out God. We will come to know him only when he reveals his Son in us, as he did with Saul of Tarsus (Galatians 1:15, 16).

Faith sees, acknowledges, confesses, trusts, and worships the risen, exalted Christ. Overwhelmed by the thought of God's greatness and power revealed in Christ, the crucified, risen Saviour, and by the infinite distance separating man and God, Agur asked a series of penetrating questions in verse 4. 'Who hath ascended up into heaven, or descended? who hath gathered the wind in his fists? who hath bound the waters in a garment? who hath established all the ends of the earth? what is his name, and what is his son's name, if thou canst tell?'

God graciously forced Job to face and deal with these same questions, laying him in the dust before him. 'Where wast thou when I laid the foundations of the earth? declare, if thou hast understanding. Who hath laid the measures thereof, if thou knowest? or who hath stretched the line upon it? Whereupon are the foundations thereof fastened? or who laid the corner stone thereof; When the morning stars sang together, and all the sons of God shouted for joy?' (Job 38:4-7).

Agur is talking about Christ, the Son of God. Verse 4 ends with a tremendous question: 'What is His name, and what is His Son's name, if thou canst tell?' God has a Son! 'In the beginning was the Word, and the Word was with God, and the Word was God' (John 1:1). Isaiah would prophesy, "For unto us a Child is born, unto us a Son is given, and the government shall be upon His shoulder; and His name shall be called Wonderful, Counsellor, The Mighty God, The Everlasting Father, The Prince of Peace' (Isaiah 9:6).

The Lord Jesus Christ, God the Son, that One in whom alone the triune God is revealed (John 1:18) is the One of whom the passage is speaking. Christ descended from heaven to save his people from their sins. This same Christ is God the Creator and Ruler of all things, who upholds all things by the Word of his power. He bound the wind in his fists and holds the waters as in a garment. It is he who established the ends of the earth. This is not a novel interpretation of Agur's words. This is precisely what Paul tells us as he sets before us the essence of saving faith (Romans 10:6-13).

Blessed is that person whom the Lord God graciously humbles before him as he did Job, Agur, and Saul of Tarsus. Such humiliation comes only when Christ is revealed, when he is made to see the glory of God shining in the face of Jesus Christ.

The faith that God gives to and works in the hearts of men comes from and rests entirely upon the pure Word of God. Taking Christ, as he is revealed in holy scripture, as our Shield and Refuge, we have peace with God. Thus, says Agur, 'Every word of God is pure: he is a shield unto them that put their trust in him'. 'Thy word is true from the beginning: and every one of thy righteous judgments endureth for ever' (Psalm 119:160). 'Thou wilt keep him in perfect peace, whose mind is stayed on thee: because he trusteth in thee' (Isaiah 26:3).

True wisdom, this wisdom that comes from Christ who is the Wisdom of God, bows to the revelation and authority of holy scripture, the Word of God. 'Add thou not unto his words, lest he reprove thee, and thou be found a liar' verse 6. 'All scripture is given by inspiration of God, and is profitable for doctrine, for reproof, for correction, for instruction in righteousness: That the man of God may be perfect, thoroughly furnished unto all good works' (2 Timothy 3:16-17).

Christ In Proverbs

The book of Proverbs, the book of Wisdom, is all about Christ. He is to be seen everywhere in the book. It is Christ who calls sinners to repentance, promising grace to all who come to him and warning rebels of the destruction they bring upon themselves by their rebellion and unbelief (1:20-33; 29:1). When Christ enters our hearts, the knowledge he gives is pleasant to our souls. He gives us understanding and protection from all evil (2:10-17). Christ is our Surety who snared himself with the words of his mouth (6:1-2).

Christ who is our Wisdom warns us to avoid 'the strange woman' (chapter 7). The harlot here spoken of is not merely the common prostitute. This harlot allures her victims upon the basis of her religious devotion (vv. 14-15). She has, by her much fair speech and flattering words, enticed many and cast many strong men into hell. 'Her house is the way to hell' (v. 27). This harlot is the same old whore described in Revelation 17 and 18. She represents all false religion, all freewill works religion.

Christ is that One called 'Wisdom' (chapter 8) by whom kings reign and princes decree justice, in whom are hid all the treasures of wisdom and knowledge, who leads in the way of righteousness, who causes us to inherit the treasures of boundless grace, who, being set up from everlasting, stood and spoke as our Wisdom in covenant grace before the world began. Christ is that One called 'Wisdom' who has built his house from hewn stones upon seven pillars of grace with the sacrifices of God (chapter 9). Christ is that One called 'Wisdom' who teaches his people how to live in this world for the glory of God in every relationship and experience (chapters 10-29). The fear of God (faith in Christ) is the source and start of all true wisdom and knowledge in every relationship and walk of life.

Christ is that One called 'Wisdom' who teaches us and convinces us of divine truth, for he is the Truth. He shows us that our God is the absolute sovereign of the universe. He who made all things for himself rules all things, including the hearts, tongues, and ways of all men, for his own glory! Even the king's heart is in his hand, absolutely controlled by him (21:1-4). It is only in and by Christ that we are made to see how God can be both 'a just God and a Saviour' (Isaiah 45:21), purging iniquity 'by mercy and truth' (Proverbs 16:6). There is no other way whereby the holy, just, and true God can forgive sin, except by the sacrifice of his darling Son, making him to be sin for us who knew no sin that we might be made the righteousness of God in him (Proverbs 17:15; Romans 3:21-26; 2 Corinthians 5:21).

In chapter 31, king Lemuel gives us a prophecy taught to him by his mother. This king Lemuel, whose name means 'to God', is commonly thought to be Solomon, and that Lemuel was a name by which his mother, Bathsheba, called him. The prophecy is given to attract our hearts to and teach us to seek out a singular virtuous woman, 'for her price is above rubies' (v. 10), whose 'husband is known in the gates' (v. 23). But, says

John Gill, the description of this virtuous woman 'is drawn up to such a pitch, and wrote in such strong lines, as cannot agree with any of the daughters of fallen Adam, literally understood'. This virtuous woman is the church of God. Her husband is Christ himself. She is set before us in direct contrast to the harlot of Babylon described in chapter 7.

Christ, who is Wisdom, calls for us to trust our God in all things, giving him our hearts. 'Trust in the LORD with all thine heart; and lean not unto thine own understanding. In all thy ways acknowledge him, and he shall direct thy paths' (Proverbs 3:5-6). 'My son, give me thine heart, and let thine eyes observe my ways' (23:26). 'Keep thy heart with all diligence; for out of it are the issues of life' (4:23).

Let us be wise, like the coney, and take refuge in Christ, the Rock of Salvation. 'The conies are but a feeble folk, yet make they their houses in the rocks' (30:26). The conies are 'an emblem of the people of God, who are a weak and feeble people, unable of themselves to perform spiritual duties, to exercise grace, to withstand the corruptions of their nature, resist the temptations of Satan, bear up under afflictive providences, and grapple with spiritual enemies, or defend themselves from them: but such heavenly wisdom is given them, as to betake themselves for refuge and shelter to Christ, the Rock of Israel; the Rock of salvation, the Rock that is higher than they; a strong one, on which the church is built, and against which the gates of hell cannot prevail: and here they are safe from the storms of divine wrath, and the avenging justice of God; from the rage and fury of men, and the fiery darts of Satan; here they dwell safely and delightfully, and have all manner of provision at hand for them; they are the inhabitants of that Rock, who have reason to sing indeed!' (John Gill).

It is written, with regard to all who trust Christ, all who take refuge in the Rock of Israel, 'He shall dwell on high: his place of defence shall be the munitions of rocks: bread shall be given him; his waters shall be sure' (Isaiah 33:16). 'Let the wilderness and the cities thereof lift up their voice, the villages that Kedar doth inhabit: let the inhabitants of the rock sing, let them shout from the top of the mountains' (Isaiah 42:11).

Do not play the part of the hypocritical spider. 'The spider taketh hold with her hands, and is in kings' palaces' (30:28). Gill suggests that the spider here represents hypocrites, 'whose hope and trust are as the spider's web, built upon their own righteousness, spun out of their own hearts; a fine, thin, slender thread, which cannot bear one stroke of the besom (broom) of divine justice. Such as these are in the palaces of Christ the King, in his churches, hypocrites in Zion'. 'So are the paths of all that forget God; and the hypocrite's hope shall perish: Whose hope shall be cut off, and whose trust shall be a spider's web' (Job 8:13-14).

Chapter 21

Ecclesiastes

All Emptiness Under the Sun All Fulness In The Son

It comes as a great surprise to many that the Word of God was deliberately written in such a way as to confuse unbelieving people. To the believer, to the sinner who has been born of God and granted eyes to see, ears to hear, and a heart to believe, it is a book unsealed, open, and clear. To the unbeliever, it is a book of confusion.

This fact is nowhere more obviously demonstrated than in the comments generally given about the book of Ecclesiastes. The vast majority of that which I have seen written about and heard spoken about this book describes it as a book of pessimism. Most tell us that this book of Solomon's wisdom is little more than the ranting of a disappointed man, frustrated with life. Nothing could be further from the truth.

One thing that makes this book so confusing to many is that it is a book full of errors. It is divinely inspired; but it is full of errors. Let me show you. In chapter three Solomon tells us that there is no difference between men and beasts, and that man dies like a dog and returns to dust (vv. 19-20). In verse 22 he tells us that the best thing a man can do is to rejoice in the works of his own hands. In chapter four he tells us that the dead are better off than the living and that non-existence is better than both (vv. 2-3).

Two Points of View

The reason many have difficulty understanding this book is that they fail to see that Solomon is here giving us the meaning of life from two points of view.

First, he shows us how the man without Christ sees things. What sad words those are. 'Without Christ!' Those who are without Christ are without God and without hope. The natural, unregenerate man lives in constant frustration. He is constantly looking for something to give him satisfaction because there is no meaning to his life. Nothing under the sun can satisfy his immortal soul. When eternity bound creatures have earth bound hearts, they live in constant frustration and misery. Such poor souls constantly feel what Solomon declares from their point of view. 'Vanity of vanities, all is vanity!' When the natural man looks over his life, he is forced to conclude, though he tries with all his might to deny it, 'all was vanity and vexation of spirit, and there was no profit under the sun' (2:11). That is how the book begins. 'The words of the Preacher, the son of David, king in Jerusalem. Vanity of vanities, saith the Preacher, vanity of vanities; all is vanity' (1:1-2).

The wisdom God gave Solomon taught him to never look for satisfaction under the sun, but to look for and find satisfaction in Christ, the Son. The person who is born of God, the person who trusts Christ, the person who is taught of the Spirit, finds meaning to his whole life and to all that is involved in life. His life has meaning because he lives in Christ and Christ lives in him. That is how the book ends. 'Let us hear the conclusion of the whole matter: Fear God, and keep his commandments: for this is the whole duty of man. For God shall bring every work into judgment, with every secret thing, whether it be good, or whether it be evil' (12:13-14). This is the whole duty of man: (1) 'Fear God' or worship God, (2) 'Keep his commandments' or believe on the Lord Jesus Christ (1 John 3:23), and (3) Live for eternity, 'For God shall bring every work into judgment, with every secret thing, whether it be good, or whether it be evil'.

Everything between shows us the emptiness of life without Christ and the vanity of seeking satisfaction in this world. This book is given as a beacon, that we may be spared the bitterness of learning the vanity of the things of earth by finding their waters to fail; that we may seek Christ and find all in him. Throughout these twelve chapters Solomon alternates between these two points of view, showing us the futility of seeking satisfaction in the things of time and sense, and teaching us to look to Christ, finding all fulness in him.

The Natural Man's View

The natural man, the unregenerate man, has a wrong view of everything. He has a wrong view of everything spiritual; but he also has a wrong view of everything in this world. This is what Solomon shows us in Ecclesiastes. In this book God chose, by divine inspiration, to preserve in his Word the carnal reasoning of the natural man 'under the sun'. Let's evaluate this man's thinking in the light of God's Word.

He has a perverted view of the universe (1:4-7; 2:24). He sees the universe as a great piece of machinery, without meaning, just existence. When he looks at himself, he sees another machine. He reasons, 'I'm just like the wind and rain; just a drop in the cycles that are ever moving'.

This perverted view of the universe gives him a perverted view of God (3:1-9, 18-22). Man has a God consciousness, from which he can never escape. But his thoughts of God are perverted. He sees God only as an impersonal force to be reckoned with, not as an almighty, gracious Redeemer to worship, trust, and love. There is a reason why reprobate men look upon God in this way. God has blinded the heart of the natural man in judgment. 'He hath set the world in their heart, so that no man can find out the work that God maketh from the beginning to the end' (3:11).

The natural man has a perverse attitude toward righteousness and wickedness. He does not understand that he is wicked; and he does not understand that righteousness is found only in Christ (Romans 10:1-4). He does not see that righteousness is the gift of God and the work of God. So he presumes that he is to balance the scales of justice by his deeds. 'In the day of prosperity be joyful, but in the day of adversity consider: God also hath set the one over against the other, to the end that man should find nothing after him. All things have I seen in the days of my vanity: there is a just man that perisheth in his righteousness, and there is a wicked man that prolongeth his life in his wickedness. Be not righteous over much; neither make thyself over wise: why shouldest thou destroy thyself? Be not over much wicked, neither be thou foolish: why shouldest thou die before thy time?' (7:14-17).

He reasons, 'If the far-away God balances things, why shouldn't I do the same?' Therefore, he adopts this attitude, 'Don't be too righteous and don't be too wicked'. The quasi-religious middle-of-the-road philosophy of our day says, 'Do the best you can under the circumstances, and God will accept you'. This is the thinking of the natural man. 'No one is perfect. We just have to do the best we can'. (7:20).

The natural man has a terribly perverted view of life and death. 'For all this I considered in my heart even to declare all this, that the righteous, and the wise, and their works, are in the hand of God: no man knoweth either love or hatred by all that is before them. All things come alike to all: there is one event to the righteous, and to the wicked; to the good and to the clean, and to the unclean; to him that sacrificeth, and to him that sacrificeth not: as is the good, so is the sinner; and he that sweareth, as he that feareth an oath. This is an evil among all things that are done under the sun, that there is one event unto all: yea, also the heart of the sons of men is full of evil, and madness is in their heart while they live, and after that they go to the dead. For to him that is joined to all the living there is hope: for a living dog is better than a dead lion. For the living know that they shall die: but the dead know not any thing, neither have they any more a reward; for the memory of them is forgotten. Also their love, and their hatred, and their envy, is now perished; neither have they any more a portion for ever in any thing that is done under the sun. Go thy way, eat thy bread with joy, and drink thy wine with a merry heart; for God now accepteth thy works'. (9:1-7).

The man 'under the sun' thinks that everyone will ultimately share a common fate. He reasons that one final end is in store for all, the righteous and the wicked, the good and the evil, the clean and the unclean, the one who sacrifices and the one who does not. His view of life is that the grave ends all. Many false religions of our day are quick to quote verse 5. But it must be understood that this statement is not divine revelation. It is merely a record given in the book of God of what men think, of the reasoning of natural men 'under the sun'.

The natural man's perverted view of things makes him a slave of the worst kind, a slave to the present, a slave to the world, a slave to his own lusts (9:7-10).

The man 'under the sun' reasons that he must make the best of every day by eating well, enjoying life, and making his heart merry. What a picture of the present age! Wear the finest threads, dress immaculately, use the most expensive perfumes, live it up! Why? Because a common fate awaits us all. But even in the midst of profane hilarity, the natural man is horribly sad, frustrated, and miserable. 'I returned, and saw under the sun, that the race is not to the swift, nor the battle to the strong, neither yet bread to the wise, nor yet riches to men of understanding, nor yet favour to men of skill; but time and chance happeneth to them all. For man also knoweth not his time: as the fishes that are taken in an evil net, and as the birds that are caught in the snare; so are the sons of men snared in an evil time, when it falleth suddenly upon them' (9:11-12) There is no song to brighten his life. No praise is heard from his lips. Just vanity! But there is another view of things!

Christ's Glory

Against this dark, dark background, Solomon sets forth the glory of our great God and Saviour. It is interspersed throughout these chapters. It is Christ alone who gives purpose and meaning to life. We find that purpose and meaning only as we find him. This book is one long exposition of our Saviour's words to the Samaritan woman, 'Whoso drinketh of this water shall thirst again'. The book presents the world in its best aspect, yet says emphatically, 'Satisfaction is not here'.

In chapter 2 we have a striking parallel to Romans 7. Both chapters are full of the personal pronoun 'I', and the result in both is failure and misery. In Ecclesiastes, Solomon says, 'I said in mine heart, Go to now, I will prove thee with mirth ... I said, I sought, I made, I builded, I planted, I got, I gathered, so I was great ... Then I looked, and behold all was vanity and vexation of spirit'.

The pronoun 'I' appears thirty-six times in this chapter, and over thirty times in Romans 7. Romans 7 is the expression of what we are in and of ourselves. In us and with us all is vanity and vexation of spirit. But in Romans 8 we look out of ourselves to Christ. Losing sight of self, we are consumed with Christ and life in him. The result is 'No condemnation ... more than conquerors ... no separation!'

A. M. Hodgkin wrote, 'When self is the centre of our life, and everything is looked at from that standpoint, all is failure. When we find in Christ a new centre and everything revolves round him, then all falls into its right place, and we find rest and satisfaction to our souls. We begin then to ask about everything – not 'How will this affect me?' but 'How will this affect my Lord and Master?' Does it touch his honour? Does it bring glory to him?'

White Robes

As was indicated before, there are dispersed through these twelve chapters many words of spiritual instruction and instructive pictures of gospel truth. 'Let thy garments be always white; and let thy head lack no ointment' (9:8). Obviously, these words, when considered from a believer's perspective, do not refer to outward, carnal things, but to inward, spiritual things (James 1:27).

How can we keep ourselves unspotted in such an evil world? How can we be continually 'unto God a sweet savour of Christ'? 'The blood of Jesus Christ his Son cleanseth us from all sin'. If we walk in the light as he is in the light, trusting Christ alone as 'the Lord our Righteousness', constantly acknowledging and confessing that we are, in and of ourselves, nothing but sin, the blood of Jesus Christ constantly cleanses us from all sin (1 John 1:6-2:2). We are kept clean before God by the merit, power, and efficacy of his sin-atoning sacrifice. Redeemed sinners, once they are born of God, 'have an unction from the Holy One ... and the anointing which ye have received of him abideth in you'(1 John 2:20, 27). This anointing is the Holy Spirit himself who seals us in grace and seals to us all the blessings of the covenant of grace (Ephesians 1:3-14).

The Little City

There is a short parable in chapter 9:13-16 with a delightful message. 'There was a little city, and few men in it'. This is a picture of the earth which the Lord God has given to the children of men; a speck in his great universe, yet he is mindful of man and visited him (Psalm 8:4-6; Hebrews 2:6-10).

'And there came a great king against it, and besieged it, and built great bulwarks against it'. Our Saviour said, 'The prince of this world cometh'. Paul tells us that the god of this world has blinded the minds of those who believe not, lest the light of the glorious Gospel should shine unto them. Thus Satan has laid siege to the city of Mansoul.

'Now there was found in it a poor wise man, and he by his wisdom delivered the city'. We know the grace of our Lord Jesus Christ, who, though he was rich, for our sakes became poor, and was found in fashion as a man, and, humbling himself, became obedient unto death, even the death of the cross. He is that wise Man who, by his Wisdom, delivers the city. The preaching of that cross is unto them that perish foolishness, but unto us who are saved it is the power of God and the wisdom of God.

'Yet no man remembered that same poor man'. It is written, 'My people have forgotten me days without number ... forgotten that they were purged from their old sins'. Again, we read in the book of God, 'Of the ten cleansed there were not found that returned to give glory to God save this stranger'. Oh, redeemed children of men, 'forget not all his benefits!'

Seed Sown

Chapter 11 contains words of encouragement as we seek to serve the interests of our God in this world by the gospel. 'Cast thy bread (seed-corn) upon the waters: for thou shalt find it after many days'. When the Nile River overflows its banks in Egypt, the rice grain is literally cast upon the fields while they are under water to spring up in due season.

In the parable of the sower, our Lord tells us plainly that, 'the seed is the word'. The ground, upon which the seed is sown, be it shallow, or trodden down, or preoccupied, or good – that is, soft and empty, and receptive – is the human heart. It contains nothing good of itself.

By the preaching of the gospel, the gospel seed is sown randomly. We cannot tell what sort of ground it will fall upon, but in this passage in Ecclesiastes God gives the faithful sower the promise of success. 'Thou knowest not whether shall prosper, either this or that, or whether they both shall be alike good;' but prosper it shall (Isaiah 55:11). Therefore, we are to be diligent in sowing, whether it be morning or evening, and whichever way the wind blows (11:6, 4). 'Preach the Word', Paul says to Timothy; 'be instant in season, out of season; reprove, rebuke, exhort, with all long-suffering and doctrine'. 'Therefore, my beloved brethren, be ye stedfast, unmoveable, always abounding in the work of the Lord, forasmuch as ye know that your labour is not in vain in the Lord' (1 Corinthians 15:58).

Remember Now
Let all who hear or read the words of wisdom given in this book heed its doctrine. Trust Christ, worship and serve him in the days of your youth, before your life of vanity utterly hardens your heart. Seek him while he may be found, in the days of your youth, because the old seldom seek him.

'Rejoice, O young man, in thy youth; and let thy heart cheer thee in the days of thy youth, and walk in the ways of thine heart, and in the sight of thine eyes: but know thou, that for all these things God will bring thee into judgment. Therefore remove sorrow from thy heart, and put away evil from thy flesh: for childhood and youth are vanity. Remember now thy Creator in the days of thy youth, while the evil days come not, nor the years draw nigh, when thou shalt say, I have no pleasure in them; While the sun, or the light, or the moon, or the stars, be not darkened, nor the clouds return after the rain: In the day when the keepers of the house shall tremble, and the strong men shall bow themselves, and the grinders cease because they are few, and those that look out of the windows be darkened, And the doors shall be shut in the streets, when the sound of the grinding is low, and he shall rise up at the voice of the bird, and all the daughters of music shall be brought low; Also when they shall be afraid of that which is high, and fears shall be in the way, and the almond tree shall flourish, and the grasshopper shall be a burden, and desire shall fail: because man goeth to his long home, and the mourners go about the streets: Or ever the silver cord be loosed, or the golden bowl be broken, or the pitcher be broken at the fountain, or the wheel broken at the cistern. Then shall the dust return to the earth as it was: and the spirit shall return unto God who gave it' (11:9-12:7).

Our Shepherd

In chapter 12 we see that our only source of wisdom, grace, salvation, fulness and security is in one Shepherd. 'The words of the wise are as goads, and as nails fastened by the masters of assemblies, which are given from one shepherd'. That Shepherd is our Lord Jesus Christ. He says of himself, 'I am the good shepherd, and know my sheep, and am known of mine. As the Father knoweth me, even so know I the Father: and I lay down my life for the sheep. And other sheep I have, which are not of this fold: them also I must bring, and they shall hear my voice; and there shall be one fold, and one shepherd ... My sheep hear my voice, and I know them, and they follow me: And I give unto them eternal life; and they shall never perish, neither shall any man pluck them out of my hand' (John 10:14-16, 27-28).

Conclusion

'Let us hear the conclusion of the whole matter.' Here is the preacher's conclusion: 'Fear God, and keep his commandments: for this is the whole duty of man. For God shall bring every work into judgment, with every secret thing, whether it be good, or whether it be evil'.

What is the whole duty of man? It comprises three parts. First, we must 'Fear God', that is, we must worship God . Second, we must 'Keep his commandments', that is, believe on the Lord Jesus Christ (1 John 3:23). Third, we must 'live for eternity', For God shall bring every work into judgment, with every secret thing, whether it be good, or whether it be evil' (2 Corinthians 4:17-5:11).

None of these 'duties' can be accomplished by men in the state of nature and our failure renders us all guilty before God. Yet, by grace ye are saved. By God's grace dead sinners are made alive in time, and for eternity. Redeemed sinners are brought by the quickening power of the Holy Spirit to newness of life, repentance before God and faith in Christ. This is the obedience of faith, and the eternal blessed state of the redeemed people of God.

Chapter 22

The Song of Solomon

I Am His and He is Mine

In many respects, this is the most precious and most refreshing of the books of inspiration. This is altogether a book about fellowship and communion with Christ. It is not to be interpreted literally. It is an allegory, a spiritual dialogue between Christ, our heavenly Bridegroom, and the church, his Bride.

John Gill wrote, 'The whole Song is figurative and allegorical; expressing, in a variety of lively metaphors, the love, union, and communion between Christ and his church; setting forth the several different frames, cases, and circumstances of believers in this life. There is no case, no circumstance, no spiritual condition which we may be in, regarding our relationship to Christ, which is not expressed in this sacred Song of Love'

C. H. Spurgeon said, 'This book stands like the tree of life in the midst of the garden, and no man shall ever be able to pluck its fruit, and eat thereof, until first he has been brought by Christ past the sword of the cherubim, and led to rejoice in the love which hath delivered him from death. The Song of Solomon is only to be comprehended by men whose standing is within the veil. The outer court worshippers, and even those who only enter the court of the priests, think the book a very strange one; but they who come very near Christ can often see in this Song of Solomon the only expression which their love to their Lord desires'.

The Song of Solomon is set in the scriptures in direct contrast to Ecclesiastes. Ecclesiastes shows us the emptiness of life without Christ. The Song of Solomon shows us the fulness of life in Christ. Ecclesiastes expounds the first part of our Lord's statement to the Samaritan woman. 'Whosoever drinketh of this water shall thirst again'. The Song of Solomon expounds the second part of his statement to her. 'Whosoever drinketh of the water that I shall give him shall never thirst'.

This is a book full of Christ. Here he is presented not only as our God, our Redeemer, our Saviour, and our King, but in the most intimate character and personal relationship imaginable: our Bridegroom, our Beloved! Here we see the Son of God in marriage union with his elect.

This sweet, precious, intimate song of love begins with the church, Christ's chosen, beloved bride speaking to him, expressing her desire for intimacy with him (1:2-4, 7).

'Let him kiss me with the kisses of his mouth: for thy love is better than wine. Because of the savour of thy good ointments thy name is as ointment poured forth, therefore do the virgins love thee. Draw me, we will run after thee: the king hath brought me into his chambers: we will be glad and rejoice in thee, we will remember thy love more than wine: the upright love thee ... Tell me, O thou whom my soul loveth, where thou feedest, where thou makest thy flock to rest at noon: for why should I be as one that turneth aside by the flocks of thy companions?'

Husband and Wife

The highest, strongest affection known to humanity is the love of a husband and wife. Our Saviour spoke of this devotion when he said, 'For this cause shall a man leave father and mother, and shall cleave to his wife, and they two shall be one flesh' (Matthew 19:5). When we understand the teaching of the Holy Spirit in Ephesians 5:22-32 that the union of a husband and wife is an earthly illustration of the heavenly relationship between Christ and his church, the Song of Solomon takes on a new meaning. We see that the love of Christ for his church and the church for him is portrayed through the love of a man for his wife and of the wife for her husband. The Song of Solomon is intimate, even passionate, because it is all about the love life of Christ and his church for each other.

The love of a man for his wife is set before us throughout the scriptures as a type and picture of Christ's love for his church, Adam and Eve, Abraham and Sarah, Jacob and Rachel, Boaz and Ruth, Hosea and Gomer. Paul said to the Corinthian saints, 'I have espoused you to one husband, that I may present you as chaste virgin to Christ'.

The Lord Jesus Christ loves his people, everlastingly, immutably, and unconditionally. All who are born of God, all who know his Son, love him. To know him is to love him. We do not love him like we should. We do not love him as we would. We do not love him as we shall. Nevertheless, we do love him (1 Corinthians 16:22; 1 John 4:19).

Christ loves us perfectly; and we want to love him perfectly. His love for us is without variation; but our love for him is not. Our love for him varies greatly, we blush with shame to acknowledge it; but acknowledge it we must. We have been forgiven much and we love much; but our love sometimes grows cold. The Song of Solomon shows us in pictures how our Beloved keeps us in his love. By experience every true believer becomes familiar with these pictures in their personal relationship with Christ.

Redemption

The Song of Solomon does not mention the word redemption or portray it openly in any way. Yet, redemption is clearly at the very heart of the relationship portrayed in this love song. In the fifth verse of the first chapter, the bride confesses both what she is by nature and what she is in Christ. 'I am black, but comely, O ye daughters of Jerusalem, as the tents of Kedar, as the curtains of Solomon.'

She says, 'I am as black as the goat hair tents of Kedar.' Blackness within and blackness without, in heart and in deed, is our nature. But in Christ every believer is as comely, as beautiful and magnificent, as the curtains of Solomon's temple. This beauty is not natural to us and was not in any way achieved by us. It is the beauty of redemption and grace. Our righteousnesses are but filthy rags; but Christ has clothed us with the robe of his righteousness (Ezekiel 16:6-14).

'O my dove, thou art in the clefts of the rock', the Beloved says to his bride. Hidden in the cleft Rock of Ages, 'crucified with Christ'. Being crucified with Christ, we are dead to the law that would condemn us, and the world that would allure us away from him.

'Behold, thou art fair, my love. Behold, thou art fair' (4:1) is our Saviour's constantly reiterated assurance to us. He tells us again and again, 'Thou art all fair, my love; there is no spot in thee' (4:7). He does not simply say, 'Soon you will be fair and one day there will be no spot in you'. He says, 'Thou art all fair, my love; there is no spot in thee'. 'For Christ also loved the church, and gave himself for it; that he might sanctify and cleanse it with the washing of water by the word; that he might present it to himself a glorious church, not having spot, or wrinkle, or any such thing; but that it should be holy, and without blemish' (Ephesians 5:25, 27).

'And you, that were sometime alienated and enemies in your mind by wicked works, yet now hath he reconciled in the body of his flesh through death, to present you holy and unblameable and unreproveable in his sight' (Colossians 1:21-22). This is talking about what Christ has done. It refers to the present state of God's saints in this world. In Christ we are both justified and sanctified, clothed with his spotless righteousness, in which we are perfectly comely, all fair, and without spot.

'My Beloved'

Throughout this song, Christ is spoken of as 'my Beloved'. His majesty, beauty, excellence, and supremacy are described in a variety of ways. He is 'the Rose of Sharon and the Lily of the Valleys' (2:1-2). The Rose of Sharon is a beautiful, fragrant, white rose. The Lily of the Valleys is a wild flower of the buttercup family, with showy flowers of brightest crimson colour. The white rose of Sharon suggests our Lord's spotless, sinless character. The crimson lily of the valleys suggests his precious blood shed for us.

'As the apple tree among the trees of the wood, so is my Beloved among the sons. I sat down under his shadow with great delight, and his fruit was sweet to my taste' (2:3). The apple tree, as it is set before us in scripture, seems to be an emblem of Christ, the Tree of Life. It (or he) provides us with shade from the heat of the sun (2:3), sweet fruit (2:3), and delightful fragrance (7:8) by His imputed righteousness. In response to the question, 'What is thy beloved more than another beloved?' the bride answers ...

'My beloved is white and ruddy, the chiefest among ten thousand. His head is as the most fine gold, his locks are bushy, and black as a raven. His eyes are as the eyes of doves by the rivers of waters, washed with milk, and fitly set. His cheeks are as a bed of spices, as sweet flowers: his lips like lilies, dropping sweet smelling myrrh. His hands are as gold rings set with the beryl: his belly is as bright ivory overlaid with sapphires. His legs are as pillars of marble, set upon sockets of fine gold: his countenance is as Lebanon, excellent as the cedars. His mouth is most sweet: yea, he is altogether lovely. This is my beloved, and this is my friend, O daughters of Jerusalem' (5:9-16). Compare this with John's vision of Christ in Revelation 1:9-18.

Deepening Love

As we read the Song of Solomon, though there are acknowledged struggles, we see the bride's love deepening with experience. So it is with us. Through our experience of grace, as we grow in the grace and knowledge of Christ, our love for him deepens. The more we enjoy sweet communion with Christ, the more we grow in love and devotion to him. Twice in these chapters, that sweet communion is interrupted for a season. But the interruptions only make us feel our need of him more fully, and graciously compel us to seek him ardently. Those seasons when our Saviour hides his face are either the result of our own declensions or times of trial, by which our Beloved wisely and graciously makes himself the more precious to us.

What we want is for Christ himself to embrace us and make his love for us known to us (1:2-3). We are fully aware that we will never seek him, except he draws us. We will never embrace him, except he embraces us first (1:4). That is how it was in our first experience of grace, when the Son of God first wed our hearts to him; and that is the way it is now. Everything depends upon him (2:4-6).

The place where communion is found is in the assembly of his saints, that place where our Saviour feeds his flocks, and causes them to rest (1:7). As we seek him, in his house, by the guidance of his watchmen, faithful gospel preachers, we find him, find him for ourselves and bring him into our mother's house, the assembly of the saints, with us (3:1-4).

Chapter 5 (vv. 1-8) describes a scene all too familiar. The lessons of that chapter are too important to merely mention. Pause briefly to consider them. The Lord Jesus speaks in verse 1. 'I am come into my garden, my sister, my spouse: I have gathered my myrrh with my spice; I have eaten my honeycomb with my honey; I have drunk my wine with my milk: eat, O friends; drink, yea, drink abundantly, O beloved'. The Bride responds ...

'I sleep, but my heart waketh: it is the voice of my beloved that knocketh, saying, Open to me, my sister, my love, my dove, my undefiled: for my head is filled with dew, and my locks with the drops of the night. I have put off my coat; how shall I put it on? I have washed my feet; how shall I defile them? My beloved put in his hand by the hole of the door, and my bowels were moved for him. I rose up to open to my beloved; and my hands dropped with myrrh, and my fingers with sweet smelling myrrh, upon the handles of the lock. I opened to my beloved; but my beloved had withdrawn himself, and was gone: my soul failed when he spake: I sought him, but I could not find him; I called him, but he gave me no answer. The watchmen that went about the city found me, they smote me, they wounded me; the keepers of the walls took away my veil from me. I charge you, O daughters of Jerusalem, if ye find my beloved, that ye tell him, that I am sick of love'.

There is within each of us a terrible tendency to become neglectful, indifferent, and lukewarm towards the Lord Jesus Christ. This common, sinful tendency of our nature must be marked, acknowledged, and avoided.

> Prone to wander, Lord, I feel it,
> Prone to leave the God I love:
> Here's my heart, Oh, take and seal it,
> Seal it for Thy courts above.

Here is a very common sin. 'I sleep'. The wise virgins often sleep with the foolish. Far too often this is the bad effect great privileges have upon our sinful hearts. When we indulge ourselves in carnal ease and security, our hearts become cold, neglectful, drowsy, and indifferent. Prayer becomes a burden. Devotion languishes. Worship sinks to nothing more than bodily exercise. Zeal dies.

Here is a hopeful sign. 'But my heart waketh'. It is a hopeful sign that there is grace in the heart when the heart struggles against that horrid, sinful sluggishness to which we are so prone. Ours is not the sleep of death. There is life within, struggling, struggling hard against sin (Romans 7:14-22).

Here is a very loving and tender call. 'It is the voice of my Beloved'. All is not lost. Though my heart sleeps so foolishly, yet Christ is my Beloved. Though my love is so fickle, so shameful, and so unworthy of him, I do love him, still. What is more, I still hear his voice and know his voice.

The Lord Jesus Christ tenderly knocks to awaken us to come and open to Him (Revelation 3:20). By his Word, by his providence, and by his Spirit, the Son of God knocks at the heart's door of his beloved, because he will not be spurned by the object of his love. He will not leave his own; neither will he let his own leave him. He has betrothed us unto himself forever (Hosea 2:19).

He not only knocks for entrance. Our beloved Redeemer graciously calls us, wooing us to himself by his grace. Whose voice is it? 'It is the voice of my Beloved that knocketh'. Who is he calling? 'My Sister!' 'My Love!' 'My Dove!' 'My Undefiled!' What does he call for? 'Open to me'. Why is he calling? 'My head is filled with dew, and my locks with the drops of the night', the night of his agony in Gethsemane, in the judgment hall, when he was crowned with thorns, piercing his brow.

Here is a most ungrateful excuse. 'I have put off my coat; how shall I put it on? I have washed my feet; how shall I defile them?' (v. 3). Because of her carnal ease, she refused the Lord's gracious invitation to communion. She did not want to trouble herself, and she did not want to be troubled, not even by him! Her heart was so cold that she preferred her ease to the fellowship of Christ. Let us be honest. We are often so wrapped up in worldly care and carnal ease that we become almost, if not altogether, indifferent to our Lord Jesus Christ!

But our Lord is gracious still. Our Redeemer's love cannot be quenched. He is longsuffering, patient, and gracious to his people, even in our most sinful rejection and denial of him. Here is a picture of our Saviour's persevering, effectual grace. 'My beloved put in his hand by the hole of the door, and my bowels were moved for him' (v. 4). It is written, 'Thy people shall be willing in the day of thy power, in the beauties of holiness from the womb of the morning: thou hast the dew of thy youth' (Psalm 110:3). How our hearts rejoice to know that Christ will not leave his people to themselves. As the hymn writer put it, 'He will never, never leave us, nor will let us quite leave Him!' His grace is effectual. His grace is persevering. His grace is irresistible. His grace is preserving. Yes, his grace is indestructible! He knocks; but we are so cold, so indifferent, so hard that we would never open to Him.

Here is a sad picture of the loving chastisement our neglect and indifference brings upon us. 'I rose up to open to my beloved; and my hands dropped with myrrh, and my fingers with sweet smelling myrrh, upon the handles of the lock. I opened to my beloved; but my beloved had withdrawn himself, and was gone: my soul failed when he spake: I sought him, but I could not find him; I called him, but he gave me no answer. The watchmen that went about the city found me, they smote me, they wounded me; the keepers of the walls took away my veil from me' (vv. 5-7; Isaiah 54:9-10). Thank God for faithful watchmen who will not allow us to hide behind any veil, excusing our indifference and sin, but faithfully expose us to ourselves and point us to Christ for mercy and grace!

Here is one last hope. 'I charge you, O daughters of Jerusalem, if ye find my beloved, that ye tell him, that I am sick of love' (v. 8). She could not find Christ for herself, so she employed the help and assistance of the Lord's people. Cherish the precious fellowship of Christ. Let nothing rob you of your rich privilege. Do nothing to drive him away (Ephesians 4:30). But when you have grieved the Spirit of God, when the Lord Jesus hides his face from you, do not despair. It is not because he has ceased to cherish you (1 John 2:1-2), but because he cherishes you so much that he is determined to make you pine for him. Are you sick of love? Does your soul long for fresh tokens of Christ's love to you? When your soul languishes, child of God, when sin robs you of Christ's manifest presence and sweet communion, as soon as he calls, open to him. 'Today, if ye will hear his voice harden not your heart'. Go back to the cross. Confess your sinful negligence. Go on seeking him. Trust him still (2 Samuel 23:5; Lamentations 3:18-33). We will find our Beloved right where we left him, in his garden, his church, gathering his lilies (6:2).

> Return, O Son of God return!
> Come knock again upon my door.
> Dear Saviour, my Beloved, return.
> Possess me and depart no more!

Assurance

Though we are fickle, weak and wavering, our marriage to Christ is firm. 'He hateth putting away.' Our communion is sometimes broken; but our union is indestructible. Why? The union is all his doing, not ours. It depends altogether upon him, not at all upon us. We can, therefore, say with confidence, 'I am his and he is mine'.

'My Beloved is mine, and I am his' (2:16). Here the Bride speaks of her possession in Christ and his possession of her. He is mine because he has given himself for me and to me. I am his because I have been bought with his blood and called by his grace, and because I have given myself to him. 'I am my Beloved's, and my Beloved is mine' (6:3). Here the thought of his ownership of her seems to hold the chief place.

'Ye are not your own. Ye are bought with a price'. 'I am my Beloved's, and his desire is toward me' (7:10). Here his ownership of and devotion to her swallows up every other thought. I am his, but more, 'His desire is toward me!'

The apostle Paul tells us in Ephesians 1 that Christ is the inheritance of his church; and we are the inheritance of Christ. 'In (Christ) we have obtained an inheritance' (v. 11); and we are 'the riches of the glory of his inheritance in the saints' (v. 18).

His Garden

'A garden enclosed is my sister, my spouse; a spring shut up, a fountain sealed' (4:12). Here our Lord gives us an idea of his inheritance in the saints. It is a quiet spot where he delights to dwell, enclosed for his use, full of all manner of precious fruits and flowers.

Our prayer must ever be that God the Holy Spirit, the Wind of heaven, will blow upon his garden and that the Lord Jesus will come into his garden, as we gather to worship him. 'Awake, O north wind; and come, thou south; blow upon my garden, that the spices thereof may flow out. Let my beloved come into his garden, and eat his pleasant fruits' (4:16). 'I am come into my garden, my sister, my spouse: I have gathered my myrrh with my spice; I have eaten my honeycomb with my honey; I have drunk my wine with my milk: eat, O friends; drink, yea, drink abundantly, O beloved' (5:1).

The church is his garden, but he shares the fruits of his garden with his chosen friends. 'Eat, O friends; drink, yea, drink abundantly, O beloved'. Christ promised both to bless Abraham's seed and to make his seed a blessing.

The sealed fountain in the midst of the garden is first for the Master's use, for he says, 'Give me to drink;' but it flows out to others. 'A fountain of gardens, a well of living waters, and streams from Lebanon' (4:15). 'Whoso drinketh of the water that I shall give him shall never thirst'. The soul's thirst quenched at the Fountain. 'The water that I shall give him shall be in him a well of water springing up unto everlasting life'. Here is an unfailing supply in the soul of every believer. But there is more. 'He that believeth on me, out of him shall flow rivers of living water', 'streams from Lebanon', flowing through the believer to thirsty souls.

Make Haste, My Beloved
As the Song of Songs, this blessed song of love, closes we have several instructive words. Here is a picture of the believer's life of faith in this world. 'Who is this that cometh up from the wilderness, leaning upon her beloved? I raised thee up under the apple tree: there thy mother brought thee forth: there she brought thee forth that bare thee' (v. 5). Here is a description of Christ's love for us. 'Set me as a seal upon thine heart, as a seal upon thine arm: for love is strong as death; jealousy is cruel as the grave: the coals thereof are coals of fire, which hath a most vehement flame. Many waters cannot quench love, neither can the floods drown it: if a man would give all the substance of his house for love, it would utterly be contemned' (vv. 6-7). Here is our Saviour calling for us to constantly call upon him. 'Thou that dwellest in the gardens, the companions hearken to thy voice: cause me to hear it' (v. 13; Hebrews 4:16). Here is the longing of our souls. 'Make haste, my beloved, and be thou like to a roe or to a young hart upon the mountains of spices' (v. 14; Revelation 22:20).

Chapter 23

Isaiah

'He shall not fail'

I am endeavouring to give a survey of the scriptures. But I want to give you more than a factual survey of the Bible. There are several good surveys of that kind available.[1] I want to show you the message of the book. Specifically, I want to clearly demonstrate the fact that the message of each book in the book of God is Christ and him crucified. I want you to see that Christ himself is 'all the counsel of God'.

We now begin looking at the prophetic books. We will, of course, begin with Isaiah's prophecy. As with other books of holy scripture, the prophetic books of the Old Testament are not arranged in chronological order. Sixteen 'holy men of God', says Peter, were chosen to write 'as they were moved by the Holy Spirit' (2 Peter 1:21). Their writings come at intervals covering a period of nearly 500 years.

Isaiah's name means 'salvation of the Lord' or 'the Lord will save'. His prophecy is prominently placed at the beginning of the prophetic books. He is often called the prophet of redemption. Isaiah's message might be summarized by the word of the Lord given in the fourth verse of chapter forty-two. After calling upon us to behold his 'Servant', the Lord God declares by the prophet, 'He shall not fail'. The Lord Jesus Christ, the Son of God, as Jehovah's righteous Servant, shall not fail to fully and perfectly accomplish the work he came to do. He shall not fail to completely save all his people (Matthew 1:21).

---

[1] It is important to understand the factual material, date, authorship and structure of each book in holy scripture. There are numerous sources from which these things can be obtained. *The Guide* by Roger Ellsworth is a fine volume serving this purpose.

The prophecies of Isaiah were delivered during the reigns of four kings of Judah: Uzziah, Jotham, Ahaz, and Hezekiah (Isaiah 1:1). He spoke primarily to Judah prior to their exile. In the opening verse he stated that he was about to relate a vision he saw concerning Judah and Jerusalem; that is to say, concerning the church and kingdom of God, represented by Judah and Jerusalem.

A Prophet

A prophet is one who receives a message from God and delivers it. The prophecy is God's revelation of his purpose to his people. As we read the prophetic books, we must understand them in three ways:

– The prophet's message was God's message to his people in their day (1:2,3).

– The prophets of the Old Testament declared, infallibly, things God would do in time to come (46:9,10).

– The prophet's message is intended for God's people in this day (in every age and place) (62:10-12).

Isaiah's Vision

Let's begin this survey of Isaiah in chapter 6.

'In the year that king Uzziah died I saw also the Lord sitting upon a throne, high and lifted up, and his train filled the temple. Above it stood the seraphims: each one had six wings; with twain he covered his face, and with twain he covered his feet, and with twain he did fly. And one cried unto another, and said, Holy, holy, holy, is the LORD of hosts: the whole earth is full of his glory. And the posts of the door moved at the voice of him that cried, and the house was filled with smoke. Then said I, Woe is me! for I am undone; because I am a man of unclean lips, and I dwell in the midst of a people of unclean lips: for mine eyes have seen the King, the LORD of hosts. Then flew one of the seraphims unto me, having a live coal in his hand, which he had taken with the tongs from off the altar: And he laid it upon my mouth, and said, Lo, this hath touched thy lips; and thine iniquity is taken away, and thy sin purged. Also I heard the voice of the Lord, saying, Whom shall I send, and who will go for us? Then said I, Here am I; send me' (vv. 1-8).

With those words the prophet of God explains his own experience of grace and ours. When Christ is revealed in a sinner's heart by the power of the Holy Spirit, the very first thing experienced is a deep sense and heartfelt confession of his own depravity, sin, and helplessness. Then the sin-atoning blood of Christ is effectually applied to the heart by the power and grace of the Spirit through the preaching of the gospel, assuring the trembling, believing soul that his iniquity is purged and his sin is taken away by the blood of Christ.

Throughout this prophecy, Isaiah speaks as a man who has seen Christ in all the fulness of his redemptive, saving glory and grace. These sixty-six chapters are full of Christ. I cannot, in this brief study, show you every picture of Christ in the book of Isaiah; but I do want to show you sufficient such that every time you read these pages in the future, you see Christ leaping through every line

The Preface

The first four chapters are introductory. They might be looked upon as the preface to the book.

Chapter 1 shows us our need of a redeemer to make us holy and acceptable to God. Isaiah begins his prophecy with a declaration of our utter depravity and corruption and the total impossibility of self salvation (vv. 2-17). In the ninth verse, he declares that there is an elect remnant who must and shall be saved. In verse eighteen sinners are called to the obedience of faith in Christ. Then we are assured of the certainty and efficacy of Christ's redeeming, saving work in verses 25-27. 'Zion shall be redeemed with judgment, and her converts with righteousness'.

In chapter 2 Isaiah tells us that the church and kingdom of God shall be established according to God's decree and that the word of grace would go out of Zion into all the world, calling God's elect out of every nation.

Chapter 3 gives us this blessed word of promise and assurance, 'Say ye to the righteous, that it shall be well with him: for they shall eat the fruit of their doings' (v. 10).

Chapter 4 declares that the result of all this shall be the exaltation and glory of our Lord Jesus Christ and the everlasting perfection and righteousness of God's elect.

'In that day shall the branch of the LORD be beautiful and glorious, and the fruit of the earth shall be excellent and comely for them that are escaped of Israel. And it shall come to pass, that he that is left in Zion, and he that remaineth in Jerusalem, shall be called holy, even every one that is written among the living in Jerusalem: When the Lord shall have washed away the filth of the daughters of Zion, and shall have purged the blood of Jerusalem from the midst thereof by the spirit of judgment, and by the spirit of burning'. (vv. 2-4)

Now, let us look at some of the delightful, instructive pictures and descriptions God the Holy Spirit gives us by the pen of his servant Isaiah.

Pictures of Christ

The prophet calls our dear Saviour, the Beloved, the Wellbeloved. 'Now will I sing to my wellbeloved a song of my beloved touching his vineyard. My wellbeloved hath a vineyard in a very fruitful hill' (5:1). What a suitable title for the Son of God. He is indeed our Wellbeloved! Our beloved Saviour is the Lord, sitting upon his throne, high and lifted up (6:1; John 12:37-41).

In the seventh chapter the prophet of God describes our Saviour as the virgin-born, incarnate God. 'Therefore the Lord himself shall give you a sign; Behold, a virgin shall conceive, and bear a son, and shall call his name Immanuel' (7:14). The incarnate Saviour is described more fully in chapter nine. 'For unto us a child is born, unto us a son is given: and the government shall be upon his shoulder: and his name shall be called Wonderful, Counsellor, The mighty God, The everlasting Father, The Prince of Peace. Of the increase of his government and peace there shall be no end, upon the throne of David, and upon his kingdom, to order it, and to establish it with judgment and with justice from henceforth even for ever. The zeal of the LORD of hosts will perform this' (9:6-7).

He who is the sanctuary of salvation to all who believe was long ago declared to be a Stone of Stumbling and a Rock of Offence to the self-righteous and unbelieving. 'And he shall be for a sanctuary; but for a stone of stumbling and for a rock of offence to both the houses of Israel, for a sign and for a snare to the inhabitants of Jerusalem. And many among them shall stumble, and fall, and be broken, and be snared, and be taken' (8:14-15).

Isaiah declared Christ to be the Light of the world. He is the Light that shines in darkness, the Light of life, the One who is the Light of the glory of God. The only light there is in this dark, dark world is our Lord Jesus Christ. 'The people that walked in darkness have seen a great light: they that dwell in the land of the shadow of death, upon them hath the light shined' (9:2). 'And he said, It is a light thing that thou shouldest be my servant to raise up the tribes of Jacob, and to restore the preserved of Israel: I will also give thee for a light to the Gentiles, that thou mayest be my salvation unto the end of the earth' (49:6).

In chapter eleven our Lord is portrayed as the Root and Branch of David, the ensign to whom chosen sinners must be gathered, and that one by whom we have both the Spirit of God and the glorious rest of faith and salvation. 'And there shall come forth a rod out of the stem of Jesse, and a Branch shall grow out of his roots. And the spirit of the LORD shall rest upon him, the spirit of wisdom and understanding, the spirit of counsel and might, the spirit of knowledge and of the fear of the LORD ... And in that day there shall be a root of Jesse, which shall stand for an ensign of the people; to it shall the Gentiles seek: and his rest shall be glorious ... And he shall set up an ensign for the nations, and shall assemble the outcasts of Israel, and gather together the dispersed of Judah from the four corners of the earth' (11:1-2, 10, 12).

Then we read that the Lord Jesus Christ is both our God and our Salvation, the Holy One of Israel in the midst of us. 'Behold, God is my salvation; I will trust, and not be afraid: for the LORD JEHOVAH is my strength and my song; he also is become my salvation ... Cry out and shout, thou inhabitant of Zion: for great is the Holy One of Israel in the midst of thee' (12:2, 6).

As said before, we cannot here go through all the pictures of Christ given by Isaiah. In chapters 13 – 21 our Redeemer is set before us as the Breaker of Babylon, the Lord of Lucifer, the Master of Moab, the Destroyer of Damascus, the Executioner of Egypt, and, the Watchman's Judge.

Let us move on to chapter 22. Still we can only pick up the highlights as we move along. Here the prophet of God describes Christ as the sovereign King of the universe. His rule and dominion, to those who know him, is as a nail in a sure place. Because he has earned and fully deserves it, he has all the glory of his Father's house. 'And the key of the house of David will I lay upon his shoulder; so he shall open, and none shall shut; and he shall shut, and none shall open. And I will fasten him as a nail in a sure place; and he shall be for a glorious throne to his father's house. And they shall hang upon him all the glory of his father's house, the offspring and the issue, all vessels of small quantity, from the vessels of cups, even to all the vessels of flagons' (22:22-24).

The Lord Jesus is the Crown of Glory and the everlasting Beauty of his people. 'In that day shall the LORD of hosts be for a crown of glory, and for a diadem of beauty, unto the residue of his people' (28:5). Again in chapter 28, the prophet declares that our Saviour is the Foundation Stone laid in Zion (28:14-18). He is a tried Foundation, a precious Foundation, and a sure Foundation. He that believes on the Son of God, he that is built upon this Foundation shall not make haste, be in confusion, be confounded, or be put to shame.

The Lord Jesus Christ is the only safe Refuge and sure Hiding Place for our souls. 'Behold, a king shall reign in righteousness, and princes shall rule in judgment. And a man shall be as an hiding place from the wind, and a covert from the tempest; as rivers of water in a dry place, as the shadow of a great rock in a weary land' (32:1-2).

Christ is the Giver of all grace. He is that one in whom chosen, redeemed sinners are made to see and experience the glory and excellence of our God (35:4-7). He is the way, the only way to God. 'And an highway shall be there, and a way, and it shall be called The way of holiness; the unclean shall not pass over it; but it shall be for those: the wayfaring men, though fools, shall not err therein. No lion shall be there, nor any ravenous beast shall go up thereon, it shall not be found there; but the redeemed shall walk there: And the ransomed of the LORD shall return, and come to Zion with songs and everlasting joy upon their heads: they shall obtain joy and gladness, and sorrow and sighing shall flee away' (35:8-10). Christ is the high way, the holy way, the safe way, the way of the redeemed, the joyful way, and the only way (John 14:6).

Christ is the Good Shepherd who rules and disposes of the world for the salvation of his sheep. 'He shall feed his flock like a shepherd: he shall gather the lambs with his arm, and carry them in his bosom, and shall gently lead those that are with young' (40:11).

The Son of God is our great Redeemer. He says, 'Fear not, thou worm Jacob, and ye men of Israel; I will help thee, saith the LORD, and thy redeemer, the Holy One of Israel' (41:14). Our Redeemer is Jehovah's Servant, chosen to be our Saviour, a Servant who 'shall not fail!' 'Behold my servant, whom I uphold; mine elect, in whom my soul delighteth; I have put my spirit upon him: he shall bring forth judgment to the Gentiles. He shall not cry, nor lift up, nor cause his voice to be heard in the street. A bruised reed shall he not break, and the smoking flax shall he not quench: he shall bring forth judgment unto truth. He shall not fail nor be discouraged, till he have set judgment in the earth: and the isles shall wait for his law' (42:1-4).

He is that Servant of whom the law of the bond slave (Exodus 21:1-6) was typical and by whom it was fulfilled (Isaiah 50:5-7). He who is Jehovah's unfailing, successful Servant, our Redeemer, is also our ever-present Lord Protector (43:1-5).

Jesus Christ is the just God, our Saviour, to whom alone we must look for salvation. 'Tell ye, and bring them near; yea, let them take counsel together: who hath declared this from ancient time? who hath told it from that time? have not I the LORD? and there is no God else beside me; a just God and a Saviour; there is none beside me. Look unto me, and be ye saved, all the ends of the earth: for I am God, and there is none else' (45:21-22).

The Son of God is our great sin-atoning Substitute, by whose stripes we are healed (53:4-11).

Our Lord Jesus Christ is that one who makes all things new. 'For, behold, I create new heavens and a new earth: and the former shall not be remembered, nor come into mind. But be ye glad and rejoice for ever in that which I create: for, behold, I create Jerusalem a rejoicing, and her people a joy. And I will rejoice in Jerusalem, and joy in my people: and the voice of weeping shall be no more heard in her, nor the voice of crying' (65:17-19).

He began making all things new when he accomplished redemption and poured out his Spirit upon all flesh (Isaiah 44:3-4). He is presently making all things new for poor sinners by his grace (2 Corinthians 5:17). Soon, he shall come again to complete his new creation (Isaiah 65:17-19; 2 Peter 3:9-14; Revelation 21:1-7).

Chapter 24

Jeremiah

'Israel hath not been forsaken of his God'.

Suppose some preacher today stood in his pulpit week after week and asserted relentlessly that God had set his face against the United States of America, that he was raising up an army in a foreign land, under the command of a barbaric dictator, to conquer this great nation and make us servants to a massive empire. Suppose the preacher asserted boldly that our Constitution and our nation were an abomination to God, that everything we value and uphold as a society is offensive to him.

Then, suppose that preacher were to go from place to place and publicly urge all Americans not to resist the will of the enemy, but to renounce the homeland and willingly move into that foreign land and bow as servants to that cruel tyrant! It would not be surprising to see that preacher publicly humiliated, ridiculed, labelled a crack-pot, even imprisoned. But he will not stop. In prison, shut up in solitary confinement, he not only refuses to retract a word, but manages to find a way to write his message in a book and have it read in every church in the land.

If you can imagine such a thing, you will have a pretty good idea what the book of Jeremiah is about. Only, Jeremiah was no crack-pot preacher. He was the prophet of God in the land of Israel in his day, the voice of God to the nation. He was, in my opinion, the boldest, most courageous, most

valiant man for truth in history. No preacher ever faced more opposition
or discouragement, with less to give him encouragement, than God's
prophet Jeremiah.

Jeremiah

Jeremiah began preaching as a very young man during the days of
King Josiah. He was God's spokesman. He was God's prophet to the
nation through the reign of four more kings until the Jews were carried
away into Babylon by the will of God. He faithfully served the Lord our
God and his own generation by the will of God for more than forty years;
and he did so in the face of relentless and almost universal opposition.

He wept much. His heart was in constant, great heaviness because of
the iniquity and rebellion of his people, and because of the impending
judgment of God upon the nation he loved. Yet, he never flinched from his
duty. He never failed to declare the Word that God put into his mouth.
Imprisoned repeatedly, put into stocks (20:2), lowered by ropes into a
miry dungeon (38:6), mocked and derided (20:7), a man of strife and
contention to the whole world (25:10), accused of treachery to his country
(38:4), opposed by false prophets (23, 28), confronted by angry mobs of
religious people (prophets and priests included) who wanted to kill him
(26), carried against his will into Egypt (43:7), under all these circumstances
Jeremiah was relentless in obedience, seeking the glory of God, delivering
the Word of God, serving the people of God from the day of his calling
until the day of his death.

He faithfully exposed Israel's sins, called them to repentance, and
warned them of judgment, asserting that the wrath coming upon them
was fully deserved. Yet, he never ceased declaring the goodness and
mercy of God. Even as he denounced Israel's wickedness and prophesied
of the nation's utter destruction, he declared the immutable faithfulness
of God to his people. He even declared that the very judgment of God
upon the nation was for the specific purpose of saving his own elect
within the nation (51:4-5; 50:33-34).

The Times

We cannot appreciate the labour or faithfulness of any man unless we
understand the times in which that man lived and served the Lord. Never
was apostasy pursued more eagerly and fully by men and women who
professed to worship the Lord our God than in Jeremiah's day.

Manasseh, Josiah's wicked grandfather, led the nation into such vile
idolatry that they never really recovered from it. Josiah's reforms were

little more than a band-aid covering a deep cancer. They only touched the surface and were but for a brief time. After Josiah's death, the nation sank back into the worst forms of idolatry and into every kind of iniquity. The whole nation was on the downward spiral of apostasy. Jeremiah's mission was to call the people back to God, but judgment was at hand.

God raised up Nebuchadnezzar to execute his wrath upon Judah. He gave him universal dominion. He even called him, 'My servant' (25:9; 27:6; 43:10). Nebuchadnezzar was the unwitting servant of the sovereign Lord God in all that he did. It was because God revealed this to Jeremiah that we find him advocating submission to Nebuchadnezzar, and it was for this that his people accused him of treachery. After the destruction of Jerusalem, Jeremiah was given his choice, whether he would go to Babylon or remain with the remnant that were left in the land. He chose the latter. Days of darkness followed. Jeremiah exhorted his people to obey the voice of the Lord and remain in the land, and not flee into Egypt. But they refused to obey, and they carried Jeremiah with them into Egypt, where, tradition says, he was stoned to death.

Jeremiah's Message

That is the story of this book; but what is its message? What does God the Holy Spirit intend for you and me to learn from this book as we read it? How does this ancient word of prophecy apply to us? We cannot in one brief summary, set forth everything that Jeremiah prophesied in forty years. But there are some things that are crystal clear.

Christ

Jeremiah's message was not gloom and doom, as most seem to think. His message was mercy and grace, salvation by God's free grace, through the sacrifice of his dear Son the Lord Jesus Christ.

Jeremiah himself was a type of Christ. This fact is so obvious that some mistook Christ, the Man of Sorrows, for Jeremiah the weeping, broken-hearted prophet (Matthew 16:14). He wept over his people as Christ wept over them (9:1). His faithfulness brought him reproach, rejection, sorrow, and suffering as it did our Lord. He compares himself to a lamb or an ox brought to the slaughter (11:19).

Throughout this book we see glimpses of our Saviour, the Lord Jesus Christ: as the Fountain of Living Waters (2:13), as the Great Physician (8:22), as the Good Shepherd (31:10, 23:4), as the Righteous Branch (23:5), as David the King (30:9), as our Redeemer (50:34), and as the Lord our Righteousness (23:6).

At the very time that David's throne appeared to be on the brink of destruction, and justice and equity were gone, the prophet announced the coming of a King of the House of David, a righteous Branch, who would reign and prosper, and execute judgment and justice in the earth. 'In his days Judah shall be saved, and Israel shall dwell safely; and this is his name whereby he shall be called, THE LORD OUR RIGHTEOUSNESS'. In this majestic name, *Jehovah-tsidkenu*, the Godhead of our Saviour is declared, and, as a descendant of David, his humanity is confirmed.

In chapter 31 the prophet of God even speaks of the incarnation of Christ for the everlasting blessedness of his people (31:20-26). With the coming of our incarnate God, the Lord declares that he will establish and fulfil a new covenant, a covenant of pure, free grace (31:31-34).

This new covenant is called 'new' because it is newly revealed and because it is ever new. But the covenant is the everlasting covenant of grace made with Christ as our Surety, ordered in all things and sure from eternity (2 Samuel 23:1-5; Hebrews 8:10). In this covenant the absolute forgiveness, everlasting righteousness, and complete salvation of God's elect (the Israel of God) was secured from eternity (Romans 8:28-30; Ephesians 1:3-6; 2 Timothy 1:9-10). This covenant was made for us because of God's everlasting love for his people (Jeremiah 31:3). In this covenant the absolute security and perseverance of God's elect in grace is secured (Jeremiah 32:37-41).

Still, all the blessings of grace promised in the covenant could never come to fruition except the Lord Jesus Christ perform his great work of redemption for us as our divinely appointed Kinsman-Redeemer. In chapter 32 Jeremiah typified Christ as our Kinsman Redeemer, exercising the right of redemption to buy back the field his uncle had lost; thereby displaying his confidence that that which God had promised his people would not and could not be lost, though the nation itself would be destroyed and carried away to Babylon.

A Prophet

Christ is the message of Jeremiah. The prophet of God is declaring the absolute certainty of grace and salvation to a chosen nation, the royal priesthood, the church of God's elect, through the Lord our Righteousness.

In chapter 1 we see how a man becomes a prophet and what a prophet is (vv. 5-9, 17-19). No man can be a spokesman for God who has not been set apart by God himself for the work. The Lord God puts his words in the mouth of his servant, sends him forth with his message, emboldened by the fact that the God who sends him will take care of him.

Judgment

Chapters 2-25 show us the cause of divine judgment. Judgment is never an arbitrary thing. It is always the just response of God to man's rebellion and sin. Blame goes first to the people who rebelled against the Lord. However, they were led in rebellion by their kings. Ultimately, people and kings were taught to rebel by their pastors, prophets, and priests.

Living In Babylon

Here is how we are to live in this world, in this generation under the wrath of God. 'Thus saith the LORD of hosts, the God of Israel, unto all that are carried away captives, whom I have caused to be carried away from Jerusalem unto Babylon; Build ye houses, and dwell in them; and plant gardens, and eat the fruit of them; Take ye wives, and beget sons and daughters; and take wives for your sons, and give your daughters to husbands, that they may bear sons and daughters; that ye may be increased there, and not diminished. And seek the peace of the city whither I have caused you to be carried away captives, and pray unto the LORD for it: for in the peace thereof shall ye have peace' (29:4-7).

Here is the hope God sets before his elect remnant. 'For thus saith the LORD, That after seventy years be accomplished at Babylon I will visit you, and perform my good word toward you, in causing you to return to this place. For I know the thoughts that I think toward you, saith the LORD, thoughts of peace, and not of evil, to give you an expected end. Then shall ye call upon me, and ye shall go and pray unto me, and I will hearken unto you. And ye shall seek me, and find me, when ye shall search for me with all your heart. And I will be found of you, saith the LORD: and I will turn away your captivity, and I will gather you from all the nations, and from all the places whither I have driven you, saith the LORD; and I will bring you again into the place whence I caused you to be carried away captive' (29:10-14).

Providence

The mystery of God's providence is unfolded in chapters 30-33. God has not forsaken his people. He is saving them (30:16). He is fulfilling his covenant (chapters 31-33). 'Behold, the days come, saith the LORD, that I will perform that good thing which I have promised unto the house of Israel and to the house of Judah. In those days, and at that time, will I cause the Branch of righteousness to grow up unto David; and he shall execute judgment and righteousness in the land. In those days shall Judah be saved, and Jerusalem shall dwell safely: and this is the name wherewith she shall be called, The LORD our righteousness' (33:14-16).

The Nations

Chapters 34-49 describe the Lord's dealing with the nations that despise him, to consume them in his wrath. In chapters 50-52 we see the mystery of Babylon unravelled wondrously. The nations of this world rise and fall exactly according to the purpose of God. Though they may appear terrifying, there is no cause for alarm. They will only serve God's purpose, the salvation of his elect. That which is true of the nations of the world is also true of the religion of the nations. Babylon, the great whore of the earth represents all antichrist religion, all free will, works religion. Babylon shall only harm the nations deceived by her. In time, she too will fall before Zion, the church and kingdom of our God (Revelation 18:3-5; 20-24). It may, at times, appear that God has forsaken his elect, that he has forgotten to be gracious, but that is never the case. 'For Israel hath not been forsaken, nor Judah of his God, of the LORD of hosts; though their land was filled with sin against the Holy One of Israel' (51:5-9).

Gospel Doctrine

There are tremendous points of gospel doctrine clearly presented in the book of Jeremiah. The only thing in which we can and must trust is the Lord our God himself. He alone must be our glory, our confidence, and our hope (9:23-24). 'Blessed is the man that trusteth in the Lord, and whose hope the Lord is' (17:7). Yet, because all men are, by nature, totally depraved, wicked at the very core of their beings (17:9), no one ever can or will know and trust the Lord God except God himself make himself known to them and do a work of grace in them, turning them unto himself in faith by omnipotent grace. Therefore, the prophet teaches us to pray, 'Heal me, O Lord, and I shall be healed; save me, and I shall be saved'. All who find him gracious will glory in him, gladly confessing, 'Thou art my praise' (17:14). Yes, all saved sinners delight to acknowledge that, 'Salvation is of the Lord!' All to whom the Lord God grants repentance readily confess, 'Surely, after that I was turned, I repented, and after that I was instructed, I smote upon my thigh: I was ashamed, yea, even confounded, because I did bear the reproach of my youth' (31:19).

In Jeremiah 50:20 we are given a marvellous declaration of the absolute, full, and everlasting forgiveness of our sin by our God. 'In those days, and in that time, saith the LORD, the iniquity of Israel shall be sought for, and there shall be none; and the sins of Judah, and they shall not be found: for I will pardon them whom I reserve'. Let every believing sinner rejoice! God himself, who charged our sins to his Son and punished him in our room and stead to the full satisfaction of justice, will never charge our sins to us.

Why has God chosen to be gracious to some and not others? Why does God save some and pass by others? The answer can only be found in one place: His own sovereign will and good pleasure. He has mercy on whom he will have mercy. He has compassion on whom he will have compassion. And whom he will he hardens. This is precisely the interpretation God the Holy Spirit gives (Romans 9:15-24) to God's instruction to Jeremiah in the potter's house (18:1-17).

Chapter 25

Lamentations

God's Strange Work Explained

When I was a nineteen-year-old boy, the Lord graciously caused a faithful gospel preacher to cross my path, who became a lifelong friend and a man of tremendous influence in my life. Bro. Harry Graham was already a fairly old man when I met him. He had pastored a small church in Ashboro, North Carolina, for most of his adult life. My wife, Shelby, and I spent many evenings in his home, with his wife, Nola, in sweet fellowship. I was never in Bro. Graham's company and did not learn something that helped me. I learned much from that faithful man! What a blessing he was, and continued to be, in my life.

One night, as I sat at his feet, Harry made this statement, 'When God deals with a sinner in mercy, he takes him to hell first'.

That is a good summary of the book of Lamentations. In this little book of masterful poetry, the Lord God explains to us, in a vivid picture, why he sends judgment upon men, specifically why he afflicts his own elect. It is because of his everlasting, unfailing compassion upon them and the multitude of his mercies toward them (Lamentations 3:31-33).

Overview

This short book of five chapters is poetry of the highest order. It is written almost entirely in an acrostic, like Psalm 119. Chapters 1, 2, and 4 each contain 22 verses. Each verse begins with a letter of the Hebrew alphabet, going through the entire alphabet. Chapter 3 contains 66 verses. In that chapter, every third verse begins with a letter from the Hebrew alphabet, going through the entire alphabet.

As the title of the book 'Lamentations' indicates, this is a book full of grief and sorrow. The grief and sorrow is caused by God's judgment upon Judah and Jerusalem. The judgment Jeremiah had faithfully warned the nation to expect had now come to pass. The Babylonians had invaded the land, destroyed Jerusalem, and carried Israel away into captivity.

There was only a small remnant left in the city of Jerusalem. Jeremiah was among that remnant. The book opens with the prophet weeping as he beholds the ruins of the city. He laments for the city and people he dearly loved and for whom he had laboured faithfully all his life. The book begins with a burst of anguish and sorrow (1:1-3).

'How doth the city sit solitary, that was full of people! how is she become as a widow! she that was great among the nations, and princess among the provinces, how is she become tributary! She weepeth sore in the night, and her tears are on her cheeks: among all her lovers she hath none to comfort her: all her friends have dealt treacherously with her, they are become her enemies. Judah is gone into captivity because of affliction, and because of great servitude: she dwelleth among the heathen, she findeth no rest: all her persecutors overtook her between the straits.'

Jeremiah seems to have been on one of the hills overlooking the city. There he sat down and wept, and lamented over Jerusalem, mourning the fall of his country and the city. The desolation of the city by the Babylonian army is described by Jeremiah in his book of Lamentations with all the vividness of an eye-witness.

Christ

Six hundred years later we see that Prophet of whom all the prophets spoke, the Lord Jesus Christ our Saviour, upon the slopes of the Mount of Olives. The sight of that proud, rebellious city, doomed by their own obstinate rebellion brought such a mighty rush of compassion to the soul of our Saviour that he wept aloud. The Man of Sorrows cried, 'O Jerusalem, Jerusalem, thou that killest the prophets, and stonest them which are sent unto thee, how often would I have gathered thy children together, even as a hen gathereth her chickens under her wings, and ye would not! Behold, your house is left unto you desolate' (Matthew 23:37-38).

It is obvious, then, at the outset, that the weeping prophet was a type of our weeping Saviour. There are pictures of Christ scattered throughout these five chapters. Both Jeremiah in his sorrow and Jerusalem under the wrath of God portray our Redeemer.

'Is it nothing to you, all ye that pass by? behold, and see if there be any sorrow like unto my sorrow, which is done unto me, wherewith the LORD hath afflicted me in the day of his fierce anger' (1:12). These words cannot be applied in their fullest meaning to anyone except our great Saviour when he hung upon the cursed tree, suffering all the horror of God's offended justice because of our sins imputed to him.

'All that pass by clap their hands at thee; they hiss and wag their head at the daughter of Jerusalem, saying, Is this the city that men call The perfection of beauty, The joy of the whole earth? All thine enemies have opened their mouth against thee: they hiss and gnash the teeth: they say, We have swallowed her up: certainly this is the day that we looked for; we have found, we have seen it'. (2:15-16). Certainly, this describes the affliction Jerusalem endured. But Jerusalem's sorrows were themselves typical of Immanuel's sorrows (Matthew 27:39).

'Also when I cry and shout, he shutteth out my prayer' (3:8) When we read those words, do they not immediately cause us to think of our Saviour crying, 'Eli, Eli, lama sabachthani? that is to say, My God, my God, why hast thou forsaken me?' (Matthew 27:46), as he endured the wrath of God for us?

'I was a derision to all my people; and their song all the day' (3:14; cf. Psalm 69:12). 'He hath filled me with bitterness, he hath made me drunken with wormwood ... Remembering mine affliction and my misery, the wormwood and the gall' (3:15, 19; cf. Psalm 69:21).

'He giveth his cheek to him that smiteth him: he is filled full with reproach' (3:30; cf. Psalm 69:20). These verses clearly speak of our Saviour. The language reminds us of Isaiah's prophetic words, 'I gave my back to the smiters, and my cheeks to them that plucked off the hair: I hid not my face from shame and spitting' (Isaiah 50:6). This was prophetic of the soldiers beating our Redeemer when he was brought before Pilate for judgment.

This little book of Lamentations captures the agony and sorrow that was so much a part of our Lord's ministry throughout his life, particularly when he was made to be sin for us and suffered all the horror of God's infinite wrath as our Substitute at Calvary. How suitable then that our Redeemer earned the title: 'A man of sorrows, and acquainted with grief' (Isaiah 53:3).

Substitution

If you read these chapters with care, you cannot avoid seeing that Jeremiah assumed the sins of his people as his own sins and spoke of God's judgment as that which had fallen upon him for sin. As it was with Jeremiah in the typical picture, it was with our Saviour, the Lord Jesus, in reality.

Our all-glorious Christ, as our sin-atoning Substitute, was made to be sin for us that we might be made the righteousness of God in him (2 Corinthians 5:21). He was cursed that we might be blessed (Galatians 3:13). He died for us, the Just for the unjust, that we might be made just and live forever.

Divine Judgment

Throughout these five chapters, we are taught that judgment is the work of God, the righteous retribution of God upon men because of wilful rebellion and sin. We are taught that all for whom the Lord God has reserved mercy are made to acknowledge that God's righteous judgments are just that, righteous and just.

In the first part of chapter 1 Jeremiah speaks of Jerusalem as a woman bereft of her husband and children. In the second part Zion speaks, and bewails her misery, identifying himself with the people, their sins, and the judgment they had earned. She acknowledges that her severe punishment is from the Lord, and confesses, 'The Lord is righteous; I have rebelled' (v. 18).

In chapter 2 the prophet gives a remarkable description of Jerusalem's ruin. No less than forty-eight times in these 22 verses, Jeremiah declares that all the things Judah suffered was God's work.

In chapter 3 Jeremiah again ascribes the judgments that befell the city as the work of God. Twenty-two times he asserts that fact. Again, he makes the miseries of the people his own. Out of the midst of the misery he stays himself upon the Lord's faithfulness and his unfailing compassion, and asserts unhesitatingly that, 'He doth not afflict willingly, nor grieve the children of men' (v. 33).

In the fourth chapter God's fearful judgments are again described. 'The Lord hath accomplished his fury' (v. 11)

In the fifth chapter it is not the prophet who speaks, not the substitute, but the people. Here we see what happens when the Lord God brings sinners to repentance. He brings his elect down to hell that he might cause them to cry to him for mercy, confessing their guilt and sin, before the holy, sovereign Lord God (vv. 1, 15-17, 19, 21-22).

The Message

The message of this book is given in chapter 3. Remember, the judgments described here did not fall upon the Philistines, the Ammonites, or the Moabites. The people here severely afflicted and brought into terrible bondage were the children of Israel, God's covenant people. They were brought down that they might be carried up. They were abased that they might be exalted. They were laid low that they might be lifted high. In all things that physical nation, the physical seed of Abraham, was representative and typical of God's elect, the spiritual seed of Abraham, the Israel of God.

Here is our hope. 'This I recall to my mind, therefore have I hope. It is of the LORD's mercies that we are not consumed, because his compassions fail not. They are new every morning: great is thy faithfulness. The LORD is my portion, saith my soul; therefore will I hope in him. The LORD is good unto them that wait for him, to the soul that seeketh him' (vv. 21-25).

Here is God's counsel. 'It is good that a man should both hope and quietly wait for the salvation of the LORD. It is good for a man that he bear the yoke in his youth. He sitteth alone and keepeth silence, because he hath borne it upon him. He putteth his mouth in the dust; if so be there may be hope. He giveth his cheek to him that smiteth him: he is filled full with reproach' (vv. 26-30).

Here is the explanation of God's strange work of judgment. Has the Lord God brought you down to hell? Has he set his holy wrath in your heart? Has he made you to see that you are a child of wrath, deserving eternal damnation in hell? Has he convinced you that if you should right now fall into everlasting torment, that is exactly what you deserve? If so, hear what God's prophet says in Lamentations 3:31-33. This was written in the book of God for you. 'For the Lord will not cast off for ever: But though he cause grief, yet will he have compassion according to the multitude of his mercies. For he doth not afflict willingly nor grieve the children of men.'

Salvation is obtained by simple, childlike faith in the Lord Jesus Christ. But any faith that does not arise from a felt need of Christ and is not accompanied by a genuine conviction of sin, of righteousness, and of judgment is not true faith (John 16:8-11). Where there is no conviction, there is no conversion. Where there is no misery, there is no mercy. Where there is no grief, there is no grace.

All who know the Lord God in the experience of his saving operations of grace freely acknowledge and frankly confess that God is strictly righteous in the exercise of his grace and truly gracious in his righteous judgments (Psalm 32:1-4; 51:1-5). These are the things that Jeremiah learned by deep, painful experience and recorded in this third chapter of Lamentations for our learning and comfort. Before God shows mercy, he causes grief; and both these works of grace; the grief that precedes it and the mercy that follows, are according to God's sovereign, eternal purpose.

Grief

'Though he cause grief.' It may seem strange; but Jeremiah declares that it is the Lord God who causes grief. He acknowledged the fact that the Lord our God is the first cause of all things. He performs all things for his people. He works all things together for good to his elect. The doctrine of God's universal providence is not some secret doctrine, hidden in the obscure pages of one of the Minor Prophets. It is a doctrine taught and illustrated throughout the Bible. It is obvious in the history of every child of grace and the confession of every sinner who is taught of God.

When you read this third chapter of Lamentations, you understand that Jeremiah was a man who had experienced terrible grief in his soul; but, being a man of God-given faith, he understood and acknowledged that the cause of all his grief was the Lord his God – 'Though he cause grief'.

The prophet of God acknowledged God in all his ways and owned him as the origin of all things. Twenty-two times, referring to his woes in verses 1-17, he said, 'God did it'. When he was afflicted, he said it was by the rod of God's wrath (v. 1). When his soul was brought into bondage, he said God had hedged him about and put a chain upon him (v. 7). When he was overwhelmed with grief, he said, he 'hath pulled me in pieces' (vv. 8-19). When he was, by these things brought to utter hopelessness in himself, he found hope in the Lord God (vv. 21-31).

Blessed are those sinners who have been brought down to utter hopelessness in themselves that they might find hope in the Lord God. The basis of hope is the Lord God himself (vv. 21-25), his abundant mercies, his unfailing compassions, his great faithfulness, his infinite fulness (v. 24), his saving goodness. The only thing an utterly helpless, hopeless sinner can do for God's salvation is wait (v. 26). The place where a sinner ought to wait and must wait for God's salvation is in the dust of repentance, before the throne of grace (vv. 27-31). We must bear the yoke of guilt in conviction (v. 27), personally doing business with the Almighty (v. 28). In repentance, we make our headquarters in the dust (v. 29), justifying God in our own condemnation (v. 30), looking to God in Christ for mercy (v. 31), crying like the publican in the parable, 'God, be merciful to me a sinner' (Luke 18:13).

This is what Jeremiah is teaching us. It cannot be explained to people who have not experienced it. But this is the experience of every heaven born soul. There is a felt darkness and confusion in the soul when God convinces a sinner of his personal vileness and hell-worthiness. This is the grief Jeremiah is talking about. It is a spiritual grief caused in the soul by God himself.

We recognize that every event of providence that brings grief is God's work. He brings the cloud over the earth as well as the sunshine. If we never saw a cloud in the sky, we could never see the bow of his covenant (Genesis 9:14). He makes peace and creates evil in the earth (Isaiah 45:7).

The eye of faith also sees that spiritual grief and sorrow are the works of God's hands. God's holy displeasure with sin is seen everywhere. It must be experienced and acknowledged. When Adam sinned in the garden, God made him feel his hot displeasure (Genesis 3:17-19). When God gave his law at Sinai, the thunder, the darkness, and the trembling made known his displeasure with sin in such a way that Israel felt it and heard it. Similarly, when God comes to a sinner in saving operations of grace, the very first thing he does is make that sinner know his displeasure. God will never give grace where he does not cause grief (John 16:8-12). As Thomas Bradbury puts it, 'When sin is not felt and hated, salvation will never be enjoyed. Where wrath has not been dreaded, love will not be experienced. The heart that is a stranger to misery must be a foreigner to mercy'. That is what the Lord used Bro. Harry Graham to teach me. 'When God deals with a sinner in mercy, he takes him to hell first'.

This is God's strange work. He causes grief so that he may bestow grace. He created 'the waster to destroy' (Isaiah 54:16) all earthly, creature comfort to bring us down to hell (Psalm 107), so that we might look to the crucified Christ and find all comfort for our souls in him alone. As Eliphaz said to Job, 'Behold, happy is the man whom God correcteth: therefore despise not thou the chastening of the Almighty: For he maketh sore, and bindeth up: he woundeth, and his hands make whole' (Job 5:17-18). Those who are grieved by God, God alone can gladden. Do what it will, the world cannot comfort when God convicts. 'Blessed are they that mourn: for they shall be comforted'.

Compassion
'Though he cause grief, yet, will he have compassion'. How sweet! How blessed! 'Though he cause grief, yet will he have compassion!' He who wounds us will heal us. God, who makes us to know and feel our ruin, will also make us to know his remedy for our ruin in Christ. 'He will have compassion!'

What is compassion? It is co-passion. It is sympathy with the sufferings and sorrows of others. It is exhibited in making one's self a companion with sufferers and mourners. The unfailing compassions of the Triune God are made known to sinners in the gospel (Ephesians 1:3-14). The Father's election, the Son's redemption, and the Spirit's operations of grace reveal our God's compassion upon his people.

When hell gaped for me as its coveted prey, when Satan roared against my soul until my very heart quaked and trembled, God Almighty in sovereign grace interposed himself. He stepped in between my soul and hell. Instead of pouring out upon me the wrath that I know I fully deserved, he showed me that he had already spent his wrath against me upon his own dear Son. Instead of pouring out wrath he embraced me in the arms of his everlasting love! (Ephesians 2:1-5).

Nothing moves God to compassion but his own purpose of grace and the sovereign inclination of his own love (Psalm 86:15; Romans 9:11-18). Because of his own, everlasting, sovereign love towards chosen sinners, the Lord God sends his messengers of compassion to them (2 Chronicles 36:15). He sent his Son to reveal it (1 John 3:16; 4:10). He sends his servants to proclaim it (Isaiah 40:1-2). He sends his Spirit into our lives to convince us of it (John 16:8).

Who can read the inspired biographies of the earthly life of the incarnate God, and doubt his compassion toward sinful men? He had compassion upon fainting souls (Matthew 9:35-36). He was moved to compassion when he saw the hungry multitude (Matthew 15:32). The blind eyes of poor sinners brought forth his compassion (Matthew 20:34). The cry of a poor leper brought forth the display of his compassion (Mark 1:40-41). The sight of the widow of Nain going to bury her son brought out the compassion of God's Son for the sons of men (Luke 7:11-15). He is the Good Samaritan who has compassion upon poor sinners (Luke 10:30-35). Our great God is full of compassion toward his sinning people (Psalm 78:38). Our great Saviour is a compassionate High Priest (Hebrews 5:2). The Holy Spirit of grace is a Spirit of compassion. We know this because we are urged not to grieve him (Ephesians 4:30). For him to be grieved by us, he must have compassion upon us.

Mercies

He causes grief that he might have compassion 'according to the multitude of his mercies'. Did you ever notice how those words 'according to' are used in the scriptures to explain God's works of grace for and in his people? Divine predestination (Ephesians 1:11), all spiritual blessings

(Ephesians 1:3-4), redemption and forgiveness (Ephesians 1:6-7), the supply of all our needs (Philippians 4:19), the grace to help (Ephesians 4:7), and all the work of God's good providence (Romans 8:28), are according to his designs of mercy. Everything God does or allows to be done is by design. He says, 'My counsel shall stand, and I will do all my pleasure' (Isaiah 46:10). He purposes. He performs. He perfects. Hell itself and all its influences do no more than serve his purpose.

> Great is the mystery, truly great,
> That hell's designs should hell defeat.
> But here eternal wisdom shines,
> For Satan works what God designs!

That misery of sin that God brings by conviction is the forerunner of mercy, which God purposed to perform in eternity. Felt misery for sins we have committed is a hopeful sign that the mercy is near which God predestinated.

Lot called God's mercy 'magnified mercy' (Genesis 19:19). Nehemiah called it 'manifold mercies' (Nehemiah 9:27). There is mercy in our God, mercy in which he delights, for sinners of every kind and clime. Jeremiah here calls it 'multitudinous mercy' (3:32). What a bountiful treasure of mercy there is in God! He is 'rich in mercy' (Ephesians 2:4). 'He delighteth in mercy' (Micah 7:18). His mercies are eternal. His mercies are sure. His mercies are free. His mercies are daily renewed upon us. His mercies bring unfailing forgiveness. God's multiplied mercies remove our multiplied miseries. God's mercies are all in his Son, our Saviour, the Lord Jesus Christ.

Chapter 26

Ezekiel

'Waters To Swim In'

Ezekiel tells us in the opening verse of his prophecy, 'the heavens were opened and I saw visions of God'. He then proceeds to tell us how he saw visions of God and his glory. When he gets to the final section of his prophecy in chapter 43, a Man stood by him, whom he heard speaking out of the house of God, as the glory of God filled the house, the place of his throne. His voice was as the voice of many waters; and Ezekiel said, 'the visions were like the vision that I saw by the river Chebar; and I fell upon my face' (43:3). Between the first vision and the last, he had seen visions of God in all his works. When he comes to the end of his prophecy and beholds the glory awaiting us, looking back over all God's wondrous works, he declares that the love of God for us in Christ is like 'waters to swim in, a river that could not be passed over' (47:1-5).

God's elect shall never pass over the river of his immutable, everlasting love. It is as immutable as it is free. It is as unquenchable as it is unpurchasable. God's elect cannot perish. Redeemed sinners cannot be damned. Once called by omnipotent mercy, saved sinners cannot be lost again. Every chosen, redeemed sinner, every sinner saved by God's almighty grace shall forever swim in the infinite length, infinite breadth, infinite depth and infinite height of the waters of his love!

God's Son

Any vision we have of God begins with the vision of his Son, the Lord Jesus Christ. We can never see the glory of God anywhere until we have seen the glory of God in the face of Christ. That is where John's vision in Revelation began. That is where Ezekiel's vision begins in chapter 1. It is where our vision must begin. We do not have to read far until we see this. First, the prophet tells us he saw 'a great cloud and a fire infolding itself' (1:4). Then he saw our Lord personified in four living creatures (vv. 5-14).

These living creatures (the same that Isaiah saw in Isaiah 6 and John saw in Revelation 4) are representative of gospel preachers. Yet, there is in them a beautiful, instructive, clear picture of our Lord Jesus Christ, too. Ezekiel saw the cherubim who 'had the likeness of a man' (v. 5). Each had four faces: the face of a lion, an ox, a man, and an eagle. Wherever cherubim are mentioned in the Bible, they are either guarding, or declaring, the holiness of God. And where but in the person of the Lord Jesus Christ is the holiness of God more fully displayed and declared?

He is the Lion of the tribe of Judah, the King who has the right to reign (Genesis 49:10). Like the beast of service, the ox, he is the Servant of Jehovah. He said that he did not come to be ministered to, but to serve, and to 'give His life a ransom for many' (Matthew 20:28). He is a Man, the Word made flesh, dwelling among us (John 1:14). He is, therefore, the perfect man. Beyond that, he soars higher than any other, and like the eagle, he looks directly into the face of God with unblinking eye. This is because he is more than perfect man. He is God manifest in the flesh. 'In the beginning was the Word, and the Word was with God, and the Word was God' (John 1:1).

Ezekiel's vision of the Lord prepared him for his ministry, as a living creature sent to proclaim God's Word to perishing sinners. Throughout the book, this phrase appears repeatedly, 'the word of the Lord came unto me'. This was his authority, and its recurrence may form the divisions of the book. Another phrase that occurs frequently is, 'they shall know that I am Jehovah'.

Then, he saw Christ on his throne, the exalted King of kings and Lord of lords, ruling over all things, just as Isaiah did before him and as John did after him. The 'Man' upon the throne (1:26) can be none other than the only-begotten Son, the representative of the invisible God. We recognize in this vision the prophetic announcement of our Lord's incarnation. The details of the vision seen by the captive on the banks of the Chebar correspond minutely with the details of the vision of the captive on the isle called Patmos.

Over eighty points of similarity may be found between the two books of Ezekiel and Revelation. As there is no doubt who is designated by John, we cannot but recognize in the vision of Ezekiel the glory of God in the person of our Lord Jesus Christ.

Both Ezekiel and John saw 'a throne set in heaven, and One sat on the throne' (1:26; Revelation 4:2, 3). They both saw the rainbow, the token of the covenant. They both saw the 'terrible crystal' of the purity of God's presence, which nothing can evade. To Ezekiel it appeared as a firmament; to John as a sea of glass (1:22; Revelation 4:6).

They both had a vision of burning lamps of the fire of God's Spirit, and of the four living creatures, whose sound was as the sound of many waters (1:24; Revelation 19:4-6). To both was given, by the One encircled by the rainbow, the roll of a book, which he was commanded to eat, and then go and prophesy (1:28; 2:1, 8-10, 3:1-4; Revelation 10:1, 2, 8-11).

'This', said Ezekiel, 'was the appearance of the likeness of the glory of the Lord' (1:28). When we read of the 'glory of the Lord' in this book, we see in it the manifested presence of God as revealed in the eternal Son, who, in the fulness of time, 'was made flesh, and dwelt amongst us, and we beheld his glory, the glory as of the only-begotten of the Father' (John 1:14).

The sight is of Christ on the throne, as the sovereign Lord accepted in heaven, and Christ upon the cross, satisfying the justice of God as our Substitute. The God-Man bringing us salvation. Then it was, Ezekiel says, that the Spirit entered into him, and then it was that he heard him that spake unto him.

As with many of the other prophets, Ezekiel himself portrayed and typified our Saviour. In chapter 4 the Lord God gave Ezekiel his message. He sent his prophet to the nation to warn them of wrath and impending judgment. But, in the midst of the warning, he gave a picture of hope. Ezekiel was required to lie on his side, first on his left side for 390 days and then on his right side for 40 days. Each of the 390 days represented the 390 years of Israel's open rebellion and idolatry in setting up the calves at Dan and Bethel. The 40 days on his right side represented the 40 years of idolatry under Manasseh's wicked, idolatrous reign in Judah. Ezekiel was required to lie on his side as one man bearing the sins of many, and bearing them to the full extent of their just punishment (v. 4). That is exactly what the Lord Jesus did for his people (2 Corinthians 5:21).

In chapters 4, 5, and 6 the prophet declares that God must and will punish sin. Sin must be punished, either in you, or in a Substitute, in a suitable man whom God himself shall send. When we get to the eighth verse of chapter six, the Lord in wrath remembers mercy and promises that some shall indeed escape his wrath through the sacrifice of that Substitute.

> v. 8 – A remnant shall escape.
> v. 9 – They shall remember me.
> v. 9 – They shall acknowledge their sin.
> v. 9 – They shall loathe themselves.
> v. 10 – They shall know that I am the Lord!

These promises find their ultimate accomplishment in the salvation of God's elect by Christ Jesus, the Lord.

God's Providence

When Ezekiel saw the glory of God upon the mercy-seat, in the face of Christ and his Sacrifice, he saw that the God of Glory is a God of absolute, unalterable purpose. In chapters 1-10 he describes the vision of wheels which the Lord gave him. It was a vision of God's marvellous works of providence. God's providence is like a great piece of machinery, wheels within a wheel (1:15-25). It appears to have many parts, but it is really one (1:16). It always moves in a straight line, according to God's unalterable, eternal purpose of grace in predestination (Romans 8:28-30). It is the sovereign work of God's throne, and the Man who sits upon it, the Lord Jesus Christ, our Saviour (1:26). This is according to the covenant made on behalf of chosen sinners before the world began (1:28). Ezekiel was overwhelmed by his vision. He says, 'This was the appearance of the likeness of the glory of the Lord! And when I saw it, I fell upon my face, and I heard the voice of one that spake' (v. 28). He withered before the glory of God and fell as one dead!

God's Grace

In chapter 2 the prophet seems to be describing his own experience of grace. He was raised, as it were, from the dead. 'And he said unto me, Son of man, stand upon thy feet, and I will speak unto thee. And the spirit entered into me when he spake unto me, and set me upon my feet, that I heard him that spake unto me' (vv. 1-2).

Then, the Lord God made him a prophet and sent him to a rebellious people (vv. 3-10). He saw a hand (v. 9), the same hand John saw (Revelation 5), the hand of the Lamb of God, the Man sitting on the throne: a hand to help him, a hand to guide him, a hand to protect him, an omnipotent hand, a pierced hand.

He saw a book (v. 10), the same one John saw, the book of God's eternal purpose! However, God is not finished teaching him yet. In chapter three God required him to eat the book (vv. 1-3). God demands reconciliation. He demands that we bow to his purpose. But we never will. Therefore God did not just tell Ezekiel to eat the book, he made him eat it (v. 2). And when he had eaten it, it was as sweet as honey (v. 3). It is the picture of a prophet, a man made strong by God (v. 8). He is a man who receives all God's Word into his heart (v. 10). He is a man moved, motivated by and consumed with the glory of God (v. 12). He is a man with a burdened, broken heart (vv. 14-15). He is a man God has made to be a watchman over the souls of men (v. 17). He is a man shut up to the will and glory of the Lord his God (vv. 22-27).

God's Judgment

In chapters seven to ten the Lord God showed his prophet the end of the matter, the judgment that must come. That which is here spoken to Israel and Judah reaches beyond those rebellious people. It reaches to all the world. The judgment here described speaks of the end of all things, the end of the world. Here four unmistakable facts about the judgment of God are obvious.

First, the judgment of God is always just. God swore to pour out his wrath upon this people because they went a-whoring after other gods. They worshipped Tammuz and the sun in the house of God (8:13-14, 17-18). No one goes to hell for what Adam did in the garden. 'The soul that sinneth, it shall die' (Ezekiel 18:4, 20). Men and women go to hell because they have personally earned the everlasting wrath of God by their own treasonous rebellion against the King of Glory. Eternal damnation, the judgment of God upon sin is that which men and women have wilfully brought upon themselves. This will be the hell of hell. The damned will know that they fully deserve all that they suffer. They will never be reconciled to it. But they will know that they deserve the just and holy wrath of God.

In chapter nine we see that judgment is preceded by a great separation of grace (vv. 3-6). A man clothed with white linen, a picture of Christ, with an inkhorn in his hand, was sent to put a mark upon the foreheads of God's chosen remnant. He commands his angels to hurt not the earth until the 144,000, the figurative sum of God's elect, have been sealed in their foreheads (Revelation 7; 2 Peter 3:9). Noah must be in the ark before the rain falls. Lot must be in Zoar before Sodom is burned. God's elect must be called before judgment falls upon the earth.

Judgment will begin at the house of God. 'Begin at my sanctuary' (9:6). 'Judgment must begin at the house of God!' (1 Peter 4:17). Judgment begins with and is most furious against those who profess to believe God, but live in rebellion against him.

Judgment shall be executed by the hands of the Mediator, the Lord Jesus Christ, so obstinately despised by men (10:4-7). Up to this point Christ is seen upon the mercy-seat. He is the mercy-seat. But now, he is taken up from between the cherubim. In that great and terrible day, when God no longer deals with sinners in mercy, there will be no mercy! Hope is gone forever. 'The Father judgeth no man, but hath committed all judgment unto the Son!' Then shall men cry, 'Hide us from the face of the Lamb!'

God's Covenant

All God's works, both in the judgment passed upon the nations and in the grace bestowed upon his elect, is but the outworking of his covenant of grace made for us with Christ our Surety before the world began. In saving us, in bringing us to Christ in faith, God brings us into the bond of the covenant (20:35-38). When his work is completely finished, he will have saved us from all our uncleanness, exactly as he swore in covenant love before the world began for the glory of his own great name (36:23-38).

God's Presence

When the Lord God has finished his work, when his house is complete, when all the tribes of the Israel of God are saved, when resurrection glory has commenced, then we will swim in the waters of his everlasting love, in his glorious presence forever. That is the scene in chapters 40-48. The river flows out of the sanctuary. It was from the south side of the altar, the place of sacrifice and the source of blessing, 'a pure river of water of life, clear as crystal, proceeding out of the throne of God and of the Lamb', or as John says, 'a Lamb as it had been slain' (Revelation 22:1). The river rises to the ankles, to the knees, and to the loins. Then it becomes 'waters to swim in, a river that I could not pass over'. Our Saviour came that we might have life, and that we might have it more abundantly. Here it is!

Christ the Giver of Life

Throughout the book of Ezekiel we see Christ as the Giver of Life. The cherubim, in the vision of the first chapter, were illustrations of the abundant life of his redeemed. The Man clothed in linen, who is the Angel of the covenant, our Great High Priest, sets the mark of life upon God's faithful ones, that their lives should be spared in the destruction of the city (9:2). His first word to the out-cast infant, which represented you and me, who became 'perfect through his comeliness' which he had put upon it, was, 'Live' (16:6). His word through the watchman was, 'I have no pleasure in the death of the wicked ... turn ye, turn ye, why will ye die, O house of Israel?' (33:11). His care as a Shepherd is over the life of his sheep in chapter 34. He answered his own question, 'Can these dry bones live?' with the words, 'Behold, I will cause breath to enter into you, and ye shall live' (37:3, 5). Finally, his promise is, 'Everything shall live whither the river cometh' (47:9).

'Son of Man'

Throughout the book, God addresses Ezekiel as the 'Son of man'. It is part of his wondrous grace that he has chosen man to be his messenger to his fellowmen, instead of choosing angels. The greatest exhibition of this grace is the fact that the Son of God became the Son of Man to fit him to be God's messenger to us. 'For verily he took not on him the nature of angels; but he took on him the seed of Abraham' (Hebrews 2:16), in all things made like unto his brethren, that he might be able to help and to save us.

The book closes with the promise of God's continual presence. 'The name of the city from that day shall be Jehovah-shammah, The Lord is there' (48:35). When God is with us and we are with him forever in that New Temple in the New Jerusalem, walking in the light of the City Foursquare, then God's work is done and both he and we shall enjoy his glory forever!

Chapter 27

Daniel

God Rules

In the 4th chapter of Daniel we read of Nebuchadnezzar's troubling dream and the interpretation of it by God's servant, Daniel.

'This is the interpretation, O king, and this is the decree of the most High, which is come upon my lord the king: That they shall drive thee from men, and thy dwelling shall be with the beasts of the field, and they shall make thee to eat grass as oxen, and they shall wet thee with the dew of heaven, and seven times shall pass over thee, till thou know that the most High ruleth in the kingdom of men, and giveth it to whomsoever he will. And whereas they commanded to leave the stump of the tree roots; thy kingdom shall be sure unto thee, after that thou shalt have known that the heavens do rule' (vv. 24-26).

Sooner or latter all men will learn what God taught Nebuchadnezzar. 'The Most High ruleth ... The heavens do rule'. That is the message of the book of Daniel. God rules! In fact, that is what the name Daniel means 'God rules' or 'God is my Judge'. The sooner we learn that fact and the more fully we are convinced of it, the better.

What does the Lord God mean for us to understand by 'God rules'? What does the Bible mean when it declares that God rules? It means just what Nebuchadnezzar confessed once he was converted (4:34-37).

'And at the end of the days I Nebuchadnezzar lifted up mine eyes unto heaven, and mine understanding returned unto me, and I blessed the most High, and I praised and honoured him that liveth for ever, whose dominion is an everlasting dominion, and his kingdom is from generation to generation: And all the inhabitants of the earth are reputed as nothing: and he doeth according to his will in the army of heaven, and among the inhabitants of the earth: and none can stay his hand, or say unto him, What doest thou? At the same time my reason returned unto me; and for the glory of my kingdom, mine honour and brightness returned unto me; and my counsellors and my lords sought unto me; and I was established in my kingdom, and excellent majesty was added unto me. Now I Nebuchadnezzar praise and extol and honour the King of heaven, all whose works are truth, and his ways judgment: and those that walk in pride he is able to abase'.

Once a person learns that 'the Most High ruleth', he will gladly extol, honour, and worship him, as Nebuchadnezzar did. No one worships except those who worship at the feet of the Lord God Almighty, the Most High, who rules the universe absolutely, always, in all places, in all things, exactly as he will. What could be more comforting to our souls? More cheering? More inspiring? More encouraging?

God Most High, who rules the universe, is God who can sustain his people in the midst of horribly evil times, as we see in Daniel 1:1-21. Our great God, from his lofty throne, gives kingdoms to men and takes them away at his pleasure, as he will, for the good of his own elect (2:37; 4:28-33; 5:1-31). The God of glory, in whom we trust, intervenes in and sovereignly manipulates all the affairs of all creatures, according to his wise, unalterable purpose, for the salvation of his elect and the glory of his own great name. Providence is but the unfolding of his purpose by a constant succession of miracles. 'He worketh signs and wonders in heaven and in earth' (6:27). He causes pagan kings to dream dreams and uses pagan witch-doctors to fetch his prophet to the king. He uses a fiery furnace to establish his servants in the place where he is pleased to put them. He uses a den of lions to exalt his servant.

Daniel's Message

Our great God shall establish his kingdom in this world, that shall never be destroyed. Though the kingdoms of men seek to destroy God's kingdom, he uses them to establish it. In the end his kingdom shall be the instrument in his hands by which the kingdoms of this world shall be crushed to pieces and annihilated. The book of Daniel is all about the establishing of God's kingdom in this world upon the foundation of his own Son's blood atonement. It reveals the everlasting triumph and glory of Christ in and by his kingdom of grace.

It is true that both the book of Daniel and its New Testament companion, the book of Revelation, speak about future things. The two books are remarkable in their symmetry and harmony. The book of Revelation illuminates and explains the book of Daniel. The book of Daniel lays the foundation for the book of Revelation. It is also true that the book of Daniel is perfectly precise in its prophetic predictions. History has verified that fact indisputably. The seventy-weeks of Daniel 9, about which everyone has heard so much and understands so little, marked the exact time when our Saviour would manifest himself in the world.

But this is much, much more than a book of prophecy. The Lord God raised up Daniel during the Babylonian captivity for a specific purpose, to fulfil a specific need, and to do a specific work. God raised up Daniel to turn the hearts of his people away from their woes to their Saviour. He raised up Daniel to show them that he was still on his throne, that his kingdom was safe, and that no real harm would ever befall them. Daniel was inspired to give a prophetic picture of redemption by Christ, setting the exact time in which it would be accomplished. He showed that God's purpose of grace included chosen sinners from among the Gentiles; that his kingdom is a spiritual kingdom reaching throughout the world; a kingdom built upon the sin-atoning sacrifice, death, and resurrection glory of the Messiah, the Christ. He declared that the ultimate accomplishment of God's purpose, the destruction of his enemies, the salvation of his people, and the everlasting glory of his Son, would, in the very last day of time, be the resurrection of the dead (Daniel 12:1-3).

Daniel's message is a message of hope, encouragement, and consolation. Though wickedness ever increases, though opposition to our God, his Son, his gospel and his people grows with unabated rage, all is well. Our God is on his throne. 'The Most High ruleth ... The heavens do rule!' Our Saviour is always triumphant, and we who are more than conquerors in him shall triumph at last over all things. The kingdom of our God cannot be destroyed. His church shall prevail. The gates of hell shall never prevail over the bulwarks of Zion.

Christ and Antichrist
The book of Daniel deals with nations and wars, specifically identifying the rise and fall of kings and kingdoms, all opposing God, opposing Christ and opposing his kingdom, the church of God. But these nations and

their kings shall fall before Christ, our King. Daniel declares, as does the book of Revelation, the sure and certain triumph of Christ over antichrist, and the equally sure triumph of God's church over Babylon. They picture the full redemption and salvation of God's elect, and the glory of Christ.

In chapter 2 Nebuchadnezzar had a dream. In his dream Nebuchadnezzar saw the image of a man. The head was made of gold, the chest and arms of silver, the stomach and thighs of brass, the legs of iron, and the feet and toes of iron mixed with clay. As Nebuchadnezzar looked, a rock was cut out, not by human hands, and thrown at the image, striking its feet. This rock then grew into a huge mountain that filled the earth. The meaning of this vision is given in verse 44. 'And in the days of these kings shall the God of heaven set up a kingdom, which shall never be destroyed: and the kingdom shall not be left to other people, but it shall break in pieces and consume all these kingdoms, and it shall stand for ever'. There must be a series of kingdoms in the earth, ruled according to man's ways, idolatrous and ungodly. But, ultimately, God's kingdom shall reduce them all to dust and fill the whole earth. The kingdoms of this world must and will crumble; but the kingdom of God shall endure forever (Revelation 11:15).

The Other Visions

I do not want to over-simplify the book, but all the rest of the visions in Daniel elaborate on this. Two rulers and two kingdoms are constantly presented. There is a lawful Ruler, the Lord Jesus Christ our Mediator, to whom God himself has given, and is giving, authority, glory, and the kingdom (7:9-14).

'I beheld till the thrones were cast down, and the Ancient of days did sit, whose garment was white as snow, and the hair of his head like the pure wool: his throne was like the fiery flame, and his wheels as burning fire. A fiery stream issued and came forth from before him: thousand thousands ministered unto him, and ten thousand times ten thousand stood before him: the judgment was set, and the books were opened. I beheld then because of the voice of the great words which the horn spake: I beheld even till the beast was slain, and his body destroyed, and given to the burning flame. As concerning the rest of the beasts, they had their dominion taken away: yet their lives were prolonged for a season and time. I saw in the night visions, and, behold, one like the Son of man came with the clouds of heaven, and came to the Ancient of days, and they brought him near before him. And there was given him dominion, and glory, and a kingdom, that all people, nations, and languages, should serve him: his dominion is an everlasting dominion, which shall not pass away, and his kingdom that which shall not be destroyed'.

The Ancient of Days is our God. The Son of Man is our all-glorious Christ, to whom he has given all dominion and glory. Daniel refers to Christ as the Prince of princes (8:25), the Anointed One (9:25), and Michael (12:1).

Then Daniel tells us of another ruler who must rise, a rebel ruler, who rises in the time of the end in vehement opposition to Christ (8:23-25). This is the antichrist described in Revelation 13, not a single man, but the whole system of false religion represented by four different beasts. These beasts represent antichrist religion, all freewill, works religion, Satan masquerading as Jesus Christ.

'And in the latter time of their kingdom, when the transgressors are come to the full, a king of fierce countenance, and understanding dark sentences, shall stand up. And his power shall be mighty, but not by his own power: and he shall destroy wonderfully, and shall prosper, and practice, and shall destroy the mighty and the holy people. And through his policy also he shall cause craft to prosper in his hand; and he shall magnify himself in his heart, and by peace shall destroy many: he shall also stand up against the Prince of princes; but he shall be broken without hand'.

God's elect, the heirs of his kingdom, bow to the rule of Christ (7:27). They will not accept the mark of the beast. They will not worship at Satan's altar. They will not worship at the altar of man's free will. They will not attempt to approach God upon an altar of works (Exodus 20:25-26). All the rest of the world follows the beasts and are in league with hell against Christ and his kingdom (8:23; 9:26). Sometimes they use peaceful, flattering words (11:21, 32, 34); but their opposition is undaunted.

References to the rebel ruler include the little horn that comes from the direction of the north (8:9), the stern-faced king (8:23), the 'ruler who will come' (9:26), the ruler who sets up the abomination that causes desolation (9:27), the king of the north (11:6), and the king who exalts himself (11:36).

The conflict between these two rulers comes to a head in the time of the end, when the world as a whole passes the point of no return in its rebellion against Christ (8:23), causing great devastation. Perhaps this refers to the age when Satan is loosed for a little season (Revelation 20) to again deceive the nations. It certainly refers to this day in which we live.

'And in the latter time of their kingdom, when the transgressors are come to the full, a king of fierce countenance, and understanding dark sentences, shall stand up. And his power shall be mighty, but not by his own power: and he shall destroy wonderfully, and shall prosper, and practice, and shall destroy the mighty and the holy people' (8:23-24).

The 'daily sacrifice', or continual ministry of Christ and the perpetual efficacy of his atonement and intercession, by which the world is now preserved from judgment (Revelation 7:1-3), is taken away (8:11-12; 11:31; 12:11). It is taken away by preachers, ministers of Satan, who transform themselves into the messengers of Christ and angels of light (2 Corinthians 11:13-15). In its place is set up the abomination that causes desolation (9:27).

Instead of preaching salvation by the righteousness of Christ, they preach salvation by a righteousness that men produce. In the time of the end, the saints of God will be severely persecuted, even to the point of death, and their power will be broken (8:24; 11:33; 12:7). That is to say, the religion of the beast shall be dominant in the earth for a divinely appointed time (2 Thessalonians 2:11-12).

Antichrist takes his stand against Christ (8:25). But our Saviour and King, the Lord Jesus Christ, shall rise to destroy the antichrist and his kingdom (Babylon shall fall!) and deliver the saints (8:25; 9:27; 12:1). All is well. When the Lord God, our Saviour and King, has finished all things, God's elect shall forever triumph over Babylon (Revelation 19:1-6).

Christ in the book of Daniel

The Lord Jesus Christ shines forth brilliantly in these twelve chapters. He is the Smiting Stone of Daniel 2:44, 45. God's Son is the One who shall come to destroy antichrist's dominion. It is He whose kingdom 'shall stand forever'.

Nebuchadnezzar looked into the fiery furnace and saw one like unto the Son of God (3:25). He did not know of whom he spoke; but this was, no doubt, a pre-incarnate appearance of the Lord Jesus.

In chapter 6 the great dilemma which perplexed Darius is a beautiful illustration of the gospel. How could Darius both keep his law and deliver Daniel? Daniel must be cast into the lion's den, or the king's throne becomes meaningless. Yet, Daniel was delivered. How can God be just and the Justifier? The only way God can maintain his absolute justice in punishing sin and yet justify his elect is by the substitutionary sacrifice of his own Son in the room and stead of his people (Romans 3:24-26). In Christ, just as Daniel suffered the king's wrath, God's elect suffered all the wrath of God to the full satisfaction of justice, and are delivered from it.

What a majestic scene in chapter 7! The Ancient of days, God the Father, is seated upon his throne. The time setting is immediately before the return of Christ. We read, 'I saw in the night visions, and, behold, one like the Son of man came with the clouds of heaven, and came to the Ancient of days...' (7:13). The verses that follow are paralleled by the description of Christ in Revelation 1:7. 'And there was given Him dominion, and glory, and a kingdom, that all people, nations, and languages should serve Him; His dominion is an everlasting dominion, which shall not pass away, and His kingdom that which shall not be destroyed' (Daniel 7:14).

Daniel 9 foretells the death of Christ and the accomplishments of it. 'Seventy weeks are determined upon thy people and upon thy holy city, to finish the transgression, and to make an end of sins, and to make reconciliation for iniquity, and to bring in everlasting righteousness, and to seal up the vision and prophecy, and to anoint the most Holy' (9:24). Our blessed Saviour has fulfilled the prophecy. He finished the transgression. He made an end of sins. He made reconciliation for iniquity. He brought in everlasting righteousness. He sealed up (fulfilled) the vision and prophecy. He is anointed of God, the most Holy.

Chapter 9 also gives us, by Daniel's example, a tremendous word of instruction about prayer. As we read Daniel's prayer, we learn how to pray. Prayer involves the confession of sin. It celebrates God's perfections. True prayer is based upon God's righteousness and seeks God's mercy. Like Daniel's, our supplications are answered before we make them (9:23). The answer is found in Christ, always in Christ, and in the revelation of God's grace and glory in him (9:24-27).

A Question

The question might be asked, 'Why does God put his people through such heavy, heavy trials?' One answer to that question is found in Daniel 11:35. It is 'to try them, and to purge, and to make them white, even to the time of the end: because it is yet for a time appointed'. 'For there must be also heresies among you, that they which are approved may be made manifest among you' (1 Corinthians 11:19). Our trials will do us no harm. (The fiery furnace only consumed the cords that bound Shadrach, Meshach, and Abednego.) Our trials are for a set time. Our trials will only make us better and heaven more glorious (2 Corinthians 4:17; 1 Peter 1:7).

Chapter 28

Hosea

'I will love them freely'.
Hosea was a prophet contemporary with Isaiah, Amos, and Micah. He was a faithful prophet of God for almost seventy years. He was God's messenger to the northern kingdom of Israel, only mentioning Judah (the southern kingdom) incidentally. This is important. You will remember that from the time that the kingdom was divided the northern kingdom was engulfed in idolatry (1 Kings 12:1-33). The practice of idolatry, as it always does, brought Israel into a state of utter moral decadence.

Hosea addresses Israel sometimes as Samaria, sometimes as Jacob, and sometimes as Ephraim, deliberately choosing names connected with failure, sin, rebellion, idolatry, and corruptions which called for wrath and judgment. Hosea speaks plainly about the wrath and judgment of God we deserve. Yet, the message of Hosea is a message of immutable grace, unfailing mercy, and indestructible love. This is seen clearly in Hosea 14:4. Here the Lord God declares his purpose of grace toward his chosen people, a purpose from which he cannot and will not be turned. 'I will heal their backsliding, I will love them freely: for mine anger is turned away from him'.

We discover a beautiful portrayal of God's immutable love to chosen sinners in chapter 11.

'And my people are bent to backsliding from me: though they called them to the most High, none at all would exalt him. How shall I give thee

up, Ephraim? how shall I deliver thee, Israel? how shall I make thee as
Admah? how shall I set thee as Zeboim? mine heart is turned within me,
my repentings are kindled together. I will not execute the fierceness of
mine anger, I will not return to destroy Ephraim: for I am God, and not man;
the Holy One in the midst of thee: and I will not enter into the city' (vv. 7-
9).

A Portrait of Grace

The book of Hosea begins with the story of Hosea and Gomer. It
describes Hosea's love for Gomer, her infidelity, her despising Hosea's
love and goodness toward her, and the gracious triumph of his love over
her. This sets the background for and tells us the meaning of the rest of
the book. What we have in the first three chapters of this book is a
tremendous, blessed portrait of God's free and sovereign grace toward
chosen sinners in Christ.

Hosea's name means 'Salvation'. He is presented in this story as a
picture of our Lord Jesus Christ. He was commanded of God to go down
to what nowadays might be called the 'red light district' of town and take
a wife from among the harlots. 'The beginning of the word of the LORD
by Hosea. And the LORD said to Hosea, Go, take unto thee a wife of
whoredoms and children of whoredoms: for the land hath committed great
whoredom, departing from the LORD' (1:2).

He chose Gomer, whose name means 'consumption'. That is a picture
of God's elect by nature, consumed with sin and consumed by sin. Gomer
was the daughter of Diblaim, whose name means raisin-cake and bears
the sense of 'dried' or 'dead'. Like Gomer, we are the dead children of a
dead father. But Gomer can also mean 'perfect' or 'complete' and that
pictures us, too. Gomer was the consummation of all Hosea's purposes
and work, the consummation of his love, so God's elect are in their ultimate
end the consummation of all God's purposes, works, and great love.

The Lord gave Hosea and Gomer three children who also represent
us. Jezreel means 'seed of God'. Loruhamah means 'no mercy'. Loammi
means 'not mine', or 'not my people'. We who were not his people and
had not obtained mercy are now his people and have obtained mercy in
Christ. That is exactly how the Holy Spirit interprets this story for us in
the book of Romans (Romans 9:25-26).

Hosea came home one day, and Gomer was gone. She had gone back
to her lovers. Chapter 2 tells us about Gomer's great fall and Hosea's
purpose of love and grace concerning her. Chapter three tells us how
Hosea's love and grace prevailed; and he fetched Gomer home again.

Here are the first three verses of chapter three:

'Then said the LORD unto me, Go yet, love a woman beloved of her friend, yet an adulteress, according to the love of the LORD toward the children of Israel, who look to other gods, and love flagons of wine. So I bought her to me for fifteen pieces of silver, and for an homer of barley, and an half homer of barley: And I said unto her, Thou shalt abide for me many days; thou shalt not play the harlot, and thou shalt not be for another man: so will I also be for thee'.

> God moves in a mysterious way,
> His wonders to perform;
> He plants His footsteps in the sea,
> And rides upon the storm.
>
> Deep in unfathomable mines,
> Of never failing skill.
> He treasures up His bright designs,
> And works His sovereign will.
>
> Ye fearful saints fresh courage take,
> The clouds ye so much dread.
> Are big with mercy, and shall break
> In blessing on your head.
>
> Judge not the Lord by feeble sense,
> But trust Him for His grace,
> Behind the frowning providence
> He hides a smiling face.
>
> His purposes will ripen fast,
> Unfolding every hour;
> The bud may have a bitter taste,
> But sweet will be the flower.
>
> Blind unbelief is sure to err,
> And scan His work in vain:
> God is His own Interpreter,
> And He will make it plain.
>
> William Cowper

Gomer had proved herself unfaithful, abandoning her husband and going after her lovers. Though she proved herself 'a wife of whoredoms', Hosea did not cease to love her. Instead, he slipped away into the haunts of shame and ill repute. There he found the object of his love, found her in the arms of her lovers. What did he do? He did not have her stoned to death, executing the just sentence of the law. He did not force her to return to him, though he might have done so. He did not leave her there, though most would have done so. What did he do? He loved her! As chapter 2 describes Gomer's horrible sin, it also describes Hosea's incomparable, indestructible love for her.

However, there is more to this story than the love of Hosea for Gomer. This is a picture of the love of Christ for us. Just as Hosea took Gomer for his wife and married a wanton woman altogether beneath him, unworthy of him, and totally without regard for him, so the Lord God our Saviour is married to his elect. Just as Gomer forsook her loving husband and went after her lovers, you and I went astray from our God as soon as we were born. Just as Gomer's pursuit of her lovers brought her into bondage, slavery, and utter ruin, so we have ruined ourselves, walking after the lusts of our own flesh. Just as Hosea hedged up Gomer's ways to force her into his arms again (2:6-7), so our God and Saviour hedged up our ways to graciously force us, to force our hearts, to return to him (Psalm 65:4; 110:3).

As Hosea secretly provided for and took care of Gomer, though she ran after her lovers (2:8), so our great God graciously took care of and provided for us throughout the days of our rebellion (Jude 1; Hebrews 1:14). As Hosea, in order to save Gomer, came to where she was and walked through the haunts of iniquity, so the Son of God, in order to save us, came into this world and walked in this land of darkness and sin. Just as Hosea redeemed Gomer with a legal ransom price, our Lord Jesus Christ redeemed us by the price of his own precious blood. Just as Hosea made Gomer his faithful wife and was faithful to her, so the Lord Jesus, by his omnipotent mercy, irresistible love, and almighty grace, makes the objects of his love his faithful bride (3:3; Jeremiah 32:38-40). Just as Hosea did all that he did for Gomer, in obedience to the will of God because of a covenant of love, so the Lord Jesus Christ does all that he does for us in obedience to the will of God as our Surety because of his covenant love for us (2:18-20).

As Hosea conquered Gomer's whorish heart by his love for her, so the Lord Jesus Christ conquers the hearts of chosen, redeemed sinners in the time of love (2:9-17).

Hosea's Message

The rest of the book of Hosea describes the sins and sinfulness, the utter debauchery of God's people, the horrible evil Israel brought upon itself, the horrible evil we bring upon ourselves by rebellion and sin, and our God's matchless, unalterable purpose of grace and love, his determination to save his elect. This is not an over-simplification of Hosea's message, but precisely the message Hosea was inspired of God to convey. In chapters 4-6 we see that Ephraim, Israel, and Judah fully deserved and constantly courted God's wrath. They would not forsake their idols (4:17). They dealt treacherously with the Lord God, often pretending in time of fear to turn to him, but clinging still to their own devices (5:4-6:6). But the pretended repentance, which comes as a result of fear and judgment, is only another mockery of God (6:4-6)

Yet, in spite of all their iniquity, in spite of all the wrath they heaped upon themselves, the Lord God would not give up his own. He declares, 'though they have hired among the nations, now will I gather them' (8:10). Why? Because he will not give them up (11:8-9). Because his love for his elect is free, unconditional, indestructible love (14:4, 7-9).

Prophecies of Christ

Prophecies of Christ in these fourteen chapters are crystal clear. Both Peter and Paul show us that the prophecy of Hosea 1:10 has been fulfilled in Christ (1 Peter 2:10; Romans 11:25-26). The book of Hosea is not talking about God's love and grace toward Abraham's physical seed. It describes, in prophetic type, God's mercy, love, and grace toward his elect in every nation, Abraham's spiritual seed, the Israel of God (Revelation 5:9,10).

After giving us the tremendous picture of his mercy, love, and grace by which we are saved (1:1-3:3), Hosea declares the meaning of the picture, assuring us that God will save his people (3:4-5).

Hosea 6:2 speaks of the resurrection of Christ; and our resurrection in him could not be more plainly foretold. The prophet expressly mentions two days, after which life should be given, and a third day, on which the resurrection should take place. Christ will come again as 'the Day-spring from on high', coming forth from the grave on the resurrection morning, and it is written of him that he shall 'come down like showers upon the mown grass' (Psalm 72:6).

Hosea 11:1 had its fulfilment in Matthew 2:15. Who can read Hosea 11:3-4 and not hear the Lord Jesus Christ speaking of his great, gracious method of grace to our poor souls? 'I taught Ephraim also to go, taking them by their arms; but they knew not that I healed them. I drew them with cords of a man, with bands of love: and I was to them as they that take off the yoke on their jaws, and I laid meat unto them'.

In chapter 13 our great God and Saviour declares his singularity as God and his gracious determination to make us know it (v. 4; Isaiah 45:22; Matthew 1:21). Verse 14 speaks again of our resurrection by Christ in the last day. 'I will ransom them from the power of the grave; I will redeem them from death: O death, I will be thy plagues; O grave, I will be thy destruction: repentance shall be hid from mine eyes'. The word translated 'ransom', means 'rescue by the payment of a price'. The word 'redeem', speaks of Christ's work as our Kinsman Redeemer. Our risen Redeemer sings triumphantly, 'O death, I will be thy plagues; O grave, I will be thy destruction!' Soon, we shall sing the same song (1 Corinthians 15:51-58).

Chapter 29

Joel

Jehovah is God

We all like to know the reason for things. Perhaps because we are naturally inquisitive, perhaps because we want someone or something to blame for things we do not like; but we all want to know the reason for things. Through the ages, men have endeavoured to discover the principle upon which history turns. Since the dawn of history, philosophers and those who think they are philosophers have continually debated what controls destiny. Is it fate or free will? Is it man, or nature, or some higher power?

Aristotle and the ancient Greek philosophers (those 'wise fools' Paul speaks of in 1 Corinthians 1) determined that history moves in cycles. Thomas Jefferson was convinced that the history of the world was determined by the political direction of nations and human government. In the late 1800s Karl Marx dipped his pen in acid and taught in his 'Communist Manifesto' that the controlling force of history is economics.

Today, multitudes today follow the thinking of men like Charles Darwen and H. G. Wells, and are convinced that evolution is the controlling force of the universe. These 'brilliant' minds, burying their heads in the sand, are convinced that man is constantly engaged in self-improvement, that man is constantly making himself better physically, mentally, morally and socially, and constantly improving history by the force of human evolution.

Of course, the Word of God reveals that which no man left to himself can ever figure out, that which no man left to himself will ever acknowledge, that which, sooner or later, everyone must acknowledge. God and God alone controls the universe. Furthermore, the God who controls the universe is Jehovah our Saviour, the Lord Jesus Christ. The hinge upon which all history turns is the cross of Christ (John 12:30-32). The hand that works the machinery of providence is God's (Romans 8:28; 11:36).

Joel's Message

That is the message of Joel's prophecy. Jehovah is God. As the book of Hosea reveals the heart of God in redemption, the book of Joel reveals the hand of God ruling the universe to save his people. The opening verses of this short prophecy tell us plainly that the prophet's message was intended for both the people to whom he spoke and to the people of future generations (1:1-3).

We know nothing at all about when Joel lived and prophesied. We know nothing of the historic circumstances of his prophecy. All we know is that his name was Joel, meaning 'Jehovah is God', and that his father's name was Pethuel, meaning 'the openheartedness' or 'sincerity of God'.

The Theme

One of the most meaningful statements ever written, and one of the most terrifying, is found in Genesis 6:3. There the Lord God declares, 'My Spirit shall not always strive with man'. The book of Joel, in my opinion, drives that fact home more forcefully than any of the other prophetic books. The theme of this prophecy is 'the Day of the Lord'. Joel speaks of 'the Day of the Lord' five times in these three short chapters. Joel tells us that history is moving constantly to an appointed end called 'the Day of the Lord' (1:15; 2:1, 11, 31; 3:14).

If you read these three chapters at one sitting, you will see that Joel does not use this phrase, 'the Day of the Lord', to refer to a specific, single day or time. In chapter 1 (v. 15) 'the Day of the Lord' is immediate. It referred to the day in which the judgment of God was seen in the land. In chapter 2 (vv. 1, 11, 31) 'the Day of the Lord' is imminent, referring to judgment that may come at any time. In chapter 3 (v. 14) 'the Day of the Lord' is future, referring to the final, consummate end of all things.

It is important that we observe this. As it is used by Joel, 'the Day of the Lord' refers to any day in which the Lord God displays his sovereignty as God. In other words, yesterday was 'the Day of the Lord'. Today is 'the Day of the Lord'. Tomorrow will be 'the Day of the Lord'. Also, there is a day coming when all creation shall acknowledge, this is 'the Day of the Lord'. Joel declares that the Lord who is God shall accomplish his purpose.

Day of Warning

First, Joel tells us that 'the Day of the Lord' is a day of warning, a day when the Lord God sends judgment to warn us of judgment. 'Alas for the day! for the day of the LORD is at hand, and as a destruction from the Almighty shall it come' (1:15).

The Lord God sent a plague of locusts upon the land of Judah because of their sin. With this plague of locusts the Lord called his people to repentance. These locusts describe an army far, far worse than any army of locusts or of men. These locusts not only destroyed the vegetation of the land, they cut off and took away the sacrifice from the house of God (1:9). Joel lived in a day much like our day, a day when God's manifest judgment had fallen upon a people who despite being called by his name had forsaken his name (1 Peter 4:17-18).

When the Lord God visits a nation, a people, a generation, or an individual in providential judgment, it is a warning of judgment to come and a merciful call to repentance (1:13-16, 19). He is saying, 'My Spirit shall not always strive with man'. 'Blow ye the trumpet in Zion, and sound an alarm in my holy mountain: let all the inhabitants of the land tremble: for the day of the LORD cometh, for it is nigh at hand' (2:1). Before this army of locusts came, the land was like the Garden of Eden. They left behind them a desolate, barren wilderness (2:3-9). A. M. Hodgkin wrote ...

> An army of locusts is incredible to those who have not watched it. They fill the air, and darken the sun like an eclipse (2:2), and spread for miles over the land. The advance columns will attack all that is green and succulent; in half an hour every leaf and blade is destroyed (1:11, 12). Others coming on in succession will strip the bark from the trees (1:6, 7). A land so devastated takes years to recover (1:17-20). The noise of their wings can be heard for miles, and the noise of the browsing is like a fire (2:5), and the land over which they have passed has the appearance of being fire-swept (2:3). Having stripped the country, they scale the walls of the cities, in serried ranks like mailed

horsemen and chariots, and marching into the houses consume everything which can be consumed in their resistless onslaught (2:4, 7-9).

Like an army of locusts, false religion devours everything and gives nothing. It eclipses the Sun of Righteousness and takes away the sacrifice. It destroys the souls of men. It comes as the judgment of God upon a people who refuse to worship him (2 Thessalonians 2:11-12). Make no mistake, this horrible army is God's army (v. 11).

Hope Given
At the close of verse 11 in chapter 2, the question is raised. 'Who can abide the day of God's wrath?' (cf. Nahum 1:2-6). Yes, the Lord God will punish sin, he must. Judgment is sure. Hell is real. Eternity is forever. But 'he delighteth in mercy!' Even now, in the face of such horrible judgment, there is hope. In wrath, he does remember mercy. We know this because the Lord God calls us to repentance, declaring himself to be 'gracious and merciful, slow to anger, and of great kindness' (2:12-14).

In verses 15-17, God's prophet pleads with his people, fathers, ministers, priests, all his people to heed the Lord's call, and plead for his mercy, as Moses' did, for the glory of his own great name (Exodus 32:11, 12; Psalm 115:1,2).

Grace Promised
Then, in the last part of chapter 2, God promises us that as surely as we seek his mercy, he will grant it (Hebrews 4:16).

'Then will the LORD be jealous for his land, and pity his people. Yea, the LORD will answer and say unto his people, Behold, I will send you corn, and wine, and oil, and ye shall be satisfied therewith: and I will no more make you a reproach among the heathen ... Fear not, O land; be glad and rejoice: for the LORD will do great things ... Be glad then, ye children of Zion, and rejoice in the LORD your God: for he hath given you the former rain moderately, and he will cause to come down for you the rain, the former rain, and the latter rain in the first month ... And I will restore to you the years that the locust hath eaten, the cankerworm, and the caterpillar, and the palmerworm, my great army which I sent among you. And ye shall eat in plenty, and be satisfied, and praise the name of the LORD your God, that hath dealt wondrously with you: and my people shall never be ashamed. And ye shall know that I am in the midst of Israel, and that I am the LORD your God, and none else: and my people shall never be ashamed' (vv. 18, 19, 21, 23, 25, 26, 27).

This promise of grace clearly involved the promise of Christ's great, accomplished redemption as our Mediator. Whether Joel understood this or not, I cannot say. But the Apostles Peter and Paul certainly did (Acts 2:16-36; Romans 10:13; Galatians 3:13-14).

'And it shall come to pass afterward, that I will pour out my spirit upon all flesh; and your sons and your daughters shall prophesy, your old men shall dream dreams, your young men shall see visions: And also upon the servants and upon the handmaids in those days will I pour out my spirit. And I will show wonders in the heavens and in the earth, blood, and fire, and pillars of smoke. The sun shall be turned into darkness, and the moon into blood, before the great and the terrible day of the LORD come. And it shall come to pass, that whosoever shall call on the name of the LORD shall be delivered: for in mount Zion and in Jerusalem shall be deliverance, as the LORD hath said, and in the remnant whom the LORD shall call'.

Deliverance Promised

In chapter 3 the Lord God promises that he will save, that he will deliver all the hosts of his elect from the nations into which he has scattered them. The battle that takes place 'in the valley of decision' (vv. 2, 14) is never in doubt. That battle is not yours, but the Lord's (2 Chronicles 20:17, 20). Though they have forsaken him, he will never forsake them. But, before the great and terrible day of the Lord shall come, he will bring again the captivity of Jerusalem. The Lord will roar out of Zion and gather his people, his heritage, his Israel out of the nations of the world. Then, his Spirit will cease to strive with man, and all Israel shall be saved. 'So shall ye know that I am the LORD your God dwelling in Zion!'

Chapter 30

Amos

A Prophet in Overalls

750 years before our Lord's incarnation the nation of Israel was a rich, thriving, prosperous kingdom. During the reign of Jeroboam II, the nation was peaceful, stable, strong, and very, very religious (Amos 3:12, 15; 4:1, 4; 5:5, 21-23; 6:3-6; 8:3-10). Many enjoyed such wealth that they had winter houses and summer houses. Others were even more wealthy, living in ivory houses on great estates.

But all was not well in Israel. The nation was morally degenerate. The land was filled with greed and corruption. The poor and weak were mercilessly oppressed by the rich and powerful (2:6; 5:11). Immorality was rampant (2:7). Rebellion, disdain of and contempt for authority, was widespread (5:11-12). Religion flourished. Religious ceremonies and activities were faithfully observed (5:21), and observed in the name of Jehovah. But the land was altogether given over to idolatry. Bethel, the house of God, had become Bethel, the house of transgression (4:4).

Into this great, proud, prosperous, religious, secure society the Lord God Almighty dropped a bombshell. A prophet by the name of Amos, a prophet wearing overalls (1:1-2). Amos was a farmer, a herdsman; one who took care of sheep, and cattle, and fig trees. He was what folks today would disdainfully call 'a redneck', 'a hayseed', or 'a country bumpkin'. Amos was a farm boy from Tekoa, which was just a few miles south of Jerusalem in the Southern Kingdom of Judah.

The Lord sent this poor, uneducated, farm boy, bibbed overalls and all, up North with his Word. Amos came storming into Samaria with a message of divine judgment, a message of impending wrath upon a people who had abandoned God and his worship, crying, 'Prepare to meet thy God, O Israel!' He spoke of drought, famine, pestilence, and earthquakes. Judgment had already begun; but it had no effect upon the hearts of the people. It would, therefore, increase and continue to increase until the nation was altogether destroyed. The Lord God swore by his prophet that because they repented not when he sent famine to their bodies, he would send a far worse, far more destructive famine, a famine of spiritual food (8:11-12). 'Behold, the days come, saith the Lord GOD, that I will send a famine in the land, not a famine of bread, nor a thirst for water, but of hearing the words of the LORD: And they shall wander from sea to sea, and from the north even to the east, they shall run to and fro to seek the word of the LORD, and shall not find it'.

The name 'Amos' means, 'Burden-bearer', and Amos bore in his soul 'the burden of the Word of the Lord' to a people who could not have cared less.

Divine Judgment

The book of Amos declares that God Almighty 'will by no means clear the guilty'. He must and shall punish sin. Because he is righteous, his rule over all the earth is righteous and just. Sin cannot be tolerated by him. It must be punished. When people sin as a social group, as a nation, the nation is punished accordingly (Proverbs 14:34). When individuals sin, they are punished accordingly as individuals (2 Corinthians 5:10-11).

Amos began his message to Israel in a strange way. In chapters one and two he describes the judgments the Lord brought upon the nations around Israel. These were the Gentiles among whom the children of Israel lived. If you look at a map of the area you will see that Amos goes around the whole nation of Israel, declaring the judgment of God upon those nations, because of their transgressions.

He begins with Damascus (1:3-5), way up in the northeast section of the map above Israel. He tells Israel that Damascus must be judged because of its cruelty. Then he speaks of Gaza, the ancient land of Philistia (1:6-8), in the opposite direction, way down on the southwest side of Israel. He tells Israel that God will destroy Gaza because they had enslaved Edom and because they were idolaters.

Then, in verses 9-10 he moves back up the coast to the land of Tyre, on the northwest side of Israel, and points out how God had judged this country because the people had broken their covenants and treated their fellow men, not as brethren, but as enemies.

Next , he moves on down to the far south of Israel to the land of Edom (1:11-12), the ancient country of Esau, and declares that God's judgment fell upon that nation because of their implacable hatred of Israel.

Then, Amos moves back up the east side of Israel to the land of Ammon (1:13-15). It is called Jordan today. Its capital, Amman, was the capital of ancient Ammon. They were punished because of their barbaric cruelty, greed, and lust for power.

Moab, on the southwest side of Israel, was to be judged because of its hatred of Israel (2:1-3). Then, he mentions the Southern nation of Judah (2:4-5), and declares that Judah must be judged because it had despised God's law.

At the end of chapter 2 (vv. 6-16), he speaks to Israel, the Northern Kingdom, and declares that God will judge them for their corruption and for injustice, corruption and injustice greater than any of the other nations. The Lord God was pressed under them, as an over-loaded cart is pressed with its load (2:13).

As we read Amos' message, it is obvious that the people of Israel were totally undisturbed, absolutely complacent, as long as he was talking about the other nations. They seem to have been thinking, 'Well, they got what was coming to them'. But when the prophet zeroed in on them, they were enraged. They said, 'Why don't you go away and preach somewhere else? We don't want to hear what you have to say'.

From verse 1 of chapter 3, Amos deals with these people exclusively, hammering home his message blow by blow to the Northern Kingdom of Israel. He begins by pointing out to them that they were a people who had a special, privileged position before God (3:1-2). That is exactly what they wanted to hear. You can picture them swelling with pride and arrogance. 'We are God's elect, his chosen, favoured, special people. We have a great history and a great heritage'. Then, the prophet hit them right between the eyes. 'Therefore I will punish you for all your iniquities'.

Privilege and Responsibility

That which was their great pride was the very reason for their great judgment. Revelation despised brings great wrath. Privilege creates responsibility. The greater our privileges are, the greater our responsibilities are. The nation of Israel had been given the greatest light, the greatest privileges of any nation. But they turned from that to walk in darkness and idolatry. Israel was the house of God. But they turned the house of God into a house of iniquity.

They had the gospel revealed to them; the Passover, the Feasts, the Sacrifices, the Priesthood, the Temple, the Altar, the Mercy-Seat. But they wilfully rejected God's revelation. Therefore, they were sentenced to the outpouring of God's wrath. This is exactly what Peter means when he says, 'Judgment must begin at the house of God' (1 Peter 4:17). It always begins there. God always starts with his professed people, and then he moves out to those round about them. They walked with God. They talked with God. But they despised him and his Word. For this reason, the prophet says, 'God is going to send judgment' (3:3-8).

The Golden Calves

Do you remember the two golden calves that were erected by the first King Jeroboam in the cities of Bethel and Dan (1 Kings 12:28)? Israel was sent to worship there and the people called those calves Jehovah. They worshipped and bowed down before those golden images. Those two calves represented three basic evils in Israel, for which God was set in judgment against them, evils for which the judgment of God continues to be manifest today.

Those golden calves, in that they were made of gold, represented the hunger of this people for material gain. They loved wealth, and made a god of gold. Then, because they were calves, or young bullocks, they were representative of power; the god of superiority. They were also symbolic of the pagan fertility gods of the nations round about them who worshiped the bull as a sign of fertility or sexual potency. Those golden calves represented Israel's enslavement to their own sensual lusts. The calves therefore symbolized material greed, shameless pride, and sensuality. One might rightly conclude that the Holy Spirit intended Amos' prophecy for our own generation.

For these things the nation of Assyria was being raised up by God to come sweeping down from the north to carry Israel away into captivity. This word of coming wrath was given almost two hundred years before that took place. God gave Israel space to repent. They refused. That is the message of chapter 4. The lesson here is very clear. Judgment never produces repentance. Time after time the Lord sent judgment that should have awakened the people (4:6-11); but they were only hardened by it.

Call to Repentance

Yet, God ever remembers mercy, even in the midst of providential wrath and judgment. So Amos delivers a message of mercy. As God's ambassador, he calls Israel to repentance. He calls for them to turn from their idols to God. The sinner's only hope is reconciliation to God (5:4-8). But Israel continued to harden their hearts, taking comfort in their refuge of lies (5:18; 6:1). There were among them two groups, just as there are today, these groups tried to hide from God in two different ways. First there was the self-righteous and then there was the presumptuous.

The self-righteous are described in chapter 5, verse 18. 'Woe unto you that desire the day of the LORD! to what end is it for you? the day of the LORD is darkness, and not light'. These self-righteous religionists went about crying, 'Oh, isn't this a terrible day. I remember the good days when people were better, more thoughtful, more spiritual, and more devoted. But things are different now. Times are so hard. Things are so bad'. They were wringing their hands, appearing to be mourning, and going through all kinds of rituals and religious ceremonies and saying, 'Oh, there is no hope for anything. Oh, if the Lord would only come! Oh, would that the day of the Lord would come. Would that we could go home to be in heaven'. Do you ever hear people talk like that?

Then the prophet thunders, 'Woe to you that desire the day of the Lord'. He says, 'Don't you know what that day will be like? Do you have any idea what you are saying? That day will be a day of darkness and doom for you' (5:18-27).

God sees through us. He sees through our religion and our rituals. He sees our hearts. He demands truth in the inward parts, in the whole of life, in the core of our being, not mere outward conformity to religious codes. God sees through all the sham and pretence, without the slightest difficulty. He is not impressed with the 'bodily exercise' of religion. He requires 'godliness'. 'Thou desirest truth in the inward part' (Psalm 51:6).

In chapter six Amos exposes the presumptuous, the carnally secure. 'Woe to them that are at ease in Zion, and trust in the mountain of Samaria'. These people cried, 'We are not concerned about these things. Let's eat, drink and be merry for tomorrow we die. Let's have as good a time as we can and make the most of life; let's enjoy it to the full while we can'. The prophet declares, 'Woe to those who are at ease in Zion'.

The ease spoken of by God's prophet Amos is a carnal ease, a fleshly security. It is not the confidence of a person who is pardoned, but the ease of a hardened wretch who has learned to despise the death chamber. It is not the assurance of one who is on the rock, but the ease of a senseless drunk, whose house is crumbling in an earthquake, falling from its sandy foundations; but he is in such a stupor that he does not know and does not care what is happening.

C. H. Spurgeon put it like this ...

This is not the calm of a soul at peace with God, but the ease of a madman, who, because he has hidden his sin from his own eyes, thinks he has concealed it from God. It is the ease and peace of one who has grown callous, hardened, brutalized, stupid, sullen, and careless, who has begun a sleep which God grant may soon be broken, or else it will surely bring him where he shall make his bed in hell.

A Prophet Indeed

In chapter seven Amos shows himself to be a true prophet. His heart was for the people to whom he spoke. Even as he pronounced God's wrath and judgment upon the people, knowing that they fully deserved it, he interceded with God on their behalf (vv. 2-6), as Moses before him (Exodus 32:30-32) and Paul after him (Romans 9:1-3). Then, when he was accused by Amaziah of being a false prophet, he acknowledged that he had no credentials or credibility as a prophet, except the call and commission of God (vv. 10-17). 'The Lord took me as I followed the flock, and the Lord said unto me, Go, prophecy unto my people Israel'.

Five Visions

In chapters 7-9 Amos describes five visions the Lord gave him concerning Israel. The first was of a plague of locusts coming to devour the land. When he saw the terrible destruction this would bring, he asked the Lord to forgive his people and withhold the plague; and the Lord granted his petition (7:1-3).

The second vision was of a devouring fire. Again, Amos sought God's mercy to spare Israel; and the Lord again repented for this and spared the people (7:4-6).

In the third vision Amos saw the Lord standing beside a wall holding a plumbline in his hand. This was a symbol of the judgment of Israel by God's righteous law. The Lord told him plainly that he was determined to execute judgment, and that Israel would not be spared. 'I will not again pass by them any more'. Amos humbly bows to God's revelation, and makes no intercession (7:7-9).

It is at this time that Amaziah, the priest of Bethel, sent a false report to the king concerning Amos, accusing him of conspiracy against the nation. With the king's authority behind him, Amaziah ordered Amos to leave the country. In response to Amaziah, Amos stated that he had not chosen to be a prophet, but God had called him to the work, and that he had no choice but to deliver the message God had given him. The chapter ends with a bold prophecy of divine judgment against Amaziah and his family because of his obstinate opposition, and a reaffirmation of judgment upon Israel (7:10-17).

In the fourth vision in chapter eight the Lord showed Amos a basket of summer fruit. The nation was described as overripe and ready for judgment. 'The end is come upon my people'. It is in connection with this vision that Amos speaks of the worst of all judgments that God can send among a people this side of hell (8:11-12). When God shuts heaven and refuses to send his Word to a people, they have no hope.

In the fifth vision (9:1-10) Amos 'saw the Lord standing upon the altar', not in mercy but in wrath to destroy the nation. Nothing would stop him.

Mercy Promised

Immediately following this last vision, as in the other prophets, the final scene declares the ultimate salvation of God's elect (9:11-15).

'In that day will I raise up the tabernacle of David that is fallen, and close up the breaches thereof; and I will raise up his ruins, and I will build it as in the days of old: That they may possess the remnant of Edom, and of all the heathen, which are called by my name, saith the LORD that doeth this' (vv. 11-12).

These verses are quoted by James (Acts 15:15-17) as referring to the fact that God's building again the tabernacle of David was not to be a reversion to Judaism, but rather the gathering of his elect from among the Gentiles by the preaching of the gospel. What a declaration of God's saving grace Amos gives at the close of his prophecy! He declares that the Lord God will raise up the fallen, that he will raise up the ruins of his people, raise up that which we have ruined, that he will deliver his captives, that he will save his elect remnant, and that he will do all his wondrous works of grace for such undeserving sinners as we are because of his covenant promises, symbolized in the promises made to Israel of possessing the land of Canaan.

Chapter 31

Obadiah

'Jacob have I loved, but Esau have I hated'.

The book of Obadiah is the shortest book in the Old Testament, just 21 verses. It can be read in just a few minutes. At first glance, it appears to be nothing but a prophecy of doom against the ancient nation of Edom, which has long ago disappeared from history. Edom is a nation buried in the dust of the past. Yet, the fact that this little book finds its place in the book of God, and that fact alone, tells us that its message is for us (Romans 15:4).

There are thirteen men in the Old Testament named Obadiah, but there is no indication that this Obadiah is the same as any of the others. His name means 'servant of the Lord', or 'worshipper of the Lord'. Like a true servant and worshipper of God, Obadiah keeps himself in the background in utter obscurity. He tells us absolutely nothing about himself. He simply steps onto the stage of history, delivers God's message, and steps down. In fact, it may be that Obadiah, rather than being his name, was simply a penname, a pseudonym used to deliberately conceal anything at all about himself. His only purpose and intent as God's prophet was to deliver God's message. What a noble example his is to all who are responsible to speak to eternity bound sinners as God's messengers!

Outline

The outline of these twenty-one verses is very easy to follow. In verses 1-9 Obadiah declares God's judgment upon Edom. Though proud, thinking themselves secure and invincible, Edom was the object of God's determined wrath and must be destroyed. Verses 10-14 display the justice of that judgment. Edom was destroyed because of their proud and cruel treatment of God's people, Israel. In verses 15 and 16 we see the result of God's judgment upon the proud nation. The Edomites were crushed by Nebuchadnezzar and later by Cyrus, who slaughtered them by the thousands, and finally brought into oblivion by the Maccabees. By the time the Romans conquered Jerusalem, Edom was nothing but a name in history. In verses 17-21 the prophet of God speaks to Edom, the house of Esau, of the sure and certain salvation of Israel 'the house of Jacob'.

Obadiah's Message

But what is Obadiah's message to us? What is the meaning of this prophecy? What does the Spirit of God here teach us? The following few passages from the inspired volume will help to make things clear. Read Genesis 3:15; Malachi 1:2-5; Romans 9:11-18. Remember, Edom is figurative of the whole house of Esau and Israel is the whole house of Jacob. Jacob was Esau's younger brother, and the object of God's everlasting love, mercy, and grace.

Obadiah's message reveals the lesson of the longstanding opposition of the children of this world to the children of God. May God give us grace to learn it, rely upon it and expect its fulfilment. Though the seed of the serpent hates, persecutes, and constantly bruises the heel of the woman's Seed, the Seed of the woman, that is Christ and his body the Church of God's elect, shall ultimately crush the serpent's head and his seed. Let me show you seven things clearly set before us in this magnificent prophecy of Obadiah.

First, learn this and rejoice. The purpose of our God cannot be hindered, thwarted, or frustrated. Before ever they were born, the Lord God declared that Esau must ever serve Jacob, that the elder must serve the younger. It shall be so until time is no more. Moses declared that Ham must serve Shem and Japheth. God's word regarding Jacob and Esau is but a declaration of God's purpose assuring chosen, redeemed sinners that the reprobate of this world can do us no harm. They only serve the interests of our souls. Jannes and Jambres fought Moses, withstanding him to the face; but they could proceed no further (Exodus 7:11; 2 Timothy 3:8-9). Those who oppose God's people in this world, who abuse, mistreat, and persecute God's elect, cannot hurt them. They only serve us.

Second, we see in the Edomites and their history that the enmity of the seed of the serpent toward the Seed of the woman shall never cease so long as time stands.

The enmity of Edom toward Israel, the enmity of Esau against his brother Jacob began long before Obadiah came on the scene. It began while the two boys were still in their mother's womb. It is an enmity manifest throughout history. It is the enmity Cain had for Abel, the enmity of Babylon against Israel, the enmity of Herod against the incarnate Son of God, the enmity of the Judaisers against Paul, the enmity of the religious world against the Kingdom of God. It is a never ceasing, unabating, ever-increasing enmity. It is the enmity of the dragon of hell against the Woman of God's choice (Revelation 12).

What is that enmity? It is the deep-seated hatred of free grace by all who proudly presume that they can be saved by their own works, saved without God. It is their antipathy to all who are saved by grace alone, trusting Christ alone, looking to him alone for redemption, righteousness and everlasting salvation. If anyone thinks this enmity is imaginary, let him read a page or two of history, it is the testimony of scripture and the history of the church.

Third, learn this. That which destroys all who perish under the wrath of God is the self-deceiving pride of their own hearts.

'The heart is deceitful above all things, and desperately wicked: who can know it?' (Jeremiah 17:9). Obadiah declares, 'The pride of thine heart hath deceived thee, thou that dwellest in the clefts of the rock, whose habitation is high; that saith in his heart, Who shall bring me down to the ground? Though thou exalt thyself as the eagle, and though thou set thy nest among the stars, thence will I bring thee down, saith the Lord' (1:3-4).

Edom represents all those vain men and women who, like Esau, despise Christ and proudly presume they can ascend to heaven by their own will, their own works, and their own goodness. They hide themselves in what they think is an impregnable rock of morality, on a high hill of experience, and say, 'All is well. I am secure. Who shall bring me down?'

Fourth, let us be reminded once more of the far reaching influence of evil. Edom, the whole nation, followed the example of their father Esau. The whole nation followed their father straight to hell! None are ever saved by the example of others; but multitudes perish forever by the example of others. What a horrible scene of the torments of the damned in hell, as the lost child looks into the eyes of his lost parents, as the lost multitudes look into the eyes of lost preachers, and curse them forever for their evil example and damning influence!

Fifth, Obadiah goes to great length in these verses of inspiration to show us that all who suffer the wrath and judgment of God perish under the just judgment of the Almighty because of their own sins (vv. 10-17).

I cannot state emphatically enough that all things are exactly according to God's purpose. The whole world is ruled and disposed of according to God's everlasting love for Jacob and hatred of Esau (Romans 9:11-24).

Vessels of mercy are vessels of mercy and shall never be vessels of wrath. Vessels of wrath are vessels of wrath and shall never be vessels of mercy. Is that clear enough?

But I state this with equal force. Those who go to hell do so because of their own sin. Vessels of mercy are prepared by grace for glory. Vessels of wrath fit themselves for destruction. Men and women go to hell because of their own obstinate, wilful rebellion and unbelief. Esau is in hell today because he despised Christ, because he preferred the world to the Son of God, because he preferred a bowl of beans to gratify his flesh to God's eternal inheritance of grace. Edom perished for exactly the same reason. That nation perished because of its hatred of God and his people, as displayed in their conduct.

In verses 17-21 we see once more that the everlasting salvation of God's elect is a matter of absolute certainty.

'But upon mount Zion shall be deliverance, and there shall be holiness; and the house of Jacob shall possess their possessions. And the house of Jacob shall be a fire, and the house of Joseph a flame, and the house of Esau for stubble, and they shall kindle in them, and devour them; and there shall not be any remaining of the house of Esau; for the LORD hath spoken it. And they of the south shall possess the mount of Esau; and they of the plain the Philistines: and they shall possess the fields of Ephraim, and the fields of Samaria: and Benjamin shall possess Gilead. And the captivity of this host of the children of Israel shall possess that of the Canaanites, even unto Zarephath; and the captivity of Jerusalem, which is in Sepharad, shall possess the cities of the south. And saviours shall come up on mount Zion to judge the mount of Esau; and the kingdom shall be the LORD's'.

Here, Obadiah, by the Spirit of prophecy, looks beyond the range of time to that last great day when Christ shall come again in his glory. In that day holiness shall be seen everywhere. The house of Jacob will possess their God-given, divinely purchased, rightful possessions. Jacob shall be a fire and Esau shall be stubble (Psalm 137). The kingdom of this world shall become the kingdom of our God (Revelation 11:15).

Seventh, the only hope for proud sinners is him who is Jacob's Portion forever, the Lord Jesus Christ.

What is your choice? Will you follow Esau to hell, choosing that which gratifies the flesh, or will you follow Jacob, choosing Christ for your everlasting portion?

Chapter 32

Jonah

'Salvation is of the Lord!'

The book of Jonah, though it is found in the minor prophets, is not really a prophecy at all. It is an inspired autobiographical sketch of a specific period in the life of Jonah. It is a book written by Jonah as he was directed by God the Holy Spirit. The purpose of the book is to show God's providence and grace in the life of his servant Jonah, and to give us a vivid picture of our Saviour's death, burial, and resurrection.

This man Jonah was the insignificant son of an insignificant man in an insignificant place. He was the son of Amittai of Gath-hepher (2 Kings 14:25) in Galilee. Gath-hepher was a city that belonged to the tribe of Zebulon in a remote corner of Israel. But God chose Jonah as an object of his grace and ordained him to be a prophet in Israel of great usefulness.

The life of Jonah, as it is recorded in this book, is a marvellous and instructive picture of God's providence and grace in the lives of his people.

As the book of Jonah opens, Jonah is already a prophet of God, a man of faith, a servant of the Lord. But he had much to learn as we see in verses 1 and 2. – 'Now the word of the Lord came to Jonah the son of Amittai, saying, Arise, go to Nineveh, that great city, and cry against it; for their wickedness is come up before me'. Why Jonah did not want to go to Nineveh we are not specifically told until we get to chapter 4. It appears that this man of God did not want to go to Nineveh because of his racial prejudice against the Assyrians who lived there. He did not *want* God to have mercy upon Nineveh (3:10-4:3).

In verse 3 we read, 'Jonah rose up to flee unto Tarshish from the presence of the Lord'. This is where Jonah's troubles began and this is where our story begins. When Jonah made up his mind to rebel against the revealed will of God, he went down to Joppa and conveniently, 'He found a ship going to Tarshish'. He probably convinced himself that it was an act of God's providence to lead him in the path he had chosen! But read the next line. 'So he paid the fare thereof!' If you choose the rebel's path, be warned. When you get on that ship, like it or not, you have to pay the price. What a great 'fare thereof' it is!

No doubt, some of us are just like Jonah. God has spoken to us. He has revealed to us what we should do. Perhaps he has spoken to us by the gospel, calling us to follow Christ. Perhaps he has called us to a specific area of service in his kingdom. Perhaps he has called us to a specific task or responsibility for the glory of his name. But we have thus far refused to hear his voice. Are you fleeing from the Lord? God may let you flee for a while. But you will have to pay the fare thereof.

A Great Wind

We read in chapter one that 'the Lord sent out a great wind into the sea'. No sooner had the ship set sail for Tarshish than a storm arose, nearly destroying the ship. Everyone was panic-stricken. In the face of death the captain and the sailors all got very religious and began to call on their gods (v. 5). But there was one man on the ship who knew what was happening. Jonah knew that this great storm had arisen for his sake (v. 12).

Be sure you learn this lesson: Everything that comes to pass in this world comes to pass by the hand of God, and comes to pass for the sake of God's elect (1 Corinthians 3:21; 2 Corinthians 4:15; 5:18).

Jonah was determined to forsake God, but God would not allow him to forsake him. 'The foundation of God standeth sure, having this seal, the Lord knoweth them that are his.' Though many times it is true of us as it was of Jonah, we turn from him in unbelief, yet, it is a faithful saying, 'If we believe not, he abideth faithful' (2 Timothy 2:19, 13).

Though Jonah sought to flee from his responsibilities as a believer, the Lord graciously forced him to confess his faith before an unbelieving mob (vv. 8-12). He confessed, 'I am an Hebrew', a child of God's election. He told these men, 'I fear God', the one true and living God; but 'I have rebelled against my Lord'. He also told them something about the mission of mercy the Lord had sent him upon, his absolute sovereignty, and his justice. In verse ten we are told that he told them what he had done. In verse fourteen we see that they knew something about who God is.

Before the day was over, God was glorified before all who were in the ship (vv. 13-16). So great is our God that even the wrath of man praises him. He sovereignly rules all things so that even the shameful deeds of his disobedient children shall ultimately cause men to praise his holy name, both for his faithfulness and for his sovereignty.

A Willing Substitute

'Behold, a greater than Jonah is here!' The Lord Jesus tells us plainly that Jonah was a type of himself. It is Christ himself who gives us the true, full meaning and significance of Jonah's experiences. Jonah, he tells us, was a sign both to the Ninevites and to all future generations (Luke 11:29-30). In this first chapter of Jonah, we see a very clear, instructive picture of our all-glorious Christ and his great sacrifice for us.

There was a mighty, tempestuous storm raging against these mariners, threatening them with immediate death (vv. 4, 11), and typical of God's wrath. When they cast lots, to determine who must be sacrificed, the lot fell on Jonah (v. 7; Proverbs 16:33; Acts 2:23-24). The Lord Jesus Christ was delivered to death by the hands of men, by the determinate counsel and foreknowledge of God. When Jonah saw that these men were about to be slain in the storm of God's wrath, he voluntarily offered himself as a substitute sacrifice to die in their stead, to suffer the wrath of God in their place, just as our Saviour volunteered to sacrifice himself for us (v. 12; John 10:17-18). As soon as Jonah was cast into the raging sea of God's wrath and judgment, 'the sea ceased from her raging' (v. 15). As soon as the Lord Jesus had suffered all the wrath of God as our Substitute, the fury of God against us was removed forever (Romans 8:1; Galatians 3:13). In verse 16 we see that all for whom Jonah gave his life were saved from death, and worshipped God.

A Great Fish

Second, we read in chapter 1 verse 17 that 'the Lord had prepared a great fish to swallow up Jonah'. God first prepared a storm. Then he prepared a fish. We do not know what kind of fish it was. Here it is called 'a great fish'. In the New Testament it is called 'a whale' (Matthew 12:40). The word used in both places refers not to specific species, but to a huge sea creature, or sea monster (a dragon). It may have been a great whale, a great shark, or a sea creature specifically prepared by God to swallow Jonah whole without killing him, a fish in which Jonah could live for three days and three nights, and a fish that would spit him out at the appointed time.

Jonah's experience in this passage is a typical representation of the accomplishment of our redemption by Christ (Matthew 12:40). Our Lord Jesus, when he was made to be sin for us, was swallowed up in the sea of God's wrath and slain as our Substitute. As a dead man, his body was cast into the heart of the earth, the tomb of death. But three days later, the Son of God, our Redeemer, arose from the tomb victorious over death, hell, and the grave. His resurrection is the proof that he has, by the sacrifice of himself as our Substitute, put away all the sins of his people, which were imputed to him. As Jonah appeared to the Ninevites as one brought back from the dead to bring them repentance and forgiveness, so the Lord Jesus Christ is revealed in the hearts of chosen sinners as One raised from the dead to give repentance and the forgiveness of sins by the merits of his sacrifice (Acts 5:30-31; Romans 1:1-6).

Jonah's deliverance from the belly of this great fish is a picture of every believer's experience of grace (2:1-10). Again, 'a greater than Jonah is here'. The Lord Jesus is obviously portrayed here. None but the incarnate God could suffer the eternity of God's wrath in a single day. He is described as suffering the very things recorded here (Psalm 69:1-4). He cried unto the Lord, just as Jonah did here (Psalm 22). He promised, in the midst of his anguish, to praise God in the congregation (Psalm 22:25). None but Christ could pay what he vowed to the Lord (Psalm 22:25). He declared the very thing Jonah did, 'Salvation is of the Lord' (Psalm 22:28; 37:39).

Still, these verses portray every believer's experience of grace. There is much debate these days about when a person is saved. In my opinion the debate is nothing but useless strife. The question, 'When were you saved?' was never raised by any apostle of Christ and never addressed to any of his saints. But this is certain, whenever a sinner is saved by the grace of God, he is taught of God. When a man is taught of God, there are some things he experiences.

A person is saved when, with the awareness of God's just wrath upon him, he calls upon God for mercy (2:1-2; see also Psalm 107). A person is saved when, from the depths of his corruption, he looks to Christ in faith (vv. 3-7). A person is saved when he comes to know the One true and living God (v. 8; John 17:3). A person is saved when God lifts him up from the miry pit of corruption by his almighty grace (v. 6). A person is saved when from the depths of his inmost soul he acknowledges and confesses that, 'Salvation is of the Lord!' (v. 9).

Once the Lord caused the great fish to spit Jonah out, the word of the Lord came to him the second time. This time Jonah hit the ground running to go to Nineveh and preach the preaching that God told him to preach

(2:10-3:10). He made the three day trip to Nineveh in one day. It is written, 'Thy people shall be willing in the day of thy power' (Psalm 110:3).

Jonah proclaimed God's message. When God intends to be gracious to sinners he sends his Word to heal them. The whole city of Nineveh, a city with 120,000 infants (4:11) repented, reasoning like any condemned sinner should, 'Who can tell if God will turn and repent, and turn away from his fierce anger, that we perish not?' (3:9).

When sinners hear God's Word and turn to him in repentance, they obtain mercy. 'And God saw their works, that they turned from their evil way; and God repented of the evil, that he had said that he would do unto them; and he did it not' (3:10). It was not that God saw their outward works of putting on sackcloth and ashes and fasting, but their inward works, their faith in him, and repentance towards him. These inward works of repentance and faith are the fruit of his grace. They were wrought in them by God and were attended with fruits and works meet for repentance in that they forsook their former idolatry and their idolatrous course of life and refrained from it. The repentance of these men is spoken of with commendation by Christ, and as that which would rise up in judgment and condemn the men of his own earthly generation (Matthew 12:41).

Then, in chapter four we read that Jonah got mad at God for his mercy upon Nineveh and went out to sulk (4:1-5).

'But it displeased Jonah exceedingly, and he was very angry. And he prayed unto the LORD, and said, I pray thee, O LORD, was not this my saying, when I was yet in my country? Therefore I fled before unto Tarshish: for I knew that thou art a gracious God, and merciful, slow to anger, and of great kindness, and repentest thee of the evil. Therefore now, O LORD, take, I beseech thee, my life from me; for it is better for me to die than to live. Then said the LORD, Doest thou well to be angry? So Jonah went out of the city, and sat on the east side of the city, and there made him a booth, and sat under it in the shadow, till he might see what would become of the city'.

A Gourd

Here is the third thing God did for Jonah. 'The Lord God prepared a gourd and made it to come up over Jonah, that it might be a shadow over his head, to deliver him from his grief'. Here is a pouting, peevish prophet. But he is the servant of a merciful and gracious God. This gourd was prepared by God for the comfort of his servant, Jonah. As we see the hand of God in grace, let us also see the hand of God in all the daily comforts of life. Every good thing we enjoy in this world, no matter how great or small it may be, comes from the hand of our God.

There is much to be learned from this comfort, this gourd that God prepared for Jonah. God sent this comfort to his servant when he was totally undeserving of comfort. The comfort God gave, though it was only a gourd, was exactly what his child needed. The Lord sent the gourd to Jonah at the right time. God's purpose in sending the gourd was to comfort and protect his beloved servant. God's purpose was perfectly fulfilled, 'Jonah was exceeding glad of the gourd'. But all earthly comforts are only temporary. We must not get too attached to them!

A Worm

Here is the fourth thing God did for Jonah. 'God prepared a worm, and it smote the gourd that it withered' (4:7). As we see the hand of God in our comforts, let us also see the hand of God in our sorrows, bereavements, and losses.

> 'Tis God that lifts our comforts high,
> Or sinks them to the grave;
> He gives, and blessed be His name!
> He takes but what He gave.

The Sun and Wind

Here is the fifth thing. 'It came to pass, when the sun did arise, that God prepared a vehement east wind: and the sun beat upon the head of Jonah' (4:8). If we are wise, we will see the hand of God in our heaviest trials. Our greatest trials sometimes come in connection with the most insignificant things; a gourd! a worm. Trials often come one on the heels of another. A worm appears. The gourd withers. The sun burns. The hot east wind beats upon Jonah's head. Our troubles sometimes appear to be downright brutal. The trials that are hardest to bear are those in which, like this trial of Jonah, there appears to be no benefit. Our heaviest trials usually come when we think we are most secure, as Jonah did, sitting under his gourd. Our trials reveal what is really in us. Jonah's trial revealed his anger against God (v. 9).

A Useful Servant

God did all of these things for his servant Jonah, so that he might prepare Jonah to be an instrument of usefulness in his kingdom. What God did for Nineveh, he was also to do for Israel, an even more undeserving people. The prophet who would carry the message was Jonah (2 Kings 14:23-27).

'Then said the LORD, Thou hast had pity on the gourd, for the which thou hast not laboured, neither madest it grow; which came up in a night, and perished in a night: And should not I spare Nineveh, that great city, wherein are more than sixscore thousand persons that cannot discern between their right hand and their left hand; and also much cattle?' (4:10-11)

The Lord God taught Jonah about mercy and taught him to be merciful. Subsequently, this man, knowing God's mercy and being merciful, was used of God as an instrument of mercy for the deliverance of many. If ever we learn to be merciful, perhaps God will use us!

Lessons

If you choose to run from God, you are running a race you cannot win. His grace is irresistible. His will is irresistible. His teaching is irresistible. The book of Jonah prefigures the fact that it is God's purpose to bring the blessings of his grace and mercy to chosen sinners throughout the world by his Righteous Servant, the Lord Jesus Christ. This little book stands as a declaration of our unceasing responsibility to proclaim the gospel of his grace to all people.

A Question

The book of Jonah ends with a question (4:10-11). We are not told how Jonah answered the Lord, or if he answered him. Perhaps the book of Jonah ends with this question so that we might be forced to answer it for ourselves. Is it right for me to ever question what God does? Is it ever right for me to be angry with my God? Is it ever right for me to prefer my own comfort, ease, and pleasure to the souls of perishing men? Is it right for me to weep over my withered, worthless gourds, while immortal souls perish without Christ? I leave it to you to answer for yourself. For my part, my heart is smitten. I pray that the Lord God will give me grace that I may be conformed to his Son, who wept not for himself but for eternity bound sinners (Luke 19:41-42; Matthew 23:37).

Chapter 33

Micah

'Who is a God like unto Thee?'

Micah, whose name means, 'who is like God', was raised up by God to be a prophet to Israel during the reigns of Jotham, Ahaz, and Hezekiah. He was a contemporary of Isaiah and Hosea. His prophecy deals with two subjects. It is a lamentation of the woeful condition of Israel and a celebration of God's abundant mercy.

The people of God were, in Micah's time, passing through a very painful trial. The nation of Israel was plagued with the incurable wound of empty, meaningless, religious ritualism. The political leaders of the people were men who devised iniquity and worked evil. The priests were men of hire. And the prophets prophesied for personal profit. Yet, all that they did was done in the name of the Lord.

Religious hucksters were in the majority and the people followed them eagerly. With confidence, they said, 'Is not the Lord among us? None evil can come upon us' (3:11). The Word of the Lord was precious in those days. There were only a few who truly spoke as prophets of God. And very few heard them. When the Lord did send a faithful prophet to them, the vast majority of the people said, 'prophesy ye not' (2:6).

All this caused Micah great pain and much sorrow. But he was a man who knew the Lord. He had a vision of God's majesty and mercy. He had received a word from the Lord. With confident joy he spoke of the latter day glory of this gospel age, when the majesty of God and the mercy of God would be revealed in Christ the Messiah (7:7-9).

'Therefore I will look unto the LORD; I will wait for the God of my salvation: my God will hear me. Rejoice not against me, O mine enemy: when I fall, I shall arise; when I sit in darkness, the LORD shall be a light unto me. I will bear the indignation of the LORD, because I have sinned against him, until he plead my cause, and execute judgment for me: he will bring me forth to the light, and I shall behold his righteousness'.

Outline

We have an excellent outline of Micah's prophesy by the chapter divisions of the book. In chapter one the Lord God gives his witness against the nations, particularly against Samaria, the capital of Israel, the ten Northern Tribes. Because of 'the sins of the house of Israel' (v. 5). doom was a matter of certainty. The Lord God declares that he will disinherit the nation, because 'her wound is incurable' (v. 9). Let us be warned (Romans 11:21-22).

In chapter two, God's prophet tells the people plainly that the cause of the wrath coming upon them is their own sin. They rose up as enemies against God. 'Therefore, thus saith the Lord; Behold, against this family do I devise an evil, from which ye shall not remove your necks'(v. 3).

In the third chapter the Lord God exposes the self-serving princes, hireling prophets, and covetous priests as the men who had led Israel into apostasy and doom. They abhorred righteousness and perverted equity in the name of God. They brought the people they claimed to serve under the sentence of doom (vv. 9-12).

'Hear this, I pray you, ye heads of the house of Jacob, and princes of the house of Israel, that abhor judgment, and pervert all equity. They build up Zion with blood, and Jerusalem with iniquity. The heads thereof judge for reward, and the priests thereof teach for hire, and the prophets thereof divine for money: yet will they lean upon the LORD, and say, Is not the LORD among us? none evil can come upon us. Therefore shall Zion for your sake be plowed as a field, and Jerusalem shall become heaps, and the mountain of the house as the high places of the forest'.

But Micah, being a faithful man, caring as he did for the souls of men, moves rapidly from announcing God's wrath upon his enemies to the proclamation of grace and salvation to chosen sinners. In the fourth chapter, he speaks of a better Prince, a better Prophet, a better Priest and a better Kingdom. The fourth chapter speaks of the coming of Christ and the establishing of his spiritual kingdom, Mount Zion, the Church of the living God, and the gathering of sinners out of every nation into his kingdom. 'The Lord shall reign over them in Mount Zion from henceforth, even forever' (v. 7). This kingdom shall triumph and prevail over all her enemies (v. 13). The gates of hell can never prevail against it!

Chapter five begins with an announcement of our Redeemer's death at the hands of his enemies, as if to indicate that his death would be the means of Israel's deliverance and the cause of his own exaltation and glory. He who was to be born at Bethlehem (The House of Bread), who must be smitten by his enemies, shall stand in glory. 'And this man shall be the Peace' (vv. 1, 2, 5). He will both gather and save his sheep, who have been scattered 'among the flocks of goats' (margin v. 8).

In chapter six the Lord God pleads with us to remember his goodness, his wondrous works of grace, 'that ye may know the righteousness of the Lord' (v. 5), teaching us that God looks on the heart (vv. 6-8), and calls us to repentance (vv. 9-16).

In the midst of the Lord's rebuke and indignation, Micah cries, 'Woe is me!' (7:1). But the hope of the Christ's coming shines like a bright star in the dark sky in this chapter. The prophecy closes with great joy and with eager anticipation of that day when God will cast Israel's sins into the depths of the sea.

'Therefore I will look unto the LORD; I will wait for the God of my salvation: my God will hear me ... According to the days of thy coming out of the land of Egypt will I show unto him marvellous things. The nations shall see and be confounded at all their might: they shall lay their hand upon their mouth, their ears shall be deaf. They shall lick the dust like a serpent, they shall move out of their holes like worms of the earth: they shall be afraid of the LORD our God, and shall fear because of thee. Who is a God like unto thee, that pardoneth iniquity, and passeth by the transgression of the remnant of his heritage? he retaineth not his anger for ever, because he delighteth in mercy. He will turn again, he will have compassion upon us; he will subdue our iniquities; and thou wilt cast all their sins into the depths of the sea. Thou wilt perform the truth to Jacob, and the mercy to Abraham, which thou hast sworn unto our fathers from the days of old'. (vv. 7, 15-20).

Prophecies of Christ

None of the Old Testament prophets spoke more clearly than Micah of our blessed Saviour. When we read Micah's prophecy, we must not fail to see that this is a prophecy of Christ our Saviour and God's great

Discovering Christ In All The Scriptures

salvation in him. Pull out a few of these jewels, hold them up in the light, and gaze upon them with wonder.

Our Saviour is spoken of in Micah 2:13 as 'the Breaker'. 'The breaker is come up before them: they have broken up, and have passed through the gate, and are gone out by it: and their king shall pass before them, and the LORD on the head of them'. Without question, this text of scripture has specific reference, historically, to the nation of Israel. If you read chapters one and two, you will see that the Lord threatened severe, but just punishment upon them because of their relentless ungodliness, idolatry, and eagerness to follow false prophets rather than those men sent of God who spoke the Word of God plainly.

Yet, in wrath our God remembers mercy. He promised those disobedient Jews deliverance; undeserved, merciful deliverance, miraculous deliverance, deliverance which had the unmistakable stamp of divinity upon it. The entire story is a clear picture of God's free grace in Christ to his elect, the true Israel of God. Like the Jews of old, we have turned aside from our God, his Word, his way, and his worship, and gone whoring after other gods, according to our own lusts.

The Lord God, in his Word, has threatened a severe, but just and everlasting punishment to be executed upon us for our sin. Yet, in wrath, our God remembers mercy. He has promised that he shall save some of Adam's fallen race by his almighty, free grace in Christ. That One who is our Saviour and Deliverer, God's dear Son, our all glorious Christ, is here called 'The Breaker'. Christ is the Breaker and all who are saved by him are described as 'the broken up'. Blessed are those who are broken by him in mercy, because he is determined not to crush them in his wrath!

The fourth chapter of Micah describes the kingdom of Christ. The destruction of Israel does not mean that God cast off his people, whom he foreordained unto everlasting salvation (Romans 11:2). Not at all! In fact, the destruction of the physical nation of Israel and of that physical kingdom made way for Christ's more glorious spiritual and everlasting kingdom, his church.

This kingdom of grace is 'established in the top of the mountains ... exalted above all hills', in heaven itself (v. 1). This kingdom is made up of God's elect from many nations. It is in this place, Mount Zion, where our God teaches us and guides us (v. 2). The church and kingdom of God is a kingdom of peace and security. Here, and here alone, men and women live together in peace, as one, because we walk together in the name of 'the Lord our God' (vv. 3-5). This is a kingdom of poor, halting sinners, gathered by Christ, healed by Christ, and ruled by Christ, a tower for sheep, a strong hold for the daughter of Zion, the place built by our God and Saviour for his redeemed ones, whom he has delivered (vv. 6-10). Though all the nations of the earth are perpetually gathered against the church and kingdom of our God, the kingdom of our God, the church of his elect, shall prevail over Babylon. Indeed, our God has consecrated all the substance of Babylon and the whole earth to the glory of Christ, our King (vv. 11-13).

In chapter five verse 1 Micah speaks of Christ's humiliation and suffering. Our blessed Saviour came here to be smitten by the rod of his enemies, and by the sword of justice as our Substitute, that he might give to us such a kingdom of grace and glory, of righteousness and everlasting salvation as is described in chapter four.

Micah verse 2 declares our Saviour's incarnation. Here the exact place of his birth is named, 'Bethlehem'. His eternal pre-existence is declared in the words, 'He shall come forth'. He could not come forth if he did not already exist. Here is the Deity of this man Micah has been describing as the man of peace, our Saviour. He is the eternal God, 'Whose goings forth have been from of old, from everlasting'.

Then, Micah speaks of the majesty of Christ in his glorious exaltation. 'And he shall stand and feed in the strength of the LORD, in the majesty of the name of the LORD his God; and they shall abide: for now shall he be great unto the ends of the earth' (v. 4).

God's Distinguishing Greatness

Though the people were turned aside unto vanity, Micah's heart was fixed upon God's promised Deliverer. He said, 'Therefore I will look unto the Lord: I will wait for the God of my salvation: my God will hear me' (7:7). With the eye of faith fixed upon Christ, believing the promises of God, Micah's heart began to swell with joy, gratitude, praise, and expectation. Unable to contain himself, the prophet of God raises his voice in exultation, closing his prophecy with a declaration of our God's distinctive greatness as God. What is it that distinguishes the true and living God from all the imaginary god's of men? Micah tells us,

'Who is a God like unto thee, that pardoneth iniquity, and passeth by the transgression of the remnant of his heritage? he retaineth not his anger for ever, because he delighteth in mercy. He will turn again, he will have compassion upon us; he will subdue our iniquities; and thou wilt cast all their sins into the depths of the sea. Thou wilt perform the truth to Jacob, and the mercy to Abraham, which thou hast sworn unto our fathers from the days of old' (7:18-20).

Here is the thing that distinguishes our God as God 'He delighteth in mercy!' Clap your hands and rejoice before him, with joy unspeakable and full of glory. This good news is pure gospel truth. It should raise a universal shout of 'Hallelujah!' The God of heaven, the God whom we have offended, the God in whose hands we are, is a God who delights in mercy! 'Who is a God like unto thee', O Lord? Micah not only declares that God is merciful, but that he delights in mercy.

Certainly, every attribute of God gives him pleasure in its exercise. But, here, mercy is singled out by inspiration as his favourite. Though all the divine attributes are eternal, mercy was the last to be revealed. His wisdom and power are seen in the creation of the world. His wrath is seen in the damnation of Satan and the angels who fell. His justice is seen in the expulsion of Adam and Eve from the Garden when his law was broken. But in mercy he spared their lives, in mercy he promised a Redeemer, in mercy he provided a sacrifice.

C. H. Spurgeon wrote, 'You might say that, mercy is God's Benjamin, and he delights most of all in it. It is the son of his right hand. But it might also be called the son of his sorrow, for the mercy of God came to be revealed in the sorrow and death of God's well-beloved Son.'

Who is a God like unto Thee, O Lord? He is gloriously sovereign. He is infinitely just. He is perfectly holy. He is omnipotent, omniscient, omnipresent, incomprehensible, and eternal. 'He delighteth in mercy.' It is the glory of God and the pleasure of God to show mercy to sinners for Christ's sake.

In Christ, for his sake, God delights in mercy. It is his glory and pleasure to be merciful. God's mercy is active, operative, and effectual. God's mercy in Christ is gloriously effectual. Take special notice of what Micah says God will do for sinners, because 'he delighteth in mercy'.

He will pardon iniquity, because 'he delighteth in mercy'. This word 'pardoneth' means that he lifts up sin and takes it away. He lifts sin up off of us and lays it upon Christ, the true scapegoat who takes it away.

The Lord God passes by the transgression of his remnant, because 'he delighteth in mercy'. Having put away sin by the sacrifice of his Son, God passes it by, taking no notice of it, as if he did not see it. He will not impute sin to his people nor call them to account for it (Romans 4:8). Through the blood of Christ sin is covered over, atoned for, and washed away. 'Our sins are so effectually removed', wrote Spurgeon, 'that we shall not ultimately suffer any loss or damage through having sinned'. Because 'he delighteth in mercy' God positively, absolutely, freely and irreversibly forgives sin through the sin-atoning sacrifice of his dear Son.

God will not retain his just anger against his people, because 'he delighteth in mercy' (Isaiah 12:1-2). God's anger, wrath, and justice, being fully satisfied in the sufferings and death of Christ, are turned away from his people.

God Almighty will turn towards us in compassion, because 'he delighteth in mercy' (vv. 19-20). He will subdue our iniquities by the blood of Christ and by the power of his Spirit. He will cast all our sins into the depth of the sea. He will perform his covenant of mercy and truth toward us (Jeremiah 31:31-34).

'God, who is rich in mercy, for his great love wherewith he loved us, even when we were dead in sins, hath quickened us together with Christ, (by grace ye are saved)'. God, who delights in mercy, is willing to be merciful, even to all who call upon him (Ephesians 2:4, 5; Ezekiel 18:31-32; 33:11). The place to obtain mercy, the only place, is at the throne of mercy, at the feet of King Jesus, the Son of God.

Here is a lesson for gospel preachers. If God delights in mercy, let his servants proclaim his mercy. Let every word of human merit be accounted as blasphemy; and let the pulpit ring with mercy. Here is a lesson for all who profess faith in Christ. If God delights in mercy, see to it that you delight in mercy too (Matthew 6:12, 14-15; Ephesians 4:32 – 5:1). Here is a lesson for you who need mercy. If God delights in mercy, you have no reason to fear seeking his mercy. There is not one hard, forbidding word in all the Bible to a sinner coming to Christ for mercy. The door is open. The invitation is free. Come to Christ for mercy. Are you willing to have his mercy? If you are, you may! Come, then; sinner, come and welcome to Jesus.

> Lord, Thou hast won, at length I yield,
> My heart by mighty grace compelled.
> Surrenders all to Thee.
> Against Thy terrors long I strove,
> But who can stand against Thy love?
> Love conquers even me.
>
> If Thou hadst bid Thy thunders roll,
> And lightning flash to blast my soul,
> I still had stubborn been.
> But mercy has my heart subdued,
> A bleeding Saviour I have viewed,
> And now I hate my sin.

Chapter 34

Nahum

'The Lord is good'.

The mercy, love, grace, and goodness of God cannot be proclaimed too fully, believed too firmly, or extolled to highly. I rejoice to declare to men and women everywhere that, 'The Lord is good'. 'The goodness of God endureth continually' (Psalm 52:1). 'I had fainted, unless I had believed to see the goodness of the Lord in the land of the living' (Psalm 27:13). 'The earth is full of the goodness of the Lord' (Psalm 33:5). 'The goodness of God leadeth thee to repentance' (Romans 2:4). 'Oh how great is thy goodness, which thou hast laid up for them that fear thee; which thou hast wrought for them that trust in thee before the sons of men!' (Psalm 31:19).

We rejoice in the knowledge of God's infinite, matchless, goodness. But, the church of this age has a terribly perverted sense of God's goodness. There is a sense of God's goodness in the church, and in the world today that is totally unbiblical. In fact, it borders upon idolatry. It is a sense of goodness that robs the Almighty of majesty. It is a concept of divine love that denies God's veracity. It is an idea of mercy that totally denies the justice of God. The modern notion of goodness totally denies God's holiness.

Those who have the idea that God is so loving, gracious, and good that he will not punish sin have no real idea of who God is. As Charles

Spurgeon once said, 'He who does not believe that God will punish sin will not believe that he will pardon it through the blood of his Son'. If we would worship God, we must be captured by a sense and awareness of the majesty, glory, and power of the omnipotent God in his glorious holiness.

If ever there was a generation that needed to hear the message of Nahum, it is this generation. In the opening verses of Nahum's prophecy we are confronted with a striking, bold declaration of God's character. Here is the one true and living God. That God before whom sinners are compelled to bow, acknowledging his awesome, infinite majesty. This great God is 'a consuming fire'!

Nahum

Nahum's name means 'comfort' or 'consolation'. We know nothing more about him than that. We do not know who Nahum was, what kind of man he was, who his parents were, how long he lived, where he died, who his descendants were, or even if he had any descendants. All we know about this man, Nahum, is that he was a prophet of God who carried in his heart the burden of the Word of the Lord and faithfully proclaimed the message God gave him to his generation. Nahum was one of those men who faithfully served the Lord God in obscurity, without fame or recognition in this world. He was a faithful man who served a faithful God. For him that was enough. God tells us virtually nothing about Nahum; but Nahum tells us much about God.

A Message of Judgment

Nahum's message was a declaration of God's determined judgment upon Nineveh. He announces it immediately (1:1, 8). About 100 years earlier the Lord had sent his prophet Jonah to this wicked city, warning them of wrath and judgment. Upon hearing Jonah's message, the city repented, turned from their idols and the ungodly ways of idolatry to worship the Lord God. God who delights in mercy, stayed his wrath. The city was spared. However, in the years that followed, the Ninevites forsook the Lord and turned again to their idols and to the ways of cruelty and lasciviousness that idolatry always produces.

Now 'the burden of Nineveh' was laid upon Nahum's heart by God. His prophecy graphically foretells the complete desolation of that people who violently persecuted God's people. The destruction came 100 years later when God in his holiness, justice, and truth rewarded the sin of Nineveh with fierce wrath.

In chapter one the judgment determined upon Nineveh is announced. In chapter two the sentence upon Nineveh is described. God was determined to utterly and permanently destroy the great, renowned city. 'Behold, I am against thee, saith the Lord of hosts' (v. 13). 'If God be for us, who can be against us?' But when God turns against us, who can be for us? In chapter three the prophet describes the execution of God's wrath upon the city. It would not come to pass for a century; but come it would. The Lord God had bruised the city with an irrevocable stroke of justice. He declares, 'There is no healing of thy bruise; thy wound is grievous' (v. 19).

Let all be warned. To despise God's mercy is to court his wrath. The Lord God had sent Jonah to Nineveh. He had displayed his grace to that wicked city, sparing them in his mercy. But they wilfully turned aside from the revelation of his goodness. Now, the reprobate city was under the irrevocable sentence of his wrath.

Nahum's prophecy describes the utter destruction of Nineveh; and the city was so utterly destroyed that every trace of its existence was covered until 1841, when some archaeologists discovered it buried beneath the sands of time.

The Ninevites thought they were impregnable. But the Almighty raises nations up and casts nations down according to his own purpose. He has his way in the whirlwind and in the sea, in the mountains and in the hills, in heaven and in earth. When the appointed time of wrath came, the Lord God raised up a pagan army to invade and destroy the city and caused it to be buried by the overflowing of the Tigris river, which had long served as its protector.

A Message Of Consolation

Nahum's message to Nineveh was a message of wrath and judgment, wrath and judgment fully deserved. However, that is not all there is to his message.

Remember, Nahum means 'comfort' or 'consolation', and his message to God's elect is a message of comfort and consolation, a message full of instruction. Observe from chapter one how fully Nahum describes the great, glorious character of our God.

Nahum began his prophecy with a declaration of God's attributes. He does not declare all the attributes of God's Being. No man could do that. But he does give us six distinct attributes of deity, six things which are essential to and descriptive of God's holy character. Who is God? What is he like? Nahum tells us ...

'God is jealous'

With God jealousy is not a fault, but an attribute. It is right for God to be jealous because he is perfect. Any assault upon his person, resistance to his will, rebellion against his rule, or objection to his work is evil. God is jealous for his Son. Ask those who crucified him! God is jealous for his own honour and glory. Ask Moses! God is jealous for his worship and ordinances. Ask Uzza! God is jealous for his people. Ask Pharaoh! God will avenge his own elect. He will avenge the honour of his name. He will avenge himself on his enemies. 'God is jealous, and the LORD revengeth; the LORD revengeth, and is furious; the LORD will take vengeance on his adversaries, and he reserveth wrath[1] for his enemies' (1:2).

Today men talk about God's love as though his love is a fluctuating passion, like ours, and altogether isolated from his other glorious attributes. The fact that 'God is love' does not in anyway diminish the fact that 'God is jealous'. In fact, it is God's love that makes him jealous, so jealous that he is 'furious' and 'reserveth wrath for his enemies'.

'The Lord is slow to anger'

In other words, this great and terrible God whose jealousy makes him furious is also patient, forgiving, and longsuffering. God is not in a hurry to punish sinners and execute judgment upon his enemies. Judgment is his strange work. He always defers it, giving sinners space for repentance. This is mercy. God is willing to be gracious. He affords opportunity for his enemies to repent and commands them to do so (Acts 17:30; 2 Peter 3:9).

'The Lord is great in power'

He is the omnipotent, almighty God. He has all power, and can do all that he is pleased to do. Our God is a great God, because he is 'great in power'. A weak, frustrated, defeated God is as useless as a bucket without a bottom, or a well without water. What is omnipotence? Omnipotence does not mean that God can do anything. Omnipotence means he has the power and ability to do everything he has purposed to do. It is the ability and power of God to do all his pleasure (Isaiah 46:9-13), to perform all his Word (Isaiah 55:11), to accomplish all his purpose (Romans 8:28-30), and to save all his people (Romans 9:13-18). A weak god is a frustration to those who worship him, because a weak god is always frustrated. The almighty Jehovah is the comfort and stay of those who trust him.

---

[1] The word 'wrath' is not in the original text. It was added by our translators. What God reserves for his enemies is inconceivably and inexpressibly horrifying! *'God is jealous'* (Nahum 1:2).

'The Lord will not at all acquit the wicked'

That is to say, God is just. Justice and truth are the habitation of his throne. Though he is longsuffering and patient, he will punish every transgressor. God's forbearance is not an indication that he lacks either the will or the ability to punish his enemies. He is great in power. He is also just. Therefore, 'the soul that sinneth, it shall die'. God will not clear the guilty. A just God cannot clear the guilty.

'The Lord will not at all acquit the wicked'. The mysteries of Calvary are bound up in this short sentence. When a known criminal is pardoned, something is desperately wrong, either with the law that condemned him or the administration of it. For God to acquit the wicked would indicate the same flaw, either in him or in his law, unless he can do so upon the grounds of justice satisfied.

How can he be just, and yet be the Justifier of sinners? If God is just and must punish sin, how can any sinner ever be saved? Will God lay aside his justice that he might be merciful? No. He cannot. Justice is essential to his character. How then can he save us? There is only one way: substitution (Job 33:24; Proverbs 16:6; Romans 3:24-26).

If God Almighty saves a guilty sinner and forgives his sins, three things must be done. First, the sinner must be punished to the full satisfaction of justice. Second, his sins and guilt must be totally removed. Third, he must become perfectly righteous. These three things can be done only by the substitutionary work of Christ. God punished all the sins of all his elect to the full satisfaction of his justice when Christ died as our Substitute (Galatians 3:13). Then he removed them from us altogether and put them away by the sacrifice of his dear Son (Hebrews 9:26). Finally, he has imputed to us Christ's perfect righteousness in exactly the same way and to the same degree as he imputed our sins to Christ (2 Corinthians 5:21).

'The Lord hath his way in the whirlwind and in the storm'

What do those words mean? They mean that the Lord our God, who is jealous, longsuffering, omnipotent, and just, is also totally sovereign. He rules all things. 'And the clouds are the dust of his feet!' (Psalm 115:3; 135:6). In all things, at all times, with all creatures, and in all places, 'The Lord hath his way!' In creation, in providence, and in grace, 'The Lord hath his way!' We rejoice in the glorious sovereignty of our great God, knowing that God always exercises his sovereignty over all things for the redemption and salvation of his people (vv. 4-6; Isaiah 45:7, 22; 50:2; 51:10-12).

As we contemplate what the Lord God did in Nineveh, let us be reminded once more that, 'Our God is in the heavens: he hath done whatsoever he hath pleased' (Psalm 115:3). 'Whatsoever the LORD pleased, that did he in heaven, and in earth, in the seas, and all deep places' (Psalm 135:6). God did not wind up the universe, start it spinning, and then leave it to see what would happen. He is not some far away observer of history. He is the God of history. He makes history. It was God who caused the wind to blow for Jonah one day, and God who picked up the elements of nature and hurled them upon Nineveh another.

Few there are who recognize these things. When some great tragedy occurs in the world, or an epidemic sweeps over the land, or pestilence strikes, no one turns to God in repentance, because no one imagines that God would do such things. Yet he declares plainly that these things are the works of his hands. 'I form the light, and create darkness: I make peace, and create evil: I the LORD do all these things' (Isaiah 45:7).

How little we see this though it should be evident to all. It was but a change in the wind that turned the tide of the battle of Gettysburg and forever altered the course of our nation's history. 'He commandeth and raiseth the stormy wind' (Psalm 107:25). Napoleon once challenged the world and God, saying, 'The Lord is on the side of the heaviest artillery'. But that proud man with his mighty artillery was stopped in his tracks and defeated by an enormous accumulation of unexpected, tiny snowflakes! 'Fire and hail; snow and vapour; stormy wind fulfilling his word' (Psalm 148:8). A century after Nahum's prophecy God turned loose his elements, and Nineveh fell to the armies of the Medes. Judgment is God's work. When we see it, let us be wise and seek his face.

Even as the prophet describes the judgment of God, the fierce anger of his wrath, he raises a question which, when answered, carries a message of hope for sinners. 'Who can stand before his indignation? And who can abide the fierceness of his anger?' Not me! Not you! God's wrath would consume us like a snowflake in a blast furnace. But the Lord Jesus Christ, our great Substitute, stood before the indignation of almighty God and consumed his wrath for us. Do you see these attributes of God? The Lord is jealous. The Lord is longsuffering. The Lord is omnipotent. The Lord is just. The Lord is sovereign. 'The Lord is good, a strong hold in the day of trouble; and he knoweth them that trust in him' (1:7).

'The Lord is good!'

Our great God is good! Goodness is as essential to God's Being as sovereignty, justice, truth, and holiness. In fact, the very name 'God' is an abbreviation of the word 'good'. Goodness is the character of our God;

and the goodness of God gives us hope, comfort, and strength in the midst of our trials and sorrows in this world. Look at what the Holy Spirit here tells us by his servant Nahum about the goodness of our God.

'The Lord is good!' Nahum has been talking about the storm of God's wrath, the terror of his justice, the greatness of his anger, whirlwinds, shaking mountains, melting hills, and burning earth. Then, he comes to a blessed, calm, serene island of rest. 'The Lord is good'.

God is essentially good. Without goodness, he would not be God. Goodness is so much the character of God that as John Gill has observed, 'There is nothing but goodness in God, and nothing but goodness comes from him' (James 1:16-17). He permits evil, but overrules it for good (Psalm 76:10). He afflicts his children and brings many evil things upon us; but he makes the evil work for good (Romans 8:28: Proverbs 12:21; Genesis 50:20). God punishes sin with vengeance; but even that punishment of sin is good as a vindication of justice and the protection of his kingdom.

God is singularly good. He is the only good One in the universe (Matthew 19:17). 'God's goodness is the root of all goodness. Our goodness, if we have any, springs out of his goodness' says William Tyndale.

God is eternally and immutably good (Malachi 3:6). The goodness of God never varies, changes, or alters. He is good, always good, good in each of his glorious Persons. God the Father is good. God the Son is good. God the Holy Spirit is good. God is good in all his acts of grace (Ephesians 1:3-14). God is good in all his works of providence (Romans 8:28). In all that he has done, is doing, and shall hereafter do, God is good. God is infinitely, incomparably, immeasurably good. Who can measure the goodness of God? To what shall his goodness be compared? He is good beyond our highest estimation of what good is. God is good to his own elect (Psalm 23:6).

'The Lord is good!' That is a sentence worthy of constant meditation. Eternity itself will not tell out the fulness of God's goodness. Note this, all his goodness is directed toward us in Christ at all times!

A Stronghold

'The Lord is a stronghold in the day of trouble'. The only place of safety in this world is the place we find beneath the shadow of his wings (Proverbs 18:10). The Lord who is good is our stronghold, our place of refuge. He is our refuge in the day of trouble (Hebrews 6:18; 4:16).

We have our days of trouble as long as we live in this world, but notice how Nahum describes them. Everyday of trouble is 'the' day of God's appointment. Every day of trouble is temporary, it is only the 'day' of trouble (2 Corinthians 4:17-18). Whatever the 'trouble' may be, the Lord is our Stronghold in the midst of every trouble (Hebrews 4:16). A stronghold is a mighty fortress for the protection of citizens against the aggressions of enemies. It is a place of safety, of peace, of residence, and of provision.

'The Lord knoweth them that trust in him'. Do you trust in him? Do you trust his Son, his finished work, his abundant grace, his many promises, his providential rule, his unerring wisdom? Do you trust this great, mighty, good God? If you do, be of good comfort 'The Lord knoweth them that trust in him'.

That word 'knoweth' is overflowing with comfort and consolation. It means that the Lord has foreordained and predestinated them that trust in him (Romans 8:29). He everlastingly loves them that trust in him (Jeremiah 31:3). He loves us without cause, without condition, without beginning, without change, and without end. The Lord is intimately acquainted with them that trust in him (Matthew 10:30). He knows who they are, where they are, and what they need. The Lord graciously approves of and accepts them that trust in him (Ephesians 1:6). The Lord holds loving communion with them that trust in him (John 15:15). The Lord tenderly cares for them that trust in him (Isaiah 43:1-7). He is with you. He will protect you. He will provide for you. He will help you. He will keep you.

Tamar may disguise herself so that Judah does not know her. Isaac, through dimness of sight, may pass over Esau and bless Jacob. Joseph may forget, or be forgotten by his brethren. Solomon may not be able to tell whose the child is. Christ may come to his own and not be received. But 'the Lord knoweth them that trust in him'. He knows Daniel in the lion's den. He knows Job on the dunghill. He knows Peter in prison. He knows Lazarus at the rich man's gate. He knows Abel falling to the ground by his brother's wrath. He knows me. He knows you (2 Timothy 2:19).

The Lord will publicly own them that trust him (Revelation 3:5). He owns us now before the throne in heaven (1 John 2:1-2). He will own us before all worlds in the last day. Let us ever trust the goodness of God, even when we cannot see his goodness. Let us flee to and abide in our mighty Stronghold. Let us ever trust our Saviour's loving care. If the Lord who is good knows us, we want nothing else to satisfy us. He knows us eternally. He knows us perfectly. He knows us universally (Psalm 107:8, 15, 21, 31). If he who is good knows us, all is well!

Chapter 35

Habakkuk

Clinging to Christ

There is an appointed day of wrath and judgment. 'It is appointed unto men once to die, but after this the judgment' (Hebrews 9:27). The God who made us has 'appointed a day, in the which he will judge the world in righteousness by that man whom he hath ordained; whereof he hath given assurance unto all men, in that he hath raised him from the dead' (Acts 17:31).

If you do not live in conscious awareness of the fact that you must soon stand before the holy Lord God in judgment, you are living in a fantasy. You are living as a fool in a dream world, refusing to face the facts of reality. Soon, you and I must stand before that august bar of divine judgment called, 'The Great White Throne' (2 Corinthians 5:10-11; Revelation 20:11-15).

To live in unbelief, to live in contempt of and rebellion against Christ is to store up for yourself wrath against the day of wrath and the righteous judgment of God (Romans 2:5). In that day there will only be two groups of people, the just and the damned, the justified and the unjustified, the righteous and the wicked, those who are eternally saved and those who are eternally damned.

If ever you come to face that fact, if ever you come to grips with reality, you will be forced to ask some questions. You will be compelled to ask, 'How can I live before God?' 'How can I escape the wrath and judgment of God in that great day when he consumes the world in his holy terror?'

'How can I be just with God?' If you are not asking yourself such questions, you live in utter naivety, with your head in the sand. If such questions have become matters of concern to you, if you would know how to escape the righteous judgment of God and the fury of his unmitigated wrath in hell, read the book of Habakkuk.

Faith

There is a statement found in Habakkuk 2:4 that is quoted three times in the New Testament. 'The just shall live by his faith'. In Romans 1:17 the emphasis is on righteousness, the righteousness of God that we receive by faith in Christ. In Galatians 3:11 the emphasis is on faith. Paul is declaring that believers do not obtain righteousness by their own works, but by faith in Christ alone. In Hebrews 10:38 the emphasis is on life, on living by faith. The Holy Spirit there declares that those who have been made righteous, receiving the righteousness of God in Christ by faith in Christ, live throughout their days on this earth by that same faith, trusting Christ.

Habakkuk seems to have all three of these ideas in mind. He tells us that sinners obtain righteousness and life by faith in Christ and that, being made righteous, God's people live by faith in Christ. We know that that is Habakkuk's message, because he sings praise to Christ our Saviour in the prophetic song of chapter 3. 'Thou wentest forth for the salvation of thy people, even for salvation with thine anointed; thou woundedst the head out of the house of the wicked, by discovering the foundation unto the neck. Selah' (v. 13; Matthew 1:21).

The Message

In a word, Habakkuk's message is *faith*. There is only one way to live. If we would live and not die, if we would escape the wrath and judgment of God, we must live by faith, clinging to Christ. Indeed, Habakkuk's name means 'embrace' or 'cling', and his message is just that. If we would live, we must live by clinging to the Lord by faith.

In chapter 1 the prophet prays for Judah, against whom the Lord God was determined to send the Chaldeans in judgment.

In chapter 2 we see the watchman upon his watchtower, receiving God's answer to his prayer.

In chapter 3 we have Habakkuk's prayer of praise and faith, in the form of a psalm to be sung in the worship of God.

The meaning of the word 'Shigionoth' in verse 1 is doubtful. Some suggest that it means 'ignorance'. Others think it means 'stringed instrument'. Here it may be interpreted both ways. Habakkuk is here declaring, 'Though I am ignorant before him, I will bow to my God, worship him, and sing praise to him upon my stringed instruments'. His song begins with a prayer, ends with contented faith, and everything between is praise.

This is the prayer with which Habakkuk begins his song. 'O LORD, I have heard thy speech, and was afraid: O LORD, revive thy work in the midst of the years, in the midst of the years make known; in wrath remember mercy' (v. 2).

He heard God's pronunciation of wrath, and was afraid, not for himself, but for those the Lord was determined to punish. God's prophet was not unmoved by the fact that multitudes were to perish forever. He bowed to God's revealed purpose; but he was terrified at the prospect of multitudes continuing under the everlasting fury of the holy Lord God.

He prays for God's church and kingdom. He prays first for the Lord to revive, that is to preserve, his work in the midst of his judgment. Then, he prays for the Lord to make himself known in the midst of the years of darkness and desolation, in the midst of his judgment. Finally, he calls for the Lord God, in wrath, to remember mercy.

The Situation

This was Habakkuk's situation. Judah was going to be invaded by the Chaldeans and Babylonians. The invasion took place at the end of the sixth century B.C., when Jerusalem fell to Nebuchadnezzar. The Lord revealed this to his prophets long before it actually took place. He told them plainly that Judah was going to be punished for her sin, and that the instrument he would use to punish Judah would be Babylon. Unlike Joel, Zephaniah, and Amos, Habakkuk does not mention the possibility that judgment might be averted. He does not call for national repentance. It is too late for repentance. Instead, he declares the inevitable destruction of Judah and, beyond that, the doom of the Chaldeans themselves.

Yet, he declares that the only way to escape the coming wrath and judgment of God is by faith, by believing God. Though judgment is certain, he declares that those who believe shall live. Carrying the heavy, heavy burden the Lord God had put upon him, Habakkuk cries out in 1:2-4 that Judah is full of violence, strife, and contention, that the nation had utterly cast aside God's holy law. 'Therefore', he says, 'judgment proceedeth'.

In verses 5-11 the prophet faithfully declares the precise method by which the Lord God would destroy the nation. He was raising up the pagan, idolatrous, ungodly, barbarian Chaldeans, a vile, immoral, wretched people, to execute his wrath against a people who professed to be his people and appeared to be far more righteous than those who would destroy them. It was a prophecy so contrary to nature and reason, that when it came to pass the people would deny that God did it, though he had plainly told them he was going to do it (v. 5).

Assurance of Life

Then in verse 12 the prophet of God speaks with absolute confidence, assuring God's true saints, the true believers, among those who professed faith in him, that God's judgment by which he would destroy the rest would not destroy them. 'Art thou not from everlasting, O LORD my God, mine Holy One? we shall not die. O LORD, thou hast ordained them for judgment; and, O mighty God, thou hast established them for correction'.

Questions

In verses 2 and 3 the prophet cried beneath the heavy weight of his burden. 'O Lord, how long shall I cry, and thou wilt not hear! ... Why dost thou show me iniquity and cause me to behold grievance?' Then, at the end of the chapter (vv. 13-17), he asked the Lord to explain to him why he would choose to use the Chaldeans to punish Judah? His question is, 'O Lord, how is it that God who is of purer eyes than to behold iniquity, will execute wrath upon Judah by a people even worse than they?'

These were not the questions of a rebel, or a reprobate unbeliever, but the questions of a faithful man perplexed by God's providential works. We might not be honest enough to put them into verbal expressions; but they are questions that frequently disturb us too. These questions remind us of Asaph's great struggle in Psalm 73.

God's Answer

We must admit that we have struggled with the same questions. The earth is filled with glaring inequity. The wicked do seem to prosper while the righteous suffer. After raising the question, Habakkuk resolves to wait for God's answer. We would be wise to do the same, and to lay the answer to heart.

In chapter 2, Habakkuk stands upon his watchtower to await God's answer, and the Lord gave it to him in a vision. He does not tell us what he saw, but it must be assumed that the rest of his prophecy is the result of the vision God gave him. I say that because God commanded him to write out the vision and make it plain (vv. 2-3). The declaration of God's vision was first and foremost a word of instruction, reproof, and assurance to Habakkuk and to us (v. 4). Let us hear the instruction, bear the reproof, and rejoice in the assurance. 'The just shall live by his faith'.

The first thing we learn is that God is running things right on schedule (v. 3). Our time and God's time are not measured by the same clock. Israel offered sacrifices for centuries in anticipation of Christ, the coming Sacrifice by whom sin would be put away. The Jews, in unbelief, fell into idolatry and were cast off by God, because, they refused to live by faith. They stumbled over the Stumbling-Stone. Going about to establish their own righteousness, they refused to submit to the righteousness of God, never realizing that, 'Christ is the end of the law for righteousness to everyone that believeth'. 'The just shall live by his faith'. But they refused to believe and perished.

Yet, 'when the fulness of the time was come, God sent forth his Son, made of a woman, made under the law, to redeem them that were under the law' (Galatians 4:4-5). You can count on it, not one thing willed, purposed, predestined, and promised by God will fail to be accomplished in exactly the way and at the precise time God has ordained. A thousand years are as a day in God's sight. He never gets in a hurry, and he is never late.

This is God's answer to all Habakkuk's question and his answer to our own questions as well. 'The just shall live by his faith' (v. 4). As mentioned at the beginning of this study, this great statement made by God to Habakkuk is repeated three times in the New Testament. Each place describes a specific aspect of Christ's all-sufficient and infallibly effectual work on behalf of his people as our Surety and Substitute.

The first New Testament quotation follows Paul's declaration, 'For I am not ashamed of the gospel of Christ: for it is the power of God unto salvation to everyone that believeth' (Romans 1:16). Then Paul says, 'For therein is the righteousness of God revealed from faith to faith; as it is written, The just shall live by faith' (Romans 1:17).

In this first chapter of Romans, Paul is standing, as it were, upon the threshold of his great epistle on justification. In it he shows us how sinners are made righteous and just before God, not by works, but by grace. In the book of God, we are given an inspired record of his wondrous work of redemption by Christ, a record of redemption accomplished by the righteousness and blood of his darling Son. Faith believes God's witness. Faith says, 'Amen', to the testimony of God concerning his Son. In believing the record God has given concerning his Son, in believing God, we receive righteousness and eternal justification. Faith does not make us righteous. Christ did that at Calvary (Romans 4:25). Faith receives the atonement and the righteousness brought in by it (Romans 5:11). Like our brother Abel, believing God, offering God the blood of his own Son, we obtain witness that we are righteous (Hebrews 11:4).

The second quote is in Galatians 3:11. 'But that no man is justified by the law in the sight of God, it is evident; for, The just shall live by faith'. Here, Paul is saying much the same thing as he wrote in Colossians 2:6. 'As ye have received Christ Jesus the Lord, so walk ye in him'. The Galatians were being tempted by false preachers, Judaizing legalists,who told them that, having been saved by grace (justified by grace), they must now keep themselves and make themselves perfect, that they must sanctify themselves by their own works.

Paul is not confusing justification and sanctification. He is clarifying them. In the context (Galatians 3:1-10) he is clearly addressing the matter of sanctification. He is telling us that both are found in Christ, that both are received by trusting Christ, that both are works of grace received by faith. He is saying, 'If you could make yourself perfect by works, you could justify yourself by your works. But that is evidently impossible, "for the just shall live by faith!"'

In Galatians 3:11 Paul is talking about the believer's walk of life in this world. Just as we are saved by faith, we continue, day by day in our life, walk and conduct to live by faith.

We see Habakkuk's words again in Hebrews 10:38. In this context, the Holy Spirit is talking about perseverance and the assurance of faith. When the night is darkest, faith pierces the darkness and, seeing the light of God's promise and grace in Christ, refuses to quit. Faith, like Habakkuk's name implies, 'embraces and clings to Christ'.

Habakkuk tells us that judgment is coming. Every proud rebel shall be destroyed. But, even in the midst of the providential calamities of divine judgment in time, and when the great and final day of wrath shall come, those who live by faith have their eyes on One who is the Anchor of their souls, knowing that he is in his holy temple (2:14, 20). 'For the earth shall be filled with the knowledge of the glory of the LORD, as the waters cover the sea'.

Certainly, this is talking about that last day, when judgment is over and God makes all things new. It is equally certain that this is talking about this gospel age, in which the gospel of God's free, sovereign, saving, grace and glory in Christ is spread over all the earth, even as God destroys the nations by the great whore of false religion, Babylon.

Still, there is more. If you have a marginal translation, you will see that the words of verse 14 might be translated, 'the earth shall be filled by knowing the glory of the Lord'. That is to say, 'We who believe God, who live by faith, knowing the glory of God in Christ, we see the fulness of God's purpose in all things through all the earth' (Romans 8:28-39). This is exactly what our Lord declares to be the case in John 11:40.

Habakkuk's Prayer

The book of Habakkuk closes with Habakkuk's great prayer of praise and faith. He gives us a fine description of God's majesty. He declares the wondrous history of God's dealings with his people in bringing them into Canaan, which portrayed the far greater blessedness that is ours in Christ, as we behold him who is the brightness of the Father's glory (Hebrews 1:3).

Three times in this prayer Habakkuk uses the exclamation, 'Selah', a word found nowhere else in the Bible except in the Psalms. This word is a call for us to pause, be silent, and consider. Someone suggested it means, 'Listen to the divine illuming, to the divine light'. How we need this silence of soul before the Lord God in these days! Let us pause and listen to the divine light.

As it was upon Mount Sinai that the whole earth was full of the glory of God (vv. 3-4), so it is now. If only we had eyes to see it, the whole earth is full of God's praise. One day soon, all things shall show forth his praise.

Even when God marches through the earth in wrath, with his glittering sword drawn, he is riding upon his 'chariots of salvation' (v. 8), and goes forth for the salvation of his people by Christ, his anointed (vv. 12-13).

We are justified by faith; we walk by faith; we will be delivered by faith. This is the vision God gave the prophet of old. Habakkuk declares, 'God is working out his eternal purpose of grace for the salvation of his people. In wrath, he does remember mercy. He is making himself known. He is preserving his church and kingdom. Blessed be his holy name!'

Habakkuk's Faith

Knowing this, the troubled, heavy-hearted prophet closes his song and his prophecy with a marvellous declaration of settled and determined faith, bowing to the wisdom, goodness and grace of God's adorable providence, even when it appears dark and difficult (vv. 17-19).

'Although the fig tree shall not blossom, neither shall fruit be in the vines; the labour of the olive shall fail, and the fields shall yield no meat; the flock shall be cut off from the fold, and there shall be no herd in the stalls: Yet I will rejoice in the LORD, I will joy in the God of my salvation. The LORD God is my strength, and he will make my feet like hinds' feet, and he will make me to walk upon mine high places. To the chief singer on my stringed instruments'.

Chapter 36

Zephaniah

'Wait ye upon me, saith the Lord'.

There is a word of counsel from our God in the opening sentence of Zephaniah 3:8 that we cannot read, or hear, or think upon too frequently. 'Wait ye upon me, saith the Lord.' It is a word of counsel that our God graciously gives us throughout the volume of holy scripture. It is a word of counsel and instruction that summarizes the message of the prophets and apostles. If the Lord God will give us grace to heed it, this word of counsel and instruction will be of immeasurable benefit to our souls as long as we live in this world. The Prophet Zephaniah announces both the execution of judgment upon the wicked and the bestowment of mercy upon God's elect, and teaches us to wait upon the Lord to perform his word. 'Wait ye upon me, saith the Lord.'

A Prophecy of Judgment

The book of Zephaniah is a prophecy of judgment. The bulk of this prophecy is taken up with identifying the sins for which God would send his wrath upon men, and announcing the horror awaiting every rebel (1:1-3:8).

Guilt must be exposed before grace can be announced. Sinners must be convinced of their guilt, or they will never seek grace. Therefore, God's prophets pointedly identify our guilt, and convince us of the wrath and judgment of God that we deserve, before declaring God's mercy and grace. Zephaniah follows that pattern. After announcing the certainty of divine judgment, he declares the certainty of God's mercy, love, and grace for his elect, and the absolute certainty of God's salvation of them (3:9-20).

Idolatry

In Zephaniah's day the professed church and kingdom of God, the nation of Judah, was in a state of unprecedented spiritual darkness. We get some idea of the condition of the land when we read 2 Kings 22:1-20.

Idolatry was rampant throughout the land. Pagan priests and those men who were supposed to be the Lord's priests were in alliance (1:4), the priests of Baal and the priests of Jehovah formed a nice, ecumenical ministerial association and worked in perfect harmony with one another to blaspheme God and destroy the souls of men. The people of Judah, for the most part, while professing to worship God, worshipped Moloch in the name of Jehovah (v. 5). There were apostates throughout the land, people who had abandoned the worship of God altogether, and yet continued to profess faith in him, people who wore Jehovah's name when it was convenient, but never inquired after him (1:6).

Moral Decadence

As is ever the case, wherever idolatry rules, moral chaos followed. Whenever men and women abandon the worship of God, ignore his Word, and despise his law, moral degeneracy is the result. It matters not what religion they adopt, their false religion and idolatry inevitably brings them into moral degeneracy.

In chapter three, Zephaniah describes his people as a filthy, polluted, and oppressing people who refused to obey God, refused to receive correction, trusted not in the Lord, would not draw near, and would not return to their God (vv. 1-2).

Corrupt Leaders

After describing the people of the land, the prophet of God faithfully exposes the corruption of Judah's political and spiritual leaders as well. Her political leaders were self-serving men who used their power and position to line their own pockets while oppressing the people. Judah's judges he describes as 'wolves' (v. 3). Her prophets were 'light and treacherous' (v. 4). They gave no thought to the Word of God, the truth of God, or the seriousness of speaking to men in the name of God. They simply gave out their own opinions and claimed to be prophesying in the name of the Lord. That made them treacherous and dangerous men. Judah's priests polluted the house of God and did violence to, or perverted, the Word of God (v. 4).

Does all of this seem familiar? It should. Zephaniah's prophecy seems to be written by a man who is describing the very day in which we live. His words present accurately the condition of the political establishment and the professed church of our day, throughout the world. Such pertinence should not surprise us. It is because this little prophecy was written by divine inspiration. It was written for us as well as for the people of Judah in his day (Romans 15:4).

Call to Repentance

Because of the spiritual and moral chaos that was rampant throughout the land, Zephaniah declares in chapter one that the Lord God will judge the earth, that he will utterly destroy it in his wrath (vv. 2-6). Yet, God says to his prophet and to all who truly worship him, 'Hold thy peace at the presence of the Lord God' (v. 7). He tells us what the Lord will do in the day of his wrath. Then, he tells us not to fret about it or murmur against it, but to hold our peace before him. 'Wait ye upon me, saith the Lord'. The God of all the earth will do right.

He declares, 'The Lord hath prepared a sacrifice'. Let us rejoice, the Lord has prepared a Sacrifice, his own darling Son, to atone for the sins of his people. He has called sinners to be his guests, to receive his Sacrifice and all the benefits of it, all the blessings of grace and salvation by his Sacrifice.

Yet, it is this Sacrifice, Christ himself, who shall execute his wrath in the day of his wrath (v. 8). The basis of salvation is the Sacrifice; and the basis of judgment is the Sacrifice. It is impossible to think that the judgment Zephaniah describes can find its fulfilment in anything short of that day when Christ comes to take vengeance upon the ungodly and make all things new, that day when it consummates the salvation of his elect in a new heavens and a new earth (vv. 14-16; Revelation 6:16). In that day of his wrath, men and women will cry out 'to the mountains and rocks, Fall on us, and hide us from the face of him that sitteth on the throne, and from the wrath of the Lamb'.

'Seeing then that all these things shall be dissolved, what manner of persons ought ye to be in all holy conversation and godliness, Looking for and hasting unto the coming of the day of God, wherein the heavens being on fire shall be dissolved, and the elements shall melt with fervent heat? Nevertheless we, according to his promise, look for new heavens and a new earth, wherein dwelleth righteousness. Wherefore, beloved, seeing that ye look for such things, be diligent that ye may be found of him in peace, without spot, and blameless' (2 Peter 3:11-14).

Zephaniah chapter two opens with a call to repentance. The faithful prophet tells us that the only way to escape the wrath of God in that great and terrible day of his wrath is to seek the Lord and find our hiding place in him, in the Sacrifice he has prepared, before that day comes (vv. 1-3).

'Gather yourselves together, yea, gather together, O nation not desired; Before the decree bring forth, before the day pass as the chaff, before the fierce anger of the LORD come upon you, before the day of the LORD's anger come upon you. Seek ye the LORD, all ye meek of the earth, which have wrought his judgment; seek righteousness, seek meekness: it may be ye shall be hid in the day of the LORD's anger'.

Salvation Promised

Zephaniah's name means, 'Jehovah hides', or 'Jehovah has hidden', or 'Jehovah's watchman'. All three meanings are manifest in this prophecy. As Jehovah's faithful watchman, he warns of judgment and wrath, and calls us to flee the wrath to come. He also assures us of the fact that God has his hidden ones in the earth, whose sins he hides and whom he will save by his matchless grace.

He describes the sins of the nations, and exposes the sins of God's people. God's elect deserve his wrath as much as anyone else. We are as guilty as the rest of the world. What evil have other men done that we have not done in thought, if not in deed?

The nature of the reprobate is our nature. His heart is our heart. His thoughts are our thoughts. His deeds are our deeds. Yet, while God pours out his wrath upon others, he pours out his love, mercy, and grace upon his elect (1 Corinthians 4:7). In chapter three, Zephaniah shows us there is a people who shall serve the Lord God willingly, with one consent (v. 9). They will come to him trusting Christ, bringing his offering to him (v. 10). They will all confess their sins, being ashamed of their doings (v. 11). This is the Lord's remnant, the remnant of Israel, whom he will cause to trust in his name (vv. 12-13).

Therefore, the prophet calls upon redeemed sinners to sing and rejoice, even in the midst of trouble. 'Sing, O daughter of Zion; shout, O Israel; be glad and rejoice with all the heart, O daughter of Jerusalem' (v. 14). He says, 'to Jerusalem, Fear thou not: and to Zion, Let not thine hands be slack' (v. 16). In verses 15 and 17 the Prophet of God gives us nine reasons to rejoice and sing, nine reasons not to fear, nine reasons to be steadfast and immovable in the work of the Lord.

1. 'The Lord hath taken away thy judgments'

The rest of the world, by reason of sin and guilt, is under the wrath of God. But 'the Lord hath taken away thy judgments'. That is good news. Zephaniah is not describing what the Lord wants to do, hopes to do, or has tried to do, but what the Lord has done. 'The Lord hath taken away thy judgments'. By the work of his free, almighty, and sovereign grace, the Lord Jesus Christ, our great God and Saviour, has taken away our judgments.

In redemption, by the sacrifice of himself, he has taken away our sins, the cause of judgment (Hebrews 9:26; Psalm 103:12; Ephesians 1:7). In the new birth, he has taken away our spiritual death, the consequence of judgment (Colossians 1:13-14). Our great God has, by the sacrifice of his own dear Son, taken away the curse of the law, the sentence of judgment (Galatians 3:13; Romans 8:1, 32-34).

Redemption was effectually accomplished, fully and completely, for God's elect when Christ died upon the cursed tree (Galatians 3:13; Hebrews 9:12). That redemption, accomplished by Christ as our Substitute, is effectually applied to the redeemed at the appointed time of love, by God the Holy Spirit in regeneration and effectual calling, by the mighty operation of his grace, creating faith in us. Thereby Christ delivered us from the bondage of guilt (Hebrews 9:14).

2. 'He hath cast out thine enemy'

Satan came into the land of man's soul by the door of sin as an invading enemy. But Christ, our mighty Man of War, the Captain of our Salvation, has cast him out. Satan was cast out of heaven as soon as he began to oppose God's purpose of grace toward us (Ezekiel 28:14-17). The Son of God broke Satan's usurped power and dominion over the nations of the world at the cross, and in that sense, cast him out when he died as our Substitute (Genesis 3:15; John 12:31; Revelation 20). Our Saviour casts Satan out of the hearts of his people in regeneration by the power of his Spirit, so that we are no longer in bondage to and under the rule of the prince of darkness (Isaiah 49:24-25; Matthew 12:28-29). Finally, the Lord Jesus Christ will cast Satan into the pit of the damned at the last day (Revelation 20:10).

3. 'The king of Israel, even the Lord, is in the midst of thee'

The Lord Jesus Christ is the King of Israel, the King of his church. He is in the midst of us. Can you grasp that? Child of God, the Lord is with you. That ought to fill us with unspeakable joy, peace, and lasting security

(Isaiah 41:10; 43:1-5). 'Rejoice in the Lord alway: and again I say, Rejoice' (Philippians 4:4).

Christ is always near at hand. He is near to support us and to supply our needs (Philippians 4:19). He is near to assist and strengthen us. He is near to protect and defend us. When Zephaniah says, 'The Lord is in the midst of thee', his meaning is threefold: He is essentially present, because he is the omnipresent God. He is providentially present, because he is determined to do us good. He is graciously present, because he promised never to leave us nor forsake us (Hebrews 13:5).

4. 'Thou shalt not see evil anymore'

What a promise this is! 'There shall no evil happen to the just' (Proverbs 12:21). 'Say ye to the righteous, that it shall be well with him' (Isaiah 3:10). The Lord God will not turn away from you to do you good! There is no bad news after you receive the good news!

5. 'The Lord thy God in the midst of thee is mighty'

When Zephaniah was delivering this message, after saying, 'The Lord is in the midst of thee', it appears that he must have thought to himself, 'Oh, I meant to say not only that the Lord is in the midst of you, but also to say, 'The Lord thy God in the midst of thee is mighty'. I am glad he was inspired to put that in. He who is in the midst of us is the Lord Jehovah, the Being of beings, the eternal, immutable, all-sufficient God.

He is the Lord thy God. He is ours by his own covenant grace. He is Emmanuel, ours by his miraculous incarnation 'God with us!' (Matthew 1:23). He is ours by his great gift of faith (Ephesians 2:8).

He who is the Lord our God is 'mighty'. He is the Almighty God, the Omnipotent Creator, and the All-Powerful Mediator and Saviour. All power in heaven and earth has been given to that Man who is our God. Therefore, he is able to save us to the uttermost, deliver us from the hand of every enemy, keep us in the midst of every temptation, sustain us in every trial, and bring us safe into his heavenly kingdom (Isaiah 9:6; Matthew 28:18).

6. 'He will save!'

The Lord our God is not only able, but also willing to save (Micah 7:18-20). He readily undertook to save us in the covenant of grace. He came in the fulness of time to seek and to save that which was lost. He has wrought out salvation for us by his obedience unto death. He sees to it that salvation is applied to every chosen, redeemed sinner. He will come again to put us in full possession of that salvation he has accomplished for us.

He saves us freely, fully, and everlastingly. He saves from sin, Satan, the law, hell, and wrath. He will save us from every temporal and every spiritual enemy in time and to eternity. 'He will save!' Sooner or later, he will save us from all our troubles (Psalm 25:22; 34:6). 'Wait ye upon me, saith the Lord'.

7. 'He will rejoice over thee with joy'
Shall God rejoice over us? Indeed he does! He rejoices over his elect with exceeding, great, inexpressible joy. The inspired prophet seems to be searching for words to describe God's joy over his people. As a bridegroom rejoices over his bride, the Lord our God, Jesus Christ, rejoices over us, his people (Isaiah 62:3-5; 61:10). When we stand before him on that great day, he will publicly rejoice over us (Revelation 19:1-9). 'Wait ye upon me, saith the Lord'.

8. 'He will rest in his love'
The Lord Jesus Christ finds great pleasure, delight, and satisfaction in loving us and in expressing his love to his people. It is pleasing to him to love us. He solaces himself in it.

There is not a greater, fuller verbal expression of Christ's love for us in all the Bible than this, 'He will rest in his love'. He says to us, 'Thou hast ravished my heart' (Song of Solomon 4:9). O what infinite, condescending grace! God not only loves us, but he loves to love us! He is pleased that he chose us as the objects of his love! Oh, my heart, be ravished with his love! Christ's love for us is without cause, without beginning, without change, and without end (Jeremiah 31:3, John 13:1).

This phrase might be translated, 'He will be silent because of his love'. Our Lord will not upbraid us because of our sins. He will never speak a word of anger or wrath to us. He will put all of our enemies to silence as well.

As one completely overwhelmed with love for another is often speechless at the sight of the one he loves, when they have been separated for a long, long time, so Christ is speechless because of his love for us.

9. 'He will joy over thee with singing'
Again, the prophet seems to be searching for words to describe Christ's love for us. He rejoices over us with joy and joys with singing! He is telling us that God himself is delighted that we are his people, his chosen, redeemed, called ones. We are his Hephzibah, in whom he delights. We are his Beulah, to whom he is married. He wants no one else. Now, in the

light of these things, Zephaniah says to us, the church and children of God, 'Be glad and rejoice with all your heart … Fear thou not … Let not thine hands be slack' (v. 16). 'Wait ye upon me, saith the Lord' (v. 8).

'I Will'

Zephaniah concludes his prophecy with six 'I will' declarations of God himself (vv. 18-20). Read them, and rejoice.

> I will gather them that are sorrowful for the solemn assembly.
> Behold, at that time I will undo all that afflict thee.
> And I will save her that halteth, and gather her that was driven out.
> And I will get them praise and fame in every land where they have been put to shame.
> At that time will I bring you again, even in the time that I gather you.
> For I will make you a name and a praise among all people of the earth, when I turn back your captivity before your eyes, saith the LORD.
>
> Wait ye upon me, saith the Lord!

Chapter 37

Haggai

'The desire of all nations shall come'.

Haggai was an exemplary prophet. His name means, 'festive' or 'festival of the Lord'. He was sent of God, along with Zechariah and Malachi, to minister to his people after they returned from the 70 years of Babylonian captivity. Haggai was exemplary as a prophet of God because he spent no time at all talking about himself. He came as God's messenger to his people. His singular authority was, 'Thus saith the Lord'. His singular desire was the glory of God. The objects of his care were the people of God. He had to rebuke; but his rebuke was full of encouragement. He had to correct; but his correction was full of comfort. He was distinctively sent of God to stir up his people, to rouse their hearts, to inspire in them devotion and consecration to their God, his glory, and his worship.

The Background

The Jews had been captives in Babylon for 70 years, just as Jeremiah had prophesied. What a sad time those seventy years of exile and bondage were for those among the Jews who truly worshipped God. They missed the assembly of God's saints in his house. While in Babylon, they hung their harps upon willows and said, 'How can we sing the Lord's song in a strange land?' (Psalm 137:1-4).

After the 70 years were fulfilled, Daniel, who prophesied in Babylon, tells us that God graciously delivered his people from Babylon and began bringing them back into their land. They came first under Zerubbabel, who is mentioned in the opening verse of Haggai. Zerubbabel was the captain of the remnant that came back from Babylon. He was appointed Governor of Judah. When they came to Jerusalem, they found the city in ruins. The walls were broken down and the temple was utterly destroyed.

The Lord sent them back specifically to rebuild the temple, to rebuild the city, and to re-establish true worship, the worship of God in the land. They began the work immediately. The first order of business was to rebuild the temple, the house of God, in Jerusalem.

At this time, they were still under Babylonian rule. But God had given them favour with the king and they were granted permission to do the work. So they started working. Imagine the enthusiasm with which they must have commenced their work. Soon, the foundation of the temple was laid. It was much smaller than the original temple Solomon had built; but the work went rapidly. In a short time, they had a row or two of stones laid on the foundation. But something happened. They stopped working. These Jews who had returned with Ezra, some 50,000 of them, specifically to build the house of God, just quit. They did nothing for more than fifteen years. This is where Haggai comes in. He was sent of God, along with Zechariah and Malachi, to speak for God to his people (Ezra 5:1-2).

Four Messages

Haggai delivered four messages to Judah. These four messages are specifically dated by him. They cover a period of about eighteen months. But everything Haggai says in these four messages is written for our learning and admonition today (Romans 15:4). His messages call for us to 'consider' some things.

He uses the word, 'consider', four times. In Haggai 1:5 he says, 'Consider your ways', telling Judah and us to give serious thought to the way we live. In verse 7 he repeats that admonition, 'Consider your ways'. But this time he is calling for us to seriously think about our present circumstances in the providence of God, showing clearly that there is a connection between the way we live in reference to God and the things we experience in the providence of God. Then, in chapter 2:15 the prophet calls for us to consider the house of God or the worship of God, in connection with the great barrenness we have experienced. In verse 18 of chapter 2 he again calls for us to consider the house of God, and the blessedness he promises in connection with it.

Let us look at Haggai's messages as they are given in these two chapters, praying that God the Holy Spirit will inscribe upon our hearts the lessons he here teaches us.

Indifference

Haggai's first message (1:1-15) is a stern word of rebuke regarding indifference to the things of God. The house of God had been left in ruins for 15 years. Of course, the people had a very good, theologically sound reason for doing nothing. The 70 years Jeremiah had spoken of were not quite finished. The predestined date of deliverance and restoration had not yet come, and some of the Jews were still in Babylon. These fine men did not want to interfere with the sovereign purpose of God. I am not stretching things. This is exactly what they said. 'Thus speaketh the LORD of hosts, saying, This people say, The time is not come, the time that the LORD'S house should be built' (Haggai 1:2).

Being the faithful prophet he was, Haggai was not about to let them off the hook. Instead of saying, 'Oh, I understand that. I had not thought of that. I see what you're saying; and we certainly do not want anyone to think we are a bunch of Arminians'. No. Haggai sticks his finger right on the sore spot and pushes hard. 'Is it time for you, O ye, to dwell in your cieled houses, and this house lie waste?' (v. 4).

In other words, the prophet says, 'The real problem here is not that you are waiting on the Lord; but that you have other things that are of such consuming concern to you that you are indifferent to the things of God. Your love of the world has made you lukewarm toward Christ'.

He appeals to our sense of shame. God's house was in ruins, while they lived in comfortable homes. They had shamefully neglected the house of the Lord. Our Master addresses this very issue in Matthew 6:33. We ought to blush with shame any time we allow ourselves to be so influenced by concern for earthly, material things, even for what we think are necessary things, that that concern takes priority over the things of God (1 Corinthians 6:19-20).

Now, let us learn the lesson. It is impossible to ignore Christ and the interests of his kingdom and glory, it is impossible to live in indifference to the things of God and prosper. We will suffer the consequences of such behaviour. Ask Bro. Jonah. The Jews sowed much and reaped little, though they looked for and expected much. They ate, but they were not filled. They drank, but they were not satisfied. They put on clothes, but they were not warm. They received wages for their labour, but they had holes in their pockets. They gathered wood, but God's breath of judgment was upon everything. Everything they did come to nothing, because they were serving themselves, not God (Haggai 1:6, 11). They made God, his worship, and his glory secondary to their own pleasure, comfort, and earthly concerns. Haggai's message had its desired effect, and the house of God was built (1:14).

Discouragement

A month later, the work stopped again. Haggai steps up to deliver his second prophetic message (2:1-9). The people had worked hard on the temple and finished it. But the restored temple appeared to be nothing compared to the great edifice Solomon built. Some of the people remembered the former temple, and wept (Ezra 3:12). They said, 'This is nice, but it is not nearly as great and glorious as Solomon's temple'. They compared the present to the past, and said to themselves, 'We cannot reproduce what our fathers did, so let's just do nothing.' 'Who is left among you that saw this house in her first glory? and how do ye see it now? is it not in your eyes in comparison of it as nothing?' (2:3). Haggai's second prophecy had a four-part message from God for the complainers:

First, the Lord said, 'I am with you' (v. 4).

Next, the Lord graciously assures his people of his continued presence, because of his steadfast covenant (v. 5).

Third, the prophet spoke of greater things than their natural eyes could see, promising the coming of Christ and the glory that would fill his house (vv. 6-7, 9).

'For thus saith the LORD of hosts; Yet once, it is a little while, and I will shake the heavens, and the earth, and the sea, and the dry land; And I will shake all nations, and the desire of all nations shall come: and I will fill this house with glory, saith the LORD of hosts ... The glory of this latter house shall be greater than of the former, saith the LORD of hosts: and in this place will I give peace, saith the LORD of hosts'.

Certainly, this prophecy was, in measure, fulfilled when Christ came into the temple at Jerusalem as an infant. He who is the embodiment of the very glory of God was brought into the temple at Jerusalem. But the ultimate fulfilment referred not to the physical temple or to our Saviour's physical appearance in it, but to the church and temple of God that that temple represented, and to the presence and glory of the Lord in it. The glory spoken of here is the glory that shall be revealed and shall be ours in the last day, when we are made partakers of his glory.

The Holy Spirit makes this clear in Hebrews 12:25-29. 'See that ye refuse not him that speaketh. For if they escaped not who refused him that spake on earth, much more shall not we escape, if we turn away from him that speaketh from heaven: Whose voice then shook the earth: but now he hath promised, saying, Yet once more I shake not the earth only, but also heaven. And this word, Yet once more, signifieth the removing of those things that are shaken, as of things that are made, that those things which cannot be shaken may remain. Wherefore we receiving a kingdom which cannot be moved, let us have grace, whereby we may serve God acceptably with reverence and godly fear: For our God is a consuming fire'.

In Hebrews 12:28 the apostle declares that we are presently receiving this kingdom and glory of which Haggai spoke. Christ is the Desire of all nations, that One who alone is the embodiment of all those things every human heart desires (Genesis 49:10; Malachi 3:1). Only in Christ; crucified, raised from the dead, ascended into heaven, and accepted, do sinners find righteousness with God, forgiveness of all sin, and that peace of conscience that flows from a well-grounded assurance of eternal life.

Let us never despise the day of small things. The Lord our God has promised that our labour is not in vain (1 Corinthians 15:58). We can never measure, by carnal means, the success of our labours in the kingdom of our God, and should never try to do so. We should never pine for former days, as if they were more desirable for us than the present. The day in which we live and serve our God and Saviour is the very best day for us to do so. We ought to say regarding the day in which the Lord has placed us, 'This is the day which the Lord hath made; we will rejoice and be glad in it' (Psalm 118:24).

We cannot do what others do, and are not responsible to do what they do. We cannot do what our forefathers did, and are not responsible for that. We can and must do what the Lord our God has given us the means and opportunity to do; and for that we are responsible. As we put our hands to the work, our God will both sustain us in it and enable us to accomplish it.

This fact ought to cheer the hearts of all those men who labour for Christ in obscure places with little apparent success, and those small assemblies of God's saints scattered across the globe who are scorned by the world as meaningless and insignificant. No child of God and no assembly of God's saints, faithfully doing what they can for Christ, ever has reason for discouragement. If, like that redeemed sinner described in Mark 14, we do what we can for him, like her, we shall be honoured by him.

The fourth part of Haggai's second message from God is in chapter two verse 8. Here the Lord God assures us that he has in his hand everything we need to do what he would have us to do. 'The silver is mine, and the gold is mine, saith the LORD of hosts'.

Our God owns all things, and rules all things. He is both the Possessor of all things and the omnipotent 'Lord of hosts', the Ruler of all things. If only we, both individual believers and local churches, used what the Lord God has put in our hands as stewards in his house; time, talents, possessions, and opportunities, for the furtherance of the gospel, the building of his kingdom, and the glory of his name, rather than for our own gratification, we would never lack the means to do his work.

Uncleanness
Haggai's third prophetic message describes our utter inability to do anything acceptable to God because of our uncleanness (2:10-19). Apparently, many who worked feverishly in restoring the house and worship of God got the idea that they were making themselves holy by their contact with the temple. So Haggai takes us back to the law of Moses to show us that we cannot be accepted of God and cannot serve him acceptably, cannot do anything acceptable in his sight, except we be made clean (vv. 11-14).

In verses 15-17 the prophet tells us to consider the temple itself, from its very foundation. Our cleanness and acceptance with God is to be found in the person and work of Christ that was portrayed in all the sacrifices and priesthood connected with the temple. As the building of the temple was God's work alone, so our salvation, our righteousness, is God's work alone.

Again, he calls for us to consider all that was typically symbolized in the temple at Jerusalem, and keep our hearts focused on that, focused on Christ and his glory, and be assured of the blessedness found in and flowing to us from him (vv. 18-19).

There is a time to sow and a time to reap. Here we are, as it were, just planting the seed. While the seed is in the ground, no one looks for the harvest. The harvest time is future. This is our sowing time. So let us sow. Soon, we shall reap. From that day, the Lord promises his blessing. Eternity shall be for God's elect, endless blessedness in the enjoyment of God's glory in the salvation of our souls by Christ.

Coming Blessedness
Haggai's last prophetic message was about that coming blessedness that awaits God's people (vv. 20-23). He spanned the ages of time and speaks of Christ even more fully.

'And again the word of the LORD came unto Haggai in the four and twentieth day of the month, saying, Speak to Zerubbabel, governor of

Judah, saying, I will shake the heavens and the earth; And I will overthrow
the throne of kingdoms, and I will destroy the strength of the kingdoms of
the heathen; and I will overthrow the chariots, and those that ride in
them; and the horses and their riders shall come down, every one by the
sword of his brother. In that day, saith the LORD of hosts, will I take thee,
O Zerubbabel, my servant, the son of Shealtiel, saith the LORD, and will
make thee as a signet: for I have chosen thee, saith the LORD of hosts'.

Zerubbabel is set before us here as a great type of our Lord Jesus
Christ. He is the Governor of Judah and the Governor of the universe,
ruling all things for his beloved Judah (Isaiah 9:6, Judges 13:18). He is the
One who shakes heaven and earth. He overthrows and subdues kingdoms.
He is Jehovah's Servant. He is the Signet, 'the express image' (Hebrews
1:1-3) of the Father. He is Jehovah's chosen One. He is the One who
builds his house.

The words of Psalm 2 and Zechariah 4 are echoed at the conclusion of
Haggai's prophecy:

'Yet have I set my king upon my holy hill of Zion. I will declare the
decree: the LORD hath said unto me, Thou art my Son; this day have I
begotten thee. Ask of me, and I shall give thee the heathen for thine
inheritance, and the uttermost parts of the earth for thy possession' (Psalm
2:6-8).

'Then he answered and spake unto me, saying, This is the word of the
LORD unto Zerubbabel, saying, Not by might, nor by power, but by my
spirit, saith the LORD of hosts. Who art thou, O great mountain? before
Zerubbabel thou shalt become a plain: and he shall bring forth the
headstone thereof with shoutings, crying, Grace, grace unto it. Moreover
the word of the LORD came unto me, saying, The hands of Zerubbabel
have laid the foundation of this house; his hands shall also finish it; and
thou shalt know that the LORD of hosts hath sent me unto you For who
hath despised the day of small things? for they shall rejoice, and shall see
the plummet in the hand of Zerubbabel with those seven; they are the
eyes of the LORD, which run to and fro through the whole earth' (Zechariah
4:6-10).

Chapter 38

Zechariah

God Remembers

It is ever the tendency of preachers, when we think God's people are becoming indifferent to the things of God, careless in ordering their lives, and lax in the service of Christ, to sternly scold them, threaten them with the whip of the law, or bribe them with the promise of blessings. We know that God's saints are no longer under the law, but under grace. We know that the scoldings, threats, and bribes of legality have no effect upon the hearts of men. Yet, when push comes to shove, we are terribly prone to revert to the use of the law.

That ought never be the case. It is Christ crucified, grace experienced, love manifest, and mercy sure that draws our hearts after our God and Saviour. Nothing inspires devotion like devotion. Nothing promotes gratitude like grace. Nothing motivates love like love.

God the Holy Spirit taught these things to his prophet Zechariah; and Zechariah used them to inspire Israel during the days of Haggai and Ezra to zealously devote themselves to the building of God's house in Jerusalem. He spoke to Israel about the sure promises of God's grace and mercy, his presence and power, and the glory that God promised would come with Christ the Messiah. In these fourteen chapters Zechariah speaks of Christ's first advent to redeem us with his blood, to put away the iniquity of his people in one day by the sacrifice of himself (3:9), and of his glorious second advent, declaring, 'the Lord my God shall come, and all his saints with thee' (14:5).

That Day

That is what the book of Zechariah is all about: Christ our God and Saviour saving his people. Yes, this prophecy was addressed to the Jews who had returned from Babylonian captivity; but its message is to God's people in this gospel day.

The phrase, 'in that day', is used by Zechariah 20 times. He uses this phrase 16 times in the last three chapters. 'That day' of which the prophet speaks is this gospel age. It began with our Saviour's first advent and extends to the end of the world when Christ comes again. In this day ...

God pours out the Spirit of grace and supplication upon chosen sinners, granting repentance to whom he will (12:10).

There is a Fountain opened (Christ crucified) for cleansing from sin (13:1-2).

Though all the world fights against us, God's church and kingdom is perfectly safe and constantly triumphant, under his constant care and protection.

And the purpose of God shall be fully accomplished in the end of the day. God's glory in Christ shall be seen in the final defeat of all his foes and in the complete salvation of all his people (14:16-21).

Can we be sure of these things? Indeed, we can, because the whole work is his work, the work of Christ our Saviour and our God, typified in mighty Zerubbabel (4:6-7, 9). 'The hands of Zerubbabel have laid the foundation of this house; his hands shall also finish it; and thou shalt know that the LORD of hosts hath sent me unto you'.

Divisions

Zechariah's prophecy really has just two divisions. Zechariah 1:1-8:23 describe the circumstances of the people during the building of the temple at Jerusalem, the present circumstances of Judah and Israel. Chapters 9-14 speak about the future, the things God would do once the temple was finished.

Visions

The book of Zechariah begins by reminding the people that it was the sin, rebellion and unbelief of their fathers that brought them into Babylon. Wrath is the response of God's justice to sin. It is never arbitrary. Yet, in wrath our God remembers mercy. Look at the third verse of chapter one. This is a word of grace and assurance the Lord God told his prophet to tell the people. 'Therefore say thou unto them, Thus saith the LORD of hosts; Turn ye unto me, saith the LORD of hosts, and I will turn unto you, saith the LORD of hosts'. What a word of grace this is from God in heaven to sinners upon the earth! He promises that he will turn to every sinner who turns to him.

After calling the people to repentance, the Lord gave his prophet eight visions to set before his people, visions full of comfort and encouragement. Four horsemen among the myrtle trees depict Israel, God's elect, scattered among the nations, but not forgotten (1:7-11). Zechariah's name means, 'God remembers;' and he reminds us that our God ever remembers his own.

Four horns are used to portray the nations and their power; but along with these four horns the prophet describes four carpenters, skilled craftsmen, as God's agents of deliverance by whom the powers of the nations, the world, shall be broken and subdued (1:18-21). Can these represent anyone other than gospel preachers, the instruments by which he sends his word of deliverance to his people (Ephesians 4:11-16)?

Then Zechariah speaks of a man with a measuring line (2:1-13) measuring Jerusalem, the City of God, his church, assuring God's people of prosperity and glory beyond measure. This is similar to what Ezekiel describes in Ezekiel 40, and to what John describes in Revelation 11. The presence of the Lord as a wall of fire round about his people makes walls unnecessary and the vastness of the City makes them impossible.

Then we see Joshua the high priest cleansed, clothed, and crowned (3:1-5), as the angel of the Lord stood by.

In chapter 4 Zechariah describes Christ, the Light of the World, as he is displayed in his church, portrayed in the vision of the golden candlestick.

The flying scroll (5:1-4) is the Word of God by which he both rules and judges the world.

The woman with a basket ('an ephah') describes both the full measure of wickedness for which God shall judge the earth, and the limitation of it by God's decree and power (5:5-11).

In chapter 6 verses 1-8 the prophet describes four chariots and the men riding in them as four spirits of the heavens, sent from the presence of the Lord to continually patrol the earth and punish evil.

Christ

There are more direct prophecies of Christ in the book of Zechariah than in any other Old Testament book except Isaiah. Zechariah speaks of our Saviour both directly and typically.

Christ is the Man who measures his church (2:1-5). He is the only man who can. He alone knows the number of God's elect. He is 'unto her a wall of fire round about, and will be the glory in the midst of her' (v. 5; Isaiah 26:1; 9:8; Isaiah 60:19; Revelation 21:23). Christ is the Angel of the Lord who commands the salvation of his people (3:1-5; Revelation 10). Christ is the Servant of God whom he shall bring forth (3:8; Mark 10:45). Christ is called 'the BRANCH' (3:8; 6:12; also Luke 1:78 - dayspring[1]).

It is our great Redeemer who is the all-seeing Foundation Stone upon which God's church and kingdom is built (3:9; 1 Corinthians 3:10-11; 1 Peter 2:6-8). It is our all-glorious God and Saviour of whom the prophet speaks, when we read in verse 9 of chapter 3, 'I will remove the iniquity of that land in one day'. Christ our Saviour is typified in Zerubbabel (4:6-9).

The Lord Jesus Christ is our Priest upon his Throne, our Priest and King, who builds his temple, bears the glory of it, and maintains the counsel of peace for us (6:13; Hebrews 6:20-7:1).

Christ is that King who came in humility, riding upon an ass's colt (9:9-12; Matthew 21:4-5; John 12:14-16). He is just, having salvation. He speaks peace to the heathen. His dominion is from sea to sea, and from the river to the ends of the earth an everlasting dominion (John 17:2). It is by the blood of his covenant that the prisoners of hope go forth from their prison. He renders to his own double for all their sins (Isaiah 40:2).

He is the Lord our God who shall save his flock and make us stones in the crown of his glory (9:16). It is Christ who was betrayed by his own friend (11:12-13; Matthew 26:47-50; 27:9). His hands were pierced in the house of his friends (12:10; John 19:37). Christ is the Fountain opened for cleansing (13:1; Revelation 1:5).

Zechariah even presents our Saviour in his dual nature as the God-man. In chapter 6 verse 12, he is called the Man. In chapter 13 verse 7, he is called Jehovah's fellow, slain by the sword of justice in our place.

Zechariah saw Christ as the Good Shepherd whose life was given for the sheep whom he came to save (13:7).

Then God's prophet speaks of our Saviour's glorious second advent (14:4-9).

Grace

Zechariah's prophecy is full of Christ and, being full of Christ, it is full of pictures of God's saving grace in Christ.

---

[1]The word ἀνατολη, here used, and translated 'the day spring', is the same which the Septuagint uses, in Jeremiah 23:5, Zechariah 3:8, 6:12 where the Messiah is spoken of, under the name of the 'BRANCH'. Undoubtedly the Messiah Jesus, is intended here, who is the man, the branch, that has grown up out of his place; not from below, but from above.

Zechariah 3:1-5 gives us a tremendous picture of God's grace displayed in the experience of conversion. Joshua the high priest of Israel stands before us in these verses as a picture of every sinner who is chosen, redeemed, called, and converted by the grace of God in Christ. The Angel of the Lord standing by is our all-glorious Saviour and Advocate, the Lord Jesus Christ, the Son of God.

Obviously, our Saviour is not one of the angelic hosts that he created. He is called 'the Angel of the Lord', because he is Jehovah's Messenger, the Angel of the covenant. This One who is called, 'the Angel of the Lord' in verse 1, is Jehovah himself. We know that because he is called, 'the Lord' (Jehovah) in verse 2. This Man who is God, the Angel of the Lord, the Lord Jesus Christ, is our almighty Advocate and effectual Intercessor (Hebrews 7:24-27; 1 John 2:1-2).

In chapter 8 (vv. 7-13) we see a prophecy regarding the sure salvation of God's elect. The Lord God declares, 'Behold, I will save my people;' and save them he will. He promises to make himself the God of his chosen 'in truth and in righteousness' in accordance with the truthfulness of his own covenant, oath, promise and character, and in perfect righteousness by the sacrifice of Christ. He promises to make his people prosperous and to make his elect remnant possessors of all things (1 Corinthians 3:21-23), and to make them who were 'a curse among the heathen … a blessing'.

In Zechariah 9:12-16 the Lord's promise of salvation to his elect is expanded. He promises his 'prisoners of hope' that he will give them 'double' (v. 12). I take that to mean the same thing promised in the gospel message in Isaiah 40:1-2. God in Christ gives believing sinners 'double' for all their sins. He gives pardon and forgiveness; and he gives justification and righteousness. Then, he makes worthless sinners saved by almighty grace instruments of great usefulness in his hands, each one 'as the sword of a mighty man' (v. 13; 1 Corinthians 1:26-29), and promises that they shall be stones in the crown of his glory (v. 16; Isaiah 62:3; Ephesians 2:7).

In chapter 10 (vv. 6-8) Zechariah's prophecy speaks of God's saving grace as the effectual, irresistible operation of his omnipotence. The Lord promises not only to 'hiss' or whistle for them, but also to 'gather them'. Grace is not merely the hissing for, but also the gathering of God's elect. Every redeemed sinner shall be gathered into the fold of mercy.

Chapter 12 tells us how it is that lost, dead, helpless sinners who will not and cannot look to Christ in faith of their own accord are made to believe by the operation of God's grace. God pours out his Spirit upon his elect, as 'the Spirit of grace and supplications' (v. 10). When he does, Christ is revealed and the sinner looks to him in repentance and faith.

God's Church

Zechariah describes the church and kingdom of God in chapters 2 (vv. 11-13), 4 (v. 2), and 8 (v. 3). Many commentators go to great lengths to try to prove their imagined theory that God's church is not to be found in the Old Testament. Precisely for that reason, it is important to point out what should be obvious. It is certainly true that the Old Testament prophets did not clearly see the full meaning of all that they wrote by inspiration (1 Peter 1:10-12). However, Zechariah, like many others, gives an unmistakable prophetic picture of God's church, family, and kingdom being made of chosen sinners from many nations in the midst of whom the Lord dwells. These blessed people, a multitude that no man can number, out of every nation, kindred, tribe and tongue are the Lord's own peculiar portion in the earth.

God's church is his candlestick in this dark world (4:2). It is the church of God that is the instrument by which he upholds, and from which he causes to shine, the Light of the world. His church is his candlestick in the earth (Revelation 1:13). Particularly, each local assembly of blood-bought sinners, saved by his omnipotent grace, is the means by which the Lord our God maintains the light of the gospel in the world from one generation to another until the end of time (1 Timothy 3:15). His holy mountain, the mountain of the Lord of hosts, that Jerusalem which is 'a city of truth' (8:3), is 'the church of the living God, the pillar and ground of the truth'.

Antichrist

Chapters 11:16-12:9 speak of God sending an idol shepherd, the man of sin, anti-christ (2 Thessalonians 2:8), and of the opposition of all the world against his church in that great battle of Armageddon that shall rage until our King comes again. Nevertheless, the Lord God declares, 'I will defend the inhabitants of Jerusalem' (12:8).

Hell

In chapter 14 we learn something about the everlasting torments of the damned, those who have opposed our God, his Christ, his gospel, and his people.

'And this shall be the plague wherewith the LORD will smite all the people that have fought against Jerusalem; Their flesh shall consume away while they stand upon their feet, and their eyes shall consume away in their holes, and their tongue shall consume away in their mouth. And it shall come to pass in that day, that a great tumult from the LORD shall be among them; and they shall lay hold every one on the hand of his neighbour, and his hand shall rise up against the hand of his neighbour' (vv. 12-13).

Oh, what a place of darkness, woe, and agony beyond description that must be in which there is nothing but everlasting, constantly increasing hatred of men and women for one another, each blaming the other for his torment!

The Feast of Tabernacles

In chapter 14 the Lord God tells us a little bit about the glory that shall be ours when Christ comes again, and the Feast of Tabernacles, the Feast of Faith in Christ, is ours forever.

'And it shall come to pass, that every one that is left of all the nations which came against Jerusalem shall even go up from year to year to worship the King, the LORD of hosts, and to keep the feast of tabernacles. And it shall be, that whoso will not come up of all the families of the earth unto Jerusalem to worship the King, the LORD of hosts, even upon them shall be no rain. And if the family of Egypt go not up, and come not, that have no rain; there shall be the plague, wherewith the LORD will smite the heathen that come not up to keep the feast of tabernacles. This shall be the punishment of Egypt, and the punishment of all nations that come not up to keep the feast of tabernacles. In that day shall there be upon the bells of the horses, HOLINESS UNTO THE LORD; and the pots in the LORD's house shall be like the bowls before the altar. Yea, every pot in Jerusalem and in Judah shall be holiness unto the LORD of hosts: and all they that sacrifice shall come and take of them, and seethe therein: and in that day there shall be no more the Canaanite in the house of the LORD of hosts' (vv. 16-21).

God required that the feast of tabernacles be kept by the Jews in the Old Testament in remembrance of their wilderness journey, when they dwelt in tents. It typified Christ's incarnation, who was made flesh, and tabernacled among us. Spiritually, we keep this feast by faith, by trusting Christ, by believing that Jesus Christ has come in the flesh (1 John 5:1). We keep the feast now; but in heavenly glory we shall keep it perfectly, ever feeding upon our Saviour, ever rejoicing in him. When the tabernacle of God is with men, when the beast is destroyed, when Babylon is fallen, when at last we are triumphant forever over the world, the flesh, and the devil, we shall worship the King, the Lord of hosts with our brethren out of all the nations of the earth, and 'keep the feast of tabernacles!'

Child of God, read the promises of God your Saviour, and begin now to enjoy the glory that soon shall be yours in perfect fulness.

Chapter 14 tells us of heaven's glory and blessedness by telling us some things that shall not be there. When Christ comes and glory begins, there shall be no more darkness (vv. 6-7), or winter (v. 8), or thirst (v. 8), or unbelief. We will worship and keep the feast (v. 16). There will be no more sin. In that great day, every pot, every gift, every service, even the bells on the horses will say, 'Holiness unto the Lord!' And 'there shall be no more the Canaanite in the house of the Lord of hosts' (v. 21). There will be no enemy to disturb us, no foe to plot against us, no evil to drive away, and no part of the land of God's promise unpossessed!

Chapter 39

Malachi

My Messenger

Malachi was another of those prophets sent of God to speak in his name, as his voice, to the children of Israel after they returned from the long years of Babylonian captivity. The rebuilding of the temple in Jerusalem was complete, the sacrifices had resumed, and the ordinances of divine worship had, to all outward appearance, been restored.

Indifference

But things were not as they seemed on the surface. Malachi spoke for God in that period following the days of Haggai and Zechariah. It was an era that corresponded in many ways with the day in which we live. Among those who wore the name of the Lord and professed to be his people, men and women who were actively involved in religion, there was a terrible coldness and indifference toward the Lord God. Unbelief was evident. The Word of God was read in his house with regularity. The form of religion was maintained. But no one, neither the priests nor the people, seemed to believe God. They maintained a form of religion, but denied the power of God. Religion with these people was nothing but a ritual, an outward exercise. Furthermore, the way they performed their religious duties demonstrated that they were a people who drew near to the Lord with their lips, but their hearts were far from him. In Malachi's day, as in the religious world today, for the most part the people who professed to be worshippers of God were 'lovers of pleasures more than lovers of God, having a form of godliness, but denying the power of it' (2 Timothy 3:4-5).

God's Messenger

Malachi was just the man for the hour. He steps in at just the right time as God's messenger. In fact, that is what his name means; and that is what he was, 'God's messenger'. We know nothing else about him. He was a man sent of God with God's message for his people in his day.

Unique book

The book of Malachi is unique in three specific ways. First, Malachi brings the Old Testament to a conclusion. His was God's last word to his people for four hundred years. For more than four hundred years the heavens would be silent until John the Baptist appeared as the voice of one crying in the wilderness, 'prepare ye the way of the Lord'. God's last word in the Old Testament was a call to repentance; and his first word in the New Testament was the same. 'Repent, for the kingdom of heaven is at hand'.

Second, unlike other prophets, Malachi's message was delivered as a dialogue. Malachi was not like the dialogue preachers of our day. His dialogue was not a dialogue between himself and those who heard him. God's prophets are never sent to carry on a dialogue with men. They are sent to deliver a message from God to men. Malachi simply presents his message in the powerful, authoritative form of a dialogue. He asked a series of questions, and he answered them. Twelve times in the first three chapters of his prophecy, he says, 'Ye say', and shows how that what the people said was in direct contrast with what God says in his Word.

The third unique quality of this prophecy is the fact that almost the entire prophecy is written as the direct word of God. Gareth Crossley points out, 'Of the fifty-five verses in this book, forty-seven are spoken by God, the highest proportion of all the prophets'.

Distinguishing Love

Malachi's prophecy begins with a declaration of God's distinguishing love and grace to his elect, as it is set forth in the scriptures (1:1-5). Yes, God's love is special, distinct, distinguishing love. He loves his elect, his Jacob. Everything he does is for his elect, for their eternal salvation and everlasting good. Esau exists only because of God's love for Jacob. The reprobate exist only to serve God's purpose of grace toward his elect.

That is exactly the meaning the Holy Spirit gives to this passage in Romans 9:11-26. Let every redeemed sinner ever remember that we owe everything we have and shall have in Christ to God's distinguishing mercy, love, and grace bestowed upon us in Christ from eternity (Jeremiah 31:3; Romans 9:15-18; 1 Corinthians 4:7).

The prophecy of Malachi was given shortly after the time of Nehemiah. Read the book of Nehemiah and you will find the setting of this prophecy and this threefold description of the corruption in Israel:

> The priesthood was defiled (Nehemiah 13:7-9, 29; Malachi 3:8), and their influence permeated the people.
>
> The children of Israel had formed an idolatrous alliance with the heathen nations around them (Nehemiah 13:23-27; Malachi 2:10-16), which resulted in mixed marriages, a mixed language, and a disregard for God's law.
>
> The support of the house of God was neglected (Nehemiah 13:10-12; Malachi 3:10).

The Levites who served in the house of God were not given their inheritance in Israel as God required. These men and their families were to be supported by the offerings and tithes of the people, so that they could give themselves to the service of the house of God. But they were working in the fields to provide for themselves, and the service of God's house was neglected.

'Even so hath the Lord ordained that they which preach the gospel should live of the gospel' (1 Corinthians 9:14). One of the great reasons why those who preach the gospel are to live by the gospel, being supported in their livelihood by the generosity of God's people, is that the Word of God and the preaching of the gospel be not neglected. When those who are responsible for the ministry of the gospel neglect prayer and study, those to whom they preach suffer.

It was at this time in these deplorable conditions that God raised up Malachi. He was not a tea-sipping socialiser. Malachi was a prophet, God's messenger. Everyone thought the prophet was old-fashioned, out-of-step with the times, and a troublemaker. They were right. Prophets are always old-fashioned, out-of-step with the times, and troublemakers for those who despise God and his Word. Yet, the faithful servant of God, like Malachi, cannot be silenced. He will, like Malachi, stick his finger directly in the middle of the sore spot in the hearts of men and press hard, forcing those who hear him to know their sin.

Seven Questions

Perhaps the saddest part of the story of Malachi is that the people were not aware of their awful condition. They were insulted by Malachi's message. This is demonstrated by seven points of dialogue between the Lord God and those who claimed to be his people.

1. 'Wherein hast thou loved us?' (1:2)

Israel's insolence in asking this question is shocking, until we are forced to acknowledge that we who are the objects of God's great love often think of God's love towards us with the same insolence (Psalm 73:2-3, 13-14). Sometimes we are so blind that we fail to see the tokens of God's amazing grace and special love for us.

'I have loved you, saith the LORD. Yet ye say, Wherein hast thou loved us? Was not Esau Jacob's brother? saith the LORD: yet I loved Jacob, And I hated Esau, and laid his mountains and his heritage waste for the dragons of the wilderness. Whereas Edom saith, We are impoverished, but we will return and build the desolate places; thus saith the LORD of hosts, They shall build, but I will throw down; and they shall call them, The border of wickedness, and, The people against whom the LORD hath indignation for ever. And your eyes shall see, and ye shall say, The LORD will be magnified from the border of Israel' (Malachi 1:2-5).

Oh, what a great lover our God is to us! The Lord God has, throughout history, protected, cared for, and provided for us, destroying our enemies on every side, because he is determined to magnify himself from upon the border of Israel, and determined to make us see and know his glory in saving us.

2. 'Wherein have we despised thy name?' (1:6)

Next, the Lord reminded Israel that a son honours his father and a servant honours his master, but they had no fear of him in their hearts. Is that not the case with many today? Is it true of you? Of me? Let us be honest. We profess that we belong to Christ, that we believe God, but where is his honour?

As I read Malachi 1:7-14, I blush with shame. How often I offer to God my Saviour that which is polluted, and lame, and sick, and worthless! David said, 'I will not sacrifice to the Lord that which doth cost me nothing'. But we have polluted our God by our demonstrative irreverence and indifference toward him. Have we not? Does that sting? Perhaps you ask, 'Wherein have we polluted thee?' That is exactly what these people did. Look at verse 7. 'Ye offer polluted bread upon mine altar; and ye say,

Wherein have we polluted thee? In that ye say, The table of the LORD is contemptible'.

3. 'Wherein have we polluted thee?'

They offered animals that were lame and sick and blind for sacrifice. They offered the most contemptible things to God and called it sacrificing, worshipping, and honouring God! No earthly ruler would tolerate such action. Men would not even treat their employer like Israel treated God, like we treat him. How often I offer to God my Saviour that which is polluted, and lame, and sick, and worthless! How much better he deserves than I give! I am tired of giving God my leftovers! Are you not? I know this. He is tired of it; and he refuses to accept such 'sacrifices!' May he graciously teach us to give him our best, the best of our time, the best of our labour, the best of our talents, and the best of our gifts. Let us determine with David, 'I will not sacrifice to the Lord that which doth cost me nothing'. I say with Malachi (1:9), 'I pray you, beseech God that he may be gracious unto us'.

Now, read chapter 2, verse 17. 'Ye have wearied the LORD with your words. Yet ye say, Wherein have we wearied him? When ye say, Every one that doeth evil is good in the sight of the LORD, and he delighteth in them; or, Where is the God of judgment?'

4. 'Wherein have we wearied him?'

Note the context of this question. The priests, who were supposed to keep knowledge, seek the word of God at his mouth, and serve as messengers of the Lord of hosts, departed out of the way, caused the people to stumble at God's law, corrupted his covenant, and led the people to deal treacherously with the Lord (vv. 7-11).

Remember, Malachi was a prophet, God's messenger. He did not speak in vague terms that might be interpreted in any way men might choose. There was no misunderstanding this man. He specifically identifies the evil into which Israel's religious leaders led them.

First, the priests led the people to profane God's holiness, that he loves, by wedding themselves to the daughters of strange gods (v. 11). They profaned God's altar, the place where his holiness was displayed in the sacrifices he required. By wedding themselves to the daughters of strange gods, they said, 'The satisfaction of justice is not really necessary. Christ's substitutionary atonement is not the only way sinners can come to God. Grace is good; but grace is not essential. As long as you are sincere, come to God any way you want to, and he will receive you'. The priests led the people in the way of Cain, ran greedily after the error of Balaam, and the gainsaying of Korah.

Second, the worship of God had become nothing more than superstitious froth, sentimentalism, and emotionalism. 'And this have ye done again, covering the altar of the LORD with tears, with weeping, and with crying out, insomuch that he regardeth not the offering any more, or receiveth it with good will at your hand' (v. 13).

Malachi's third charge proved that these people were mere hypocrites, pretending to worship God, while living according to their own brute lusts. They utterly disregarded the word of God and their moral responsibilities before him, as was manifest in their disregard for marriage (vv. 14-16).

Marriage

I know that some who read these words are divorced, and some are divorced and remarried. For some, your circumstances are not of your choosing, but what another forced upon you. For some, the whole thing took place before God saved you. For others, it was a matter of utter disregard for the glory of God on your part.

I preface my next comments with this word. It needs to be understood by all. That which is past is past. Leave it there. You cannot correct the past. If Christ has forgiven your sin, it is forgiven. The people of God ought not to hold it over your head.

Be sure you understand this, too. There is no such thing as a biblical divorce. Marriage is for life. And there is no such thing as a divorce that is 'best' for all involved, or 'best' for the children. Hear what God says.

'Yet ye say, Wherefore? Because the LORD hath been witness between thee and the wife of thy youth, against whom thou hast dealt treacherously: yet is she thy companion, and the wife of thy covenant. And did not he make one? Yet had he the residue of the spirit. And wherefore one? That he might seek a godly seed. Therefore take heed to your spirit, and let none deal treacherously against the wife of his youth. For the LORD, the God of Israel, saith that he hateth putting away: for one covereth violence with his garment, saith the LORD of hosts: therefore take heed to your spirit, that ye deal not treacherously' (Malachi 2:14-16).

The marriage vow I took 35 years ago was not simply a nice phrase repeated before men, but a vow made before my God. The covenant I entered into on that day was not just a marriage covenant with my wife, but a covenant made with my God. Anyone who takes such things lightly is a fool. I hear people offer many excuses for abandoning their families. They are all just excuses for rebellion and irresponsibility.

Some say, 'I'm just not happy any more'. The fact is our happiness has absolutely nothing to do with our responsibility. Others seek to excuse their behaviour by declaring, 'I just don't love him (or her) any more'. Most of the time that means, 'I have found someone else to love'. But, even if that is not the case, the excuse is lame. It is a man's responsibility to love his wife and a woman's responsibility to reverence her husband. Frequently, people try to lay the blame for their own behaviour on their husband or wife, saying, 'He (or she) is not the kind of husband (or wife) he (or she) ought to be'. Again, the excuse is lame. My responsibility as a husband to my wife has nothing to do with the kind of wife she is. My wife's responsibility as my wife has nothing to do with the kind of husband I am.

Multitudes obtain divorces upon the grounds of 'incompatibility', declaring, 'We are not compatible with one another'. That may be true, but it is far better to live incompatibly with a man or woman than to live incompatibly with God!

I repeat, 'Marriage is for life'. Malachi declares that God made Adam 'one', that is one wife, and 'he hateth putting away'. The Lord God made Adam one wife, made Adam and Eve one before him, and instituted the union of one man and one woman in marriage for the moral preservation of humanity (1 Corinthians 7:14). For any to dissolve that union is to 'deal treacherously' with their husband or wife, to 'deal treacherously' with their children, to 'deal treacherously' with society, and (above all) to 'deal treacherously' with the Lord our God.

In verse 17, the faithful prophet declares that the religion of such people is nothing but lip service, and that it is a weariness to God. 'Ye have wearied the LORD with your words. Yet ye say, Wherein have we wearied him? When ye say, Every one that doeth evil is good in the sight of the LORD, and he delighteth in them; or, Where is the God of judgment?' When men and women abandon the authority of God, despise his law, and disregard his Word, there is no standard by which to live. When everyone does that which is right in his own eyes, they call evil good and good evil, and justice is gone.

Christ

But blessed be our God, he will never abandon his own. Look at chapter 3. Here we see our Saviour, in whom alone we have hope, by whose grace we are saved and kept. Christ is our all-glorious Substitute, in whom God has established his covenant, and in whom he delights (v. 1). He sits as a refiner and purifier, and he will purify all his own (vv. 2-3).

Our sacrifices are made acceptable and pleasant to our God in and by our Substitute (v. 4; 1 Peter 2:5). He is the Lord our God who changes not; and 'he hateth putting away'. Therefore we are not consumed (v. 6).

5. 'Wherein shall we return?' (3:7)

'Even from the days of your fathers ye are gone away from mine ordinances, and have not kept them. Return unto me, and I will return unto you, saith the LORD of hosts. But ye said, Wherein shall we return?' Their attitude suggests that they did not even know they had strayed from the Lord. They actually thought they were doing God a service.

6. 'Wherein have we robbed thee?' (3:8)

'Will a man rob God? Yet ye have robbed me. But ye say, Wherein have we robbed thee? In tithes and offerings'. 'Will a man rob God?' It is almost as if they respond, 'Preposterous! A man will not even rob a fellow man'. But God said, 'Ye have robbed me' in tithes and offerings.

In Malachi's day the people of Israel robbed God of his divine honour in their half-hearted worship. Therefore, it is not surprising to learn that they robbed him in tithes and offerings. The tithe was one tenth of a person's income. It was devoted to God, to his worship and service, by the requirement of the law in the Old Testament for the maintenance of the tabernacle and temple and for the livelihood of the priestly families (Leviticus 27:30-32; Deuteronomy 14:22-26; Numbers 18:21-32). Even before the law was given requiring it, Abraham and Jacob voluntarily tithed as a response to God's goodness, acknowledging that they belonged to him and owed all to him (Genesis 14:20; 28:22).

As a display of repentance, the Lord calls for Israel to bring their tithes into the storehouse (the temple), and promises to pour out his blessing upon those who honoured him in such an act of worship (vv. 9-12). It is his promise that he will honour those who honour him (1 Samuel 2:30; Proverbs 3:9-10).

The tithe is mentioned only eight times in the New Testament (Matthew 23:23; Luke 11:42; 18:12; Hebrews 7:5, 6, 8, 9). In each place the passage refers to the Old Testament practice. In the New Testament that law is never applied to believers in this gospel age, not even once, because we are not under the law but under grace, and grace has nothing to do with law. The gospel teaches believers to give generously and willingly, both for the support of the poor, particularly poor brethren of the household of faith, and for the support to the gospel ministry (Acts 2:44-45; 4:32-37; 2 Corinthians 9:6-8).

The example we are to follow for such free generosity is Christ himself. As he proved the sincerity of his love for us by freely giving himself to redeem us, we prove the sincerity of our love for him by giving in his name (2 Corinthians 8:7-9).

The Old Testament tithe was, in principle, an act of faith. The tithe was given as the first fruits. As such, it declared that the tither trusted God for the full harvest. The gift of the tithe asserted that the tither acknowledged that he and all he possessed was God's property. Our gifts in this gospel age express the same thing. By honouring the Lord God with our gifts, we express the same faith, acknowledging that all we are belongs to our God and that all we possess we possess as stewards, into whose hands our Master has entrusted that which he would have us use for his glory, his people, and his gospel. Let us be faithful stewards, honour God our Master and Saviour in all things (1 Corinthians 16:1-3; 2 Corinthians 8:1-9:15; Matthew 6:24).

The promise is still true, 'Them that honour me I will honour' (1 Samuel 2:30; Galatians 6:6-10). A. M. Hodgkin wrote,

> The tithe was the outward recognition that everything belonged to God. We are to bring him our whole selves, body, soul and spirit, all that we have and all that we are, all that we know about in our lives, and all that we do not know about yet. If we thus honestly keep nothing back from him, we may be certain that he will accept us and will open the windows of heaven, and pour us out such a blessing that there shall not be room enough to receive it, but it shall flow out to all around. 'All nations shall call you blessed, for ye shall be a delightsome land, saith the Lord of hosts'.

7. 'What have we spoken so much against thee?' (3:13)

'Your words have been stout against me, saith the LORD. Yet ye say, What have we spoken so much against thee? Ye have said, It is vain to serve God: and what profit is it that we have kept his ordinance, and that we have walked mournfully before the LORD of hosts?' (vv. 13-14).

The context in verse 14 indicates that they had spoken against the Lord in both word and action. Though they had kept up their religious ceremonies, they did not worship God in their hearts. All the while, despite their protests, they were bringing torn, lame animals for sacrifice. They were trying to outdo each other in making money, procuring divorces, and indulging their lusts.

The Faithful Remnant

In the midst of all these people with an empty profession of faith there was a faithful remnant that feared God. They 'spoke often one to another; and the Lord hearkened, and heard it, and a book of remembrance was written before him for them that feared the Lord, and that thought upon his name' (3:16).

Then Malachi leaped the centuries and saw the time when men shall be rewarded. A remnant of Israel, the 'hidden treasure' of Matthew 13, God's elect, will experience the fulfilment of Jehovah's words: 'And they shall be mine, saith the Lord of hosts, in that day when I make up my jewels; and I will spare them, as a man spareth his own son that serveth him' (3:17).

The Day

Chapter 4 speaks of that day of Christ's coming when the proud and the wicked shall be like stubble. But to those who fear his name, the appearing of Christ will be the 'Sun of righteousness' (v. 2), arising with healing in his wings.

Thus the Old Testament canon is brought to a close. In every book, the person and work of the Lord Jesus is spoken of, pointing forward to his incarnation, his righteous life, his sacrificial death for our sins, his victorious resurrection, and his glorious return to defeat Satan, to purge the world of evil. We have seen that One of whom it is written, 'It pleased the Father that in him should all fulness dwell' (Colossians 1:19). In these thirty-nine books of inspiration 'We have found him, of whom Moses in the law, and the prophets, did write, Jesus of Nazareth, the son of Joseph'. (John 1:45).

The New Testament

Chapter 40

Matthew

Christ the King

I cannot stress this fact often enough or forcefully enough. The Bible, the Word of God, is in its entirety a book about Christ. It is a Him book. It is all about Him who loved us and gave himself for us. I do not mean by that that the Bible is a Christ centred book. I do not mean that Christ is the primary aspect of divine revelation in these pages. I mean that Christ is the message of holy scripture.

This is exactly what God the Holy Spirit tells us in Luke 24:27. Our Saviour said to those two disciples on the Emmaus road, 'O fools and slow of heart to believe all that the prophets have spoken' (v. 25). Then, we read in verse 27, 'And beginning at Moses and all the prophets, he expounded unto them in all the scriptures the things concerning himself'.

The message of this book is Jesus Christ and him crucified. This book is not a book about history, or a book about morality, or a book about religious dogma. This is a book about Christ and redemption by his blood. That is precisely what the apostle Peter tells us in Acts 10:43. The apostle Paul states exactly the same thing, declaring that the one message he preached, everywhere to all people, was Jesus Christ and him crucified. This message, he declares, is 'all the counsel of God', the whole of divine revelation.

In 1 Corinthians 2:1-2, Paul writes 'And I, brethren, when I came to you, came not with excellency of speech or of wisdom, declaring unto you the testimony of God. For I determined not to know any thing among you, save Jesus Christ, and him crucified'. Now, look at Acts 20. Paul is about to leave his brethren at Ephesus, never to see them again. They urged him not to go to Jerusalem for fear that the Jews would kill him. Yet he declares, 'I go bound in the spirit unto Jerusalem ... that I might finish my course with joy, and the ministry which I have received of the Lord Jesus'. Then he tells us exactly what his course and ministry was, which he had received from the Saviour. It was 'to testify the gospel of the grace of God' (Acts 20:22-24). Now, look at verses 26 and 27. Here Paul defines what it is to preach the gospel. 'Wherefore I take you to record this day, that I am pure from the blood of all men. For I have not shunned to declare unto you all the counsel of God'.

The book of God is a book about Christ. In the Old Testament, the law, the prophets, and the Psalms declare, 'Someone is coming'. When we open the book of Matthew, that blessed Someone steps onto the stage of history and identifies himself as the incarnate God, our Saviour (Matthew 1:18-23).

One Object of Faith

The Old Testament saints believed God just as we do, trusting Christ just as we do, and were saved by grace, trusting the crucified Lamb of God in exactly the same way we are. Christ was not then fully revealed. He was not personally identified. Yet, he was known and trusted as God the Saviour, the Christ, the Anointed One, the promised Seed.

Beginning with the Gospel of Matthew, we move from the realm of shadow, type, and prophecy into the full sunshine of the Sun of Righteousness, the Son of God.

As we have seen, the Old Testament speaks of him on every page, but speaks in shadows, in types, in symbols, and in prophecies, all looking forward to the coming of that Someone whom Abel, Enoch, Noah, and Abraham trusted. You cannot read the Old Testament without a sense of anticipation, thinking to yourself, this book is talking about Someone who is yet to appear, who is a woman's Seed, an Ark of salvation, a sin-atoning Lamb, a man who is God, a Redeemer, a King like David, a Prophet like Moses, a Priest like Melchizedek, a divine Substitute, and a Saviour.

Matthew, Mark, Luke, and John say, 'Here he is!' When we come to read the four gospels, we say with Andrew and Phillip, 'We have found the Messiah ... the Christ ... We have found him of whom Moses in the law, and the prophets did write, Jesus of Nazareth, the son of Joseph' (John 1:41-45). 'And the Word was made flesh, and dwelt among us, (and we beheld his glory, the glory as of the only begotten of the Father,) full of grace and truth' (John 1:14). 'Thou shalt call his name JESUS: for he shall save his people from their sins' (Matthew 1:21).

Here we see Christ as he is. Remember, what he was is what he is; and what he is, is what we have. All the fulness of his character and being and life and glory (John 17:22) is ours. That makes the four gospels uniquely important. They tell us exactly who our Saviour is.

The Sun of Righteousness has arisen with healing in his wings (Malachi 4:2). In the 39 books of the Old Testament we have been watching the unfolding of the dawn of that day which Abraham rejoiced to see, the rising of that Star of whom Balaam spoke, and of the great Light promised in Isaiah. We have been watching one cloud after another dissipate by the rising Sun. Now, the King of Glory, of whom David sang, has come. 'We have seen his star in the east' (in the Old Testament) 'and are come' (in the New Testament) 'to worship him'. We have 'seen the Lord's Christ'. As we pick up the New Testament, we say with old Simeon, who waited for the Consolation of Israel, our 'eyes have seen thy salvation, which thou hast prepared before the face of all people; a light to lighten the Gentiles, and the glory of thy people Israel' (Luke 2:30-32).

Why Four Gospels?

People sometimes wonder why we have four gospel narratives. The reason is really very simple. Matthew, Mark, Luke, and John show us our Saviour's full character, his full person and work from four angles. They do not give us four different pictures, but four different views of the same picture. Really, they present the Lord Jesus like a statue, each allowing us to view the statue from a different side. I say that because in some ways a statue is better than a picture. A statue allows us to see the image it represents from all sides. The four gospels have been compared to the four cherubim of Ezekiel and Revelation.

Matthew shows Christ as the King, as the Lion of the Tribe of Judah, who has come to save his people from their sins.

Mark presents him as Jehovah's Servant, who has come to fulfil his Father's will, the ox ready to serve and ready to be sacrificed upon the altar.

Luke, the beloved Physician, presents him as the Son of Man, full of human sympathy and tenderness, as the cherub with the face of a man suggests.

John, like the eagle soaring into the heavens, sets the Saviour before us as the Son of God, with a majesty that transcends all our thoughts and imagination.

Christ the King

Let us take a brief view of Matthew's gospel, and worship the Lord Jesus Christ, our King. Here we see the royal majesty of our heavenly King and his great kingdom.

Matthew, more than all the other gospel writers, sets forth the Mosaic law, referring constantly to the Old Testament scriptures, and shows that both the law and the scriptures of the Old Testament find their fulfilment in Christ, the King.

The Genealogy

Matthew 1:1-17 gives us our Lord's genealogy, tracing it back to Abraham. We read in verse 1, 'The book of the generations of Jesus Christ, the Son of David, the Son of Abraham.' He is set before us in verse 1 as the Son of Abraham to show us that he is that One with whom God's covenant was made, and as Abraham's promised Seed in whom all the covenant is fulfilled. He is set before us as the son of David (v. 6) to show us that he is the rightful Heir to David's throne, and that he has come to take possession of David's true kingdom and throne.

The Jews carped about many things, raised many questions, and made many accusations in their attempts to discredit our Saviour's claims as the Christ, as God's Messiah; but never once did they question his genealogy. Why? Because it was a matter of public and biblical record that could not be disputed.

The Sinner's Saviour

There is something especially precious in our Saviour's genealogy that is commonly overlooked. Here, just before we are told that he came to save his people from their sins, three of his ancestral mothers are named who had a smear upon their names. Tamar was Judah's daughter-in-law, who played the harlot and committed incest. Ruth was a Moabitess, a woman of a cursed race, a race that came into existence by Lot's incestuous behaviour.

Bathsheba was the adulteress wife of Uriah. Add to that the fact that our Saviour is here identified specifically as the son of David by Bathsheba; and you can almost hear him saying, 'Behold, I have come to save poor sinners!'

The Incarnation

Our Saviour's wondrous divinity is immediately presented in Matthew's record of the incarnation and virgin birth (1:18-25). Here is a picture of the New Birth. The Lord Jesus Christ was conceived in a sinner, conceived by the work of God the Holy Spirit, and conceived without the aid of a man. That is exactly how Christ is formed in us in the new birth.

Here is our Saviour's name, 'Jesus'. Here is his mission, 'He shall save his people from their sins'. Here is the character of his people, sinners. Note that they were already his people before he came to save them, chosen in eternal election, given to him as a Surety. Here is his divinity, the certainty of his success. Our Saviour is God in human flesh, Emmanuel!

Old Testament Prophecies

Matthew 1 and 2 set before us a number of Old Testament prophecies fulfilled by our Saviour's incarnation. He is Immanuel, the virgin born Saviour (Isaiah 7:14; Matthew 1:22-23). He is a Nazarene (Judges 13:5; 1 Samuel 1:11; Matthew 2:23). He fulfilled Jeremiah's prophecy of weeping in Ramah (Jeremiah 31:15; Matthew 2:17-18). He was called out of Egypt (Hosea 11:1; Matthew 2:15). He was born at Bethlehem (Micah 5:2; Matthew 2:5-6).

Wise Men

Matthew alone describes the visit of the wise men (chapter 2:1-13). The whole world at this time was expecting the advent of some Great One. These wise men came to Jerusalem asking, 'Where is he that is born King of the Jews?' Their adoration of the newborn King foreshadowed his universal dominion (John 17:2; Romans 14:9). Matthew tells us how Herod, the usurper of David's dominion, sought to slay the heir to David's throne (vv. 14-23).

John The Baptist

In this Gospel John the Baptist appears preaching repentance and introducing the Lord Jesus as the mighty Judge who shall purge his floor with tremendous judgment (3:10-17). Our Lord Jesus Christ was immersed by John to fulfil all righteousness.

At first John was reluctant to immerse the Saviour because he recognized who it was that stood before him, and was humbled in his presence. But, when the Master said, 'Suffer it to be so now: for thus it becometh us to fulfil all righteousness. Then he suffered him', and immersed the incarnate God in the Jordan River.

The question is sometimes asked, 'How did Christ's baptism fulfil all righteousness?' There can be but one answer. By his baptism, and by believer's baptism today, righteousness is fulfilled symbolically. By our baptism (immersion), we symbolically testify how it is that sinners are made righteous before God. Our sins are washed away and we are made righteous by our death, burial, and resurrection with Christ, our Substitute.

This man is owned at his immersion as the Son of God. When our Lord was baptized John saw the Spirit of God descending and abiding upon him, thereby identifying him as the Son of God and the Messiah. This is he in whom the Father takes pleasure. When he came up out of the watery grave, the Father spoke from heaven, declaring, 'This is my beloved Son in whom I am well pleased'. This same word from heaven was heard at the transfiguration (17:5). By these two things, the Lord God tells us that Christ, our ascended, exalted Saviour, is that One in whom alone we find acceptance with God. As the Holy Lord God is well pleased with his Son, so he is well pleased with his elect in his Son, our Substitute.

The Temptation

Matthew's account of the temptation is detailed and instructive (4:1-11). Our Lord was tempted in all points like as we are, yet without sin. The devil came and found nothing in him. The word 'tempted' would be better translated 'tested'. Temptations, tests and trials, do not make any change in anyone. They simply reveal what the person is (James 1:12-15).

There is some debate about whether our Lord's temptations were real, and whether it was possible for him to sin. The temptations were real. Yet, there was no possibility of the holy, incarnate God sinning. The temptations proved that there was no evil in him (John 14:30). If you run a test to establish the purity of water, the test is real; but the fact that the test is real does not imply that there is impurity in the water. The test will simply show the water pure or corrupt. So it was with our Master's temptations. They showed him 'holy, harmless, undefiled, and separate from sinners'.

Christ's Kingdom

Beginning in Matthew 4:17, our Lord began to preach, saying, 'Repent, for the kingdom of heaven is at hand'. The word 'kingdom' appears fifty-three times in Matthew. Thirty-five times Christ's kingdom is called, 'the kingdom of heaven', an expression found nowhere else in the Gospels.

Chapters 5-7 give us our Saviour's Sermon on the Mount. Here he tells us the nature of his kingdom. The Jews, because of their perverted understanding of the Old Testament, expected the Messiah to establish a physical, Jewish kingdom in the earth. Our Saviour dispelled that notion at the very outset of his public ministry in this tremendous sermon.

He opens his sermon (5:3-13) with the beatitudes, declaring that those who are his servants, his people, those who enter into his kingdom are identified not by outward ceremonies but by inward grace (Philippians 3:3). The kingdom of heaven is inward, not outward.

The service of his kingdom (chapter 6) is inward, heart service, not an outward show. Every form of religion with which I am familiar tells its adherents to show their religion to men by outward deeds. The Son of God tells his disciples never to attempt to show their religion by outward deeds that are seen, approved of, and applauded by men. Our giving, our prayers, our fastings are to be things arising spontaneously, kept in strict secrecy, and performed for God and before God.

True religion is a matter of faith in Christ, a matter of the heart. The only thing our Saviour tells us to show is mercy, love, and grace. That is what is discussed in the latter part of this chapter. The law of his kingdom is love; and love is best displayed in forbearance, forgiveness, and uprightness.

Chapter 7 continues with the same subject, teaching us to guard against rash judgment concerning others. We ought to embrace as brethren all who profess faith in Christ (who profess to believe the gospel of God's free and sovereign grace in him), without doubtful disputations (Romans 14:1). Then, our Lord brings his message to a pointed conclusion, urging us all to make certain we trust him alone, to make certain we have entered in 'at the strait gate'.

Miracles

In chapters 8 and 9 our Lord performed numerous, unparalleled miracles, displaying his omnipotent grace. He healed a leper, who came worshiping him, with a touch. He healed the centurion's servant by the mere exercise of his will. He touched Peter's mother-in-law and raised her from her sickbed. 'When the even was come, they brought unto him many that were possessed with devils: and he cast out the spirits with his word, and healed all that were sick: That it might be fulfilled which was spoken by Esaias the prophet, saying, Himself took our infirmities, and bare our sicknesses' (Matthew 8:16-17).

He calmed the raging tempest by his word, healed a paralyzed man and forgave his sins, raised a man's daughter from the dead, healed a woman who had been diseased with an issue of blood for twelve years, and gave two blind men their sight. There can be no question about it, this man was and is God the Son!

Conversion

In chapter 10 our Lord names his apostles and sends them out to preach the gospel. In the eleventh chapter he confirms himself to John the Baptist's disciples. In chapter 12 he shows himself to be Jehovah's Servant spoken of in Isaiah 42:1-4, that is the Lord of the sabbath, and declares that the sabbath was made for man, not man for the sabbath. Healing the man with a withered hand on the sabbath, he hints that the sabbath of the Old Testament portrayed the believer's experience of grace, finding life and rest in him. Then, our Lord shows us that conversion is nothing less than his own entrance into a man's heart, casting Satan out, and setting up his own throne in the heart by omnipotent grace.

The Parables

We have seven parables of the Kingdom in chapter 13, each beginning with 'The kingdom of heaven is like', except that of the sower, where we have the word 'kingdom' in verse 11. Numerous other parables are recorded by Matthew, all describing the spiritual nature of Christ's kingdom, and the establishment of it by grace alone.

The parable of the sower tells us of the necessity of the Holy Spirit's work, making the heart good ground to receive the gospel. It also warns us of those things that rob men's souls of the blessings of the gospel.

The parable of the tares teaches us that we must never try to separate the tares from the wheat. That work is performed by Christ himself, through the preaching of the gospel.

The mustard seed and leaven parables tell us that the kingdom of God grows secretly, almost imperceptibly, but constantly until all God's elect are gathered in by his grace.

The parable of the treasure hid in the field speaks of Christ's purchased dominion over and possession of the whole world as the God-man Mediator (John 17:2), that he might obtain the treasure of it, the church of his elect.

The parable of the pearl of great price teaches that we must forsake all for Christ, who is the Pearl of great price.

The parable of the great net, like that of the tares, tells us that as long as time stands the kingdom of heaven (the outward, visible kingdom and every local church) is a mixed multitude of good fish and bad, true believers and those who merely profess to be believers.

The parable of the lost sheep (18:10-14) portrays our Saviour's determination to save his elect and his joy in saving them. That of the wicked servant (18:23-35) portrays our Redeemer's teaching (vv. 15-22) on the necessity and blessedness of believers forgiving those who offend them.

The parable of the labourers (20:1-16) is our Lord's picture of grace, displaying the fact that all God's elect are perfectly accepted in him. This parable is preceded in chapter 18 and followed in chapter 20 by strife among the disciples regarding who shall be greatest in the kingdom of God. Because salvation is by grace alone, because there are no degrees of acceptance with God, because the whole of our salvation is bestowed freely for Christ's sake, there can be no degrees of reward in heaven.

The parable of the vineyard (21:33-43) portrays the wrath of God to be visited upon the Jewish nation for slaughtering his Son.

The marriage supper parable sets before us the freeness of grace proclaimed by the gospel (22:2-14).

The parable of the ten virgins warns us of the danger of religion without Christ, outward religion without inward grace, and the great need of diligence in personally watching over our own souls (25:1-13).

The parable of talents (25:14-30) shows us our responsibility to be faithful stewards of that which the Lord God has put in our hands to use for his glory.

Divine Sovereignty

In all these parables the absolute sovereignty of God our Saviour over all things is clearly exemplified. Our Saviour declares that he has the right to do with his own what he will (20:15; Romans 9:15-18). In this opening book of the New Testament he asserts that he came specifically to redeem and that he effectually calls the 'many' in this world who are his own elect (20:28; 22:14; 1:21), and only them.

Promises To The Church

In Matthew 16 and 18 the Lord Jesus identifies himself as the only Foundation upon which his church is built, and that the building of his church is his work alone. Immediately after making this declaration, he tells us that the way he would build his church is by the merit, power, and efficacy of his sin-atoning sacrifice (16:13-21).

Then in chapter 18 (v. 20) he promises that he is always with his assembled saints when they gather for worship in his name. This church, this kingdom that Christ builds, he protects, provides for, and shall make triumphant over hell itself.

Transfiguration

Along with Mark and Luke, Matthew tells us of the unveiled glory of the King in his transfiguration, foreshadowing his resurrection glory as

Zion's King. He adds this touch, 'His face did shine as the sun', and these words, 'in whom I am well pleased', showing how perfectly our Lord fulfilled God's Law as a Representative Man (Matthew 17:1-13; Mark 9:2-13; Luke 9:28-36).

Meaningless Questions

In chapter 22 the Pharisees, Sadducees, and lawyers come asking meaningless questions about political matters, the resurrection, and the law. Their questions were made meaningless by the fact that they ignored the one great question 'What think ye of Christ?' (v. 42). In chapter 23 our Lord condemns them and all who follow their path.

The Crucifixion

Chapters 26 and 27 give us a brief account of our Lord's betrayal, his mock trial, and the agony of his crucifixion and death as our sin-atoning Substitute. Forsaken by heaven and earth, alone he endured all the wrath of God for us when he was made to be sin. Darkness covered the earth for three hours. Upon the cursed tree, he vanquished sin, death, Satan, and hell.

As Paul puts it in Colossians, he made a show of them openly, triumphing over them, and leading them behind him as a conqueror would lead a train of captives in open display before the people. When at last he gave up the ghost, the veil of the temple was ripped apart, showing that he had opened the way for sinners to come to God. Many were raised from their graves, showing that the sentence of death can never be executed upon those for whom he died.

Substitution is beautifully portrayed in the fact that Christ died in the place of Barabbas. Barabbas went free because a Substitute died in his place; and God's elect must and shall go free because Christ died in their place (Romans 8:1; 33-34).

The Resurrection

In his account of the resurrection (chapter 28) Matthew tells of the great earthquake, the angel whose face was like lightning; for fear of whom the keepers did shake and became as dead men, and of the Lord's bodily appearance to his disciples after he arose. He was sent to the tomb as a guilty criminal, worthy of death. He was released as a free man, without sin, 'justified in the Spirit' and 'declared to be the Son of God' our Saviour, because he had accomplished our justification by the sacrifice of himself (Romans 4:25).

Our Commission

Finally, this Gospel gives us, as no other, our Lord's last royal commission. The risen Lord says to you and me, 'Go tell the world what I have done'. 'And Jesus came and spake unto them, saying, All power is given unto me in heaven and in earth. Go ye therefore, and teach all nations, baptizing them in the name of the Father, and of the Son, and of the Holy Ghost: teaching them to observe all things whatsoever I have commanded you: and, lo, I am with you alway, even unto the end of the world. Amen' (Matthew 28:18-20).

Chapter 41

Mark

Christ the Servant

The words of our Saviour in Mark 10:45 give us a clear summary of Mark's Gospel. Remember, Mark's object is to present our Saviour in his character as Jehovah's righteous Servant; and that is exactly how our Lord describes himself. 'For even the Son of man came not to be ministered unto, but to minister, and to give his life a ransom for many'.

Distinct Purpose

Each of the four gospel narratives is distinct. Each one presents our Saviour in a specific character. It is a mistake to read Matthew, Mark, Luke, and John as four biographies of the Lord Jesus. They are not biographies at all. They are biographical character sketches. Each is intended to be different from the other. Each presents our Saviour from a distinct different point of view. The four Gospels give us four distinct views of our Lord and of his work.

The Gospel of Matthew is written to present Christ as the King. The Gospel of Mark presents his character as Jehovah's Servant. The Gospel of Luke presents him as the Son of Man. The Gospel of John presents him as the Son of God.

No Genealogy

Have you ever wondered why there is no record of our Lord's ascension in Matthew and John, and why there is no record of his genealogy in Mark? Luke gives his own record of our Lord's genealogy as a man; but John gives us neither a record of his genealogy nor his ascension. Why? The answer is obvious when you remember the distinct purpose of each.

Matthew presents Christ as the King, and Luke presents him as the man promised in the Old Testament. In both cases a genealogical record is needed. Because Christ is the King from eternity, a record of his ascension in Matthew's case would be redundant. John presents the Saviour as the incarnate God, that One who is immutably God over all and blessed forever. In his case, a record of our Lord's genealogy or his ascension would be contrary to his purpose. Mark only mentions the ascension, because his intent is to show us that as Jehovah's Servant, our Saviour's mission is complete, successful, and accepted by the Father. Having finished his work, he sat down on the right hand of the Majesty on High (Hebrews 1:1-3; 10:10-14).

Christ the Servant

Mark's Gospel narrative is 'a joyful account of the ministry, miracles, actions, and sufferings of Christ' says John Gill. It is all about the obedience of our Saviour to the will of God. He tells us nothing about the birth and early life of our Lord. He gives us very few details about our Master's sermons. Yet he gives greater details than others about his miracles. Mark's is the shortest of the four Gospels yet it is not in any way less significant. Mark used greater brevity than the others; but his narrative is just as important. Those who suggest that Mark simply copied down some facts from Matthew, or that he wrote what Peter told him to write both miss the purpose of Mark's work and undermine the inspiration and authority of holy scripture. Without question, he got information from those men who taught him the gospel; but he wrote by divine inspiration.

J.C. Ryle very properly observed that Mark's Gospel is 'The independent narrative of an independent witness, who was inspired to write a history of our Lord's works, rather than of his words ... Like all the rest of scripture, every word of St. Mark is "given by inspiration of God", and every word is "profitable".'

Mark Himself

The man God used to give us this inspired narrative of our Saviour's obedience as our Representative, as the One who worked out righteousness for us, was a man like us, not always dependable, a sinner saved by grace, just like we are.

In other places he is called John Mark. He was the man who accompanied Paul on his first missionary journey and proved himself at that time an unfaithful servant. He could not take the pressure of the work: the constant opposition, the thankless labour, and the relentless long, lonely hours. Tired and frustrated he left Paul and ran back home. This is not the only time we see Mark displaying such weakness.

If you want to meet Bro. Mark turn to chapter 14. There is an unnamed young man here, who is probably Mark himself. I say that because Mark does not give us the man's name and because this is the only time this incident is mentioned in scripture. After our Lord's arrest in Gethsemane, we are told that the disciples forsook him. But Mark adds what is found in verses 51 and 52. 'And there followed him a certain young man, having a linen cloth cast about his naked body; and the young men laid hold on him: And he left the linen cloth, and fled from them naked'.

Yet, this is the man God chose to use to give us this portion of his Word. A less than dependable servant, a man who was at times very weak, was nevertheless chosen to record for us the perfect faithfulness of that Servant of God of whom it is written, 'He shall not fail', the Lord Jesus Christ. I am thankful for that fact. Are you not? If the Lord used one failure, maybe he will use another (1 Corinthians 1:26-29).

Peter's Influence

Mark was Peter's son in the faith (1 Peter 5:13). He was converted under the influence of Peter's ministry and taught by Peter. He was, as well he should have been, greatly influenced by his pastor, Peter. His Gospel narrative naturally reflects the teachings and viewpoints we see in Peter.

In fact, if you will look at Acts 10:38, you will see that Peter gives us a very brief summary of all that is recorded for us in the Gospel of Mark. Speaking in the house of Cornelius, we read that Peter stood among them and told them exactly what Mark tells us in these 16 chapters. 'How God anointed Jesus of Nazareth with the Holy Ghost and with power: who went about doing good, and healing all that were oppressed of the devil; for God was with him.'

Matthew and John, like Peter and Paul, were apostles of Christ. As such, they learned the gospel from the Master himself. Neither Mark nor Luke was an apostle. What they learned of Christ, they learned, like us, through the preaching of others and the teaching of the Holy Spirit through the preached Word (Romans 10:17).

Profitable Mark

John Mark was also the son of Barnabas' sister, Mary (Acts 12:12, 25; Colossians 4:10). Probably as a result of Paul's earlier experience with Mark, Paul and Barnabas eventually had a falling out because Paul refused to take Mark with them on his second missionary journey (Acts 15:36-41). But that is not the end of the story. At some point, Paul and Mark did some fence mending, and in his latter days Paul found Mark to be one of the few who were loyal to the gospel. As he was awaiting execution, he wrote to Timothy and said, 'Take Mark, and bring him with thee: for he is profitable to me for the ministry' (2 Timothy 4:11).

Mark's Message

Instead of opening with a record of our Lord's incarnation and birth, instead of telling us about his youth and early years, Mark begins at once with Christ's ministry. Look at verse 1 of chapter 1 'The beginning of the gospel of Jesus Christ, the Son of God'. This is the beginning, but not the end, for there is no end to the story Mark tells. He is telling us the God-story of redemption, grace, and salvation by God's Servant, 'Jesus Christ, the Son of God'.

Our Lord tells us that the story will go on forever, even in eternity. This is too wondrous to grasp; but our Lord tells us that in that great day called 'eternity', 'he shall gird himself and make (us) to sit down to meat, and will come forth and serve (us)' (Luke 12:37). We will never come to the end of the story. The gospel of Jesus Christ, the Son of God is everlasting.

Time Fulfilled

After describing the ministry of John the Baptist and our Lord's baptism by him (1:2-13), Mark gives a very brief description of the wilderness temptation (vv. 12-13). Yet, even in his brevity, Mark adds some things that show the greatness of that trial by which the faithfulness of Jehovah's Servant was proved.

Matthew and Luke tell us that our Lord was 'led' of the Spirit into the wilderness. Mark's words are stronger. 'The Spirit driveth him into the wilderness'. It is Mark who tells us the temptation lasted forty days, and that the Lord was 'with the wild beasts' in the wilderness.

Then, he begins to describe our Lord's earthly ministry in verses 14 and 15 of chapter 1. 'Now after that John was put in prison, Jesus came into Galilee, preaching the gospel of the kingdom of God, And saying, The time is fulfilled, and the kingdom of God is at hand: repent ye, and believe the gospel'.

Mark tells us that our Lord stepped onto the scene of history and declared that the time God had promised for the accomplishment of his promises of redemption were fulfilled. That meant that the kingdom of God was now in the midst of men. If we enter into that kingdom, we must enter in by faith's door, believing on the Lord Jesus Christ. In due time, Christ came here to die for the ungodly (Romans 5:6; Galatians 4:4-5). 'When the fulness of the time was come, God sent forth his Son, made of a woman, made under the law, to redeem them that were under the law, that we might receive the adoption of sons.' Christ came here as Jehovah's Servant (Philippians 2:5-8).

First Disciples

Immediately after announcing our Lord's appearance in Galilee, calling sinners to repentance, Mark shows us what is meant by that. In verses 16-18 we are told how that the Lord Jesus called his first disciples, Simon and Andrew, James and John. Those who repent and believe, those who come to and follow Christ, those who are born into his kingdom are called by him. Those who are called by him forsake all and follow him.

Full of Activity

The Gospel of Mark is a book full of activity. Mark moves rapidly from one place to another and from one miracle to another. The words 'immediately', 'forthwith', 'anon', and 'straightway', meet us constantly in these 16 chapters. Many of the chapters begin with the word 'And'. If Mark were telling us his story orally, we might say, 'Slow down. Catch your breath. You're moving too fast'. That is exactly the sense the Holy Spirit intends to give us in this book. Mark is describing God's faithful Servant, our all-glorious Christ, whose meat and drink it was to do the will of his Father. He had nothing to call his own, not even his time. O Lord, my God, give me grace to be such a servant!

Mark moves like lightning as he declares our Lord's works in Galilee, casting out demons and healing the sick (1:21-3:12; 5:25-34; 6:53-56; 7:24-37). He gives us display after display of our Lord's power and authority as that Servant into whose hands the Father has given all things. After giving us four kingdom parables in chapter 4, he calmed the raging sea and the troubled hearts of his disciples with his mere word (4:35-41). He cast demons out of the poor Gadarene (5:1-20). A woman was healed of her twelve-year issue of blood by the touch of his garment (5:25-34). He raised Jairus' twelve year old daughter from the dead (5:35-43). He fed hungry multitudes by miraculously multiplying little (6:34-44; 8:1-9). Twice we read of him giving sight to the blind. Repeatedly, we read of our tender Saviour having 'compassion' upon needy souls.

Pictures of Grace

These miracles were intended to display our Saviour's power and authority as that man who is Jehovah's Servant, that man who is God, to show that he has power and authority by virtue of who he is and by virtue of the sacrifice he made in eternity and was about to make at Calvary, to forgive sins (2:9-10).

It is therefore obvious that these miracles were intended to be pictures of his wondrous works of grace in saving lost sinners. Like the leper, saved sinners have been made whole by Christ, the Priest, who touched us and made himself unclean to make us clean. We are made whole by the omnipotent touch of his grace. Like the woman with that twelve-year issue of blood, who had spent all she had on physicians of no value, we are made whole by virtue we get from touching him. Like the Syrophenician woman, we who have no claim on the children's bread have obtained mercy by faith in Christ. Like the Gadarene, we have been made whole and set free by the Master's word of grace. Like the blind men, our Lord has given us eyes to see him and to see 'every man clearly'. Like Jairus' daughter, the Lord Jesus Christ raised us up from the dead.

Determination to Die

Beginning in chapter 8 (v. 31), we see a marked determination in our Saviour, Jehovah's Servant. He set his face like a flint to go up to Jerusalem, to suffer all the wrath of God as our Substitute (Isaiah 50:5-7). 'And he began to teach them, that the Son of man must suffer many things, and be rejected of the elders, and of the chief priests, and scribes, and be killed, and after three days rise again.'

The Lord Jesus did not come here hoping that the Jews would allow him to be their king, sitting on a physical throne in Jerusalem. He came here as the King to suffer and die, rise again the third day, and ascend to his throne to give eternal life to his elect by the virtue and efficacy of his blood atonement. He came here to do the will of his Father, suffering death as our Substitute at Jerusalem, and nothing could deter or hinder him from accomplishing his purpose.

Peter's Reaction

Look at Peter's response to the Lord's declared purpose (v. 32). 'Peter took him, and began to rebuke him'. Matthew gives a fuller quotation of

Peter's words. 'Then Peter took him, and began to rebuke him, saying, Be it far from thee, Lord: this shall not be unto thee' (Matthew 16:22). Peter said, 'Spare yourself of this, Lord'. That is always the response of the flesh to trouble. 'Spare yourself.' The Master sternly rebuked Peter, saying, 'Get thee behind me, Satan: for thou savourest not the things that be of God, but the things that be of men' (v. 33).

Gill suggests, I think accurately, that, 'the Lord rebuked him in a very severe, though just manner; being touched in his most tender part, and dissuaded from that which his heart was set upon, and he came into the world for; whose keen resentment is seen by using a phrase he never did but to the devil himself'. The Master knew the source and cause of Peter's comments. The flesh, like Satan, is always opposed to the will of God. The flesh always chooses that which is easiest on, and most appealing to, the flesh.

That this is the meaning of this conversation between Christ and his errant disciple is obvious because of what follows in verses 34-38. If we would follow Christ, if we would be his disciples, if we would be God's servants (that is what it is to be a believer!) we must give up our will to his will. We must surrender the rule of our lives to the rule of God our Saviour. That is what Jehovah's righteous Servant did in the example he left us in the rest of Mark's Gospel (1 Peter 2:21).

Transfiguration

In chapter 9 we have Mark's account of the Transfiguration. 'And he said unto them, Verily I say unto you, That there be some of them that stand here, which shall not taste of death, till they have seen the kingdom of God come with power' (v. 1). Six days later Christ led Peter, James, and John up on the mountain. Quite literally, they did not taste of death till they saw the King coming in glory. Peter refers to this in 2 Peter 1:16-18.

'For we have not followed cunningly devised fables, when we made known unto you the power and coming of our Lord Jesus Christ, but were eyewitnesses of his majesty. For he received from God the Father honour and glory, when there came such a voice to him from the excellent glory, This is my beloved Son, in whom I am well pleased. And this voice which came from heaven we heard, when we were with him in the holy mount'.

The suggestion is that God's purpose for his elect and the purpose of Christ's redemptive work is that we should not taste of death. He came to deliver us from the awful taste of death. Our all-glorious Saviour tasted death for everyone he came to save that we might never taste it (Hebrews 2:9), that we might ever behold and be the recipients of his glory as Jehovah's righteous Servant (John 17:22-26).

Then the Lord identifies his family, those who shall behold and enjoy his glory forever, his children, the citizens and heirs of his kingdom. They are those who, in this world, cast all their care on him (vv. 17-24), becoming as little children taken into his omnipotent arms, trusting him as Lord and Saviour (vv. 36-37), and blessed in and by him. Mark alone tells us that he took the little children up in his arms when he blessed them (10:13-16).

Money Changers

Our Lord's last week on earth before the crucifixion begins in chapter 11. Here again Mark tells us about a very significant event the other Gospel writers were not inspired to record. 'And they come to Jerusalem: and Jesus went into the temple, and began to cast out them that sold and bought in the temple, and overthrew the tables of the moneychangers, and the seats of them that sold doves; and would not suffer that any man should carry any vessel through the temple' (vv. 15-16).

This is not the same event John spoke of in John 2:13-16. That event took place at the beginning of our Lord's ministry. That which Mark records took place at the end of his ministry. For the second time, the Lord Jesus overthrows the tables of the money-changers, and cleanses the temple. Mark says, he 'would not suffer that any man should carry any vessel through the temple'.

According to the Mosaic law, it was the responsibility of the priests to catch the blood of the sacrifices on the brazen altar in the outer court and carry it into the holy place before the altar. Once each year the high priest would go into the Holy of Holies and sprinkle that blood upon the mercy seat. All of this was highly symbolic of Christ's sin-atoning work.

He of whom the priests and the sacrifices were types had come to put an end to all this. He would not allow any man to carry anything through the temple. In other words, he ended the sacrifices. He is the end of the law (Romans 10:4). In this act our Lord was saying, 'The Lamb of God has come to put away sin by the sacrifice of himself'.

More Questions

Mark chapters 10-13 are primarily concerned with the questions people asked the Saviour. In chapter 10 he answers the Pharisees' questions about divorce, the rich young ruler's question, the disciples' question about salvation, and James and John's question about greatness. He tells the Pharisees that marriage is forever. He told the rich young ruler that the way to eternal life is faith alone, that faith that surrenders all to Christ as Lord and God.

When the disciples heard the conversation between Christ and the rich young ruler, and heard the Master's explanation of why that man so rich in material property and religious morality did not believe, they said, 'Who then can be saved?' The Master answered, 'With men it is impossible, but not with God: for with God all things are possible'.

In chapter 11 he answers the questions of the priests, the scribes, and the elders who come out of hatred for him and try to trap him with their questions about his authority to purge the temple. He answered them by refusing to answer them.

In chapter 12 the Pharisees, Herodians, Sadducees, and a scribe tried to trap him with their questions. The Lord Jesus saw through their hypocrisy and answered them accordingly. The Pharisees and Herodians were trying to get him to say something that could be used to accuse him of stirring insurrection against Caesar. The Sadducees tried to trick him into saying something that might be twisted into a denial of the resurrection. Then a scribe tried to trick him into speaking a word against the law.

In chapter 13, as they sat on the Mount of Olives, Peter, James, John, and Andrew ask the Lord Jesus what he meant when he spoke of the destruction of the temple. They said, 'Tell us, when shall these things be? and what shall be the sign when all these things shall be fulfilled' (v. 4). The rest of the chapter is taken up with our Saviour's answer, warning them and us of the great danger of following false christs.

A Good Work

Multitudes talk about good works. Usually their intent is to defend their pretended good works of self-righteousness. In chapter 14 Mark shows us an event that displays what a good work is. 'A woman having an alabaster box of ointment of spikenard very precious; and she brake the box, and poured it on his head' (v. 3). Others, including the disciples, sharply criticized her.

'And Jesus said, Let her alone; why trouble ye her? she hath wrought a good work on me. For ye have the poor with you always, and whensoever ye will ye may do them good: but me ye have not always. She hath done what she could: she is come aforehand to anoint my body to the burying. Verily I say unto you, Wheresoever this gospel shall be preached throughout the whole world, this also that she hath done shall be spoken of for a memorial of her' (vv. 6-9).

The Master said, 'She hath wrought a good work on me'. That is the only time in the Bible anything done by a sinful human being is specifically called 'a good work' by our Lord. That fact is very instructive. Good works are not what most people imagine they are. A good work is a work of faith. This dear lady seems to have been the only person who understood and believed what the Lord had said about his death and resurrection. A good work involves personal sacrifice. It is always costly. A good work is a work of spontaneous love wrought for Christ. A good work is doing what you can for the Saviour. A good work is a work that God our Saviour never forgets.

The Crucifixion

Beginning with chapter 15, we have the account of the crucifixion. Mark describes this as an act of horrible brutality done in the name of justice and righteousness. The Lord Jesus appears to be a defeated man, a tragic failure, and his cause hopelessly lost. He is hounded, bludgeoned and spat upon. Finally, he is crucified upon the cursed tree between two thieves. Is this Jehovah's Servant?

No wonder the high priests, as they saw him hanging naked upon the tree, covered in his own blood and the abuse of men, laughed and said, 'He saved others; himself cannot save' (v. 31).

That is a strange statement. Yet it is one of the most remarkable statements of gospel truth ever to fall from the lips of men. It shows that God is able to make even his enemies praise him.

Three Things

As we read this account, we see three things that they could not make our Lord do. First, they could not make our Lord speak. 'And Pilate asked him again, saying, Answerest thou nothing? behold how many things they witness against thee' (v. 4). He could have called twelve legions of angels to deliver him; but the Master said nothing, and Pilate wondered.

Second, they could not make him drink. 'And they gave him to drink wine mingled with myrrh: but he received it not' (v. 23). Why not? The mixture offered him would have relieved our Lord of some of the agony he endured. Had he drunk what they gave him, he would have saved himself the effect of the agony of the cross and the weight of the burden of all hell and all the wrath of God pressing upon him; but he would not. He would not spare himself.

Then, third, they could not make him die. 'And Jesus cried with a loud voice, and gave up the ghost' (v. 37). He 'unspirited' himself. He dismissed his spirit. He did not die at the hands of the Jews or the Romans. He died at the hand of God, by his own voluntary will, as Jehovah's Righteous Servant (John 10:17-18).

'And being found in fashion as a man, he humbled himself, and became obedient unto death, even the death of the cross. Wherefore God also hath highly exalted him, and given him a name which is above every name: that at the name of Jesus every knee should bow, of things in heaven, and things in earth, and things under the earth and that every tongue should confess that Jesus Christ is Lord, to the glory of God the Father' (Philippians 2:8-11).

The Resurrection

When we get to the last chapter and the resurrection of our Lord, we see his reason. He was silent and refused to appeal to Pilate or the crowd, because he was laying the basis for a coming day, when in resurrection power and glory every knee will bow and every tongue will confess that Jesus Christ is Lord to the glory of God the Father.

He would not drink to dull his senses, because he was laying a basis upon which even those who stood around the cross might enter into a life eternal. He was laying the foundation upon which God can be just and the Justifier of all who believe. He was determined to die, that he might be exalted as Lord of all, to give eternal life to as many as the Father had given him.

He would not let men take his life; but he voluntarily laid it down himself in order that he might overcome our greatest enemy, death, and forever deliver all who would believe in him from the power and awful sting of death. That is the Gospel. He saved others, but himself he could not save. That is Mark's story.

My Favourite Verse

Let me give you my favourite verse in Mark's Gospel. It is not surprising to me that it is Mark and Mark alone who says what he does here (16:7). In this verse, he who was himself a follower who had been unfaithful, speaks a word about his beloved friend and father in the faith, his pastor, Peter. He tells us that the young man who stood by the tomb of the risen Lord said to Mary Magdalene and Mary the mother of James, 'Go your way, tell his disciples and Peter that he goeth before you into Galilee: there shall ye see him, as he said unto you'.

It is as though he was reminding Peter, and all of us who are like Peter (weak, faltering, failing, sinful followers of Christ), that God's forgiveness of our sins in Christ is full, absolute, and complete. Christ died for our sins. That means, between us and our God and Saviour, everything is all right!

The book of Mark began with the words 'the beginning of the gospel of Jesus Christ, the Son of God'. In the last two verses of chapter 16 we have the continuation. The Lord Jesus Christ, Jehovah's Servant, is still carrying on his work, working through the preaching of the gospel by his church. 'So then, after the Lord had spoken unto them, he was received up into the heaven, and sat on the right hand of God. And they went forth, and preached everywhere, the Lord working with them, and confirming the word with signs following.'

Chapter 42

Luke

Christ the Son of Man

As we have seen in our studies of Matthew and Mark, each of the four gospels was written by divine inspiration, each revealed the person and work of our Lord Jesus Christ, but each one was intended by the Holy Spirit to set forth a particular, distinct aspect of our Saviour's person and work. None of the gospel narratives give us a complete view of Christ; but all four taken together tell us plainly and fully who the Lord Jesus Christ is, what he did, why he did it, and where he is now.

Matthew was written to show us that our Lord Jesus Christ is the divine Messiah, the Redeemer-King promised in the Old Testament scriptures. Mark was inspired to present the Lord Jesus as Jehovah's righteous Servant. John's gospel sets forth the glorious divinity of the Lord Jesus Christ as God the Son, the second person in the holy trinity.

Luke's gospel was designed and written to show us the perfect and glorious humanity of our Saviour. Just as John shows us that our Redeemer is the Son of God, Luke shows us that he is the Son of Man.

Son of Man

Luke was inspired of God to present our Saviour distinctly as 'the Son of man'. That is the title our Lord used to describe himself more than any other. As we read the Gospel of Luke, the One we meet here is the Redeemer-

King whom Matthew described, the Righteous Servant Mark portrayed, and the incarnate God John declares. He is the same Person; but Luke presents him primarily as the Man who is God, while John presents him as the God who is also man.

Luke gives us more details than either Matthew or Mark about our Saviour's birth. Luke alone tells us a little bit about our Lord's childhood. He stresses, more than the other gospel writers, our Redeemer's dependence upon his Father in prayer, his poverty, and his sympathy with men. He does this because it is his purpose to show us that our Saviour's perfect humanity is just as essential to his saving work as his divinity. He could not accomplish his mission were he not both God and man in one glorious person. Luke's message is essentially contained in the words of our Lord in chapter 19. 'For the Son of man is come to seek and to save that which was lost' (v. 10).

Luke and Acts

Luke specifically wrote his gospel to a man named 'Theophilus'. This is the same man to whom he addressed the book of Acts. Both Luke and Acts were written specifically for Theophilus (Acts 1:1-2). We know nothing about him, except what Luke, himself, tells us. This Theophilus was a man of rank and honour. Luke calls him 'most excellent Theophilus'. Not many noble are called (1 Corinthians 1:26), but some are. God has chosen some of all ranks. The name Theophilus means either 'lover of God' or 'loved of God'. The book of Acts is really a continuation of Luke's Gospel, as he indicates in the opening verses of the opening chapter. The Gospel of Luke describes the works of Christ while he was on the earth. In the book of Acts, Luke picks up right where he left off in his Gospel narrative, only in Acts he describes the works of the ascended Christ through his church.

'Forasmuch as many have taken in hand to set forth in order a declaration of those things which are most surely believed among us, Even as they delivered them unto us, which from the beginning were eyewitnesses, and ministers of the word; It seemed good to me also, having had perfect understanding of all things from the very first, to write unto thee in order, most excellent Theophilus, That thou mightest know the certainty of those things, wherein thou hast been instructed' (Luke 1:1-4).

'The former treatise have I made, O Theophilus, of all that Jesus began both to do and teach, Until the day in which he was taken up, after that he through the Holy Ghost had given commandments unto the apostles whom he had chosen: To whom also he showed himself alive after his passion by many infallible proofs, being seen of them forty days, and speaking of the things pertaining to the kingdom of God: And, being assembled together with them, commanded them that they should not depart from Jerusalem, but wait for the promise of the Father, which, saith he, ye have heard of me' (Acts 1:1-4).

In Acts chapter 1, Luke describes his gospel as 'a treatise of all that Jesus began both to do and teach, until the day in which he was taken up'. Though they did not record every word and deed of Christ (John 21:25), Luke and the other gospel writers did record all that the Holy Spirit inspired, all that we need to know, particularly all that Christ did and said relating to the salvation of his people. They wrote clearly of his obedience to the Father, his conformity to the law, and his death as our Substitute, by which he brought in everlasting righteousness and obtained eternal redemption for us.

Things Most Surely Believed

Then Luke tells us that the Lord Jesus Christ gave his commandments by the Holy Spirit to chosen apostles, and by them to his church. All the doctrines and ordinances, faith and practice of the church are by the commandment of Christ, laid down in the Word of God (2 Timothy 3:16). Both in Acts and here, at the very outset of his Gospel, Luke tells us that his intention in writing this gospel narrative is to 'set forth in order a declaration of those things which are most surely believed among us' (1:1).

Contrary to popular opinion, believers are people who believe some things, some specific things, and all believers believe them. All Christians do, most assuredly, believe some specific things. We believe those things revealed in the book of God. Anyone who does not believe that which God reveals in the inspired volume of holy scripture is not a Christian, is not a believer and does not know God, no matter what he may profess. Roger Ellsworth wrote, 'The church is a community of faith, a community that tenaciously holds with overpowering conviction to a distinct body of truths'.

Yes, there are some things all true Christians believe. Luke makes no bones about this. Neither should we. Let men accuse us of being narrow-minded dogmatists, out of step with the rest of the religious world, and heap upon us whatever ugly names they choose, the Word of God plainly declares that some things are vital. Some things must be known and believed. Those who do not believe these things are not saved.

Luke tells us that he wrote his gospel 'to set forth in order those things which are most surely believed among us'. All who are, like Theophilus, lovers of God love those things most surely believed among us. What are those things? Luke does not leave us to decide for ourselves what they are. He tells us plainly some of those things most assuredly believed by all who know and love, trust and worship the God of Glory.

Luke shows us that all men are sinners in need of God's salvation, — lost, ruined, dead in trespasses and sins, under the curse of God's holy law, and totally incapable of changing their condition. He tells us that the Lord Jesus Christ came to seek and to save that which was lost, like the lost coin, the lost sheep, and the lost Son (chapter 15).

Luke also shows us that the Man, Jesus, is the Christ and that he is the incarnate God. All who are taught of God believe that the Son of God came into this world in the flesh (1:35; 9:20).

Every believer gladly confesses, with Zechariah, that the Lord Jesus Christ has effectually accomplished and obtained salvation for sinners by his obedience and death as the sinners' Substitute (1:68). Remember, that which Zechariah spoke concerning the accomplishments of Christ, he spoke being filled with the Holy Ghost. He tells us that Christ accomplished redemption and explains exactly what that means (1:67-79).

This salvation which Christ obtained for his elect by his blood atonement, by effectual, accomplished redemption, comes to sinners by the gift of God, according to his own sovereign, eternal purpose of grace in Christ, as a matter of pure grace (4:25-27).

And Luke shows us that God's grace in Christ is so abundantly free that every sinner in this world who needs it has it (9:11). It is still true today the Lord Jesus Christ heals all who have need of healing. That is to say, he saves all who need salvation.

Luke's Distinctives

As we read the Gospel of Luke, we cannot help noticing that Luke tells us many precious things that are not even mentioned by any of the other inspired writers. Luke alone gives us historic information about Zechariah and Elizabeth, the parents of John the Baptist, and tells us about John's birth. Only Luke tells us about the angel's announcement to Mary of our Saviour's birth. It is only in Luke's Gospel that we read of Simeon, Anna, and Mary's song. Luke alone gives us information about our Redeemer's childhood. None of the other Gospel narratives tell us about the conversions of Zacchaeus and the dying thief. Only Luke gives us the parables of The Good Samaritan, The Pharisee and the Publican, The

Prodigal Son, and The Rich Man and Lazarus. Only Luke tells us about the Lord's walk with two of his disciples along the Emmaus road after his resurrection. How thankful we are for these things! For these things we are indebted to Luke, 'the beloved physician'.

Luke Himself

Who was this man, Luke? As we have seen, both this gospel narrative and the book of Acts were written by Luke. But who was Luke? He was a man of such modesty that he never mentioned his own name, even when he wrote about events in which he played a prominent role. Yet, he was, obviously, a man of remarkable usefulness in the early church.

Paul calls him, 'Luke the beloved physician' (Colossians 4:14). As was remarked concerning Theophilus, not many of the wise and noble of this world are called, but some are; and Luke was one of them. He was Paul's constant, faithful companion. He accompanied Paul on his second missionary journey as far as Philippi. There, after the Lord raised up a gospel church, Luke stayed behind, probably to take care of and further instruct the young saints at Philippi in the things of God.

Seven years later, while Paul was on his third missionary journey, he and Luke joined up again at Philippi. As Paul went on his way to Jerusalem, Luke went with him. When Paul was arrested at Caesarea, Luke was with him. Luke was still by Paul's side when they sailed for Rome. He went with his friend through the perils of the sea and stayed by his side when he was arrested at Rome. Luke alone stayed with Paul to the end. When Paul was about to lay down his life as a martyr for Christ, he wrote, 'Only Luke is with me' (2 Timothy 4:11).

Luke was a Gentile, as his name indicates, the only Gentile who was chosen of God to write a portion of the inspired volume of holy scripture.

The Son of Man

Luke gives us a portrait of the Son of Man, the Man Christ Jesus. All the gospel writers show us both the divinity and the humanity of Christ; but John was distinctly written to set forth our Lord's eternal deity; and Luke was distinctly written to show us his perfect humanity. Let us never forget that our Lord Jesus Christ lived upon this earth the life of a perfect man, completely obedient to the will of God, as our Surety, Representative, Mediator, and Substitute, without sin in nature, thought, word, or deed. Had he not been a perfect man, he could not have been our Saviour. Therefore, Luke was inspired of God to show us the perfection of our Saviour as a real man.

The Lord Jesus Christ was a Man of great courage. He was not a hard, abrasive man; but he was a courageous man. This boldness and courage is seen most distinctly in our Lord's preaching. He knew that he was his Father's Servant. Therefore, he spoke the Word of God with unflinching courage (chapter 4). When he was advised to flee from Herod, he basically said, 'Go tell that old fox that I am doing what I came here to do, and that he can't stop me' (13:32).

When the time came for him to lay down his life as our sin-atoning Substitute, our Saviour set his face like a flint to go up to Jerusalem, that he might accomplish the will of him that sent him (9:51). Fearlessly and unfalteringly, our Saviour walked, step by step, with determined resolve, up to Mount Calvary to lay down his life for us, according to the will of God, not in defeat but in victory, not to be pitied but worshipped.

Our Lord Jesus Christ was also a Man of great tenderness, compassion, and sympathy. He declared in his very first sermon, that he came here to preach the gospel to the poor, to set the captive free, and to give sight to the blind (4:18-19). Luke constantly portrays the Lord Jesus as a man full of compassion, drying tears of sorrow, pitying the outcast, entertaining despised publicans, receiving sinners, healing all who had need of healing. Let every man learn from the Master. Manhood, real manhood involves both courage and compassion.

Moreover, and this is very, very important, as the perfect Man, our Lord Jesus Christ was a Man of implicit faith. He believed God perfectly. He lived in constant fellowship with God as a Man. What an example of consecration and faith he gave us! His very first recorded words were, 'I must be about my Father's business' (2:49). His last words before his final breath of mortality were, 'Father, into thy hands I commend my spirit' (23:46).

On at least eight other occasions, Luke describes our Lord Jesus as a Man of faith, calling upon God his Father, and our Father, in prayer.

> At his baptism (3:21)
> After healing the leper (5:16)
> Before choosing his disciples (6:12)
> Before Peter's great confession (9:18)
> At his transfiguration (9:29)
> Before teaching his disciples how to pray (11:1)
> In Gethsemane (22:42)
> As he hung upon the cross (23:34)

As God's servants in this world, we all must confess, with shame and sorrow, that we are often weak, hard hearted, and unbelieving. But, blessed be God, that Man who is our divine Saviour lived before God in the perfection of manhood for us – perfect in courage, perfect in tenderness, mercy and compassion, perfect in faith! But he is more than an exemplary Man.

Luke presents this holy Man, the Lord Jesus Christ, to us as God's Salvation. He brought salvation to sinners. He won it by his obedience. He bought it with his blood. He secured it by his ascension into heaven. He gives it by his grace. But Luke tells us more. He tells us that the Lord Jesus Christ himself is Salvation (2:25-32).

Salvation is not a creed, a confession, a church, or an experience. Salvation is a Person, the Lord Jesus Christ. We rejoice in the blood and righteousness of Christ and adore his doctrine; but it is the Lord Jesus Christ himself that we trust, love, honour and worship. 'Unto you that believe, *He* is precious'.

The gospel we preach is the good news of salvation accomplished and secured by the obedience and death of the God-man, Christ Jesus. Luke, speaking in perfect harmony with all the prophets and apostles, tells us that this salvation is God's Salvation; his work, his property, his gift. It is a finished work.

Salvation is a work accomplished for sinners of every race, Jew and Gentile, everywhere. This salvation demands faith in Christ, a faith that only God himself can give, a faith that willingly bows to Christ as Lord, a salvation to be preached to all the world.

Luke's object is to show us the humanity of our Saviour; but his humanity would be of no value to us if he is not God. All that he was and did as a man would be totally without benefit to us, if he is not God. So Luke shows us that this great man is much more than that. He shows us that this great Man is the Almighty God.

Christ is omnipotent. He has all power over all things and exercises it all the time. The God-man, our Mediator, has complete authority over all evil (4:12, 35; 9:38; 11:14). He controls all of what men call 'the elements of nature' (8:22-25; 9:12-17; 5:4-11). He has total dominion over life and death (8:41-42; 7:11-15). He has total dominion over sickness, disease, and trouble (Luke 5:12-13; 7:1-10; 4:38-35; 5:18-25; 6:6-10; 18:35-43). He has power in heaven and in earth to forgive sins (5:24; 7:48). He has the power and authority to bless people (6:20-22), and to give eternal life in heaven to whomsoever he chooses (23:43; 24:46-47). All things are in his hands (John 17:2).

Gospel For Sinners

The gospel of God is a gospel for sinners; the good news of redemption obtained and salvation finished is for poor, needy, lost sinners. Luke's Gospel is just that. It is good news for needy sinners. Luke shows us the compassionate love of Christ in becoming Man to save us. He traces our Lord's descent back to Adam, and shows him as the Son of Man and the Son of God, the Saviour of men. He is both the 'Son of the Highest' and the Son of the lowest.

Like Matthew, Luke gives us our Lord's genealogy (3:23-38); but it is not the same. Matthew's account of the genealogy begins with Abraham and traces the Saviour's lineage up to Joseph. Luke begins with the Saviour himself and traces his lineage back to Adam, and then to God himself. Matthew shows us our Saviour's lineage through Joseph, him 'being (as was supposed) the son of Joseph' (Luke 3:23). Luke traces his lineage through Mary.

The Shepherds

Instead of the visit of the Magi, Luke tells us of the common shepherds to whom the Saviour's birth was announced as glad-tidings of peace to all people, 'To you is born a Saviour, which is Christ the Lord'.

Simeon and Anna

Aged Simeon said, 'Mine eyes have seen thy salvation', as he took the Holy Child in his arms. And Anna 'spake of him to all that looked for Redemption in Israel'. Luke records his compassion to the Widow of Nain (7:11-18), and of his tenderness and mercy toward the woman that was a sinner (7:36-50). Luke tells us the story of Zacchaeus and of the consequent murmuring of the Pharisees because he had gone to be a guest with a man which was a sinner (19:1-10).

The Parables

The parables recorded in Luke's Gospel are intended to display both our Redeemer's compassion and his saving power and efficacy. The parable of the Good Samaritan shows us how condescending Christ is in the exercise of his saving mercy. The parable of the Pharisee and the Publican show the contempt of our Saviour for self-righteous religionists and his great mercy, love, and grace to needy sinners. The parable of the Importunate Widow shows us how that all who need and seek his grace find it at the throne of grace. The Parable of the Lost Sheep, the Lost Coin, and the Lost Son show us the great joy there is in the very heart of God over the lost one that is found. In the parable of the Great Supper (14:16-24; Matthew 22:1-14), it is Luke who tells us of the Lord's command to go out into the highways and hedges and compel them to come in. The words, 'Yet there is room', seem to echo throughout these 24 chapters.

Luke alone tells us that when our Lord beheld the city, he wept over it (19:41-44). It is Luke who describes the Saviour's bloody sweat in Gethsemane (22:39-46). Luke tells us of the saving power possessed by our Saviour as he hung upon the cursed tree, displayed in saving the dying thief, gathering as it were, even in his agony, the first-fruits of his atonement (23:39-43).

Luke alone gives us the account of our Lord's walk along the Emmaus road with two of his troubled disciples after his resurrection (chapter 24). It may be, as some have suggested, that Luke was one of those two disciples. He tells of our Lord eating a piece of broiled fish and some honey to show us his perfect humanity, even after his resurrection. Yes, blessed be his name, that Man, who is risen and exalted, is still a man touched with the feeling of our infirmities, full of sympathy, and yet is the omnipotent God, able to help in time of need!

The Last Scene

The last scene in the Gospel of Luke is a scene that Luke alone gives us (chapter 24). First, in verses 44-47, the Saviour condescends to confirm the shaken faith of his fearful disciples and opens their understanding to comprehend the scriptures.

'And he said unto them, These are the words which I spake unto you, while I was yet with you, that all things must be fulfilled, which were written in the law of Moses, and in the prophets, and in the psalms, concerning me. Then opened he their understanding, that they might understand the scriptures, And said unto them, Thus it is written, and thus it behoved Christ to suffer, and to rise from the dead the third day: And that repentance and remission of sins should be preached in his name among all nations, beginning at Jerusalem.'

Then, he issues his commission to his church, assuring us of the power of his Spirit to do his work (vv. 48-49). 'And ye are witnesses of these things. And, behold, I send the promise of my Father upon you: but tarry ye in the city of Jerusalem, until ye be endued with power from on high'. Then in verses 50-53 the crucified, risen Son of Man ascends to Glory to take his place on his throne as the God-man, and blesses his people as he ascends his throne. As he did, we read, 'And he led them out as far as to Bethany, and he lifted up his hands', those nail pierced hands into which the Lord God has placed the reigns of the universe as our Mediator, 'and blessed them', as the High Priest whose sacrifice God had accepted. 'And it came to pass, while he blessed them, he was parted from them, and carried up into heaven'. There he sits, King forever (Romans 9:5), our almighty and all-prevailing Advocate, God over all, full of mercy, love and grace. 'And they worshipped him, and returned to Jerusalem with great joy: And were continually in the temple, praising and blessing God'. Let us worship him, obey him with great joy, and ever be found praising and blessing our God because of this Man who is our Saviour. 'Amen'.

Chapter 43

John

Christ the Son of God

The apostle John tells us exactly what his purpose was in writing his gospel narrative, 'Many other signs truly did Jesus in the presence of his disciples, which are not written in this book: But these are written, that ye might believe that Jesus is the Christ, the Son of God; and that believing ye might have life through his name' (20:30-31). John wrote his Gospel to show us that Jesus of Nazareth is the Christ, the Son of God; and he begins his message by stating that fact clearly, emphatically, and beautifully. 'In the beginning was the Word, and the Word was with God, and the Word was God. The same was in the beginning with God' (1:1-2).

There is one word used repeatedly throughout these 21 chapters. That one word is the key to all things spiritual, the key to spiritual life, spiritual knowledge, and spiritual understanding. The word is 'believe'. John uses it 98 times in this Gospel. His intention is that 'we might believe that Jesus is the Christ, the Son of God; and that believing, we might have life through his name'. May the God of all grace give us grace to go on believing 'that Jesus is the Christ, the Son of God'.

Distinctive Features

Matthew, Mark, and Luke are called 'The Synoptic Gospels' because they each give us an orderly, well-arranged narrative of our Saviour's earthly life and ministry, describing (for the most part) the same events in different ways and for different purposes. John's Gospel is different. It was written much later than the other three. In the Gospel of John we are given the inspired reflections of an old man who had faithfully served the Son of God many, many years. With one foot in heaven, he tells us of his all-glorious Saviour, the Son of God, that we might believe him. John's Gospel is neither a historical biography nor a theological textbook. Rather, what we have here is the loving adoration of a saved sinner for his great Saviour, describing the greatness, grace, and glory of the Son of God as he had experienced it.

There are several things that stand out as distinctive features of John's Gospel. Unlike Matthew, Mark, and Luke, John does not mention any of our Lord's parables. Yet, he was inspired to describe miracles not recorded by the other writers. John alone tells us about the Lord Jesus turning water into wine at the marriage feast in Cana (2:1-11), the healing of the nobleman's son (4:46-54), the healing of the lame man at the Pool of Bethesda (5:1-9), the feeding of the five thousand (6:1-14), the Lord Jesus coming to his disciples walking across the stormy sea (6:15-21), the healing of the man born blind (9:1-7), and the resurrection of Lazarus (11:38-44).

The miracles described by John seem to have been specifically intended to lay the foundation for something our Lord was about to teach. When the Master was about to teach some great truth, he performed a miracle to illustrate what he was about to say. He had a way of getting people's attention.

Just before he drove the money changers out of the temple and told how that he was about to build a greater, more glorious temple by his death and resurrection, our Saviour turned water into wine. 'This beginning of miracles did Jesus in Cana of Galilee, and manifested forth his glory; and his disciples believed on him' (2:11). Just before declaring himself to be the Son of God, into whose hands the Father has committed all things in chapter 5, our Lord healed the nobleman's son and the impotent man. Just before telling us that he is the Bread of Life in chapter 6, our Saviour fed five thousand men with five loaves of bread and two small fish. The Lord Jesus came walking across the stormy sea, showing his dominion over all things, teaching us to trust him, just before his disciples saw the multitudes abandon him because of the gospel he preached (chapter 6). In John 8:12 our Saviour declared, 'I am the light of the world: he that followeth me shall not walk in darkness, but shall have the light of life'. Then, in chapter 9 he healed the man who was born blind and said, 'I am the light of the world'. After declaring to Martha, 'I am the resurrection and the life' (11:25), the Master went out to the tomb and raised Lazarus from the dead.

'I AM'

Another distinctive feature of John's Gospel is the fact that he alone gives us the seven 'I AM' sayings of Christ. Seven times the Lord says, 'I AM'. These sayings are very precious and give us a delightful, instructive picture of our Redeemer. 'I AM' is the name by which the Lord God revealed himself to Moses in Exodus 3:13-14. By taking this title and name as his own the Lord Jesus declared himself to be God, and did so at least seven times.

'I am the bread of life' (6:35). If we would live, we must eat this Bread.

'I am the light of the world' (8:12). If we would see, we must have this Light.

'I am the door of the sheep' (10:7). If we would enter into life, we must enter by this Door.

'I am the good shepherd' (10:11). If we are saved, we must be saved by this Shepherd.

'I am the resurrection and the life' (11:25). If we would be partakers of resurrection glory and eternal life, he who is the Resurrection and the Life must be ours. We must trust him.

'I am the way, the truth, and the life' (14:6). If we would have eternal life, we must be in the Way, know the Truth, and be given the Life.

'I am the true vine' (15:1). If we would bring forth fruit unto God, we must be grafted into this Vine.

The significance of our Lord using the words 'I AM' with reference to himself must not be overlooked. This enraged the Jews because they understood exactly what he meant by this description. He was saying, 'I am the eternal God, Jehovah, the Redeemer and Deliverer. I am all, for I am God'. Using these two words, 'I AM', with reference to himself, he identified himself as the covenant God of Israel. Liberals and religious infidels today may not recognize that fact; but the Jews who heard the Master understood him perfectly (John 8:58-59; 10:31-33).

John also gives a distinct emphasis to the fact that the Lord Jesus spoke of a specific time and hour for which he came into the world (2:4; 7:6, 8, 30; 8:20; 12:23, 27-28; 13:1; 17:1).

Divisions

In chapters 1-12 John tells us who Christ is, giving highlights of his life and ministry during the three years of public, earthly ministry. In chapters 13-21 the apostle gives an account (an account none could give except a tender-hearted old man, full of love for Christ) of our Lord's last night upon the earth, his death as our Substitute, and his resurrection.

Christ our God

That *Man* Luke described, the *Servant* Mark portrayed, and the *King* Matthew declared, Jesus of Nazareth, is himself the Christ, the Son of God, our eternal God and Saviour. That is what John asserts with utter dogmatism in chapter 1. John declares that this man is the Word who is God (v. 1), the second person of the holy trinity, altogether equal with the Father (v. 2), the Creator of all things (v. 3), and the incarnate God our Saviour (vv. 10-18, 29). This Man who is God is the Lamb of God, spoken of and typified throughout the Old Testament, by whose sacrifice our sins are taken away.

Best Things Last

In chapter 2, when our Lord turned the water into wine and began to show forth his glory, the governor of the feast said to the bridegroom, 'Every man at the beginning doth set forth good wine; and when men have well drunk, then that which is worse: but thou hast kept the good wine until now' (v. 10). That is exactly what our Saviour does in his wondrous works of grace. He saves the best wine until the last (1 Corinthians 2:9). As good as the experience of God's grace in Christ is here, it is but a foretaste of that which awaits us in heaven's glory.

The New Birth

In the first chapter we are told that sinners are made to be the sons of God and are born again by the will of God alone (11-13). In chapter 3 we have our Lord's discourse on the new birth with Nicodemus. Here he shows us both the nature and necessity of the new birth. Until a person is born again he can neither see nor enter into the kingdom of God (vv. 3, 5). This spiritual new birth is altogether the work of God the Holy Spirit sovereignly giving life and faith to whom he will (v. 8). Then, the Master told Nicodemus that the only way any sinner can live before God, the only way we can be saved is by trusting him as our sin-atoning Substitute (vv. 14-18).

All grace, all salvation, all life, all hope is in Christ. Do you believe on the Son of God? Do you trust Christ alone as your Saviour? That is the one thing that must be settled. To believe Christ is to have life. To abide in unbelief is to abide in death, under the wrath of God. That was John the

Baptist's message and that is the message of God's preachers in every age and place, 'The Father loveth the Son, and hath given all things into his hand. He that believeth on the Son hath everlasting life: and he that believeth not the Son shall not see life; but the wrath of God abideth on him' (vv. 35-36). 'He that hath the Son hath life; and he that hath not the Son of God hath not life' (1 John 5:12).

The Samaritan Woman

In chapter 4 John gives us a tremendous picture of God's grace. Our Lord Jesus 'must needs go through Samaria' because there was an elect sinner there for whom the time of love had come. Grace chose her. Grace marked the place at which grace would be given. Grace brought the Samaritan woman to the appointed place at the time of love. Grace brought Christ to the sinner. And grace brought the sinner to Christ and gave her faith.

The Impotent Man

In chapter 5 our Saviour came to the Pool of Bethesda. There were many around the pool who were impotent, blind, halt, and withered. But the sovereign Saviour came there to show mercy to one certain individual, a particular, chosen sinner who had been impotent for thirty-eight years. 'And immediately the man was made whole' (v. 9).

That is another picture of God's saving grace. It is sovereign, distinguishing, effectual grace. Spiritually, God's elect are totally impotent. We could never be saved if any part of salvation depended on us. But it does not. The Lord Jesus saves poor, impotent sinners by his own almighty arm of omnipotent mercy (Ephesians 2:1-5).

Witnesses to Christ

In the second half of chapter 5 our Lord Jesus shows himself to be the Christ by numerous witnesses. As we read these verses and others like them (10:16-18), we must not imagine that our Lord is declaring anything that might suggest him being inferior to the Father. Rather, our Lord is declaring his voluntary subjection to the will of his Father (Isaiah 50:5-7) as our Mediator and Surety.

'Then answered Jesus and said unto them, Verily, verily, I say unto you, The Son can do nothing of himself, but what he seeth the Father do: for what things soever he doeth, these also doeth the Son likewise. For the Father loveth the Son, and sheweth him all things that himself doeth: and he will show him greater works than these, that ye may marvel. For as the Father raiseth up the dead, and quickeneth them; even so the Son quickeneth whom he will. For the Father judgeth no man, but hath committed all judgment unto the Son: That all men should honour the Son, even as they honour the Father. He that honoureth not the Son honoureth not the Father which hath sent him. Verily, verily, I say unto you, He that heareth my word, and believeth on him that sent me, hath everlasting life, and shall not come into condemnation; but is passed from death unto life. Verily, verily, I say unto you, The hour is coming, and now is, when the dead shall hear the voice of the Son of God: and they that hear shall live. For as the Father hath life in himself; so hath he given to the Son to have life in himself; And hath given him authority to execute judgment also, because he is the Son of man. Marvel not at this: for the hour is coming, in the which all that are in the graves shall hear his voice, And shall come forth; they that have done good, unto the resurrection of life; and they that have done evil, unto the resurrection of damnation. I can of mine own self do nothing: as I hear, I judge: and my judgment is just; because I seek not mine own will, but the will of the Father which hath sent me. If I bear witness of myself, my witness is not true' (5:19-31).

John the Baptist bore witness to him as the Christ, the Lamb of God, the eternal Saviour (vv. 33-35). His own works; his miracles, his satisfaction, the rent veil, all bear witness that he is the Christ, the Son of God, our Saviour (v. 36). The Father bore witness to Christ (v. 37) at his baptism and at his transfiguration, trusting him as our Surety (Ephesians 1:12), putting all things in his hands as the Son of Man (v. 27), and giving him all pre-eminence (Colossians 1:18; Philippians 2:8-11). And the book of God bears witness to him, that he is indeed the Christ (vv. 37-39). Moses, in all the books of the law, bore witness to him, typically and prophetically, and by the veil being rent, witness is made that he had fulfilled the whole law, satisfying the wrath and justice of God as our Representative (vv. 46-47).

The Offence of the Gospel

Multitudes followed our Saviour, not because they were converted by his grace, but because they had eaten the loaves and fish. They were religious because they found religion profitable. They followed Christ outwardly because of what they gained by doing so. But, then, our Lord preached a message that offended the crowd. We read in John 6:66 'From that time many of his disciples went back, and walked no more with him'. What did he preach? What was it that so greatly offended the multitudes? It was the message of God's free, sovereign, saving grace, the same message that offends lost religious crowds throughout the world today.

It was the declaration that salvation is by the will of God alone (vv. 37-40). He asserted that fallen man's natural, total depravity makes salvation by the will of man impossible (v. 44). Our Master declared that salvation is altogether the work of God's free, sovereign, irresistible grace (v. 45) and this salvation can be possessed only by faith in Christ, eating his flesh and drinking his blood, trusting his righteousness and his atonement as our only ground of acceptance with God (vv. 47-58). This salvation was obtained by Christ laying down his life for chosen sinners scattered throughout the world (v. 51).

'These things said he in the synagogue, as he taught in Capernaum. Many therefore of his disciples, when they had heard this, said, This is an hard saying; who can hear it? When Jesus knew in himself that his disciples murmured at it, he said unto them, Doth this offend you? What and if ye shall see the Son of man ascend up where he was before? It is the spirit that quickeneth; the flesh profiteth nothing: the words that I speak unto you, they are spirit, and they are life. But there are some of you that believe not. For Jesus knew from the beginning who they were that believed not, and who should betray him. And he said, Therefore said I unto you, that no man can come unto me, except it were given unto him of my Father. From that time many of his disciples went back, and walked no more with him' (6:59-66).

These were the same people who sought just a short while earlier, to take him by force and make him a king (6:15).

'If Any Man Thirst'

In the seventh chapter "the Jews' feast of tabernacles was at hand". His brethren tried to get the Lord to go up to the feast, to show himself to the world, but he refused. Later, he went up to the feast privately. Then, on the last day of the feast, as our Master beheld the multitudes going home from their religious ritual, he proclaimed a great, magnanimous, gracious, invitation to needy souls that is echoed around the world to this day, wherever the gospel is preached.

'In the last day, that great day of the feast, Jesus stood and cried, saying, If any man thirst, let him come unto me, and drink. He that believeth on me, as the scripture hath said, out of his belly shall flow rivers of living water' (vv. 37-38).

The Adulterous Woman

The eighth chapter opens (vv. 1-11) with a tremendous picture of redemption and grace in Christ. A woman taken in adultery, scorned by men and condemned by God's holy law, is freely and fully forgiven of all sin by the Son of God who stooped to the earth and rose again.

Disciples Indeed

Beginning in verse 31 of chapter 8 our Lord gives us four unmistakable marks by which true disciples, true children of Abraham are identified in this world: (1.) They do the works of Abraham (v. 39). That is to say, they believe God. (2.) True disciples love Christ (v. 42; 1 John 4:19). (3.) They receive, bow to, and believe God's Word (v. 47). (4.) They keep Christ's doctrine (v. 51), they continue in his Word (v. 31) and holdfast the gospel.

The Good Shepherd

In the ninth chapter our Lord healed a man who was born blind. Because of this the Jewish authorities excommunicated the man. They kicked him out of their church because the Son of God gave him sight. His parents, out of fear of the same treatment, virtually disowned him. But the Lord took him into his arms, into the sheepfold of his grace. Now, John gives us our Saviour's great discourse on the Good Shepherd (chapter 10). Christ is the Good Shepherd and he has sheep. He voluntarily laid down his life for his sheep. He calls his sheep by name. He must and shall save his sheep. He gives his sheep eternal life. His sheep shall never perish!

Lazarus

The eleventh chapter tells us about Mary, Martha, and Lazarus, our Lord's beloved friends, and the sickness and death of Lazarus by the will of God and for the glory of God. Then, we see the Son of God raise Lazarus from the dead by the Word of his omnipotence. What a picture this is of God's saving operations of grace! Like Lazarus, I was dead. Like Lazarus, the Lord Jesus loved me. He came to where I was. He called me by name. I came forth to him and he set me free.

Chapter 12 opens with our Lord in the home of his friends Martha, Mary, and Lazarus again. Mary anoints him for his burial. As he sets his face toward Calvary, our Lord declares that which he would there accomplish by the sacrifice of himself 'Now is the judgment of this world: now shall the prince of this world be cast out. And I, if I be lifted up from the earth, will draw all men unto me. This he said, signifying what death he should die' (vv. 31-33).

Foot Washing

Chapter 13 begins the second section of John's Gospel. Everything, from here through to the end of chapter 19 took place in the last hours of our Saviour's earthly life. In chapter 13 he gives us an example of how we ought to love one another by washing his disciples' feet. He did not do this to establish foot washing as a church ordinance, but to show us how to love one another. Love involves action, not sentimental words. Love bows low and gladly performs the most menial task for the sheer comfort of its object. 'By this shall all men know that ye are my disciples, if ye have love one to another' (v. 35).

Then our Lord told Peter how that he would deny him three times before the morning sun arose. 'Simon Peter said unto him, Lord, whither goest thou? Jesus answered him, Whither I go, thou canst not follow me now; but thou shalt follow me afterwards. Peter said unto him, Lord, why cannot I follow thee now? I will lay down my life for thy sake. Jesus answered him, Wilt thou lay down thy life for my sake? Verily, verily, I say unto thee, The cock shall not crow, till thou hast denied me thrice' (vv. 36-38).

Immediately after that, we read those sweet, sweet words of comfort and assurance in John 14:1-3. 'Let not your heart be troubled: ye believe in God, believe also in me. In my Father's house are many mansions: if it were not so, I would have told you. I go to prepare a place for you. And if I go and prepare a place for you, I will come again, and receive you unto myself; that where I am, there ye may be also'. How Peter must have cherished those words after his fall and restoration!

Comfort

Chapters 14, 15, and 16 are filled with words of tender comfort and instruction for God's people in this world in which we must endure constant sorrow and tribulation. 'These things I have spoken unto you, that in me ye might have peace. In the world ye shall have tribulation: but be of good cheer; I have overcome the world' (16:33).

The Lord's Prayer

Then, in chapter 17 John gives us the Lord's great, high priestly prayer for us, in which he prays not for the world but for his elect, asking his Father to keep us throughout our days on earth, through all our tribulations, and then to bring us safe to glory. Only in eternity can we know the full scope of our Lord's words recorded here.

'And the glory which thou gavest me I have given them; that they may be one, even as we are one: I in them, and thou in me, that they may be made perfect in one; and that the world may know that thou hast sent me, and hast loved them, as thou hast loved me. Father, I will that they also, whom thou hast given me, be with me where I am; that they may behold my glory, which thou hast given me: for thou lovedst me before the foundation of the world. O righteous Father, the world hath not known thee: but I have known thee, and these have known that thou hast sent me. And I have declared unto them thy name, and will declare it: that the love wherewith thou hast loved me may be in them, and I in them' (17:22-26)

When I compare John 17:5 with John 17:22, I am utterly overwhelmed. Can it be true? Has the Lord Jesus Christ, the Son of God, our all-glorious Redeemer given to everyone of his elect all the glory the Father gave to him as our covenant Surety and Mediator, all the glory that he now possesses as the God-man in heaven? Are we really and truly so perfectly one with him and so perfectly accepted in him that we shall all fully possess all the glory the Father gave him as the reward of his obedience unto death? Yes, O my soul, yes, it is true! He who is God and cannot lie declares it to be so!

Gethsemane

Chapter 18 brings us with our all-glorious Christ into Gethsemane. But John leaves out most of the things described by Matthew and Luke. Instead, he tells us of our Saviour's care for his disciples when the soldiers came to arrest him, emphasizing the fact that he is God in total control, even over those who arrested him. Here again, we have a picture of redemption and grace. As if to demonstrate that he is God over all, not a helpless victim, the Saviour takes the initiative. He asked the soldiers, 'Whom seek ye?' When they told him they had come for that man called Jesus, he declared, 'I AM', and they fell down as dead men. Those men, representing the law by which he was to be executed, were slain before him. Then, the Master said, 'I AM' ('he' is in italics), 'If therefore ye seek me, let these go their way'. That is exactly what our Saviour says to the law of God. You can't have me and my sheep. If you take me, you must let my people go free (vv. 4-9; cf. Exodus 3:14, 15).

'It is Finished'

In chapter 19 our Saviour is crucified. In verse 30 we read these great, triumphant words of our victorious Redeemer, 'It is finished!' 'When Jesus therefore had received the vinegar, he said, It is finished: and he bowed his head, and gave up the ghost'. What was finished? The law was finished, being satisfied (Romans 10:4). The prophets were finished, being fulfilled. All the work he came to do (Matthew 1:21; John 1:45) was finished. Atonement was finished. Righteousness was finished. Judgment was finished. Sin was finished.

Restoration

Chapters 20 and 21 tell us about our Lord's resurrection and his appearances to his disciples after the resurrection. By his death and resurrection as our Substitute, our Lord Jesus reconciled us to our God, restored all that we had lost by the sin and fall of our father Adam, and restored us entirely to our God. Is it not most fitting that John shows us the restoration of his fallen disciple in this context? The Lord Jesus came to Peter in grace, assuring him of his love and forgiveness, and assuring Peter of his love for his Saviour.

Conclusion

We read in John 21:25, 'And there are also many other things which Jesus did, the which, if they should be written every one, I suppose that even the world itself could not contain the books that should be written. Amen'. When John says, 'I suppose', he is still writing by inspiration. It is as though the Lord God is telling us, 'You cannot imagine how big my Son is, how great he is, and what wonders he has accomplished. If you go into every detail of who he is and what he has done, the world itself would not hold the books it would take to declare it all'. There could not be a more fitting conclusion of the Gospel of the Son of God.

Chapter 44

The Acts Of The Apostles

The Unfinished Story

Some things are finished. How we ought to rejoice in that blessed fact! When our Saviour cried, 'It is finished', all the work he intended to accomplish on earth was finished. Nothing was left undone that he came here to do.

> Nothing, either great or small;
> Nothing, sinner, no;
> Jesus did it, did it all,
> Long, long ago!
>
> When He, from His lofty throne,
> Stooped to do and die,
> Everything was fully done;
> Hearken to His cry –
>
> 'It is finished!' Yes indeed,
> Finished every jot.
> Sinner, this is all you need.
> Tell me, is it not?

Weary, working, plodding one,
Why toil you so?
Cease your doing, all was done,
Long, long ago!

Till to Jesus' work you cling
By a simple faith,
Doing is a deadly thing.
Doing ends in death!

Cast your deadly 'doing' down,
Down at Jesus' feet.
Stand in Him, in Him alone,
Gloriously complete!

Since Christ died and rose again for all God's elect, righteousness is finished, sin is finished, atonement is finished, satisfaction is finished, the law is finished, the curse is finished, judgment is finished, condemnation is finished. Our all-glorious Christ has put away our sins by the sacrifice of himself. 'By his own blood he entered in once into the holy place, having obtained eternal redemption for us' (Hebrews 9:12).

But the work of Christ as our Mediator and Surety is not yet finished. It will not be finished until he has brought all his sheep into the fold of his grace and presents all God's elect unto the Father, holy, unblameable, and unreproveable in everlasting glory. His work will not be finished until the Father has put all his enemies under his feet, until every knee bows and every tongue confesses, of things in heaven, and things in earth, and things under the earth, that Jesus Christ is Lord.

It is this ongoing work of the risen Christ in the earth that the book of Acts describes. In his Gospel narrative Luke told us all that our Lord Jesus Christ 'began to do'. Here, in the book of Acts, he tells us what our risen, exalted Lord and Saviour continues to do in the earth, through his church, by the preaching of the gospel, and the power and grace of the Holy Ghost.

'The former treatise have I made, O Theophilus, of all that Jesus began both to do and teach, Until the day in which he was taken up, after that he through the Holy Ghost had given commandments unto the apostles whom he had chosen: To whom also he showed himself alive after his passion by many infallible proofs, being seen of them forty days, and speaking of the things pertaining to the kingdom of God: And, being assembled together with them, commanded them that they should not depart from Jerusalem, but wait for the promise of the Father, which, saith he, ye have heard of me. For John truly baptized with water; but ye shall be baptized with the Holy Ghost not many days hence' (1:1-5).

The book of Acts is an inspired history of the apostolic ministry of the early church, covering a period of thirty to thirty-five years. The central theme throughout the book is the ascension and Lordship of the crucified Christ, our Saviour and King.

Twofold Witness

Peter declares, in Acts 5:32, 'We are his witnesses of these things, and so is also the Holy Ghost, whom God hath given to them that obey him'. Throughout these 28 chapters, we see the mighty work of the ascended Christ in this world, by the gospel through the twofold witness of his church and his Spirit. It was Christ who shed forth the Holy Spirit at Pentecost (2:33). It was Christ who chose the men who were sent forth to preach the gospel and chose their various fields of service.

Our Saviour's last words to his church before he ascended into heaven were, 'Ye shall be witnesses unto me both in Jerusalem, and in all Judea, and in Samaria, and unto the uttermost part of the earth' (1:8). But those men, as is so often the case with God's church today, failed to see the breadth of the work the Lord had given them to do. And, again, as is so often the case today, their unwillingness to put aside social, racial prejudices greatly hindered their usefulness.

Though the Lord Jesus plainly told them to carry the gospel to all men, they confined their preaching of the gospel to Jerusalem until the Lord graciously forced them to obey him by sending persecutions that scattered the disciples everywhere. 'Therefore they that were scattered abroad went every where preaching the word' (8:4). The blood of the first New Testament martyr, Stephen (chapter 7), proved to be, as our God assures us all things are, according to his purpose for the salvation of his elect (Romans 8:28-30). It was one of the means used in the purpose of our all-wise God to prepare Saul of Tarsus to be the great Apostle of the Gentiles (8:1-4).

Preaching

The book of Acts tells us much about preaching. Those who were scattered abroad went everywhere preaching the Word. Philip preached Christ in Samaria and the Lord gathered many sheep into his fold. Soon,

Caesarea (8:40), Phenice, Cyprus, Antioch (11:19), and Damascus (9:2) all heard the gospel.

The disciples went everywhere preaching the Word; but what does that mean? What did these disciples preach? The words, 'preach', 'preached', and 'preaching', are used thirty-seven times in the book of Acts. It is not insignificant that every time they are used the subject preached was Jesus Christ and the resurrection. If the book of Acts is to be taken for our standard (and it is), it must be concluded that unless Christ has been preached no preaching has been done. The book of Acts demonstrates that our Lord Jesus Christ was the singular subject of preaching in the earliest days of Christianity (1 Corinthians 1:23; 2 Corinthians 4:5). We see our Saviour's direct, sovereign intervention in bringing chosen Gentiles into his kingdom. Peter carried the Gospel to the Jews at Pentecost (chapter 2), and to the Gentiles in the house of Cornelius (chapter 10), and so fulfilled his promise concerning 'the keys of the kingdom of heaven' (Matthew 16:18-19).

If you read the book of Acts in one sitting, you will find that the history recorded here moves rapidly. It is, as Roger Ellsworth puts it, 'exhilarating reading', as our God's wondrous works are set before us one after the other, in city after city. On one day the Lord graciously added about three thousand souls to his kingdom, all confessing Christ in believer's baptism (2:41). On another day about five thousand, hearing the gospel, believed on the Son of God (4:4).

Witnesses

In chapter 1:8 our Saviour tells us plainly what the lifelong work and responsibility of every believer is. 'Ye shall be witnesses unto me' (Isaiah 43:10, 12; 44:8; Luke 24:48). First, we read, 'Ye shall receive power after that the Holy Ghost is come upon you'. Without question, this refers to the special, apostolic power that came upon those men chosen to be our Lord's apostles. Yet, it certainly has meaning for us today. No one can ever be saved, serve God, or lay down his life in the cause of Christ as his witness until the life-giving power of the Holy Spirit comes upon him in regeneration. 'Salvation is of the Lord!' It is by God's grace alone (Romans 11:6; Ephesians 2:8-9). Then, when the life-giving power of the Holy Spirit comes upon you, the Son of God says, 'Ye shall be witnesses unto me'.

A witness is one who accurately and honestly relates to others that which he has heard with his own ears, seen with his own eyes, and felt and experienced in his own heart. He does not relate second-hand information. He declares only what he himself personally knows to be true (1 John 1:1-3). It is the privilege, responsibility, and honour of every believer to be a witness for Christ in his generation. This is every believer's calling and vocation in this world. Every true Christian is a missionary. Every true believer is an evangelist. Every true follower of Christ is a preacher. Every true child of God is his witness.

The word 'witness' is the word from which we get the word 'martyr'. Christ's witnesses are his martyrs, people who lay down their lives in the cause of Christ. Go ahead and work your job so that you can pay the expenses of life; but do not forget that your calling, your life's work, is to be his witness. Let nothing interfere with that.

After making that great promise of grace that is given in chapter 1 verse 8, promising to immerse his church and kingdom into his Spirit, promising to give his church the abiding unction and power of the Holy Spirit, the Lord Jesus ascended up into heaven before the eyes of his disciples, as if to say, 'I am going to my throne, be assured of my promise'.

Faithful, but Fallible

The very next thing we see in the book of Acts is the fact that God's servants, his witnesses in this world, all of them, are sinful, fallible mortals. As someone said, 'the best of men are but men at best'.

Acts 1:12-26 covers a brief waiting period, just 10 days, between the ascension of Christ and the outpouring of the Holy Spirit on the Day of Pentecost. The things that are recorded here were written by Luke by divine inspiration for our learning and admonition. If we are wise, we will lay them to heart.

First, the Lord Jesus Christ fulfilled every prophecy of the Old Testament scriptures relating to his incarnation, life, earthly ministry, crucifixion, resurrection, and ascension. When Luke tells us that the disciples returned from the mount called Olivet to Jerusalem (v. 12), he is, almost casually, telling us that Christ stood upon Mount Olivet when he ascended to heaven, just like the prophet Zechariah said he would (Zechariah 14:4; Ezekiel 11:23). The mount had been divided in two parts by a great earthquake in the days of Uzziah. Our Lord ascended from that part of it which was near Bethany (Luke 24:50). It was there that he began his sufferings (Luke 22:39). It was most fitting, therefore, that he should cast off the reproach of his sufferings there by his glorious ascension.

Second, the path of blessedness and usefulness is the path of obedience (vv. 12-14). The disciples returned to Jerusalem because the Lord commanded them to do so (v. 4). There their enemies awaited them. There they were most likely to suffer and be persecuted. But the Lord's commandment was clear. So they returned (Proverbs 3:5-6).

There, in a large upper room, they met together in prayer, united in heart, waiting for the promise of the Holy Spirit. Much needed to be done. They had a message to proclaim. Sinners were perishing. But the Lord had commanded them to wait. So they waited. They were waiting upon the Lord, waiting for God to move, waiting for God to come upon them, waiting for God to open the door before them (Psalm 27:14; 62:5-7; 1 Chronicles 15:13).

We must obey his Word and wait for his direction. In all things the point of our responsibility is the commandment of God. We must obey him. Obeying his Word, the disciples were filled with the Spirit and greatly used of God for much good.

Third, even the best of men are only men at best (vv. 15-26). So long as we are in this world we will be prone to error and sin. We stray in many ways and err in many things. Even true, faithful servants of God are weak, fallible men of flesh and blood. This is manifest in the fact that Peter led the disciples to choose an apostle God had not chosen.

Peter's Mistake

Most certainly, Peter was a faithful man. He had the heart of a true pastor. On other occasions he acted rashly from bad motives, but not here. His motives were good. He wanted what was best for the glory of God, the people of God, and the gospel of God. The sin of Judas had made a vacancy in the apostolic office. Twelve apostles were originally chosen and ordained. As there were twelve tribes in Israel, descended from the twelve patriarchs, so there were twelve apostles. They are the twelve stars, which make up the church's crown (Revelation 12:1). For them, twelve thrones were reserved (Matthew 19:28). Peter read Psalm 69:25 and concluded that it was the responsibility of the church to fill the vacancy left by Judas' apostasy. His error was an error of judgment, not of motive or principle.

He humbly recognized the sovereignty of God in all that had happened (v. 16). He understood that the death of Christ was the work of God for the redemption of his people (2:23; 4:27-28). He realized that God had sovereignly overruled the evil deeds of Judas to accomplish his own eternal purpose (Psalm 41:9).

Peter sorrowfully remembered the fall of his former friend and companion (vv. 17-19). He said no more about the subject than was necessary. Though he and Judas had been close friends, he bowed to the will of God and honoured the judgment of God upon his friend. Peter knew that the only difference between him and Judas was the grace of God (1 Corinthians 4:7).

He reverenced and honoured the Word of God (v. 20). Peter sincerely wanted to obey the scriptures. He thought he was doing what God would have him do. He was motivated by an earnest desire for the glory of God. With genuine reverence, he sought the will of God (vv. 21-25).

Peter should have sought the Lord before he appointed Justus and Matthias. Never say to God, 'Lord, I am going to do this or that, you choose which you want me to do'. Rather, go to God and say, 'What will you have me to do?'

When the lots were cast, Peter led the church to ordain an apostle God had not chosen (v. 26). It was true; the Lord's intention was for his church to have twelve apostles, twelve and only twelve. David's prophecy must be fulfilled. Another apostle must take Judas' place. But, like the others, he must be personally chosen and ordained to the office by Christ himself. The Lord had not chosen Justus or Matthias for this office. He had chosen Paul (1 Corinthians 15:8).

How could Peter have made such a mistake? He sought to determine the will of God by casting lots. Like David, he made the mistake of seeking to determine the will of God by seeking the will of the people (1 Chronicles 13:1-4). He tried to accomplish the will and work of God by the wisdom and energy of the flesh. As a result, Matthias was chosen to do what God had neither called him to do, nor gifted him to do.

Still, Peter was God's appointed leader for that early church. In spite of his many errors, faults, and failures, Peter was God's man, and the people of God rightfully submitted to his rule as their pastor (Hebrews 13:7, 17). Though he was a fallible man, he was a faithful man. He preached the gospel of Christ, sought the will of God, lived for the glory of God, and served the people of God. Blessed is that congregation who has been given such a pastor after God's own heart (Jeremiah 3:15). Faithful pastors do sin. Faithful pastors do err in judgment. Faithful pastors do even err in doctrine. Faithful pastors do make mistakes. Faithful pastors need the prayers and the love of God's people (1 Thessalonians 5:12, 13, 25; Hebrews 13:18).

Pentecost

Acts 2 records the fulfilment of Joel's prophecy (Joel 2), of John the Baptist's message, and of our Saviour's promise in Acts 1:8. The Jews were gathered in Jerusalem for the annual observance of the Feast of Pentecost. That Old Testament, legal observance was highly symbolical. The feast of Pentecost was a picture of the ingathering of God's elect by the mighty operations of God the Holy Spirit.

On this day the Lord Jesus immersed his church and kingdom into the Holy Spirit. This, Peter tells us, was God's declaration that Christ, of whom David was a type, had ascended to his throne as King in Zion. This signal event was identified, as Joel had prophesied, by the disciples proclaiming the gospel in the languages of those who heard them (2:5-11), and the resulting ingathering of souls was great (2:41). Those three thousand souls were but the firstfruits of that great harvest that is sure to come. When all the elect are gathered from all the nations of the world unto Christ, they shall be a multitude more numerous than the stars of heaven and the sands upon the shore.

Deacons

Acts 6 records the next great event in the history of the early church. Seven deacons were chosen by divine order to take care of the material and physical affairs of the church, so that the apostles could give themselves to prayer, study, and preaching. That this was done by divine order is evident from the fact that Paul was later inspired to instruct Timothy (1 Timothy 3) about the men and their work who are ordained as deacons. Though they may, like Stephen and Philip, be teachers and preachers, the purpose of deacons in the local church is to serve the Lord by serving his church and their pastor, relieving the pastor as much as possible of anything that might interfere with his labour in the gospel.

It should be noted that there is no requirement here, or elsewhere in the New Testament, that every local church must have deacons, or that the deacons must be seven in number. Circumstances must determine the need. This local church had about 10,000 members before any deacons were needed. Each local assembly must decide for itself when deacons are needed, how many are needed, and which men in the assembly are gifted for the work of a deacon.

Saul of Tarsus

The offence of the gospel was so great and persecution became so intense that one of the first deacons, Stephen, was stoned to death, while preaching the message of redemption and grace by Christ (7:1-60). In chapter 8 another deacon, Philip, preached the gospel in Samaria and saw many converted. Then, he was carried away by the Holy Spirit to proclaim Christ to a solitary Ethiopian. When the time comes for one of God's chosen to be called, he will by one means or another cause the chosen, redeemed sinner to hear the gospel (Romans 10:17). Our God works in ways beyond our imagination. By leaving the great scene of revival in

Samaria and preaching Christ to this one Eunuch from Ethiopia, Philip was used of God to send the gospel into and through Africa!

Then, we come to chapter 9 and the conversion of Saul of Tarsus, one of the chief persecutors of Christ, his church, and his gospel. Saul the persecutor was transformed by grace into Paul the angel of God by whom the gospel would be carried to the Gentles.

The apostle Paul tells us plainly that his conversion experience was an example and pattern of all true conversions (1 Timothy 1:16). Because his conversion is the pattern by which all conversions must be examined, it is recorded in great detail three times in the book of Acts (9:1-22; 22:4-16; 26:9-19). If you and I are saved by the grace of God, we have experienced the same thing Paul experienced on the Damascus Road.

Salvation begins with divine election (9:15). Saul was saved in time because he was chosen in eternity. Were there no election, there would be no salvation. We would not and could not choose the Lord, but he chose us, and his choice of us made certain that we would choose him (John 15:16). Election is the cause of faith. Faith in Christ is the fruit and evidence of election.

Salvation comes and faith is wrought in the chosen sinner by divine revelation (9:3; 22:14; 2 Corinthians 4:6). Paul was made to see the Lord Jesus Christ and the glory of God in him. He saw how that God could be both just and the Justifier of all who believe, through the substitutionary sacrifice and blood atonement of the Lord Jesus Christ. He saw Christ and heard his voice.

Salvation is the result of a divine call (9:4-9). Saul of Tarsus heard God's call. It was the irresistible call of grace. All the chosen, redeemed sheep of Christ, at the appointed time of love, hear his voice and follow him. The call of the Spirit that comes to chosen sinners by the preaching of the gospel is always effectual (Psalm 65:4). It causes dead sinners to live and come to Christ. This is the pattern of all true conversions. Do you follow the pattern?

Cornelius

In the tenth chapter the Lord God sent Peter to preach the gospel to Cornelius, a Gentile, and his household. When Cornelius and his friends heard the gospel, the same thing happened in Joppa that had happened when Peter preached at Jerusalem. God poured out his Spirit there upon the Gentiles, just as he had in Jerusalem on the Day of Pentecost. This was the second and last outpouring of the Holy Spirit. It was done here to confirm to Peter and the Jewish believers with him that God is no respecter of persons, and that his elect are found among all people (10:34-38).

This is exactly the meaning Peter gave of this, when he got back to Judea and found his friends upset because he had gone to eat with and preach to Gentiles, and that some of the Gentiles had received the Word (11:1-2, 15-18).

'And as I began to speak, the Holy Ghost fell on them, as on us at the beginning. Then remembered I the word of the Lord, how that he said, John indeed baptized with water; but ye shall be baptized with the Holy Ghost. Forasmuch then as God gave them the like gift as he did unto us, who believed on the Lord Jesus Christ; what was I, that I could withstand God? When they heard these things, they held their peace, and glorified God, saying, Then hath God also to the Gentiles granted repentance unto life'.

Peter and Paul

The book of Acts primarily moves around the labours of two men: Peter and Paul. The Lord Jesus appeared to Saul of Tarsus to make him 'a minister and a witness' (26:16), to send him 'far hence unto the Gentiles' (22:21). In Paul's three great missionary journeys the Lord made his will known to his servant with unmistakable clarity.

Peter was primarily the Apostle to the Jews. Paul was primarily the Apostle to the Gentiles. He was the last apostle to be called. It was Paul, not Matthias, who was ordained of God to take Judas' place. The book opens with Peter preaching the gospel in Jerusalem, the great centre of the Jewish nation. It closes with Paul preaching the gospel in Rome, the great centre of the world power.

Missions

No book has ever been written about missions that compares with the book of Acts. Those the Lord had chosen were recognized by the local church in which they served him, and were sent out by God through his church, without a mission board, without deputation (going from church to church begging for bread); and wherever God sent them, when they preached the gospel, 'as many as were ordained to eternal life believed' (13:1-3, 48).

The Lord opened the way before his servants, directed them to his elect, prospered his Word, provided for them, and protected them wherever they went. When Paul wanted to carry the gospel to Asia, the Holy Spirit refused to let him go. When he tried to go to Bithynia to preach Christ there, 'the Spirit suffered them not'. At last, they were sent to Philippi (16:6-13). Why? There were some elect sinners there for whom the time of love had come. Yes, God sovereignly hides the gospel from some and reveals it to others, as he will (Matthew 11:25-26; Romans 9:15-18). At Philippi Paul preached to some women by a river's side, and the Lord opened Lydia's heart to receive the Word. Then, Paul and Silas were arrested, because the time had come for God to save the Philippian jailer and his household.

In chapter 17, they entered into Athens. When Paul beheld a 'city wholly given to idolatry', he preached the same gospel to the 'wise and learned' idolatrous Greek philosophers that he had preached to Lydia and the jailer. A faithful man's message is never adapted to suit his hearers. It is always the same. At Corinth in chapter 18 there was such an uproar in the city because of the gospel that Paul's life appeared to be in jeopardy. 'Then spake the Lord to Paul in the night by a vision, Be not afraid, but speak, and hold not thy peace: For I am with thee, and no man shall set on thee to hurt thee: for I have much people in this city' (vv. 9-10).

Directed by the Spirit of God, the early church pursued a specific method. They went everywhere preaching the gospel. They did not go out building schools and hospitals. 'They went everywhere preaching the word'. They went from one city to another preaching the gospel. 'Some believed and some believed not;' but neither the message nor the method varied. Jerusalem, Samaria, Antioch, Cyprus, Iconium, Lystra, Derbe, Philippi, Thessalonica, Berea, Athens, Corinth, Ephesus, and Rome all heard the message of redemption and grace in Christ. These early preachers were steadfast, straightforward, and successful. They went out in utter dependence upon the living God, with unquenchable zeal and undaunted courage. Their one aim was to fetch God's elect home to their Saviour. Their only message was Christ and him crucified. The only weapon of their warfare was the gospel of the grace of God.

Jerusalem Conference

In Acts 15 Luke gives us the historical narrative of the conference at Jerusalem. Paul explains the theological issues of the conference in Galatians 2 and it is helpful to read these passages together. This conference was not a church council to debate and determine what doctrine should be believed and preached. When Paul went up to Jerusalem, his mind was already made up. He refused to budge an inch, or give any ground at all to the legalists (Galatians 2:5, 21). He went to Jerusalem only so that the doctrine of the believer's absolute freedom in Christ from the law of Moses might be publicly avowed, even by those whose primary sphere of ministry was among the Jews. At the Jerusalem conference, the

apostles and elders, and the church as a whole, being led by the Holy
Spirit (v. 28), publicly denounced legalism and stripped every preacher of
law and legality of all credibility.

Predestination and Responsibility

When we get to Acts 27 Paul is a prisoner on board a ship headed to
Rome. During the voyage a tremendous storm arises. Here we are given a
very instructive lesson with regard to divine predestination and human
responsibility. As far as anyone could tell, all hope of salvation was gone
(v. 18). But that was not the case at all. God had purposed that every man
on board the ship would be saved from the storm and that Paul would be
brought to Rome. He assured Paul of this, and Paul assured the people on
board the doomed ship that they would all come to land without harm (vv.
21-25).

'After long abstinence Paul stood forth in the midst of them, and said,
Sirs, ye should have hearkened unto me, and not have loosed from Crete,
and to have gained this harm and loss. And now I exhort you to be of
good cheer: for there shall be no loss of any man's life among you, but of
the ship. For there stood by me this night the angel of God, whose I am,
and whom I serve, Saying, Fear not, Paul; thou must be brought before
Caesar: and, lo, God hath given thee all them that sail with thee. Wherefore,
sirs, be of good cheer: for I believe God, that it shall be even as it was told
me'.

Later, when he saw the shipmen about to abandon the ship, he told
the centurion and the soldiers that if any left the ship they would perish,
urging them to believe God, relax, and take some nourishment. (vv. 31-35).

'Paul said to the centurion and to the soldiers, Except these abide in
the ship, ye cannot be saved. Then the soldiers cut off the ropes of the
boat, and let her fall off. And while the day was coming on, Paul besought
them all to take meat, saying, This day is the fourteenth day that ye have
tarried and continued fasting, having taken nothing. Wherefore I pray
you to take some meat: for this is for your health: for there shall not an hair
fall from the head of any of you. And when he had thus spoken, he took
bread, and gave thanks to God in presence of them all: and when he had
broken it, he began to eat'.

Why did Paul appear to make the sailor's safety dependent upon
staying aboard ship after declaring the absolute certainty of God's purpose
and promise? He fully understood that the point of man's responsibility
is the command of God, not the purpose of God. He understood that God
has not only ordained the ultimate end of all things, but also every means
by which he will accomplish the end. He understood that every man is

responsible to obey God's command. And he understood that disobedience to the revealed will of God ends in death.

Broken Pieces

Would you be used of God as these men and women were? Read Acts 27:44, and let us observe one more lesson. 'And the rest, some on boards, and some on broken pieces of the ship. And so it came to pass, that they escaped all safe to land'.

God uses raging storms, wrecked ships, broken pieces, and snake bitten men for the building of his kingdom (28:1-10). Brokenness, humility, and contrition of heart are essential to usefulness in the kingdom of God. Only broken hearts know God and walk with God. Rowland Hill once said, 'If you want to see the height of the hill of God's love you must go down into the valley of humility.'

Brokenness, contrition, humility is nothing but a just estimate of ourselves. It is neither more nor less than an honest, heartfelt sense of our utter nothingness. Humility and contrition are the knees of the soul. Christ will never take us into his arms until we lay ourselves at his feet, as David did in Psalms 32 and 51, broken with a sense of real personal sinfulness.

Pray for a broken, contrite heart. God uses broken things (27:44). Brokenness is the beginning of the life of faith. Brokenness is the root of all true revival in the soul. It is painful. Our flesh opposes it. But we must be broken. We will never break ourselves. We must be broken by grace. Our wills must be broken to God's will. Brokenness is dying to self. It is the response of the renewed heart to Holy Spirit conviction (Zechariah 12:10). Because conviction is continual, brokenness is continual.

Brokenness is the spirit of Christ. Christ, who is God, took upon himself the form of a servant. He willingly gave up everything for us. As a Servant he had no rights of his own, no home of his own, no possessions of his own, no will of his own. He did not have so much as an hour to call his own. When he was reviled, he reviled not again, but committed himself to God. He went willingly, but with broken heart, to Calvary, where he was made to be sin for us. Brokenness is found only at the foot of the cross.

Lord, bend this proud and stiffnecked I,
Help me to bow my head and die,
Beholding Him on Calvary
Who bowed His head and died for me!

Brokenness means having no plans, no time, no possessions, no money, no life of my own. It is to be crucified with Christ. It is a constant yielding of ourselves to God. We must seek it; but only God can give it. If we are his, he will. He receives none, but those whom he breaks. Only God can break us.

If he uses us, he will break us. And if he breaks us, he will use us. Paul, along with his shipwrecked companions, came to shore on an 'island called Melita', modern day Malta, wet and cold. As they gathered wood and built a fire, a deadly snake bit Paul on the hand. When he shook it off, without suffering any harm from the viper (Mark 16:18), the barbarians thought he was a god. As a result of all that took place, the Lord God miraculously opened the door, by using venomous self-righteous Jews, barbaric Romans, a storm at sea, a ship wreck, some broken ship timbers, a snake bite, and even the idolatry of a barbaric island tribe, to open the way for the gospel of Christ to be preached among the tribesmen of Malta. Let us ever adore the wisdom and sovereignty of our God. 'Surely the wrath of man shall praise thee: the remainder of wrath shalt thou restrain' (Psalm 76:10).

Chapter 45

Romans

'I am not Ashamed of the Gospel'

The book of Romans is considered by many to be the most profound piece of literature in existence. It is, without question, an epistle of pure gold from beginning to end. It has powerfully influenced and altered the lives of countless men and women for nearly two thousand years. John Calvin said, 'When anyone gains a knowledge of this Epistle, he has an entrance opened to him to all the most hidden treasures of scripture.'

The importance of this epistle cannot be overstated. Martin Luther called the book of Romans 'the perfect Gospel' and referred to it as 'the true masterpiece of the New Testament'. He wrote, 'This letter is truly the most important piece in the New Testament. It is purest Gospel. It is well worth a Christian's while not only to memorize it word for word but also to occupy himself with it daily, as though it were the daily bread of the soul. It is impossible to read or to meditate on this letter too much or too well. The more one deals with it, the more precious it becomes and the better it tastes'.

It was this book, Paul's Epistle to the Romans, that God used to cause 'the light of the glorious gospel of Christ' to shine in Luther's heart and light the fire that lit up the world, that we call 'the Reformation'.

Background

Paul wrote this epistle to the saints at Rome while he was in Corinth. It was not the first of Paul's inspired epistles. In fact, it was one of Paul's latter epistles. It is particularly placed where it is in within the New

Testament by the arrangement of divine providence, perhaps because of its tremendous importance.

We do not know how the church in Rome was started. Paul wrote to them because he had heard of their faith in Christ, and he wanted to serve their souls. He wanted all God's elect to be firmly grounded in the truth. What a magnanimous heart he must have possessed! He took the time, under the pressure of immense responsibilities, to write this masterpiece of pure gospel doctrine to people he had never seen. These things make the book of Romans all the more interesting.

The Gospel

The book is important because it reveals every essential aspect of Gospel doctrine. In the first chapter Paul clearly defines the gospel. Remember, there is but one gospel (Galatians 1:6-9). The New Testament does not reveal a gospel. It reveals the gospel. Here the gospel is defined by a man writing under divine inspiration. All other definitions and descriptions of the gospel given by men must be judged in the light of this definition.

'Paul, a servant of Jesus Christ, called to be an apostle, separated unto the gospel of God, (Which he had promised afore by his prophets in the holy scriptures,) Concerning his Son Jesus Christ our Lord, which was made of the seed of David according to the flesh; And declared to be the Son of God with power, according to the spirit of holiness, by the resurrection from the dead: By whom we have received grace and apostleship, for obedience to the faith among all nations, for his name: Among whom are ye also the called of Jesus Christ' (vv. 1-6).

The Gospel is of God. It is defined here as 'the gospel of God' for at least these four reasons: (1) God is the Author of it, (2) God is the Subject of it, (3) God is the Revealer of it, and (4) God is the Executor of it (Ephesians 1:3-14). The Gospel we believe and preach was 'Promised afore by his prophets in the holy scriptures'. It is not a novel doctrine. This is the everlasting gospel. It was conceived in the heart of God from all eternity. It was ordained before the world was. It was hid in Christ, the Wisdom of God, from the beginning (Proverbs 8). It was revealed to the sons of men in promise, by the prophets, in pictures, in type and in ceremony throughout the Old Testament (Acts 10:43; Hebrews 1:1, 2; Luke 24:44, 45). It was manifested in time by the coming of our Lord (2 Timothy 1:9, 10).

It is 'concerning his Son'. The gospel of God is all about Christ. The gospel is not about baptism, morality, or religious reformation and ritualism of any kind. The gospel is all about Christ. Christ is the express and solitary subject of the gospel. Christ is the gospel. The gospel concerns his person and his work. The whole gospel is included in Christ; and if a man removes one step from Christ, he departs from the gospel (2 Corinthians 11:3; 1 John 5:11-13, 20).

It is all about Christ, who was 'declared to be the Son of God with power, according to the spirit of holiness, by the resurrection from the dead' (v. 4). Be sure you get this. Christ was made or became a man, the seed of David (Galatians 4:4); but he was not made the Son of God. He was 'declared to be the Son of God' (John 10:30). He is declared to be the Son of God with power (Hebrews 1:2,3; Matthew 28:18; John 17:2; 5:36). He was declared to be the Son of God with power, 'according to the spirit of holiness', by whom he was justified when he raised him from the dead (1 Timothy 3:16).

He was declared to be the Son of God by the resurrection from the dead. It is upon this great fact, the fact of his resurrection from the dead that the whole gospel rests (1 Corinthians 15:12-19). Our Lord's resurrection from the dead declares visibly and undeniably that he is all that he claimed. His resurrection is the declaration of our justification (Romans 4:25-5:1). And his resurrection from the dead is the guarantee of ours.

Then, Paul tells us (vv. 5-6) that it is in Christ and by the gospel that we receive grace unto the obedience of faith, being called of God by the irresistible grace and power of his Spirit. It is against this backdrop that Paul declares, 'So, as much as in me is, I am ready to preach the gospel to you that are at Rome also. For I am not ashamed of the gospel of Christ: for it is the power of God unto salvation to every one that believeth; to the Jew first, and also to the Greek. For therein is the righteousness of God revealed from faith to faith: as it is written, The just shall live by faith' (vv. 15-17).

Total Depravity

Beginning with verse 18 in chapter 1 and going through to chapter 3 verse 19, Paul shows us the universal need of the gospel by setting forth the utter depravity and total inability of all men to know God or attain salvation without the gospel. All men by nature are condemned and under the wrath of God because all 'hold (hold down and suppress) the truth of God in unrighteousness' (1:18).

The heathen know the truth of God by the light of nature and conscience, but suppress and pervert it according to their own lusts. The Jews know the truth of God, both by the light of nature and conscience and by the revelation of God in the Old Testament scriptures, but suppress and pervert it according to their own lusts.

Men and women the world over who have the inspired volume of holy scripture, and who have heard the gospel preached in this day are in a position of even greater responsibility. Yet, the world over, fallen men and women sin against the light of creation, the light of conscience, and the light of inspiration in holy scripture, suppressing and perverting the truth of God in unrighteousness according to their own lusts. 'Therefore thou art inexcusable, O man ... For as many as have sinned without law shall also perish without law: and as many as have sinned in the law shall be judged by the law' (2:1, 12).

That simply means that salvation by the works of men is utterly impossible. Salvation must come by the gospel. 'Now we know that what things soever the law saith, it saith to them who are under the law: that every mouth may be stopped, and all the world may become guilty before God' (3:19).

Justification

Beginning in verse 20 of chapter 3 and going through chapter 5, the Holy Spirit shows us that justification is altogether the work of God's free grace in Jesus Christ, without works of any kind on our part. The gospel of Christ is the proclamation of free justification by Christ, the declaration of redemption accomplished, showing forth the righteousness of God, righteousness earned by the faithful obedience of Christ unto death as the sinner's Substitute. It is the proclamation of the good news that the God of heaven is 'a just God and a Saviour' (Isaiah 45:21).

'Therefore by the deeds of the law there shall no flesh be justified in his sight: for by the law is the knowledge of sin. But now the righteousness of God without the law is manifested, being witnessed by the law and the prophets; Even the righteousness of God which is by faith of Jesus Christ unto all and upon all them that believe: for there is no difference: For all have sinned, and come short of the glory of God; Being justified freely by his grace through the redemption that is in Christ Jesus: Whom God hath set forth to be a propitiation through faith in his blood, to declare his righteousness for the remission of sins that are past, through the forbearance of God; To declare, I say, at this time his righteousness: that he might be just, and the justifier of him which believeth in Jesus' (3:20-26).

Abraham and David

In the fourth chapter Paul uses both Abraham and David as examples of this free justification. Both Abraham and David received justification by faith in Christ, just as believers do today. Believing on Christ, God declared them righteous, without any righteousness or righteous works of their own.

'For what saith the scripture? Abraham believed God, and it was counted unto him for righteousness. Now to him that worketh is the reward not reckoned of grace, but of debt. But to him that worketh not, but believeth on him that justifieth the ungodly, his faith is counted for righteousness. Even as David also describeth the blessedness of the man, unto whom God imputeth righteousness without works, Saying, Blessed are they whose iniquities are forgiven, and whose sins are covered. Blessed is the man to whom the Lord will not impute sin' (4:3-8).

Justification is not accomplished by faith. If faith added anything to justification, Paul's statement in 4:16 would not make any sense. Rather, faith receives the blessedness of free justification accomplished by Christ. 'Therefore', we read, 'it is of faith, that it might be by grace; to the end the promise might be sure to all the seed' (v. 16).

When we read in 4:22 that God imputed the righteousness of Christ to Abraham, Paul tells us that that was not written for Abraham's sake alone, 'but for us also, to whom it is being imputed, if we believe on him that raised up Jesus our Lord from the dead' (v. 24, my translation). In verse 25 Paul tells us that justification was accomplished by Christ at Calvary. He was delivered unto death as our Substitute because of our sins imputed to him. On the third day he was raised from the dead because he had accomplished our justification. In 5:1-11, building upon what he has just declared, Paul assures us of justification accomplished and eternal salvation made certain by Christ's finished work.

'Therefore being justified,[1] by faith we have peace with God through our Lord Jesus Christ: By whom also we have access by faith into this grace wherein we stand, and rejoice in hope of the glory of God. And not only so, but we glory in tribulations also: knowing that tribulation worketh patience; And patience, experience; and experience, hope: And hope

---

[1] In my opinion the most serious flaw in our English translation of the New Testament is the placing of the comma after faith rather than after justification. With the comma being placed after faith, it makes it appear that Paul is telling us that justification is conditioned upon our believing, which is diametrically opposed to what he has just declared. The comma should be placed after justified. Faith in Christ brings us the joy and peace of justification; but faith has nothing to do with the accomplishment of justification. Faith is one of the fruits of justification, not the cause.

maketh not ashamed; because the love of God is shed abroad in our hearts by the Holy Ghost which is given unto us. For when we were yet without strength, in due time Christ died for the ungodly. For scarcely for a righteous man will one die: yet peradventure for a good man some would even dare to die. But God commendeth his love toward us, in that, while we were yet sinners, Christ died for us. Much more then, being now justified by his blood, we shall be saved from wrath through him. For if, when we were enemies, we were reconciled to God by the death of his Son, much more, being reconciled, we shall be saved by his life. And not only so, but we also joy in God through our Lord Jesus Christ, by whom we have now received the atonement' (5:1-11).

Two Men

In 5:12-21 Paul shows that our father Adam, and the sin and fall of our race in and by him, was typical and representative of our salvation by Christ. Just as all the human race were made sinners by what Adam did as our representative before God, so all God's elect are made righteous before God by what Christ did as the last Adam, our all-glorious Federal Head, Substitute and Representative before God.

'Wherefore, as by one man sin entered into the world, and death by sin; and so death passed upon all men, for that all have sinned ... Therefore as by the offence of one judgment came upon all men to condemnation; even so by the righteousness of one the free gift came upon all men unto justification of life. For as by one man's disobedience many were made sinners, so by the obedience of one shall many be made righteous. Moreover the law entered, that the offence might abound. But where sin abounded, grace did much more abound: That as sin hath reigned unto death, even so might grace reign through righteousness unto eternal life by Jesus Christ our Lord' (5:12, 18-21).

Paul's message here is very simple and very clear. Righteousness and justification are things accomplished for us by Christ, totally and completely outside our experience and altogether without contribution of any kind from us.

Sanctification

Chapter 6 begins with a brief discussion of believer's baptism, declaring that by baptism every believer is symbolically baptized into Christ and into his death, asserting that when Christ died as our Substitute, we died with him and in him. Rising up from the watery grave, we declare that when Christ arose, we arose with him and in him. Then, Paul draws this conclusion to our symbolic profession of faith in Christ, 'Even so, we also should walk in newness of life'. With that, he begins to tell us about our new life in Christ which we refer to as 'sanctification'.

Being sanctified, separated from all men by the grace of God and made righteous in Christ, we must not serve sin (vv. 6-11). Having assured us that God reckons every believer dead to sin in free justification, he tells us that we who believe ought to use God's reckoning with reference to ourselves. 'Likewise reckon ye also yourselves to be dead indeed unto sin, but alive unto God through Jesus Christ our Lord'.

Being saved by the grace of God, we are free in Christ. We do not live as slaves under the yoke of legal bondage, but as sons and daughters of our God and heavenly Father. Twice in two verses Paul declares that we 'are not under the law' (vv. 14-15).

Then, in the seventh chapter he tells us that we are free from the law in exactly the same way as a woman whose husband is dead is free from the law of her husband. 'Wherefore, my brethren, ye also are become dead to the law by the body of Christ; that ye should be married to another, even to him who is raised from the dead, that we should bring forth fruit unto God' (7:1-4).

Yet, as long as we live in this body of flesh, God's saints in this world live in a constant struggle with sin. Believers are men and women constantly at war with themselves. We would love God with all our hearts and our neighbours as ourselves; but we simply are not able (yet) to do so. We would never sin against our God; but we cannot (yet) live without sin.

'For we know that the law is spiritual: but I am carnal, sold under sin. For that which I do I allow not: for what I would, that do I not; but what I hate, that do I. If then I do that which I would not, I consent unto the law that it is good. Now then it is no more I that do it, but sin that dwelleth in me. For I know that in me (that is, in my flesh,) dwelleth no good thing: for to will is present with me; but how to perform that which is good I find not. For the good that I would I do not: but the evil which I would not, that I do. Now if I do that I would not, it is no more I that do it, but sin that dwelleth in me. I find then a law, that, when I would do good, evil is present with me. For I delight in the law of God after the inward man: But I see another law in my members, warring against the law of my mind, and bringing me into captivity to the law of sin which is in my members. O wretched man that I am! who shall deliver me from the body of this death? I thank God through Jesus Christ our Lord. So then with the mind I myself serve the law of God; but with the flesh the law of sin' (7:14-25).

This subject of our sanctification continues in chapter 8 (vv. 1-27). Sanctification is life in the Spirit, and life in the Spirit is neither more nor less than living by faith, walking with God by faith in Christ Jesus. Those who are born of God no longer live after the flesh. That is to say, we do not live by the bondage of the law, but in the blessed liberty of grace. And living by grace, trusting Christ alone as our righteousness before God, the law of God is fulfilled in us (3:31).

'There is therefore now no condemnation to them which are in Christ Jesus, who walk not after the flesh, but after the Spirit. For the law of the Spirit of life in Christ Jesus hath made me free from the law of sin and death. For what the law could not do, in that it was weak through the flesh, God sending his own Son in the likeness of sinful flesh, and for sin, condemned sin in the flesh: That the righteousness of the law might be fulfilled in us, who walk not after the flesh, but after the Spirit. For they that are after the flesh do mind the things of the flesh; but they that are after the Spirit the things of the Spirit. For to be carnally minded is death; but to be spiritually minded is life and peace. Because the carnal mind is enmity against God: for it is not subject to the law of God, neither indeed can be. So then they that are in the flesh cannot please God. But ye are not in the flesh, but in the Spirit, if so be that the Spirit of God dwell in you. Now if any man have not the Spirit of Christ, he is none of his. And if Christ be in you, the body is dead because of sin; but the Spirit is life because of righteousness' (8:1-10).

Paul proceeds to tell us that all who live by faith in Christ; who walk not after the flesh but after the Spirit, being totally free from all fear of condemnation, or even the possibility of it, live in the constant, immediate hope and expectancy of the glorious liberty of the sons of God, as 'heirs of God and joint-heirs with Christ'.

God's Purpose

Many modern commentators, preachers, and religious leaders tell us that, 'The book of Romans reveals God's great plan of salvation'. Nothing could be further from the truth. God Almighty does not have a plan of salvation! I make plans; and you make plans. But, we all know that 'the best laid plans of mice and men often go awry'. God Almighty does not have a plan. He has an eternal, unalterable purpose of grace called divine predestination, by which he sovereignly rules the universe all the time. That is the grorious subject of Romans 8:28-11:36.

Chapter 8 verse 28 gives us the sweet assurance of God's wise, adorable, unerring providence, which is but the execution of his eternal purpose of grace in predestination. God's eternal purpose of grace in predestination secured the eternal glory of God's elect before the world began and assures every believing sinner of the certainty of eternal glory with Christ, even while we live in this world, struggling with our own unbelief and sin.

'And we know that all things work together for good to them that love God, to them who are the called according to his purpose. For whom he did foreknow, he also did predestinate to be conformed to the image of his Son, that he might be the firstborn among many brethren. Moreover whom he did predestinate, them he also called: and whom he called, them he also justified: and whom he justified, them he also glorified. What shall we then say to these things? If God be for us, who can be against us? He that spared not his own Son, but delivered him up for us all, how shall he not with him also freely give us all things? Who shall lay any thing to the charge of God's elect? It is God that justifieth. Who is he that condemneth? It is Christ that died, yea rather, that is risen again, who is even at the right hand of God, who also maketh intercession for us. Who shall separate us from the love of Christ? shall tribulation, or distress, or persecution, or famine, or nakedness, or peril, or sword? As it is written, For thy sake we are killed all the day long; we are accounted as sheep for the slaughter. Nay, in all these things we are more than conquerors through him that loved us. For I am persuaded, that neither death, nor life, nor angels, nor principalities, nor powers, nor things present, nor things to come, Nor height, nor depth, nor any other creature, shall be able to separate us from the love of God, which is in Christ Jesus our Lord' (8:28-39).

No passage in the book of God is sweeter to the tastes of believing hearts, no pillow can be found that is more soft and restful for our aching heads, there are no words from our God in which our souls more greatly rejoice than Romans 8:28-39, unless it is Romans 9. Romans 8:28-39 declares God's purpose of grace, his determination to save the people of his love. Romans 9 declares that nothing in that great purpose of grace is ever in jeopardy, because nothing in the purpose of God hinges upon the will and work of men. Nothing depends upon what we call the good choices and works of men or the evil choices and works of men. Everything hinges upon, is determined by, and comes to pass according to God's sovereign will, according to his good purpose of grace.

'(For the children being not yet born, neither having done any good or evil, that the purpose of God according to election might stand, not of works, but of him that calleth;) It was said unto her, The elder shall serve the younger. As it is written, Jacob have I loved, but Esau have I hated. What shall we say then? Is there unrighteousness with God? God forbid.

For he saith to Moses, I will have mercy on whom I will have mercy, and I will have compassion on whom I will have compassion. So then it is not of him that willeth, nor of him that runneth, but of God that sheweth mercy. For the scripture saith unto Pharaoh, Even for this same purpose have I raised thee up, that I might show my power in thee, and that my name might be declared throughout all the earth. Therefore hath he mercy on whom he will have mercy, and whom he will he hardeneth' (9:11-18).

'Whosoever'

Does that mean that men have no responsibility? Does that mean that some cannot be saved? Perish the thought! This all means that some men most certainly shall be saved. This means that every sinner in the world who believes on Christ has eternal life. This is a matter of certainty because the work is already done. That is what Paul tells us in chapter 10 verses 4-8. In verse 13 he declares, 'whosoever shall call upon the name of the Lord shall be saved'. Then, he tells us that God has determined that all he has purposed to save, he has purposed to save by the hearing of the gospel (vv. 14-17). But what if they live in a heathen land? What if no one in that land has ever heard of Christ? That would create a problem for the planning of men, but not for the purpose of God!

Chapter 11 describes how the Lord raised up the nation of Israel and used their rebellion and unbelief, and his judgment upon them, called 'the casting away' of Israel after the flesh, to send the Gospel into all the world to save his elect out of every nation, his true Israel, the Israel of God.

'For I would not, brethren, that ye should be ignorant of this mystery, lest ye should be wise in your own conceits; that blindness in part is happened to Israel, until the fulness of the Gentiles be come in. And so all Israel shall be saved: as it is written, There shall come out of Sion the Deliverer, and shall turn away ungodliness from Jacob: For this is my covenant unto them, when I shall take away their sins' (11:25-27).

Yes, God raises up men and nations and tears them down, precisely according to his own eternal, sovereign, good, wise, and adorable purpose of grace toward his elect (Isaiah 43:3-7). Paul was simply overwhelmed by this fact. Let every redeemed sinner who reads this epistle join him in his adulation of our great God

'O the depth of the riches both of the wisdom and knowledge of God! how unsearchable are his judgments, and his ways past finding out! For who hath known the mind of the Lord? or who hath been his counsellor? Or who hath first given to him, and it shall be recompensed unto him again? For of him, and through him, and to him, are all things: to whom be glory for ever. Amen' (11:33-36).

Something Very Reasonable

In chapters 12-16 the Apostle Paul calls upon all of us who are the objects of God's eternal love and the recipients of his saving operations of grace to devote our lives entirely to him, to the glory of his name and the welfare of his people, and tells us that this entire consecration of our lives to God is the only reasonable thing that can be expected from saved sinners.

'I beseech you therefore, brethren, by the mercies of God, that ye present your bodies a living sacrifice, holy, acceptable unto God, which is your reasonable service. And be not conformed to this world: but be ye transformed by the renewing of your mind, that ye may prove what is that good, and acceptable, and perfect, will of God. For I say, through the grace given unto me, to every man that is among you, not to think of himself more highly than he ought to think; but to think soberly, according as God hath dealt to every man the measure of faith' (12:1-3).

In the rest of chapter 12 he tells us to love one another. In chapter 13 he tells us to live as good citizens in this world, rendering evil to none, not even our most implacable enemies, but only good. In chapters 14 and 15 he teaches us to bend over backwards to get along with our brethren, never despising the young and the weak, but nurturing them as the children of God, following the example of Christ

'Let every one of us please his neighbour for his good to edification. For even Christ pleased not himself; but, as it is written, The reproaches of them that reproached thee fell on me. For whatsoever things were written aforetime were written for our learning, that we through patience and comfort of the scriptures might have hope. Now the God of patience and consolation grant you to be likeminded one toward another according to Christ Jesus: That ye may with one mind and one mouth glorify God, even the Father of our Lord Jesus Christ. Wherefore receive ye one another, as Christ also received us to the glory of God' (15:2-7).

In the sixteenth chapter Paul closes this epistle with a sweet, blessed promise of grace. 'And the God of peace shall bruise Satan under your feet shortly. The grace of our Lord Jesus Christ be with you. Amen' (v. 20). Then, he adds ...

'The grace of our Lord Jesus Christ be with you all. Amen. Now to him that is of power to stablish you according to my gospel, and the preaching of Jesus Christ, according to the revelation of the mystery, which was kept secret since the world began, But now is made manifest, and by the scriptures of the prophets, according to the commandment of the everlasting God, made known to all nations for the obedience of faith: To God only wise, be glory through Jesus Christ for ever. Amen' (16:24-27).

A Precious Book

The book of Romans is very interesting when we see how the Lord has been pleased to use it. It is very important because of its content and message. But it has become precious to those who have experienced its message. As I read this great epistle, I identify with what I read. Do you?

I am not ashamed of the gospel (1:1-17). Though I am, by nature, a guilty sinner, without excuse before God (1:18-3:19), I am completely, freely, forever justified in Christ (3:20-5:21). As I am justified by the grace of God, so too, I am sanctified by the grace of God (chapter 6). Yet, I am a man at war with myself (chapter 7). Though I am a man at war with myself, I am a man without guilt before God, free from all possibility of condemnation, living in hope of eternal life, and assured of eternal glory with Christ (chapter 8). I am a chosen vessel of mercy (chapter 9). I know that I am because I believe on the Lord Jesus Christ (chapter 10). I am amazed as I stand in awe before my all-wise, ever-gracious, sovereign God and Saviour (chapter 11). I belong to God my Saviour by the sweet constraint of his grace. I belong to him. All the world belongs to him. All my brothers and sisters in Christ belong to him (chapters 12-16). 'O the depth of the riches both of the wisdom and knowledge of God! how unsearchable are his judgments, and his ways past finding out! ... For of him, and through him, and to him, are all things: to whom be glory for ever. Amen'.

Chapter 46

1 Corinthians

'Is Christ Divided?'

Paul began this epistle to the church at Corinth by reminding them that he is 'an apostle of Jesus Christ through the will of God' (1:1). That fact had been challenged. So Paul simply states the fact of his apostleship as the basis of his authority in writing to them about their souls and the things of God. Then (1:2-9), before addressing the many things that had to be addressed, he reminded the Corinthian believers who they were, lest they or anyone else misinterpret the stern rebukes of this epistle as declarations of condemnation.

He begins by reminding the Corinthians that they had been sanctified in Christ and been called of God. The apostle assures them of continued grace and peace from God the Father and from the Lord Jesus Christ, and of his continual thanksgiving to God for the grace bestowed upon them by Christ (vv. 3-4). He then proceeds to assure them of his complete confidence that the gospel and the boundless grace of God had been confirmed to them by the operations of God the Holy Spirit upon them in effectual calling, causing them to ever look for Christ's coming (vv. 5-6). He goes so far as to assure these Corinthian believers that our ever-faithful God, who had called them into the fellowship of Christ, would at last bring them blameless into glory in the resurrection (vv. 8-9).

The Corinthian Church

All these assurances of grace and glory were given by divine inspiration to the church at Corinth. I cannot imagine a local church anywhere in the world, at any time in history, plagued with more evil than the church at Corinth. Among these saints, horrid immorality was winked at as a matter of indifference (chapter 5). Yet, they embraced the notion that by abstaining from physical pleasure they could make themselves more holy and spiritual (chapter 7).

God's faithful servant, by whom they were taught the gospel, was scorned among them. Pride caused them to disdain the poor and the weak. Those who possessed, or thought they possessed, great spiritual gifts looked down their noses at those they considered less spiritual. Though the Corinthian church was probably the wealthiest of the New Testament churches, it was the most miserly in giving. They horribly abused the ordinances of God, making the person by whom they were baptized a matter of pride and spiritual superiority, and turning the Lord's Table into a carnal, religious feast. And they denied the resurrection of our Lord.

All these things divided the local church at Corinth into factions, threatening to destroy it. Yet, when Paul wrote this epistle to them, he addressed them as 'them that are sanctified (having been sanctified) in Christ, called to be saints' (1:2), assuring them that God would confirm them unto the end and make them 'blameless in the day of our Lord Jesus Christ' (v. 8).

A Needful Lesson

I call your attention to these things because they set before us a very, very important lesson, a lesson of which we need to be constantly reminded. God's saints in this world are often plagued with moral weaknesses, poor judgment, spiritual evil, and doctrinal error. So long as we are in this world, God's saints – all of us – are sinners still. We dare not make excuse for our own sins or the sins of others, giving license to evil.

But, even more importantly, we dare not make ourselves judges over our brethren, pronouncing those whom God has sanctified accursed. If men and women profess to believe the gospel of God's free and sovereign grace in Christ, they are to be received and embraced by us as our brothers and sisters in Christ, 'not to doubtful disputations' (Romans 14:1). 'Who art thou that judgest another man's servant? to his own master he standeth or falleth. Yea, he shall be holden up: for God is able to make him stand' (Romans 14:4).

God's Work, Not Ours

Such judgment is God's work, not ours. There are many who think they have the ability to distinguish between sheep and goats, between tares and wheat, between good fish and bad, and try to make it their business to separate the one from the other. They foolishly and arrogantly think they have the ability to determine who is saved and who is lost. The fact is: no one has that ability. Our Lord Jesus pointedly tells us to let the wheat and tares grow together (Matthew 13:30).

If we try to separate the good from the bad, we will do so basing our judgment upon the outward appearance. We have no other basis of judgment. That means, our judgment is always wrong. 'For the LORD seeth not as man seeth; for man looketh on the outward appearance, but the LORD looketh on the heart' (1 Samuel 16:7).[1]

If it were left to us, we would always run off the sheep and hug the goats, pull up the wheat and cultivate the tares, throw out the good fish and keep the bad (Matthew 13:28-30). Our business is to cast out the gospel net, gathering in fish, both good and bad, as the Lord determines, knowing that where Christ plants his wheat, Satan plants tares, and where Christ gathers his sheep, Satan brings in goats. It is the business of God's church and his servants to faithfully preach the gospel. As we do, God will, by the preaching of the gospel, separate 'the precious from the vile' (Jeremiah 15:19), gather his wheat into his barn and bind up the tares for the burning. The gospel fan is in our Lord's hand. 'He will thoroughly purge his floor, and gather his wheat into the garner; but he will burn up the chaff with unquenchable fire' (Matthew 3:12).

Four Letters

It was during Paul's two years in Ephesus that he became aware of the problems in Corinth and began corresponding with them about their problems. He actually appears to have written four letters to them. Two of these were not inspired and are lost. First and Second Corinthians, his second and fourth letters, were written by divine inspiration and are preserved for us, for our learning and edification.

In the first letter he had written, which he mentions in 1 Corinthians 5:9, Paul had obviously rebuked the saints at Corinth sharply because of

---

[1] I do not suggest or imply that we are to embrace as our brothers and sisters in Christ those who deny the gospel of God's free and sovereign grace in Christ. Anyone who does not believe the gospel of Christ is lost, no matter what he professes, how loudly he claims to believe on the Son of God, or how pious and devoted he may appear to be in his outward behaviour (2 John 9-10).

the many things by which they brought reproach upon the name of Christ and the gospel of his grace. But the evil practices continued. However, it did at least get their attention, and they wrote to Paul asking him a number of questions (7:1), which he answers by divine inspiration in this epistle.

Problems Addressed

Before answering their questions, Paul confronted the issues dividing the church, urging them to unite their hearts in the cause of Christ for the glory of God (1:10-6:20). 'Now I beseech you, brethren, by the name of our Lord Jesus Christ, that ye all speak the same thing, and that there be no divisions among you; but that ye be perfectly joined together in the same mind and in the same judgment' (v. 10).

He asked in verse 13, 'Is Christ divided?' Of course not. Therefore, God's people must not allow anything to divide them. Let us ever go the extra mile to preserve unity. Let us swallow our shameful, sinful pride, the cause of division, to promote the unity of God's church (Ephesians 4:1-6). Anytime a person causes division in the body of Christ, specifically in a local assembly of God's saints, he is courting divine judgment (1 Corinthians 3:16-17). The problems dividing the saints at Corinth were basically twofold.

First, the members of the church were divided according to their admiration of one preacher over another (1:10-4:21). Some claimed to be followers of Apollos, the great orator, others of Peter, the apostle to the Jews, others of Paul, the apostle to the Gentiles, and others of Christ. Roger Ellsworth correctly observes, 'These "Christ-boasters" were claiming that Christ belonged exclusively to them'. In fact, it appears that each group thought it had a corner on divine truth the others all lacked.

The cause of the division was clearly an infatuation with carnal, worldly wisdom and an utter failure to understand that the preaching of the gospel is the wisdom of God. The Corinthians vainly imagined (as many do today) that men and women could be persuaded to believe on Christ, converted, and attain spiritual knowledge by carnal means.

One Message

In chapter 1:18-25, Paul declares that it is only by the preaching of the gospel that God calls out, saves, and teaches his elect. This, and this alone, is 'the power of God and the wisdom of God'. In verses 26-31 he tells us that the instruments God is pleased to use as his voices in this great work are themselves nothing (3:7). He uses nothings and nobodies to call out his elect specifically for the purpose 'that no flesh should glory in his presence'.

In chapter 2 Paul tells us that the power of the gospel preached is neither in the intellectual ability or rhetorical ability of the preacher, but in the gospel message itself (2:1-5). 'And I, brethren, when I came to you, came not with excellency of speech or of wisdom, declaring unto you the testimony of God. For I determined not to know any thing among you, save Jesus Christ, and him crucified. And I was with you in weakness, and in fear, and in much trembling. And my speech and my preaching was not with enticing words of man's wisdom, but in demonstration of the Spirit and of power: That your faith should not stand in the wisdom of men, but in the power of God' (2:1-5).

In chapters 3 and 4 Paul shows us clearly who God's servants are and how they serve the cause of Christ. He has shown that God's servants are all men with one message, 'Jesus Christ and him crucified'. In chapter 3 he tells us that they are all totally insignificant and meaningless in themselves. Gospel preachers are but hoes and hoses by which God tills, and plants, and waters his garden.

'For while one saith, I am of Paul; and another, I am of Apollos; are ye not carnal? Who then is Paul, and who is Apollos, but ministers by whom ye believed, even as the Lord gave to every man? I have planted, Apollos watered; but God gave the increase. So then neither is he that planteth any thing, neither he that watereth; but God that giveth the increase. Now he that planteth and he that watereth are one: and every man shall receive his own reward according to his own labour' (3:4-8).

Yet, he carefully points out that those instruments God uses are to be respected as his instruments of good to the souls of men. God's servants are not to be idolized; and they are not to be despised. They are to be respected, honoured, and received as God's servants; and each is to be equally respected, honoured, and received as God's servant. Though nothing in themselves, Paul says, we are 'ministers by whom ye believed' (3:5) and 'labourers together with God' (3:9).

Then he tells us that the only labour that shall be of any lasting value is gospel preaching. God's servants all have one Foundation upon which to build and the church and kingdom of God is built on that one Foundation, which is Christ. Everything that passes for religious exercise, everything else that is brought into the church, every other means by which anyone attempts to build the church and kingdom of God is just wood, hay, and stubble and will be burned in the fire of God's wrath.

Stewards of God

In the fourth chapter Paul asserts that God's servants are but stewards in the house of God. As such they must have no concern for any man's approval or disapproval, but of God's only, knowing that all things will soon be revealed in their true light.

'Let a man so account of us, as of the ministers of Christ, and stewards of the mysteries of God. Moreover it is required in stewards, that a man be found faithful. But with me it is a very small thing that I should be judged of you, or of man's judgment: yea, I judge not mine own self. For I know nothing by myself; yet am I not hereby justified: but he that judgeth me is the Lord. Therefore judge nothing before the time, until the Lord come, who both will bring to light the hidden things of darkness, and will make manifest the counsels of the hearts: and then shall every man have praise of God' (4:1-5).

Only one thing is required of stewards: faithfulness. God's servants are not required to be brilliant or even smart, impressive or even mediocre, successful or even useful in the eyes of men. The one thing required of them is that they be found faithful, faithful to God, faithful to his glory, faithful to the gospel, and faithful to the souls of men. If one man is more useful or less useful than another as the steward of God, more talented or less talented than another, there is no cause for pride or division. God alone makes the difference (4:7).

Worldliness

The second problem and cause of division at Corinth was worldliness, the love of this world (5:1-6:20).

Worldliness, contrary to popular religious opinion, is not dressing like the world, eating and drinking like the world, or doing business where the world does business. Worldliness is the love of the world. Nothing is more dangerous to our souls than that which our Lord calls 'the care of this world and the deceitfulness of riches ... and the lusts of other things' (Matthew 13:22; Mark 4:19).

It was the love of the world that caused the Corinthian believers to wink at one of their own living in incest with his father's wife (chapter 5). Such a thing was commonly accepted in the Roman world; and they did not wish to offend or appear judgmental of ungodliness.

Paul demanded that the man be put out of the assembly, so that he might be converted from the error of his ways and to prevent him from corrupting the lives of others by the church's apparent approval of his conduct.

As Christ our Passover was sacrificed for us, we must sacrifice ourselves to him if we would keep the feast of faith and of the Lord's Table 'with the unleavened bread of sincerity and truth'. Sometimes that means saying publicly, 'We do not approve of the evil the world embraces', thereby inviting the world's frowns and sneers.

Lust after material wealth which is love of the world, further stirred strife in the church, so much so that they were suing one another in courts of law (chapter 6). Men who were destined to sit in judgment over angels were bickering about money and property before unbelievers!

How does Paul seek to correct the evil? Does he bring out the whip of the law? Never! He was addressing believers, people who live by a far higher rule and are motivated by a far higher principle. He seeks to correct the evil of their conduct, not by threatening them with punishment, but by reminding these Corinthian saints of what God had done for them in Christ by his marvellous grace (6:9-11, 19-20).

Questions Answered

Beginning in chapter 7, Paul answers the questions the Corinthian church had asked in their letter to him.

Asceticism

Someone had persuaded some of these saints that if they would deprive themselves of natural, physical pleasure they would be more holy and spiritual.

The particular thing about which they raised a question was marriage. Would a brother or sister be more spiritual and useful if he or she chose not to enjoy the privileges of marriage? If so, then should married couples live as celibates? Should those who are married get a divorce, so that they can be more devoted to the Lord?

Ridiculous as these questions may appear to us, they were serious to the Corinthians. Once a person embraces the idea that evil is outside himself, there is no limit to the incredible extremes into which he will run to make himself appear more holy, devoted, and spiritual than another. I once knew a man who moved his family into a remote mountainous place, more than a hundred miles from the nearest neighbour (literally). When I asked him why he had done so, he answered, 'I want to keep myself and my family holy'! Granted, such cases are extreme, but the evil behind such extreme separatism is very real and very common. The Holy Spirit warns us of it and urges us to avoid it in the strongest terms possible (Colossians 2:16-23).

The essence of Paul's reply to such foolish notions is just this. Holiness is not outward, but inward. Marriage, the privileges of marriage, and all other things in this world, except those things prohibited by God in his Word, are perfectly lawful and right. God did not save you to make life in this world miserable, but useful and meaningful.

Meats Offered to Idols

The same thing applies to meats offered to idols (chapter 8). If the Corinthian believer went to the meat market and bought a piece of meat, he did not need to ask whether it was meat left over from a pagan religious ceremony. If the person selling the meat made a point of the matter, or if one of his weaker brethren pointed out the fact that that was the case, he ought to choose something else to avoid offence.

In other words, the idol is nothing and its meat is nothing. We are at perfect liberty to use and enjoy anything in God's creation for its intended purpose. But we must not use our liberty in a way that puts a stumbling block before our brethren.

Paul's Apostleship

Many at Corinth questioned Paul's credibility as an apostle. He displays the folly of such judgment in those who had been converted under his ministry, who had learned the things of God from his lips in chapter 9.

Paul had laboured with his hands at Corinth, making tents for his livelihood, lest any should accuse him of serving himself and preaching for personal gain. But he found that men who are determined to make evil accusations are never concerned with facts. Some at Corinth used Paul's willingness to labour for his own bread as a reason to be suspicious of his genuineness as an apostle of Christ. So he seized the opportunity to teach them, and us, that God's servants ought never be allowed, much less required, to provide for themselves. They are to be provided for and supported through the generosity of God's people (vv. 7-14).

Yet, a faithful man will never allow the unfaithfulness of others to keep him from doing what God has called him to do. 'For though I preach the gospel, I have nothing to glory of: for necessity is laid upon me; yea, woe is unto me, if I preach not the gospel' (v. 16, Haggai 1:13).

Worship

The Corinthian church had so perverted the ordinances of our Lord that every aspect of worship in their public assemblies was wrong. They appear to have mixed both the laws and ceremonies of the Old Testament and the practices of their pagan neighbours with the worship of God, much like churches do today.

In chapter 10 Paul tells us that all that happened to Israel in the history recorded in the Old Testament happened to teach us spiritual, gospel truths. As the Jews were baptized symbolically with reference to Moses, believers are baptized with reference to Christ. The Rock that followed them through the wilderness was Christ. The Water of Life that flowed to them from the smitten Rock portrayed the grace of God flowing to sinners through the Lamb of God smitten and crucified by the law of God as our Substitute. As that Rock could be smitten but once, so Christ was 'once slain to put away sin by the sacrifice of himself'. As God was faithful to bring his chosen through all their temptations and trials into the land of promise, so he is faithful to keep and preserve his elect today. As Israel in all their sacrifices professed themselves to be one with the altar, so all who worship God in Christ are one with Christ, and we symbolically show that oneness at the Lord's Table.

'The cup of blessing which we bless, is it not the communion of the blood of Christ? The bread which we break, is it not the communion of the body of Christ? For we being many are one bread, and one body: for we are all partakers of that one bread' (vv. 16-17).

Chapters 11-14 address the matter of order in the worship of God. Paul had been asked about the role of women in public worship, the observance of the Lord's Supper, and spiritual gifts. All these things the Corinthian church was perverting. Paul commands that women are to keep silent in the church and show proper respect for men before God, particularly for their own husbands. He told the church to observe the Lord's Supper in faith, discerning the Lord's body, in remembrance of Christ, not as a religious party. And he required that in all things the worship services of the public assembly were to be in a decent, reverent, orderly manner. The rule in all these things must be the glory of God and brotherly love (10:31; 12:31- 13:8).

The Resurrection

In chapter 15 the apostle displays his utter shock that some of the Corinthians had doubts about the resurrection of Christ. He tells us that there is but one gospel and that Christ's resurrection is vital to its message (vv. 1-4). Then he declares that our Lord's resurrection from the dead is an undeniable fact of history (vv. 5-11). Next, Paul assures us that Christ's resurrection guarantees the resurrection of all God's elect in and by him unto everlasting glory and immortality (vv. 17-58).

'But now is Christ risen from the dead, and become the firstfruits of them that slept. For since by man came death, by man came also the resurrection of the dead. For as in Adam all die, even so in Christ shall all be made alive. But every man in his own order: Christ the firstfruits; afterward they that are Christ's at his coming. Then cometh the end, when he shall have delivered up the kingdom to God, even the Father; when he shall have put down all rule and all authority and power. For he must reign, till he hath put all enemies under his feet' (vv. 20-25).

'Behold, I show you a mystery; We shall not all sleep, but we shall all be changed, In a moment, in the twinkling of an eye, at the last trump: for the trumpet shall sound, and the dead shall be raised incorruptible, and we shall be changed. For this corruptible must put on incorruption, and this mortal must put on immortality. So when this corruptible shall have put on incorruption, and this mortal shall have put on immortality, then shall be brought to pass the saying that is written, Death is swallowed up in victory. O death, where is thy sting? O grave, where is thy victory? The sting of death is sin; and the strength of sin is the law. But thanks be to God, which giveth us the victory through our Lord Jesus Christ. Therefore, my beloved brethren, be ye stedfast, unmoveable, always abounding in the work of the Lord, forasmuch as ye know that your labour is not in vain in the Lord' (vv. 51-58).

Giving

As is ever the case with those who look for an excuse to be miserly in giving, the Corinthians asked Paul how much each should give and how. In chapter 16 he tells them and us that our giving is to be done as an act of worship in the house of God, as we gather in his house on the first day of the week, and that the measure of our giving is to be the liberality of love (vv. 1-3, 14).

Paul closes this epistle urging us to 'stand fast in the faith and be strong' (v. 13), to do all things in love (v. 14), and to addict ourselves to serving our brethren (v. 15). His very last word is an inspired word of condemnation against all who do not love the Lord Jesus Christ, and an inspired benediction of grace upon all who do. 'If any man love not the Lord Jesus Christ, let him be Anathema Maranatha. The grace of our Lord Jesus Christ be with you. My love be with you all in Christ Jesus. Amen' (vv. 22-24).

Chapter 47

2 Corinthians

For the Glory of Christ

Pastor Roger Ellsworth gives an excellent introduction to 2 Corinthians in his very helpful book, *The Guide – The Bible Book by Book*. He writes, 'In the conclusion of 1 Corinthians we find Paul anticipating Timothy making a visit to the church of Corinth (1 Corinthians 16:10). That visit apparently took place and yielded the bad news of considerable opposition to the apostle. Paul responded to this report by visiting Corinth himself. His visit, while not reported in the book of Acts, can be inferred from Paul's own statements (2 Corinthians 2:1; 12:14; 13:1-2). This visit is known as "the painful visit" because it evidently featured an ugly incident in which one of the congregation insulted Paul while the other members sat idly by.

After returning to Ephesus, Paul sorrowfully wrote to the church and sent the 'letter of tears' with Titus. In this letter, which we do not possess, the apostle called the church to discipline the man who had opposed him. Paul was so eager to receive Titus' report on the reception of this letter that he left Ephesus and went first to Troas (2:12) and then to Macedonia to meet him (7:6,13). He was greatly relieved to learn that most of the Corinthians had repented of their opposition, and the man who so vigorously opposed Paul had been disciplined by the congregation and had repented. While in Macedonia, Paul wrote 2 Corinthians and dispatched Titus and another brother (12:18) to carry it to Corinth.'

Key Verse

The central theme in 2 Corinthians is the sacrifice of our Lord Jesus Christ as our great Substitute. We cannot understand the message of this book until we understand the message of its key verse (5:21). Indeed, we cannot properly understand the Bible until we understand this message. 'For he hath made him to be sin for us, who knew no sin; that we might be made the righteousness of God in him'.

What profound truth, what stupendous grace, what wondrous mystery those words contain! 'He', God the Father, 'hath', in holy justice and infinite mercy, 'made', by divine imputation, 'him', the Lord Jesus Christ, his infinite, well-beloved, only begotten, immaculate Son, 'to be sin', an awful mass of iniquity, 'for us', God's elect, helpless, condemned, sinful rebels! Now, as the result of Christ being made sin for us, and suffering all the horrid wrath of God as our Substitute to the full satisfaction of divine justice, all for whom he died are made to be the very righteousness of God in him by that same divine imputation.

Substitution

Chapter 5 verse 21 declares the great, glorious, and effectual substitutionary work of Christ upon the cross, as he 'bare our sins in his own body on the tree, that we, being dead to sins, should live unto righteousness: by whose stripes ye were healed' (1 Peter 2:24). This is the foundation truth of Christianity, the rock upon which our hopes are built. This is the only hope of the sinner, and the only joy of the true believer.

'The heart of the gospel', wrote C. H. Spurgeon, 'is redemption, and the essence of redemption is the substitutionary sacrifice of Christ'. The great substitutionary work of Christ, the mighty transfer of sin from the sinner to the sinner's Surety, the punishment of the Surety in the sinner's place, the pouring out of the infinite, indescribable wrath of God, which was due to us, upon our Substitute. This is the greatest transaction that ever took place upon the earth, the most marvellous sight that men ever beheld, and the most stupendous wonder that heaven ever executed. Jesus Christ was made to be sin for us, that we might be made the righteousness of God in him. Jesus Christ, the spotless Son of God was made to be sin; and every sinner who trusts him is made the righteousness of God in him!

Personal Letter

Second Corinthians is clearly the most personal and emotional of all Paul's letters. These thirteen chapters are filled with passion. They contain far more personal information about Paul and his labours for the gospel than any of his other epistles. But it is a great mistake to imagine that Paul wrote this epistle merely to defend himself, or to give us an account of what he did, accomplished and suffered for Christ. Paul was far too concerned for the glory of God, the souls of men, and the gospel of Christ than that. His defence of himself and his ministry was not a personal defence. Rather, it was the defence of Christ and the gospel of his grace that Paul preached.

Christ Crucified

Jesus Christ and him crucified is the message of 2 Corinthians. The theme throughout these thirteen chapters is, as in all his epistles, the glory of Christ in redemption and grace.

The book is filled with Christ and the glory of God's free grace in Christ. Every argument for obedience, every promise of grace, every hope set before us in these chapters, and every motivation by which Paul inspires us to live in this world for the glory of God is built upon the mercy, grace, and love of God in our all-glorious Christ.

When Paul speaks of grace and peace from God the Father, he tells us that it is 'from the Lord Jesus Christ' (1:2). When he speaks of the blessedness of God, 'the Father of mercies and the God of all comfort, who comforteth us in all our tribulations', he tells us that our mercies and consolations come to us and abound from our Lord Jesus Christ and his sufferings for us (1:3-5), and that as surely as he was raised from the dead, our God will deliver us from all our woes by his grace (1:8-10). What blessed titles Paul here gives to our God: 'the Father of mercies and the God of all comfort'.

The Tenses

In the tenth verse of chapter 1 Paul speaks of God's gracious deliverance in three tenses. He is telling us how the Lord continually delivered him from death. Though he had the sentence of death in himself and was so troubled that he 'despaired even of life', he learned not to trust in himself, but 'in God which raiseth the dead'. Then he tells us how the Lord had delivered him, was delivering him, and would deliver him. 'Who delivered us from so great a death, and doth deliver: in whom we trust that he will yet deliver us'.

In these things we have a magnificent picture of every believer's experience of grace. Though we once despaired of life, living under the sentence of death in ourselves, the Lord God graciously saved us. But it

Discovering Christ In All The Scriptures

is a great mistake to think of salvation only as something we experienced in the past. 'Salvation' is a very big word. It includes all the work of God in bringing his elect from the ruins of fallen humanity into 'the glorious liberty of the sons of God' in heaven.

Salvation includes God's past works of grace, his present works of grace, and his future works of grace. A proper grasp of these threefold tenses will help us to understand the nature and significance of our eternal salvation in the purpose of God the Father, the accomplished work of God the Son and the continuing care and comfort of the saints by God the Holy Spirit.

The Lord our God has saved us. There is a very real sense in which it must be said that every believer's salvation is a completed work in the past. Our God saved his elect in his eternal purpose of grace in Christ, the Lamb of God slain from the foundation of the world (Romans 8:28-30; Ephesians 1:3-6; Revelation 13:8). Election, predestination, and adoption are works by which God saved us in eternity. He saved us by the sin-atoning sacrifice of Christ at Calvary, too. When the Son of God cried, 'It is finished!' redemption's work was done. Sin was put away and 'we were reconciled to God by the death of his Son' (Romans 5:10). Then, at the appointed time of love, the Lord God saved us in regeneration by the effectual, irresistible work of his Holy Spirit in omnipotent grace, giving us life and faith in Christ (Ephesians 2:1-5).

The Lord is saving us now, ever supplying us with grace, preserving and keeping us, because he has declared that we 'shall never perish' (John 10:28). His daily providence and his all-sufficient grace are constantly engaged in saving us.

There is also a sense in which it must be said that our salvation is future, 'for now is our salvation nearer than when we believed' (Romans 13:11). There is a day appointed when Christ shall come again. When he does, our salvation will be complete in resurrection glory. All who have been saved are being saved, and shall yet be saved. He who has kept us will keep us unto the end. And, at the last day, he will raise us up into heaven in the perfection of resurrection glory.

The Promises of God

When Paul declares his own veracity as the servant of God, he turns our attention immediately away from himself to the veracity of God our Saviour and all the promises of God in him (1:18-22). He declares, 'all the promises of God in Christ are yea, and in him Amen, unto the glory of God by us'. Then, he tells us of four great works of grace, by which all the promises of God are verified to us (vv. 21-22). (1.) He has established us in Christ. (2.) He has anointed us with his Spirit. (3.) He has sealed us in his grace. And (4.) he has 'given us the earnest of the Spirit in our hearts'.

Always Triumphant

In chapter 2, when Paul asserts the certain and constant acceptance and triumph of gospel preachers and their message, he says, 'For we are unto God a sweet savour of Christ' (vv. 14-16). He asserts that this is true regardless of the response of men to the message of the gospel. 'For we are unto God a sweet savour of Christ in them that are saved, and in them that perish: To the one we are the savour of death unto death; and to the other the savour of life unto life'.

Then, in the light of this awesome fact, the apostle declares his own sense of utter insufficiency to engage in such a labour by raising the question, 'And who is sufficient for these things?' The answer to that question is given in chapter 3. 'And such trust have we through Christ to God-ward: Not that we are sufficient of ourselves to think any thing as of ourselves; but our sufficiency is of God' (vv. 4-5). The gospel is a trust given into the hands of men made sufficient to the work by God's grace.

When he declares that unbelieving men and women read the scriptures with a blindfold over their eyes, and therefore cannot see the things of God, he asserts that the 'veil is done away in Christ'. Once God gives faith in Christ, the blindfold is taken away, and we are able to see and enter into the kingdom of God.

'Now the Lord is that Spirit: and where the Spirit of the Lord is, there is liberty. But we all, with open face beholding as in a glass the glory of the Lord, are changed into the same image from glory to glory, even as by the Spirit of the Lord' (3:14, 17, 18).

A Trusted Treasure

Paul looked upon the ministry God had given him as a heavenly treasure entrusted to his care, and to which he was determined to be faithful. In chapter 4 he declares that the message he preached, the message we must preach, is 'the glorious gospel of Christ', that by which God gives light and grace to chosen sinners.

'But if our gospel be hid, it is hid to them that are lost: In whom the god of this world hath blinded the minds of them which believe not, lest the light of the glorious gospel of Christ, who is the image of God, should shine unto them. For we preach not ourselves, but Christ Jesus the Lord; and ourselves your servants for Jesus' sake. For God, who commanded the light to shine out of darkness, hath shined in our hearts, to give the light of the knowledge of the glory of God in the face of Jesus Christ. But we have this treasure in earthen vessels, that the excellency of the power may be of God, and not of us' (4:3-7).

Trouble Everywhere

Beginning with chapter 4 verse 8, Paul tells us that he had trouble everywhere, all the time. For him, heartache and woe were relentless. He was 'always bearing about in the body the dying of the Lord Jesus' (4:10). Yet, when he speaks of his countless afflictions, he declares them to be but light afflictions and momentary compared to the glory awaiting us in heaven with Christ (4:8-5:9). Blessed is that man or woman who learns to live constantly in the immediate prospect of eternity. It would lighten our load, brighten our days, drive away our gloom, and cheer our hearts to live every day as though we were on the doorstep of heaven.

'Knowing that he which raised up the Lord Jesus shall raise up us also by Jesus, and shall present us with you. For all things are for your sakes, that the abundant grace might through the thanksgiving of many redound to the glory of God. For which cause we faint not; but though our outward man perish, yet the inward man is renewed day by day. For our light affliction, which is but for a moment, worketh for us a far more exceeding and eternal weight of glory; While we look not at the things which are seen, but at the things which are not seen: for the things which are seen are temporal; but the things which are not seen are eternal. For we know that if our earthly house of this tabernacle were dissolved, we have a building of God, an house not made with hands, eternal in the heavens'. (4:14-5:1).

Persuasions

In chapter 5, knowing the terror of the Lord awaiting sinners at the judgment seat of Christ, the apostle seeks to persuade all who read this epistle to be reconciled to God. How does the inspired writer persuade sinners to trust Christ? By declaring to them the finished work of and redemption accomplished by the crucified Son of God (5:14-6:2).

'For the love of Christ constraineth us; because we thus judge, that if one died for all, then were all dead: And that he died for all, that they which live should not henceforth live unto themselves, but unto him which died for them, and rose again. Wherefore henceforth know we no man after the flesh: yea, though we have known Christ after the flesh, yet now henceforth know we him no more. Therefore if any man be in Christ, he is a new creature: old things are passed away; behold, all things are become new. And all things are of God, who hath reconciled us to himself by Jesus Christ, and hath given to us the ministry of reconciliation; To wit, that God was in Christ, reconciling the world unto himself, not imputing their trespasses unto them; and hath committed unto us the word of reconciliation. Now then we are ambassadors for Christ, as though God did beseech you by us: we pray you in Christ's stead, be ye reconciled to God. For he hath made him to be sin for us, who knew no sin; that we might be made the righteousness of God in him. We then, as workers together with him, beseech you also that ye receive not the grace of God in vain. (For he saith, I have heard thee in a time accepted, and in the day of salvation have I succoured thee: behold, now is the accepted time; behold, now is the day of salvation.)'

Unequal Yoke

Paul's words in 6:14-7:1 have been terribly misapplied by many to teach that believers are to separate themselves from unbelievers in their daily lives and normal earthly connections. That is not the meaning of this passage. Paul is calling for all who trust Christ to come out of Babylon, to make a clean break with all false religion. Here, the apostle Paul promises, by divine inspiration, that God will receive all who abandon the religion of the world; all freewill, works religion, trusting Christ alone as Saviour and Lord. He promises that all who trust Christ shall be received by God as his own sons and daughters. 'Having therefore these promises, dearly beloved, let us cleanse ourselves from all filthiness of the flesh and spirit, perfecting holiness in the fear of God'. As we relentlessly separate ourselves from the filth of Babylon's religion, we are continually perfecting (bringing to its end and completion) our separation from the world by our God and our separation unto our God.

Christian Giving

When Paul instructs the saints at Corinth about giving, he inspires and motivates generosity in them by reminding them, and us, of Christ's great love for us, and the unspeakable gift of God in him (8:7-9; 9:15).

There is an abundance of instruction in the New Testament about Christian giving. All of 1 Corinthians chapter 9 and 2 Corinthians chapters 8 and 9 are taken up with this subject. However, there are no commands to the people of God anywhere in the New Testament about how much we are to give. Tithing and all systems like it are things altogether foreign to the New Testament. Like all other acts of worship, giving is an act of grace. It must be free and voluntary. But there are some plain, simple guidelines laid down in 1 Corinthians and here in 2 Corinthians for us to follow. Christian giving must be motivated by love and gratitude towards Christ (8:8-9). Love needs no law. It is a law unto itself. It is the most powerful and most generous of all motives.

Our gifts must arise from willing hearts (8:12). If that which we give arises from a willing heart, if it is given freely and cheerfully, it is accepted of God. The Lord is not concerned with the amount of our gift, be it great or small; he looks to the motive behind it.

We should give to the work of the gospel in proportion to our blessings from the Lord (1 Corinthians 16:2). We are expected to give generously in accordance with our own ability.

All of God's people should give ('everyone', 1 Corinthians 16:2; 'every man', 2 Corinthians 9:7). Men and women, rich and poor, old and young, all who are saved by the grace of God are expected to give for the support of God's church and kingdom.

We should be both liberal and sacrificial in our giving (9:5-6). We have not really given anything until we have taken that which we need, want, and have use for and have given it to the Lord (Mark 12:41-44).

Our gifts must be voluntary (9:7). Our gifts must be purposeful 'Every man according as he purposeth in his heart, so let him give' (9:7).

We are to give as unto the Lord (9:7; Matthew 6:1-5). We give, not to be seen of men, but for the honour of Christ, hoping for nothing in return.

This kind of giving is well-pleasing to God. 'God loveth a cheerful giver' (9:7; Philippians 4:18; Hebrews 13:16).

Our Warfare

In the tenth chapter Paul tells us that the weapons of our warfare; prayer, faith, and gospel preaching, by which we bring rebels to the obedience of faith, are not carnal, but spiritual (vv. 3-5). God's church is an army at war in hostile, enemy territory. Our battle is not political or social, but spiritual. We are engaged in a war for the souls of men and the glory of God. In this great army there are five ranks of soldiers: the foolish, the weak, the base, the despised, and the things which are not (1 Corinthians 1:26-29). The weapon by which the church of God shall march over the gates of hell and prevail is the gospel of Christ.

Paul's Fear

In chapter 11 the apostle Paul shows great concern, lest anyone be 'corrupted from the simplicity that is in Christ', by those who preach another Jesus, another, spirit, another gospel, and another righteousness (vv. 2-5, 13-15). He was fearful that the influence of false apostles, men who claimed to speak as God's messengers, but were really Satan's messengers, might turn some away from the singular hope of faith, Christ.

It is very important that we see how Paul describes these messengers of hell, by whom the souls of men are deceived with a false gospel, preaching 'another Jesus' and 'another spirit'. They are not described as promoters of licentiousness, immorality, and open blasphemy. They are far more subtle than that. These men are wicked men who, as 'Satan himself is transformed into an angel of light', present themselves as 'the ministers of righteousness'. They promote righteousness, devotion, morality, and religious works. But the righteousness they preach and promote is self-righteousness. It is righteousness produced by men, not the righteousness of God in Christ.

Abundant Revelations

When Paul describes his temporary translation into heaven, he says very little about that experience and focuses our attention instead upon the lessons he had learned about the all-sufficient grace of God in Christ (12:2-10). The things he saw and heard in Paradise were things that no tongue could describe. When the experience ended, lest he 'should be exalted above measure through the abundance of the revelations' given to him, the Lord gave him a 'thorn in the flesh'. He sent Satan to him as a messenger, constantly beating him in the face, to keep him from glorying in what he had experienced.

Prayer

Though he did not look upon it as such at the time, Paul tells us that this thorn in the flesh was God's gift to him (Philippians 1:29). At the time, it was so aggravating, painful, and hard to bear that Paul earnestly prayed for the Lord to take this thorn from him.

We must not miss the lesson here given about prayer. None of us knows what is best for the glory of God, the good of our own souls, or the accomplishment of God's purpose of grace in Christ (v. 8). Because we do not know what is best, we do not know how to pray for anything as we ought. It is written, 'We know not what we should pray for as we ought' (Romans 8:26). Prayer is not for the gratification of our carnal lusts. It is not the means by which we obtain what we want from the Lord. Prayer, true prayer, involves submission to the will of God. It is the cry of the believer's heart to his heavenly Father to do what is right and best. If I am

God's child, if truly I know him and trust him, I want what he has purposed. I bow to him, surrendering my will to his will, my desires to his purpose, my pleasure to his glory, knowing that his will is best. Therefore, when we pray in our ignorance the Holy Spirit cleans up our prayers and presents to the Father the true groanings of our hearts (Romans 8:26).

Our Lord Jesus taught us ever to surrender our will to the Father's will. When the will of God appears to contradict that which might appear to be most pleasing to our flesh, we ought always to follow our Master's example, saying, 'Not my will, thy will be done'. See John 12:27-28.

In chapter 12:2-10 Paul says that, though the Lord graciously refused to give him what he asked for, he graciously granted him what he really wanted and needed. John Gill says, 'The Lord always hears and answers his people sooner or later, in one form or another, though not always in the way and manner they desire; but yet in such a way as is most for his glory and their good. The apostle had not his request granted, that Satan might immediately depart from him, only he is assured of a sufficiency of grace to support him under the exercise, so long as it should last'.

All-sufficient Grace

The Lord graciously assured Paul of his all-sufficient grace. 'He said unto me, My grace is sufficient for thee: for my strength is made perfect in weakness' (v. 9). Here God's elect are assured of his grace in Christ and the absolute sufficiency of it always and in all things. One of the names of our great God is El-Shaddai, which means God All-sufficient. The grace of God in Christ and that alone is our sufficiency. Nothing but the grace of God in Christ is sufficient grace; and it is sufficient for all his elect, all the time, and in all circumstances.

Look at verse 9 again. In the second part of the verse our Saviour declares that his strength is made perfect in our weakness. Obviously, our weakness contributes nothing to the perfection of Christ's strength. He is the omnipotent God. The meaning of this statement is that the strength of our Lord and Saviour Jesus Christ appears to be, or is manifestly perfect through the weakness of those sinners who are saved by his grace. Paul writes in another place, 'When we were yet without strength, in due time, Christ died for the ungodly'.

Read the last sentence of verse 9 one more time. 'Most gladly therefore will I rather glory in my infirmities, that the power of Christ may rest upon me'. It is only when we are brought to acknowledge our weakness, infirmity, frailty, nothingness, and insufficiency that the power of Christ and his all sufficient grace rests upon us. The moment we flex our muscles, straighten our backs, lift our chins and say, 'I can do this', we are in trouble.

Pleasure in Infirmity

In chapter 12 verse 10 we read, 'Therefore I take pleasure in infirmities, in reproaches, in necessities, in persecutions, in distresses for Christ's sake: for when I am weak, then am I strong'. Here, writing by inspiration, Paul obeys the admonition given in Joel 3:10, where it is written, 'Let the weak say, I am strong'. He that is weak and sees himself to be so is strong in Christ, and has the blessed experience of renewed strength from him day by day. May God give us grace, always, in all things, to know our weakness, that we may have his strength.

Self-examination

When he calls for us to examine ourselves (13:5-6), the one thing to be determined is whether or not we are in the faith, whether or not we trust Christ. 'Examine yourselves, whether ye be in the faith; prove your own selves. Know ye not your own selves, how that Jesus Christ is in you, except ye be reprobates? But I trust that ye shall know that we are not reprobates'.

We are not to examine one another and we are not to subject ourselves to the examination of others. If we examine others, we will become hardened in self-righteousness, harsh and judgmental, arrogantly making ourselves the standard by which we judge others. If we subject ourselves to the examinations of others, we will have nothing but the words and opinions of men as the basis of our faith. Our assurance, if we get any, will be nothing but a temporary, self-righteous confidence, varying with the opinions of the person to whom we are listening.

The point of examination is this one thing: 'Whether ye be in the faith'. It does not matter when, where, or how you came to be in the faith, or even who was preaching when you believed. It only matters that 'ye be in the faith'. For most of God's people conversion is not a climactic experience, but a gradual process. Some, like Saul of Tarsus, have great, climactic experiences. But most are brought to Christ one faltering step at a time. Even those who have Damascus road experiences must be gently led into the knowledge of Christ by one like Ananias (Acts 9:6-18). Are you, or are you not, now in the faith? That is the only issue of examination. If you are in the faith, you are saved. If you are not, you are lost.

'Prove your own selves'. The only way to know 'whether ye be in the faith' is to bring your faith to the Word of God, crying with David, 'Search me, O God, and know my heart: try (prove) me, and know my thoughts: and see if there be any wicked way in me (see if I am in the way of the wicked), and lead me in the way everlasting' (Psalm 139:23-24).

If God will 'say unto my soul, I am thy salvation' (Psalm 35:3), I want no other proof. Does the Lord God give such a word to believing sinners, a word by which we may be assured of his grace? Indeed, he does. 'Whosoever believeth that Jesus is the Christ is born of God ... He that believeth on the Son of God hath the witness in himself: he that believeth not God hath made him a liar; because he believeth not the record that God gave of his Son. And this is the record, that God hath given to us eternal life, and this life is in his Son. He that hath the Son hath life; and he that hath not the Son of God hath not life. These things have I written unto you that believe on the name of the Son of God; that ye may know that ye have eternal life, and that ye may believe on the name of the Son of God' (1 John 5:1-13).

Chapter 48

Galatians

'I do not frustrate the grace of God'.

If I had opportunity to address all the preachers, church leaders, theologians, and religious people of this world at one time, who believe and teach that salvation is in any way, to any degree dependent upon or determined by the will or work of man, I would lay this solemn charge, this horrible indictment against them: You frustrate the grace of God and make the death of the Lord Jesus Christ an insignificant, meaningless, useless thing. That is precisely the charge Paul laid against those who taught such heresy in Galatia. Then, he declared, as spokesman for all who believe and preach the gospel of God's free, sovereign, saving grace in Christ, 'I do not frustrate the grace of God: for if righteousness come by the law, then Christ is dead in vain' (2:21). That is just how serious the book of Galatians is.

When Paul sat down to write this epistle, he was clearly provoked and angry. This book was intended by Paul and by God the Holy Spirit who inspired it, to be a deliberate, forceful confrontation. There are no friendly greetings, no gentle salutations, no kind, soothing reflections in this book. Everything in these six chapters is 'in your face' confrontation.

An Angry Apostle

To say the least, the apostle was a little hot under the collar. Why? What provoked Paul and stirred his anger? The Galatian churches, churches God raised up under the influence of Paul's ministry among them, were being led away from Christ and his gospel by false teachers in their midst. These men, professing to be the servants of Christ, were slandering Paul, accusing him of being a false prophet, and denying the gospel of God's free and sovereign grace in Christ. All the while they pretending to promote and defend the gospel. They were trying to make Christianity a mere extension of Judaism, just as multitudes do today.

They did not openly deny that salvation is by the free grace of God in Christ. They did not openly state that Christ is not enough, that Christ is not sufficient, or even that works must be mixed with faith. The messengers of Satan are far too subtle for that. They were teaching salvation by grace through works; but they did not state it quite that way. The Galatian heretics taught that true faith is a faith that expresses itself in the observance of the Mosaic law and that any faith that did not express itself in law obedience was a false faith. These men and their heresy were being embraced by the Galatian churches.

Paul was shocked. How could they be confused about this? If salvation is by grace, it cannot be by works. If salvation is by works, it cannot be by grace. 'If by grace, then is it no more of works: otherwise grace is no more grace. But if it be of works, then is it no more grace: otherwise work is no more work'. (Romans 11:6). There can be no mixture of the two.

The issue at Galatia, unlike the issues at Corinth, horrible as they were, was the gospel of God, the glory of God, the finished work of Christ, and the souls of men. Therefore, Paul jumped in, as one writer put it, 'with both fists flying'. Paul had reason to be provoked. His anger was completely justified.

One Gospel

It is ever the practice of those who oppose the gospel of God's free grace to slander the men who preach it. The legalists at Galatia knew they could not refute Paul's doctrine by scripture. If they were to turn men away from Paul's message, they must turn them away from him. Therefore, they sought to discredit Paul as God's messenger.

For this reason, the opening verses of chapter one identify Paul decisively as an apostle of God, not an apostle of men, or an apostle by the authority of men, but of and by the Lord Jesus Christ and God the Father. With that as his authority, Paul denounces as false every rival gospel. He tells us that every 'gospel' that teaches the sinner to look for righteousness and salvation anywhere except in Christ alone is no gospel at all, but a frustration of the grace of God; and with regard to those who preach another 'gospel' he says, 'let him be accursed' 'Let him be damned forever'. Paul could not have used stronger language to convey his thoughts on this matter.

'I marvel that ye are so soon removed from him that called you into the grace of Christ unto another gospel: Which is not another; but there be some that trouble you, and would pervert the gospel of Christ. But though we, or an angel from heaven, preach any other gospel unto you than that which we have preached unto you, let him be accursed. As we said before, so say I now again, If any man preach any other gospel unto you than that ye have received, let him be accursed' (vv. 6-9).

The gospel of God is good news about something done, not good advice about something you must do. The gospel is the good news of redemption obtained, righteousness brought in, sin put away, and salvation secured by the obedience and death of Christ as the sinner's Substitute (Daniel 9:24; John 19:30; Hebrews 1:1-3; 9:12, 26, 28; 10:10-14). Anyone who asserts that something must be done by the sinner before these things can be accomplished is a false prophet, preaching a false gospel, and those who follow him follow him to hell.

That is just how serious this matter is and Paul is leaving his readers under no misapprehension. Having said that, the fat was now in the fire. This was a full frontal attack on these enemies of truth. In verses 10-24 Paul asserts that contrary to the accusations of his detractors at Galatia, he had no desire to please men and made no effort to do so. The gospel of God was not something he learned from men. He learned it by divine revelation. His authority as an apostle and preacher, though confirmed by the other apostles (2:1-10), did not come from them, but from Christ himself.

Peter's Compromise

So far was Paul from being a compromising man-pleaser that when Peter compromised the gospel by his actions at Antioch Paul withstood him to the face (2:11-17). While at Antioch, Peter enjoyed a good barbeque dinner with the Gentile brethren there, until he saw some of his Jewish brethren approaching. At the sight of these men, Peter got up from the table and separated himself from the Gentiles, as if to say, 'Oh, I should not have done that. The law of Moses forbids eating good barbeque'.

When he did that, by his mere act, he led many into error, even Barnabas. By his action, Peter led others to believe that righteousness, justification, salvation, and acceptance with God is not totally the work of God's grace, but is in some way dependent upon our own obedience to the law of God.

Frustrating Grace

Peter's actions were far more evil than most imagine. His implied doctrine was a frustration of the grace of God. He implied that justifying righteousness can be obtained by the works of men. Therefore, Paul publicly withstood him to the face before both the Jews and the Gentiles at Antioch.

'But when I saw that they walked not uprightly according to the truth of the gospel, I said unto Peter before them all, If thou, being a Jew, livest after the manner of Gentiles, and not as do the Jews, why compellest thou the Gentiles to live as do the Jews? We who are Jews by nature, and not sinners of the Gentiles, Knowing that a man is not justified by the works of the law, but by the faith of Jesus Christ, even we have believed in Jesus Christ, that we might be justified by the faith of Christ, and not by the works of the law: for by the works of the law shall no flesh be justified. But if, while we seek to be justified by Christ, we ourselves also are found sinners, is therefore Christ the minister of sin? God forbid' (vv. 14-17).

Justification

We are justified by the faith of Christ, not by our faith in Christ, but by the faith and faithful obedience of Christ himself unto death as our Substitute (Romans 4:25). By our faith in Christ we receive and enjoy the blessedness of justification. We are not justified by something we do, but by Christ alone. To suggest, or imply in any way that our works, or even our experience, have anything at all to do with making us righteous before God for justification is to deny the gospel altogether. Paul puts it this way: 'I do not frustrate the grace of God: for if righteousness come by the law, then Christ is dead in vain' (v. 21). If righteousness could be established by something men do, then Christ died for nothing! Again, Paul could not have used stronger language to denounce the heresy of mixing works with grace for justification. Salvation is by grace alone, in Christ alone, received by faith alone, without works of any kind.

Antinomianism

Paul understood exactly what he was saying, and understood exactly what his detractors would say about his doctrine. He could almost hear them screaming with clinched fists, 'Antinomianism! That is antinomianism! If our works have nothing to do with righteousness, if we can be saved without obeying God's law and doing good works ourselves, you are telling us that we can go out and live like we want to in lawlessness, licentiousness, and lasciviousness'.

I know that is what they said, both because that is what Paul says they said (v. 17), and because I have heard those words countless times. The legalist never really wants to live as he pretends to live. The very language he uses to denounce free grace betrays the fact that if he could be saved without serving God, he would not serve him. The fact is, any man who preaches salvation by grace alone, without works, will be accused of antinomianism and of promoting licentiousness; but the charge is baseless and false (v. 17).

Sanctification

In chapter 3 Paul moves from justification to sanctification. He argues with the Galatians (and us) that their experience of grace forbids the idea that righteousness can be obtained by their works. He writes, 'O foolish Galatians, who hath bewitched you, that ye should not obey the truth, before whose eyes Jesus Christ hath been evidently set forth, crucified among you? This only would I learn of you, Received ye the Spirit by the works of the law, or by the hearing of faith? Are ye so foolish? having begun in the Spirit, are ye now made perfect by the flesh?' (vv. 1-3)

Sanctification and justification are two distinct works of God's grace; but the two cannot be separated. Those who are justified are also sanctified. Furthermore, sanctification as well as justification is a work of grace alone. Once we have received righteousness in justification by faith in Christ, we do not make ourselves more holy, more righteous before God by our works in sanctification. Believers grow in grace: in faith, in love, and in consecration to God. But believers do not become more holy and righteous before God as they grow in grace. The only time the word 'holy' is used in the scriptures in connection with a man in a relative sense is in Isaiah 65:5. There the Lord God says such people who think they are holier than others 'are a smoke in my nose'.

Christ is both our justification and sanctification (Obadiah 1:17, 1 Corinthians 1:30; Hebrews 10:10-14). His name is Jehovah-tsidkenu 'The Lord our Righteousness' (Jeremiah 23:6). We have no righteousness before God but him. To suggest that we make ourselves righteous by our works in sanctification is to mix grace and works; and that is a frustration of the grace of God. 'I do not frustrate the grace of God: for if righteousness come by the law, then Christ is dead in vain' (v. 21).

No Mixture

In a word, Paul's doctrine is this: Any mixture of grace and works in the matter of righteousness is a total denial of grace, for it is a frustration of grace. Therefore in chapters 3:19-4:31 he tells us that the whole purpose of the law was fulfilled when Christ suffered, died, and rose again as our Substitute. The law was our schoolmaster unto Christ. Once Christ came and fulfilled it, the law's work was finished. 'Christ is the end of the law for righteousness to everyone that believeth' (Romans 10:4).

There is no place for legal bondage in the household of faith. Those who would bring God's saints under the yoke of legal bondage deny the whole gospel of the grace of God and every believer's experience of grace. All who attempt to make themselves righteous by the works of the law are still under the curse of the law.

'For as many as are of the works of the law are under the curse: for it is written, Cursed is every one that continueth not in all things which are written in the book of the law to do them. But that no man is justified by the law in the sight of God, it is evident: for, The just shall live by faith' (vv. 10-11).

Those who would bring believers under the yoke of legal bondage deny every believer's experience of grace (vv. 1-5). They deny the Old Testament scriptures, which assert that Abraham was justified by faith without works (vv. 6-9). They deny the efficacy of Christ's atonement, asserting that Christ died in vain, that he did not actually secure the blessing of grace for God's elect by his death (vv. 13-14). They deny the whole purpose of the law as a schoolmaster unto Christ (vv. 15-29). And, he shows in chapter 4, they deny the blessed liberty of the gospel and the grace of God, the very liberty Christ obtained for us by his obedience to the law and his death by the law, by attempting to bring us back under the yoke of bondage (vv. 1-11).

'But when the fulness of the time was come, God sent forth his Son, made of a woman, made under the law, To redeem them that were under the law, that we might receive the adoption of sons. And because ye are sons, God hath sent forth the Spirit of his Son into your hearts, crying, Abba, Father. Wherefore thou art no more a servant, but a son; and if a son, then an heir of God through Christ' (vv. 4-7).

Christ died for God's elect, his eternally adopted children, that we might receive the Spirit of adoption in regeneration, giving us faith to look upon God through the blood of our Saviour with confidence as our heavenly Father (Hebrews 10:19-22). Trusting Christ, we are no longer servants, but sons. The promoters of law righteousness would have us swap sonship for slavery! No wonder Paul was fearful for their souls! No wonder he stood in doubt of them (v. 19). These Gentile believers, to whom the law was never given, were being duped by their false teachers to swap the liberty of Christ for the bondage of Moses.

'But now, after that ye have known God, or rather are known of God, how turn ye again to the weak and beggarly elements, whereunto ye desire again to be in bondage? Ye observe days, and months, and times, and years. I am afraid of you, lest I have bestowed upon you labour in vain' (vv. 9-11).

In the latter part of chapter 4 (vv. 21-31) Paul uses Sarah and Hagar and their sons Isaac and Ishmael as an allegory. The allegory teaches us, that as Hagar and Ishmael, the fruit of Abraham's shameful works by which he attempted to perform God's righteous promise, had to be cast out of Abraham's house, so all our own works righteousness, all attempts to make ourselves righteous before God, must be cast out as filthy rags. It is written, 'Cast out the bond woman and her son'. There is no room in the house of grace for the works of the flesh, for legal obedience.

Stand Fast

In the fifth chapter Paul urges us to stand fast in the blessed liberty of the gospel, warning us that if we do anything by which we hope to gain God's favour, improve our standing in God's favour, or keep ourselves in God's favour, we have abandoned the gospel and abandoned grace altogether. He says, 'Christ is of no value to anyone who attempts to make himself righteous before God'.

'Stand fast therefore in the liberty wherewith Christ hath made us free, and be not entangled again with the yoke of bondage. Behold, I Paul say unto you, that if ye be circumcised, Christ shall profit you nothing. For I testify again to every man that is circumcised, that he is a debtor to do the whole law. Christ is become of no effect unto you, whosoever of you are justified by the law; ye are fallen from grace' (vv. 1-4).

There is no antinomianism here, no licentiousness, no encouragement to sin. Far from it! The rest of the book of Galatians is a declaration that this liberty of grace is life in the Spirit. As we walk in the Spirit, looking to Christ alone for righteousness and salvation, we will not fulfil the lusts of the flesh. It is self-righteousness and legalism that causes men and women to bite and devour one another and that in the name of righteousness! Grace teaches believers to restore their fallen brethren, to bear one another's burdens, to love one another, and so to fulfil the law of Christ. Grace teaches us not to sow to the flesh and reap corruption, but to sow to the Spirit and reap life everlasting.

Our only hope is the cross of Christ. Our only motivation, our only rule of life is the cross. All who have this hope and live by this rule are blessed as 'the Israel of God'.

'But God forbid that I should glory, save in the cross of our Lord Jesus Christ, by whom the world is crucified unto me, and I unto the world. For in Christ Jesus neither circumcision availeth any thing, nor uncircumcision, but a new creature. And as many as walk according to this rule, peace be on them, and mercy, and upon the Israel of God' (6:14-16).

The Cross

The sum and essence of all true doctrine, the essence of all true Christianity, and of all motivation in the lives of God's elect in this world is the cross of our Lord Jesus Christ (6:14). When Paul writes, 'God forbid that I should glory, save in the cross of our Lord Jesus Christ', he is telling us that his only trust, his only hope before God is that which Christ accomplished as our all-sufficient, effectual Redeemer at Calvary.

Throughout the book of Galatians the cross of Christ is central. The cross, as Paul uses it, refers not to the wooden cross upon which Christ died, or the historic fact of the cross, but the doctrine of the cross. Redemption and salvation by the death of our Lord Jesus Christ as our sin-atoning Substitute.

The cross is deliverance by blood atonement (1:3-5). The cross is life (2:19-20). The cross is righteousness (2:21). The cross is the removal of our curse (3:13). The cross is the certainty of God's blessing (3:14). The cross is the centre of our faith (3:22). The cross is the ground of our adoption (4:4-7). The cross is an offence to the unbelieving (5:11). The cross is the source of all grace (5:22-24). The cross is that by which we are crucified unto the world and the world unto us (6:14-15). The cross is our rule, our peace, our mercy, and our life (6:16-18).

> I must needs go home by the way of the cross,
> There's no other way but this;
> I shall ne'er get sight of the gates of light,
> If the way of the cross I miss.
>
> I must needs go on in the blood sprinkled way,
> The path that the Saviour trod,
> If I ever climb to the heights sublime,
> Where the soul is at home with God.
>
> So I bid farewell to the way of the world,
> To walk in it never more;
> For the Lord says, 'Come', and I seek my home,
> Where He waits at the open door.
>
> The way of the cross leads home,
> The way of the cross leads home,
> It is sweet to know as I onward go,
> The way of the cross leads home.

Chapter 49

Ephesians

'To the Praise of His Glory'

In the very first chapter of Ephesians we are brought immediately into the counsel chambers of the triune God, caused to think about electing love, blood atonement, effectual grace, and preserving mercy, and made to worship before the august throne of our triune, covenant-keeping God, our Father in heaven, our beloved Saviour, and our divine Comforter. Unless it is the book of Psalms, there is, perhaps, no section of holy scripture to which I turn more often and meditate upon more constantly than Paul's Epistle to the Ephesians. I find it delightful. I never read these pages without coming away with something fresh for my heart from the throne of God.

Speaks of Christ

I love this book because of the Person of whom it speaks. When I open the book of Ephesians, no matter where I am reading, no matter where I sit down, no matter where I walk in this treasure house, I feel as if I am immediately in the presence of our Lord Jesus Christ. The words 'in Christ', 'in him', 'by Christ', 'through Christ', and 'for Christ', or other words with the same meaning, are used fifty-five times in this book. Fifty-five times the Holy Spirit reminds us that everything we have from God, everything we are by grace, and everything we hope to enjoy in heavenly glory is in Christ. In Christ, God has given us all that he can give and all that we can enjoy. He has given us himself!

The Ephesians

I love to muse upon the things written in these pages because of the people to whom this book was written, The Ephesians. Ephesus was a large, wealthy, metropolitan city of Asia Minor. It was called, 'The Light of Asia'. It was a city filled with brilliant, wealthy people. It was the envy of the world in its day. Tradesmen, scholars, philosophers, and orators flocked to Ephesus. They thought it had everything a man could want, but Ephesus was a godless society. Actually, that is not true. They had gods galore. However, they were altogether without the knowledge of God. Like the society in which we live, idolatrous, man-centred religion walked hand in hand with superstition, immorality, lasciviousness, and utter decadence. The worshipers at the great temple of Diana at Ephesus, just like many religious people in our day, openly promoted every moral perversity imaginable. Yet, from among these hell-bent pagans, the Lord God was pleased to raise up a people, objects of his everlasting love, to whom he revealed his gospel, in whom he revealed his Son, and by whom he made known his grace.

Contrast

What a contrast there is in the very first verse of the epistle between the person who wrote it and the people to whom it was written. It is a contrast that singularly displays the great sovereignty of our God in the exercise of his grace. 'Paul, an apostle of Jesus Christ by the will of God, to the saints (those who are sanctified) which are at Ephesus, and to the faithful (those who have been and are made faithful) in Christ Jesus'.

Not many of the wise, the mighty, and the noble are called, but a few are. Most of God's servants, most of the prophets of the Old Testament, most of the apostles in the New Testament, and most gospel preachers today were nobodies and nothings when God called them, just shepherds and fishermen. But Paul was one of the most brilliant and most highly educated men of his day. Like Isaiah in the king's court, this man was a man whose words were respected and heard. Before God saved him, Saul of Tarsus would not have allowed himself to even come into contact with these pagan Gentiles at Ephesus. Now for he risked his life for them, that he might preach the gospel to them!

Truly, God is no respecter of persons. He has mercy on whom he will have mercy. God's servants are just messengers. It matters not whether the messenger has an eloquent, trained and polished, baritone voice, and uses perfect grammar, or has a coarse, gravelly voice and obviously does not know the difference between an adverb and an adjective. God's messengers are not sent to impress, but to instruct, to deliver his message.

Paul considered himself nothing but God's messenger, and counted it his highest honour to be such. 'Unto me, who am less than the least of all saints, is this grace given, that I should preach among the Gentiles the unsearchable riches of Christ' (3:8).

Heavenly Places

I love the book of Ephesians because it brings me into 'heavenly places'. The words 'heavenly places' are found nowhere else in the Bible, except in the book of Ephesians. The Holy Spirit inspired Paul to use this term repeatedly (1:3; 1:20; 2:6; 3:10; see also 6:12). Some prefer to translate the word used in these places 'heavenlies' instead of 'heavenly places'. Whichever way it is translated, this term, 'heavenly places', refers to heavenly things, heavenly words, heavenly doctrines, heavenly promises, heavenly possessions, and heavenly experiences belonging to God's elect in Christ.

'Heavenly places' refer to the place of eternal, covenant blessings in Christ. 'Blessed be the God and Father of our Lord Jesus Christ, who hath blessed us with all spiritual blessings in heavenly places in Christ' (1:3).

'Heavenly places' speak of the place of our great High Priest's royal, kingly intercession, advocacy, and sovereign dominion. 'And what is the exceeding greatness of his power to us-ward who believe, according to the working of his mighty power, Which he wrought in Christ, when he raised him from the dead, and set him at his own right hand in the heavenly places, Far above all principality, and power, and might, and dominion, and every name that is named, not only in this world, but also in that which is to come' (1:19-21).

'Heavenly places' identify our spiritual union and communion with Christ as well. 'And hath raised us up together, and made us sit together in heavenly places in Christ Jesus' (2:6). There he is, yonder, at the Father's right hand, seated, accepted, and blessed. But here is something more. Yonder, 'in heavenly places', I am, seated, accepted, and blessed at the Father's right hand. Frequently, I do not feel so close to my God. Indeed, I often feel far off from him. But my faith does not rest in my feelings. My comfort and assurance are not derived from the cracked cistern of my feelings. My faith is in, and my comfort, hope, and assurance are founded upon the Word of God. And God says in his Word, right here in Ephesians 2:6, that I am with Christ 'in heavenly places'. I prefer what God says to what my deceitful hearts says.

> Near, so very near to God, nearer I cannot be,
> For in the Person of His Son, I am as near as He!

'Heavenly places' are those places in which we are taught of God by divine revelation. 'To the intent that now unto the principalities and powers in heavenly places might be known by the church the manifold wisdom of God' (3:10). This passage of scripture refers to the gathered assemblies of God's saints around the world as 'heavenly places' of spiritual instruction. Here, as we sing, and pray, and worship, and receive instruction in the knowledge of Christ by the gospel of the grace of God, the angels of God are also instructed in the wonders of blood atonement, pardoning love, and saving grace!

'Heavenly places' are the place of spiritual privilege and stern perplexity, blessed assurance and bothersome anxiety, sweet communion and stubborn conflict. 'For we wrestle not against flesh and blood, but against principalities, against powers, against the rulers of the darkness of this world, against spiritual wickedness in heavenly places' (6:12 marginal translation). The world is the enemy of our Father. The devil is at arms against our Master. The flesh is at war with the Spirit and our carnal hearts are enmity against God. Therefore, we need not be surprised to find our daily experience an experience of unceasing, constant warfare.

Grace

I also love this blessed book of Ephesians because it talks so much about grace, God's free, sovereign, saving grace in Christ. All grace is ours in Christ by divine purpose and joyful experience, to use for our own comfort and peace, and for one another's good, and for the glory of our great God and Saviour, the Lord Jesus Christ.

The Explanation of Grace

In the first chapter of Ephesians Paul explains what God has done for us by his wonderful, free, saving grace in Christ. He begins this epistle by telling us what the triune God has done for us, according to his own sovereign will and eternal purpose, for the praise of his glory. The grace of God flows to us from the three persons of the Holy Trinity, Father, Son, and Holy Spirit. Grace comes to sinners according to the Father's purpose, the Son's purchase, and the Spirit's power (Jonah 2:9).

All Spiritual Blessings

The apostle assures us that all God's elect have been blessed of God with all spiritual blessings in Christ from eternity (1:3), and that all the blessings of grace come to chosen sinners according to God's eternal purpose of grace in election (1:4). At the very outset of his letter, he declares that there is no possibility of grace, salvation, and spiritual blessedness apart from God's eternal election and sovereign, loving predestination. Having asserted that all the blessings of God's grace are the eternal, unalterable possession of every sinner who believes on the Lord Jesus Christ, Paul proceeds in chapter one to name ten of those great, spiritual blessings (vv. 3-14).

Election is the first blessing named (vv. 3-4) The Lord God chose a vast multitude of sinners unto salvation in Christ before the world began. He chose us to make us 'holy and without blame before him'. And he will accomplish his purpose (5:27; Jude 24-25).

The second great blessing of grace is divine predestination (vv. 4-5). In eternal love for us our heavenly Father predestined all his elect to what Paul calls in the book of Romans 'the glorious liberty of the sons of God'.

The third blessing of grace Paul names is adoption (v. 5). Imagine that, the God and Father of our Lord Jesus Christ adopted us into his family in and by Christ before he called the world into existence (1 John 3:1). Why? Just because he would! He did it 'according to the good pleasure of his will, to the praise of the glory of his grace' (vv. 5-6).

Next, the apostle tells us that our great God 'hath made us accepted in the Beloved' (v. 6), not acceptable, accepted! (Esther 5:1-3). By an act of free and sovereign grace, he accepted all the objects of his eternal love in Christ before the world began. Those he accepted in eternity can never be made unaccepted in time.

Redemption is named as the fifth bounty of God's grace possessed by all who are in Christ (v. 7). Redemption is deliverance from all sin, all condemnation, and all the consequences of our sin and fall in Adam, deliverance into 'the glorious liberty of the sons of God'. This redemption is that which was accomplished and obtained for us by the precious, sin-atoning blood of Christ (Hebrews 9:12).

Then, sixth, Paul tells us that the forgiveness of sins is ours in Christ (v. 7). Where there is redemption accomplished there is also pardon. In fact, Paul explains what he means by redemption by saying, redemption means forgiveness. 'In whom we have redemption through his blood, the forgiveness of sins, according to the riches of his grace'. Grace does not proclaim a redemption that offers pardon, but a redemption that demands pardon. Justice satisfied means pardon granted. This acceptance with God, this redemption by the blood of Christ, this blessed forgiveness is ours 'according to the riches of his grace'.

In verses 9 and 10 Paul tells us seventhly that God has given to every believer the knowledge of 'the mystery of his will'. The secret things belong to God; but he has revealed his purpose of grace to his children. He has made 'his good pleasure' known to us in his Word and by his

Spirit. It is the purpose and good pleasure of God to save all his elect; and that is what he is doing in his daily works of providence and grace. When time is fulfilled, he will 'gather together in one all things in Christ'.

In Christ, who took possession of heavenly glory for us as our Forerunner (Hebrews 6:20), we have obtained an eternal inheritance in heaven, 'being predestinated according to the purpose of him who worketh all things after the counsel of his own will' (1:11-12). Yes, the inheritance of heavenly glory is the present and eternal possession of every sinner who trusts the Son of God (John 17:5, 22). We are 'heirs of God and joint-heirs with Jesus Christ'.

Eighth, in verse 13 the apostle tells us that every believer has been sealed by God the Holy Spirit. We believe by the almighty operations of God the Holy Spirit, and believing we are sealed.

Grace is not a proposition, but a performance. Grace is not something God offers, but something God does. We do not believe as the result of God's offer, but as the result of God's operation. This operation of grace, by which we believe, has an intimate, indivisible relationship to the word of truth, the gospel of salvation accomplished in Christ.

The gospel is called 'the word of truth' because it reveals Christ who is the Truth. It is called 'the gospel of your salvation' because it reveals salvation accomplished by Christ. It is called 'the word of life' because it is the means by which God the Holy Spirit conveys life to dead sinners (1 Peter 1:23-25). Do you believe on the Lord Jesus Christ? If you do, it is because God the Holy Spirit has revealed Christ to you and in you by the gospel (2 Timothy 1:9-10).

Where the Holy Spirit has performed his work of grace in regeneration, he also performs his work of grace in preservation. He seals all the blessings of covenant grace to us and seals us in the covenant (vv. 13-14). A seal implies three things. (1.) Property – That which is sealed is the property of the one whose seal is upon it. (2.) Preciousness – Any item that is sealed is of great value. (3.) Preservation – When a thing is sealed it is preserved from harm or spoilage. This is the ninth blessing in Paul's list.

The tenth blessing of God's boundless grace possessed by every sinner who believes on the Lord Jesus Christ, is 'the earnest of the Spirit' (v. 14). The Holy Spirit dwelling in us as the Spirit of adoption, by whom we believe, is the pledge and guarantee of our eternal inheritance in heaven.

A Prayer for Understanding

These great riches of God's boundless grace in Christ are the present possession of all believers; but none of us knows how rich we are in

Christ. Therefore, Paul prayed that the Lord God would grant us some understanding of our vast spiritual wealth as the sons of God (vv. 15-23). Here are three things hidden from all natural men, that Paul asked God to cause his believing people to see and understand. (1.) What is the hope of his calling? It is Christ's obedience unto death as our Substitute. (2.) What are the riches of the glory of his inheritance in the saints? They are the complete satisfaction of the Father's purpose, Christ's finished work of redemption, and the Holy Spirit's mighty operations of grace. (3.) What is the exceeding greatness of his power to usward who believe? It is the sovereign, irresistible power of God's omnipotent grace by which we are called from death to life in Christ. It is the very power by which God raised his Son from the dead (v. 20).

Grace is power; sovereign, omnipotent, effectual, irresistible power. According to the words of the Holy Spirit, it takes the very same power to cause a dead sinner to live and believe on the Lord Jesus Christ as it took to raise the dead body of our crucified Redeemer from the grave.

The Fulness of Christ

In verses 20-23 Paul declares the greatness, glory, supremacy, and dominion of our exalted Saviour as the Head of his church. Then, at the end of chapter one, he makes a statement that is as comforting as it is astounding. He tells us that the church of God's elect, the body of Christ, is 'the fulness of him that filleth all in all' (v. 23). Paul is speaking of Christ in his mediatorial capacity. As he is the fulness of all things, so his church is his fulness as the God-man Mediator. What does that mean? It means that he cannot be complete as a Mediator and Saviour if even one chosen member of his body is lost. It means that the salvation of every chosen, adopted, predestined, redeemed, called, and sealed sinner is a matter of absolute certainty. The fulness of Christ as our Mediator could never be accomplished without the salvation of his people. 'He shall see of the travail of his soul, and shall be satisfied'.

The Experience of Grace

In chapter 2 the Holy Spirit inspired the Apostle to give us a detailed description of every believer's experience of grace. The grace of God, as we experience it in this world, involves two things. It involves the new birth and the consequent reconciliation of our hearts to God in Christ. We must be born again because we were all born in spiritual death by nature. And we must be reconciled to God because we all hate God by nature. Ephesians 2 deals with these two aspects of grace.

Regeneration

Regeneration is the sovereign work and operation of grace performed in the hearts of chosen, redeemed sinners by God the Holy Spirit, sinners who are by nature both dead and depraved. The new birth is not achieved or accomplished by man's will, but by God's power, not by man's choice, but by God's purpose.

Once again, it is not something God offers, but something he does. The new birth is a resurrection from the dead. It is that first resurrection spoken of in Revelation 20:6, of which we are told, 'Blessed and holy is he that hath part in the first resurrection: on such the second death hath no power, but they shall be priests of God and of Christ, and shall reign with him a thousand years'.

Look at Ephesians 2:1-10 and the condition of all men by nature. 'And you hath he quickened, who were dead in trespasses and sins; Wherein in time past ye walked according to the course of this world, according to the prince of the power of the air, the spirit that now worketh in the children of disobedience: Among whom also we all had our conversation in times past in the lusts of our flesh, fulfilling the desires of the flesh and of the mind; and were by nature the children of wrath, even as other' (vv. 1-3). Natural man is spiritually depraved and spiritually dead.

Here is the mighty work of God in the new birth, in raising us from our spiritual death to life in Christ. 'But God, who is rich in mercy, for his great love wherewith he loved us, even when we were dead in trespasses and in sins, hath quickened us together with Christ, (by grace ye are saved)' (vv. 4-5). The reason for all this is the love of God (v. 4). The new birth is the effect of God's work in us (v. 5). The result of it is union, communion, and fellowship with Christ in the power of his resurrection. 'And hath raised us up together, and made us sit together in heavenly places in Christ Jesus' (v. 6). As we were raised together with Christ representatively, we have been raised together with him spiritually in the new birth (John 5:24-26).

Why has the Lord been so gracious to such sinners as we are? Paul answers that question in verse 7. 'That in the ages to come he might shew the exceeding riches of his grace in his kindness toward us through Christ Jesus'. Then, in verses 8-10 he summarizes all that he has said in the first seven verses of chapter two.

'For by grace are ye saved through faith; and that not of yourselves: it is the gift of God: Not of works, lest any man should boast. For we are his workmanship, created in Christ Jesus unto good works, which God hath before ordained that we should walk in them'.

Reconciliation

The result of regeneration is reconciliation (vv. 11-22). Remember, Paul is dealing with the believer's experience of grace. We were legally reconciled to God at Calvary by the death of his Son (Romans 5:10-11). But our hearts were still enmity against God until he conquered us by his grace and graciously forced us to bow to him in reconciliation.

Here is a fact we must never forget. 'Wherefore remember, that ye being in time past Gentiles in the flesh, who are called Uncircumcision by that which is called the Circumcision in the flesh made by hands; That at that time ye were without Christ, being aliens from the commonwealth of Israel, and strangers from the covenants of promise, having no hope, and without God in the world' (vv. 11-12; Isaiah 51:1-2). 'But now in Christ Jesus ye who sometimes were far off are made nigh by the blood of Christ' (v. 13). There is that blessed phrase again *in Christ*. To be in Christ is to be ...

Chosen in him.
Redeemed in him.
Justified in him.
Called in him.
Sanctified in him.
United to him.
Accepted in him.

Connection

In verses 14-21, Paul tells us that the grace of God experienced in the soul, not only unites and reconciles us to God in Christ, it also unites and reconciles us to one another in Christ. All stones in a building, built upon one foundation and connected to one cornerstone, are united to and connected to one another. So, too, all who are built on Christ are fitted together.

This is Paul's doctrine in Ephesians and in all his writings. That which God requires of us God alone can do for us!

Atonement for sin (2 Corinthians 5:21).
Perfect righteousness (Matthew 5:20).
Spiritual life, a spiritual nature, the new birth (John 3:7).
Faith in Christ (Hebrews 11:6).

These are the things the Lord God Almighty has done for us and in us by his grace in Christ.

The Enjoyment of Grace

In chapter 3 Paul describes what I call the enjoyment of grace. There comes a time, sometime after you are converted, as you grow in the grace and knowledge of our Lord Jesus Christ, that you begin to really enjoy the grace of God. Much like a husband and wife really begin to truly enjoy one another, comfortably and confidently enjoy one another only after they have been married for a while, believers, while never getting over the wonder of grace, do not really enjoy grace until they have lived in it and experienced it a while.

A Mystery Revealed

The gospel of the grace of God is a wondrous mystery revealed. It is the revelation of how God justified sinners and reconciles them to himself and to one another, in one body with Christ as our Head. Though it cost him his very life, as it will every faithful gospel preacher, Paul considered it his greatest honour, highest privilege, and most delightful joy to be made a preacher of this gospel (vv. 7-8).

'Whereof I was made a minister, according to the gift of the grace of God given unto me by the effectual working of his power. Unto me, who am less than the least of all saints, is this grace given, that I should preach among the Gentiles the unsearchable riches of Christ'.

A Pastor's Heart

As a faithful gospel preacher, as a pastor with a pastor's heart, Paul wanted those people to whom he preached to know in the fullest way possible, by experience, all the blessedness of God's abundant, free grace in Christ (vv. 9-21, 3 John 1:4). It was the desire and burning passion of his heart that these Ephesian saints might be made to see ...

The manifold wisdom of God in the scheme of grace. 'And to make all men see what is the fellowship of the mystery, which from the beginning of the world hath been hid in God, who created all things by Jesus Christ: To the intent that now unto the principalities and powers in heavenly places might be known by the church the manifold wisdom of God' (vv. 9-10). The eternal purpose of his grace. 'According to the eternal purpose which he purposed in Christ Jesus our Lord'(v. 11). And the free accessibility we have to our God in Christ by his grace. 'In whom we have boldness and access with confidence by the faith of him'(v. 12; Hebrews 10:19-22).

A Pastor's Prayer

In verses 14-19 Paul tells the Ephesians his heart's prayer to God for them; but there is more here than Paul's prayer for the saints at Ephesus. This was his prayer for all God's elect, even you and me. As a true under shepherd of Christ, Paul laboured for the good of those under his immediate influence and for the good of God's church as a whole. Read his prayer and ask the Lord to answer it for you.

'For this cause I bow my knees unto the Father of our Lord Jesus Christ, Of whom the whole family in heaven and earth is named, That he would grant you, according to the riches of his glory, to be strengthened with might by his Spirit in the inner man; That Christ may dwell in your hearts by faith; that ye, being rooted and grounded in love, May be able to comprehend with all saints what is the breadth, and length, and depth, and height; And to know the love of Christ, which passeth knowledge, that ye might be filled with all the fulness of God'.

In all his labours and in all his desire, his confidence was in Christ and his aim was the glory of Christ. 'Now unto him that is able to do exceeding abundantly above all that we ask or think, according to the power that worketh in us, Unto him be glory in the church by Christ Jesus throughout all ages, world without end. Amen' (vv. 20-21).

The Education of Grace

The fourth chapter of Ephesians shows us the education of grace. Paul urges us to labour at maintaining the blessed unity of God's church and kingdom, the unity of all true believers in Christ by the Spirit of God. All that we know and experience of God's grace teaches us that God's people are one and that we ought to cherish and promote that oneness. The way to do that is to walk before God and with one another in humility, with longsuffering, forbearing one another and forgiving one another relentlessly.

'I therefore, the prisoner of the Lord, beseech you that ye walk worthy of the vocation wherewith ye are called, With all lowliness and meekness, with longsuffering, forbearing one another in love; Endeavouring to keep the unity of the Spirit in the bond of peace. There is one body, and one Spirit, even as ye are called in one hope of your calling; One Lord, one faith, one baptism, One God and Father of all, who is above all, and through all, and in you all' (vv. 1-6).

Then he tells us that in the church and kingdom of God there is no room for and no basis for envy and jealousy. Each of us are given specific gifts to use for the glory of Christ, the interests of the gospel, and the benefit of God's elect (4:7). When the Lord Jesus Christ ascended up into heaven and took his seat at the right hand of the majesty on high, he received gifts for men and gives those gifts to men, as he will. One of the gifts, with which he has endowed his church, is the gift of the ministry (vv. 8-16). Read verses 11-14.

'And he gave some, apostles; and some, prophets; and some, evangelists; and some, pastors and teachers; For the perfecting of the saints, for the work of the ministry, for the edifying of the body of Christ: Till we all come in the unity of the faith, and of the knowledge of the Son of God, unto a perfect man, unto the measure of the stature of the fulness of Christ: That we henceforth be no more children, tossed to and fro, and carried about with every wind of doctrine, by the sleight of men, and cunning craftiness, whereby they lie in wait to deceive'.

No Licentiousness

Grace does not cause or promote licentiousness, but true godliness (vv. 17-24). The gospel of the grace of God and the grace of God experienced in the soul teaches believing men and women to live soberly, righteously, and godly in this present evil world for the glory of Christ. We are totally free from the law; but believers are not lawless. Saved sinners seek to glorify God in all things. If a person's religion promotes, permits, or allows room for lasciviousness, greed, and deceitful lusts, his religion is not the religion of grace. Grace teaches people to bridle their passions and their tongues (vv. 25-29). Grace causes saved sinners to fear the thought of grieving the Holy Spirit (v. 30).

In a word, grace makes people gracious. 'Let all bitterness, and wrath, and anger, and clamour, and evil speaking, be put away from you, with all malice: And be ye kind one to another, tender-hearted, forgiving one another, even as God for Christ's sake hath forgiven you' (vv. 31-32).

The Exercise of Grace

Ephesians chapter 5 describes the exercise of grace by people who have experienced it and have been taught by it. We who have been the recipients of grace ought to always take care to magnify the grace of God in our deeds, as well as with our words. As we have been loved of God, we ought to walk in love with one another. 'Be ye therefore followers of God, as dear children; And walk in love, as Christ also hath loved us, and hath given himself for us an offering and a sacrifice to God for a sweetsmelling savour' (vv. 1-2). As people who are called to be saints, we should always seek to live in a manner becoming saints (vv. 3-13).

We must endeavour, for Christ's sake, to shake ourselves from our natural tendency toward lukewarmness, indifference, and indolence in spiritual things, and buy up every opportunity to worship and serve our Master. 'Wherefore he saith, Awake thou that sleepest, and arise from the dead, and Christ shall give thee light. See then that ye walk circumspectly, not as fools, but as wise, Redeeming the time, because the days are evil. Wherefore be ye not unwise, but understanding what the will of the Lord is' (v 14-17).

If we would live for Christ in this world, we must ever seek to be filled with the Spirit (5:18-6:9). Being filled with the Spirit is not some charismatic fit or Pentecostal spasm. To be filled with the Spirit is exactly what verses 18-33 tell us it is. To be filled with the Spirit is to ...

> – offer thanks and praise to God in all things and for all things, in your heart.
> – submit to one another in the will of God.
> – imitate Christ in all things: as husbands, as fathers, as masters, as servants.

The Exhortation of Grace

The latter half of chapter 6 concludes this blessed book with the exhortation of grace (vv. 10-24). Paul urges us to be strong in the Lord and to stand firm in the gospel and in the cause of Christ. 'Having done all stand!' He tells us to put on, as our continual, daily clothing, 'the whole armour of God, that you may be able to stand against the wiles of the devil'. In verses 14-21 Paul tells us what the believer's complete, sevenfold armour is:

> The Girdle of Truth is the firm, settled conviction regarding the Revelation of God in his Word.
>
> The Breastplate of Righteousness is not the breastplate of our own pretence of righteousness, but the righteousness that is ours in Christ. We put it on by continually looking away from ourselves to Christ, and reminding ourselves continually of what we are in him and what he has done for us by his grace.
>
> Gospel Shoes are to be put on every day, standing firm in the grace and peace revealed and given to us by the gospel
>
> The Shield of Faith is reliance upon the promises of God. 'My Grace is sufficient for thee. Him that cometh unto me, I will in no wise cast out! I am with thee! I will never leave thee, nor forsake thee!'

The Sword of the Spirit is the Word of God. We are to use it to protect ourselves from the assaults of Satan.

Praying always for ourselves, but more importantly for one another, we war a good warfare in this world.

Finally, if we would serve our God and Saviour and the interests of his kingdom, let us make it our heart's ambition that all God's people in this world have and enjoy his peace and love with faith, and his boundless grace continually. Let us make it our life's ambition to promote these things, for the glory of God our Saviour. 'Peace be to the brethren, and love with faith, from God the Father and the Lord Jesus Christ. Grace be with all them that love our Lord Jesus Christ in sincerity. Amen' (vv. 23-24).

Chapter 50

Philippians

'Rejoice in the Lord'

The book of Philippians was written to the saints at Philippi while Paul was a prisoner at Rome. In fact, four of Paul's epistles were written while he was a prisoner at Rome (Ephesians, Philippians, Colossians, and Philemon). It is striking that the book of Philippians was written at that time because this is an epistle of joy. The central message of these four chapters is found in this blessed admonition: 'Rejoice in the Lord always: and again I say, Rejoice' (4:4).

In the midst of terribly difficult circumstances, even in the prospect of being put to death because of his faithfulness in preaching the gospel, Paul repeatedly speaks of his unbridled joy in Christ and calls upon us to 'rejoice in the Lord always'.

Roger Ellsworth points out that the words 'joy' and 'rejoice' appear sixteen times in this brief letter, and references to Christ, including pronouns, are found 61 times in its 104 verses. It is obvious that Christ, not circumstances, was the source of Paul's joy.

In the midst of great heaviness Paul here teaches us to rejoice in Christ. In the midst of great tribulation he teaches us to be content in our Saviour. The Philippians might well remember that he and Silas rejoiced as they sang praises to God with bleeding backs when they were prisoners at Philippi (Acts 16:25). Here, he calls upon them and us to follow his example.

Matters of Joy

Pause to consider the examples presented in these chapters as things in which Paul rejoiced and for which he tells us we ought to rejoice. He rejoiced in the sweet fellowship of God's saints. Paul counted the church of God his family. He rejoiced in fond memories, sweet experiences, and loving fellowship with his brothers and sisters in Christ (1:3-11; 4:1). In chapter 1 verse 6 Paul gives a word of confident assurance to his brethren. He says to these saints at Philippi and to every sinner who trusts Christ as his Saviour and Lord, I am 'confident of this very thing, that he which hath begun a good work in you will perform it until the day of Jesus Christ'. Salvation is altogether the work of God. That makes the security and ultimate resurrection glory of God's elect a matter of absolute certainty (Ecclesiastes 3:14). Those to whom the Son of God gives eternal life 'shall never perish' (John 10:28).

Paul was confident that these Philippian believers, and all believers, would persevere unto the end, because he was confident that the work of God cannot be overturned. In verse 7 he says it was right for him to think this way, because they had been made partakers of the same grace of God he had experienced and proclaimed.

Look at the tender words he uses to describe his feelings for these saints he had not seen in a long, long time. 'I thank my God upon every remembrance of you' (v. 3). 'I have you in my heart' (v. 7). 'I long after you all in the bowels of Jesus Christ' (v. 8). I pray for you, that you may be 'filled with the fruits of righteousness, which are by Jesus Christ, unto the glory and praise of God' (v. 11).

Look too at the matters that brought joy to the apostle. He rejoiced that, in God's good providence, his sufferings for the gospel were one means by which the Lord God was pleased to advance the gospel (1:12-20; 2:17).

Paul rejoiced and was completely happy to suffer, or to die, or to live, as the Lord willed, because he knew that Christ would be magnified and the best interests of his people served, as God graciously accomplished his will (1:19-26).

This faithful servant of God found his joy full when he knew that God's saints walked and worshipped together as one (2:1-2). The unity of God's people is something Paul mentions in all his epistles. It was a great grief to him when the fellowship of God's saints was interrupted and a great joy when he saw it being promoted.

Paul also rejoiced in the company and ministries of his fellow-labourers in the gospel. He is truly the servant of Christ who rejoices in and promotes the labours of other servants of Christ, as labourers together with him. In chapter 2, Paul specifically mentions Timothy and Epaphroditus (vv. 19-30). He could not have spoken more highly than he did of his young friend Timothy (vv. 19-23). He could not have spoken more honourably and tenderly of his old friend Epaphroditus, who was, apparently, the pastor of the Philippian church (vv. 25-30).

How could a man in the midst of such adversities express such joy in so many directions? How could a man who was about to be executed on trumped up charges be joyful and content? What was the secret of his joy? We discover the answer in Philippians 4:4-7.

'Rejoice in the Lord alway: and again I say, Rejoice. Let your moderation be known unto all men. The Lord is at hand. Be careful for nothing; but in every thing by prayer and supplication with thanksgiving let your requests be made known unto God. And the peace of God, which passeth all understanding, shall keep your hearts and minds through Christ Jesus'.

Paul rejoiced in, and would have us rejoice in, the Lord. If ever we learn to rejoice in the Lord, we will be able to rejoice in the Lord always, no matter what our circumstances may be. 'Rejoice in the Lord'. If we learn to rejoice in the Lord, we will learn to 'rejoice in the Lord always'. I cannot rejoice in my sorrows; but I can rejoice in the Lord who sent them. I cannot rejoice in my bed of languishing; but I can rejoice in the Lord who makes my bed. I cannot rejoice in bereavement; but I can rejoice in the Lord who gives and takes away as he will. I cannot rejoice in my emptiness; but I can rejoice in the Lord's fulness. I cannot rejoice in my pain; but I can rejoice in his presence.

Life and Death

In the first chapter Paul teaches us, by his own marvellous example, what our attitude ought to be about life and death as believers (vv. 20-24). Of this one thing, every believer ought to be certain. 'Christ shall be magnified in my body, whether it be by life, or by death'. If we are confident of this, what more can we want?

'For to me to live is Christ, and to die is gain. But if I live in the flesh, this is the fruit of my labour: yet what I shall choose I wot not. For I am in a strait betwixt two, having a desire to depart, and to be with Christ; which is far better: Nevertheless to abide in the flesh is more needful for you'.

The Mind of Christ

In chapter 2, Paul admonishes us ever to have the mind of Christ. In verses 5-11 he tells us of the matchless goodness and grace of our Saviour as the voluntary Servant of God, descending step by step in humiliation, until he had fulfilled all the will of God as our Redeemer in this world, telling us that Christ's humiliation under the hand of God was not only the accomplishment of our salvation, but also his path to exaltation.

'Let this mind be in you, which was also in Christ Jesus: Who, being in the form of God, thought it not robbery to be equal with God: But made himself of no reputation, and took upon him the form of a servant, and was made in the likeness of men: And being found in fashion as a man, he humbled himself, and became obedient unto death, even the death of the cross. Wherefore God also hath highly exalted him, and given him a name which is above every name: That at the name of Jesus every knee should bow, of things in heaven, and things in earth, and things under the earth; And that every tongue should confess that Jesus Christ is Lord, to the glory of God the Father'.

May God give us grace to have the mind of Christ. That is the secret to unity and fellowship in the kingdom of God. If we live with the mind of Christ, we will walk in sweet fellowship, each preferring the other better than himself (vv. 1-5).

Rejoice

In chapter 3 we come to the heart of this epistle. The chapter begins with another call to rejoice. Paul says, 'Finally, my brethren, rejoice in the Lord'. We ought always, in the depths of our hearts and souls, to rejoice in the Lord.

No matter what our providential experiences and circumstances are, we always have reason to rejoice in the Lord. Here is an exhortation to joy. What a blessed command! 'Rejoice in the Lord alway: and again I say rejoice!' Rejoice in the greatness of his person as our all-sufficient Substitute.

Rejoice in the power of his blood, which cleanses us from all sin. Rejoice in the perfection of his righteousness, which is imputed to us for justification. Rejoice in the abundance of his grace, which is always sufficient for us.

Rejoice in the immutability of his love, which never fails. Rejoice in the rule of his providence, which works all things together for our good. Rejoice in the fact of his intercession, continual and effectual on our behalf. Rejoice in the fact that your names are written in heaven.

This is the exhortation with which Paul opens this chapter. 'Rejoice in the Lord!' May God give us grace ever to do so for the glory of Christ and the good of his people. This is the 'joy of faith' (1:25).

Beware

In verse 2, the apostle gives us a serious warning. 'Beware of dogs'. He warns us to beware of false prophets. He calls them dogs because that is what the Word of God calls male prostitutes. False prophets are men who have, for their own sakes, prostituted the gospel of Christ and the glory of God (Deuteronomy 23:18; Isaiah 56:10-11). He continues, 'beware of evil workers'. This is a warning against those who teach, preach, and promote any system of man centred, works based, free will religion. Our Saviour calls such people workers of iniquity (Matthew 7:22-23). Paul is not finished with his warning yet.

Verse 2 concludes with 'beware of the concision'. Those who are of the concision are men and women who cut, mutilate, and torture their bodies in hope of winning God's favour. He specifically refers to those who taught that believers had to be circumcised. But the warning reaches to all who teach that holiness is to be attained by depriving ourselves of things created for us and observing religious ceremonies and taboos (Colossians 2:16-23).

In essence Paul is saying, 'Beware of Christless religion'. Beware of any religious custom, doctrine, or service that is centred in yourself and encourages attention on yourself.

True Religion

In verse 3 we are given a description of true religion. 'For we are the circumcision, which worship God in the spirit, and rejoice in Christ Jesus, and have no confidence in the flesh'.

True religion is not man centred, but Christ centred. True religion is not ceremonial, but spiritual. True religion is not a matter of creed, but of conviction. True religion is not outward, but inward. 'For we are the circumcision', God's true, covenant people, the Israel of God, Abraham's true children, which 'worship God in the Spirit'. We worship God as he is revealed in the scriptures, by the power of his Holy Spirit, in our spirits, and in a spiritual manner. True worship is spiritual worship, not carnal, ceremonial ritualism (John 4:23-24, Romans 2:29; 9:6,7).

God's elect are people who 'rejoice in Christ Jesus'. We trust the Lord Jesus Christ alone, placing all our confidence in him as our Saviour. We are complete in him (1 Corinthians 1:30-31; Colossians 2:9-10). 'And have no confidence in the flesh'. We place absolutely no confidence in our flesh, the experiences, emotions, or (imaginary) excellencies of our flesh. The privileges of the flesh, the feelings of the flesh, and the works of the flesh are no basis of confidence before God.

Self-denial

In verses 4-8 Paul is set before us as an example of self-denial. Self-denial is an essential aspect of saving faith. Though it increasingly comprehends all aspects of life as we grow in the grace and knowledge of our Lord Jesus Christ, self-denial begins with and is essentially a denial of all personal worth and merit as a grounds of hope before God.

Here is a legalist of the highest order laying aside the filthy rags of his self-righteousness for the blessed, pure, perfect righteousness of Christ. Paul counted all his fleshy, carnal, natural privileges, religious distinctiveness, and educational advantages as nothing but dung before God. He placed no confidence in his flesh. He found that one 'Pearl of Great Price', and sold everything he had to get it (Matthew 13:45-46). This was done on the Damascus Road when the Lord saved him (v. 7). And this was a decision he made everyday with increasing, growing commitment and consecration to Christ. He counted all things but dung for Christ.

Why? What was the cause of this man's self-denial, consecration, and commitment? What made this man willing to forsake everything and follow Christ? Paul was inspired, motivated, and driven to the point of utter obsession by four great ambitions of faith.

Ambitions of Faith

He gives us those four great ambitions in verses 8-11.

First, look at the last phrase of verse 8: 'That I may win Christ!' What an ambition! The life of faith is the lifelong pursuit of Christ. Faith looks upon Christ as the most precious, most desirable, most lovely, and most valuable Person and Object in the world. The more he is known, the more he is wanted. Therefore true faith willingly forsakes all to follow him. Christ is the Treasure hidden in the field, for which we would gladly spend all. He is that Pearl, for which we must sell all. Jesus Christ is the 'one thing needful' who must be chosen. Christ is the one thing we must have. Blessed are those who can say with Paul, 'I count all things loss that I may win Christ'.

Then Paul reveals his second great ambition, he continues, 'And be found in him, not having mine own righteousness, which is of the law, but that which is through the faith of Christ, the righteousness which is of God by faith' (v. 9).

This is the believer's standing. We are in Christ. This is Christianity. This is salvation. To be in Christ, nothing less, nothing more, nothing different. It is not partly in Christ and partly in the law, or partly in the ordinances, or partly in the church. To be saved is to be in Christ. Religion is knowing doctrines and facts. Salvation is knowing God (John 17:3; 1 John 5:20). Religion is knowing what I believe. Christianity is knowing whom I believe (2 Timothy 1:12). Religion is being reformed. Salvation is being regenerated (John 3:3). Religion makes men new converts. Christianity makes us new creatures (2 Corinthians 5:17). Religion is being in the church. Salvation is being in Christ (John 15:5; Ephesians 5:30). Believers are people who are in Christ by God's eternal decree, the Holy Spirit's operations of grace, and by personal faith in the Son of God.

To be in Christ is to have perfect righteousness before God. Our righteousness is not something we establish by performing good works, but something Christ established for us as our Representative before God. We do not make ourselves righteous by our obedience. Christ made us righteous by his obedience to the law, satisfying its every demand for us as our Substitute (Romans 5:19). Our righteousness before God is the righteousness of God in Christ imputed to us by God himself.

As we stand before the holy Lord God, we want to be found in Christ, while we live in this world, as we offer our services, prayers, and sacrifices to him. We want also to be found in Christ when we leave this world, and when we stand before his great bar of judgment.

Third, Paul's ambition is 'That I may know him, and the power of his resurrection, and the fellowship of his sufferings, being made conformable unto his death' (v. 10).

To know Christ in the power of his resurrection is to know that his resurrection is the assurance of our justification (Romans 4:25). It is to be born of God, living by that same power that raised Christ from the dead (Ephesians 1:19). The power of his resurrection guarantees our resurrection (1 Corinthians 15:47-49). To know Christ in the power of his resurrection is to live everyday, experimentally, walking in the knowledge of the power of his resurrection. Walking with Christ in the newness of life, we want the power of his resurrection to dominate, control, and direct our lives in all things. We want to be continually made new by him. To know Christ 'in the fellowship of his sufferings' is to know our personal interests in his sin-atoning sufferings unto death as our Substitute. It is to know that he died for me. There is only one way that anyone can know that, and that is by trusting him.

Furthermore, to know him in the fellowship of sufferings is to know, being convinced by God the Holy Spirit through the revelation of the gospel, that he has put away my sin by the sacrifice of himself. It is to know that he has brought in everlasting righteousness for me by his obedience unto death and that he has fully redeemed me from the judgment and condemnation of God's holy law by his sin-atoning death as my Substitute (John 16:8-11). It is to know that he has obtained eternal redemption for me (Hebrews 9:12).

As his sufferings are Christ's glory, Paul wanted Christ's sufferings to be his glory (Galatians 6:14). He wanted to know Christ and the fellowship of his sufferings to such an extent that he was ever 'being made conformable unto his death'. He wanted to be conformed to Christ in his death, to be entirely consecrated to the glory of God, perfectly submissive to the will of God, and motivated by nothing but love for his God and his people.

Fourth, Paul desires 'If by any means I might attain unto the resurrection of the dead' (vv. 11-14)

Certainly, this includes a great desire for the resurrection of his body at the last day. But, primarily, the yearning spoken of here is a yearning for that moral, spiritual resurrection of grace that lifts us out of the death and darkness of sin. The world, the flesh, and all human life are death. In Christ there is life, real life, eternal life, a life of righteousness, peace and joy in communion with God. This is what Paul wanted. This is the thing he continually sought (2 Corinthians 5:1-9). He wanted all that the Lord God purposed for him in eternity and Christ purchased for him at Calvary (Ephesians 1:3-6). He wanted to be like Christ.

These are the ambitions of every believer's heart, the goals he seeks, the things for which he lives. Children of God, set your hearts upon these things and, by the grace of God, you shall have them. 'For our conversation is in heaven; from whence also we look for the Saviour, the Lord Jesus Christ: Who shall change our vile body, that it may be fashioned like unto his glorious body, according to the working whereby he is able even to subdue all things unto himself' (vv. 20-21). These are the things Paul has in mind, which he urges us to think upon continually, that we might have peace and joy and contentment in this world (4:8-13).

An Acceptable Sacrifice

In the latter part of chapter 4 Paul speaks of the thoughtful, loving gift the saints at Philippi sent to him by Epaphroditus, assuring them that their gift to him was 'an odour of a sweet smell, a sacrifice acceptable, well-pleasing to God' (v. 18). Then, he assures them that as they had ministered to him according to their ability, so the Lord God would supply all their needs according to his ability. 'But my God shall supply all your need according to his riches in glory by Christ Jesus' (v. 19). Notice, Paul promises that God will supply the needs of his saints, not 'out of', but 'according to his riches in glory by Christ Jesus'. That means that he supplies our needs according to his infinite ability and infinite goodness in Christ.

Three Great Comforts

Go back to chapter 1 and look at three great facts revealed in this chapter that sustained and comforted Paul as he lived in this world and as he prepared to leave it. Let us learn them, and they will comfort and sustain us as well. Paul understood that everything that happened to him was brought to pass by the will of God and would serve the cause of Christ's gospel (v. 12). He knew that everything he experienced in this world was for the good of his soul and worked for his own eternal salvation (v. 19). And Paul knew that everything he suffered in this world, he suffered by the will of God (v. 29).

Chapter 51

Colossians

'Christ is All'

Three words are found in Colossians 3:11 that need to be emblazoned upon the hearts of all who would seek to understand, interpret, and proclaim the message of holy scripture. Those three, simple, one-syllable words are:

Christ is all.

These three words are the essence and substance of all true Christianity. Christ is the foundation of all true doctrine and motive for all godliness. Christ is the message of all true preaching and the object of all true worship. In what sense does the Holy Spirit mean for us to understand that 'Christ is all'? How far are we to take those words? In all things concerning our souls, eternity, the will of God, the knowledge of God, and the glory of God 'Christ is all'. The book of Colossians is all about Christ, our all-glorious Saviour.

This letter to the church at Colosse was written while Paul was a prisoner at Rome, about thirty years after our Saviour died at Calvary. Paul wrote this epistle about the same time that he wrote Ephesians, Philippians, and Philemon.

We do not know who first brought the gospel to the city of Colosse. Though some in this assembly had never seen Paul's face (2:1), Luke tells us that some years earlier he and Paul went throughout the region of Phrygia (Asia Minor) preaching the gospel (Acts 16:6 and 18:23). While preaching in that region, many were converted by the grace of God and turned from their idols to worship the true and living God (Acts 19:11, 22, and 26).

After he had sown the seed of the gospel, Satan sowed his tares among the wheat. As it is now, so it was then. Wherever Paul preached the gospel of God's free and sovereign grace in Christ, workmongers came behind him preaching freewill and works religion.

Epaphras' Concern

When, Epaphras (called Epaphroditus in Philippians 2:25 and 4:18), the pastor of the church, came to visit Paul in Rome, he told Paul of the faithfulness of God's saints at Colosse and of his concern for their souls because of the heretics who sought to corrupt the gospel and turn the hearts of the saints away from Christ.

They came in the name of Christ, pretending to be the servants of Christ, but they were in reality the messengers of Satan. Judaisers tried to mix law and grace, mingling Moses and Christ, teaching that works must play some part in salvation.

Others sought to corrupt the gospel by mixing vain philosophy with the revelation of God, teaching for doctrine the commandments, superstitions, and reasoning of men. Some even taught the veneration, or worship, of angels and saints, and taught for mortification the punishing of the body!

Still others crept in among God's saints teaching the proud Gnostic notion that salvation is to be attained by knowledge, teaching that men arrived at Christ by knowledge.

They all preached righteousness. They all called it the righteousness of Christ; but the message they preached was the righteousness of man, a righteousness that was ultimately gained by something man must do, experience, feel, or know. It was not that righteousness sinners have by faith alone.

Paul, inspired by God the Holy Spirit, wrote this epistle to confirm God's elect in the gospel of Christ, to warn them of the heresies by which Satan's messengers sought to pervert the gospel, and to urge them to 'continue in the faith grounded and settled, and be not moved away from the hope of the gospel' (1:23).

An Encouraging Salutation

This letter, like most of Paul's epistles, opens with a gracious, encouraging salutation (1:1-8). 'Paul, an apostle of Jesus Christ, by the will of God'. Paul refers to himself as 'an apostle of Jesus Christ', not 'the apostle of Jesus Christ'. Paul was one voice among many; and he looked upon himself that way. In the beginning of this gospel age there were twelve apostles. Paul was the apostle born out of season, the one God had chosen to take Judas' place. The apostles were men chosen by Christ. They saw the Lord personally. They had infallible knowledge of the gospel as they wrote the words of holy scripture, being inspired by the Holy Spirit. They were gifted to work miracles for the confirmation of their doctrine (2 Corinthians 12:12). When the last of the apostles went to glory, the apostolic age and the apostolic gifts, by which the apostles were identified as God's inspired messengers, ended. This was all done 'by the will of God'. There are no apostles in the church today. There are many preachers sent as messengers of God to his people, but no apostles.

'And Timothy, our brother'. Though Timothy was not an apostle Paul included him in this salutation, because God's servants are all brethren, fellow-labourers, and workers together in his vineyard. Commenting on this verse, Henry Mahan wrote, 'The highest office-bearer in the church recognizes even the least as being a brother and worthy of respect and recognition. In Christ we are one, and he that is greatest is but a servant'. God's servants are not rivals, but fellow labourers in the Master's vineyard. There is no such thing as 'Big Me' and 'Little You' in the kingdom of God.

'To the saints and faithful brethren in Christ'. All believers are saints; sanctified men and women. All believers are faithful. All believers are brethren. We are sanctified by God the Father in election, God the Son in redemption, and God the Holy Spirit in the new birth. We are brethren because we have the same Father, because we are in one body and family, and because we have one elder brother, Christ Jesus. All who are born of God are 'in Christ'. We are saints, we are brethren, and we are faithful only because we are 'in Christ'.

'Grace be unto you and peace'. Believers seek that which is best for one another and truly wish one another well. We cannot desire anything better for anyone than this: 'Grace be unto you, and peace'. Grace saves us. Peace makes us know that we are saved. Grace is the root of every blessing. Peace is the flower that makes life sweet and fragrant. 'Grace be unto you and peace from God our Father and the Lord Jesus Christ'. There is no grace for anyone and no peace except that which is freely bestowed upon needy sinners by God the Father through the mediation of our Lord Jesus Christ.

'We give thanks to God'. Because grace, peace, faith and love, and all things pertaining to salvation are the gifts of God, he alone is to be thanked and praised for them. It is right for us to recognize and commend these things in our brothers and sisters in Christ; but thanks and praise goes to our God alone (Psalm 103:1-5). Every gift of grace is from God through our Lord Jesus Christ (John 3:27; James 1:17).

Faith, hope, and love always go hand in hand. Where one is found, the other two are always present. All are the gifts of God's grace. Faith is that gift of grace that unites us to Christ and gives us peace with God. Love is that gift of grace that unites us to one another and gives us peace. Hope is that gift of grace that unites us to Christ in eternity and gives us peace.

'Whereof ye heard before in the word of the truth of the gospel, Which is come unto you, as it is in all the world; and bringeth forth fruit, as it doth also in you, since the day ye heard of it, and knew the grace of God in truth'. We do not know the grace of God in truth unless it brings forth fruit in us. We may know it in our heads, but we do not really know it at all if it does not affect our lives, and bring forth faith, love, and hope: faith, which lifts us above the world; love, which preserves us from selfishness; and hope, which keeps us up under all trials.

'Dear Fellowservant'

In verses 7 and 8 the Holy Spirit inspired Paul to commend to this church their beloved pastor, thereby encouraging them to highly esteem him and hear him. 'As ye also learned of Epaphras our dear fellowservant, who is for you a faithful minister of Christ; Who also declared unto us your love in the Spirit'. Epaphras was Paul's fellow-servant. He was a faithful minister of Christ. And he loved and spoke well of those people whose souls he served.

How I rejoiced to read of Epaphras speaking well of God's people and of Paul speaking well of Epaphras! Many these days seem to think godliness requires them to pick holes in the armour of others, point out their faults, and castigate them for their failures. Grace teaches men, who experience it, better. Grace teaches us to honour our brethren, cover their faults, extol their virtues, forgive their offences, and help and lift them up when they fall.

Paul made it his business to remind the saints at Colosse what a great blessing of God they had in their faithful pastor and promoted his honour in their eyes. Every preacher ought to follow his example when speaking of other faithful pastors (4:12-13).

Fit for Heaven

In verses 9-14 the apostle Paul declares that the Lord our God has, by the almighty, effectual operation of his grace, made us fit for heaven. Here Paul tells these saints, 'Since the day Bro. Epaphras came here and told me about you and God's grace in you, I have not ceased to give thanks to God for you and have not ceased to pray for God's grace ever to be upon you and work in you'.

'That ye may be filled with the knowledge of his will'; his revealed will, his purposed will, his providential will, his redemptive will. Paul prayed not only that they might have a knowledge of these, but that they might be 'filled with the knowledge of his will in all wisdom and spiritual understanding'.

'That ye might walk worthy of the Lord unto all pleasing'. This is talking about our conduct and behaviour in the church, in our homes, in the job, and on the street. Let us seek to live, and walk, and talk as those who are in Christ, seeking to please and glorify God.

'Being fruitful in every good work'. Believers are trees of righteousness, planted by the Lord to bear the fruit of the Spirit and to walk in good works in the kingdom of Christ (Galatians 5:22-23; Ephesians 2:10).

'Increasing in the knowledge of God'. We honour God by believing him and by living for him as we grow in the knowledge of him. We cannot grow in grace if we do not grow in knowledge of Christ. And we cannot grow in the knowledge of Christ without growing in grace (2 Peter 3:18).

'Strengthened with all might according to his glorious power'. We do not and cannot attain these things or do these things by our own strength and power, but by his (2 Corinthians 12:9).

We read in verse 12 that our great God has made all who trust his Son 'meet to be partakers of the inheritance of the saints in light'. Pastor Epaphras spoke to Paul in glowing terms of the Colossian saints, of their faith and hope in Christ, and their love for Christ, his gospel, and his people. The Lord our God has, by his almighty, free, saving grace in Christ, qualified us, has made us fit, to enter into and possess heaven itself, the bright and glorious inheritance of the saints. By nature we are fit for hell. Grace has made us fit for heaven in Christ, by his blood atonement and perfect righteousness (1 Corinthians 1:30).

In verses 13 and 14 he tells us that this fitness for heaven is altogether the work of God's free grace in Christ. 'Who hath delivered us from the power of darkness, and hath translated us into the kingdom of his dear Son: In whom we have redemption through his blood, even the forgiveness of sins'.

What a Great Saviour

Having barely declared what Christ did for us at Calvary, Paul was inspired by the Holy Spirit to extol, magnify, honour, and praise him as our all-glorious Saviour and Lord (1:15-29). Several years ago one of our deacons read these fifteen verses in my office one night before we had prayer together. As soon as he finished reading them, another of our deacons quietly exclaimed, 'What a great Saviour!' That is as good a summary of the passage as I have ever seen or heard. Here Paul is showing us what a great Saviour our Lord Jesus Christ is. Throughout the chapter, he plays a symphony on just one string: 'He!'

Christ is exactly what God is, for he is God. He is that One, the only One in whom God is seen and known. He is 'the image of the invisible God' (v. 15) and 'the express image of his person' (Hebrews 1:3). He is himself God (John 1:1-3). 'For in him dwelleth all the fulness of the Godhead bodily' (Colossians 2:9)

He is the firstborn of every creature (v. 15). That is to say, he is 'the Beginning of the creation of God' (Revelation 3:14). We know that is what this means because the next verse, verse 16, tells us so. 'For by him were all things created, that are in heaven, and that are in earth, visible and invisible, whether they be thrones, or dominions, or principalities, or powers: all things were created by him, and for him'. He is the eternal Creator of all things. 'He is before all things and by him all things consist' (v. 17).

He is the Head of the Church, the beginning of all things, the firstborn from the dead, the upholder of all things, that he might have the pre-eminence. 'And he is the head of the body, the church: who is the beginning, the firstborn from the dead; that in all things he might have the pre-eminence' (v. 18).

Christ is fulness (v. 19) 'For it pleased the Father that in him should all fulness dwell:' All divine fulness (Colossians 2:9), all mediatoral fulness, all covenant fulness, all saving fulness, all everlasting fulness, undiminishable fulness!

He is reconciliation (vv. 20-22). It is Christ who has reconciled all the elect to God in redemption, and who reconciles them to God in conversion, and who shall reconcile all things to the glory of God in eternity. That is to say, he will cause all things to show forth the praise of God forever (Revelation 5:13-14).

Christ is our hope of glory (v. 27). He is the One 'whom' we preach, because he is the revelation of the great mystery hid in ages past under the pictures, types and shadows of the law, and hidden from all unbelievers (2 Corinthians 4:3-4), but is revealed in every believer as our only and all-sufficient hope of glory (vv. 23-29).

Complete in Christ

In chapter 1 Paul has shown us that Christ is a complete Saviour. In the second chapter he shows us that every believer is complete in him. Many had crept into the church who denied the gospel of Christ and, with great subtlety, endeavoured to turn the people of God away from 'the simplicity that is in Christ' (2 Corinthians 11:3). In Colossians 2:1-15 Paul communicates his concern to the Colossians and instructs them to be steadfast in the faith of Christ.

The instruction Paul gives in these verses is just as applicable to the church today as it was to the saints at Colosse. Many today would turn us away from the simplicity that is in Christ. They tell us that we must have more than Christ, do more than simply trust Christ, experience more than the grace of God in Christ, and seek more than the fulness that is in Christ. Any doctrine that turns you away from Christ, any doctrine that turns your eyes away from Christ, is not of God. I admonish you to flee from such doctrine as you would flee the plague. The doctrine that turns you away from Christ will land your soul in hell!

'In him are hid all the treasures of wisdom and knowledge' (v. 3). God has put all the riches of grace and glory, all the treasures of divine wisdom and spiritual knowledge in his Son, the Lord Jesus Christ our Saviour. Do not look for God's mercy, grace, and righteousness anywhere but in Christ. All the knowledge of God and everything pertaining to salvation is in Christ (1 John 5:12, 20).

'And this I say, lest any man should beguile you with enticing words' (v. 4). Satan tries to sow seeds of error wherever the gospel of Christ is preached. His messengers do not openly deny Christ and salvation by grace. They mix the work of Christ with the works of men. They mix law and grace. If Satan can get you to look to yourself and trust your own works, experiences, feelings, or emotions even partially he has ruined your soul altogether (Galatians 5:2, 4).

Though Paul was absent from them physically, his heart was with the people of God. Their orderly manner of life, orderly worship, and steadfastness in the faith of Christ caused him great joy (v. 5). These men and women had not yet been moved away from the hope of the gospel and Paul was very concerned to do what he could to promote their continued steadfastness. His instructions are very simple and clear and vital to the interests of our souls.

'As' and 'So'

'As ye have therefore received Christ Jesus the Lord, so walk ye in him' (v. 6). How did you first receive Christ? You received him by faith alone, without any works whatsoever of your own. You had no experiences upon which to lean, no works, no feelings, no resolutions. You had nothing to bring to Christ but your sin. You received Christ alone as the sum and substance of all truth, the fulfilment of all promises, the fountain of all grace, the singular object of faith and love, and the only foundation of your hope before God. You trusted his blood alone for atonement, his righteousness alone for acceptance, and his intercession alone for salvation. In exactly the same manner as you first received Christ, now walk in him.

Continue living by the same faith, as a sinner trusting Christ alone for all things. If you get above this, you will forsake Christ altogether. We do not begin with Christ and then go on to perfection in the strength of the flesh. The true believer begins by faith, lives by faith, and dies by faith, trusting Christ, only Christ, and nothing but Christ, all the way from the gates of hell to his entrance into glory.

If we would live in faith, constantly trusting Christ, we must be 'rooted and built up in him, and stablished in the faith, as ye have been taught, abounding therein with thanksgiving' (v. 7). Like a tree, deeply rooted in the fertile earth, faith takes hold of Christ, draws all strength, nourishment, and life from him, and bears fruit by the constant supply of his grace. As a building is built upon and shaped according to its foundation, the believer is built upon Christ alone, and his life is moulded to Christ. Child of God, see to it that you abound in this faith. Never forsake it. Never weary of it. Never look for any other source of comfort, strength, hope, or assurance than faith in Christ. Trusting Christ alone, you have abundant reason for thanksgiving before God. But be warned, there are many who would turn you away from the simplicity of the faith.

Beware

'Beware lest any man spoil you through philosophy and vain deceit, after the tradition of men, after the rudiments of the world, and not after Christ' (v. 8). Do not allow anyone to turn you away from Christ by a show of intellectualism, philosophy, and human reason. Our faith must be ruled by the Word of God alone. We build our doctrine only upon 'thus saith the Lord'. Let no one impose upon you the traditions of men, no matter how impressive and popular they are. There is no place for human tradition in the worship of the living God. Exactly in proportion as we receive the traditions of men, we depart from the worship of God.

And we must never allow anyone to bring us back under the 'rudiments of the world', Mosaic ordinances. The rites and ceremonies of the Mosaic law: circumcision, abstaining from certain meats, sabbath observance, and all such things were altogether typical. Christ has fulfilled them all. Any observance of such things today is sinful. All true worship is spiritual. God is not worshipped where dead men and women observe dead, carnal ordinances. There is absolutely no need for men to observe these things, seek any other foundation of hope before God, or look anywhere else for acceptance with God. Christ is all we need.

'For in him dwelleth all the fulness of the Godhead bodily' (v. 9). All that God is, is in Christ, for he is himself God. All that God requires of sinners is in Christ. All that God gives to men and women is in Christ. And all that we can need, or desire, for time and eternity, is in Christ. All grace, all mercy, all love, all peace, all wisdom, all righteousness, all redemption, all sanctification, all salvation, all life is in Christ alone. And it is all in him in all fulness. You cannot add anything to fulness.

'And are complete in him, which is the head of all principality and power' (v. 10). The Lord Jesus Christ is the head of all things. By virtue of his obedience to God as our Mediator, Christ has been given the place of supremacy, dominion, and rule over the entire universe. All who believe are complete in him. As all the fulness of the triune Godhead resides in Christ our Mediator, so all the fulness of Christ, the Mediator, is ours by faith; and we are complete in him.

In Him

What does it mean to be in Christ? Many answers are given to that question in the Word of God. We who believe are in Christ by God's elective purpose. We are in the heart of our Saviour's love, in the hand of his protective power, and in the eye of his constant care. Here Paul tells us what it is to be in Christ experimentally.

To be in Christ is to be born again, by God's sovereign grace (v. 11). Paul uses the word 'circumcised' to represent the new birth, because that is what circumcision symbolized in the Old Testament. Circumcision was instituted by God, as the token and seal of his covenant with Abraham (Genesis 17:10-13). It was a mark by which Israel was distinguished from all other nations and it was a picture of what happens in a man's heart in regeneration (Romans 2:28-29; Philippians 3:3). In the Old Testament a child was named at the time of his circumcision (Luke 1:59; 2:21); and in regeneration we have been given a new name. We have been made the sons of God (Galatians 4:6-7; 1 John 3:1-3). Circumcision gave the children of Israel the right to eat the Passover (Exodus 12:48). This spiritual circumcision is made without hands. It is altogether a matter of the heart. It is the work of God the Holy Spirit.

To be in Christ is to trust him (v. 12). All who are born of God are given faith in Christ. The one certain mark of the new birth is faith in the Lord Jesus Christ. Faith in Christ is publicly confessed by believer's baptism. Baptism is the ordinance of God by which we confess the faith of the gospel. It is described by Paul as a burial and a resurrection (Romans 6:4-6). In baptism we confess to both the church of God and the world, our faith in the finished work of Christ and our allegiance to him as our sovereign Lord. This faith in Christ, which we confess in our baptism, is the gift of the operation of God (Ephesians 2:8), the fruit of the Holy Spirit (Galatians 5:22) and the effectual work of his omnipotent grace in regeneration (Ephesians 1:19).

To be in Christ is to be the object and recipient of God's immutable, saving grace in him (vv. 13-15). When God raised his Son from the dead, he was raised as our Representative. Christ lived, died, and rose again as the Representative and Substitute of God's elect. As the result of his finished work, the blessings of God's saving grace have been effectually secured to his people. We all by nature are born dead in sin because of our sin and fall in our father Adam (Romans 5:12). But God has been gracious to us through Christ.

He quickened us, gave us life, and raised us up, together with Christ. That means two things, first, when Christ arose from the dead, we rose in him representatively, and second, in the new birth we were raised from spiritual death to spiritual life by the power of Christ, our risen Saviour.

God has freely and completely forgiven us of all sin through the merits of Christ's righteousness and shed blood. All our sins, past, present and future, sins of youth and old age, sins of omission and sins of commission, sins of deed and sins of heart, all are freely and eternally forgiven by God through the merits of Christ our Substitute.

God's forgiveness of our sins is a just and righteous forgiveness. He does not simply ignore or excuse our sins. He removed our sins from us entirely by punishing them to the full extent of his own justice in Christ (Romans 3:24-26). The oracles and ordinances of God's holy law, being broken by us, were against us. The law of God demanded our execution. But Christ, by his blood, blotted out the law's accusations, and blotted out all our sins, nailing them to his cross (Isaiah 43:25; 44:22). 'There is therefore now no condemnation to them that are in Christ Jesus' (Romans 8:1).

Are you, or are you not in Christ? If you knew the value of your soul, if you knew the riches of his grace, if you knew the love of Christ, you would give no rest to your eyes until you found yourself to be in Christ. God help you to seek him. If you seek him with all your heart, you will find him. If you are in Christ, it is all because of God's free grace toward you. And if you are in Christ, 'Ye are complete in him' (v. 10).

Complete in Him

What does it mean to be complete in Christ? The word 'complete' means 'entire, finished, made full, perfect'. Essentially, it is the same word used in verse 9, where Paul says, 'In him dwelleth all the fulness of the Godhead bodily'. As all the fulness of the eternal God is Christ's, all the fulness of Christ as the Mediator for sinners is ours in him. This is astonishing grace indeed.

If I am complete in Christ, I have in Christ all that God requires of man (1 Corinthians 1:30). Whatever God, in his holiness, righteousness, justice and truth, requires of fallen men, we have in Christ. God cannot require more than he has given us in Christ. When he gave us his dear Son, our heavenly Father freely gave us all things in his Son.

If I am in Christ, I possess all that God can or will bestow upon man (Ephesians 1:3). God is the Author and Giver of all blessings. He alone can bless. If he blesses not, none can bless. But if he blesses, we are blessed indeed. Paul tells us plainly that God has blessed us with all spiritual blessings in Christ Jesus. Nothing good, nothing of real spiritual value, nothing we require is omitted. All the fulness of grace, all the blessings of the covenant, all the sure mercies of God, all things pertaining to life and godliness in this world and in the world to come have been bestowed upon all who trust the Son of God.

This is what it means to be complete in Christ. In him we have been given justification, sanctification, peace, pardon, eternal life, and title deed to heaven. All these blessings were given to us irrevocably by the gift of God's sovereign grace in Christ before the world began (Ephesians 1:4-5). We are members of Christ. He is our Head and Representative. We are members of his body and partakers of him. We are blessed in him, through him, and for his sake. Christ himself is the Substance of all blessing and blessedness. He received the blessings of grace in our name in the covenant of grace. All the blessings bestowed upon us are dependent upon Christ's obedience, not ours. We already possess every blessing of grace in Christ (Romans 8:28-30). We may not yet enjoy all the blessings of the covenant experimentally, but they are already ours in Christ. As surely as he has received them for us, we shall receive them from him.

This is the glorious heritage of the sons of God. 'Ye are complete in him!' There is nothing lacking. Everything God can or will give to man he has from eternity given to all who are in Christ. Every blessing of grace in Christ is secure to all God's elect forever.

If I am in Christ, I am complete in him. That means I have in Christ all that I need to carry me through this world and bring me safe to heaven (Isaiah 40:29; 2 Peter 2:9). I do not know what lies ahead, what forces of darkness lie in wait for me, what trials or temptations shall meet me. But our great God and Saviour declares, 'My grace is sufficient for thee'. No matter what I need of earthly good, my God shall supply my need (Philippians 4:19). No matter what temptation I meet, my God shall give me grace to escape it (1 Corinthians 10:13). No matter what trial I face, my God shall sustain me with grace to endure the trial (Isaiah 41:10). No matter how I may fail him, sin against him, and dishonour his name, as I often do, my faithful Saviour shall not fail me.

Fail him, I often do. Fail me, he never shall. He will lift me up when I fall. He will pray for me when I am tempted. He will plead for me when I sin. He will preserve me and keep me to the end and bring me safe to heaven. If left to myself, I know, I would forsake him. But, blessed be his name, Christ will not leave me to myself (Jeremiah 32:38-40).

Being complete in Christ, I shall have all that I need to satisfy my heart in the world to come. 'The desire of the righteous shall be granted' (Proverbs 10:24). Child of God, what do you desire? Do you desire to be free from all sin? It shall be granted. Do you desire to be perfectly obedient to Christ? It shall be granted. Do you desire to know, love, and worship Christ perfectly? It shall be granted. Do you desire to be like Christ entirely? It shall be granted. Do you desire to be free of all fear? It shall be granted. Do you desire to be free of all trouble? It shall be granted. Do you desire to see the glory of God your Saviour? It shall be granted. Do you desire to glorify your beloved Lord? It shall be granted.

Whatever it is that your renewed, sanctified heart desires, it shall be granted to you in heaven's eternal glory. If even one small desire were left unfulfilled, you would not be complete in Christ; but 'ye are complete in him'.

Practical Results

What are the practical results of our being complete in Christ? Are you in Christ, united to him by a living union of faith? If you are, you are complete in him. Before God, in the sight of God, you are complete, perfect, full, and entire. You lack nothing. Nothing! Let no man sit as judge over you, beguile you with false doctrine, bring you into bondage, move you from your steadfastness, or turn your eyes away from Christ.

If we are complete in Christ, we are entirely free in him (vv. 16-23). We are entirely free from the curse of God's holy law (v. 14). We are entirely free from the rule of the Mosaic law as a system of life, government, or motivation for service to God. And, being in Christ, we are entirely free from the traditions, commandments, and doctrines of men (vv. 20-22). We are complete in Christ. What do we care for the religious customs and traditions of men? Christ is our only Lord, Master, and Lawgiver. We obey none but him. Christ is our only Prophet. We get our doctrine and practices from no one but him. Our religion is the religion of Christ. We have no regard for the religion of men.

If we are complete in Christ, we should be steadfast in him (vv. 8-9). Though others are carried about with every wind of doctrine, seeking new, deeper, more emotional experiences, we are content to seek the old paths and walk in them (Jeremiah 6:16). Nothing is more exciting to our hearts than that which is most substantial. Only those who have no sure foundation for their souls need to be constantly seeking some new experience.

Being complete in Christ, we have a settled assurance of our acceptance and eternal salvation in him. Our assurance before God is not based in any way upon anything done, felt, or experienced by us. We delight in times of reviving, in the sweet manifestations of Christ to our hearts, those blessed times of spiritual communion with our God. We delight in those times when the Spirit of God comes upon us and enables us to worship and serve him with exceptional liberty. There is no experience on earth so delightful to my heart as that of being enabled to preach the gospel with the power of the Spirit, or worship God in the Spirit. But our hope and assurance rests in none of these things. Our assurance is Christ alone (2 Timothy 1:12).

Hearts Set

All believers are one with Christ; 'and ye are complete in him'. He is our hope. We are dead, buried, and risen with him. Therefore, Paul admonishes us to put off the old and to put on the new (1:27; 2:10, 12; 3:1-11), setting our hearts upon those great, glorious things above, which he has been declaring to us in chapters 1 and 2, realizing that 'Christ is all and in all'.

'If ye then be risen with Christ, seek those things which are above, where Christ sitteth on the right hand of God. Set your affection on things above, not on things on the earth. For ye are dead, and your life is hid with Christ in God. When Christ, who is our life, shall appear, then shall ye also appear with him in glory' (3:1-4).

As was his custom, Paul concludes the book of Colossians in chapters three and four, by giving us very practical applications of gospel doctrine. Our union with Christ demands that we set our hearts on him, devoting ourselves to his honour in our daily lives (3:1-8; Romans 12:1-2), in the church of God (3:9-17), in our homes (3:18-4:1; Ephesians 5:22-6:9), and in the world (4:2-6).

Let no one imagine that God's boundless, free grace in Christ leads to licentiousness. It is the love and grace of God that we have experienced that constrains us both to love and serve one another and to love, serve, and honour him. That is precisely Paul's argument. Because 'Christ is all and in all', we are inspired and motivated to these things to the glory of God our Saviour.

'Put on therefore, as the elect of God, holy and beloved, bowels of mercies, kindness, humbleness of mind, meekness, longsuffering; Forbearing one another, and forgiving one another, if any man have a quarrel against any: even as Christ forgave you, so also do ye. And above all these things put on charity, which is the bond of perfectness. And let the peace of God rule in your hearts, to the which also ye are called in one body; and be ye thankful. Let the word of Christ dwell in you richly in all wisdom; teaching and admonishing one another in psalms and hymns and spiritual songs, singing with grace in your hearts to the Lord. And whatsoever ye do in word or deed, do all in the name of the Lord Jesus, giving thanks to God and the Father by him' (3:12-17).

Chapter 52

1 Thessalonians

'How Ye Ought to Walk and to Please God'

As believers, our lives are a constant disappointment to us. We want to walk in this world in a way that honours our God. We want to please him in all things. How miserably we fail! God the Holy Spirit gives us plain, clear instructions in the book of 1 Thessalonians about 'how we ought to walk and to please God' (4:1).

Paul wrote his first letter to the church at Thessalonica specifically to communicate to them his love for them and his desire to return to them, that he might again preach the gospel to them. How he rejoiced when he thought about God's goodness and grace in his people! He told the Thessalonians that he prayed for them night and day, exceedingly desiring to see them, that he 'might perfect that which is lacking in your faith' (3:10), that is, that he might be an instrument through which the Lord God would graciously cause them, through the preaching of the gospel, to grow in grace and in the knowledge of Christ into the full maturity of faith (3:11-13).

Background

Thessalonica was the capital city of the Roman province of Macedonia. When Paul and Silas came there preaching the gospel of Christ, telling them all 'that Christ must needs have suffered and risen again from the dead', and asserting that Jesus of Nazareth whom we preach is the Christ, after three weeks of gospel preaching, a riot broke out and Paul and Silas were run out of town (Acts 17:1-10). But the Word of God is never preached in vain. Though many opposed Christ and his gospel, and were enraged by it, a great multitude believed (Acts 17:4). In time a gospel church was established in Thessalonica. It is to this church that Paul wrote 1 and 2 Thessalonians.

1 Thessalonians was written specifically to teach God's saints, 'how ye ought to walk and to please God'. Paul's salutation (1:1) is very similar to his salutations in other epistles, with one notable exception. Here Paul makes no mention of his apostolic office. There was no need for him to do so, because there were none in that church who were even slightly suspicious of him.

Election Known

In chapter 1 Paul tells the saints of God at Thessalonica how very thankful he was to God for them and for the manifest grace of God in them (vv. 2-3). Then, he makes what may appear to some a very strange statement. He says in verse 4 'Knowing, brethren beloved, your election of God'. He tells these saints at Thessalonica that they were numbered among that vast multitude of sinners chosen to salvation in Christ before the world began. How could he have known that? Is it possible to know who the elect are? Indeed, it is. If you believe on the Lord Jesus Christ, your faith in him is the result of 'your election of God'.

Election is a blessed doctrine of holy scripture. It is taught in every book of the Bible, on almost every page of inspiration. Hundreds of texts could be quoted to show this. Look up the words, 'choose', 'chosen', 'elect', and 'election' in a concordance. You will be astounded at the prominence of this doctrine in the Word of God. It cannot be denied that election is a Bible doctrine (John 15:16; Acts 13:48; Ephesians 1:3-4; 2 Thessalonians 2:13-14; 2 Timothy 1:9; Psalm 65:4). It is a blessed doctrine, full of consolation.

Election was an act of God's eternal sovereignty (Romans 9:11-23), an act of free, unconditional grace (Matthew 11:25-26), unalterable, immutable, and irreversible (Malachi 3:6; Romans 11:29), infallibly effectual, securing the salvation of all whom God has chosen (Romans 8:28-30), and the fountain of all other grace (Ephesians 1:3-4). Our election by God was personal and distinguishing. It was in Christ and the only cause for our election was the everlasting love of God for us (Jeremiah 31:3; Ephesians 1:4).

But election is a doctrine that is often misrepresented and, therefore, misunderstood by many. Some people oppose the doctrine of election, simply because they have never heard it taught as the Bible teaches it. Election is not in anyway contrary to, or inconsistent with, the promises of God in the gospel (Matthew 11:28; John 3:36; Romans 10:9-13; Acts 16:31; Mark 16:16). Furthermore, election does not diminish man's responsibility before God. God commands all to repent and trust his Son and all are responsible to do so (Isaiah 45:22; John 6:29; 1 John 3:23; 5:10-13).

The Holy Spirit here tells us that our election of God is something that may be known (1:3-10). Repentance, faith, conversion, and good works are the fruit and the evidence of election. If you are born of God, if you trust Christ, you are one of God's elect.

No mere man can open and read the Lamb's book of life. No mortal can ever know who the elect are until they are regenerated and called by God the Holy Spirit. However, each of us can prove our own selves. We can make our calling and election sure. In 1 Thessalonians the Apostle Paul, writing by divine inspiration, tells us that he knew these men and women in the Church at Thessalonica were elect, chosen of God, and precious by five distinct marks of grace upon them. If you are one of God's elect, these five marks are upon you. If I am one of the elect, these marks are upon me. Who are God's elect? Look into the Word of God and you will see. There is no need for guesswork about this matter. The Holy Spirit shows us five evidences of God's election in 1 Thessalonians chapter one. Here the Holy Spirit holds up these saints at Thessalonica as examples to all who believe of what God's electing grace does for sinners (v. 7).

God's elect are people who hear the gospel preached and receive the gospel as it is preached in the power of God the Holy Spirit (v. 5). The elect are those who are called by the effectual, irresistible power and grace of God the Holy Spirit. They are called by the Spirit through the preaching of the gospel (Romans 1:15-17; 10:13-17; 1 Corinthians 1:21-23; 15:1-3; Hebrews 4:12; James 1:18; 1 Peter 1:23-25).

God's elect are those who follow Christ (vv. 3, 6). Chosen sinners, when saved by the grace of God, are made disciples, followers of Christ, voluntary servants of King Jesus. Believers are not perfect, and never pretend to be. They know something of the corruption of their own hearts. Yet, in the tenor of their lives those who are born of God follow Christ.

God's elect are a people who are committed to Christ and the gospel of his grace (v. 8). As the saints at Thessalonica sounded out the gospel to perishing sinners in their generation, so God's saints today make it their business to make the gospel known for the glory of God.

God's elect experience repentance and conversion by the power of his grace. They turn from their idols to serve the living God (v. 9). Believers forsake their idols and the idolatrous religious practices of their former manner of life. They will not be found worshipping a false god. You will not find a child of God kneeling before a pagan deity, kissing a crucifix, or professing faith in a helpless, frustrated god whose purpose, will, and work are prevented by man's imaginary free-will.

God's elect are waiting for Christ (v. 10). Believers live upon the high ground of faith, looking for that blessed hope, the glorious appearing of the great God, our Saviour, the Lord Jesus Christ. Believing his Word, we live in hope and expectation of the resurrection, being confident that he who died for us and rose again has, by his blood atonement, effectually 'delivered us from the wrath to come'.

An Overwhelming Trust

In the second chapter Paul tells us that he looked upon the ministry God had given him, the blessed work of preaching the gospel, as a great trust committed to him by God. He was simply overwhelmed by the fact that he was 'allowed of God to be put in trust with the gospel' (v. 4).

Paul's attitude toward the work of the ministry stands before us, throughout his writings, as a constant challenge to all those men in every age to whom the Lord God has granted this great trust (Ephesians 3:8). He came to Thessalonica with the deep conviction that the Lord God himself had sent him there to preach the gospel (vv. 2, 7; Acts 16:6-10). His goal in doing so was the honour of God and the good of their immortal souls (v. 4). Therefore, he did not use flattering, deceitful words to please his hearers. He was not motivated by covetousness and self-interest, and did not seek the honour that men might give him (vv. 3-6). As a faithful servant of God, he dealt with their souls with all the tenderness and affection of a nursing mother caring for her children, labouring night and day for them as a father for his family (vv. 7-12).

'But we were gentle among you, even as a nurse cherisheth her children: So being affectionately desirous of you, we were willing to have imparted unto you, not the gospel of God only, but also our own souls, because ye were dear unto us. For ye remember, brethren, our labour and travail: for labouring night and day, because we would not be chargeable unto any of you, we preached unto you the gospel of God. Ye are witnesses, and God also, how holily and justly and unblameably we behaved ourselves among you that believe: As ye know how we exhorted and comforted and charged every one of you, as a father doth his children, That ye would walk worthy of God, who hath called you unto his kingdom and glory'.

The saints at Thessalonica received Paul as God's messenger to their souls and treated him with the love and honour that reflected their gratitude to God for sending his gospel and his servant to them (vv. 13-14; Isaiah 52:7). It is not surprising to see Paul saying to them, 'Ye are our glory and joy' (v. 20). Paul was absent from them physically, but very much present with them in heart, and longed to be with them again physically (vv. 17-19).

'These Afflictions'
In the third chapter the apostle Paul gives us very tender and wise instruction concerning the things that all believers suffer in this world for Christ's sake. He would have come again to them already, had Satan not hindered him (2:18). When he could not come himself, he sent Timothy to establish them and comfort them in the midst of their trials and temptations, and was greatly encouraged by the grace manifest in them in the face of those things (3:1-9).

'Wherefore when we could no longer forbear, we thought it good to be left at Athens alone; And sent Timotheus, our brother, and minister of God, and our fellowlabourer in the gospel of Christ, to establish you, and to comfort you concerning your faith: That no man should be moved by these afflictions: for yourselves know that we are appointed thereunto. For verily, when we were with you, we told you before that we should suffer tribulation; even as it came to pass, and ye know. For this cause, when I could no longer forbear, I sent to know your faith, lest by some means the tempter have tempted you, and our labour be in vain. But now when Timotheus came from you unto us, and brought us good tidings of your faith and charity, and that ye have good remembrance of us always, desiring greatly to see us, as we also to see you: Therefore, brethren, we were comforted over you in all our affliction and distress by your faith: For now we live, if ye stand fast in the Lord. For what thanks can we render to God again for you, for all the joy wherewith we joy for your sakes before our God'.

Did you catch Paul's words in verse three? 'That no man should be moved by these afflictions: for yourselves know that we are appointed thereunto'. He told the Thessalonians that these things would come. They should not have been surprised by them. Neither should we. Our Lord said, 'In the world ye shall have tribulation; but be of good cheer; I have overcome the world'. 'These afflictions' are things appointed by our God, and are things to which we are appointed by him. They are for an appointed time, an appointed purpose, and have an appointed end.

How We Ought to Walk

In chapter 4 Paul follows his instruction about our afflictions with a word of instruction about how we ought to walk and to please God in the midst of all 'these afflictions'. Let it be our goal in all things and at all times to walk in this world in a manner that is pleasing to our great God and Saviour, by whom we have been saved (3 John 1:11).

It must be stated that the only way we can please God is by faith in Christ (Hebrews 11:5-6; Colossians 2:6). Yet, we must never imagine that our personal behaviour in this world is a matter of indifference. We must never forget who we are and whose we are. Everything we say and do reflects either positively or negatively upon the honour of our God and the gospel we believe. Therefore, Paul urges us to live for the glory of God, ruled by the Word of God, possessing our vessels in sanctification and honour (vv. 1-4).

'Furthermore then we beseech you, brethren, and exhort you by the Lord Jesus, that as ye have received of us how ye ought to walk and to please God, so ye would abound more and more. For ye know what commandments we gave you by the Lord Jesus. For this is the will of God, even your sanctification, that ye should abstain from fornication: That every one of you should know how to possess his vessel in sanctification and honour'.

Paul specifically urges us to abstain from fornication, sexual perversity (v. 3), and to live in moral uprightness (vv. 5-8). Then he tells us who have been taught of God to love one another, and to increase loving one another more and more (vv. 9-10). In verses 11 and 12 he tells us to pursue a quiet, industrious life of honesty, not prying into other people's affairs.

'Them Which Are Asleep'

In the last part of the chapter (vv. 13-18) the apostle turns our minds to eternity, and tells us to live in the sweet comfort of resurrection glory, particularly encouraging us to honour God in times of bereavement. Let us ever remember, the Holy Spirit does not here tell us that we must not sorrow when loved ones are taken from us, but urges us not to sorrow as others, 'who have no hope'.

'But I would not have you to be ignorant, brethren, concerning them which are asleep, that ye sorrow not, even as others which have no hope. For if we believe that Jesus died and rose again, even so them also which sleep in Jesus will God bring with him. For this we say unto you by the word of the Lord, that we which are alive and remain unto the coming of the Lord shall not prevent them which are asleep. For the Lord himself shall descend from heaven with a shout, with the voice of the archangel, and with the trump of God: and the dead in Christ shall rise first: Then we which are alive and remain shall be caught up together with them in the clouds, to meet the Lord in the air: and so shall we ever be with the Lord. Wherefore comfort one another with these words'.

'The Day of The Lord'

In the fifth chapter Paul continues with his instructions concerning Christ's glorious second advent. He urges us to live in the constant, immediate anticipation of Christ's second coming with watchfulness and sobriety, as children of God walking in the light, 'putting on the breastplate of faith and love, and for an helmet, the hope of salvation. For God hath not appointed us to wrath, but to obtain salvation by our Lord Jesus Christ' (vv. 7-11).

High Esteem

The saints at Thessalonica highly esteemed Paul as God's servant and messenger to them. The Apostle urges them and the saints of God in every age to give that same honour to all those men who faithfully preach the gospel, labouring in the Word of God and labouring for their souls. 'And we beseech you, brethren, to know them which labour among you, and are over you in the Lord, and admonish you; And to esteem them very highly in love for their work's sake. And be at peace among yourselves' (vv. 12-13).

God's saints are to highly esteem and give honour to those men who faithfully labour in the Word and preach the gospel to them (Isaiah 52:7; Romans 10:15; 1 Timothy 5:17). Only those preachers who faithfully preach the gospel of God's free and sovereign grace in Christ are worthy of this high esteem. All heretical work-mongers and promoters of will-worship are to be held in utter contempt (Galatians 1:6-8). But God's servants are to be honoured. This honour is to be extended beyond the local church and beyond one's own pastor, to all who faithfully preach the gospel: pastors, elders, missionaries, evangelists, etc.. Here the Holy Spirit shows us three things about God's servants and the honour they are to be given.

First, faithful pastors are men who 'labour among you'. The work of the ministry involves labour. I readily grant that many self-serving men use the pastoral office only to please themselves; and lazily go about their pastoral duties doing only what is required of them. God's servants labour in the Word and in doctrine. They study diligently, pray earnestly, and preach with urgency, using every gift and opportunity God bestows upon them for the furtherance of the gospel, the glory of Christ, and the benefit of his people (1 Timothy 4:12-16).

Second, they are 'over you in the Lord'. Pastors are not bullish tyrants; but they are the spiritual rulers of God's house in exactly the same sense that a man is the ruler of his house in the Lord (1 Timothy 3:4-5; Acts 20:28; Hebrews 13:7, 17). As such they must take the oversight of the flock, ruling in the name of God, by the Word of God (1 Peter 5:1-3).

Third, as overseers in the family of God, God's servants faithfully 'admonish you', teaching you the Word of God, the will of God, and the ways of God. They teach you what to believe and how to live for the glory of God.

The believer's responsibility to his pastor is also set before us as involving three things.

'Know them which labour among you'. Make yourself acquainted with God's servants. Seek to understand their labours and burdens. Find out what they need. Learn how best to assist them in their work.

'Esteem them very highly'. This high esteem is not esteem given to the man because he is intelligent, an unusually gifted preacher, or a well-liked man, but for his 'work's sake' as God's faithful servant. As such, he is a man worthy of your honour, worthy of your financial support, and worthy of respectful. Speak honourably when you talk about him.

This high esteem is to be given 'in love'. Let every child of God see that he loves and promotes love for his pastor.

The result of this high esteem and honour of believers for God's servants is peace. In the churches of Christ you will 'be at peace among yourselves' exactly in proportion to your love for and high esteem of God's servants.

'That Which is Good'

In verses 14 and 15 Paul urges us to take care to exercise patience toward all men, rendering to none evil for evil. Then, he urges us to follow that which is good, both among ourselves and with regard to all men (vv. 15-22). 'Rejoice evermore'. Let us ever be found rejoicing in the Lord. 'Pray without ceasing'. His is not an admonition to spend all our time on our knees literally, but to spend all our days on our knees spiritually, constantly living by faith in Christ, trusting him for all things. 'In every thing give thanks: for this is the will of God in Christ Jesus concerning you'. Everything that comes to pass is the will of God in Christ concerning you; and it is his will that we give thanks to him in everything.

'Quench not the Spirit'. Let us take care that we do not quench the Holy Spirit within us by evil deeds, particularly by hardness and bitterness toward one another (Ephesians 4:30). 'Despise not prophesyings'. Nothing so quickly and effectually quenches the Spirit of God as the wilful neglect of gospel preaching, by which we are taught of God and led in the worship of God. 'Prove all things; hold fast that which is good. Abstain from all appearance of evil'. It is our responsibility to prove all things spiritual by the gospel, holding firmly those things that honour our God and Saviour. Anything, be it doctrine, ordinance, ceremony, or practice, that appears in any way to contradict the gospel of God's free and sovereign grace in Christ and his great glory in salvation, or appears to promote the flesh, we must refuse to embrace.

In verse 23 Paul tells the Thessalonian saints of his prayer for them. What a prayer this is! 'And the very God of peace sanctify you wholly; and I pray God your whole spirit and soul and body be preserved blameless unto the coming of our Lord Jesus Christ'. In verse 24 he gives them and all believers a great, inspired word of assurance regarding our salvation. 'Faithful is he that calleth you, who also will do it'. Then, he closes this great epistle with these final, tender, affectionate words. 'Brethren, pray for us. Greet all the brethren with an holy kiss. I charge you by the Lord that this epistle be read unto all the holy brethren. The grace of our Lord Jesus Christ be with you. Amen' (vv. 25-28).

Chapter 53

2 Thessalonians

'The Lord Jesus Shall be Revealed from Heaven'

In 1 Thessalonians Paul gave a word of comfort to God's saints regarding those who have died in faith, assuring us of their resurrection and ours when the Lord Jesus comes again. In this epistle he picks up that same theme, assuring us again that 'the Lord Jesus shall be revealed from heaven' (1:7).

Before he ascended back into heaven, our blessed Saviour promised that he would return. He also assured us that before his second coming there would be a time of 'great tribulation', widespread lawlessness, and apostasy. He described that time in horrific terms. One writer put it in these words: 'The seams of society would come apart, and disorders, violence and riot would be so widespread that men's hearts would literally fail them for fear of the things that were coming on the face of the earth'. Our Saviour put it this way: 'For then shall be great tribulation, such as was not since the beginning of the world to this time, no, nor ever shall be' (Matthew 24:21).

The saints at Thessalonica were enduring such great persecutions and tribulations because of their faith in Christ that they appear to have been convinced that the day of the Lord was at hand in their day. Some had even quit their jobs, because they were convinced that the Lord Jesus was about to appear. In the three chapters of this epistle Paul corrects very common errors that many people still have regarding Christ's second coming.

Our Trials and Christ's Coming

In the first chapter Paul assures us that the trials and persecutions we endure in this world shall be corrected when Christ comes again. In that great day everything will be set in order and manifest in its proper light. Soon, the Lord God our Saviour will avenge his elect.

The epistle begins with a gracious commendation of the saints at Thessalonica for their obvious growth in grace, for which Paul gave thanks to God. The grace of God was obviously working in them. That fact was reflected in their growing faith, love for one another, and patience in trials, persecutions, and tribulation (vv. 1-5).

'We are bound to thank God always for you, brethren, as it is meet, because that your faith groweth exceedingly, and the charity of every one of you all toward each other aboundeth; So that we ourselves glory in you in the churches of God for your patience and faith in all your persecutions and tribulations that ye endure: Which is a manifest token of the righteous judgment of God, that ye may be counted worthy of the kingdom of God, for which ye also suffer'.

A Day of Recompense

Then he assures them of the glorious second advent of our Lord Jesus Christ.

'Seeing it is a righteous thing with God to recompense tribulation to them that trouble you; And to you who are troubled rest with us, when the Lord Jesus shall be revealed from heaven with his mighty angels, In flaming fire taking vengeance on them that know not God, and that obey not the gospel of our Lord Jesus Christ: Who shall be punished with everlasting destruction from the presence of the Lord, and from the glory of his power; When he shall come to be glorified in his saints, and to be admired in all them that believe (because our testimony among you was believed) in that day' (vv. 6-10).

When Christ comes again, we shall be well recompensed for anything and everything we suffer in this world for Christ's sake (Matthew 19:26-28; Romans 8:17; 1 Peter 1:3-9). Paul is reminding God's troubled, afflicted, and persecuted saints that our God has not forgotten us. He is going to straighten things out in that great day. He tells us that those things we suffer here, in God's providence, particularly those things that we suffer because of our faith in Christ, both demonstrate that God has made us 'worthy of the kingdom of God', and that soon we shall inherit it with Christ. God has made us worthy of his kingdom. He has made us worthy to inherit heavenly glory (Colossians 1:12) by Christ's blood atonement, his imputed righteousness, and his grace in the new birth. That thought ought to be enough to comfort and sustain us amidst our temporary troubles in this world (2 Corinthians 4:14-5:1).

Our Lord's glorious second advent will also bring a day of recompense to unbelieving rebels. There is a day coming when God will set them straight, when those who oppose him, his gospel, and his people will stand before that Man who is our God and Saviour, the Judge of all the earth who must do right.

This is not to be a secret thing, no secret rapture, but the glorious appearing of the great God and our Saviour. Our Lord will be revealed 'in flaming fire, taking vengeance on them that know not God and obey not the gospel'.

They shall be punished 'with everlasting destruction from the presence of the Lord and from the glory of his power'. What horrible terror awaits all who refuse to obey the gospel! Hell is everlasting destruction! Hell is everlasting banishment from the presence of the Lord.

For unbelievers Christ's second coming will be a terrifying thing, terrifying beyond description. But for believers it shall be the consummation of all hope and indescribably glorious. When our Lord Jesus appears in that day, 'he shall come to be glorified in his saints, and to be admired in all them that believe' (v. 10).

Paul does not say that Christ is going to be glorified 'by' his saints. But as the world sees the wisdom, the power, and the righteousness of God's great grace in the salvation of his elect, our great God and Saviour shall be glorified in his saints. In that great day our God will show all the universe 'the exceeding riches of his grace, in his kindness toward us, through Christ Jesus' (Ephesians 2:7).

In the last two verses of the first chapter he assures them of his unceasing prayers on their behalf (vv. 11-12).

Great Apostasy and Christ's Coming

In chapter 2 Paul tells the Thessalonians that there would be a time of great apostasy, 'a falling away', a departure from the gospel that shall engulf the professed church of Christ in darkness. Apparently, someone had written to the Church there, or visited it, and told them that Paul said, 'The Lord Jesus is coming soon'.

'Now we beseech you, brethren, by the coming of our Lord Jesus Christ, and by our gathering together unto him, That ye be not soon shaken in mind, or be troubled, neither by spirit, nor by word, nor by letter as from us, as that the day of Christ is at hand'. (vv. 1-2)

In these first two verses five things are obvious. (1) Our Lord Jesus Christ is coming again. He is on his way back at this very moment. 'Behold, he cometh!' (2) There are no signs or prophecies yet to be fulfilled before the Lord's return. (3) We are never told to look for signs, but always to look for Christ himself. (4) We should live every day upon the tiptoe of faith, looking for Christ at any moment, while labouring in his vineyard as responsible servants. (5) Our Lord may appear at any moment; but we must never allow anyone to dupe us into thinking he knows when. He may not return for another thousand years.

Throughout church history there have been some who predicted the second coming of Christ, setting dates, and trying to scare people into the Kingdom of God. Do not be fooled by such things. No one has an inside track on God's purpose. No one knows when Christ shall appear. No one knows the day or the hour of our Lord's glorious second advent, or, for that matter, the month, or year, or century!

Anyone who makes such predictions does not speak by the authority of God. Our Saviour told his disciples, 'It is not for you to know the times or the seasons, which the Father hath put in his own power' (Acts 1:7).

The Apostasy

'Let no man deceive you by any means: for that day shall not come, except there come a falling away first, and that man of sin be revealed, the son of perdition' (v. 3). While there are no visible signs or prophecies to be fulfilled before our Lord's return, the Apostle does tell us that before Christ's second advent, there will be a wholesale, universal apostasy and departure from the faith.

Paul is not talking here about liberals, open heretics, and vile ungodliness. He talks about those things in other places. Here he is talking about a departure of men and women from the faith who claim to be in the faith, a subtle, deceiving, damning departure from the faith by professed believers throughout the world. Look at this third verse. Here the Holy Spirit tells us that heresies must come. They had already begun in apostolic times; and they only get worse as time passes (1 Corinthians 11:19; 1 Timothy 4:1-3; 2 Timothy 3:1-9; 1 John 4:1-3). In this way the man of sin, antichrist, will be revealed.

Forget about what you see coming out of Hollywood and read in books of fiction, masquerading as books on Bible prophecy. This man of sin will not be revealed to the world. He is not some hideous looking, green-eyed monster in a red suit, with horns and a pitch fork. He is so smooth and slick that unless God himself enables you to recognize him, you cannot recognize him. However, he shall be revealed to God's elect.

Antichrist Revealed

'Who opposeth and exalteth himself above all that is called God, or that is worshipped; so that he as God sitteth in the temple of God, showing himself that he is God' (v. 4). Here the Apostle identifies the antichrist, this man of sin. The antichrist is not one man.

I have no problem at all in stating as many of our forefathers did, in great faithfulness, that the pope is antichrist and the church of Rome is antichrist. I do not mean that is the way it used to be. I mean that 'his unholiness', the pope, is antichrist. I mean that Roman Catholicism is antichrist. That cannot be stated too often, or too emphatically. However, it is a serious mistake to limit antichrist to one man, or one religious sect. Antichrist was already at work in the Apostolic age. John said many antichrists had gone out into the world. Paul had to contend with antichrists at Galatia, Colosse, Corinth, and Jerusalem.

Notice how Paul describes this thing called 'the man of sin, the son of perdition'. He is one who opposes God, exalts himself above God, and sets himself up in the temple of God and is worshipped as God, showing that he is God.

Antichrist is any system of religion, any man, any preacher, any church, any denomination that makes salvation to be dependent upon or determined by the will, works, and worth of man, rather than the will, works, and worth of Christ. It does not matter whether that system of religion is conservative or liberal, a mainline Protestant Church or a wild cult, Baptist or Methodist, Pentecostal or Presbyterian. Any church, doctrine, preacher, or religious system that makes man the centre-piece is antichrist.

Those who teach that God's will can be altered, hindered, or thwarted by man's will are, according to Colossians 2, will worshippers and not God worshippers. They are antichrists. Those who teach that the merit and efficacy of Christ's atonement resides in man's will, man's decision, and man's faith are antichrists.

Those who teach that the gracious operations of God the Holy Spirit may be successfully resisted by man are antichrists. Those who teach that grace can be forfeited or taken away as the result of something a man does are antichrists.

Satan Loosed

'Remember ye not, that, when I was yet with you, I told you these things? And now ye know what withholdeth that he might be revealed in his time. For the mystery of iniquity doth already work: only he who now letteth will let, until he be taken out of the way' (vv. 5-7). Paul told these saints at Thessalonica that the Holy Spirit now restrains, or withholds, the power and influence of antichrist. However, the time shall come, he wrote, when the Lord God will turn all hell loose to deceive the nations of the world again. At the end of the age, he said, Satan shall be loosed for a little season (Revelation 20:1-7).

Signs and Wonders

'And then shall that Wicked be revealed, whom the Lord shall consume with the spirit of his mouth, and shall destroy with the brightness of his coming: Even him, whose coming is after the working of Satan with all power and signs and lying wonders, And with all deceivableness of unrighteousness in them that perish; because they received not the love of the truth, that they might be saved' (v. 8).

Read the Apostle's inspired words with care. Do not allow a single syllable to pass before your eyes without prayerful thought and consideration. Here are five things revealed in these three verses.

Antichrist arises, is revealed, consumed, and destroyed exactly according to the purpose of God. Signs, wonders, and miracles are as certainly marks of antichrists in the last days as they were of Christ and his Apostles in the Apostolic Era. The deception of antichrist is tremendous, so tremendous that were it possible, the very elect of God would be deceived (Matthew 24:24, Mark 13:22).

Teaching unrighteousness

The religion of antichrist, self-righteousness, is here called 'unrighteousness'. Those who teach men to work out their own righteousness before God are promoting and teaching unrighteousness.

The reason for the delusion of men is their own, wilful rejection of truth. It is not that they do not receive the truth, theoretically, but that 'they received not the love of the truth, that they might be saved'.

It is not merely giving mental assent to truth that is evidence of saving faith. Saul of Tarsus had that. Judas had that. The demons who confessed Christ had that. Saving faith not only embraces truth, it loves the truth. We love Christ, the embodiment of truth; and we love the truth of the gospel revealed in and by him. All believers do.

Strong Delusion

'And for this cause God shall send them strong delusion, that they should believe a lie: That they all might be damned who believed not the truth, but had pleasure in unrighteousness' (vv. 12-13).

Do not imagine that things are out of control. We do get a little fearful. Sometimes we act as though the circumstances in which we are living are overwhelming. We must never entertain such thoughts. This day of religious deception and delusion is no more outside God's plan, purpose, and power than the formation of a rose. Things are coming to pass as they are exactly according to God's sovereign purpose. God sends blindness in judgment, just as he sends light in grace. He gives unbelievers the fruit of their own way, even sending them to hell singing, 'blessed assurance, Jesus is mine' (Proverbs 1:31; 16:25). Again, the Apostle tells us that the religion of man, free will, works religion, which men think is righteousness, is unrighteousness before God.

A Cause for Thanksgiving
Can you imagine what shouts of 'Hallelujah!' 'Glory!' and 'Bless God!' must have gone up from the hearts of these people when they read these next lines? 'But we are bound to give thanks alway to God for you, brethren beloved of the Lord, because God hath from the beginning chosen you to salvation through sanctification of the Spirit and belief of the truth: Whereunto he called you by our gospel, to the obtaining of the glory of our Lord Jesus Christ' (vv. 13-14).

Be sure you get the message contained in these two glorious verses of scripture. Here the Holy Spirit is telling us that the only reason you and I are not lost and ruined, the only reason we are no longer under the spell of antichrist, trusting our dead works of self-righteousness, the only reason we are not worshipping at the altar of our own free will, the only reason we are not reeling to and fro in drunkenness, intoxicated with the wine of Babylon's fornications is God's sovereign election. Every time we hear or read the words election, electing love, and electing grace we ought to lift our hearts to our great, gracious, and all-glorious God with thankful praise and say, 'Thank God, for electing love!'

Election is God's sovereign work. We give thanks to God for it because God did it. The cause of election is God's free, sovereign, everlasting love. All who are 'beloved of the Lord' were chosen to salvation in Christ. Election took place in eternity. 'God hath from the beginning chosen you' (Ephesians 1:3-6).

Election is unto salvation. 'God hath from the beginning chosen you to salvation'. Those who were chosen to salvation must be saved. Else, the purpose of God is meaningless. God's elect were chosen to be saved 'through sanctification of the Spirit'. God will not save sinners apart from or without the regenerating work of the Holy Spirit, by which all the chosen are made 'partakers of the divine nature'. We were chosen to salvation by the instrumentality of specific means: 'Belief of the Truth!'

Not only has God chosen and predestinated us to salvation, he has also ordained that every chosen sinner be saved by 'belief of the truth'. God does not use religious lies to save sinners. He uses the truth. It is not the delusion of free will, works religion that sets sinners free, but the truth, not truth, but the truth! Christ is the Truth. We are saved as we are brought to know him who is the Truth through the preaching of the gospel (John 6:44-45; Ephesians 1:12-14).

God never by-passes the use of means in accomplishing his purpose of grace. The only way a person can ever come to believe the truth is by the effectual, irresistible call of the Holy Spirit, which comes to chosen, redeemed sinners through the preaching of the gospel. 'Whereunto he called you by our gospel'.

Every saved sinner has been chosen, redeemed, and called 'to the obtaining of the glory of our Lord Jesus Christ!' Whatever that glory is which our Lord Jesus Christ now possesses as our Mediator, we shall obtain in all its fulness and blessedness, because of God's sovereign election (John 17:5, 22). The glory of Christ has something to do with the perfection of holiness, the possession of power, and the totality of satisfaction. These things shall be ours forever in that blessedness that awaits us at the throne of our God!

The Traditions

In verse 15 Paul says, 'Therefore, brethren, stand fast, and hold the traditions which ye have been taught, whether by word, or our epistle'. In these days of wholesale apostasy, in these days of spiritual darkness, famine, and utter perversion we who have been taught of God must stand fast in the traditions, not in the traditions of religious custom and superstition, but in the traditions of holy scripture and gospel truth. Let others say and do what they will, for those who have experienced grace, all hesitation, shifting, shirking, shrinking, evading, and compromise would be treason to the Son of God! We must stand fast (2 Timothy 1:13; Jeremiah 6:16).

In verses 16 and 17 we read, 'Now our Lord Jesus Christ himself, and God, even our Father, which hath loved us, and hath given us everlasting consolation and good hope through grace, Comfort your hearts, and stablish you in every good word and work'. This was Paul's benediction, his inspired declaration of divine blessing upon God's elect. This is God's word of promise to every sinner who trusts Christ alone as Saviour and

Lord. The Triune God 'hath loved us'. The Lord God has given us 'everlasting consolation' through the everlasting gospel of his everlasting grace (Isaiah 40:1-2). God has given us a 'good hope through grace'. Christ is our Hope! 'The Lord is my portion, saith my soul. Therefore will I hope in him'. The God of all grace will 'comfort your hearts, and stablish you in every good word and work', for Christ's sake. With those words of blessing and grace, Paul brings us to the very practical instructions of chapter three.

Waiting For Christ

In the first chapter of 1 Thessalonians the apostle tells us that believers are to be constantly waiting for Christ's glorious return. He commended the Thessalonian saints for doing so (v. 10). But some at Thessalonica had become fanatically obsessed with the thought of Christ's coming. They decided that, since we are to live in constant anticipation of Christ's return, they would quit their jobs and just pray, read their Bibles, and sing hymns until the Lord returned.

You may think, 'No sensible person would do that'. You are mistaken. The error of these saints at Thessalonica has been repeated many times. I know several people who were duped by a preacher just a few years ago, who had persuaded multitudes across the country and around the world that the Lord Jesus would return on September 4, 1994. Many sold their homes, quit their jobs, and sent him their money. They were convinced that they were acting in faith, doing what devotion to Christ required. They were not heretics. They believed the gospel and still do. But they were duped by a man.

That is exactly what happened to some in Thessalonica. 'For we hear that there are some which walk among you disorderly, working not at all, but are busybodies' (v. 11). Therefore, after requesting prayer for himself, Paul assures the Thessalonians of God's faithfulness and of his confidence that the Lord would teach them to patiently wait for Christ, not in slothful, uselessness, but as faithful servants.

'Finally, brethren, pray for us, that the word of the Lord may have free course, and be glorified, even as it is with you: And that we may be delivered from unreasonable and wicked men: for all men have not faith. But the Lord is faithful, who shall stablish you, and keep you from evil. And we have confidence in the Lord touching you, that ye both do and will do the things which we command you. And the Lord direct your hearts into the love of God, and into the patient waiting for Christ' (vv. 1-5).

Let me try to illustrate this. I am often away from home for several days at a time preaching the gospel. Usually my wife stays at home to take care of things in my absence. When the time nears for me to return home, you might, if you were in the house and did not know what was happening, think my wife was behaving rather strangely. She will finish up all her cleaning, get all dolled up, and go look out the front widow. By this time she has already started preparing one of my favourite meals. She will set the table, and go look out the front window. Then she will stir everything that needs stirring, put on a pot of coffee, and go look out the window. If you were to call her and ask, 'Shelby, what are you doing?' I know exactly what her answer would be. She would say, 'Oh, nothing. I'm just waiting for Don to get home'. Then, she would look out the front window again. This time she sees me driving up the road. If she were talking to the President of the United States, she would say, 'Oh, Don's here. I've got to go', and run outside to meet me.

That is what Paul teaches us in 2 Thessalonians 3. We are to wait for our Saviour's glorious second advent every moment while we go about our business as his stewards in this world serving him. 'Blessed is that servant, whom his lord when he cometh shall find so doing' (Luke 12:43).

Chapter 54

1 Timothy

'Teach No Other Doctrine'

Up to this point, all of Paul's letters have been addressed to local churches. However, First and Second Timothy and Titus are what we call Pastoral Epistles. They were written by divine inspiration to give us specific, clear instructions about how we are to behave ourselves in the house of God (1 Timothy 3:15). These three epistles are specifically addressed to Timothy and Titus, divinely appointed pastors of local churches, because it is the pastor's responsibility in any local church to guide God's people in the worship and service of Christ.

Timothy

The first two of these very important, Pastoral Epistles was written to Paul's friend and faithful co-labourer in the gospel, Timothy. Timothy had enjoyed the rare, blessed privilege of being raised under the influence of holy scripture. He was taught the Word of God as a child, both by his mother and his grandmother (2 Timothy 1:5; 3:15); and he was converted when he was just a young man.

Because Paul speaks of Timothy as his 'own son in the faith' (1:2), many have thought he was converted under the influence of Paul's ministry. But that does not appear to have been the case. In Acts 16:1-2 we discover that Timothy was already converted when Paul first met him. Though he was but a very young man, he was already a disciple 'well reported of by the brethren'.

Paul calls Timothy his 'own son in the faith', because he was to Timothy, in the family of God, like a father. Paul was the man through whom Timothy was taught, by whom his spiritual life was directed. Timothy for his part served Paul with all the love, loyalty, and faithfulness of a son serving his father, though Timothy was himself a faithful gospel preacher.

Paul had sent Timothy to Ephesus; but for some reason he wanted Paul's approval (if not permission) to leave there and go to another place. We are not told why he wanted to leave; but Paul urged him to stay, that he might charge those who were wavering from the faith 'that they teach no other doctrine' (1:3).

Christ in the Letter

It will be edifying, I am sure, to see how Paul sets forth the person, work, and glory of our Lord Jesus Christ in this book. He tells us in the very first verse of the first chapter that Christ is our Hope. We have no hope before God but him. His blood, his righteousness, and his intercession give us a good hope. The Lord Jesus Christ is the Saviour of sinners. He came into this world specifically to save sinners (1:15). What blessed good news this is! This great Saviour is God, the Eternal King (1:17). He is also our Mediator, the one Mediator between God and men (2:5), our Daysman, our Advocate with the Father. The Lord Jesus Christ is our Ransom. He gave himself a ransom for our souls and ransomed us out from under the curse of the law (2:6). This all-glorious Christ, our great Saviour, has been received up into Glory as our Ransom and Mediator (3:14-16). Our exalted Redeemer is the Saviour and Preserver of all men in providence, and he is specially, distinctly, the Saviour and preserver of all who trust him (4:9-10). Christ, in whom we trust, is the Blessed and only Potentate (the only Possessor of power), King, and Lord of the universe (6:13-16).

'No Other Doctrine'

In chapter 1 Paul tells Timothy to 'charge' (command, order, or demand) that those under his care 'teach no other doctrine' than the gospel of God's pure, free, sovereign grace in Christ (vv. 3-20). The errors and heresies Timothy had to resist in Ephesus in his day are the same as those the church of God faces in every generation and in every part of the world. Some added to the revelation of God in holy scripture the moral fables of human wisdom and philosophy. Others claimed to find secret codes and meanings hidden away in the genealogical records of the Old Testament. They taught nothing that was comforting and edifying. Their doctrine only raised questions and stirred strife and division in the church. Also, there were legalists at Ephesus, as there are everywhere, who tried to put God's saints back under the yoke of bondage to the Mosaic law.

Paul tells us that such people 'have turned aside unto vain jangling, desiring to be teachers of the law; but they simply do not know what they are talking about. They try to put righteous men and women, the saints of God, under the terror of the law, not knowing that the law was made for the unrighteous (vv. 8-11). Paul tells us that all such doctrine is 'contrary to sound doctrine', contrary to 'the glorious gospel of the blessed God'.

After telling Timothy to command that no one in the church of God be allowed to teach such things, having just mentioned 'the glorious gospel of the blessed God', Paul tells us what great things the Lord God had wrought in him by the gospel (vv. 12-17), assuring us of its reliability (v. 15).

First Charge

Paul gave Timothy (and every gospel preacher) four distinct charges in this epistle (1:18-20; 4:11-16; 5:21-25; 6:11-16). The first chapter closes with a charge issued to all who preach the gospel to 'war a good warfare, holding faith with a good conscience' (vv. 18-20).

Orderly Worship

In chapters 2 and 3 Paul tells us that all matters involved in the worship of God must be orderly and ordered by the Word of God. It is clear that he considered the matter of public worship to be a matter of highest priority in the lives of God's saints. He specifically discusses three things in these two chapters: (1) Prayer, (2) The Role of Women, and (3) The Qualifications for Pastors and Deacons.

With regard to the matter of prayer, specifically public prayer in the house of God, Paul tells us that we ought always to pray for all men, that is for men of every rank and order in society, particularly for those who are in authority over us (2:1-8).

In verses 9-15 of chapter 2 he tells us that women ought to display a conscientious awareness of the fact that they are women, behaving as ladies in the house of God, filled with modesty and observing God's order in creation. When women come to the house of God, they are to dress modestly, as 'women professing godliness', 'learn in silence, with all subjection', never teaching or usurping authority over men, but always 'to be in silence'.

In chapter 3, verses 1-13 the apostle tells us that pastors and deacons must be men of proven faith and faithfulness. He concludes the chapter with a tremendous statement concerning the purpose and message of God's church in this world.

'These things write I unto thee, hoping to come unto thee shortly: But if I tarry long, that thou mayest know how thou oughtest to behave thyself in the house of God, which is the church of the living God, the pillar and ground of the truth. And without controversy great is the mystery of godliness: God was manifest in the flesh, justified in the Spirit, seen of angels, preached unto the Gentiles, believed on in the world, received up into glory' (vv. 14-16).

Instructions to Preachers

The whole of the second half of 1 Timothy (chapters 4-6) is taken up with instructions to preachers. In these chapters he tells Timothy and all who are trusted with the blessed work of preaching the gospel the kind of men they should aspire to be as the servants of God. He begins this section by telling us that God's servants in this world must constantly deal with and help God's people to resist an ever-increasing departure from the gospel.

'Now the Spirit speaketh expressly, that in the latter times some shall depart from the faith, giving heed to seducing spirits, and doctrines of devils; Speaking lies in hypocrisy; having their conscience seared with a hot iron; Forbidding to marry, and commanding to abstain from meats, which God hath created to be received with thanksgiving of them which believe and know the truth. For every creature of God is good, and nothing to be refused, if it be received with thanksgiving: For it is sanctified by the word of God and prayer' (4:1-5).

He tells us that a good preacher will both constantly put the brethren in remembrance of these things and steadfastly resist every temptation to turn away from the message of the gospel (vv. 6-8).

Second Charge

In verses 11-16 Paul urges Timothy, and every man to whom God has given the blessed privilege of preaching the gospel of Christ, to give himself in wholehearted devotion to the work of the ministry. This is Paul's second charge to Timothy.

'These things command and teach. Let no man despise thy youth; but be thou an example of the believers, in word, in conversation, in charity, in spirit, in faith, in purity. Till I come, give attendance to reading, to exhortation, to doctrine. Neglect not the gift that is in thee, which was given thee by prophecy, with the laying on of the hands of the presbytery. Meditate upon these things; give thyself wholly to them; that thy profiting may appear to all. Take heed unto thyself, and unto the doctrine; continue in them: for in doing this thou shalt both save thyself, and them that hear thee'.

Third Charge

In the fifth chapter we are told how we are to respect and care for God's saints, particularly those who are widows (widows in deed), and those elders who labour in the Word and doctrine. The chapter concludes with a third charge, demanding that these things be done, that God's saints and his preachers be cared for without partiality. 'I charge thee before God, and the Lord Jesus Christ, and the elect angels, that thou observe these things without preferring one before another, doing nothing by partiality'. (v. 21).

Preachers and Money

One of the greatest difficulties preachers have is the handling of money. Faithful men are often in a position to abuse the gifts of others; and greed and covetousness are powerful lusts of the flesh that must be constantly resisted. Therefore, the Holy Spirit speaking by Paul commands every gospel preacher to flee from the love of money and the will to enrich himself.

'But godliness with contentment is great gain. For we brought nothing into this world, and it is certain we can carry nothing out. And having food and raiment let us be therewith content. But they that will be rich fall into temptation and a snare, and into many foolish and hurtful lusts, which drown men in destruction and perdition. For the love of money is the root of all evil: which while some coveted after, they have erred from the faith, and pierced themselves through with many sorrows. But thou, O man of God, flee these things; and follow after righteousness, godliness, faith, love, patience, meekness. Fight the good fight of faith, lay hold on eternal life, whereunto thou art also called, and hast professed a good profession before many witnesses' (6:6-12)

Fourth Charge

Paul's fourth charge to Timothy, his fourth charge to all who preach the gospel, is that we keep this commandment with regard to money and material things as those who are indeed the servants of the King of kings.

'I give thee charge in the sight of God, who quickeneth all things, and before Christ Jesus, who before Pontius Pilate witnessed a good confession; That thou keep this commandment without spot, unrebukeable, until the appearing of our Lord Jesus Christ: Which in his times he shall show, who is the blessed and only Potentate, the King of kings, and Lord of lords; Who only hath immortality, dwelling in the light which no man can approach unto; whom no man hath seen, nor can see: to whom be honour and power everlasting. Amen' (vv. 13-16).

'Them that Are Rich'

In verses 17-19 the apostle moves from the preacher and his attitude toward money to the people who actually are rich, and tells Timothy to instruct those of God's saints in this world who are entrusted with material wealth to use it wisely and graciously for the glory of God and the good of his people.

'Charge them that are rich in this world, that they be not highminded, nor trust in uncertain riches, but in the living God, who giveth us richly all things to enjoy; That they do good, that they be rich in good works, ready to distribute, willing to communicate; Laying up in store for themselves a good foundation against the time to come, that they may lay hold on eternal life'.

This instructive epistle closes with a passionate appeal to Timothy, 'O Timothy, keep that which is committed to thy trust, avoiding profane and vain babblings, and oppositions of science falsely so called: Which some professing have erred concerning the faith. Grace be with thee. Amen' (vv 20-21).

Timothy is to look upon the gospel of the grace of God as a great treasure trusted to his hands, a treasure to be faithfully guarded as one would guard his life. For, 'We have this treasure in earthen vessels, that the excellency of the power may be of God, and not of us' (2 Corinthians 4:5-7).

Chapter 55

2 Timothy

'Endure Hardness as a Good Soldier of Christ'.

Second Timothy was the last epistle written by the Apostle Paul before he was put to death for preaching the gospel of Christ. This epistle was written primarily to encourage Timothy to remain loyal and faithful as the servant of God. I find it remarkable that this man, knowing that his executioner was at the door, as one of his last acts, writes to a friend and fellow labourer in the gospel to encourage him to be steadfast in the midst of trial and opposition, to, as he puts it, 'endure hardness as a good soldier of Jesus Christ'. What a remarkable man Paul must have been!

The aged Apostle is sitting alone in the dark, miserable Roman prison, the imminent flash of the swordsman's blade etched in his mind's eye. Yet, his heart is full of concern for his dear son in the ministry, Timothy, who was serving as pastor of the local church at Ephesus. Timothy was being confronted with the onslaught of grievous wolves entering from without and with corrupt men arising from within the assembly (Acts 20:29-32). The flagship church of Asia Minor had become the battleground for the gospel of God and the cause of Christ.

The church of God, the truth of God, and the glory of God were under assault. The souls of men were at stake. Thus, before leaving this world, Paul wanted to encourage his friend and God's faithful servant to remain faithful. Can you picture Timothy reading this powerful, emotion filled

letter from his cherished and admired mentor? His eyes must have been
full of tears. As he got to the last chapter, he understood clearly that this
was Paul's last will and testament to him.

It is likely that even before this letter reached Timothy, Paul's head
had been severed from his body. This great man of God died just as he
had lived as a living sacrifice to his God (Romans 12:1). A more fitting
epitaph could not have been written for him than that which the Holy
Spirit inspired him to write at the end of this epistle, 'I have fought a good
fight, I have finished my course, I have kept the faith' (4:7).

For Us

But these four chapters were not written for Timothy alone. They
were written for us (Romans 15:4), particularly for God's servants who
labour as gospel preachers in the midst of relentless opposition. This
great epistle is written to encourage us to be faithful to our God. As 'he
abideth faithful', let us be faithful to him. The contents of this letter can
be summed up in three words: personal, pastoral, and practical.

Second Timothy is a very personal letter. It displays the great, personal
affection Paul had for Timothy. He prayed for him night and day (1:3-6).
He calls Timothy his 'dearly beloved son', looking upon him as one as
dear to him as a son (1:2; 2:1). He longed to see him one more time before
leaving this world (4:9, 21). Such personal love and concern ought to ever
be manifest in God's saints toward one another, and should be distinctly
manifest in gospel preachers toward one another.

This is also a pastoral letter, along with First Timothy and Titus.
Timothy was pastor of the church in Ephesus during very disturbing
times. His was not an easy task (1 Timothy 1:3-4, 18; 2 Timothy 1:6-8).
Paul wrote this epistle to encourage and exhort him to continue faithful in
all things, to make a full proof of his ministry (4:5).

Second Timothy is also a very practical letter. Of course, all the book
of God is practical; but this epistle distinctly concentrates on the practical
aspects of daily taking up our cross and following Christ. In 1 Timothy
6:12 we are encouraged to 'fight the good fight of faith', and here we are
told how to do it. Second Timothy is indispensable.

'A Sound Mind'

In the opening verses of chapter 1 Paul expresses his love for Timothy
and tells him how thankful to God he is for him (vv. 1-7). He assures his
dear friend that he prayed for him continually, and urged him to 'stir up
the gift of God' that was in him. Timothy was a man gifted of God for the

work of the ministry; and the gifts God had given him he was responsible to use. If nothing else will rouse a gospel preacher to faithfulness in the work trusted to his hands and courage in performing it, the bare fact that God has made him his servant ought to do it (Ephesians 3:8-12).

But Paul would leave no stone unturned as he sought for arguments that would encourage Timothy to continue faithful in the cause of Christ. He reminds him of his mother's faith in Christ, his grandmother's faith in Christ, and of his own unflinching faithfulness in serving God with a pure conscience. Then, he tells Timothy and us that there is never a reason for us to give way to cowardice and fear before men or before hell itself, because our God has given us the spirit of power, love, and a sound mind needed to serve him (1:6-7). Having the Spirit of God ('power from on high') dwelling in us, having our hearts motivated by love for Christ and his people, and having our minds established firmly by the gospel, we have no reason to be afraid as we go about our lives doing the will of God.

'Hold Fast'

Beginning in verse 8 and going to the end of chapter 1, Paul urges Timothy, and thereby the Spirit of God urges us, to hold fast and remain faithful in believing and proclaiming the gospel in the very teeth of hell itself. Remember, Paul was writing from prison. Many who pretended to be the servants of Christ, and some who truly were the servants of Christ, were intimidated and cowed by his imprisonment and had abandoned him, just as our Lord's disciples abandoned him. He was particularly hurt by Phygellus and Hermogenes who had turned away from him (v. 15). Yet, there were others like Onesiphorus who comforted and refreshed him.

Paul understood well that Timothy's strength would not come from himself. To inspire his strength he turned Timothy's attention to the gospel of Christ. He says in verses 8-12, 'Timothy, let me remind you that I am here, in these chains, because of the gospel I have preached. You do the same'. He knew, as Roger Ellsworth puts it, 'our willingness to stand for the gospel will be in direct proportion to our understanding of it'. He tells us exactly what that gospel is for which he was imprisoned and put to death. This is that form of sound words we must hold fast (vv. 9-10).

The gospel is a declaration that salvation is entirely God's work. God 'hath saved us'. It is the declaration of salvation done. God 'hath saved us, and called us'. It declares that salvation is altogether God's work, without the aid of man, 'not according to our works'. The gospel is the blessed good news that salvation is a matter of free grace, God's work alone, accomplished according to God's eternal, unalterable purpose.

Salvation comes to chosen sinners 'according to his own purpose and grace'. The gospel is the revelation of the fact that God's salvation and grace were given to chosen sinners in Christ before the world began. God's saving grace 'was given us in Christ Jesus before the world began'. The gospel of Christ is the declaration, the manifestation, the revelation of light, life, and immortality in and by Christ, in whom is 'the promise of life' (v. 1). 'Who hath saved us, and called us with an holy calling, not according to our works, but according to his own purpose and grace, which was given us in Christ Jesus before the world began, But is now made manifest by the appearing of our Saviour Jesus Christ, who hath abolished death, and hath brought life and immortality to light through the gospel' (vv. 9-10).

Though imprisoned and facing imminent execution, Paul was not ashamed, shaken, confused, or confounded by his circumstances in the good providence of God, or with regard to the gospel for which he was about to die. In fact, that was his only comfort and peace. He says, 'I am not ashamed: for I know whom I have believed, and am persuaded that he is able to keep that which I have committed unto him against that day' (v. 12).

It is against this backdrop that Paul calls for Timothy and us to 'hold fast'. With that as the backdrop, how dare we do otherwise? 'Hold fast the form of sound words, which thou hast heard of me, in faith and love which is in Christ Jesus. That good thing which was committed unto thee keep by the Holy Ghost which dwelleth in us' (vv. 13-14).

'Be Strong'

In chapter 2 Paul calls for us to 'be strong in the grace that is in Christ Jesus'. Like Timothy, we are not only to hold the gospel firmly ourselves, we are to commit it to others. Faithful men learn the gospel from faithful men, and then teach it to other faithful men, generation after generation. This is a continuing obligation upon gospel preachers.

Clearly, Paul is passing the torch to Timothy. He is urging him to continue to depend upon God, assuring him that he would find the strength needed and the grace sufficient in Christ. Paul's long ministry with Timothy had included many hardships, and as Timothy took up the mantle he could expect more of the same. So Paul urged him to submit to difficulties as a good soldier.

In verses 3-6 we are given examples of how we are to 'be strong in the grace that is in Christ Jesus'. He uses three examples to help him and us understand the responsibilities upon us in this world. First, he tells us that, like good soldiers, we must remain free from entanglement with other lesser goals and activities while serving the cause of Christ in this world (vv. 3-4). Then, he tells us that we must, as disciplined athletes, do the work of building Christ's kingdom, spreading his gospel, and ministering to his people according to the rule of his Word (v. 5). Third, Paul tells us that as labourers in God's vineyard, we must give ourselves to the constant toil of tending the vineyard, like any good farmer tends his ground (v. 6).

In a word, that which is required in the service of Christ (required of gospel preachers and required of all who serve Christ in their own place) is dogged, relentless persistence. If ever this dogged persistence was exemplified in a mere man, that man was the apostle Paul (vv. 8-10).

Then, Paul assures us that 'the Word of God is not bound' and cannot be bound (v. 9). He assures us that our great God is ever faithful. He does so to inspire our dogged persistence in faithfulness to him, no matter the temporary cost or opposition (vv. 11-13).

Requirements for Preachers

In the remaining portion of chapter 2 (vv. 14-26) Paul tells us what is required of those who preach the gospel. Remember, however, this book was not written only to instruct preachers. If we are to instruct eternity bound men and women in the truth of God, if we are to teach people the things of God as his witnesses in this world, whether preaching from the pulpit or discussing the gospel with our barber or hair-dresser, we must heed these requirements.

We must avoid strife about words (v. 14); and we must study the Word of God (v. 15). We must shun the profane and vain babblings of men about the things of God, being confident that 'the foundation of God standeth sure', that God will save his elect (vv. 16-19). We must purge ourselves of all false religion and the vain babblings of it (vv. 20-21). We must flee those youthful lusts that inspire religious debate, following righteousness, faith, love, and peace (vv. 22-23). We must instruct those who hear us with gentleness, meekness, and patience (vv. 24-26).

'This Know Also'

In chapter 3 Paul continues telling us what is necessary for us to know and understand if we are to be useful as God's witnesses in the day and generation we have been put here to serve. We cannot possibly minister to our generation if we fail to understand it. Therefore this third chapter begins with a plain declaration of what we face in these 'last days'.

'This know also, that in the last days perilous times shall come. For men shall be lovers of their own selves, covetous, boasters, proud, blasphemers, disobedient to parents, unthankful, unholy, Without natural affection, trucebreakers, false accusers, incontinent, fierce, despisers of those that are good, Traitors, heady, highminded, lovers of pleasures more than lovers of God; Having a form of godliness, but denying the power thereof: from such turn away. For of this sort are they which creep into houses, and lead captive silly women laden with sins, led away with divers lusts, Ever learning, and never able to come to the knowledge of the truth' (vv. 1-7).

'The last days' began with our Lord's first advent and will continue until his second coming (Acts 2:14-17; Hebrews 1:1-2; 1 John 2:18). They are days of continually increasing ungodliness, self-centredness, and rebellion accepted and practiced by religious people who have a form of godliness (v. 5), but deny the gospel which is the power of God (Romans 1:16).

Lest we be discouraged, intimidated or overwhelmed at the realization of these things, Paul assures us that the cause of Christ and the purpose of God cannot and will not be hindered by them (vv. 8-9).

'Now as Jannes and Jambres withstood Moses, so do these also resist the truth: men of corrupt minds, reprobate concerning the faith. But they shall proceed no further: for their folly shall be manifest unto all men, as theirs also was'.

All that those 'men of corrupt minds, reprobate concerning the faith', who oppose God, his gospel, and his church can do is resist the truth. They shall not prevail over it, even momentarily. It is certain that 'evil men and seducers shall wax worse and worse, deceiving, and being deceived' (v. 13); but as Aaron's rod swallowed up the rods of Jannes and Jambres when they turned them into snakes, so the Word of God will swallow up all who oppose it. Therefore, Paul writes, 'Continue thou in the things which thou hast learned and hast been assured of, knowing of whom thou hast learned them; and that from a child thou hast known the holy scriptures, which are able to make thee wise unto salvation through faith which is in Christ Jesus. All scripture is given by inspiration of God, and is profitable for doctrine, for reproof, for correction, for instruction in righteousness' (vv. 14-16).

The Word of God and the Word of God alone is sufficient as the means by which we are to know all things spiritual and withstand the evil influence of false religion. It is profitable for doctrine, to teach us everything we need to know about God, salvation, and ourselves. It is profitable for reproof, refuting error and false religion. It is profitable for correction, correcting our own misunderstandings and wayward behaviour. It is profitable for instruction in righteousness, teaching us the way of life, faith, and righteousness in Christ.

'Preach the Word'

Paul's last word to Timothy in chapter four, and to us is this: 'Preach the Word!' God's remedy for the wickedness of this age and every age is gospel preaching.

'I charge thee therefore before God, and the Lord Jesus Christ, who shall judge the quick and the dead at his appearing and his kingdom; Preach the word; be instant in season, out of season; reprove, rebuke, exhort with all longsuffering and doctrine. For the time will come when they will not endure sound doctrine; but after their own lusts shall they heap to themselves teachers, having itching ears; And they shall turn away their ears from the truth, and shall be turned unto fables. But watch thou in all things, endure afflictions, do the work of an evangelist, make full proof of thy ministry' (vv. 1-5).

Then, he concludes this epistle and his life with a description of his own life and ministry as the servant of God, and calls upon Timothy to come to him quickly, desiring to see him one more time before leaving this earth for heavenly glory (vv. 6-22).

'I am now ready to be offered, and the time of my departure is at hand. I have fought a good fight, I have finished my course, I have kept the faith: Henceforth there is laid up for me a crown of righteousness, which the Lord, the righteous judge, shall give me at that day: and not to me only, but unto all them also that love his appearing' (vv. 6-8).

Paul knew that his execution was at hand. He had already appeared before Nero once. Now he must appear before the monstrous wretch again, and he knew what the outcome would be. But he is looking beyond all that. He is about to depart from this world, about to enter into a 'house not made with hands, eternal in the heavens' with Christ. Yet, he was cold and lonely. He says ...

'Do thy diligence to come shortly unto me: For Demas hath forsaken me, having loved this present world, and is departed unto Thessalonica; Crescens to Galatia, Titus unto Dalmatia. Only Luke is with me. Take Mark, and bring him with thee: for he is profitable to me for the ministry. And Tychicus have I sent to Ephesus' (9-12).

He asked Timothy to bring him his coat, his books, and the scriptures, desiring to the end to learn more of Christ (v. 13). He had been greatly injured by Alexander the coppersmith (vv. 14-15). When he first stood before Nero, no one stood with him. All forsook him. Still, the Lord stood with him and delivered him out of the mouth of the lion (vv. 16-17). Though he knew that Nero (the monstrous raging lion), from whom he had been delivered, would have him killed this time, he tells Timothy and us that God had indeed given him the spirit 'of power, and of love, and of a sound mind'. Nero would kill his body; but by Nero's hand, he declares confidently, 'the Lord shall deliver me from every evil work, and will preserve me unto his heavenly kingdom: to whom be glory for ever and ever' (v. 18).

Paul closes this epistle with some personal words to his friends. What a delightful letter this is! What a challenge and comfort it must have been to Timothy. But remember, this was written to you and me as much as it was to Timothy. Paul wrote this, his last epistle, to encourage us to stand firm, to hold fast to the form of sound words given to us in the gospel of Christ, to endure hardness as good soldiers of Christ, remembering that he is able to keep that which we have committed to him, and he will.

Chapter 56

Titus

'Adorn the Doctrine of God'

This epistle was addressed to Titus, the pastor of the church at Crete. Paul sent Titus to Corinth to settle the difficulties that threatened the survival of that congregation (2 Corinthians 2:13; 12:18; 7:6-15). This is the last of Paul's very short, but very important and instructive Pastoral epistles. It begins with a salutation that is more lengthy than most of Paul's salutations. The salutation itself is illuminating (1:1-5).

Election

Have you ever noticed that one of the most common names used in the New Testament referring to believers in general is 'elect'? Divine election was in the New Testament era such a commonly understood thing that saved sinners were commonly addressed as 'the elect'. In the opening verse of this epistle Paul speaks of the saints of God as 'God's elect'. Among the early churches, election was so readily talked about that God's elect became synonymous with believers. Our Lord declared that the elect cannot be deceived by antichrists (Matthew 24:24), and that God gathers his elect from the four corners of the earth (Matthew 24:31). We are told that God shall avenge his own elect (Luke 18:7). Paul calls upon 'the elect of God' to put on Christ (Colossians 3:12.). Peter addressed his first epistle to God's elect (1 Peter 1:2). John addressed his second epistle to 'the elect lady' (2 John 1) and spoke of her 'elect sister' (2 John 13). In those days everyone who professed to be followers of Christ rejoiced in the electing love of God our Saviour and understood the blessedness of his great grace, who declared, 'Ye have not chosen me, but I have chosen you' (John 15:16).

Our Faith

Paul declares himself to be God's servant and an apostle of Christ 'according to the faith of God's elect, and the acknowledging of the truth which is after godliness'. The faith of God's elect is one. That is to say, all God's elect have the same faith. In verse 4 he calls it 'the common faith'. We all have our faith from one common source. It is the gift of God's grace (Ephesians 2:8-9) and the operation of God the Holy Spirit in us (Colossians 2:12). The faith that God gives his elect embodies and acknowledges one common truth, 'the truth' of the gospel: redemption, grace, and salvation by Christ's substitutionary accomplishments (1 Corinthians 15:1-3; Galatians 1:6-9). This is the faith 'which is after godliness'. Religion will produce morality; but only the gospel of Christ will produce godliness – the worship of God.

Believing the gospel, we have 'hope of eternal life, which God, that cannot lie, promised before the world began' (v. 2). Without Christ, we are 'without hope'. Believing Christ, trusting his blood and righteousness, we have 'a good hope through grace' of eternal life. We have every reason to confidently expect eternal life, because 'God, that cannot lie', promised it to all who are in Christ 'before the world began'. This promise of our salvation is a promise that was made by God the Father to God the Son as our Surety in eternity (Psalm 2:8). The Father promised our Surety, the Lord Jesus Christ, that he would give eternal life to his elect by virtue of his obedience unto death as our Substitute. This word of promise is now made manifest by the preaching of the gospel: 'But hath in due times manifested his word through preaching, according to the commandment of God our Saviour' (v. 3; 2 Timothy 1:9-10).

Our Saviour

Titus was Paul's son in the faith. That is to say, he was one of many who were converted under the influence of Paul's ministry. We see this in verse 4. There we also see a combination of titles used in all three chapters in the book of Titus that must not be overlooked. Paul speaks of 'God our Saviour' and of 'Christ our Saviour' in that order in 1:3-4, in 2:10 and 13, and in 3:4 and 6. His obvious intent is to emphasize the eternal deity of our Lord Jesus Christ. He who is our Saviour is himself the eternal God.

Set In Order

Paul left Titus in Crete 'to set in order the things that were wanting', and to ordain elders in every city in which God raised up an assembly of believers (v. 5). His purpose in writing this epistle was to give his son in the faith instructions about setting things in order in the churches of Christ.

The first matter of order in every local church involves the man who serves as pastor. The church is only as strong as the man who leads it. Therefore, the Holy Spirit again gives us a description of the kind of man who is to be set aside for the work of the gospel ministry (vv. 5-9). Along with all the other qualifications for a pastor, Paul asserts that he must be one who holds fast 'the faithful word'. He must be a man who is thoroughly convinced of and committed to the gospel of God's free and sovereign grace in Christ, 'that he may be able by sound doctrine both to exhort and to convince the gainsayers'. The reason for this is clear. He will always have plenty of 'gainsayers' to convince (vv. 10-16).

Gainsayers

The man who leads God's saints in the worship and service of Christ must never allow false teachers to go uncorrected and unrebuked. They are here called 'gainsayers' because those who preach any other gospel oppose and speak against the gospel of Christ. Paul specifically identifies those in Crete of whom he spoke. They were men who taught that faith in Christ is not enough, that the blood of Christ is not enough, that the righteousness of Christ is not enough, that we must add to his righteousness our own righteousness if we would really be pure in the eyes of God.

All who teach such doctrine are, in the words of inspiration, 'unruly, vain talkers, deceivers, liars, and evil beasts'. They are motivated by gain, and their 'mouths must be stopped'. Paul specifically names those who are 'of the circumcision', those who seek to impose the yoke of the law upon God's saints. Having turned from the truth, they teach 'Jewish fables and the commandments of men'. Do not miss what Paul here declares. Those who attempt to make our obedience to the law of God the basis of righteousness, either for justification or sanctification, subvert the law and turn it into nothing but 'Jewish fables and the commandments of men'. Of all such false teachers, Paul writes, 'They profess that they know God; but in works they deny him, being abominable, and disobedient, and unto every good work reprobate' (v. 16). In their works of self-righteousness (their attempts to establish their own righteousness) they deny God, his grace, and his salvation altogether.

Grace Teaches

In chapter 2 Paul shows us that the gospel of the grace of God, not the law of Moses, teaches all to whom it is revealed that salvation is by grace alone and teaches us how to live in this world for the glory of God. In this chapter the apostle is urging us to adorn the doctrine of the grace of God that we profess to believe by the way we live in this world. As he does, he makes no appeal to the law, but only to grace.

In verses 1-10 he tells both the man who preaches the gospel and the people who hear and believe the gospel how to adorn the gospel. He is telling us how to behave ourselves so that we may 'adorn the doctrine of God our Saviour in all things' (v. 10).

This is both our personal responsibility and our privilege. I hope it is your desire and my own. We are to 'adorn the doctrine of God our Saviour in all things'. That is to say, we are to set forth in our lives, as well as in our doctrine, the beauty, glory, and attractiveness of the gospel of Christ. If we hope to persuade men and women to believe the gospel we preach, we must show them, by our lives, the beauty of the gospel. If we would honour Christ and his gospel in the eyes of men, we must have our lives regulated and governed by the gospel.

The Pastor

Every pastor, every man who speaks to men in the name of God, is responsible to adorn the gospel by faithfully preaching it. 'But speak thou the things which become sound doctrine' (v. 1). Every preacher has a mandate from God and the preacher's mandate is always the same. All who are sent of God as his messengers to eternity bound men and women are sent to preach the gospel, to constantly declare those 'things which become sound doctrine' (2 Timothy 4:1-5).

The doctrine we preach is the doctrine of grace, which is the doctrine of Christ. Those things which become sound doctrine are those things that are consistent with and honouring to the gospel: Divine Sovereignty, Effectual, Substitutionary Redemption, Satisfaction by the Blood of Christ, Ruin by the Fall, Redemption by the Blood, Regeneration by the Holy Spirit.

Specifically, gospel preachers are responsible to pointedly apply the gospel to the daily affairs and responsibilities of men and women in this world. It is a pastor's responsibility to faithfully teach people how to live in this world for the glory of Christ, applying the Word of God to every area of life. It is the responsibility of God's saints to personally obey the gospel, applying it to every area of their lives.

I realize that many people prefer to ignore this fact; but it is a fact nonetheless. God Almighty does interfere with people's lives. If the God of glory is pleased to open the windows of heaven and drop his saving grace into our hearts, he takes over. He insists on it. Christ will either be Lord of all or he will not receive you at all. This is what Paul teaches in verses 2-10. The apostle has a word here for just about everyone.

Aged men: 'That the aged men be sober, grave, temperate, sound in faith, in charity, in patience' (v. 2).

Aged women: 'The aged women likewise, that they be in behaviour as becometh holiness, not false accusers, not given to much wine, teachers of good things; That they may teach the young women to be sober, to love their husbands, to love their children' (vv. 3-4).

Young women: 'To be discreet, chaste, keepers at home, good, obedient to their own husbands, that the word of God be not blasphemed' (v. 5).

Young men: 'Young men likewise exhort to be sober minded' (v. 6).

Pastors: 'In all things showing thyself a pattern of good works: in doctrine showing uncorruptness, gravity, sincerity, Sound speech, that cannot be condemned; that he that is of the contrary part may be ashamed, having no evil thing to say of you' (vv. 7-8).

Employees: 'Exhort servants to be obedient unto their own masters, and to please them well in all things; not answering again; Not purloining, but showing all good fidelity; that they may adorn the doctrine of God our Saviour in all things' (vv. 9-10).

The Holy Spirit here calls for all who believe the gospel of the grace of God to adorn it, to show forth the beauty and grace of the gospel in all things for the glory of God (1 Corinthians 10:31). If we are indeed born of God, if we truly are believers, if we have really experienced the grace of God, we know that grace teaches us so to live.

The Work of Grace
'For the grace of God that bringeth salvation hath appeared to all men' (v. 11). As Paul uses the phrase, 'the grace of God', in this place he is referring to 'the doctrine of God our Saviour'. 'The grace of God' in this verse means 'the gospel of the grace of God'. The gospel we preach, 'the doctrine of God our Saviour', is 'the gospel of the grace of God'.

The doctrine of the gospel is the message of grace; not freewill, not works, not grace and works, but grace alone. Grace is the origin of the gospel. Grace is the message of the gospel. Grace is conveyed by the gospel (1 John 1:1; 1 Peter 1:23-25). Grace is the rule of the gospel (Romans 6:12-14; 2 Corinthians 5:14-15).

This gospel, the grace of God, brings salvation. Salvation is by God's sovereign, omnipotent operations of grace. It is an act and work of grace that is almighty and irresistible. In this context 'the grace of God' is used as a synonym for 'the gospel of God'. The Holy Spirit is telling us that the gospel is the means by which salvation is brought to and wrought in chosen, redeemed sinners. The gospel of the grace of God shows us the way of salvation. It proclaims the person and work of Christ, who is salvation. It is the announcement of salvation accomplished by Christ. The gospel of the grace of God is the means by which God the Holy Spirit brings salvation to elect sinners (Romans 10:13-17). No sinner is given life, faith, and salvation in Christ apart from the preaching of the gospel.

This gospel of the grace of God has appeared unto all men. Certainly, Paul does not mean for us to understand that every person in the world has heard the gospel. Obviously, that is not so. There are many who have never heard the gospel. What Paul is telling us is that the gospel has been and is preached freely to all men and women, people of every rank, race, and region (Romans 16:25-26). God has his elect among all people. It is our responsibility to preach the gospel to all men (Matthew 28:19-20). We are assured that the gospel we preach brings salvation to all who believe. 'It is the power of God unto salvation to everyone that believeth' (Romans 1:16).

The Teaching of Grace
'Teaching us that, denying ungodliness and worldly lusts, we should live soberly, righteously, and godly, in this present world' (v. 12). Whenever the gospel of the grace of God comes into a sinner's heart by the life giving, regenerating power and grace of God the Holy Spirit, it effectually teaches him some things.

The grace of God does not simply give out the lesson and leave it to us to get the lesson. Grace sees to it that we get the lesson. It teaches us to whom we must look for eternal life (Isaiah 45:22), what we must believe (Galatians 1:6-9), and how to live in this world.

The gospel is not given for intellectual speculation, but for practical direction. It is given for our eternal salvation and for the ordering of our lives. It tells us plainly what we are to do and what we are not to do. It tells us what to follow and what to shun.

The grace of God effectually teaches saved sinners to deny ungodliness and worldly lusts. The gospel teaches us to say 'No' to unbelief and the neglect of God. It teaches us to love and value his Word, his worship, and his will. It teaches us to say 'No' to worldly lusts, sensuality, covetousness, ambition, and the desire for recognition and praise. The grace of God teaches people to live right. It teaches us to live soberly (with temperance and moderation) with respect to ourselves, righteously (doing what is right) with respect to others, and godly with respect to God, worshipping him in the totality of our lives (Romans 12:1-2; 1 Corinthians 6:19-20).

The Expectation of Grace

'Looking for that blessed hope, and the glorious appearing of the great God and our Saviour Jesus Christ' (v. 13). Paul does not tell us to set dates, or even to speculate about when the time of our Lord's coming may be. He does not tell us to look for signs of the end time, or to even think about when the end time may be. Grace teaches us to look for Christ himself, and to do so in faith and expectation. Grace gives us a good, well-grounded hope, a hope that breeds anticipation and desire.

There is one common and blessed hope for all believers. There is not one hope for one group or catagory of believer, and another hope for another group. We all have the same hope, upon the same ground. It is a glorious, blessed hope, a hope that no mortal eye has seen, no mortal ear has heard, and no natural mind has imagined. The basis of our hope is grace, free grace through a crucified Substitute (Ephesians 1:18). The thing hoped for is glory with Christ. It is the design of the gospel to set our hearts upon the hope laid up for us with Christ in heaven, not upon the things of this world (Matthew 6:33; Colossians 3:1-4).

> Fade, fade each earthly joy, Jesus is mine.
> Break every tender tie, Jesus is mine!
> Dark is this wilderness,
> Earth has no resting place
> Jesus alone can bless. Jesus is mine!
>
> Farewell, mortality, Jesus is mine!
> Welcome, eternity, Jesus is mine!
> Welcome, oh loved and blest!
> Welcome sweet scenes of rest!
> Welcome my Saviour's breast! Jesus is mine!

Our hope of eternal glory with Christ, if we trust him, is a well-grounded hope. Our Father promised it (Titus 1:2). Our Saviour purchased it (Hebrews 9:12). Our Substitute possesses it (Hebrews 6:20). We have the earnest of it (Ephesians 1:14). In Christ we are worthy of it (Colossians 1:12). Our blessedness will be attained when Christ, who is our hope, appears. Notice how Paul describes our Saviour. He appears unable to find words worthy of him. Jesus Christ is 'the great God'. He is the great God and 'our Saviour'. Soon, this great God, who is our Saviour, 'shall appear'. Then, 'we also shall appear with him in glory' (Colossians 3:4). This is the expectation of grace (1 John 3:1-3).

The Motivation of Grace

Paul is calling for us, in every aspect of our lives, to 'adorn the doctrine of God our Saviour'. How does he induce us to obey his admonition? How does he persuade us? How does he motivate us? He does not threaten us with punishment or loss of reward. He does not entice us with promises of rewards, or higher degrees of glory in heaven. There are no higher decrees of salvation! Rather, the apostle induces us to love and serve our great God and Saviour, to seek in all things to honour him, simply by reminding us of what he has done for us by his matchless grace. 'Who gave himself for us, that he might redeem us from all iniquity, and purify unto himself a peculiar people, zealous of good works' (v. 14). Christ loved us and gave himself for us, that he might redeem and deliver us from all iniquity, from all sin and all the consequences of it, that he might purify us (by blood and by grace) unto himself a peculiar people, zealous of good works.

God's saints are a peculiar people. We are loved with a peculiar love, objects of God's peculiar delight, blessed with peculiar blessings, supplied with peculiar provisions, and separated from the world by peculiar grace (1 Corinthians 4:7). The word 'peculiar' means 'distinctively excellent, valuable, and honourable'. We are Christ's portion, his bride (Ruth 4:6-10), the lot of his inheritance, the jewels of his crown, his fulness (Ephesians 1:23), his peculiar people.

Christ's peculiar people are made, by the grace of God, to be zealous of good works. God the Father ordained that we should walk in good works (Ephesians 2:10). God the Son redeemed us that we should walk in good works. God the Holy Spirit effectually teaches every chosen, ransomed sinner to be zealous of good works. The gospel teaches us to 'maintain good works' (3:8). Let us, therefore, 'learn to maintain good works', not for salvation, not for justification, not to make ourselves more holy and acceptable to God, but 'for necessary uses' (3:14), that we may honour our great God and Saviour and the gospel of his grace in all things, not being unfruitful.

This is Paul's admonition to Titus; and this is the Word of God the Holy Spirit to every preacher of the gospel. 'These things speak, and exhort, and rebuke with all authority. Let no man despise thee'. He is to declare the doctrine of the gospel, pointedly applying it to every area of life. The pastor is to exhort, to press with earnestness the claims of Christ upon his people. He is responsible to 'rebuke', too, to reprove all who neglect, oppose, contradict, and deny these things, these doctrines and duties of grace. He must do so 'with all authority', speaking as he does in God's name, with God's authority, and with God's approval. Then, Paul says, 'Let no man despise thee'. The preacher must give no one reason to despise him because of his conduct. When people despise him because of the gospel he preaches, he is to have no regard for the opinions of disobedient men. Paul shows us by his own example what he means in 1 Corinthians 4:1-3.

A Re-enforcement
    In chapter 3 Paul gives a re-enforcement to all that he has said in chapter 2. Why? Because these things need to be constantly pressed upon our hearts. 'Whether therefore ye eat, or drink, or whatsoever ye do, do all to the glory of God' (1 Corinthians 10:31). In all things Paul urges us to honour our God and the gospel of his grace, reminding us to even be gentle in our dealings with the base and the wicked, remembering that we were once exactly as they are.
    'Put them in mind to be subject to principalities and powers, to obey magistrates, to be ready to every good work, To speak evil of no man, to be no brawlers, but gentle, showing all meekness unto all men. For we ourselves also were sometimes foolish, disobedient, deceived, serving divers lusts and pleasures, living in malice and envy, hateful, and hating one another' (vv. 1-3).

Our Motivation
    Then, once more, he motivates us to heed these tremendous admonitions, contrary as they are to human flesh, by reminding us of what our God has done for us in Christ by his matchless grace. Always, he uses grace, never the whip of the law, to motivate God's people.
    'But after that the kindness and love of God our Saviour toward man appeared, Not by works of righteousness which we have done, but according to his mercy he saved us, by the washing of regeneration, and renewing of the Holy Ghost; Which he shed on us abundantly through Jesus Christ our Saviour; That being justified by his grace, we should be made heirs according to the hope of eternal life' (vv. 4-7).

Discovering Christ In All The Scriptures

The question is often asked, 'If you do not preach the law, how do you get people to live right, to do what they ought to do?' The answer is, 'Preach up Christ and free grace. It is the grace of God that brings salvation, and that alone, that effectually teaches all who have experienced it to say no to ungodliness and worldly lusts, and to live soberly, righteously, and godly in this present world'. This is certain. If the whip of the law can get a person to do what the grace of God does not inspire him to do, he has simply never known the grace of God.

That makes all 'contentions and strivings about the law' unprofitable and vain (v. 9). Those who persistently refuse to heed these things, who will not cease from legalism, who will not give up their own righteousness, trusting Christ alone as Jehovah-tsidkenu, 'The Lord our Righteousness' (Jeremiah 23:6), are heretics who are condemned by their own doctrine.

There is no motive to godliness like the assurance of free salvation, complete redemption, and perfect righteousness in Christ by the grace of God (Jeremiah 23:6; 33:16; 50:20; 1 Corinthians 6:9-11, 19-20). 'This is a faithful saying, and these things I will that thou affirm constantly, that they which have believed in God might be careful to maintain good works. These things are good and profitable unto men' (3:8).

Chapter 57

Philemon

'Put That On My Account'

The book of Philemon is a personal letter written by Paul while he was a prisoner at Rome to a man at Colosse by the name of Philemon. It is a personal letter, dealing with a very personal matter; but it was written by divine inspiration to teach us things concerning our Lord Jesus Christ and the gospel of God's free grace in him.

Paul wrote to Philemon, a believer in Christ, about one of his slaves, Onesimus, who had robbed Philemon then run away to Rome. While in Rome, Onesimus came into contact with Paul, heard the gospel, and was converted by the grace of God. After his conversion, Paul sent Onesimus back to Philemon with this letter urging Philemon to receive Onesimus as his brother in Christ, just as he would receive Paul himself, assuring him that he would gladly pay whatever Onesimus owed him.

'I beseech thee for my son Onesimus, whom I have begotten in my bonds: Which in time past was to thee unprofitable, but now profitable to thee and to me: Whom I have sent again: thou therefore receive him, that is, mine own bowels: Whom I would have retained with me, that in thy stead he might have ministered unto me in the bonds of the gospel: But without thy mind would I do nothing; that thy benefit should not be as it were of necessity, but willingly. For perhaps he therefore departed for a season, that thou shouldest receive him for ever; Not now as a servant, but above a servant, a brother beloved, specially to me, but how much more unto thee, both in the flesh, and in the Lord? If thou count me therefore a partner, receive him as myself. If he hath wronged thee, or oweth thee ought, put that on mine account' (vv. 10-18).

The story we have before us in this short epistle is a beautiful picture of what the Lord Jesus does for every chosen, redeemed sinner. He has paid our debt, all that we owed to the law and justice of God. He intercedes for us with God, against whom we have sinned, from whom we have gone astray. Our blessed Saviour said to the offended justice and inflexible law of God, regarding all his people and our sins, 'put that on mine account', and, with his one great sacrifice for sin as our substitute, he paid our debt. Because Christ is our Mediator, Substitute, and Surety, because all God's elect are one with him, the Father receives and accepts every believing sinner as he receives and accepts Christ himself (Ephesians 1:6).

Philemon

Philemon was a truly gracious man. 'Hearing of thy love and faith, which thou hast toward the Lord Jesus, and toward all saints' (v. 5). He maintained a church in his house (v. 2). He loved Christ and his people (v. 7). He was a benevolent friend to the Apostle Paul. He treated his servants kindly and graciously. Paul was confident that he would be obedient to the word of God, the word of God sent to Philemon by his servant Paul (v. 21).

Onesimus

Onesimus was a slave Philemon had come to trust. He had given Onesimus charge over at least some of his household goods. He trusted his treasures to the care of this slave as a steward. But Onesimus betrayed his master's trust. Knowing his guilt and fearing his master's wrath, Onesimus ran away to Rome. There he must have hoped to lose himself in the crowded streets among the vagabonds and street people. Then, by one means or another, in God's good providence Onesimus was brought into that room where God's servant, Paul, was a prisoner. He heard Paul preach the gospel of God's saving grace in Christ; and this poor runaway slave was arrested by God's omnipotent grace, converted by the power of his Spirit, born again by the 'word of God' (1 Peter 1:23), and made to be a believer, a child of God.

Nevertheless, Onesimus still belonged to Philemon. He was a wanted man. His master had a lawful right to have him executed. The only right thing for this slave to do was to return to his master and hope that he would be gracious.

The Picture

What a picture the Lord here gives us of his amazing grace! We who are now converted by God's omnipotent mercy were once just like Onesimus. We went astray from the womb speaking lies (Psalm 58:3). We robbed God, or attempted to, of his glory as God. We despised him and his goodness; but we still belonged to God. If we had what we deserved, we would have perished under his wrath. It would be lawful, righteous, and just for the holy Lord God to slay us in his fury. Our only hope was and continues to be, his mercy. Fleeing to him for mercy, pleading for mercy in Christ, he received us graciously in Christ, for Christ's sake, even as he receives Christ.

Sinner

All men belong to God. We are his property. It is right for him to do with us whatever he will (Matthew 20:15). The unbelieving sinner belongs to God. Though he refuses to acknowledge it, he is God's property. He is a wanted man. Justice cries out for his execution. It would be lawful, righteous, and just for God to slay him. But, if he pleases, he can have mercy upon him. The only thing for the sinner to do is to go to God, confessing his guilt and sin, pleading the merits of God's own dear Son, the Lord Jesus Christ, and hope that he will be gracious.

> Come, humble sinner, in whose breast
> A thousand thoughts revolve,
> Come, with your guilt and fear oppressed,
> And make this last resolve.

> 'I'll go to Jesus, though my sin
> Hath like a mountain rose:
> I know His courts I'll enter in,
> Whatever may oppose.

> Prostrate, I'll lie before His throne,
> And there my guilt confess.
> I'll tell Him I'm a wretch undone
> Without His sovereign grace.

> I'll to the gracious King approach,
> Whose sceptre pardon gives.
> Perhaps He may command my touch,
> And then the suppliant lives.

Perhaps He will admit my plea,
Perhaps will hear my prayer;
But if I perish I will pray
And perish only there.

I can but perish if I go,
I am resolved to try;
For if I stay away I know,
I must forever die.

But if I die with mercy sought,
When I the King have tried,
This were to die, (delightful thought!)
As sinner never died!

Once Onesimus was converted, the Apostle Paul took down his pen and paper, and by the inspiration of God the Holy Spirit, he wrote this little epistle to Philemon with his own hand, with the hope of both preserving Onesimus' life and making reconciliation between Onesimus and Philemon.

Christian Love
Here is an example of true Christian love (v. 5). Indeed, there is no true love in the hearts of men except Christian love, the love that Christ gives to and creates in his saints by his grace. Paul showed great love in his regard for Onesimus. He took this degraded, loathsome creature in. Once he had been converted by the grace of God, Paul regarded him and treated him as his own son. Onesimus and Timothy were very different men before they were converted. Timothy was a moral, upright young man, one who believed God from his youth. Onesimus was the offscouring of society. After they were converted, they were both equal in Paul's eyes. This is a lovely picture of Christ's regard for his brethren. In Christ there is no such thing as rank. In Christ our past is irrelevant.

Philemon showed great brotherly love in his reception of Onesimus. Though Philemon had been greatly wronged by this man, he received him again into his household, freely forgiving him the wrong he had done (Matthew 6:14-15; Ephesians 4:32).

If God forgives us, surely we ought to forgive one another. If Christ receives us, surely we ought to receive one another. This kind of love is the law that rules God's elect. It is the principle by which saved people live (John 13:34-35).

Substitutionary Redemption

Here is an example of substitutionary redemption. Onesimus had wronged Philemon. He had betrayed his master's trust, despised his master's goodness, and stolen his master's goods. Onesimus owed much to Philemon. But Paul says, 'If thou count me therefore a partner, receive him as myself. If he hath wronged thee, or oweth thee ought, put that on mine account' (vv. 17-18). That is exactly what the Lord Jesus Christ has done for us (Isaiah 53:4-10).

Divine Forgiveness

Here is an example of divine forgiveness. Paul says, 'If thou count me therefore a partner, receive him as myself' (v. 17). Onesimus was forgiven through the intercession of another. He was accepted, not as a slave, but as a brother, an equal. Furthermore, he was accepted because of another. The God of Glory receives every sinner who trusts his dear Son as he receives Christ himself. We are 'accepted in the Beloved'. We have been forgiven through the intercession of Christ. We have been accepted as the sons of God, in every way equal to Christ in God's sight (1 John 3:1). We have been accepted because of another, accepted because of the Lord Jesus Christ, and accepted as Christ is accepted.

> Near, so very near to God,
> Nearer I cannot be,
> For in the Person of His Son
> I am as near as He!
>
> Dear, so very dear to God,
> Dearer I cannot be,
> For in the Person of His Son
> I am as dear as He!

Wondrous Grace

Perhaps the thing that stands out most beautifully in the book of Philemon is the picture it gives us of God's wondrous, amazing, irresistible grace. In the case of Onesimus, we see clear evidence that the grace of God is always effectual and irresistible, and can never be thwarted in its purpose. Grace is not merely God's will to save. Grace is God's act of saving. In the matter of salvation grace is always first! The grace of God always takes the initiative in salvation.

Grace first contrived the way
To save rebellious man;
And all the steps that grace display
Which drew the wondrous plan.

Grace first inscribed my name
In God's eternal book:
'Twas grace that gave me to the Lamb,
Who all my sorrows took.

Onesimus was the object of sovereign election. This poor slave did not know it, but he was the chosen object of God's eternal, electing love. He was not worthy of God's love. He did not desire God's love. He did not seek God's love.

Nevertheless, he was loved of God from eternity. God had said concerning Onesimus, 'I will be his God and he shall be my son'. And so it came to pass. God passed by many slaves who were just like Onesimus, and chose him. The Lord God passed by many men and women at Colosse who were far nobler than Onesimus, and chose him.

As a general rule, the most unworthy of the unworthy, the most loathsome of the loathsome, the most useless of the useless, the most vile of the vile are the objects of God's grace (1 Corinthians 1:26-29; Jeremiah 31:3). What are you, and what am I, that God should be merciful to us? Let us never forget where we were, who we were, and what we were when the grace of God found us and called us by his grace (1 Corinthians 1:26-28; 6:9-11; Isaiah 51:1).

Sovereign Grace

Be sure you understand this. The grace of God is always sovereign (Romans 9:15-16). Man has no claim upon the grace of God. God is in no way obliged to show anyone his mercy. He can save us if he will, or he can damn us if he will. It is entirely up to him. God is not in our hands. We are in God's hands.

The Lord God is sovereign. He does as it pleases him. God chooses some, and passes by others (Romans 9:11-13). God sent his Son to redeem some, but not others (John 10:11, 15, 26). God sends the gospel to some, and refuses to send it to others (Acts 16:6-13). God sends his Spirit to call some, and leaves the rest to their own chosen darkness and ignorance (Acts 13:48, see also Amos 3:2). This is God's right as God. Believers gladly submit to his total, absolute sovereignty (Romans 9:18-21).

Mortals, be dumb; what creature dares
Dispute His sovereign will?
Ask no account of His affairs,
But tremble and be still.
Just like His nature is His grace,
All sovereign, and all free;
Great God, how searchless are Thy ways,
How deep thy judgments be!

The grace of God sought Onesimus. Onesimus did not seek God. God sought Onesimus. Onesimus was not looking for the Lord. The Lord was looking for Onesimus. Onesimus did not want grace. Grace wanted Onesimus. Onesimus did not come to grace. Grace came to Onesimus. Onesimus did not find the Lord. The Lord found Onesimus. The name of God's church is 'Sought Out' (Isaiah 62:12). The Lord God declares, 'I am found of them that sought me not' (Isaiah 65:1).

Modern religion says to the sinner, 'You take the first step, and God will do the rest'. God says to the sinner, "Without me, ye can do nothing'. You have no ability and no will to come to me. I will come and be gracious to whom I will be gracious'. Grace always takes the initiative in salvation. God chose us; we did not choose him. God gave us life; we did not give life to ourselves. God sought us; we did not seek him. God came to us; we did not come to him. Josiah Conder wrote,

'Tis not that I did choose Thee,
For, Lord, that could not be,
This heart would still refuse Thee,
Hadst Thou not chosen me.
Thou from the sin that stained me
Hast cleansed and set me free,
Of old Thou hast ordained me,
That I should live to Thee.

'Twas sovereign mercy called me,
And taught my opening mind;
The world had else enthralled me,
To heavenly glories blind:
My heart owns none above Thee,
For Thy rich grace I thirst;
This knowing, if I love Thee,
Thou must have loved me first.

Prevenient Grace

Grace is always on time. It is never before time, and it is never behind time, but always on time. The grace of God rules and overrules all things to accomplish its purpose (Psalm 76:10; John 17:1-2; Romans 8:28). Onesimus had no right to rob his master and runaway; but God was pleased to make use of Onesimus's sin to accomplish his conversion. In the wise arrangement of divine providence, Onesimus's evil deed brought him to the place where God was determined to be gracious to him (Psalm 76:10). 'For perhaps he therefore departed for a season, that thou shouldest receive him for ever' (v. 15).

Onesimus did exactly what he wanted to do. He freely exercised his 'free-will' and chose the path of wickedness. Still, God had a hand in the whole affair. This is what the old writers used to call prevenient grace, grace that goes before and prepares the way for grace (Acts 2:23; 4:27-28; 13:29).

Onesimus madly ran the sinful course of his own 'freewill'. Had not the Lord God sovereignly intervened, this man's actions would surely have brought him to ruin and to hell. But God's purpose of grace could not and would not be overturned. Onesimus must come to Rome. Onesimus must hear the gospel from Paul's lips, hear it at precisely the time he heard it, in the place where he heard it, and in the exact circumstances in which he heard it. That meant that Paul and Onesimus had to be brought to Rome at the same time, at 'the time of love' (Ezekiel 16:8) the Lord God had ordained for Onesimus from eternity.

How will it all happen? The Lord God called the old serpent, Satan, into his service. Satan is not God's rival, but his devil. He is not a wild beast out of control, but a conquered lion on the chain of omnipotence. Satan is under the total dominion of God our Saviour (Revelation 20:1-3). Satan tempted Onesimus, just at the right time, and persuaded him to steal his master's goods. At about the same time, he led an angry mob to have Paul arrested at Jerusalem. Having robbed his master, Onesimus was filled with fear and fled to Rome. Paul, too, is en route to Rome, as a prisoner. At last, on the appointed day, through many apparently random events, Onesimus comes before Paul, and Paul preaches the gospel to him in the power of the Holy Spirit. Onesimus is converted.

God almighty, when he intends to be gracious to a sinner, always brings the sinner, whom he has chosen, to the preacher, whom he has chosen, to receive the good news (Romans 10:14-17). Perhaps Onesimus had been arrested. Perhaps he came to Paul for help. We are not told. But Onesimus and Paul meet face to face at the appointed time, in the appointed place, for the appointed purpose. It is still true ...

God moves in a mysterious way
His wonders to perform;
He plants His footsteps in the sea,
And rides upon the storm.

Deep in unfathomable mines
Of never failing skill,
He treasures up His vast designs
And works His sovereign will.

Here is a word of comfort and encouragement for you whose sons and daughters break your hearts through their rebellion and waywardness. Sometimes this is God's appointed way of grace. It is far better to lose them for a season and gain them for eternity, than to keep them at home in self-righteousness and to lose them for eternity. The chosen sinner must, by one means or another, be brought down; and God knows exactly the best way to bring his own down before him (Psalm 107:1-43). The wise thing for us to do is to humbly submit to the wise and good will of our God. 'It is the Lord, let him do what seemeth him good'.

Are you not glad to know that the grace of God rules and overrules all things to accomplish its purpose? Grace is always on time.

Successful Grace

The grace of God is always successful. Grace cannot be defeated. Grace cannot be thwarted. Grace cannot be overturned. Grace cannot be resisted. God had chosen Onesimus, and Onesimus must be saved. Grace preserved him, provided for him, protected him, and led him all the days of his life, even in his rebellion (Hebrews 1:14; Hosea 2:8; Jude 1). And at the appointed time, grace conquered Onesimus' heart (Ezekiel 16:3-8).

By the power of God's grace, Onesimus was made a new man in Christ. Behold the wondrous, transforming power of the grace of our God! He who was an unprofitable wretch, a common thief, was transformed into a profitable servant of God and a profitable servant among men. Grace changes a man's character, and grace changes his behaviour; at home, at work, in all things! Rowland Hill once said, 'I would not give half a penny for a man's piety if his dog and cat were not better off after he is converted'.

The grace of God is efficacious. It gloriously achieves what it is sent to do. The grace of God is successful. It is always successful (Romans 8:29-30). The good Shepherd goes seeking his sheep. He never gives up the search until he finds his sheep. He always fetches his sheep home.

God Honouring

Grace honours God. Grace always gives God the glory. This is the reason why God does things the way he does them, so that we might be 'to the praise of the glory of his grace ... to the praise of his glory who first trusted in Christ' (Ezekiel 16:62-63; Ephesians 1:3-14). 'Salvation is of the Lord'. It was the Lord God who chose Onesimus, who redeemed him, sought him, called him, gave him life and faith in Christ, and who kept him.

Gives Hope

Grace gives us hope. The grace of God is a door of hope for perishing sinners. The God of all grace is he that 'delighteth in mercy'. Let all who need grace come to the throne of grace to obtain mercy and find grace to help in time of need (Hebrews 4:16). Oh, what a difference grace makes in the lives of sinners! It is grace alone that makes the difference. 'For who maketh thee to differ from another? and what hast thou that thou didst not receive? now if thou didst receive it, why dost thou glory, as if thou hadst not received it?' (1 Corinthians 4:7).

Chapter 58

Hebrews

Christ is Better

The Psalmist David, speaking prophetically of Christ's great accomplishments as our Saviour, sang, 'His glory is great in thy salvation: honour and majesty hast thou laid upon him. For thou hast made him most blessed for ever' (Psalm 21:5-6). In the book of Hebrews the Holy Spirit tells us something of the great glory of our God and Saviour, the Lord Jesus Christ. In the opening words of this magnificent epistle we see that this is the theme of the book.

'God, who at sundry times and in divers manners spake in time past unto the fathers by the prophets, Hath in these last days spoken unto us by his Son, whom he hath appointed heir of all things, by whom also he made the worlds; Who being the brightness of his glory, and the express image of his person, and upholding all things by the word of his power, when he had by himself purged our sins, sat down on the right hand of the Majesty on high; Being made so much better than the angels, as he hath by inheritance obtained a more excellent name than they' (1:1-4).

Truly his glory is great in salvation

We are not told who wrote this epistle, when it was written, or to whom it was written. It was obviously written to men and women of

Jewish ancestry who were born of God; but we have no indication where they were located. This lack of information is not accidental. God the Holy Spirit, whose Word this is, intended for every person who picks it up and reads it to read it as God's Word specifically to him.

These Jewish believers, being constantly pressured by family and friends to go back to their former religion, to go back to Judaism, needed encouragement to remain stedfast, to 'hold fast the confidence and the rejoicing of hope firm unto the end' (3:6). As with the saints at Galatia, Judaisers were trying to get these Hebrew belivers to go back to the Mosaic law, back to Jewish ritualism, back to empty, meaningless religious activity, to give up the way of life and faith in Christ. Everywhere, on every side, they were harassed, pressured, and persecuted for the gospel's sake and because they had abandoned the religion of their father's and trusted Christ alone for righteousness with God.

In a word, they faced the same pressures God's saints face in all places and in all ages. This epistle was written by divine inspiration to God's saints everywhere. It is intended to draw forth steadfast devotion to Christ, by showing us his great glory in salvation.

Christ's Work

As we read these 13 chapters we should not be at all surprised to see that the focus of the entire epistle is the glorious salvation which the Lord Jesus Christ, the Son of God, has accomplished. We are reminded of four great facts about Christ and his work as our Mediator throughout this epistle.

First, everything that the Lord Jesus Christ did for us as our Substitute and Saviour he did by himself, alone (1:3; 2:14, 18; 7:27; 9:12-14, 25-26; 12:3).

There was none to help him. He purged our sins by himself, offered himself, gave himself, and obtained eternal redemption for us by himself. His glory is great in salvation precisely because it is his work alone.

Second, everything that the Lord Jesus Christ did for us, as our Substitute and Saviour, he did just once (7:27; 9:12, 26-28; 10:10).

There was no need for anything he did to be done twice. Once was enough. He lived once. He obeyed once. He brought in righteousness once. He died once. He arose once. He obtained eternal redemption once. Once is enough.

Third, everything the Son of God did as the God-man our Saviour, our Substitute, everything he did for the salvation of God's elect, he did for us all alike (2:9; 6:20; 9:12; 10:10, 20; 11:40).

He tasted death for us all (2:9). The Son of God died to bring all God's elect to glory. He entered into heaven for us as a forerunner (6:20). He sanctified every sinner for whom he died by his blood, and perfected us all forever by his once for all sacrifice on our behalf (10:10, 14). The Lord Jesus has made a way for us all to approach and find acceptance with God (10:20). All God's elect, every sinner in the universe who believes on the Lord Jesus Christ, shall obtain the same eternal inheritance in Christ (11:40). Abraham, Isaac, and Jacob, Peter, James, and John, Paul, and you, and I shall all be made perfect together.

Fourth, everything that our Saviour did for our salvation, he did perfectly. Nothing needs to be, and nothing can be, added to it (10:10-14).

The Lord Jesus Christ is the perfect God, the perfect Man, the perfect Son, the perfect priest, the perfect Sacrifice, the perfect Altar, the perfect Tabernacle, the perfect Captain of our Salvation, and the perfect Surety. He has 'perfected for ever them that are sanctified!'

Because everything he did, he did perfectly, and because he is the perfect God-man, because all that he did, he did as our Representative, Substitute, and Surety, everything he did is of infinite value and efficacy.

That simply means everything he did has everlasting consequence. It is forever (1:8; 5:6; 6:20; 7:17, 21; 10:12-14; 13:20). His throne is forever. His priesthood is forever. He has perfected and sanctified his people forever. His covenant is an everlasting covenant.

God-man

Nowhere in scripture is our Saviour's eternal deity and glorious humanity more clearly set forth than in the first two chapters of Hebrews. Remember, the purpose of this epistle is to show forth the greatness of Christ's glory in the accomplishment of our salvation and to encourage us to remain steadfast in the confidence of our faith in him. What better way could this goal be accomplished than by reminding us at the outset that he who is our Saviour is both God and man in one glorious person? Because he is a man like us in all things, sin alone excepted, he is able to understand all our needs. Because he is God over all, he is able to meet all our needs.

Central Doctrine

The central doctrine of this epistle is Christ's eternal priesthood and his finished, efficacious sacrifice for the redemption and salvation of his people. The book of Hebrews stresses the infinite importance and efficacious power of Christ's sin-atoning blood in obtaining eternal redemption for us, in purging the conscience, and in opening to us the heavenly sanctuary.

Better

The key word in the book of Hebrews is 'better' (1:4; 6:9; 7:7, 19, 22; 8:6; 9:23; 10:34; 11:16, 35, 40; 12:24). One purpose of this book is to show us that Christ is 'better' than all who came before him. He is better than the prophets, better than the angels, better than Moses, better than Joshua, and better than Aaron.

He is Surety of a better covenant, established upon better promises, giving a better hope. Christ our Saviour is better than the tabernacle, the altar, and the mercy-seat. He is a better Sacrifice, offering better blood, giving us a better access to and better standing before the holy Lord God. In all things Christ is better than all others. He is infinitely better. He is the best!

Better than the Prophets

Christ is better than the prophets (1:1-4). Each of the prophets gave us a partial revelation of God and his purpose. Reading the prophets and studying their messages, we leave each one thinking (as they intended), 'This is not the final word. There is more to be revealed'. Christ is the perfect, complete, full, and final revelation of God.

The prophets were mere messengers. Christ is the Message. The prophets were mere men. Christ is the Creator, Ruler, Redeemer, and Saviour of men. The prophets were sinners in need of atonement. Christ is atonement. By his one sacrifice, 'he purged our sins' and 'sat down on the right hand of the Majesty on high', because his work was finished and accepted.

Better than the Angels

Christ is better than the angels (1:4-2:18). The angels are creatures of God. He is the Son of God (v. 5). The angels were commanded of God to worship the Lord Jesus Christ, his incarnate Son, as God, even in his humiliation as he came into the world (v. 6). God never commanded an angel to sit with him on his throne; but he said to his Son, when he had finished his work of redemption as our Substitute, 'Sit thou on my right hand, until I make thine enemies thy footstool' (vv. 7-13). Christ is one with the Father, in every way his equal. But the angels are 'all ministering spirits, sent forth to minister for them who shall be heirs of salvation' (v. 14).

They minister for those who shall be the heirs of salvation; but Christ is our Saviour (2:6-18). He visited the earth in human flesh, made a little lower than the angels, that he might taste death for all his elect (referred to by the words 'every man' in verse 9). His elect are every man numbered among the many sons he shall bring to glory (v. 10). His elect are those who are sanctified by him, whom he calls brethren (v. 11). His elect are the children the Father gave him to redeem and save (v. 13). His elect, the every man for whom he tasted death, are the seed of Abraham, on whom he took hold to redeem and save (v. 16).

Better than Moses
Christ is better than Moses (3:1-19). Moses, of course, represents the law of God. He was a servant in the house. Christ is Builder and the Master of the house. God's elect, his church and kingdom, are his house (3:6). In this house Moses was a servant for a season. But Moses could not bring the children of Israel into the land of promise because he represented the law, and the law cannot save. It cannot give rest. Moses had to die in the wilderness. Joshua was raised up to take his place and to lead Israel into Canaan, into the land of rest. But Joshua, too, was but a man typical of Christ.

Better than Joshua
Christ is better than Joshua (4:1-16). As Joshua brought Israel into the typical land of promise, the land of blessedness, bounty, and rest, so the Lord Jesus Christ brings God's elect into rest by his omnipotent grace. As Israel's enemies were conquered by the hand of God in Joshua's day, so our enemies were conquered by God our Saviour, our Joshua, the Lord Jesus Christ (Colossians 2:13-15).

Better than the Sabbath
Christ is better than the sabbath (4:9-11). The Old Testament sabbath was, like everything else in Old Testament worship, typical of Christ who is our true Sabbath. The sabbath rest of faith in Christ was typified by God ceasing from his works of creation and resting on the seventh day, and in Israel resting in Canaan. As the Lord God ceased from his works, sinners enter into rest when they cease from their works and trust Christ alone for acceptance with God. Just as surely as Christ our Substitute has entered into his rest in glory, there is a vast multitude of sinners in this world who must also enter into his rest. They must enter in because God ordained it, and because Christ has obtained it for us.

Better than Aaron

Christ is better than Aaron (4:14-7:28). Beginning at the end of chapter 4 and going through chapter 7, the Holy Spirit tells us that the Lord Jesus Christ is our great High Priest, and that he is a Priest better than Aaron, with a better priesthood than Aaron's typical priesthood in Israel.

'Seeing then that we have a great high priest, that is passed into the heavens, Jesus the Son of God, let us hold fast our profession. For we have not an high priest which cannot be touched with the feeling of our infirmities; but was in all points tempted like as we are, yet without sin. Let us therefore come boldly unto the throne of grace, that we may obtain mercy, and find grace to help in time of need' (4:14-16).

All Aaron could do was offer typical sacrifices and make ceremonial cleansings. Christ is a better Priest. His work is neither typical nor ceremonial, but real and sure. He is a Priest who is able to save and save to the uttermost all who come to God by him. He who is our Priest is the omnipotent Lion of the tribe of Judah (7:11-27). If our Lord, who came not from the tribe of Levi but from the tribe of Judah, was to be our High Priest, 'there is made of necessity a change also of the law' (7:12). The law regarding these things was disannulled because of its weakness and unprofitableness (7:18; Romans 8:4).

The Lord Jesus Christ could not be our great High Priest before God, except the Levitical law which required the priests to be of the tribe of Levi be set aside and be made of no effect. That legal system under which the Jews lived and worshipped God in the Old Testament was only temporary and typical. Once Christ came and fulfilled it in its entirety, he put and end to the typical, Levitical system altogether (Romans 10:4).

'It is yet far more evident' that our Lord Jesus Christ is a great High Priest infinitely superior to Aaron because those priests were temporary, made priests 'after the law of a carnal commandment', without an oath, for a limited time. Christ was made a Priest forever after the order of Melchizedek and the oath of God in his eternal decree, by the power of an endless life (Hebrews 7:11-27).

A Better Covenant

Our Lord and Saviour Jesus Christ, is the Surety and Mediator of a better covenant (8:1-13). The old covenant was a conditional covenant of human effort, law and works. In that covenant the whole weight of responsibility was upon the shoulders of men. The new covenant, of which Christ is the Surety, is an unconditional covenant of pure, free grace. In this covenant nothing depends upon frail and fickle men. In this covenant the whole weight of responsibility was laid upon the shoulders of One who is mighty, our great Surety, the Lord Jesus Christ. This new covenant of grace is that of which the prophet Jeremiah spoke (Jeremiah 31:31-34).

'But now hath he obtained a more excellent ministry, by how much also he is the mediator of a better covenant, which was established upon better promises. For if that first covenant had been faultless, then should no place have been sought for the second. For finding fault with them, he saith, Behold, the days come, saith the Lord, when I will make a new covenant with the house of Israel and with the house of Judah: Not according to the covenant that I made with their fathers in the day when I took them by the hand to lead them out of the land of Egypt; because they continued not in my covenant, and I regarded them not, saith the Lord. For this is the covenant that I will make with the house of Israel after those days, saith the Lord; I will put my laws into their mind, and write them in their hearts: and I will be to them a God, and they shall be to me a people: And they shall not teach every man his neighbour, and every man his brother, saying, Know the Lord: for all shall know me, from the least to the greatest. For I will be merciful to their unrighteousness, and their sins and their iniquities will I remember no more' (8:6-12).

A Better Tabernacle

Christ is a better Tabernacle (9:1-28). Everything in the Old Testament tabernacle, and later the temple, was typical of the Lord Jesus Christ. They were but 'a figure for the time then present ... until the time of reformation'. Christ is the true Tabernacle. He is the true place of worship and blessing.

'Christ being come an high priest of good things to come, by a greater and more perfect tabernacle, not made with hands, that is to say, not of this building; Neither by the blood of goats and calves, but by his own blood he entered in once into the holy place, having obtained eternal redemption for us. For if the blood of bulls and of goats, and the ashes of an heifer sprinkling the unclean, sanctifieth to the purifying of the flesh: How much more shall the blood of Christ, who through the eternal Spirit offered himself without spot to God, purge your conscience from dead works to serve the living God? And for this cause he is the mediator of the new testament, that by means of death, for the redemption of the transgressions that were under the first testament, they which are called might receive the promise of eternal inheritance. For where a testament is, there must also of necessity be the death of the testator' (9:11-16).

A Better Sacrifice

Christ is a better Sacrifice (10:1-39). All the laws, sacrifices, holy days, and religious observances of the Old Testament were only typical rituals. They could never take away sin or give sinners acceptance with God. Christ did and does!

> Not all the blood of beasts
> On Jewish altars slain,
> Could give the guilty conscience peace,
> Or wash away the stain.
>
> But Christ, the heavenly Lamb,
> Takes all our sins away:
> A Sacrifice of nobler name
> And richer blood than they.
>
> Believing, we rejoice
> To see the curse remove:
> We bless the Lamb with cheerful voice,
> And sing redeeming love!

Christ and his sacrifice, his finished work as our Substitute and Saviour is the whole of our acceptance with God, the whole of our peace from God, and the whole of our assurance before God (10:4-22).

A Better Object of Faith

Christ is the better Object of Faith (11:1-40). In chapter 11 the Apostle shows us that Christ is the better Object of Faith, better than any that any man may choose, for he is the only Object of Faith among God's saints throughout the ages.

He is the One by whom Abel worshipped God and by whom Enoch walked with God and pleased him. Christ is the Ark of Salvation in whom Noah trusted. He is the One with whom Abraham, Isaac, and Jacob walked. Joseph, Moses, Joshua, Rahab, Samson, and David, all God's saints of old believed in him, lived by him, died in him, and reign with him today.

Let us, like those countless multitudes of old, trust Christ alone as our Saviour. It is only by believing in him that we can know our election by him (11:1-2). It is only by faith in him that we can understand the things of God. (11:3). It is only by believing in him that we can please God (11:6).

A Better Motive

Christ is the better motive (12:1-29). The book of Hebrews calls for perseverance in faith, urging us to continue in the grace of God. We have many examples to follow. But our best and only real inspiration and motive is Christ himself.

'Wherefore seeing we also are compassed about with so great a cloud of witnesses, let us lay aside every weight, and the sin which doth so easily beset us, and let us run with patience the race that is set before us, Looking unto Jesus the author and finisher of our faith; who for the joy that was set before him endured the cross, despising the shame, and is set down at the right hand of the throne of God. For consider him that endured such contradiction of sinners against himself, lest ye be wearied and faint in your minds' (12:1-3).

In a word Christ is a better Saviour than any to whom we might look (13:1-25). For Jesus is the only Saviour there is, 'the same yesterday, and today, and for ever' (v. 8). Those who serve at the altar of freewill, of works religion, cannot eat at this Altar (v. 10). As he suffered outside the city for us, bearing our reproach, 'Let us go forth therefore unto him without the camp, bearing his reproach' (v. 13). 'By him therefore let us offer the sacrifice of praise to God continually, that is, the fruit of our lips giving thanks to his name' (v. 15). Truly, his glory is great in salvation!

'Now the God of peace, that brought again from the dead our Lord Jesus, that great shepherd of the sheep, through the blood of the everlasting covenant, Make you perfect in every good work to do his will, working in you that which is wellpleasing in his sight, through Jesus Christ; to whom be glory for ever and ever. Amen'. (13:20-21).

Chapter 59

James

'Be Ye Doers of the Word'

The book of James is thought to be the earliest of all the New Testament epistles. It was written by James, the half-brother of our Saviour. The epistle was written to Jewish believers who had been greatly scattered in God's good providence (1:1).

In these five short chapters James addresses those to whom he writes as 'brethren' fifteen times (1:2, 16, 19; 2:1, 5, 15; 3:1, 10, 12; 4:11; 5:7, 9, 10, 12, 19). He is writing to men and women who were born of God, to people who believe on the Lord Jesus Christ. This epistle was written to all in every place who are washed in the blood of Christ and robed in his righteousness, to all who trust the Lord Jesus Christ.

In these five chapters James gives us divinely inspired instructions about how we are to live in this world for the glory of God. He is not writing as a counsellor offering advice, but as God's messenger giving authoritative instruction. Throughout the book, James speaks in imperatives.

Our Trials

In chapter 1:2-12 James tells us that we are to always look upon our trials, those things that try, test, and prove the reality of our faith in Christ, as tokens of God's grace. Those heartaches and troubles God's saints experience in this world are not evidence of anger, wrath, and judgment, but evidence of mercy, love, and grace (Hebrews 12:5-14). This is particularly true when the things we suffer are the result of our faith in Christ (2 Timothy 2:12).

In Acts 8:1 we read, 'And at that time there was a great persecution against the church which was at Jerusalem; and they were all scattered abroad throughout the regions of Judea and Samaria, except the apostles'. In chapter 11 we are told that the persecuted saints were scattered 'as far as Phoenicia, and Cyprus, and Antioch', and that they went everywhere 'preaching the word' (Acts 11:19). Our Saviour said, 'Blessed are they which are persecuted for righteousness' sake: for theirs is the kingdom of heaven. Blessed are ye, when men shall revile you, and persecute you, and shall say all manner of evil against you falsely, for my sake. Rejoice, and be exceeding glad: for great is your reward in heaven: for so persecuted they the prophets which were before you' (Matthew 5:10-12).

James seems to have those very words in mind, as he writes the opening verses of his epistle. He urges us to always count it our honour as the children of God to suffer anything at the hands of wicked men for Christ's sake. Yet, what he says to us applies to anything we suffer in this world in the good and wise providence of our God.

'My brethren, count it all joy when ye fall into divers temptations; Knowing this, that the trying of your faith worketh patience ... Blessed is the man that endureth temptation: for when he is tried, he shall receive the crown of life, which the Lord hath promised to them that love him' (1:2, 3, 12).

> God in Israel sows the seeds
> Of affliction, pain, and toil;
> These spring up and choke the weeds
> That would else o'erspread the soil.
> Trials make the promise sweet;
> Trials give new life to prayer;
> Trials bring me to His feet;
> Lay me low and keep me there.

The word 'temptation', as it is used in these verses, refers to a test or a trial by which our fidelity is proved, by which our faith is proved. In verses 13-16 the same word is used, but it is obvious that it is used in a different sense. In verses 13-16 the word 'tempted' refers to an enticement to evil.

Our Temptations

Our trials are always to be ascribe to the work of our heavenly Father and his goodness. They are always the blessings of his grace and favour. Our temptations to evil we must never ascribe to or blame on God. James makes this distinction with great clarity.

'Let no man say when he is tempted, I am tempted of God: for God cannot be tempted with evil, neither tempteth he any man: But every man is tempted, when he is drawn away of his own lust, and enticed. Then when lust hath conceived, it bringeth forth sin: and sin, when it is finished, bringeth forth death. Do not err, my beloved brethren' (vv. 13-16).

God sends us trials to teach us patience (v. 3), to cause us to grow in grace and in faith; but God never tempts anyone to sin (v. 13). Yes, God has ordained from eternity all things that come to pass in time (Ephesians 1:11). Yes, God works all things together for the good of his elect (Romans 8:28). And, yes, God graciously and wisely rules and overrules the evil deeds of men and devils to sovereignly accomplish his will (Psalm 76:10). But the holy Lord God cannot be tempted with evil and he does not tempt any to evil.

When we sin, we have no one to blame but ourselves. Let us never seek to excuse our sin by attributing it to God's sovereign purpose. We are tempted to evil when we are drawn away by our own wicked lusts. It is our lust, nothing else that is to be blamed for our sin (vv. 14-15). 'Do not err, my beloved brethren' (v. 16). Your sin is your fault no one else's, your responsibility no one else's.

God's Work

In verses 17-25 James tells us that God's work is good. He tells us that every good thing in this world comes down from our Father in heaven. Just as all the evil there is in this world erupts from the festering corruption of our vile hearts (Mark 7:20-23), every good thing there is in this world comes down from the throne of God and is the gift of his grace. 'Every good gift and every perfect gift is from above, and cometh down from the Father of lights, with whom is no variableness, neither shadow of turning' (v. 17).

Then, in verse 18 James tells us that it is by the work and good gift of God's omnipotent grace that chosen, redeemed sinners are born again, born again by the good gift of the gospel. 'Of his own will begat he us with the word of truth, that we should be a kind of firstfruits of his creatures'. What a blessed good gift the preaching of the gospel, 'the Word of truth', is! Let us ever cherish it. By it God has been pleased to save us (Romans 10:10-17; 1 Peter 1:23-25). He has done so 'of his own will' (Romans 9:15-16), 'that we should be a kind of firstfruits of his creatures'. Firstfruits are the best. Firstfruits belong to God. Firstfruits are the pledge of the full harvest (Exodus 34:22; Deuteronomy 15:19; 1 Corinthians 15:23).

The Power of Godliness

'The Word of Truth' is the whole volume of sacred scripture, which is the revelation of Christ, redemption, grace, and salvation by him. The Word of Truth is the whole revelation of God in holy scripture, the gospel of his free grace in Christ. This is the power of God unto salvation (Romans 1:16-17), and the power of godliness, by which we live in this world for the glory of God (2 Timothy 3:5).

If we would live in this world for the glory of God in the exercise of true religion, our lives must be ruled and guided by the gospel of Christ. If we would live under the influence of God's powerful grace, by the power of godliness, we must hear the gospel (vv. 19-20), receive the message of God (v. 21), and obey it (vv. 22-25).

Whenever we come into the house of God, it should be with an intense desire to hear the Word of God. Thomas Manton made this wise observation, 'If we were as swift to hear as we are ready to speak there would be less wrath and more profit in our meetings'.

Usually, I find that when men do not profit from the ministry of the Word it is because they practice exactly the opposite of what James commands in James 1:19, 'Wherefore, my beloved brethren, let every man be swift to hear, slow to speak, slow to wrath'. They are slow to hear, swift to speak, and swift to anger. There are men who seem to come to church for no other reason than to find some point of disagreement. They can hardly wait for the preacher to finish his message so they can point out his errors.

Such men are a continual source of strife and division. They do not worship, and they try to keep others from worshipping. Let us guard against this tendency of proud, self-willed flesh. May God make us swift to hear and slow to speak.

Hearing the Word

Here is some practical advice on hearing the Word of God. First, prepare yourself to hear the Word (Ecclesiastes 5:1-2). Then, before you go to the place of worship, spend some time in prayer. Ask God to speak to you. Ask God to enable his servant to speak with clarity and power. Go seeking a message from heaven.

Submit yourself to the Word of God. When you are sitting in the assembly, listen personally for yourself. Submit your ideas, your traditions, and your doctrines to the scriptures. Be willing to forsake anything that is not plainly taught in the Bible. Be willing to obey everything that is required by the gospel. Meditate upon the Word. Do not swiftly speak against what you hear. Do not become angered by what you hear. Instead, meditate upon it. Ask God to apply the Word to your heart and give you understanding. Seek the glory of Christ in your response to his Word.

True Religion
Beginning in verse 26 of chapter 1 and going through chapter 5, James tells us how we are to live in this world for the glory of God. He tells us what true religion is in verses 26-27 of the first chapter. 'If any man among you seem to be religious, and bridleth not his tongue, but deceiveth his own heart, this man's religion is vain. Pure religion and undefiled before God and the Father is this, To visit the fatherless and widows in their affliction, and to keep himself unspotted from the world'. Then, beginning in chapter 2, he explains the details.

True religion involves caring for one another, particularly caring for our needy brethren (vv. 1-26). You will notice that James speaks of good works, as they are ever spoken of in the New Testament, as works of faith and love. By these things we justify our professed faith in Christ before one another.

There is no contradiction between James and Paul. James is not teaching that we justify ourselves before our God by our works. Rather, the Holy Spirit here teaches us that we justify our professed faith in Christ before one another by our works. Any professed faith that does not cause a person to take care of the needs of his brethren, be it ever so orthodox, is a useless, dead profession.

'What doth it profit, my brethren, though a man say he hath faith, and have not works? can faith save him? If a brother or sister be naked, and destitute of daily food, And one of you say unto them, Depart in peace, be ye warmed and filled; notwithstanding ye give them not those things which are needful to the body; what doth it profit? Even so faith, if it hath not works, is dead, being alone. Yea, a man may say, Thou hast faith, and I have works: show me thy faith without thy works, and I will show thee my faith by my works. Thou believest that there is one God; thou doest well: the devils also believe, and tremble. But wilt thou know, O vain man, that faith without works is dead?' (vv. 14-20)

True religion necessitates the bridling of our tongues (3:1-12). Gossip and slander, speaking evil to or about our brothers and sisters in Christ, is totally inconsistent with a profession of faith in Christ (Ephesians 4:17-5:2). We do more to hurt one another and do more harm by the use of our tongues than in any other way. If the Lord will give us grace and wisdom to control our tongues, we will be useful, not harmful to one another. The person who has learned when to speak, what to speak, and how to speak for the glory of God and the good of the church is mature in faith. His actions justify his professed faith. He is controlled in his life by grace and love.

True religion demands grace, grace that only God our Saviour can supply (3:13-5:6). We must drink from the right Fountain: Christ (3:13-18). We must recognize that our greatest foe is ourselves (4:1-5:6). That will put an end to warring among ourselves. Let us resist the devil and submit to our God in all things, and be at peace. Loving one another, let us carefully guard against gossip and slander, hardness and unkindness, and protect one another. Let us particularly take care to protect one another's name (4:11).

If we would honour our God, if we would do all things for the glory of our Saviour, we must seek by his grace to be patient (5:7-12), pray for one another (5:13-18), and seek to restore one another (5:19-20). 'Brethren, if a man be overtaken in a fault, ye which are spiritual, restore such an one in the spirit of meekness; considering thyself, lest thou also be tempted. Bear ye one another's burdens, and so fulfil the law of Christ. For if a man think himself to be something, when he is nothing, he deceiveth himself' (Galatians 6:1-3).

Chapter 60

1 Peter

'The Salvation of Your Souls'

It is commonly agreed that Peter wrote his first epistle in the year 65
A.D. within a year after the Emperor Nero burned the city of Rome to the
ground. That happened in July of 64 A.D.

A fire broke out in the city of Rome that eventually engulfed the whole
city in flames, leaving it a virtual heap of ashes. The devastation was
immense. Historians believe that the fire was started intentionally by the
Roman Emperor, Nero. He wanted to make space in the city to build some
great palaces that would give his name an unforgettable place in history.

It was from this time that the saying arose, 'Nero fiddled while Rome
burned'. Actually, the violin had not yet been invented but Nero was
seen looking over the city, playing some kind of instrument, as he watched
the devastation with delight. Of course, he was never charged with the
crime; but historians are generally agreed that he was the man responsible.

For their part, the inhabitants of Rome were convinced that Nero was
responsible and were enraged. The population of the city were on the
brink of anarchy and ready to overthrow the Emperor. Nero needed a
scapegoat, someone he could blame for the fire.

There was a group of people in Rome who were just suited for his
wicked scheme. They were called 'Christians'. They followed a man called

554 Discovering Christ In All The Scriptures

Jesus Christ. They were a strange society of people, a minority group, commonly disliked and mistrusted by the masses. Rumours about this strange religious sect abounded. It was commonly reported that they drank blood. It was suggested they were cannibals because they ate someone's body. They worshipped secretly in each other's homes and greeted each other with 'an holy kiss'.

Of course, such familiarity, mutual care and affection amongst the believers led to more rumours. Christians were commonly accused of engaging in many evil practices. In fact, they were regarded with such suspicion that when Nero needed a scapegoat and started the rumour that the Christians had burned down the city of Rome, it was readily accepted and believed.

So began the fierce persecutions that took place under Nero's infamous reign as Emperor of Rome. Believers were hunted, arrested, tortured, and put to death by the hundreds. They were dipped in tar and burned as torches to light Nero's courtyards while he threw an outdoor party. They were tied to chariots and dragged to death through the streets of Rome. They were thrown to the lions. They were tied up in leather bags and thrown into pools of water. In countless other ways the saints of God were persecuted and killed as the most despicable people in the world.

Peter's Epistle to the Strangers

It was during this time of persecution that Peter wrote this blessed epistle to God's suffering saints scattered as 'strangers throughout Pontus, Galatia, Cappadocia, Asia, and Bithynia'. Peter wrote a letter of hope to his suffering brothers and sisters in Christ, encouraging them to endure the things they suffered as Christians, knowing that even the brutalities they endured at the hands of wicked men were according to the purpose of God (2:21-24).

How can people endure evil and hardship patiently? What will inspire them to persevere? How can they be comforted? Peter knew exactly what they needed. In chapter 1 he wrote to them about redemption and grace in Christ, about the salvation of their souls.

'Peter, an apostle of Jesus Christ, to the strangers scattered throughout Pontus, Galatia, Cappadocia, Asia, and Bithynia, Elect according to the foreknowledge of God the Father, through sanctification of the Spirit, unto obedience and sprinkling of the blood of Jesus Christ: Grace unto you, and peace, be multiplied. Blessed be the God and Father of our Lord Jesus Christ, which according to his abundant mercy hath begotten us again unto a lively hope by the resurrection of Jesus Christ from the dead,

To an inheritance incorruptible, and undefiled, and that fadeth not away, reserved in heaven for you, Who are kept by the power of God through faith unto salvation ready to be revealed in the last time. Wherein ye greatly rejoice, though now for a season, if need be, ye are in heaviness through manifold temptations: That the trial of your faith, being much more precious than of gold that perisheth, though it be tried with fire, might be found unto praise and honour and glory at the appearing of Jesus Christ: Whom having not seen, ye love; in whom, though now ye see him not, yet believing, ye rejoice with joy unspeakable and full of glory: Receiving the end of your faith, even the salvation of your souls'.

Salvation

The first part of this epistle (1:1-2:12) beautifully describes God's free, saving grace in Christ, 'the salvation of your souls'. Multitudes live in frustration because they think their lives are meaningless. They know nothing of redemption, salvation and grace. Life is meaningless until we find its true meaning in Christ.

There is nothing of greater importance than the salvation of your soul. You are a living soul. You have a body; but you are a living soul. You will spend eternity somewhere, in some state. You will live forever, either in the eternal bliss of salvation in heaven, or in the eternal state of death, the second death, in the torment of divine wrath in hell.

The salvation of a soul involves the very glory of God himself. If the Lord God is pleased to save you by his almighty, free and sovereign grace in Christ, it will be to show forth the praise of the glory of his grace. God saves sinners for his own name's sake (Ephesians 1:3-14). He says, 'For mine own sake, even for mine own sake, will I do it' (Isaiah 48:11; Psalm 106:8), thus, 'the salvation of your souls' is the subject of Peter's first epistle.

Because the salvation of our soul is of such immense importance, we are admonished in the scriptures to make our calling and election sure, lest we be deceived with one of Satan's devices to the damning of our souls. May God the Holy Spirit make us honest with ourselves and honest before him. As we look at the salvation described in this book, let us ask ourselves one question 'Is this the salvation I possess?'

If the salvation described here is your salvation, you have reason to give thanks to God continually. If the salvation you think you have is not described in these terms, then your imagined salvation is a vain delusion. Many professors hide behind a refuge of lies that will crush their souls down to hell forever, unless the Lord delivers them.

Ten Things About Salvation

In the first twelve verses of this epistle God the Holy Spirit describes what salvation is. If we are saved by the grace of God, this is the salvation we have experienced. If we have not experienced this salvation, we have not yet been saved by the grace of God. Here Peter tells us ten things about God's great gift of salvation in Christ.

1. In Bible terms salvation is a radical thing (v. 1). Salvation is something so radical, so life altering that it makes every saved sinner a stranger in this world. Certainly, religion makes people strange; but grace makes believers strangers to the world. 'Therefore the world knoweth us not, because it knew him not'. Believers are strangers to the people of the world. We are a paradox, Christians are people who are puzzling to the world. The world can never understand what makes us tick, why we do what we do, how we live, or what motivates us. The world can understand and explain any and every form of human religion. But the world can never understand a child of God. It's a grace thing. They just can't get it. Grace experienced in the soul makes a person a stranger in this world.

2. Salvation is the work of the triune God alone (v. 2). Salvation begins in that blessed, eternal work of God the Father called, 'election'. It is wrought in us by the regenerating, sanctifying work of God the Holy Spirit by irresistible grace. This salvation was earned and purchased for us by the obedience and death of God the Son, our Lord Jesus Christ in effectual redemption.

3. God's salvation brings both grace and peace. It brings every gift and blessing of divine favour as a matter of pure, free grace. Where there is grace, there is peace; peace with God, peace from God, the peace of God. Grace and peace are added and multiplied to saved sinners in Christ, never subtracted or divided.

4. Salvation, as it is described in the Bible, both honours God and gives all praise and honour to God (vv. 3-4). 'Blessed be the God and Father of our Lord Jesus Christ, which according to his abundant mercy hath begotten us again unto a lively hope by the resurrection of Jesus Christ from the dead, To an inheritance incorruptible, and undefiled, and that fadeth not away, reserved in heaven for you'. See Ephesians 1:3-6.

5. That salvation which is described in the book of God gives hope. Grace gives us a living hope. That hope is 'Christ in you, the hope of glory'. It is a hope that is based upon and found in God's abundant mercy in a risen Saviour. It is a hope for eternity, the hope of an inheritance, an incorruptible inheritance, an undefiled inheritance, an inheritance that fadeth not away, an inheritance reserved in heaven for us.

6. God's salvation is a salvation that keeps all by grace who are in grace (v. 5). Believers are a people 'kept by the power of God through faith unto salvation ready to be revealed in the last time'. Grace chose us. Grace found us. Grace put us in the way. Grace keeps us in the way. Grace keeps us through faith. Yes; and it is grace that gives us the faith through which we are kept.

7. This great salvation, great as it is now, in this present, earthly experience of it, is a salvation 'ready to be revealed' (v. 5).

8. Salvation, real salvation, causes saved sinners to rejoice in the Lord, always (v. 6). 'Wherein ye greatly rejoice, though now for a season, if need be, ye are in heaviness through manifold temptations'. This is real joy, joy in the very depths of our hearts and souls, joy in God our Saviour. When we have nothing else in which to rejoice, we can and should rejoice in our God and in his salvation (Philippians 4:4-5).

'Wherein ye greatly rejoice, though now for a season, if need be, ye are in heaviness through manifold temptations: That the trial of your faith, being much more precious than of gold that perisheth, though it be tried with fire, might be found unto praise and honour and glory at the appearing of Jesus Christ: Whom having not seen, ye love; in whom, though now ye see him not, yet believing, ye rejoice with joy unspeakable and full of glory: Receiving the end of your faith, even the salvation of your souls' (1:6-9).

Believers have joy in the midst of heavy trials. Notice that we are here told three things about our trials in this world. Let us not forget them. First, they are only for a season. Second, there is a 'need be' for them all. Third, they will make heaven more glorious and blessed than it otherwise would be, or could be (v. 7).

Believers have joy because of Christ (v. 8). 'Whom having not seen, ye love; in whom, though now ye see him not, yet believing, ye rejoice with joy unspeakable and full of glory'.

Believers have joy because of the end (v. 9). 'Receiving the end of your faith, even the salvation of your souls'.

9. This salvation is a salvation which is consistent with all the scriptures (vv. 10-11).

10. This salvation that God performs and gives freely to chosen sinners in Christ is the fulfilment of all the Old Testament scriptures. The prophets of old inquired and searched diligently for it (v. 10). He who taught them was the Spirit of Christ, who was in them and 'testified beforehand the sufferings of Christ, and the glory that should follow' (v. 11).

Revelation from above

This is what we see in verse 12. The only way any sinner can ever know and experience this salvation is by divine revelation. Those prophets in the Old Testament era wrote the things they wrote by divine inspiration, not just for themselves, but for us also. 'Unto whom it was revealed, that not unto themselves, but unto us they did minister the things, which are now reported unto you by them that have preached the gospel unto you with the Holy Ghost sent down from heaven; which things the angels desire to look into'. The salvation they received was the salvation we receive. It is salvation revealed unto us by the grace of God. It is revealed by type, shadow, promise, and prophecy in the Old Testament through the report of the gospel by the Holy Ghost sent down from heaven. This great salvation is a salvation that the angels desire to look into (v. 12; Ephesians 3:8-10).

Our Response

That is how the Word of God describes this thing we call 'salvation'. Does this describe your salvation? If it does, how thankful you ought to be! How you ought to love our God! That is what we are told in 1 Peter 1:13-2:12.

Peter declares we ought to consecrate ourselves to our Saviour, remembering that we have been saved from a meaningless, useless existence (1:13-15). The holy Lord God of Heaven is our Father and we are his dear children (1:16-17). We have been redeemed by the precious blood of Christ (1:18-20). He who loved us and redeemed us has given us faith and hope in God (1:21-22). We have been born again by the Word of God (1 Peter 1:23-25). We are living stones in the temple of God, built upon the Foundation Stone, Christ Jesus (2:5-12).

This is what Peter says to you and me. Hear the motives he gives for us to live in utter consecration to our God. Begin at verse 10 and go backwards to verse 5. We are the recipients of mercy (2:10), saved to show forth the praises of him who called us (2:9), God's own, special, distinct, peculiar people (2:9), a holy nation (2:9), a royal priesthood (2:9), a nation of kings and priests unto God, a chosen generation (2:9), and a royal priesthood offering up spiritual sacrifices acceptable to God by the merits and mediation of Christ (2:5).

Not only is it true that our prayers and gifts, our specific deeds of worship and love are accepted of God as spiritual sacrifices, so too are our very lives (Romans 12:1-2; Ecclesiastes 9:7). What greater motivation could there be?

The Will of God

Perhaps you are thinking, 'I want to live for Christ, I want to honour God. I just do not know how. I just do not know what I should do and not do'. If you are a believer, I know that it is your soul's desire to live for Christ, to honour God in your life. I also know that it is the nature of man to desire rules and laws by which he can measure his success. However, the Holy Spirit, instead of giving us rules and laws and commandments to fulfil, gives us a principle by which our lives, that is, all areas of our lives, are to be governed. That principle by which grace governs the lives of God's saints in this world is submission, submission to the will of God. That is what Peter shows us in chapter 2:13-3:12.

Grace teaches us to submit to all God ordained authority; particularly, Peter tells us to submit to our political, civil rulers for Christ's sake (2:13-17). If the saints, to whom this epistle was addressed, were expected to honour and submit to Nero and the Roman rulers under him, it certainly applies to us today. Where there is no honour given to government, there is no fear of God.

Grace teaches us to submit to our employers (2:18-19). Peter is not here giving approval to the inhuman, horrid practice of slavery that was so common throughout the world in that day. He is simply using the common practice to teach submission to the will of God. He tells even those who were slaves with wicked masters to be subject to them for Christ's sake. Believers ought to be the best, most dependable, most trustworthy workers in any place of employment.

Grace teaches us to patiently endure suffering, even from wicked men, just as our Saviour did, knowing that the things we suffer are according to the will of God and ordained by him for our eternal good (2:20-25).

Grace teaches us to honour God in our homes, submitting one to another (3:1-7). Wives, even those married to unbelieving men, are to live in submission to their husband as their heads. One reason given for this is that their unbelieving husbands might be converted because they observe true grace manifest in their wives, 'even the ornament of a meek and quiet spirit, which is in the sight of God of great price'.

Chapter 3:3-4 is not a prohibition to women fixing their hair and wearing make up and jewellery. It is simply a declaration that the believing woman is to be more concerned about living in godliness than about dressing in gaudiness

Husbands are to love their wives, submitting to their needs as the weaker vessel. Believing husbands and wives ought always to live together 'as heirs together of the grace of life'.

Grace teaches us to live together in the church of God as brethren, submitting our own wills and preferences to one another (3:8-12) 'Let nothing be done through strife or vain glory; but in lowliness of mind let each esteem other better than themselves' (Philippians 2:3). The church of God ought to be the one place in this world where God's saints find nothing to hurt them. It ought to be a blessed habitation of peace, a household of faith and grace in which every person is treated with pity, kindness, and courtesy, in which none should ever experience gossip, slander, reproach or abuse of any kind.

Suffer Well

Even when we are called upon by God's good and wise providence to suffer evil at the hands of men, let us suffer well, as those who believe God. Peter teaches us how to do so in chapter 3:13-4:9. In circumstances such as these persecuted saints found themselves, he asks, 'Who is he that will harm you, if ye be followers of that which is good?' Let us behave in such a way that we do not suffer as evil men. When we do suffer for the gospel's sake, let us sanctify the Lord God in our hearts, not murmur against him. Let us ever be ready to give reason for the hope that is in us (v. 15). Let us remember that Christ suffered much more for us (v. 18). And let us remember that he who suffered and died for us, that he who loved us and gave himself for us is seated in heaven and has dominion over all things, even over those who cause us to suffer by their evil deeds (v. 22).

'Beloved, think it not strange concerning the fiery trial which is to try you, as though some strange thing happened unto you: But rejoice, inasmuch as ye are partakers of Christ's sufferings; that, when his glory shall be revealed, ye may be glad also with exceeding joy. If ye be reproached for the name of Christ, happy are ye; for the spirit of glory and of God resteth upon you: on their part he is evil spoken of, but on your part he is glorified. But let none of you suffer as a murderer, or as a thief, or as an evildoer, or as a busybody in other men's matters. Yet if any man suffer as a Christian, let him not be ashamed; but let him glorify God on this behalf' (4:12-16).

Serving God in His House

In chapter 5 Peter moves directly from the matter of how we are to endure suffering from the hands of wicked men to how we are to serve God in his house. It is as though he is telling us to make certain that none of God's elect suffer anything in his house, but that we should labour together as one body in peace for the glory of God, strengthening one another for life in this world.

Let every pastor in the church of God be a faithful shepherd, tenderly caring for Christ's sheep, feeding them, watching over them, guiding them, and showing them by example how to live for the honour of God in a world of woe (vv. 1-4). Let every child of God walk in loving submission to our God and to one another, casting all our care upon him, knowing that he cares for us (vv. 5-9). Let us ever remind ourselves and each other of God's boundless, sure and certain grace in Christ, keeping our hearts fixed upon eternity, not upon our temporary trials here (vv. 10-11; 2 Corinthians 4:18-5:1).

You will notice that, at the close of this letter, Peter says he wrote it from Babylon. Many imagine that Peter is here using the word Babylon as a metaphor or even a spiritual term for Rome. But there is no foundation for that supposition. There is no historical or biblical evidence that Peter ever visited Rome. Peter says he was in Babylon, or modern day Baghdad, on the Euphrates River in Assyria.

Chapter 61

2 Peter

Grow in Grace and Knowledge

The apostle Peter wrote his first epistle to God's saints who were suffering the horrible trial of persecution under the Roman Emperor, Nero. His second epistle was written shortly afterward, just before his death (1:14), and is addressed to the same suffering saints. Their circumstances had not changed.

The first epistle dealt with the hard, hard trial of persecution, of suffering for Christ's sake. In that epistle Peter urges us to persevere in the faith, assuring us of God's great grace in Christ and urging us to follow the example our Saviour set before us (1 Peter 2:21-24).

In 2 Peter the inspired apostle deals with a trial even more difficult to endure, and urges us to remain steadfast in faith in the face of the ever-increasing onslaught of false religion. In these three chapters Peter urges us to persevere in the faith, assuring us again of God's great grace to us in Christ, and urging us to 'grow in grace, and in the knowledge of our Lord and Saviour Jesus Christ' (3:18). In 1 Peter we are taught to rejoice in hope in the face of great trials. Here, in 2 Peter, we are taught to remain faithful to the truth in the midst of great falsehood.

Precious Things

In these two epistles the apostle Peter reminds us of the many blessings of grace our God has given us in Christ. In fact, he tells us that the Lord God has, according to his divine power, 'given unto us all things that pertain unto life and godliness, through the knowledge of him that hath called us to glory and virtue' (1:3). Among these many gifts of grace, Peter names six that he calls 'precious'.

He tells us that the trial of our faith is more precious than gold that perishes, because the trials of our faith in this world will make heaven more glorious than it could otherwise have been (1 Peter 1:7).

In 1 Peter 1:19 he tells us that the blood of Christ, by which we have been redeemed, is 'the precious blood of Christ', because it is the effectual, sin-atoning blood of the Lamb of God, who was foreordained as our Redeemer.

He tells us (1 Peter 2:6) that we who are God's spiritual temple are living stones in the house of God, built upon Christ, the precious Corner Stone and Foundation Stone laid in Zion.

Then, he says, 'Unto you therefore which believe he is precious' (1 Peter 2:7). Truly, Christ is precious to all who believe! Everything about him, all that he is, all that he has done and is doing is precious!

Peter begins this second epistle by telling us that the great gift and grace of faith that we have obtained from the Lord is 'precious faith' (1:1). It is that which we have obtained 'through the righteousness of God and (even) our Saviour Jesus Christ'.

Then, in 1:4 he tells us that the promises of God given to us in Christ are 'precious promises', precious because they are 'yea and amen in him', because they are unalterable and sure.

As we read these three chapters, we think to ourselves, 'Bro. Peter, you could not have written anything more suited to the needs of God's saints in this present day'. It is as though Peter knew, way back then, what we would need today. That is because this book, the Word of God, is written by divine inspiration and is written specifically for God's saints in every place, circumstance, and time. Its message is God's message for you and me right now. Every word in these three chapters is pertinent to us and filled with instruction for us. It is specifically addressed 'to them that have obtained like precious faith with us through the righteousness of God and our Saviour Jesus Christ'. May God give us grace to receive and obey his message to us.

Grow in Grace

In chapter 1 Peter's admonition to us is to grow in the grace and knowledge of Christ. He knew that the secret to spiritual strength is Christ. Knowing Christ, who is the source of spiritual strength and knowledge, is the grace of God.

If we would be strong in faith, we must have an ever-increasing knowledge of our utter weakness in ourselves. A knowledge that our only acceptance with God is Christ, and that our only hope of salvation is the grace of God feely bestowed upon us and given to us in Christ. Paul said, 'When I am weak, then am I strong', and that is true of all believers. If we would be strong in faith, if we would grow in the grace and knowledge of Christ, 'He must increase, and (we) must decrease' (John 3:30).

The Same Gifts

Peter begins this epistle by assuring us that all believers have the same gifts of grace. We do not all possess the same gifts of ministry and service; but all believers do possess the same gifts of grace (Ephesians 1:3-6). We tend to think of the apostles and prophets as men who had greater grace than we have; but that was not the case. They were all, just like us, sinners saved by grace. Peter tells us in verse one that he is writing to people just like himself, who 'have obtained like precious faith with us', and have obtained it in exactly the same way, through the merit, virtue, and efficacy of Christ.

Then, in verse 3 he tells us that God has 'given unto us all things that pertain unto life and godliness'. Someone once said, 'Even the weakest believer holds in his hands all that the mightiest saint ever possessed'. That is exactly what Peter tells us here. All that we need to live forever before God is ours in Christ. And all that we need to live in this world in godliness is ours in Christ, too. In other words, Peter is telling us that God has given us in Christ everything needed to handle whatever comes up in life, and to handle it with grace.

Do we understand that? Very few do. Multitudes there are who are always looking for something more than Christ and the grace of God in him. They want something new, something different, some new experience, some new revelation, something greater than grace! Something greater than Christ! May God save us from such folly. If Christ is all, and he is, then Christ is enough!

This is what that means in the context of 2 Peter. If we have everything in Christ, we only need to know more of him, and we will have all that it takes to handle the problems we deal with in this world. Having Christ, we have all we need for 'life and godliness'.

Faith in Christ is the gift of God's grace. The faith we have obtained of God comes through the righteousness of God. The grace and peace that sustains us in life comes to us 'through the knowledge of God and (even) of Jesus our Lord' (v. 2). Believing on the Lord Jesus Christ, God has given us 'exceeding great and precious promises: that by these we might be partakers of the divine nature, having escaped the corruption that is in the world through lust' (v. 4). In other words, Peter tells us that being born of God, believing on Christ, we have (past tense) escaped everything in the world that once held us in corruption through our lust.

The Influence of Grace

In verses 5-11 Peter calls for us to grow in grace, and faith, and the knowledge of Christ. He calls us to give diligence in making our calling and election sure, as Paul puts it, working out our own salvation, because it is God who works in us to will and to do of his own good pleasure. The grace of God that brings salvation teaches us how we are to live in this world (Titus 2:10-14). John Gill wrote ...

'The Gospel, and the precious promises, being graciously bestowed and powerfully applied, have an influence on purity of heart and conversation, and teach men to deny ungodliness and worldly lusts, and to live soberly, righteously, and godly; such are the powerful effects of Gospel promises, under divine influence, as to make men inwardly partakers of the divine nature, and outwardly to abstain from and avoid the prevailing corruptions and vices of the times.'

Peter continues, 'And beside this, giving all diligence, add to your faith virtue; and to virtue knowledge; And to knowledge temperance; and to temperance patience; and to patience godliness; And to godliness brotherly kindness; and to brotherly kindness charity. For if these things be in you, and abound, they make you that ye shall neither be barren nor unfruitful in the knowledge of our Lord Jesus Christ' (vv. 5-8). If we are born of God we have all this in Christ; but we must diligently work at discovering it and applying it in our lives. The secret to enjoying peace in this world is faith in and obedience to God our Saviour.

> Trust and obey, for there's no other way
> To be happy in Jesus, but to trust and obey.

The knowledge of God's grace and promises in Christ, and the application of them to our lives will keep us from being barren and unfruitful. There is a knowledge of Christ that is barren and unfruitful. As James tells us, 'Faith without works is dead'. Those who have a dead faith are spiritually dead. That is what Peter tells us in verse 9, 'But he that lacketh these things is blind, and cannot see afar off, and hath forgotten that he was purged from his old sins'. Their professed faith is just that, a profession of faith that has cleaned up their lives outwardly; but they are still spiritually blind.

Make Sure

'Wherefore the rather, brethren, give diligence to make your calling and election sure: for if ye do these things, ye shall never fall' (v. 10). We do not make our calling and election sure to ourselves by these evidences of grace. It is God the Holy Spirit who makes our calling and election sure to us by giving us faith in Christ (Hebrews 11:1). As James speaks of us justifying our profession of faith before men by our works, Peter here tells us that we make our faith in Christ manifest and sure before one another in the same way. 'For so an entrance shall be ministered unto you abundantly into the everlasting kingdom of our Lord and Saviour Jesus Christ' (v. 11). If you and I have that faith which is made manifest and shows itself by love, these graces: virtue, knowledge, temperance, patience, godliness, brotherly kindness, and love, (vv. 5-7) shall be added to us abundantly as we leave this world and enter into heavenly glory.

The Basis of Faith

In verses 12-21 Peter directs our hearts to the source and basis of our faith: The Word of God. If we would grow in faith and in the knowledge of Christ, we must ever be established in the revealed truth of God, ever remembering that which God reveals to us in his Word. The apostle reminds us that the gospel we have received is the testimony of men who were eye-witnesses of Christ's divine majesty (vv. 16-18). Peter, James, and John saw the glory of Christ on the Mount of Transfiguration (John 1:14). They heard the testimony of God from heaven (Matthew 17:1-5).

Yet, we have an even more sure Word than the mere eye-witness account of those faithful men. In fact, Peter says in verses 19-21 that the basis of his faith in Christ was something far more sure and dependable than his own experience upon the Mount of Transfiguration. The basis of all true faith, the authority for all that we believe as the children of God is not our experience, but the written Word of inspiration.

This is Peter's doctrine in verses 19-21. We believe that Jesus of Nazareth is the Christ, the Son of God, in whom alone God is well-pleased and in and by whom alone God is well-pleased with us, because he has perfectly fulfilled everything written in the Old Testament.

False Prophets

In chapter 2 Peter identifies false prophets and warns us of their subtlety. He is not talking here about atheists and agnostics. He is talking about wolves in sheep's clothing. He is talking about men who claim to be the servants of God and preachers of the gospel, who profess to love and serve the Lord Jesus Christ. Watch how he describes them (vv. 1-3).

'But there were false prophets also among the people, even as there shall be false teachers among you, who privily shall bring in damnable heresies, even denying the Lord that bought them, and bring upon themselves swift destruction. And many shall follow their pernicious ways; by reason of whom the way of truth shall be evil spoken of. And through covetousness shall they with feigned words make merchandise of you: whose judgment now of a long time lingereth not, and their damnation slumbereth not'.

They are sneaky, deceitful men. They bring in damnable heresies. They deny the Lord Jesus Christ by denying the efficacy of his work and his dominion as Lord. The ways they preach are pernicious ways to hell (Proverbs 14:12; 16:25).

They speak evil of the Way, the Way of Truth, of Christ and his finished work. They are motivated by covetousness. They make merchandise of men's souls. They shall be damned.

Because there are many (following the very men of whom Peter here speaks, who point to this passage as a 'proof text' to deny Christ's effectual atonement for the sins of God's elect, and his effectual redemption of his people, and to prove the blasphemy of universal atonement and universal redemption, we must give attention to the language Peter uses here.

The word used for 'Lord' in verse 1 is δεσποτησ (despotes). The word translated 'bought' is αγοραζω (agoradzo). Peter is not suggesting that there is some sense in which Christ made atonement for or died to make salvation possible for reprobate men. He is telling us that as a man, as the God-man our Mediator, Christ bought the right to rule over and dispose of all things for the salvation of his own elect (John 17:2; Romans 14:9; Philippians 2:9-11). As our Mediator, our Saviour bought the field of the world that he might redeem and save the treasure of his elect hidden in the field (Matthew 13:44).

Remember, these are men who profess to believe, love, worship, and preach the Lord Jesus Christ in all his fulness. Yet, they deny him in the very message they preach. Those who preach conditional grace deny his effectual grace. Those who preach conditional election deny his effectual election. Those who preach conditional atonement deny his effectual atonement. Those who preach conditional salvation deny his effectual salvation. Those who preach salvation by man's works deny his redeeming work. Those who preach salvation by man's will deny his sovereign will. And those who deny the efficacy of his work and accomplishments as the sinners' Substitute deny him altogether, no matter how loudly they profess to love him.

In verses 10-21 Peter gives us a more detailed description of these false prophets. He tells us that all such men are presumptuous, self-willed, and ignorant men who speak evil of God's true servants and of the gospel of his grace that his servants preach, because these are 'things they understand not'. They are men with eyes full of adultery, who cease not from sin, ever 'sporting themselves with their own deceivings'. Like Balaam, they 'have forsaken the right way' because they love 'the wages of unrighteousness'. Be warned! All preachers of free-will, works religion are a curse to your children, beguiling unstable souls. They promise liberty, but bring bondage, the bondage of corruption. If you follow them, you will follow them to hell.

Word of Comfort

Yet, even as he describes the horrible perversity of false religion and warns us that those who follow the false prophets will perish with them, Peter assures us that trusting Christ, following him, God's saints need not be alarmed (vv. 4-9). God knows exactly what he is doing. He is saving his own elect. His purpose is sure (Ruth 4:14). He spared not the angels that fell; but he saved his elect angels. He spared not the old world; but he saved Noah and his family. He spared not Sodom and Gomorrah; but he saved Lot. Though he will destroy all who 'stumble at the Word, being disobedient, whereunto also they were appointed' (1 Peter 2:8), 'the Lord knoweth how to deliver the godly out of temptations' (2 Peter 2:9).

Christ's Coming

In chapter 3 Peter concludes his epistle by assuring us of the certainty of Christ's coming and the certain salvation of all God's elect before Christ comes again in his glory, urging us to live in anticipation of eternal glory.

In the opening verses of this chapter he reminds us again of false prophets, 'walking after their own lusts, and saying, Where is the promise of his coming?' He tells us that these scoffers are willingly ignorant of the scriptures (v. 5). Then he explains to us that the reason Christ has not yet returned to the earth. It is simply this, God has not yet saved all his elect (vv. 9, 15).

The elect family is not all in the Ark. God's Lots have not all yet been brought out of Sodom, but they will be! Then, Christ will come and make all things new (vv. 8-14). Be patient. God does not judge time like we do. He is not in a hurry.

'But, beloved, be not ignorant of this one thing, that one day is with the Lord as a thousand years, and a thousand years as one day. The Lord is not slack concerning his promise, as some men count slackness; but is longsuffering to us-ward, not willing that any should perish, but that all should come to repentance. But the day of the Lord will come as a thief in the night; in the which the heavens shall pass away with a great noise, and the elements shall melt with fervent heat, the earth also and the works that are therein shall be burned up. Seeing then that all these things shall be dissolved, what manner of persons ought ye to be in all holy conversation and godliness, Looking for and hasting unto the coming of the day of God, wherein the heavens being on fire shall be dissolved, and the elements shall melt with fervent heat? Nevertheless we, according to his promise, look for new heavens and a new earth, wherein dwelleth righteousness. Wherefore, beloved, seeing that ye look for such things, be diligent that ye may be found of him in peace, without spot, and blameless' (vv. 8-14).

Final Admonition

Peter's final admonition is found in verses 17-18 of chapter 3. It is twofold. First, he urges us to be steadfast in the faith of the gospel. 'Ye therefore, beloved, seeing ye know these things before, beware lest ye also, being led away with the error of the wicked, fall from your own stedfastness' (v. 17). We must ever guard against the influence of false prophets. The surest way to avoid the subtle influence of false doctrine is to cling to plainly revealed truth, refusing to even give an ear to anything new.

Second, he urges us to 'grow in grace, and in the knowledge of our Lord and Saviour Jesus Christ' (v. 18). Here the apostle re-emphasizes what he said in chapter one. As we cling tenaciously to that which we know, let us constantly seek grace to grow in grace, in the gifts of grace; in faith, in hope, in love, etc. and in the exercise of grace. We grow in grace only as we grow 'in the knowledge of our Lord and Saviour Jesus Christ'. Learn everything you can about Christ. Look for him in his Word (John 5:39). Seek not only to know all you can about him, but also to know him (Philippians 3:10), growing continually in the knowledge of your need of him and the bounteous grace of God that is yours in him, ever seeking his glory. 'To him be glory both now and for ever. Amen'.

Chapter 62

1 John

The Church of God His Family

The church of God is set before us in many ways in the scriptures. It is the kingdom of God. It is the bride of Christ. And it is the family of God. It is as the family of God that God's saints are addressed in 1 John. This is an intimate, family epistle. John was an old man when the book was written, an old man who had faithfully served Christ and his church for many years. Though this epistle is not specifically addressed to an individual local church, John writes in these five chapters as a father to his beloved children. It is obvious that he wrote this letter to an assembly in which he was in very close, personal relationship, an assembly that loved and respected him as children do a good and faithful father. The fact that this epistle is not addressed to any specific local church indicates that it is the intent of the Holy Spirit that every gospel church receive it as a Word from God our Father specifically to his family, to his beloved children in this world.

Robert Hawker wrote of this epistle, 'One sweet feature runs through the whole of it, in relation to the church, namely, the apostle's testimony to the Father's love, the Son's grace, and the Holy Spirit's fellowship'.

Heresy

Like the apostles Peter, Paul, and James, John was very concerned with the evil influence of false teachers and false religion. John specifically exposes the Gnostic heresy so prevalent in his day, and increasingly so in our day. Gnostics claim to have a special degree of knowledge, by which they have arrived at salvation. However, salvation does not come by superior knowledge or wisdom, but by divine revelation. Salvation is not in what we know, but who. 'This is life eternal, that they might know thee the only true God, and Jesus Christ, whom thou hast sent' (John 17:3). John deals with this decisively (1:1-3; 4:1-3; 5:1, 7).

Another heresy common in John's day, and increasingly so in ours, is the teaching that that which is physical is evil. This leads many to deny that the Lord Jesus Christ is truly God in human flesh. It also gives rise to the ascetic heresy that righteousness is to be obtained by denying ourselves of natural, physical pleasure. The grace of God teaches us to deny ungodliness and worldly lusts, and to live soberly, righteously, and godly in this world; but godliness is nowhere associated in the book of God with what we eat, or drink, or wear. Rather, it has everything to do with 'faith which worketh by love' (Galatians 5:6).

In John's day, as in ours, there were also many who taught perfectionism They asserted that sinless perfection was attainable by diligent self-denial, that one could and must increase in holiness and sanctification until he has eradicated sin from his life. Of course, such heretics always deny that their doctrine is in any way a doctrine of works. They insist that their notion of 'progressive holiness' is the result of God working in us by his Spirit and grace. But John asserts that their doctrine is a total denial of all gospel truth (1:8-10). Believers know and confess their sin, looking to Christ alone for righteousness.

Then there are always those who teach that a believer's character and conduct are of no consequence, that as long as we have knowledge of and confess the right doctrine, we may live in licentiousness, gratifying the flesh, and live in communion with God at the same time. Such crass antinomianism has plagued the church from its beginning. But John declares that all who live in licentiousness are children of the devil, not children of God, no matter what they profess to believe (3:10).

A Pastor's Concern

John obviously did not write as a detached academic. Everything in these five chapters displays the gentle concern of a faithful, loving pastor's heart. Throughout the book he addresses his readers as his 'little children' (2:1, 12, 13, 28; 3:7, 18; 4:4; 5:21), first stating something and then repeating it again and again, as one would instruct a small child.

The gospel of John was written that we might believe that Jesus is the Christ, the Son of God, and that believing we might have life through his name (John 20:31). John wrote this epistle because he wanted every believer to know, to be confidently assured of the fact, that he has eternal life in Christ (5:9-13).

The Word of God

In chapter 1 the apostle assures us that the Lord Jesus Christ, our Saviour, that One in whom we trust, is the eternal Word of God. He is the Word of life, by whom we live (vv. 1-3; John 1:1-4).

What a mammoth volume of theology John gives us in the first three verses of this epistle. He tells us that the man Christ Jesus is eternal, 'That which was from the beginning'. He is eternal life, 'That eternal life, which was with the Father'. The Lord Jesus is the Word of Life that One by whom and in whom God who is life resides and is revealed. That One who is life and gives life. That One in whom and by whom we have life. The Lord Jesus Christ is the incarnate God 'For the life was manifested, and we have seen it', heard it, gazed upon it with wonder, and handled it.

John wants all who believe to live together in the sweet, blessed fellowship of Christ. He tells us the basis and the essence of all true fellowship in verse 3. 'That which we have seen and heard declare we unto you, that ye also may have fellowship with us: and truly our fellowship is with the Father, and with his Son Jesus Christ'. This fellowship rises from the knowledge of God in Christ and the blessed life that is ours by the sin-atoning sacrifice of Christ our Saviour (1:7, 9; 2:1-2, 12; 3:5, 16; 4:9-10, 14; 5:11-13). It is the fellowship of light and knowledge (1:5-7; 2:20). It is the fellowship of faith in Christ (3:23; 5:1, 13). This blessed fellowship is the fellowship of life, righteousness, hope, and love in Christ (2:29; 3:1-3, 9-10; 4:7-11; 5:1).

By faith in Christ, John tells us, we walk together in life with God. All who are born of God, all who believe on the Lord Jesus Christ are the possessors of God's boundless free grace in Christ. We are forgiven of all sin (1:7, 9; 2:12; 3:5), possessors of eternal life, and never can perish (2:25). We are taught of God (2:20-27), adopted as the children of God (3:1), loved of God and made to be lovers of God (4:19), and forever accepted of God (5:11-15).

The Grace of God

In chapter 2 John gives a clear and assuring declaration of the grace of God that is ours in Christ. He begins the chapter by dealing with that which is most perplexing and troubling to God's saints in this world: our sins! What happens when the believer sins? Do our sins destroy our relationship with God? Do our sins destroy our fellowship with God?

In the first verse John tells us that the things he has told us, and the things he is about to tell us are written for the express purpose of preventing us from sinning. Then, he immediately assures us that our sins do not and cannot in anyway destroy our relationship with our Father. Do not misunderstand what John is declaring here. Yes, our sins do, very greatly, interrupt our enjoyment of God's favour. But our sins do not and cannot destroy or lessen our acceptance with God, because the whole of our acceptance with God is in Christ, who is our unceasing, unfailing Advocate with the Father. 'My little children, these things write I unto you, that ye sin not. And if any man sin, we have an advocate with the Father, Jesus Christ the righteous: And he is the propitiation for our sins: and not for ours only, but also for the sins of the whole world' (vv. 1-2).

These are two of the most precious, most comforting, most soul-cheering verses to be found in the whole Word of God. Yet they remind us of a very sad fact, which we must never forget. All of God's children in this world, at their very best, are still sinners. John says, 'My little children, these things write I unto you, that ye sin not'. Children of God, do not sin! We should never sin. We must oppose sin and resist it. It is an astonishing thing to realize that men and women who are loved of God, redeemed by the blood of Christ and regenerated by the power and grace of God the Holy Spirit need to be urged not to sin. But the admonition is needed by us all. Do not sin!

Still, John knew very well that all of God's saints in this world do sin. Therefore, he says, 'If any man sin'. The apostle uses gentle language, but he knew that we would sin. It was John who said, 'If we say that we have no sin, we deceive ourselves, and the truth is not in us' (1:8). So long as we live in this world, in this body of flesh, we shall sin. Sin is what we are by nature. Sin is mixed with all we do. Sin mars even our best deeds. 'We are all as an unclean thing; and all our righteousnesses are as filthy rags' (Isaiah 64:6). All of God's people in this world have learned to confess, with the apostle Paul, 'I know that in me (that is, in my flesh) dwelleth no good thing' (Romans 7:18). Every believer mournfully cries, 'O wretched man that I am!' (Romans 7:24), because every believer knows himself to be a vile sinner.

We do sin, but John assures us that our sins will never deprive us of our interest in Christ. Notice John's words: 'If any man sin, we have an advocate with the Father'. Yes, though we do sin, we have an Advocate with the Father still. The text does not read, 'If any man sin, he has forfeited his Advocate with the Father'. It says, 'We have an Advocate', sinners though we are.

All the sin a believer ever has committed, or ever can commit, cannot destroy his interest in Christ. We may, any one of us, fall into some dreadful, shameful, sorrowful transgression. God forbid that it should ever happen. But there is no sin, no evil thought, imagination, or deed of which you and I are not capable. Yet when we do sin, these horrible, treasonable acts can never tear us from our Saviour's heart. What a wonderful, blessed and liberating truth this is. Are you not glad that God 'hath not dealt with us after our sins; nor rewarded us according to our iniquities'? (Psalm 103: 10).

Child of God, I tell you plainly that the Lord Jesus Christ will never forsake his wandering sheep. He will not leave his erring child. I say, with John, 'Do not sin'. May God strengthen you with grace to resist sin and to hate evil. But when you do sin, do not despair. God still declares, 'I am the Lord, I change not; therefore ye sons of Jacob are not consumed' (Malachi 3:6).

Mark this down as a solid pillar of gospel truth: notwithstanding all our sin, we are perfectly justified, completely accepted, wholly righteous, and graciously beloved in Christ. Let every believer in God's blessed, sovereign grace lay hold on this mercy, ever drawing comfort, and assurance from it.

John also gives us a reason for this blessed assurance. God has provided his Son, the Lord Jesus Christ, as an Advocate for his sinning people. 'We have an Advocate with the Father, Jesus Christ the righteous: and he is the propitiation for our sins'. God will never charge his believing children with sin, because Christ has completely satisfied the justice of God for us, and he pleads the merits of his righteousness and blood for us in heaven.

The Son of God ever bears our names before the Father, pleading the merits of his own blood and righteousness for our eternal salvation. We need never fear wrath and condemnation from God, because 'We have an Advocate with the Father, Jesus Christ the righteous: and he is the propitiation for our sins'. We know that our Advocate in heaven is an effectual Advocate, because he is 'Jesus', the 'Christ', 'the Righteous', 'and he is the propitiation for our sins'.

Because Christ is our Advocate, though we face countless enemies to our souls in this world, within and without, enemies by which multitudes are destroyed, God's elect shall abide forever (v. 17). The grace of God shall remain in you, and you 'shall continue in the Son, and in the Father' (v. 24). 'And this is the promise that he hath promised us, even eternal life' (v. 25). Our Saviour said, 'I give unto them eternal life, and they shall never perish'.

The Sons of God

In chapter 3 the apostle John sets before us the great and glorious privilege that is ours in Christ as 'the sons of God'. Here is a cause for great wonder. 'Behold, what manner of love the Father hath bestowed upon us, that we should be called the sons of God'. God Almighty so loved us that he has made us his own dear children (vv. 1-3). John Gill wrote:

'This is a privilege that exceeds all others. It is better to be a son than to be a saint. Angels are saints, but not sons. They are servants. It is better to be a child of God than to be redeemed, pardoned, and justified. It is great grace to redeem from slavery, to pardon criminals, and justify the ungodly; but it is another and a higher act of grace to make them sons; and which makes them infinitely more honourable, than to be the sons and daughters of the greatest potentate upon earth; yea, gives them an honour which Adam had not in innocence, nor the angels in heaven, who though sons by creation, yet not by adoption.'

Here is a cause for grave concern. Our every sin is the transgression of God's holy law and calls for judgment, wrath, and condemnation. 'Whosoever committeth sin transgresseth also the law: for sin is the transgression of the law' (v. 4).

Here is a cause for unceasing joy and praise. 'And ye know that he was manifested to take away our sins; and in him is no sin' (v. 5). Christ has taken away our sins, all our sins: past, present, and future.

> There's pardon for transgressions past:
> It matters not how black their cast.
> And, Oh, my soul, with wonder view,
> For sins to come there's pardon too!

Here is a cause for constant thanksgiving and earnest prayer. The Lord Jesus Christ, our great God, so loved us that he laid down his life for us, to save us; and we ought to love each other just that way. 'Hereby perceive we the love of God, because he laid down his life for us: and we ought to lay down our lives for the brethren' (v. 16).

The Servants of God

In chapter 4 John tells us to test, try, and prove every preacher who claims to speak for God, distinguishing the servants of God from the messengers of Satan and antichrist by one specific thing. What they have to say concerning the person and work of Christ (vv. 1-3). Every true servant of God confesses in public as well as in private that the Lord Jesus Christ is God the Son, come in the flesh. Having accomplished all that he came here to accomplish, having accomplished fully everything written in the prophets concerning the Christ, he brought in righteousness. He made an end of sin. He magnified the law and made it honourable. He saved his people from their sins. He accomplished and obtained eternal redemption and salvation for all his people by the sacrifice of himself.

Every false prophet, every messenger of Satan, every servant of antichrist, while professing to believe in and worship Christ, denies that he has accomplished redemption by the sacrifice of himself. Every false prophet declares that you must do something to make up for that which Christ did not complete, that you must do something to make his redemption complete and effectual. Every one of them say that you must do something to make yourself righteous, that you must do something to atone for your own sin.

'We Love Him'

Then, John assures us both of God's great love for us and of every believer's love for him, telling us that our love for him is the response of our hearts to his love for us, not the other way around (vv. 9-10, 19).

'In this was manifested the love of God toward us, because that God sent his only begotten Son into the world, that we might live through him. Herein is love, not that we loved God, but that he loved us, and sent his Son to be the propitiation for our sins ... We love him, because he first loved us'.

Consider this wonderful truth. 'We love him, because he first loved us'. God's saints differ on many points. But in this one thing every true child of God is like every other child of God: 'We love him'. We do not love him as we desire. We do not love him as we know we should. We do not love him as we soon shall. But we really do love him. It is not possible for a person to experience the grace of God in salvation and not love the God of all grace. It is not possible for a person to know the efficacy of Christ's blood in his own soul and not love his gracious Redeemer. It is not possible for a person to have his heart renewed by the power and grace of the Holy Spirit and not love the Spirit of life. In spite of our many weaknesses, sins, and failures we do honestly and sincerely confess, 'Lord, thou knowest all things, thou knowest that I love thee'.

We know also that we would never have loved him if he had not loved us first. The love of God for us precedes our love for him. 'He first loved us'. He loved us before we had any desire to be loved by him. He loved us before we sought his grace. He loved us before we had any repentance or faith. He loved us before we had any being. He loved us eternally. Does he not say, 'I have loved thee with an everlasting love, therefore with lovingkindness have I drawn thee'? He chose us, redeemed us, and called us because he loved us.

Not only does God's love for us precede our love for God; but God's love for us is the cause of our love for him. 'We love him, because he first loved us'. We would never have loved the Lord, if he had not intervened to conquer us with his love. In the midst of our sins and corruption, he passed by, and behold it was 'the time of love' (Ezekiel 16:8). He revealed his great love for us in Christ. As we beheld the crucified Christ dying in the place of sinners, the love of God conquered our rebel hearts. Trusting Christ as our only Saviour, we are compelled to love him because he first loved us. Now we know that whatever we are, by the grace of God, we are because he loved us.

The Witness of God

In the fifth chapter John gives us the witness of God, by which our hearts are assured of salvation in Christ and acceptance with him. In the opening verses of this chapter he declares plainly that all who trust Christ are born of God and love God (vv. 1-3). Then, he assures us that all who trust Christ overcome the world (vv. 4-5). Beginning in verse 6, John tells us of the re-assuring witnesses God has given concerning his Son and the efficacy of his grace and salvation in his Son.

There are three witnesses in the earth (vv. 6 and 8). The witness of the water has reference to our Saviour's baptism, in which he symbolically fulfilled all righteousness for us, and the Father spoke from heaven declaring him to be the Son of God. The witness of the blood has reference to our Lord's sin-atoning sacrifice, which he accomplished at Calvary. The witness of the Spirit is the witness of God the Holy Spirit to the finished work of Christ in the scriptures and in that conviction that creates faith in God's elect (John 16:7-11).

There are also three witnesses in heaven. 'For there are three that bear record in heaven, the Father, the Word, and the Holy Ghost: and these three are one' (v. 7).[1] God the Father bears witness to the accomplishments of Christ, having accepted him as our sin-atoning Sacrifice. God the Son bears witness to his own accomplishments as our Mediator, pleading the merits of his blood and righteousness before God for us. And God the Holy Spirit bears witness, convincing sinners to come to the throne of grace for mercy, through faith in Christ alone.

---

[1] See Appendix 1 (p 621) for John Gill's excellent comments on this verse.

God's Witness Within

In verses 9-15 John concludes that if we receive anything at the mouth of two or three witnesses among men, we surely ought to receive the infinitely greater witness of our God, and be assured of his grace.

'If we receive the witness of men, the witness of God is greater: for this is the witness of God which he hath testified of his Son. He that believeth on the Son of God hath the witness in himself: he that believeth not God hath made him a liar; because he believeth not the record that God gave of his Son. And this is the record, that God hath given to us eternal life, and this life is in his Son. He that hath the Son hath life; and he that hath not the Son of God hath not life. These things have I written unto you that believe on the name of the Son of God; that ye may know that ye have eternal life, and that ye may believe on the name of the Son of God. And this is the confidence that we have in him, that, if we ask any thing according to his will, he heareth us: And if we know that he hear us, whatsoever we ask, we know that we have the petitions that we desired of him'.

The apostle gives us one final word of assurance in verse 20. 'And we know that the Son of God is come, and hath given us an understanding, that we may know him that is true, and we are in him that is true, even in his Son Jesus Christ. This is the true God, and eternal life'. Then he gives us a tender, but much needed, admonition in verse 21. 'Little children, keep yourselves from idols. Amen.'

Chapter 63

2 John

'For the Truth's Sake'

Though it does not bear his name, it is evident that this epistle was written by the apostle John. When we compare its language (2 John 1:5-9) with that of 1 John (1 John 2:7-8; 3:23; 4:1-3; 5:3), we see that the language used here is the same. John's purpose in writing this brief epistle is to exhort and encourage us to continue in the truth and faith of the gospel, to walk in love to God and his people, and to avoid false teachers and their doctrines.

The Elect Lady

John addresses this epistle to 'the elect lady'. Did you ever pause to think about what name is used most often in the New Testament to describe God's people? They are called 'saints' forty times, 'sons of God' sixteen times, 'strangers' six times, 'Christians' just three times, and 'believers' just twice. But the term that is used more often than any other, except for 'saints', to describe the people of God in the New Testament is 'the elect'. In fact, the word 'saints' is but another way of saying, 'elect'. God's saints are those separated from others, separated unto God from eternity by electing love.

Election was such a commonly known and commonly discussed theme in the early church that when believers spoke to and about one another they used the word 'elect' to distinguish God's people from the rest of the world. Many suggest that this 'elect lady' was a certain, believing woman, and that John wrote this epistle to her and her believing children. Perhaps that is the case. In Christ there is neither male nor female. Both are one in him. It is not unlikely that one of the epistles of the New Testament might be addressed to a woman.

It is certain that our Lord gave special attention to and showed special care for certain women: the Samaritan woman, Mary and Martha, the woman with an issue of blood, the Syrophenician, and the woman who anointed him for his burial. After his resurrection he appeared to a woman and sent her to tell the disciples that he was alive. If we think of Miriam, Ruth, Deborah, Esther, Dorcas, Lydia, Priscilla, Lois, and Eunice, we should not be at all surprised to see the Holy Spirit honour and distinguish a certain woman by addressing an apostolic epistle to her.

If the epistle was written to an individual woman and her children, it should be noted that her children were addressed as grown, mature children who were found 'walking in truth' (v. 4). They were children who had themselves professed faith in Christ and walked in truth.

I think, however, that John uses the term, 'the elect lady', to refer to a local church. It really does not matter which. Neither is there any need for us to know which. The epistle was written by divine inspiration for and to all who walk in truth. It is certain that John's words are written to every child of God in this world, for God's children are God's elect. His church is his 'elect lady'. God's elect are those chosen by his grace to eternal life in Christ before the world was made (Matthew 24:31; Romans 8:33; Ephesians 1:3-6; Colossians 3:12; 1 Thessalonians 1:4; 2 Thessalonians 2:13-14; 1 Peter 1:2).

We are not told when the epistle was written, or where John was when he wrote it. Again, such things are not material, had they been we would have been told. This is God's Word to us today. May he teach us its message and make it sweet to our souls.

The Truth
'The elder unto the elect lady and her children, whom I love in the truth; and not I only, but also all they that have known the truth' (v. 1). John calls himself an Elder because he was both a pastor and an old man. At the time he wrote this epistle, he was at least a hundred years old. He expresses his sincere and heartfelt love for this elect lady and her children, whom he and his companions loved in the truth. He speaks of the joy he and his companions, who were lovers of the truth, found in these who walked in the truth.

Believers love all men as men, but God gives his elect a special love for those who are in the family of faith (Galatians 6:10; Titus 3:15). Notice the connection between John's love for God's saints and their love for the truth. Those who love Christ, who is the Truth, love all who walk in the Truth. We love one another for Christ's sake. It is he who dwells in us and abides in us forever.

Notice this too, John speaks to God's elect with great confidence and assurance as well as with great tenderness and affection. 'The elect lady', as John calls her, had in her election all the blessings, benefits, and effects of election. As the bud contains all the future blossoms and foliage of the flower, so God's elect have all the blessings of grace in Christ (Ephesians 1:3-6), 'according as he hath chosen us in him before the foundation of the world'. Robert Hawker wrote on this passage in *The Poor Man's Commentary*:

'Together with this electing grace, there is the calling grace appointed also. "For whom he did predestinate, them he also called" (Romans 8:30). And in the season of that call, there is given the pardoning grace to all sins. So blessedly speaks the Apostle. "And you being dead in your sins, and the uncircumcision of your flesh, hath he quickened together with him, having forgiven you all trespasses" (Colossians 2:13).

And neither doth the blessing stop here. For justification immediately follows. "Being justified freely by his grace, through the redemption which is in Christ Jesus" (Romans 3:24). And both sanctification and glory bring up the rear, in the sure events involved in the blessed act of God's sovereign love, when, from all eternity, the Lord chose the church in Christ Jesus (Ephesians 1:4; 1 Corinthians 1:30; 2 Timothy 1:9; Romans 8:30, 31).'

The Truth's Sake

'For the truth's sake, which dwelleth in us, and shall be with us for ever' (v. 2). The word 'truth' occurs five times in the first four verses of this epistle. It refers both to Christ and to the doctrine of Christ. The two cannot be separated. Truth is more than facts about Christ. Truth is Christ himself (John 14:6; 4:24; 8:32; 18:37). Christ dwells in us and his Word dwells in us, as an inward principle of grace which lasts forever (John 15:4-7; 17:17).

John's Salutation

'Grace be with you, mercy, and peace, from God the Father, and from the Lord Jesus Christ, the Son of the Father, in truth and love' (v. 3).

John's salutation is like that used by other apostles (1 Timothy 1:2; Romans 1:7), but he characteristically adds, with respect to Christ, that he is the Son of God. This was a special issue to John and it appears that he never missed a chance to state it emphatically (John 1:1, 18; 10:30; 1 John 1:3, 7; 4:2, 15).

'In truth and love'. These two words, 'truth' and 'love', are used repeatedly in this epistle. They are companions. They cannot be separated. God is light (truth) and God is love. Let them ever be united in our minds and hearts. Truth without love becomes stern, cold, and even cruel. Love without truth, if such were possible, would be unstable and without foundation.

Great Joy

'I rejoiced greatly that I found of thy children walking in truth, as we have received a commandment from the Father' (v. 4). God's children rejoice when they find others who are God's children. The Psalmist sang, with regard to God's church, his 'elect lady', 'Lo! Children are an heritage of the Lord, and the fruit of the womb is a reward' (Psalm 127:3).

Apply these words, as we may to an individual household, and see cause for great joy to any parent. To see our natural children walking spiritually in truth is, perhaps, the greatest boon we can experience in this world as believers. When they are blessed with grace, we are blessed with grace!

Even when that is not the case, even when we must, like David, look over our sons and daughters with sorrow, seeing nothing but Absaloms, Adonijahs, and Amnons coming from our loins, let us, as we sigh, 'although my house is not so with God', take solace in God's covenant grace 'ordered in all things and sure' (2 Samuel 23:5).

Apply this to a pastor looking over a local church he has served or a church with which he has had some connection, and the same joy is discovered. John's joy is the expression of a faithful pastor's heart and love. God's servants dance in their hearts when we see his children walking in truth, walking with Christ in the blessed truth of Christ revealed in the gospel.

It brought great joy to the apostles to find the children of this elect lady 'walking in truth', living day by day in a continual, progressive spirit, attitude, and conversation which revealed that Christ was in them. They not only professed to know Christ, but their conduct and conversation revealed a living union with him. This is the commandment we have received from the Father (Micah 6:8; 1 John 3:18).

Love One Another

'And now I beseech thee, lady, not as though I wrote a new commandment unto thee, but that which we had from the beginning, that we love one another' (v. 5). This is the same thing John told us in 1 John 2:7, 8. He is probably referring to the words of our Saviour in John 13:34. It is that which our Lord taught from the beginning. How sweetly the life of grace in Christ leads to a life of love. 'As ye have received Christ Jesus the Lord, so walk ye in him, rooted and built up in him' (Colossians 2:6-7). It is impossible to be otherwise. Where Christ is, there must be fruitfulness in Christ. Where the Spirit of God is, the love of Christ shines.

The love John is talking about is much more than warm feelings and emotions about God and one another. We cannot love one another and walk in love if we do not walk in truth. We cannot so love if we do not walk with Christ in the truth he reveals in his Word, 'And this is love, that we walk after his commandments. This is the commandment, That, as ye have heard from the beginning, ye should walk in it' (v. 6).

Antichrist

'For many deceivers are entered into the world, who confess not that Jesus Christ is come in the flesh. This is a deceiver and an antichrist' (v. 7). John is referring to false teachers and preachers, who are described by their character and work. They are seducers, who cause others to go astray. They pretend to be gospel preachers, to love the truth, to be concerned for men's souls, and to desire the glory of God. But they handle the Word deceitfully. They are impostors (1 John 2:18; Matthew 7:15, 16; 2 Peter 2:1-3).

The primary error of these false prophets is their denial of the person and work of Christ. They profess to believe in Christ as a prophet, teacher, healer, a messenger from God, and even the Messiah and the Son of God. However, they deny him altogether by denying that he has come in the flesh and accomplished all that the scriptures declare he would accomplish: the redemption and salvation of his people (Daniel 9:24; Isaiah 53:10-11; Matthew 1:21; Hebrews 9:12). They do not necessarily deny that he came. They deny that he has effectually accomplished what he came to do, but assert that he merely made redemption and salvation possible. These whom John describes as antichrists deny that the Lord Jesus finished the transgression and made an end of sins. They deny that he brought in everlasting righteousness, that he fulfilled all the prophets, 'sealed up the vision', and that he was anointed as Lord over all because he finished the work.

He who is the Christ 'shall see of the travail of his soul, and shall be satisfied'. The cross of our Lord Jesus Christ shall never be discovered a miscarriage! He satisfied the justice of God and the justice of God shall satisfy him. 'He shall see his seed' brought out — out of captivity, prison, bondage, and the world, brought in — into his kingdom, brought up — taught and cared for, and brought home!

All who deny, either in word or in doctrine, by statement or implication, that Jesus Christ is God are deceivers and anti-Christ (John 10:30-33; Matthew 1:21-23).

Look to Yourselves

'Look to yourselves, that we lose not those things which we have wrought, but that we receive a full reward' (v. 8). This is an exhortation to the elect lady and her children to look about them, be aware of these antichrists and their doctrine. They must take care of themselves and beware of false teachers and false doctrines (2 Corinthians 11:1-4).

We must take care not to lose, or throw away, those things that we have wrought by faith, those things that we profess have been wrought in us by grace, and in the end lose our own souls. What tragedy! If we depart from the gospel of Christ, there remains no sacrifice for sin (Hebrews 10:26; 6:4-6).

Christ is our wisdom, righteousness, sanctification, and redemption (1 Corinthians 1:30). If we are not redeemed in him, we have no life or hope (Galatians 4:4, 5). Let us persevere in the faith of Christ until we are made like him. This shall be our full reward (Hebrews 3:6, 14; Colossians 1:19-23).

The Doctrine of Christ

'Whosoever transgresseth, and abideth not in the doctrine of Christ, hath not God. He that abideth in the doctrine of Christ, he hath both the Father and the Son' (v. 9). Anyone who denies the doctrine of Christ, the Messiah, has not, knows not, and believes not God. 'The doctrine of Christ' has to do with the following characteristics and glorious attributes of our Lord.

First, Christ's person as the Son of God, as truly God, and the union of the two natures divine and human, in one person. Second, Christ's offices as Mediator, Surety, Prophet, Priest, and King. Third, Christ's redemptive work: his obedience, suffering, death, resurrection, and ascension, by which he obtained eternal redemption for his people. Fourth, Christ's return to judge and to reign.

This is the doctrine of grace, redemption, and eternal glory. The man who abides in the truth of Christ has both the Father and the Son. He has an interest in them and a knowledge of them (John 17:3; 1 John 5:11-13).

Receive Them Not

'If there come any unto you, and bring not this doctrine, receive him not into your house, neither bid him God speed' (v. 10). If anyone comes to your church or your home, pretending to be a gospel preacher, one who does not preach this doctrine but despises and denies it, do not allow him to preach in the house of God and do not entertain him in your home' (Romans 16:17; Galatians 1:8, 9).

'Neither bid him God speed'. Do not help him, encourage him, or pray for him. Do not give him the impression that you are sympathetic to him or his efforts.

'For he that biddeth him God speed is partaker of his evil deeds' (v. 11). Those who wish false teachers well, who encourage them, or who converse with them in a friendly and familiar way instead of reproving them and shunning them as they ought, are aiding and abetting them, supporting them in their attacks on Christ and can be considered partakers in their evil deeds.

Conclusion

John concludes this epistle very graciously, expressing his love for these dear saints, and his desire to see them face to face, and by conveying to them the greetings of another gospel church, the elect sister of this elect lady. 'Having many things to write unto you, I would not write with paper and ink: but I trust to come unto you, and speak face to face, that our joy may be full' (v. 12).

Although he had many things to write to them and teach them, he preferred not to do so with paper and ink. This blessed old man hoped to visit God's dear saints and talk to them personally, so that their joy may be complete. There is a great value in correspondence between believers; but nothing replaces personal fellowship, exhortation, and encouragement (Hebrews 10:24, 25; 3:13; Colossians 3:16).

'The children of thy elect sister greet thee. Amen' (v. 13). Let us learn, especially gospel preachers, from this short, but gracious epistle of John the elder, how to address God's elect with words of comfort and consolation in Christ. They are to be spoken to graciously and affectionately, for comfort and edification, to build them up in mutual love, in the fellowship of the Truth, in the fellowship of Christ. There is no need to speak harshly and bitterly. Robert Hawker again wrote:

Discovering Christ In All The Scriptures

'There is nothing more strengthening to the Church of God, than when old disciples speak to young ones, concerning God's purposes in Christ, as manifested in his electing, converting, redeeming, establishing grace! It is blessedly said by one of old, 'the righteous shall bring forth fruit in his old age, to show that the Lord is upright'. Did not the Lord the Spirit cause this epistle to be sent by John to one Elect Lady, to be recorded in the Church, and handed down, through the several ages, to the present hour, on purpose to teach old saints, and especially faithful old ministers, how to speak to the elect children of Christ, in the several stations and characters as they stand in grace?'

Chapter 64

3 John

Gaius, Diotrephes, and Demetrius

Here is a letter written by the apostle John to his beloved son in the faith, Gaius. Gaius was not a pastor, preacher, or elder. He was a man whom God had saved, a believer, a member of a local church, which had been visited by some missionaries. These missionaries were travelling about, preaching the gospel to the Gentiles. In their journeys they stopped at the town where Gaius lived to visit the brethren there. Gaius took them into his house, fed them, entertained them, and lodged them for several days, perhaps for several weeks. When they left, he gave them some travelling money to help with their expenses.

When they got back to the church of which John was the pastor, these travelling evangelists, these missionaries, could not stop talking about Gaius. They told John about him. They told their friends about him. They told the whole church about Gaius. When John heard these men talking about his spiritual son, his heart bubbled up with joy and gratitude. He wrote this letter, by the inspiration of God the Holy Spirit, to commend Gaius. And he does commend him! He tells us that Gaius loved the gospel (vv. 3-4), that he was faithful in all things, and that he was generous, charitable, and hospitable to his brethren, even to those who were total strangers (vv. 5-6). Like Abraham, Gaius entertained strangers who came to him in the name of Christ, and in so doing he entertained angels unawares (Genesis 18:3; Hebrews 13:2).

John's second epistle was written to the elect lady, whom John loved in the truth. This epistle is addressed to a man named 'Gaius', 'whom', John also says, 'I love in the truth'. Truth and love are companions, twin graces that can never be separated. This epistle commends truth and love displayed in Gaius' deeds. For it is 'faith which worketh by love' (Galatians 5:6).

In this epistle we have a clear contrast of three men, Gaius, a very gracious man, to whom the epistle is addressed, and Diotrephes, who was a proud deceiver, and Demetrius, who was a man of good report. God the Holy Spirit directed John's heart and pen to write this brief epistle for our learning and admonition. He has preserved it for us in the sacred volume.

Gaius

'The elder unto the well beloved Gaius, whom I love in the truth' (v. 1). We see the name 'Gaius' four other times in the New Testament (Acts 19:29; 20:4; Romans 16:23; 1 Corinthians 1:14). Each time it refers to different men. This man's name was common in the Roman Empire, perhaps as the name 'John' is today. The Gaius to whom this epistle is addressed was a beloved brother, who was converted under John's ministry, one of his children in the faith and dearly beloved (v. 4). Not only did John love him, Gaius was a man 'well-beloved'. He was beloved of God and chosen unto eternal salvation in Christ (Jeremiah 31:3; Ephesians 1:3-6; 2 Thessalonians 2:13), and beloved of his brethren.

Gaius was beloved of those saints who knew him because he was a man of great faith, integrity, and generosity. He had experienced the grace of God; and that made him gracious. He was sound in doctrine and sound in heart. Gaius was a loving and lovable man.

Prosperity

'Beloved, I wish above all things that thou mayest prosper and be in health, even as thy soul prospereth' (v. 2). The word 'above' would be better translated 'in'. That is obvious in the context in which the word is used. John would not desire prosperity in temporal things above Gaius' prosperity in spiritual and eternal things. Yet, his love for Gaius and his desires for him included temporal things. What he is saying here is 'I wish that you may have a prosperous journey through this world and be in good health, even as your soul prospers. I pray that the Lord will grant his continual, manifest blessings upon you'. The Amplified Bible interprets verse 2 this way: 'Beloved, I pray that you may prosper in every way and [that your body] may keep well, even as [I know] your soul keeps well and prospers'.

Physical health is a great blessing and is altogether the gift of God's providential goodness. Among the countless promises of God to his people, there are many that relate to temporal things (Deuteronomy 28:1-14). The scriptures teach us that, with regard to all who are called of God by the effectual, irresistible grace and power of God the Holy Spirit to life and faith in Christ, everything for time and eternity prospers and is the blessing of God upon us (Romans 8:28). He that spared not his own Son, but delivered him up for us all, will with him freely give us all things (Romans 8:32).

Temporal Things

God's saints in this world are given liberty to use all things temporal as we live to serve and honour God our Saviour. It is written, 'all things are yours ... and ye are Christ's' (1 Corinthians 3:21-23). If the Lord causes us to abound in earthly goods and in good health, he accompanies those blessings with grace sufficient to make them prosperous to our souls. When that is the case, let us, like Gaius, use such blessings of providence 'faithfully in whatsoever' we do (v. 5), both in connection with our brethren in the church and kingdom of God, and in connection with the world, doing good to all men, and especially to them who are of the household of faith.

If the Lord sends adversity he takes out all the bitterness of it, still his grace is sufficient. He assures us that this, too, is his blessing, the very best thing for us. So that, though the fig-tree does not blossom and fruit is not found in the vine, though the labour of the olive fail and the fields yield no meat, though the flock be cut off from the fold and there be no herds in the stall, yet, the child of God can, and will say, I will rejoice in the Lord, I will joy in the God of my salvation (Habakkuk 3:17, 18).

Spiritual Things

As in temporal things, so, too, in spiritual things, the child of God is always blessed and prospers. It is written,

'Blessed be the God and Father of our Lord Jesus Christ, who hath blessed us with all spiritual blessings in heavenly places in Christ: According as he hath chosen us in him before the foundation of the world, that we should be holy and without blame before him: In love having predestinated us unto the adoption of children by Jesus Christ to himself, according to the good pleasure of his will, To the praise of the glory of his grace, wherein he hath made us accepted in the beloved'. (Ephesians 1:3-6)

We are blessed, in time and to all eternity, with the Father's love, the Saviour's redemption, and the Holy Spirit's grace. All the blessings of grace, so boundlessly bestowed upon us from eternity in Christ, are gifts of God which shall not be taken away neither in this world nor in the world to come (Romans 11:29). Our God has given us peace and pardon through the blood of the cross. He gives us continual manifestations of his boundless love. The Lord Jesus comes to bless, comfort, and encourage us, and to make himself known to us in ways with which he does not deal with the world (John 14:18-23). 'Who shall describe', asks Robert Hawker, 'the outpourings of divine love, or the incomings of divine grace, the child of God is continually receiving from the Lord, who is blessing him with all spiritual blessings in Christ Jesus?'

Eternal Things

Regarding eternal blessings, our God has not only given us the promise of the life that now is, but of that which is to come. Indeed, eternal life is ours now. It is already begun in our souls. 'He that hath the Son of God hath life'. He enjoys it now by faith. 'For faith is the substance of things hoped for, the evidence of things not seen' (Hebrews 11:1). And faith in Christ is the earnest given by the Spirit of glory to come.

Gaius' Testimony

'For I rejoiced greatly, when the brethren came and testified of the truth that is in thee, even as thou walkest in the truth' (v. 3). Some brethren came to John from the place where Gaius lived and told him that Gaius was a man who believed the truth of the gospel and that he was a man of a truly gracious spirit. He walked before God, and men, in such a way that he was known by God's saints as one who lived for the glory of God. His life was a life that adorned the doctrine of God our Saviour in all things (Titus 2:10). The report of these men concerning Gaius filled the old pastor with joy.

'I have no greater joy than to hear that my children walk in truth' (v. 4). Nothing makes a faithful gospel preacher happier than to hear that those to whom he has preached the gospel, and for whom he has been the means God used to bring them to the knowledge of Christ, believe and walk in the truth. We can bestow no greater gift upon our friends, and no greater inheritance upon our families than the gospel of Christ. And they can bring no greater joy and satisfaction to our hearts than to receive the truth and walk therein (Acts 3:2-6; Philemon 20-21).

Proper Honour

'Beloved, thou doest faithfully whatsoever thou doest to the brethren, and to strangers' (v. 5). The Holy Spirit teaches us to give honour to whom honour is due (Romans 13:7). We are not to flatter men, but it is altogether proper to honour and commend one another. Here John commends Gaius for his hospitality and charity to God's saints and to strangers who crossed his path. He was a kind and generous man, who cared for and ministered to the needs of others. Both his heart and his home were open to men. He used that which God had given him for the benefit of others. Thus, he both blessed the lives of many and was blessed of God in his own life (Hebrews 13:1-2).

Gaius did 'faithfully' that which he did. He did not do things in a hypocritical and pretentious way to be seen of men and gain their applause. He did what he did because he loved the Lord and the Lord's people (Matthew 6:1-4).

'Which have borne witness of thy charity before the church: whom if thou bring forward on their journey after a godly sort, thou shalt do well' (v. 6). This verse makes it clear that the 'strangers' referred to in verse 5 were travelling preachers, evangelists (missionaries), who were strangers to Gaius before they came to his town. They testified before the church at Ephesus of his love, friendship, and care of them. They were greatly moved by his spirit of grace and love and gave thanks to God for the grace of God in him.

Supporting Missionaries

Notice what John tells us here about the support of gospel preachers, particularly about the support of missionaries. 'Whom if thou bring forward on their journey after a godly sort, thou shalt do well'. In 2 John, he warned us not to support those false teachers and preachers who come preaching 'another gospel' (2 John 10-11; cf. Acts 20:28-30). Here he tells us that we do well to aid God's children and to help make their journey through this world to be more pleasant especially those who are travelling missionaries (Matthew 10:42; 2 Kings 4:8-10).

In verses 7 and 8 he tells us why we do well in supporting those brethren who go forth in the name of Christ preaching the gospel. Such men have gone out from home and family for Christ's sake. They are not supported by the heathen to whom they preach, taking nothing from them, lest the gospel be reproached. Freely we have received and freely we give. We ought to support and provide for such men. In doing so we are fellow-labourers and fellow-helpers to the truth. It is a great privilege to preach the gospel and an equal privilege and blessing to provide for those who preach it, for in doing so we also serve the cause of the gospel.

The only proper reason for the existence of any local church in this world is the furtherance of the gospel. The church exists on earth only for the preaching of the gospel of the Lord Jesus Christ. The church of God is a sounding board for the gospel. It is our responsibility to use every means at our disposal to proclaim the gospel of Christ as fully and universally as we possibly can to the generation in which we live. We have no other commission (Matthew 28:18-20; Mark 16:15-16; Luke 24:46-48; Acts 1:8). One of the most effective means we have of preaching the gospel in any age is gospel missions, sending out missionaries to preach the good news of redemption and grace in Christ around the world.

Missionaries are men called and gifted of God to establish churches, train pastors, and help establish those pastors and churches in the gospel of the grace of God, so that they might carry on the work of the gospel for the years to come. Medical missionaries, educational missionaries, and cultural missionaries are not true missionaries, and should not be supported by local churches. Missionaries are men who have a mission from God, and their mission is to preach the gospel of Christ.

With these things in mind, let us examine what the Spirit of God teaches in these verses about the church's responsibility to missionaries. After highly commending this man, Gaius, for all that he had done, John urged him to do even more. Realizing that God's servants are to be supported entirely by the generous, free, voluntary gifts of his people, John gave Gaius, and us, four reasons why we should support missionaries.

1. It is pleasing to God for us to do so

John told Gaius that when God's servants come to town, we are not only to care for them while they are with us, but we are to 'bring (them) forward on their journey after a godly sort' (v. 6). It is the responsibility of local churches to provide all those things that God's servants need to carry on their work. Missionaries have all the earthly needs that the rest of us have and many that we do not have. They must have homes, food and clothing for their families. They must provide health care for their households. They have to educate their children, and they have to have some means of transportation, just like we do. In addition to these things, every expense for the work on the field comes out of the missionary's pocket! Whatever it takes to keep faithful men free of earthly care, so that they may give themselves whole-heartedly to the work of the ministry, we must do!

John tells us that this is a 'godly sort' of work. The marginal translation of these words is: this is a work 'worthy of God'. It is a work becoming to those who serve God. If we do this, if we support God's servants in the work of the gospel, we do well. This is a work pleasing to God. God delights to see those who love Christ showing their love by generosity towards his servants (2 Corinthians 9:7).

2. We should give 'for his name's sake'

'For his name's sake they went forth' (v. 7). And 'for his name's sake' we must supply their needs. There is only one thing that compels the true servant of God to take his wife and children to a remote, far distant country to preach the gospel, leaving behind the comforts of his homeland, the company of his friends, and the warmth of his family: he is motivated by a burning jealousy for the name of Christ (Romans 1:5, 16-17) and desires to serve Christ with all he has.

That same burning jealousy for Christ's name inspires God's saints to give of their means to supply those men with the support they need. Every believer wants all men and women to hear the gospel of Christ, so that our great Saviour may be known, trusted, worshipped, and glorified throughout the world. The best means we have of accomplishing that great goal is giving of our means to support faithful gospel-preaching missionaries.

Our Lord is so highly honoured by the service of those whom he sends out to preach the gospel that he counts anything we do for them as having been done for him (Matthew 10:40-42), and indeed it is. God's servants are his ambassadors. Those men who faithfully preach the gospel of God's free and sovereign grace in Christ, the gospel of his electing love, accomplished redemption, effectual grace, and saving fulness, are God's representatives and spokesmen in this world (2 Corinthians 5:18-21).

Anything we do to one of God's ambassadors, we do to him. Anything done for God's ambassador is done for him; and anything done against God's ambassador is done against him.

3. Faithful men have no other means of support

'Because that for his name's sake they went forth, taking nothing of the Gentiles' (v. 7). These men preached to the Gentiles freely, refusing to seek, or even take financial support from unbelievers. Because they are faithful to Christ, the gospel of his grace, and the souls of men, they have no means of support other than the generosity of God's people.

4. Fellow-helpers to the Truth

By our loving, free, generous support of God's faithful servants, we become 'fellow-helpers to the truth'. When we supply a man's needs, so that he can preach the gospel of Christ freely to others, we become allies with him in the work of preaching the gospel. What a privilege! The work of the ministry is God's work; but God does his work through the labours of faithful men, through the preaching of the gospel. These men do their work by the generosity of faithful men and women, who work hard and freely give of their means, so that the gospel may be preached freely around the world.

God's church is one, and we are one with those missionaries we are privileged to support. Their cause is our cause; their work is our work, and their reward is our reward. The next time we have the opportunity to show hospitality to, entertain, give to, or do anything for one of God's servants, let us remember these things: This is a work that is pleasing to God. This is a work that is done by faith in and for the honour of Christ's name. This is a work done for worthy men, men who have forsaken all to preach the gospel. They are worthy to live by the gospel. By these things we are 'fellow-helpers to the truth'.

Diotrephes

'I wrote unto the church: but Diotrephes, who loveth to have the pre-eminence among them, receiveth us not' (v. 9). John wrote a letter to the church of which Gaius was a member. It was a letter of instruction, counsel, and apostolic orders. But Diotrephes, who was evidently an officer in the church, perhaps the pastor, refused to accept John's instruction and counsel, because he loved to have pre-eminence. He wanted people to honour and follow him. He craved recognition. Pastor Henry Mahan wrote, 'Everything in a church ought to be done by pastor and people in love, meekness and with mutual consent, with each seeking the glory of Christ and the good of all (Philippians 2:3-8; Romans 12:3, 10:1; 1 Corinthians 4:6,7)'. Diotrephes did what he did for the glory of Diotrephes! He was one of those wolves in sheep's clothing Paul told the church at Ephesus would arise from their midst 'speaking perverse things to draw away disciples after them' (Acts 20:30).

'Wherefore, if I come, I will remember his deeds which he doeth, prating against us with malicious words: and not content therewith, neither doth he himself receive the brethren, and forbiddeth them that would, and casteth them out of the church' (v. 10). John was determined, when he next visited the church, to expose this wicked man to the church and reprove him for his deeds (Galatians 2:11). He describes Diotrephes as one who spoke prating, empty things against him and other faithful servants of God.

How common Diotrephes' behaviour is to this day among self-serving preachers! True servants of God, true preachers of the gospel are prated against, not only by men of the world, but also by professors of religion. That which is spoken against them is just 'prating', silly, idle, and empty slanders. Such slanders take up any little matter and rail against faithful men in order to hurt their character, spoil their usefulness, and render their labours ineffective. But all their railing and prating is only to exalt themselves in the eyes of the people (1 Timothy 5:19; 2 Corinthians 10:10).

Diotrephes was not satisfied with speaking against John and his ministry. He refused to receive the preachers and missionaries sent by John. He threatened to cast those who received them out of the church.

'Beloved, follow not that which is evil, but that which is good. He that doeth good is of God: but he that doeth evil hath not seen God' (v. 11). The apostle here tells Gaius and us not to follow Diotrephes' wickedness. Such pride, ambition, love of pre-eminence, and self-exaltation is to be rebuked; and those who engage in it are to be rejected as evil men (Titus 3:1,2; James 4:11; Ephesians 4:31, 32). He who manifests the grace and spirit of Christ in attitude and action is of God, and he who does not has evidently not experienced the grace of God and does not know God at all (1 John 4:6-8, 20-21).

Demetrius

'Demetrius hath good report of all men, and of the truth itself: yea, and we also bear record; and ye know that our record is true' (v. 12). Demetrius was a man whose character, like that of Gaius, was exactly opposite to that of Diotrephes. His was an example to be followed. Demetrius was kind, considerate, and gracious. He had a good reputation and report. He was loved and respected by all who knew him.

It is sad, but terribly common, that trouble makers and those of a critical spirit find many followers. Let those who are wise mark the man of a Christ-like attitude and a loving spirit and follow his example. John bore record to the character of Demetrius, and we know that his word is true and dependable.

Diotrephes and Demetrius are known to us only by name. Robert Hawker wrote of them, 'How different their characters were! How opposed while they lived! How differently regarded when they died. How opposite in the esteem of the church, through all ages! And how everlastingly opposite, if dying as they are here said to have lived, through all the eternal world? How blessed to have a good report of all men; yea, and of the truth itself, which is Christ (John 14:6). Oh! For the whisper of Jesus, in a dying hour, to confirm his grace in the soul, as manifested in a living hour; that both in life and in death the soul be found in him (Isaiah 43:1-4)'.

The tender-hearted Apostle concludes his epistle with these words. 'I had many things to write, but I will not with ink and pen write unto thee: But I trust I shall shortly see thee, and we shall speak face to face. Peace be to thee. Our friends salute thee. Greet the friends by name' (vv. 13-14).

Reflections

We cannot conclude this study of 3 John in a more edifying way than by reflecting on Robert Hawker's summary statement upon these fourteen verses of inspiration.

'What a beautiful view is here afforded, of the beloved Apostle in his pastoral office, addressing the faithful Gaius, beloved in the Lord. To behold the venerable saint of God, amidst all the infirmities of declining years, thus blessing God, and blessing the servant of God, in his wishes both for spiritual and temporal prosperity.

But while we look at John, who justly commands our veneration and our love, let us look infinitely above John, and behold John's Lord still blessing all his church; and every Gaius of his redeemed family below, with blessings in himself.

Precious, precious Jesus! We desire to praise thee for all that is lovely, in the disciple whom Jesus loved; for all that is lovely in John, was, and is derived from thee! Lord! Hasten on thy blessed purposes, and bring on thy glorious day when thou wilt come to be glorified in thy saints, and to be admired in all that believe! To thee, Lord, it belongs, to keep thy Church from falling, and to present it faultless before the presence of thy glory with exceeding joy. In the blessed hope of thy appearing, may all thy Church in thee, and through thee, daily ascribe to Father, Son, and Holy Ghost, Israel's God in covenant, endless praises. Amen'.

Chapter 65

Jude

'Certain Men Crept in Unawares'

Jude was one of our Saviour's half-brothers (Matthew 13:55), and James' full brother. He out-lived all the Apostles, except John. His epistle was written no more than 30-35 years after our Lord's ascension. The purpose of God the Holy Spirit in giving this epistle to the church is evident from its contents. Heresies had already sprung up and the church was infested with them (v. 4).

It is a great mercy to us that both Jude and John lived to see those things come to pass that our Lord Jesus, the Apostle Paul, and the Apostle Peter had prophesied. Had they not lived to see the heresies and heretics prophesied filling the church in those early days, we would never have had the instructive epistles they were inspired to write, equipping us to deal with them. Indeed, the Apostle Paul tells us plainly that heresies must come that the truth of God and the people of God might be made manifest (1 Corinthians 11:19).

Common Salvation

Jude addresses all he has to say to the church of God's elect, to all who are born of God (vv. 1-3). Then, through the greater part of these twenty-five verses (vv. 4-19), he describes the terrible character and state of the reprobate. Yet, these things are written to God's saints for our consolation and instruction. At the end of his letter (vv. 20-25), he reminds us of the safety, security, and blessedness of God's elect and ascribes all praise to our all-glorious Christ, our God and Saviour.

Jude begins his epistle by describing the common salvation of all God's elect. He calls it 'the common salvation', because all who are saved by the free and sovereign grace of God in Christ enjoy all the blessings and privileges of grace in common and all embrace one faith, the faith of the gospel.

'Jude, the servant of Jesus Christ, and brother of James, to them that are sanctified by God the Father, and preserved in Jesus Christ, and called: Mercy unto you, and peace, and love, be multiplied. Beloved, when I gave all diligence to write unto you of the common salvation, it was needful for me to write unto you, and exhort you that ye should earnestly contend for the faith which was once delivered unto the saints' (vv. 1-3).

'The faith which was once delivered unto the saints', is the faith of the gospel, the faith that God gives to all his people by the teaching of his Holy Spirit in effectual grace. This faith involves certain doctrines – though commonly unknown in today's religious world – that are now and have always been commonly embraced and proclaimed among those who believe God. These are the doctrines of election, preservation, effectual calling, and the trinity of persons in the Godhead.

In verse one Jude writes, 'Jude, the servant of Jesus Christ, and brother of James, to them that are sanctified by God the Father, and preserved in Jesus Christ, and called', indicating that the doctrines are such common things in the household of faith that he, like Peter, uses them as a salutation.

God the Holy Spirit inspired his servant Jude to open his epistle with words of tender affection and grace. He speaks of the most weighty, soul-cheering, and essential truths of the gospel in simple, brief, unmistakable terms. In this one, short verse, Jude declares that ...

All who believe God in time were sanctified by God the Father in eternal election, separated unto God, declared and made to be holy in Christ, and accepted in the Beloved! All who were sanctified by God in election were, are, and shall forever be preserved in Christ, our Mediator, unto the time of love, when they are called: preserved in eternity, preserved through Adam's fall, preserved in the days of their rebellion, preserved after conversion, and preserved unto eternal glory! Blessed be God, those who are preserved in Christ Jesus shall never perish!

Who can describe such grace? God's elect are preserved in Jesus Christ, before they are called to Jesus Christ, and preserved in all the after stages of life, until grace is finished in glory. We ought to meditate on these things continually. To do so we must enter into eternity, and look back over the everlasting hills, through all the pathways by which the Lord has brought us on our way, before we can have any real sense and apprehension of the unspeakable blessings contained in these four words, 'preserved in Jesus Christ'.

All who were set apart by the Father unto himself in Christ and preserved in Christ, the Lamb slain before the foundation of the world, are, at the appointed time of love, graciously, irresistibly, and effectually called to life and faith in Christ by the omnipotent mercy of God the Holy Spirit. Robert Hawker wrote:

'So infinitely blessed and important is this great grace of the Holy Spirit, in calling, that, until it is wrought, no child of God can have any apprehension, either of God the Father's love in election, or God the Son's grace in redemption. It is by regeneration that we are made partakers of the divine nature, having escaped the corruption that is in the world, through lust! (2 Peter 1:4, 5).'

Just as the other apostles (Ephesians 1:3-14; 1 Peter 1:2-9), Jude opens his epistle with a declaration that salvation is the work of God alone, the eternal, indestructible, effectual work of God alone, and the work of God in the trinity of his holy persons: Father, Son, and Holy Spirit. Jude knew that all who worshipped God would know and rejoice in that which he declared (1 John 5:7-12; 2 Timothy 1:9-10; Titus 3:3-7).

We date all our mercies from eternity. We find their source in the election of grace. It was in Christ that we were chosen, accepted, blessed with all spiritual blessings, and given all grace and salvation before the world began. It is in Christ that we are preserved and 'kept by the power of God'. Therefore, we delight to say, with Paul, concerning all who believe on the Lord Jesus Christ, 'We are bound to give thanks always to God, for you, brethren, beloved of the Lord, because God hath from the beginning chosen you to salvation, through sanctification of the Spirit, and belief of the truth; whereunto he called you by our Gospel, to the obtaining of the glory of our Lord Jesus Christ' (2 Thessalonians 2:13, 14). 'Thanks be unto God for his unspeakable gift!'

Common Blessings

In verse 2 Jude assures us that this common salvation, about which he is writing, brings common mercies to every believer. 'Mercy unto you, and peace, and love, be multiplied'. Mercy from the Father, peace in and from Jesus Christ, and love in and by the Holy Spirit, sweetly flow to us in streams of grace as the fruits and effects of those glorious acts of the Triune God described in verse 1.

Common Faith

Verse 3 speaks of that common faith possessed by all who have God's gift of faith in Christ. 'Beloved, when I gave all diligence to write unto you of the common salvation, it was needful for me to write unto you, and exhort you that ye should earnestly contend for the faith which was once delivered unto the saints'.

What is that faith? The scriptures show us the answer plainly and fully. The great and leading doctrines of the gospel in the everlasting love of the Father, Son, and Holy Spirit are written on every page. The Person, glory, blood shedding, and righteousness of the Lord Jesus Christ, with redemption only in his blood, and regeneration only by God the Holy Spirit are the foundation of all our mercies. To contend for these, and with earnestness, is to contend for the very life of our souls. Any reluctance on our part to openly profess these glorious truths, or any denial of them by others, is the wounding of the Redeemer in the house of his friends and high treason against the Majesty of God.

The Distinction

Jude draws a clear line of distinction between the elect and the reprobate, between the believer and the religious unbeliever. In verses 1-3 he speaks of God's elect. In verses 4-19 he speaks only of apostates, describing them as those who walk after their own ungodly lusts, who were of old ordained to this condemnation, sensual, and having not the Spirit. These are two distinct classes of people: the elect and the reprobate.

Common Foes

In verses 4-19 Jude describes those men who are the common foes of God's elect in every age. In these verses we have one horrid portrait of apostasy drawn out in many characters. The language Jude uses describes one specific class of men who come under the same condemnation. Taken together, as Jude sets them before us, in one view, these apostates form one picture. And they all come to the same condemnation. We shall do well, under God the Spirit's teaching, to look both at their persons, and their features, and mark them one by one.

'For there are certain men crept in unawares, who were before of old ordained to this condemnation, ungodly men, turning the grace of our God into lasciviousness, and denying the only Lord God, and our Lord Jesus Christ. I will therefore put you in remembrance, though ye once knew this, how that the Lord, having saved the people out of the land of Egypt, afterward destroyed them that believed not. And the angels which kept not their first estate, but left their own habitation, he hath reserved in everlasting chains under darkness unto the judgment of the great day. Even as Sodom and Gomorrha, and the cities about them in like manner, giving themselves over to fornication, and going after strange flesh, are set forth for an example, suffering the vengeance of eternal fire' (vv. 4-7).

'Likewise also these filthy dreamers defile the flesh, despise dominion, and speak evil of dignities. Yet Michael the archangel, when contending with the devil he disputed about the body of Moses, durst not bring against him a railing accusation, but said, The Lord rebuke thee. But these speak evil of those things which they know not: but what they know naturally, as brute beasts, in those things they corrupt themselves. Woe unto them! for they have gone in the way of Cain, and ran greedily after the error of Balaam for reward, and perished in the gainsaying of Core. These are spots in your feasts of charity, when they feast with you, feeding themselves without fear: clouds they are without water, carried about of winds; trees whose fruit withereth, without fruit, twice dead, plucked up by the roots; Raging waves of the sea, foaming out their own shame; wandering stars, to whom is reserved the blackness of darkness for ever' (vv. 8-13).

'And Enoch also, the seventh from Adam, prophesied of these, saying, Behold, the Lord cometh with ten thousands of his saints. To execute judgment upon all, and to convince all that are ungodly among them of all their ungodly deeds which they have ungodly committed, and of all their hard speeches which ungodly sinners have spoken against him. These are murmurers, complainers, walking after their own lusts; and their mouth speaketh great swelling words, having men's persons in admiration because of advantage. But, beloved, remember ye the words which were spoken before of the apostles of our Lord Jesus Christ; How that they told you there should be mockers in the last time, who should walk after their own ungodly lusts. These be they who separate themselves, sensual, having not the Spirit' (vv. 14-19).

Certain Men

First, they are said to have been 'certain men' (v. 4), which had crept in unawares. Jude is not speaking of infidels, men who totally disown Christ. He is describing certain men, who had crept into the church, men who professed to believe in Christ. These are the very apostates Paul warned us to beware of (Acts 20:29, 30). Peter also gave us warning concerning them (2 Peter 2:13). But Jude had lived to see some of them arise among the saints of God.

Crept In

Second, Jude says, they have 'crept in unawares'. Like slithering serpents, they come into the church, professing to be lovers of Christ. They worm themselves into the church under the guise of believers. As Satan transformed himself into an angel of light, that he might more successfully deceive, his ministers appear as ministers of righteousness, in a pretence of love for Christ before his people that they might destroy the souls of men (2 Corinthians 11:14, 15).

Jude is talking about well-known, highly esteemed men, not just church members, but preachers, teachers, and religious leaders. They were the Korahs and Balaams (Numbers 16 and 22) of their day, famous in the churches, men of reputation.

What swarms have followed those apostates Jude describes! They blaze like comets for a while. Like 'wandering stars' as Jude calls them, they make a big show for a time. To them 'is reserved the blackness of darkness for ever'. They are full of promises, empty promises, like 'clouds without water'. Like 'clouds without water, carried about of winds', there is no grace in their hearts and no work of regeneration upon their souls. They have a name to live, but are dead before God, 'twice dead', spiritually dead and under the sentence of the second death, 'of old ordained to this condemnation' (Revelation 20:6).

Ungodly Men

Third, they are described as 'ungodly men, turning the grace of our God into lasciviousness, and denying the only Lord God, and our Lord Jesus Christ'. Notice that there are no charges of immorality. Had their lives been notorious for any breaches of the moral law, surely such would have been mentioned. Had their conduct been notoriously corrupt in any flagrant acts of licentiousness, they would soon have been discovered.

These men are called 'ungodly men' because their doctrine was directly levelled against the gospel of God's free and sovereign grace in Christ. They turned 'the grace of God into lasciviousness', not by using grace as an excuse for ungodly behaviour, but by daring to charge the grace of God that brings salvation with leading to lasciviousness, asserting that the gospel of free, absolute, unconditional grace promotes evil behaviour among those who believe it. They turned the grace of God into lasciviousness by asserting that the glorious gospel of God's free grace, which proclaims free, full, complete, irrevocable pardon to sinners through the blood and righteousness of Christ alone, opens the floodgates of sin (Romans 3:8; 6:1-2). Again, I say, what swarms follow them!

This 'turning the grace of God into lasciviousness' was accompanied with 'denying the only Lord God, and our Lord Jesus Christ'. As we have seen, it is not possible that these men openly denied God's Being, or the fact that our Lord Jesus Christ lived, died, and rose again. Had that been the case, they could not have crept into the church.

How could they be said to deny the only Lord God, except by denying his free grace? Yet, by denying, as multitudes do today, the absolute efficacy of God's purpose and work, by denying the absolute efficacy of the Father's purpose and love, the Son's blood atonement, and the Spirit's omnipotent call. By denying that our Lord Jesus Christ actually redeemed and saves all God's elect by his finished work of redemption, they do in effect deny the very being of God. Robert Hawker issued the following challenge in his excellent commentary on Jude:

'Look at this scripture in every way and direction in which it can be placed, and look for grace from the Almighty Author of inspiration, to have a right understanding of it. And then ask your own heart, what was Jude directed by the Holy Spirit to give all diligence to write to the Church of the common salvation, unless to have guarded the minds of the faithful against the creeping in of such certain men as are here described? What faith but the faith of God's elect, in God the Father's everlasting love, and God the Son's complete, and finished salvation, could the Apostle mean, when he exhorted the Church, "earnestly to contend for the faith once delivered unto the saints"?'

Their Condemnation

Fourth, the judgment such ungodly men shall forever endure is exactly correspondent to their conduct. 'And Enoch also, the seventh from Adam, prophesied of these, saying, Behold, the Lord cometh with ten thousands of his saints, To execute judgment upon all, and to convince all that are ungodly among them of all their ungodly deeds which they have ungodly committed, and of all their hard speeches which ungodly sinners have spoken against him' (vv. 14-15).

When the Lord Jesus comes with his saints; he will convince them all, not only of their ungodly deeds, but also of all their hard speeches, which ungodly sinners have spoken against him (John 5:22-23; Acts 10:42; 17:31; 2 Thessalonians 1:7-10). Every place in holy scripture, which describes the day of judgment, speaks of Christ the Son of God, as the Judge in that day (Matthew 25:31, 32; Acts 10:42; 2 Thessalonians 1:7-10). He, whose eyes are as a flame of fire, 'shall judge the quick and the dead, at his appearing and his kingdom' (2 Timothy 4:1).

Read these solemn verses again and again. Ask God the Holy Spirit to burn them into your heart that you may be able in the light of holy scripture to understand what is going on in the religious world around us today. Do we not daily hear and read the hard speeches spoken against Christ, and by certain men crept in unawares into the church? Multitudes of famous religious leaders, verbally deny our Saviour's being as God. Others, who would never openly assert such, just as fully deny it by denying the merit and efficacy of his blood and righteousness and intercession, asserting that all is vain without some contribution from man.

Such doctrine is the blasphemous assertion that the Son of God is a failure! But that shall never be (Isaiah 42:4; 53:11-12). The cross of our Lord Jesus Christ shall never be discovered a miscarriage. His grace shall never be frustrated. 'He shall see of the travail of his soul and shall be satisfied'. He who satisfied the justice of God for his elect, shall be satisfied by the justice of God in the salvation of his elect.

Nothing could be more suitable than the punishment here denounced upon all such blasphemy. When the Lord Jesus comes in his glory with all his holy angels, showing forth the glory of his grace in the salvation of all his people, he shall, by the overwhelming brightness of his glory, convince all who oppose him who he is and what he has done to their everlasting horror in hell. He shall, in that great day, 'execute judgment upon all and convince all of their hard speeches', which they have spoken against him.

Sensual Men

Fifth, Jude tells us that these men are 'sensual, having not the Spirit' (v. 19). This is the thing that in all ages distinguishes 'between the righteous and the wicked; between him that serveth God, and him that serveth him not' (Malachi 3:18).

Here the Holy Spirit tells us plainly that all who oppose the gospel of God's free and sovereign grace in our Lord Jesus Christ are unregenerate and have not been given the gift of eternal life and salvation in Christ by God the Holy Spirit. Such men, as we might expect, 'speak evil of those things which they know not; but what they know naturally as brute beasts, in those things they corrupt themselves. They have gone into the way of Cain; they have ran greedily after the error of Balaam, for reward; and perished in the gainsaying of Core. These are spots in your feasts of charity. Their mouth speaketh great swelling words, having men's persons in admiration, because of advantage'.

These are different descriptions of the same, sensual, unregenerate men who have not the Spirit, and yet profess to be worshippers of God and disciples of Christ. Like their father, the devil, they rage against the authority and dominion of God.[1] Like Cain, they presume that their works can and do give them some measure of righteousness and acceptance with God. Like Balaam, they mingle the worship of God with the worship of idols, compromising the truth of God in the name of unity, peace, and brotherly love. Like Korah, they are ambitious, motivated by the gratification of their own lusts, 'feeding themselves without fear'.

Divine Sovereignty

Jude began his description of these apostate false prophets by telling us that they were 'before of old ordained to this condemnation' (v. 4; 2 Thessalonians 2:13-14). This testimony to God's sovereignty, so offensive to those sensual people who have not the Spirit of God and so precious to every believer who knows by distinguishing grace his acceptance with the holy Lord God in Christ, his Beloved, is a clear display of the fact that the only distinction there is between the righteous and the wicked is the distinction our God has made by his distinguishing grace (1 Corinthians 4:7). For this we shall forever praise him.

Every child of God, in this present Christ-despising generation, is a wonder of grace, a testimony to God's infallible mercy. We ought to esteem it our highest honour to bear testimony to God's holy name and wondrous grace in Christ. Our great and gracious God has reserved to himself thousands who have not and will not bow the knee to Baal. 'Even so now, at this present time also, there is a remnant according to the election of grace' (Romans 11:4-5).

Israel, Angels and Sodom

Jude reminds us of the apostates among the children of Israel who came out of Egypt and perished in the wilderness in unbelief (v. 5). Though they had all the advantages of a temporal salvation, yet, having no part nor lot in the matter of grace and eternal salvation in Christ, their carcasses fell in the wilderness (Romans 9:6, 7; Hebrews 3:16-19).

'The angels, which kept not their first estate', not being elect angels, were left to the mutability of their own will, fell, and in that fall, were everlastingly condemned. Here again, we find cause for endless praise. Had we not been sanctified and preserved in Christ Jesus by God's eternal grace, we too would be everlastingly condemned. Had the Lord God left us to our own wills, as he did those angels, we would perish forever

---

[1] See Appendix 2 (p 623) for comments on Michael the archangel.

(Romans 9:16). Were it not for the fact that we are yet 'preserved in Jesus Christ' even now, we would perish immediately.

What cause we are given for unceasing thanksgiving and praise for God's electing, preserving grace in Christ! And truly, we may say with the prophet, 'except the Lord of hosts had left unto us a very small remnant, we should have been as Sodom, and we should have been like unto Gomorrah' (Isaiah 1:9).

Enoch

The Holy Spirit has given us no record of Enoch's prophecy. It may have been an oral, rather than a written prophecy. All we know concerning it is the account Jude gives in verses 14-15. But it is a blessed prophecy of our Lord's glorious second advent. When Enoch is called 'the seventh from Adam', the meaning is that his was the seventh generation of believing men in the earth: Adam, Seth, Enosh, Kenan, Mahalaleel, Jered, Enoch (1 Chronicles 1:1-2).

Blessed Safety

'But ye, beloved, building up yourselves on your most holy faith, praying in the Holy Ghost, Keep yourselves in the love of God, looking for the mercy of our Lord Jesus Christ unto eternal life' (vv. 20-21). Here Jude assures us of the absolute safety of God's elect, being 'preserved in Jesus Christ', even in the midst of a reprobate age. This is much the same as Paul's declaration to the Thessalonian saints in 2 Thessalonians 2:1-14.

When he tells us that we must build up ourselves in our 'most holy faith, praying in the Holy Spirit, and keep' ourselves in the love of God, 'looking for the mercy of our Lord Jesus Christ unto eternal life', Jude does not mean that we are our own keepers, or that we can create faith in our own hearts. The scriptures everywhere teach us that all who are kept are kept by the power of God unto eternal life. Our Lord declares regarding his church, 'In that day, sing ye to her a vineyard of red wine. I the Lord do keep it. I will water it every moment: lest any hurt it, I will keep it night and day' (Isaiah 27:2-3; 1 Peter 1:5).

Jude is telling us that we must ever wait for the grace and power of God the Holy Spirit. Ever aware of our need of Christ, we must abide in him, looking to him alone for life, grace, and eternal salvation (Colossians 2:6-7). Let us have a sure, fixed, and certain hope in him regarding all the blessed and glorious events of that great day of God our Saviour, ever expecting 'the mercy of our Lord Jesus Christ unto eternal life'.

It is nothing but mercy, mercy alone, and mercy sure that is the hope and expectation of every believing soul. For chosen, redeemed, believing sinners, justified, sanctified, called, and kept in Christ, there is nothing doubtful about the issue of that day (2 Peter 1:3-4; 1 Corinthians 1:30; 6:11; Isaiah 45:24-25). Jude would not have been inspired by the Holy Spirit to give us this confidence were it a matter of uncertainty (Titus 2:13; 2 Peter 3:12).

Compassion

The mercy, love, and grace we have experienced, we are to show to one another. Jude writes, 'And of some have compassion, making a difference: And others save with fear, pulling them out of the fire; hating even the garment spotted by the flesh' (vv. 22-23).

There is nothing found among men so affectionate and tender as the love of brethren in Jesus. The compassion God's saints show to wanderers and backsliders, to those who are tempted and fallen, and to those who are ignorant and out of the way is sweetness itself. Saved sinners are compelled by the grace we experience to stretch out the helping hand in any way and every way we can to raise up the fallen (2 Corinthians 5:14; Galatians 6:1-2). Because we cannot know who God's elect are, until they are called by his grace and given faith in Christ, we seek to save, as from the fire, all who are tottering upon the brink of hell. Though we loathe their sins as we loathe our own garments, which are defiled and spotted when we put them upon our corrupt bodies, we earnestly desire their eternal salvation in Christ.

To God Be The Glory

'Now unto Him that is able to keep you from falling, and to present you faultless before the presence of his glory, with exceeding joy; to the only wise God, our Saviour, be glory, and majesty, dominion, and power, both now and ever. Amen' (vv. 24-25).

He who has all along preserved us is the One who keeps us from falling. It shall be the special and personal joy and glory of Christ our Surety and Substitute to present his Church to himself at the last day. We nowhere read in scripture of God the Father or God the Holy Spirit presenting the Church before the throne. It shall be God the Son's, our all-glorious Saviour's, final work as our Mediator to bring his church home as a bride adorned for her husband, and present her to himself before the Father (1 Corinthians 15:24-28). He 'loved the Church and gave himself for it, that he might sanctify and cleanse it with the washing of water by the word; that he might present it to himself a glorious Church, not having spot or wrinkle, or any such thing, but that it should be holy, and without blemish (Ephesians 5:25-27).

Chapter 66

Revelation

'The Revelation of Jesus Christ'

It has been my singular object in these surveys of the Bible to show clearly that the singular subject, theme, and message of the entire book of God, the Old Testament and the New, is the Person, work, and glory of the Lord Jesus Christ. As in creation, providence, and redemption, so in the holy scriptures, it is the purpose of God 'that in all things he might have the pre-eminence' (Colossians 1:18).

Him book

The book of God is a book all about Christ (Luke 24:27, 44-48). The Bible is a Him book. It is all about Him. All the promises and blessings of God given to sinful men and women are in Christ (Ephesians 1:3). Apart from Christ, God promises nothing but wrath; and every supposed blessing will prove to be a curse. All the love, mercy, and grace of God is in Christ. All the revelation and knowledge of the triune God is in Christ. Christ is not only the central message of holy scripture; he is *the* message of holy scripture. To understand that is to have the key that opens the Word of God and reveals its treasures.

That which is true of the whole volume of inspiration is especially and gloriously true of the last, closing chapters of the volume, the book of Revelation. This last book of the Bible is Christ's revelation of himself to his servants. This book is 'The Revelation of Jesus Christ' (1:1). It is not the revelation of St John, but 'the Revelation of Jesus Christ' given to and recorded by John. It is not the book of revelations (plural). It does not contain many revelations. It contains one revelation seen in many things. It is 'the Revelation of Jesus Christ'.

Two Points

In his book, *More Than Conquerors*, William Hendriksen made two points that are crucial to a proper understanding of the book of Revelation. First, 'the theme of this book is: the Victory of Christ and of his Church over the Dragon (Satan) and his helpers. The Apocalypse intends to show you, dear believer, that things are not what they seem!' God's purpose is not in jeopardy. Christ, his church, and his truth will be triumphant at last.

The second point Hendriksen made is about the visions John describes. Each vision, or section of this book, must be interpreted as a vision covering the entire gospel age. 'Each section', Hendriksen wrote, 'gives us a description of the entire Gospel Age, from the first to the second coming of Christ, and is rooted in Israel's history under the old dispensation to which there are frequent references'. Confusion comes when men try to mix the visions together and make them form a prophetic history of world events. Each vision is a picture of the Person and work of Christ in redemption, grace, and judgment throughout the gospel age.

Follow that basic, simple guide and you will not greatly err in interpreting the book of Revelation, and your heart will be comforted and thrilled in reading what God has determined to do for you and with you in Christ. A general survey of these twenty-two chapters of inspiration will give the reader a clear understanding of the fact that the revelation given to John and recorded in this book is 'The Revelation of Jesus Christ'.

Faithful Witness

Christ is 'the faithful witness' (1:5). This title refers to our Saviour's prophetic office. He is that Prophet of whom Moses spoke (Deuteronomy 18:15; John 6:14), both faithful and true. He is the faithful witness of God to his people (John 1:14, 18), and our faithful witness before the holy Lord God, as our Advocate with the Father (1 John 2:1).

First Begotten

Our Saviour is 'the first begotten of the dead' (1:5). This refers to our Redeemer's priestly office. If he is 'the first begotten of the dead', then he must have once died. He died for the sins of his people and rose again for their justification. When he arose as our Head and Representative, 'he entered in once into the holy place, having obtained eternal redemption for us' (Hebrews 9:12). With his own precious blood, our great High Priest has opened for us a way of free access to God (Hebrews 10:19-22).

Prince of Kings

Our Redeemer is 'the prince of the kings of the earth' (1:5). By virtue of his finished work of redemption, the God-man, our Mediator, has been made the sovereign Monarch of the universe (John 17:2; Romans 14:9; Philippians 2:9-11). He is Lord and King even over his enemies. The kings of the earth have their crowns and kingdoms from him; they rule by his decree, doing his will (Proverbs 21:1); and one day soon they will all bow before his throne and glorify him as King.

Him that Loved Us

The Lord Jesus is 'him that loved us, and washed us from our sins in his own blood, and made us kings and priests unto God' (1:5-6). He 'loved us' particularly and distinctively, with an everlasting, immutable love. Because he loved us, he chose us in eternal election, became our Surety in the covenant of grace, and with his Father, predestinated us unto heavenly glory.

Therefore, he 'washed us from our sins in his own blood'. By the shedding of his blood, the Lord Jesus Christ effectually washed away the sins of God's elect. He washed our sins from the record of heaven, from the memory of God, and washed us from our sins, making us holy and righteous in the sight of God! That is the work of Christ in redemption.

All whom he loved, he washed; and in the fulness of time, he makes them 'kings and priests unto God'. That speaks of regeneration and conversion. Christ, sending his Spirit to redeem sinners, gives us a new, holy nature by which we are made to reign over the lusts of our flesh, so that we are no longer under the dominion of sin. As priests, consecrated to God, we have direct access to God through his blood.

Him that Liveth

The Son of God says, 'I am he that liveth' (1:18). He lives forever because he is Life! Apart from him there is no life. He lives forever because he is the living God. But here he is talking about himself as the God-man, our Mediator, who once was dead, having died as our Substitute for the satisfaction of divine justice. He died! We thank God for that; but he is now alive for evermore. Christ Jesus lives forever on behalf of his elect, those for whom he died. He lives to make intercession for us (Hebrews 7:25). He lives to give eternal life to all his redeemed ones (John 17:2). Because He lives, we live also. We live in him, by the virtue of his death and by the power of his life.

Holds the Keys

Our all-glorious Lord Jesus Christ holds 'the keys of hell and of death' (1:18). Hell in this place simply refers to the grave. The Lord Jesus Christ, by the virtue of his resurrection, has power, authority, and dominion over death and the grave (Psalm 68:18-20; 1 Corinthians 15:51-58). He conquered death, hell, and the grave when he died for us and rose again. Therefore, these great terrors have no power over us to do us harm, and should cause us no fear (Hebrews 2:14-15). Christ has delivered us from spiritual death in regeneration, the first resurrection (John 5:25), and shall deliver us from death and the grave in the resurrection of our bodies at the last day. It is written, 'Blessed and holy is he that hath part in the first resurrection: on such the second death hath no power' (20:6).

Holds the Stars

He who is the Head of the church is 'he that holdeth the seven stars in his right hand, who walketh in the midst of the seven golden candlesticks' (2:1). These seven golden candlesticks are the churches of Christ in this world. How blessed are those people who are privileged to gather with God's saints in public worship (Matthew 18:20). The Lord Jesus Christ, the Son of God, walks in the midst of his churches!

The seven stars are gospel preachers, God's appointed pastors, who are the angels, messengers of God, to his churches. The Lord Jesus Christ holds them in his right hand, puts them where he wants them, gives them the messages they are responsible to deliver, uses them as he sees fit, and protects them as they go about his business. Let every true gospel preacher be esteemed by God's saints as an angel of God sent with a message from God for their souls (1 Thessalonians 5:12-13).

Lion of Judah

He who is our Saviour is 'the Lion of the tribe of Judah' (5:5). Our Saviour sprang from the tribe of Judah and is comparable to a lion. Like a lion, he is strong and courageous. Like a lion, he devours his enemies. Like a lion, he always prevails. He prevailed over our enemies. He prevailed with God as our Surety and Substitute. And he prevails over the hearts of chosen sinners in saving grace.

Root of David

Our Saviour is called 'the Root of David' (5:5). Later, he is called 'the Root and offspring of David' (22:16). He is both the God from whom David obtained his life and the Man who came from the root of David's house. As a Man, our Saviour arose 'as a root out of a dry ground' (Isaiah 53:2). Yet, he is the Root from which all his people draw their life. The Root of our family tree is Jesus Christ himself!

The Lamb on the Throne

'In the midst of the throne stood a Lamb' (5:6). That Lamb standing in the midst of the throne of God is Christ our Saviour, who was slain for us. He is seen standing in the midst of the throne because he is the centre of God's decrees and works and the One who executes all God's purposes. He alone is worthy and able to open the book of divine predestination and fulfil it. Christ stands in the midst of the throne and of the twenty-four elders (the church of God) and the four beasts (the preachers of the gospel) as the Saviour of all his people and the One of whom all his servants speak. The throne John saw represents the glory of God as well as the dominion of God; and Christ, as the Lamb of God, is the revelation and accomplishment of God's glory.

The Mighty Angel

In chapter 10 we see our Lord Jesus Christ as the 'the mighty Angel come down from heaven' (10:1-3). Our blessed Saviour is the Angel of the Covenant (Malachi 3:1), the Angel of the Lord's Presence (Isaiah 63:9), the Archangel (Jude 9), and the mighty Angel of the Lord who rules the universe, fulfilling the book of God's decrees. To the wicked and unbelieving, he is the Angel of Judgment. But on behalf of his covenant people, he is seen as the Angel of Providence. He is the Messenger sent by God to reveal his will, accomplish his purpose, and redeem his people.

In the chapter 20 we see our Saviour as the mighty Angel again, binding Satan and casting him into the bottomless pit (20:1-3; John 12:31). This great and mighty Angel is God our Saviour (18:1). He alone has the keys of death and hell (1:18). No creature could ever bind the devil, or even hinder his influence. He was the greatest, most powerful creature of the Almighty. None but Christ, the Creator, could bind him. In order to accomplish our salvation Satan had to be bound. Here we see Christ coming with the key of the bottomless pit and a great chain in his hand. He came to shackle a treasonous rebel and lock him away. The scriptures plainly tell us that one purpose of our Lord's incarnation and birth was to make war with, conquer, and bind the prince of darkness (Genesis 3:15; 1 John 3:8; Revelation 12:5-11). Christ has won that war!

The Lamb Slain

The Lamb we saw standing in the midst of the throne (5:6) is 'the Lamb slain from the foundation of the world' (13:8). In the purpose and decree of God, in anticipation of the fall, for the fulfilling of God's covenant, Christ was looked upon by God the Father as our all-sufficient, sin-atoning sacrifice before ever the world was made. God's elect were looked upon in him as being saved from eternity (Romans 8:28-31; Ephesians 1:3-6; 2 Timothy 1:9). All that we experience in time of God's redeeming grace was done for us in eternity in God's decrees. Before the world was made, in the mind and purpose of almighty God, Christ was the Lamb slain. That means that in the mind of God, from all eternity, the covenant of grace was fulfilled, the ransom price was paid, the Surety was exalted, and God's elect were saved.

Faithful and True

The Lord Jesus Christ is called 'Faithful and True' (19:11). What a name for the Son of God! He well deserves it, for he is faithful and true in all things. He is Faithful to his people, to his covenant, to his promises, and to himself. He is True. He is both the Truth and the True One. Jesus Christ is a true Friend and Brother (Proverbs 17:17), a true Saviour (1 John 1:9; 2:1-2), and a true Husband (Song of Solomon 5:1-9). So true is this Husband to his bride that he will never leave her and will never let her leave him.

The Word of God

He is 'The Word of God' (19:13). 'In the beginning was the Word, and the Word was with God, and the Word was God' (John 1:1). Christ is the Word, by which God reveals himself and through which the triune God performs all his works. He is the eternal, creating Word, by whom all things were made (John 1:3; Hebrews 1:1-2). He is the incarnate, revealing Word, by whom God is revealed to man (John 1:14, 18). And he is the almighty, saving Word (Hebrews 4:12-13), by whom God calls out and saves his people in regenerating grace.

King of Kings

Our Saviour is the 'King of kings and Lord of lords' (19:16). As we saw in chapter 1, verse 5, the Lord Jesus Christ is the absolute, singular, rightful, sovereign Monarch of heaven and earth (Acts 2:32-36).

Makes All Things New

The Lord Jesus Christ is that one who declares, 'behold, I make all things new' (21:5-6). In grace he makes all things new. 'Therefore if any man be in Christ, he is a new creature: old things are passed away; behold, all things are become new' (2 Corinthians 5:17). In heavenly glory he makes all things new, granting to his people a new name and a new life, without the possibility of sin, sorrow, or death. In the last days he will create 'a new heavens and a new earth, wherein dwelleth righteousness' (2 Peter 3:13).

Alpha and Omega

So great and glorious, so full and perfect is our Lord Jesus that he is declared to be the 'Alpha and Omega' (22:13). He is the 'A' and the 'Z', the first and the last, the beginning and the end of all things. The covenant of grace begins and ends with Christ. The whole of creation has its origin in Christ and shall find its consummation in Christ. Every event of providence comes from Christ and shall glorify Christ. The entire volume of holy scripture, from beginning to end, speaks of Christ. In the salvation of God's elect Jesus Christ is the beginning, the end, and everything between (1 Corinthians 1:30-31).

Bright and Morning Star

Our Redeemer is 'The Bright and Morning Star' (22:16). He is the Light that shines in darkness, that shines in our hearts to give the light of the knowledge of the glory of God. He is the Day Star of grace, the Sun of Righteousness, risen over this sin-cursed earth, with healing in his wings. He is the Star of that great eternal day yet to come. In the natural world men talk of the glory of the sunrise at dawn. How much more glorious will be the dawn of that resurrection morn.

Come Quickly

Our dear Saviour, the Lord Jesus Christ, declares, 'Surely, I come quickly' (22:20). Soon he shall appear! Suddenly, without warning, the King of glory shall come again to destroy his enemies, save his people, restore his creation, and glorify his Father. Time is short. 'Then cometh the end', when the God-man Mediator will perform his last mediatoral work. He shall deliver up the kingdom, all the hosts of his elect unto God the Father, saying, 'Behold I and the children which God hath given me!' And God shall be 'all in all' (Isaiah 8:18; Hebrews 2:13; 1 Corinthians 15:24-28).

No More Tears

Then, we shall see his face, 'and God shall wipe away all tears from our eyes; and there shall be no more death, neither sorrow, nor crying, neither shall there be any more pain: for the former things are passed away' (21:4).

Impossible as it is for us to imagine, there is a time coming when we shall weep no more, when we shall have no cause to weep! Heaven is a place of sure, eternal, ever-increasing bliss; and the cause of that bliss is our God! Heaven is a place of joy without sorrow, laughter without weeping, pleasantness without pain! In heaven there are no regrets, no remorseful tears, no second thoughts, no lost causes, no sorrows of any kind!

If God did not wipe away all tears from our eyes, there would be much weeping in heaven. We would surely weep much over our past sins, unconverted loved ones forever lost in hell, wasted opportunities while we were upon the earth, our many acts of unkindness toward our brethren here, and the terrible price of our redemption! But God will wipe away all tears from our eyes; all of them! In heaven's glory there will be no more death to part loving hearts. There will be no more sorrow of any kind. There will be no more crying for any reason. There will be no more pain of any sort. Why? How can these things be? 'The former things are passed away!'

Our great God shall, in heaven's glory, remove us from all sin, remove all sin from us, and remove us from all the evil consequences of sin. He will remove us from every cause of grief. He will bring us at last into the perfection of complete salvation and every desire of our hearts will be completely gratified. Then, we will be like Christ. We will be with Christ. We will see Christ. We will love Christ perfectly. We will serve Christ unceasingly. We will worship Christ without sin. We will rest in Christ completely. We will enjoy Christ fully. We will have Christ entirely. These things shall be our everlasting experience, without interruption!

Face to Face

We are told in Revelation 22:4, 'And they shall see his face'. What a blessed, glorious prospect this is! This is the great object of our hope, the great desire of our hearts, the great joy of heaven, and the great fulness of our heavenly reward. The very Christ who died in our place at Calvary, fully satisfying the wrath and justice of God for us, will be seen by us.

We shall literally see his face. It is delightfully true that we shall see and enjoy many things in heaven. But that which is now desired, and will then be enjoyed above all else is the sight of Christ himself. It seems that our text also implies a spiritual sight of Christ, which is far sweeter. In the next world we shall have a greater ability to see Christ than we now possess. We shall see him perfectly and know him fully. Our vision of him will be uninterrupted. The paradise of God is a heaven of pure, intense, eternal, perfect, spiritual fellowship with Christ.

In that future estate of glory and bliss we shall have a clear, undimmed vision of Christ, because everything that now hinders our sight of him will be removed. Our many sins, our earthly cares, and our sorrows in this world now prevent us from seeing our Lord as we desire. But then there will be nothing between us and our Saviour. In glory there will be nothing in our hearts to rival Christ. We will love him as he ought to be loved, perfectly. Christ will not only be supreme, he will be all.

Why do we consider this vision of Christ the greatest bliss of heaven? Why do we place such importance upon this one aspect of our heavenly inheritance? The reason is just this: When we see the Lord's face our salvation will be complete. Every evil thing will be completely eradicated from us. When we see his face we shall be forever conscious of his favour. And when these eyes see his face a complete transformation will take place. 'We shall be like him, for we shall see him as he is' (1 John 3:2). We shall see things as he sees them. We shall think as he thinks. Our will will be one with his will. Our hearts will be one with his heart. Then, when we see his face, we shall be perfectly satisfied.

How sweet, then, is this promise of our Saviour, 'Surely, I come quickly!' How earnestly our souls ought to pray, 'Even so, come, Lord Jesus'.

Amen

Appendix 1

John Gill on 1 John 5:7

John Gill's comments on 1 John 5:7 are so important that they cannot be omitted, even from a brief survey of 1 John. Gill writes:

'This is not only a proof of the Deity of each of these three persons, inasmuch as they, are not only said to be *'one'*, that is, one God; and their witness is called the witness of God (1 John 5:9), but of a Trinity of Persons, in the unity of the divine essence. This unity of essence, or nature, is asserted and secured, by their being said to be one. This respects not a mere unity of testimony, but of nature.

It is not said of them, as of the witnesses on earth, that they *'agree in one'*; but that they *'are one'*. And they may be called a Trinity, inasmuch as they are *'three'*; and a Trinity of Persons, since they are not only spoken of as distinct from each other, the Father from the Word and Holy Ghost, the Word from the Father and the Holy Ghost, and the Holy Ghost from the Father and the Word; but a personal action is ascribed to each of them.

They are all three said to be testifiers, or to bear record; which cannot be said of mere names and characters; nor be understood of one person under different names. If the one living and true God only bears record, first under the character of a Father, then under the character of a Son, or the Word, and then under the character of the Holy Ghost; testimony, indeed, would be given three times, but there would be but one testifier, not three, as the apostle asserts.

Suppose one man should, for one man may bear the characters, and stand in the relations of father, son, and master; of a father to a child of his own; of a son, his father being living; and of a master to servants under him; suppose, I say, this man should come into a court of judicature, and be admitted to bear testimony in an affair there depending, and should give his testimony first under the character of a father, then under the character of a son, and next under the character of a master; every one will conclude, that though there was a testimony three times given, yet there was but one, and not three, that bore record.

This text is so glaring a proof of the doctrine of the Trinity, that the enemies of it have done all they can to weaken its authority, and have pushed hard to extirpate it from a place in the sacred writings'.

Appendix 2

Comments on Jude 9

It might be helpful for me to give some additional explanation of Jude verse 9. Michael the archangel can be, in my opinion, none other than Christ himself, the Angel of the Covenant, the Angel of the Lord. There is but one Archangel, or Prince of Angels (Daniel 10:13, 21), and that is Christ, the Head of all principality and power. The name by which he is here spoken of, 'Michael', means 'one who is as God'. We find this name, 'Archangel', only twice in the whole book of God (1 Thessalonians 4:16 and Jude 9). In both places there can be little question that it has reference to our Lord Jesus Christ in his mediatoral office.

The only place in the book of God to which this passage might have reference is Zechariah 3:1-10. The explanation John Gill gave of Jude 9 is, in my opinion, the best I have read. I say that simply because it is completely consistent with the whole teaching of Scripture and specifically with Jude's message. Gill explains:

'It was to show that the law of Moses was to be abolished and buried by Christ, never to rise again ... The law of Moses is sometimes called Moses himself (John 5:45; Acts 15:21; 21:21; 2 Corinthians 3:15) and so the body of Moses ... The law of Moses was restored in the time of Joshua the high priest, by Ezra and Nehemiah. Joshua broke the law and was charged by Satan as guilty, who contended and insisted upon it that he should suffer for it. So that this dispute or contention might be said to be about the body of Moses, that is, the body of Moses' law, which Joshua had broken'.

In the dispute Michael, or the Angel of the Lord, our the Lord Jesus Christ, chose not to '*bring a railing accusation, but said, The Lord rebuke thee*' (Jude 9; Zechariah 3:2). Pointing to his finished work of redemption and righteousness as the sole basis of Joshua's acceptance with God, the Lord Jesus Christ spoke as our Mediator, just as he did in the flesh in John 17 and does now as our Advocate in heaven (1 John 2:1-2), and called upon the Father to rebuke Joshua's accuser (Romans 8:1, 33-34).

Index of Bible Verses

Old Testament

New Testament

Mark	page
1:40-41	232
4:19	420
7:20-23	549
8:34-35	88
9:2-13	352
9:49-50	119
10:45	326
12:10	178
12:41-44	432
13:22	498
14	319
16:15-16	594
16:16	26, 485
16:18	402

Luke	page
1:31-33	128
1:59	477
1:74	97
1:78	326
2:21	477
2:30-32	345
3:22	186
4:22	185
4:24-26	111
7:11-15	232
7:37-38	82
9:28-36	352
10:21	185
10:30-35	232
10:39	82
11:29-30	277
11:42	338
12:37	358
13:43	502
14:25-33	60, 114
18:7	517
18:12	338
18:13	134, 230
19:41-42	281
20:17	178
22:39	393
23:35-36	179
24:25-27	175
24:27	343, 160, 611
24:44	404
24:44-45	160
24:44-47	175

Luke	page
24:44-48	611
24:46-48	594
24:48	392
24:50	393

John	page
1:1	186, 188, 236, 584
1:1-3	16, 474
1:1-4	573
1:3	186, 616
1:14	236, 237, 567, 612, 616
1:18	188, 612, 616
1:41-45	345
1:45	23, 340
1:47-52	44
2:17	178
3:3	465
3:7	453
3:14-16	43
3:27	472
3:30	565
3:35	81
3:36	485
4:23-24	463
4:24	583
5:22-23	605
5:24-26	452
5:25	614
5:36	405
5:39	570
5:45	623
5:45-47	47
6:14	612
6:29	485
6:35	186
6:44-45	500
6:47	186
6:48-58	27
7:37	185
8:32	583
10:11	180, 532
10:14-16	198
10:15	532
10:17-18	277, 364
10:26	532
10:27-28	198
10:28	428
10:30	405, 584

Acts	page	Romans	page
20:28	490	7	195
20:28-30	593	7:1-4	28
20:29-30	603	7:4	50
20:29-32	509	7:6-9	49
20:30	596	7:14-22	204
21:21	23, 623	7:14-23	34, 76, 94
		7:18	574
Romans		7:24	574
1:1-6	278	8:1	28, 74, 277, 311, 352,
1:3-4	43		478, 623
1:5	595	8:1-4	50
1:7	584	8:2-4	58
1:15-17	485	8:4	542
1:16	303, 514, 522	8:8-10	51
1:16-17	550, 595	8:17	119, 494
1:17	300, 303	8:21	21
1:18	514, 522	8:23	50
1:18-32	137	8:26	86, 433, 434
2:4	132, 291	8:28	53, 71, 233, 297, 258,
2:5	299		591, 534, 549
2:28-29	477	8:28-30	34, 90, 159, 238, 294,
3:3-4	111, 125		391, 428, 479, 484
3:8	604	8:28-39	304
3:10-19	80	8:29	298
3:18	184	8:29-30	24, 535
3:19	49	8:30	583
3:19-20	83	8:30-31	583
3:19-26	49	8:32	591
3:20-28	94	8:32-34	311
3:21-26	189	8:32-39	50, 138
3:24	583	8:33	582
3:24-26	82, 248, 295, 478	8:33-34	352, 623
3:31	98	9:1-3	268
4:8	99, 288	9:5	376
4:25	303, 352, 440, 465	9:6-7	607
4:25-5:1	405	9:11-13	125, 532
5:6	359	9:11-18	232, 272, 294
5:10	428	9:11-23	484
5:10-11	50, 453	9:11-26	333
5:11	303	9:15-16	532, 550
5:12	16, 17, 80, 478	9:15-18	25, 333, 351, 399
5:12-19	19	9:15-24	223
5:19	79, 465	9:16	608
6:1-2	604	9:18-21	532
6:4-6	119, 478	9:25-26	252
6:11	138	10:1-4	193
6:12-14	521	10:4	28, 50, 55, 362, 386,
6:14	161		441, 542
6:14-15	28, 50	10:5-13	54